the essentials of...

LITER🪰TURE

IN ENGLISH POST–1914

Ian Mackean

Hodder Arnold

A MEMBER OF THE HODDER HEADLINE GROUP

First published in Great Britain in 2005 by
Arnold, a member of the Hodder Headline Group,
338 Euston Road, London NW1 3BH

http://www.arnoldpublishers.com

Distributed in the United States of America by
Oxford University Press Inc.
198 Madison Avenue, New York, NY10016

British Library Cataloguing in Publication Data
A catalogue record for this book is available from the British Library

Library of Congress Cataloging-in-Publication Data
A catalog record for this book is available from the Library of Congress

ISBN–10: 0 340 88268 9

ISBN–13: 978 0 340 88268 9

1 2 3 4 5 6 7 8 9 10

Typeset in 9pt New Baskerville by Dorchester Typesetting Group Ltd
Printed and bound in Spain

What do you think about this book? Or any other Arnold title?
Please send your comments to feedback.arnold@hodder.co.uk

Contents

Introduction

The purpose of this book is to provide an introduction to literature in English of the modern period – approximately 1914 to the present day – from around the world. The first of the book's four sections, 'Major authors', presents articles on important modern authors. Given the large number of eligible authors and the limitation on space, difficult choices had to be made about which authors to include. I have aimed to offer a representative selection in terms of nationality, time period and gender.

The second and third sections present articles on aspects of modern literature. Here I have included a representative selection in terms of both subject matter and type of article. Articles about literature can take many forms, such as a biographically based study of an author's life and works, a close analysis of a single text, a broad historical survey of a country's output, an analysis of the political and historical background to a country's literature, an overview of worldwide trends or any combination of these. Literary criticism can also deal with its subject at many levels, from the basic introduction to the postgraduate thesis. I have presented articles of a variety of types and levels in order that the reader can experience a wide range of approaches. Thus, while being a source of information about literature, this book also offers examples of the range of forms which writing about literature can take. The book draws together the knowledge and enthusiasm of a large number of contributors from all over the world, most of them university lecturers or postgraduate students currently active in the field of literary studies.

The fourth section, 'Reference materials', contains the glossary, a list of poets laureate and winners of prizes, and a time chart.

Within articles, names of authors about whom there is a separate entry have been printed in blue. Important terms have also been highlighted in blue, to indicate that there is an entry on them in the glossary.

The editor welcomes feedback on the book at IanMackean@hotmail.com or IanMackean@Bigfoot.com

For links to internet resources on literature, visit www.english-literature.org/resources/

Ian Mackean BA (Hons) (University of Reading), Dip Lib, 2004

Acknowledgements

Many people have helped in the production of this book. I should like to express my thanks to all who have contributed articles. In addition I should like to thank the following: Ronald Knowles of the University of Reading, Trenton Hickman of Brigham Young University, Steven Barfield of the University of Westminster, my parents for help in numerous ways, Helen Jefferson-Brown for invaluable proofreading and constructive criticism, and Petri Liukkonen of Kuusankoski Library www.kirjasto.sci.fi

List of contributors

Dr Maria-Sabina Draga Alexandru is an Associate Tutor at the School of Literature and Creative Writing, Faculty of Arts and Humanities, University of East Anglia, Norwich and Lecturer in twentieth-century British and American Studies at the Department of English, Faculty of Foreign Languages and Literatures, University of Bucharest Romania. She has published a book entitled *The Postmodern Condition: Towards an Aesthetic of Cultural Identities*, as well as articles on contemporary fiction in English. She is co-editing a collective volume entitled *Women's Voices in Postcommunist Eastern Europe*. She is currently completing a second PhD focusing on contemporary Indian fiction in English at the University of East Anglia.

Levi Asher is webmaster of Literary Kicks www.litkicks.com

Tathagata Banerjee, MA.

Steven Barfield is Senior Lecturer in English Literature at the University of Westminster. He has published articles and chapters on Samuel Beckett, contemporary British theatre and critical theory and is currently working on co-edited collections on Samuel Beckett's drama and on contemporary British theatre companies. He is Deputy Director of the UK Network of Modern Fiction Studies. He is Deputy Director of the UK Network of Modern Fiction Studies. His web page is www.wmin.ac.uk/sshl/new/englit/barfield.htm

Siddartha Biswas is a lecturer at St Paul's Cathedral Mission College, Kolkata, West Bengal, India. He has published articles on John Keats, on the sonnet form and on contemporary films. His principal interest lies in the field of drama and cinema. He has worked extensively on Synge and Oscar Wilde. His ongoing research is on the dynamics of exchange between the text and the screen.

Gary Blohm has just completed a PhD, and has taught English studies at the University of Exeter. He has published work on Charles Bukowski in a collection dedicated to American cultural and historical criticism. His other interests include the works of Raymond Carver and cultural influence on the self in twentieth-century American fiction.

Drs Bram de Bruin has been a teacher of English since 1968. He has taught English as a foreign language at a variety of schools in the Netherlands. He specialises in English literature for sixth form students, and has presided over the English department of the Dutch Association of Teachers of Foreign Languages since 2000.

Debanjan Chakrabarti PhD is head of Communications and Literature at the British Council, East India. A Felix Research Scholar at the School of English and American Literature at Reading University, England, he did his PhD on Graham Greene. He has also taught courses on Modernism and films at Reading. Debanjan did his MA and BA in English at Jadavpur University, Kolkata, India. Having started his career as a journalist for *The Telegraph* (Kolkata), he regularly contributes to several English newspapers, magazines, and webzines in India and abroad.

Stephen Colbourn retired from full-time teaching at the age of fifty. After studying Russian and English as a Foreign Language at the University of Reading he worked abroad for twenty years. Currently he is based in Thailand where he is a freelance writer. He has written widely on ELT and has published articles on literature, linguistics and computers in various journals.

Hugh Croydon Before he retired, Hugh Croydon was Head of English in a large Comprehensive School in Hertfordshire. An enthusiastic student of the American Theatre, he has directed or acted in plays by Eugene O'Neill, Arthur Miller, Tennessee Williams, Edward Albee and David Mamet. Until recently he examined in English for the International Baccalaureate.

Dr Selwyn R. Cudjoe is a professor of Literature at Wellesley College, Massachusetts, USA. He is also a visiting scholar at the Afro-American Studies Department at Harvard University. He has published extensively on Caribbean literature, including the book, *Beyond Boundaries: The Intellectual Tradition of Trinidad and Tobago in the Nineteenth Century*. His article was first published on www.trinicenter.com/Cudjoe/

Dr Santanu Das is research Fellow in English at St. John's College, Cambridge, and his book *Touch and Intimacy in First World War Literature* will be published in 2005.

Pilar Cuder Domínguez Universidad de Huelva, Spain. www.uhu.es/37158/. Her book *Margaret Atwood: A Beginner's Guide* was published in 2003.

Dr Julie Ellam, PhD, is a tutor for the English Department, University of Hull, England. For her PhD, Julie Ellam wrote about love in Jeanette Winterson's main novels. She is currently writing a book-length study of this topic.

Dr Jonathan Ellis holds a Leverhulme Early Career Fellowship at the School of English and American Literature, University of Reading, England. He specialises in modern poetry and film studies. He has published articles on Simon Armitage, Amy Clampitt and Paul Durcan, with further work on Philip Larkin and Stevie Smith forthcoming. He has recently completed a book on Elizabeth Bishop.

Victoria J. Essary, Brigham Young University-Idaho, USA.

Ian Foakes is an English teacher with a keen interest in post colonial studies. A graduate of the Open University, he teaches English at Forest School in Snaresbrook, East London. www.forest.org.uk/contactmap.htm

Kristina Gashler, Brigham Young University, Utah, USA.

Amy Glauser Bankhead, Brigham Young University, Utah, USA.

Holly Hancey, Brigham Young University-Idaho, USA.

Trenton Hickman is Assistant Professor of English at Brigham Young University, Utah, USA.

Karen C. Holt is a professor of English at Brigham Young University in Rexburg, Idaho, where she was the Reading Center Director for ten years. Karen teaches literature, rhetoric, and advanced composition and recently published an article on Charles Frazier's *Cold Mountain*. Karen also reviews textbooks and is currently writing her dissertation for the University of Idaho.

Carole Jones, PhD, is a freelance writer, researcher and teacher. Carole's main areas of research are Victorian literature and ideas, and writing by women. Her doctoral thesis is a study of George Eliot's sympathy and duty in relation to nineteenth-century theories of altruism. Carole Jones has edited *Daniel Deronda* and co-edited *Vanity Fair*. She is currently writing a biography of Jane Anderson, while also attempting to publish fiction!

Sarah Jones has a degree in Accounting and has studied English Literature with the London School of Journalism. She has worked in Human Resources and lived in various countries overseas during the past fifteen years.

Alison Kelly, MA, Oxon is a postgraduate student in the School of English and American Literature, University of Reading, England. She teaches courses in contemporary North American literature and is writing a PhD on the work of Lorrie Moore.

Michael King, a graduate of the University of Hertfordshire in Literature and History, has been for many years a lecturer with the Workers' Educational Association, specialising in twentieth-century British poetry, the modern short story and George Orwell. He also lectures for the Institute for the International Education of Students and is a teacher of English as a second language.

Nil Korkut is a teaching and research assistant at the Department of Foreign Language Education, Middle East Technical University, Ankara Turkey. Her research interests include fiction, parody, literary theory and narrative theory, and she has presented a number of papers on related topics at various conferences. Nil Korkut is currently writing her PhD dissertation on literary parody.

Jayne Lendrum As a postgraduate student at the School of English, Queen's University, Belfast, Jayne Lendrum contributed to The Imperial Archive, a project supervised by Dr Leon Litvack. www.qub.ac.uk/en/imperial/imperial.htm

Petri Liukkonen, MA is Director of Kuusankoski Library, Kuusankoski, Finland, and has created the web site Books and Writers. at www.kirjasto.sci.fi

Ian Mackean has an Honours Degree in English Literature from the University of Reading, and a Postgraduate Diploma in Librarianship. He is currently a tutor with The London School of Journalism, and webmaster of English Literature Resources. www.english-literature.org/resources

Mark Mills is an English MA candidate at Brigham Young University, in Provo, Utah. His research interests include modern and postmodern American literature and critical theory. He is currently working on his masters thesis, a study of Cormac McCarthy's border trilogy.

Andy Morrison As a postgraduate student at the School of English, Queen's University, Belfast, Andy Morrison contributed to The Imperial Archive, a project supervised by Dr Leon Litvack. www.qub.ac.uk/en/imperial/imperial.htm

Dr Bernice M. Murphy completed her PhD at Trinity College Dublin in 2003. She has edited a collection of essays on the American Gothic writer Shirley Jackson and is contributing an essay on Stephen King to the forthcoming *Dictionary of Literary Biography* volume on American Gothic and Romance Writers. She has also written entries on Shirley Jackson, Peter Straub, Stephen King, Richard Matheson, H.P. Lovecraft and the Horror genre itself for the online *Literary Encyclopedia*: www.litencyc.com

Antonia Navarro-Tejero, PhD is an Associate Professor at the Universidad de Cordoba (Spain) and formerly a Visiting Professor at the Central Institute of English and Foreign Languages, Hyderabad, India. She holds a PhD in English (Indian women authors), and has published widely on caste and gender issues in India. She has lived and lectured in the USA, India and Spain. She is the author of the books *Matrimonio y patriarcado en autoras de la diaspora hindz* (2001), *Gender and Caste in South-Asian*

Women Authors, and is currently completing a monograph on Githa Hariharan. She is a 2004-2005 Fulbright scholar at University of California, Berkeley.

Dr Ünal Norman is an Associate Professor of English Literature at the Faculty of Education, Middle East technical University, Ankara, Tyrkey. Ünal Norman has been teaching drama for over thirty years. She has published articles on Shakespeare, Modern British Drama and American Drama. She is currently researching the "rewriting" of Shakespeare's plays by 20th century writers.

Dr Tatiani Rapatzikou is a lecturer at the School of English in the department of American Literature and Culture at the Aristotle University of Thessaloniki, Greece. She is the author of *Gothic Motifs in the Fiction of William Gibson* has published articles on the technological uncanny, digital culture and multimedia performance. She has collaborated with Penguin Classics for the 2003 edition of *Edgar Allan Poe: The Fall of the House of Usher and other Writings.* She is now teaching twentieth-century American fiction and poetry.

Katie Richie is a graduate student at Brigham Young University. She is currently working on a MA in American Literature.

Pat Righelato, BA, PhD, is a lecturer at the School of English and American Literature, University of Reading, England. She has published articles on American fiction and poetry and has edited texts of Henry James and Harriet Beecher Stowe. She was for a number of years joint contributor to 'American Poetry: the Twentieth Century' in *The Year's Work in English Studies.* She is currently working on a book-length study of Rita Dove.

Midori Saito is a PhD student at Goldsmiths College, University of London, England and Hitotsubashi University, Japan. Her field of research is Caribbean Literature, Colonial/Postcolonial Literature and Comparative Literature. She has published an article on Lafcadio Hearn in the Lafcadio Hearn Dictionary and is currently writing her PhD thesis on Jean Rhys.

Ana María Sánchez-Arce teaches at The University of Reading. She has co-edited *European Intertexts: Women's Writing in English in a European Context* with Patsy Stoneman, published articles on contemporary British and postcolonial fiction and co-translated an anthology of Anglophone women's writings about the Spanish Civil War (ed. A. Usandizaga). She is currently finishing her doctoral thesis on authenticity in contemporary literature at the University of Hull, England.

Ann Severn is a tutor for the Workers' Educational Association for whom she teaches English and drama, fiction and poetry. She lectures in Literature to the Barts Society in association with the Buckinghamshire Chilterns University College based in High Wycombe, England. Previous publications have been for the National Primary Centre and have dealt with educational issues concerning continuity and progression within the state educational system.

Dr Margaret J-M Sonmez is a lecturer at the Department of Foreign Language Education, Middle East Technical University, in Ankara, Turkey. She has published a number of articles on variation and change in Early Modern English Language, on a variety of literary subjects.

Helen Soteriou, BSc (Hons), MSc is a psychologist. She has recently completed her Masters Degree in Mental Health Studies' Occupational Psychiatry & Psychology at King's College, London. She has spent a number of years at the Institute of psychiatry and Institute of Neurology working on various research projects. She is currently working at the Royal Free Hospital, as a Neuropsychologist and as an associate for a Management consultancy company. She hopes to begin a PhD in the area of gambling addictions later this year.

David Stock, Brigham Young University, Utah, USA.

Margaret Tarner, now retired, worked for the British Council as Inspectress, Teacher Trainer and Teacher of EFL in Africa and the Far and Middle East. She has published numerous guided readers and data sheets for Foreign Learners of English.

Thomas Thale was formerly deputy head of English at Vista Soweto and a lecturer in the African Literature Department of the University of the Witwatersrand. He has a Masters degree in African literature. His article was first published on SouthAfrica.info at www.safrica.info

Angela M. Thompson, Brigham Young University, Utah, USA.

Amanda Thursfield is Director of Information for the British Council in Italy, and has contributed articles to Contemporary Writers in the UK: www.contemporarywriters.com

Gareth Vaughan has a Degree in English and History and a Postgraduate Diploma in Librarianship. He works in publishing.

Part 1

Major modern authors A–Z

ACHEBE, CHINUA (1930–)

I would be quite satisfied if my novels (especially the ones I set in the past) did no more than teach my readers that their past – with all its imperfections – was not one long night of savagery from which the first Europeans acting on God's behalf delivered them.

Morning Yet on Creation Day

Albert Chinualumogu Achebe, regarded by some as 'the founding father of modern African literature',[1] is famous for his novels describing the effects of Western customs and values on traditional African society. His satire and his keen ear for spoken language have made him one of the most highly esteemed African writers in English.

While his mother tongue was Igbo, Achebe was educated in English and his literary language is standard English blended with Igbo vocabulary, proverbs, images and speech patterns. He has defended the use of English in the production of African fiction, insisting that the African novelist has an obligation to educate, and has criticised European critics for failing to understand African literature on its own terms. Achebe has defined himself as a cultural nationalist with a revolutionary mission 'to help my society regain belief in itself and put away the complexes of the years of denigration and self-abasement'. But he is also critical of postcolonial African leaders who have pillaged economies, and during the military dictatorship of Sani Abacha he left Nigeria several times.

Achebe was born in Ogidi, Nigeria, the son of a teacher in a missionary school. His parents, though they instilled in him many of the values of their traditional Igbo culture, were devout evangelical Protestants and christened him Albert after Prince Albert, consort of Queen Victoria. In 1944 Achebe attended Government College in Umuahia, then went to the University College of Ibadan, where he studied English, history and theology,

graduating in 1953. While at university he rejected his British name and took his indigenous name, Chinua. After university he travelled in Africa and America and worked for a short time as a teacher. In 1954 he joined the Nigerian Broadcasting Company in Lagos, and in the 1960s he was the director of External Services for The Voice of Nigeria.

During the Nigerian Civil War (1967–70) Achebe served in the Biafran government service and then taught at universities in the USA and Nigeria. In 1967 he co-founded a publishing company at Enugu with the poet Christopher Okigbo, and since 1971 he has edited *Okike*, the leading journal of new Nigerian writing. Achebe was appointed research fellow at the University of Nigeria, later becoming a professor of English, and has been a professor emeritus since 1985. He also held the post of Professor of English at the University of Massachusetts, where he met **James Baldwin**, also a faculty member, who was Professor of African Studies at the University of Connecticut. Achebe then became a faculty member at Bard College, New York, deciding to remain there rather than returning to his homeland in part because, having been confined to a wheelchair since a car accident in 1990, he needed medical attention which may not have been available in Nigeria.[2]

Achebe's first novel, *Things Fall Apart* (1958), a central text of **postcolonial** literature, is set in the 1890s when missionaries and colonial government imposed themselves on Igbo society. Part of Achebe's aim in writing the novel was to 'write back' to novels such as Joyce Cary's *Mister Johnson* (1939) to present an insider's view on his country and its people which he felt had been misrepresented.[3] The story depicts the life of Okonkwo, the ambitious and powerful leader of an Igbo community, who relies on his physical strength and courage. Okonkwo's life is good: his compound is large, he has no troubles with his wives, his garden grows yams, and he is respected by his fellow villagers. When he accidentally kills a clansman he is banished from the village for seven years. The ultimate causes of his downfall are his blindness to circumstances and the influence of the missionary church, which brings with it the new authority of the British District Commissioner.

His unwillingness to change sets him apart from the community, and he tries to fight colonialism single-handedly. Achebe took the novel's title from a line from the poem 'The Second Coming' by **W. B. Yeats**: 'Things fall apart; the centre cannot hold.'

No Longer At Ease (1960), set in the 1950s, examines the interaction between native and colonial cultures in the urban setting of Lagos. *Arrow of God* (1964) returns to the tribal setting of *Things Fall Apart* but, being set in the 1920s, explores a later stage of colonialism. The central character is Ezeulu, a priest, who sends one of his sons to missionary school and gains a measure of approval from the English district superintendent. However, Ezeulu is doomed because when defending the traditions of his people he is afraid of losing his authority and unable to reach a compromise.

A Man of the People (1966) satirises the power struggles and corruption in a post-independence African state in the 1960s. The two central characters are Nanga, the Minister of Culture, and the teacher Odili, who tells the story. Odili takes a stand against the government, not for ideological reasons but because Nanga has seduced his girlfriend. Their political confrontation becomes violent, Nanga's thugs cause havoc and the army responds by staging a coup. The novel reflects Achebe's deep personal disappointment with what Nigeria has become since independence.

Anthills of the Savannah (1987) is a polyvocal text with multiple narrators. The story is set in an imaginary West African state where Sam, a Sandhurst-trained military officer, has become president. Chris Oriko and Ikem Osodi, his friends, die while resisting brutal abuse of power. A military coup eliminates Sam and Beatrice Okah – Chris's London-educated girlfriend – is entrusted, with her community of women, with restoring political sanity.

In 1983, upon the death of Mallan Aminu Kano, Achebe was elected deputy national president of the People's Redemption Party. As the director of Heinemann Educational Books in Nigeria, he has encouraged and published the work of dozens of African writers. In 1984 he founded the bilingual magazine *Uwa ndi Igbo*, a valuable source for Igbo studies.

Achebe has also published collections of short stories, poetry and books for children. His collections of essays include *Beware, Soul Brother* (1971) on his experiences during the civil war, *Morning Yet on Creation Day* (1975), *Hopes and Impediments* (1988) and his long essay 'The Trouble With Nigeria' (1983). In the essay 'An Image of Africa: Racism in Conrad's Heart of Darkness' (1975) he argues that while Joseph Conrad's *Heart of Darkness* is a condemnation of imperial exploitation, it also displays racist attitudes. On Achebe's 70th birthday in November 2000, Wole Soyinka said: 'Achebe never hesitates to lay blame for the woes of the African continent squarely where it belongs.'

References

1. **Sengupta, Somini** (2000) *Chinua Achebe: A Storyteller Far From Home.* The New York Times on the Web, www.nytimes.com/learning/general/featured_articles/000112wednesday.html (accessed 19.6.04)

2. Ibid.

3. **Slattery, Katharine** (1998) *The African Trilogy – 'writing back' to Mister Johnson.* From The Imperial Archive, Queen's University, Belfast. www.qub.ac.uk/en/imperial/nigeria/writback.htm (accessed 21.6.04)

Selected works:

Things Fall Apart (1958); No Longer At Ease (1960); The Sacrificial Egg And Other Stories (1962); Arrow of God (1964); A Man of The People (1966); Kansan Mies Chike And The River (1966); Beware, Soul Brother (1971); Girls at War (1972); How the Leopard got his Claws (1972); Christmas in Biafra and other Poems (1973); Morning Yet on Creation Day (1975); The Drum (1977); The Flute (1977); Literature and Society (1980); The Trouble With Nigeria (1983); The World of Ogbanje (1986); Anthills of the Savanna (1987); The University and The Leadership Factor in Nigerian Politics (1988); Hopes and Impediments (1989); Nigerian Topics (1989); The Heinemann Book of Contemporary African Short Stories (ed. with C. L. Innes) (1992); Home and Exile (2000).

Further reading

Emenyonu, Ernest N., *Emerging Perspectives on Chinua Achebe.* Africa World Press, 2004.

Okpewho, Isidore (ed.) *Chinua Achebe's 'Things Fall Apart': A Casebook*, Oxford University Press Inc, USA, 2003.

Contributors: Petri Liukkonen, Ian Mackean

This entry is an edited version of an article originally published on 'Books and Writers' at www.kirjasto.sci.fi

ALBEE, EDWARD (1928–)

We neither love nor hurt because we do not try to reach each other.

The Zoo Story

Edward Albee has written and directed some of the greatest plays of modern American drama. He won a New York Drama Critics' Circle Award for *Who's Afraid Of Virginia Woolf?* (1962) and went on to win three Pulitzer Prizes, for *A Delicate Balance* (1966), *Seascape* (1975) and *Three Tall Women* (1994). *The Goat, or Who is Sylvia?* (2002) also won a New York Drama Critics' Circle Award.

Albee was born in Virginia and adopted as an infant by a wealthy theatrical family. Although brought up in luxury, he did not have a happy childhood, finding the rigidity of his strong-minded adoptive mother suffocating. He attended various private schools, where his chief interest was writing poetry and fiction. He moved to New York City at the age of 20 and lived there in relative poverty, working at odd jobs.

In his early plays such as *The Zoo Story* (1958) and *The American Dream* (1961), Albee experimented with the **Theatre of the Absurd**. *The Zoo Story* is essentially an extended monologue by a drifter who seeks out human contact, however one-sided, to relieve his isolation. Desperate to prove his existence he gets himself killed with the unintentional help of a stranger he meets in a park. The play was designed to shock audiences out of complacency and bring them face to face with the painful facts of life. The appearance on the American stage of this tragically alienated character, Jerry, with his powerful rhetoric, had a similar effect to that of John Osborne's Jimmy Porter in *Look Back in Anger* (1956) on the British stage. Albee was hailed as the new voice of contemporary American life and the leader of a new theatrical movement. He

gained a reputation for displaying the suffering of a host of lonely characters previously ignored by American drama.

Following *The Zoo Story*, Albee wrote a series of one-act plays: *The Death of Bessie Smith* (1960), *The Sand Box* (1960) and *The American Dream*, which exemplifies Albee's trademark of a middle-class American family living on illusion and dominated by an overbearing woman. It is a dark and grotesque comedy, a satire on, and condemnation of, impoverished American values and emptiness of spirit. On the one hand it resembles *Death of a Salesman* by **Arthur Miller**, having a domestic setting; on the other it resembles Ionesco's *Bald Soprano* in its depiction of highly exaggerated characters.

Albee's first full-length play, *Who's Afraid of Virginia Woolf?*, is unquestionably his best and holds a place beside the best of Eugene O'Neill, **Tennessee Williams** and Arthur Miller in the history of American drama. It portrays the venomous marriage of one of the most memorable couples of western literature, George and Martha. The couple treat each other, and their guests, to a night of heavy drinking, accompanied by dangerous and psychologically twisted verbal games. By the end of the night a shocking truth emerges – having blamed each other for their adult son leaving home, it emerges that the son is a figment of their combined fantasy, which they have maintained for 21 years as a defence against fear, alienation and the disappointments of life. Dominated by insecurity, like Jerry of *The Zoo Story*, their hateful behaviour and uncontrolled expression of emotions are their way of dealing with the challenges of survival. The play is superbly constructed in its intellectual dialogue, violent emotional outbursts and the way it gradually exposes the social pretence of the couple. Albee's message is that living under illusions becomes destructive to any relationship. The title is unconnected with **Virginia Woolf**, but is borrowed from the children's song 'Who's Afraid of the Big Bad Wolf?', which symbolises the fears and insecurities of modern life. The themes of the play do, however, have resonances with those explored in Woolf's work.

The passionate quality and theatrical power of *The Zoo Story* and *Who's Afraid of Virginia Woolf?* began to fade in Albee's subsequent plays, being replaced by dry intellectuality, although his wit and cutting dialogue remained undiminished. *A Delicate Balance* dealt with issues similar to those explored in *Who's Afraid of Virginia Woolf?*, but in a more moderate manner. The two plays are linked in the way they recognise that social norms, family rituals and even devious behaviour are defence mechanisms against an **existential** fear that cannot be named. *A Delicate Balance* is about a married couple, Tobias and Agnes, who unexpectedly have to give refuge to some friends whose presence disrupts the precarious peace and civility and the illusion of normality in the household. The result is a display of antisocial, hysterical, aggressive and altogether grotesque behaviour by the family members. The line between sanity and insanity becomes very thin. The premise of the first part of the play has an affinity with *The Iceman Cometh* by Eugene O'Neill – it is better to live an illusion than to suffer a disrupting influence.

With *Seascape,* a charming and entertaining fantasy, Albee produced a liveliness and lightness that had been absent from his plays for over a decade. A middle-aged couple, Nancy and Charlie, meet Sarah and Leslie, two amphibians who are about to evolve. The amphibians are very much like humans, with middle-class human values and friction in their marriage. The creatures have doubts about evolving when they realise that human emotions can be painful. The evolution is a metaphor for the uncertainty about what to do when one stage of human life comes to an end. The play ends with Nancy and Charlie promising to help the amphibians with their quest to become human, their commitment arising from their recognition that the end of one stage in life can be the entry into another.

In the 1970s and 1980s, Albee's production slowed down and his plays were not commercially successful. He became frustrated with the theatre and felt audiences did not understand him. The plays of this period continued to be studies in cold intellectuality, lacking dramatic vitality, giving the impression that the dramatist was talking to himself in a private discourse. In contrast to the feverish emotions and struggle for survival of his earlier characters, the people inhabiting his plays now avoided emotional engagement with life.

In 1994 Albee recaptured the verve of his earlier plays with *Three Tall Women*, which was a success. The storyline is very simple: a haughty, bitter old woman lies dying, attended by two other women and visited by a young man. The play, with **postmodern** tensions, has three separate women in the first act, who become the same 'everywoman', at different stages of her life, in the second act. Albee's frank dialogue probes old age without sentimentality. The play is about forgiveness, reconciliation and fate, presented through Albee's black sense of humour. The women expose the bare truths of life – how people live and love, what they settle for and how they die.

The Goat, or Who is Sylvia? (2002), a witty and hilarious but disturbing play, is his most controversial to date. Martin, a successful architect living harmoniously with his wife Stevie and their homosexual son, falls in love with Sylvia, a goat, and when his bizarre secret comes out the whole family structure is destroyed. What starts as a drawing-room comedy turns into a tragedy of marital infidelity with a shocking difference. There is also a hint of incest between the father and son. The play's concern is to test our limits of tolerance. By transgressing taboos it challenges us to question whether the limits our civilisation enforces are arbitrary, what the nature and meaning of love is and who decides what behaviour is normal and acceptable.

Albee's varied work shows the influence of **Samuel Beckett**, Eugene Ionesco, Tennessee Williams and Arthur Miller. He depicts humankind's inability to communicate, and the human need for integration and involvement with others. He attacks the replacement of real values with artificial ones in American society; condemns complacency, cruelty and emasculation; and challenges his audience to form opinions on various social issues. He favours the structural pattern of realistic opening, increasing emotional entanglement, peak of intensity and quick ending. To label him would impoverish a dramatist who explored and expanded the boundaries of American drama.

Selected works:

The Zoo Story (1958); *The Death of Bessie Smith* (1960); *The American Dream* (1961); *Who's Afraid of Virginia Woolf?* (1962); *The Ballad of* the Sad Café (1963); Tiny Alice (1964); A Delicate Balance (1966); Seascape (1975); Three Tall Women (1994); The Goat, or Who is Sylvia? (2002).

Further reading

Bloom, Harold (ed.) Edward Albee (Modern Critical Views), NY: Chelsea House, 2000.

Mann, Bruce J. (ed.) Edward Albee: A Casebook, NY: Taylor and Francis, 2001.

Contributor: Ünal Norman

AMIS, SIR KINGSLEY (1922–95)

It was a perfect title, in that it crystallized the article's niggling mindlessness, its funereal parade of yawn-enforcing facts, the pseudo-light it threw upon non-problems.

Lucky Jim

Kingsley Amis's novel *Lucky Jim* (1954) earned him a place among the first of the writers known in the 1950s as the **Angry Young Men**. However, while John Osborne, in *Look Back in Anger* (1956), the play which gave the group its name, expressed rebellious resentment and bitterness, Amis channelled his energies into comedy and social satire. As well as novels and essays Amis wrote literary criticism and several volumes of poetry. He was awarded the Booker Prize for *The Old Devils* in 1986 and was knighted in 1990. His son is the successful novelist **Martin Amis**.

Amis was born in Norbury, a suburb south of London, and educated at the City of London School and St John's College, Oxford. He served as a lieutenant in the Second World War and later taught at universities in England, Wales and America.

His first novel, *Lucky Jim*, a satire on academia and campus life, achieved immediate popularity on its publication in 1954 and won a Somerset Maugham Award the following year. The social background to the novel, and to the work of the Angry Young Men as a group, was the rise of a generation of young people from middle- and lower-class backgrounds who had gained access to higher edu-

cation as a result of changes in the English education system brought about by the Education Act of 1944. Having risen in society they then challenged the existing establishment, both social and literary, which was controlled by those from more privileged and traditional backgrounds.

In the story, the protagonist, Jim Dixon, has risen from his lower-middle-class background and begun a career as a lecturer at a provincial university but finds himself frustrated and infuriated by an academic establishment dominated by those from more privileged backgrounds than his own. Jim's colleagues, his social 'superiors' against whom the satire is directed, are shown to be pretentious and hypocritical, in both their social behaviour and their academic work.

Jim finds his way through the pretensions of others by following his instincts about what is worthwhile and what is false, and by learning to trust in his luck. The theme of luck is relevant in a number of ways, from the luck which determines one's social status to the good and bad luck in Jim's day-to-day affairs which provide much of the humour of the novel. When, at the end, he finally gains a better job and wins the girl of his choice, luck has played a part, but his honesty has helped to bring the luck his way and his courage has helped him grasp it.

Jim Dixon appears again in two other novels which satirise pretension and snobbery. In *That Uncertain Feeling* (1955) he is a small-town librarian in Wales, and in *I Like It Here* (1958), which drew on Amis's experience of visiting Portugal, he is a writer abroad.

Lucky Jim is sometimes called a 'campus novel', having the theme of university life in common with John Wain's first novel, *Hurry on Down*, published a few months earlier in 1954, and later novels such as *The Masters* (1951) by C. P. Snow, *The History Man* (1975) by Malcolm Bradbury, and a number of novels by David Lodge, including *Changing Places* (1975).

At Oxford Amis met and became friends with **Philip Larkin**. They shared a love of jazz music, discussed their writing projects, and *Lucky Jim* was published with a dedication to Larkin. The two remained lifelong friends and had similar views on poetry, which resulted in their both having poems published in anthologies which became known as key works of **The Movement**: *Poets of the 1950s* (1955), edited by D. J. Enright, and *New Lines* (1956), edited by Robert Conquest. The Movement poets, in reaction against what they saw as the elitism and pretension of **Modernist** writers, such as those of the **Bloomsbury Group**, and the unrestrained experimentation of poets such as **Dylan Thomas**, wrote careful, disciplined verse. Other Movement poets included Thom Gunn, D. J. Enright, John Wain and Elizabeth Jennings.

After the death of Ian Fleming, Amis wrote a James Bond novel, *Colonel Sun* (1968), under the pseudonym Robert Markham. In his later novels he moved away from social comedy to explore other types of fiction. *The Riverside Villas Murder* (1973) is a detective story which reconstructs a murder which took place in the 1930s, the era of Amis's childhood. *Ending Up* (1974) deals with old age, while *The Alteration* (1976) explores the prospect of the Reformation never having taken place and the Papacy retaining its power.

Amis also published several works of literary criticism, including a critique of science fiction, *New Maps of Hell* (1960), *The James Bond Dossier* (1965), *What Became of Jane Austen?* (1975) and *Rudyard Kipling and His World* (1975).

Selected works:

Bright November (1947); *A Frame of Mind* (1953); *Poems: Fantasy Portraits* (1954); *Lucky Jim* (1954); *That Uncertain Feeling* (1955); *A Case of Samples: Poems 1946–1956* (1956); *I Like It Here* (1958); *Take A Girl Like You* (1960); *New Maps of Hell* (1960); *My Enemy's Enemy* (1962); *The Evans County* (1962); *One Fat Englishman* (1963); *The Egyptologist* – with Robert Conquest (1965); *The James Bond Dossier* (1965); *The Anti-Death League* (1966); *A Look Around the Estate* (1967); *I Want It Now* (1968); *Colonel Sun* – as Robert Markham (1968); *The Green Man* (1969); *Girl, 20* (1971); *On Drink* (1972); *The Riverside Villas Murder* (1973); *Ending Up* (1974); *Rudyard Kipling and His World* (1975); *What Became of Jane Austen and Other Questions* (1975); *The Alteration* (1976); *Jake's Thing* (1978); *Russian Hide and Seek* (1980); *Every Day Drinking* (1983); *How's Your Glass?* (1984); *Stanley and The Women* (1984); *The Old Devils* (1986); *Difficulties With Girls* (1988); *The Folks That Live on the Hill* (1990);

Memoirs (1991); *Mr Barrett's Secret and Other Stories* (1993); *The Russian Girl* (1994); *You Can't Do Both* (1994); *The King's English: A Guide to Modern Usage* (1998); *The Letters of Kingsley Amis* – edited by Zachary Leader (2002).

Further reading

Carpenter, Humphrey, *The Angry Young Men: a Literary Comedy of the 1950s*, Allen Lane, 2002.

McDermott, John, *Kingsley Amis, an English Moralist*, Palgrave Macmillan, 1989.

Contributor: Ian Mackean

AMIS, MARTIN (1949–)

If you are interested in ugliness and sleaze, and the comedy of that, then London is absolutely the place to be.[1]

Martin Louis Amis, who has been one of the most prominent English writers since the 1970s, is the son of Hilary Bardwell and the late **Sir Kingsley Amis**. His step-mother is the novelist Elizabeth Jane Howard. In 1983 he was listed as one of the 'Best Young British Novelists' by *Granta* magazine, along with fellow authors such as Julian Barnes, **Ian McEwan** and **Salman Rushdie**.

Amis's writing is notable for its dark humour and surprising moral undercurrents, and a recurring, but not exclusive, interest in metropolitan life in contemporary England. In the context of London settings, Amis explores the darker aspects of English society, in particular the violence implicit in some areas of youth culture, and the cruelty arising from envy between friends and between different classes. His style is expansive, revealing his admiration of American writers such as **Saul Bellow** and **Vladimir Nabokov**.

Amis graduated with first class honours in English from Exeter College, Oxford. From 1972 to 1975 he was an editorial assistant for *The Times Literary Supplement*, later becoming the assistant editor. Between 1977 and 1979 he was the literary editor of *The New Statesman* and he continues to contribute articles regularly to newspapers and magazines. His first novel, *The Rachel Papers* (1973), a story of adolescence, won a Somerset Maugham

Award in 1974 and was filmed in 1989. His second novel, *Dead Babies* (1975), about a group of young people indulging in sex and drugs over a weekend, was also filmed, in 2001.

Success (1978), and *Other People: A Mystery Story* (1981), were quickly followed by one of his best-known novels, *Money: A Suicide Note* (1984), which satirises the amoral value system of Britain in the 1980s under Margaret Thatcher. There is a **postmodern** element in all of Amis's fiction, and *Money* includes an appearance by the author in a self-reflexive excursion into **metafiction**. This twist is furthered by the name of the first-person narrator – John Self – adding a dimension of self-parody. But Self, a typical Amis **antihero**, should not be taken entirely as a self-portrait. In *Experience* (2000) Amis comments:

It would be a ferocious slander of Martin Amis (who was, incidentally, a minor character in this book) if I called *Money* autobiographical. It certainly wasn't *higher* autobiography. But I see now that the story turned on my own preoccupations: it is about tiring of being single; and it is about the fear that childlessness will condemn you to childishness.[2]

In 1987 Amis published a volume of short stories, *Einstein's Monsters*, which considers the dangers of the nuclear age, and the sense of impending apocalypse was continued in his next novel, *London Fields* (1989), which, like much of his fiction, was set in contemporary London.

Time's Arrow: or the Nature of the Offence (1991) is the only one of Amis's novels to date that has been short-listed for the Booker Prize. The novel is narrated by what appears to be the soul of a man who is initially called 'Tod Friendly', although as the novel progresses it is revealed that Tod is a pseudonym. Tod's life story is told backwards, from death to birth, and the reader eventually learns that he had been a doctor at Auschwitz. Amis said that he inverted time, by beginning at the end, 'because Auschwitz is a psychotically inverted world and one of the bedrocks of Nazism was the complete inversion of the doctor's role.'[3]

The Information (1995) is based on the differing fortunes of, and rivalry between, two male friends who are both novelists. As a novel about novel-writing it self-consciously exploits the technique of metafiction. It also mocks the publishing and writing industry, and humorously sabotages the possibility of friendship between authors. *Night Train* (1997) marks a departure in style, being a pastiche of American detective fiction. *Yellow Dog* (2003) is set in England and the United States and is typical of Amis's work in its sharp humour, its interest in class difference and privilege, and its focus on criminal behaviour.

In 2002 Amis published his autobiography, *Experience*, which won the James Tait Black Memorial Prize for biography. Other non-fiction works include *Koba the Dread: Laughter and the Twenty Million* (2002), which analyses the effects of Stalin's power, and also examines his father's attitudes towards Communism. Three collections of his non-fiction essays have been published: *The Moronic Inferno and Other Visits to America* (1986), *Visiting Mrs Nabokov and Other Excursions* (1993) and *The War Against Cliché* (2001).

References

1. **Amis, Martin** (2000) quoted in Bigsby, Christopher. *Writers in Conversation Volume One With Christopher Bigsby.* University of East Anglia: EAS Publishing, p. 44. (Hereafter referred to as 'Bigsby'.)

2. **Amis, Martin** (2000) *Experience.* London: Jonathan Cape, p. 177.

3. **Bigsby**, p. 33.

Selected works:
The Rachel Papers (1973); *Dead Babies* (1975); *Success* (1978); *Other People: A Mystery Story* (1981); *The Invasion of the Space Invaders* (1982); *Money: A Suicide Note* (1984); *The Moronic Inferno and Other Visits to America* (1986); *Einstein's Monsters* (1987); *London Fields* (1989); *Time's Arrow: or the Nature of the Offence* (1991); *Visiting Mrs Nabokov and Other Excursions* (1993); *The Information* (1995); *Night Train* (1997); *Heavy Water and Other Stories* (1998); *Experience* (2000); *Koba the Dread: Laughter and the Twenty Million* (2002); *Yellow Dog* (2003).

Contributor: Julie Ellam

**ATWOOD,
MARGARET (1939–)**

*Fiction is where individual
memory and experience
and collective memory and
experience come together.*[1]

Photo credit: © PA Photos-EPA

Margaret Eleanor Atwood ranks among the foremost modern Canadian authors, as well as being one of the most prominent Canadian cultural figures of all time. She has excelled in both poetry and fiction, her work having been awarded many literary prizes both in Canada and abroad.

Born in Ottawa, Atwood spent long periods of her childhood with her family in the Quebec bush, where her entomologist father carried out his fieldwork for months at a time. Her later childhood and adolescence were spent in Toronto, a city which features frequently in her work. Having developed an interest in writing while at high school, she felt inspired to pursue it further when, while studying at the University of Toronto, she came into contact with celebrated Canadians of the 1950s and 1960s, such as the critic Northrop Frye, and the poet Jay Macpherson. After obtaining her B.A. in 1961, she went to Radcliffe College, in Cambridge, Massachusetts, to study for an M.A.

Atwood first made her reputation as a poet, gaining recognition with *The Circle Game*, which won the Governor General's Award for Poetry in 1967. Several other collections followed throughout the 1970s, earning her a name as a representative poetic voice of a new generation of Canadian writers. Particularly notable was *The Journals of Susanna Moodie* (1970), which used the poetic persona of a well-known writer of Victorian Canada to explore the representation of gender and national identity. This productive period culminated with the publication of an anthology, *Selected Poems*, in 1976. Thereafter Atwood continued to publish poetry, but not as abundantly as before, as she was turning her attention to fiction. Two further anthologies collected her later poetic output: *Selected Poems II: Poems Selected and New, 1976–1986* (1986) and *Eating Fire: Selected*

Poems 1965–1995 (1998).

Atwood's first novel, *The Edible Woman* (1969), was well received, but it was *Surfacing* (1972) that gave her a name as a novelist in critical circles, mainly due to its stylistic innovations. Both novels are set in contemporary Canada and deal with the problems of young women in western societies. In *The Edible Woman*, Marian MacAlpin, after becoming engaged, is beset by emotional distress which escalates into anorexia nervosa. In *Surfacing*, an unnamed first-person narrator travels to the Quebec wilderness in search of her missing father, and in the process undergoes a deep personal transformation. Atwood's two other novels of the 1970s, *Lady Oracle* and *Life Before Man*, were also popular, keeping her in the spotlight as one of Canada's most outstanding young writers. Her first collection of short stories, *Dancing Girls*, was published in 1977, and has been followed by further compilations.

International acclaim came for Atwood in the 1980s with her novel *The Handmaid's Tale* (1985), which won the Governor General's Award for Fiction in English (1986), was shortlisted for the Booker Prize, and was made into a film (1990). Set in the future, *The Handmaid's Tale* describes a totalitarian society where women are wholly dependent on men, and classified according to their function. The 'handmaids' of the title are used for breeding in a world where births have become scarce. The narrator, Offred, is a handmaid, and her struggle to survive in the hostile circumstances forms the basis of Atwood's examination of the past, present, and possible future of western society. The novel has been compared to other famous **dystopian** fictions of the twentieth century, such as *Brave New World* (1932) by **Aldous Huxley** and *Nineteen Eighty-four* (1948) by **George Orwell**, but Atwood's **feminist** perspective was unique.

In the 1990s Atwood's international reputation went beyond that of any other Canadian writer, as her books were translated into many languages, and she continued to receive major awards for her fiction and poetry, such as the Commonwealth Writer's Prize for her 1993 novel *The Robber Bride*, and the Booker Prize for *The Blind Assassin* in 2000.

From early in her career Atwood strove to make Canadian literature better known and more respected both within and without her country. In 1972 her book *Survival: A Thematic Guide to Canadian Literature* posed questions about the existence and make-up of a distinctive Canadian literature. The work was controversial, because the Canadian public of the time did not care much for the national literature, and at school and university it was the English and American classics that were taught. In this and in her later critical pieces, *Second Words* (1982), *Strange Things* (1995) and *Negotiating with the Dead* (2002), Atwood has sought to promote Canadian literature, and to reflect on the writer's role in society. Atwood is committed to social issues, being involved in environmental and humanitarian causes.

Atwood's fictional style reflects her concerns with the role of writers and the function of storytelling. Her novels implicitly raise questions concerning the perspective of the narrator, usually by providing a first-person narrator with whom readers can identify, but who proves to be an **unreliable narrator**. Moreover, her stories tend to be open-ended. As a result of these techniques, readers are often puzzled because they fail to find a simple answer, or a clear resolution of the situations and problems described. This is Atwood's way of involving the reader in the act of fiction-making, an approach she shares with other **postmodernist** writers. Atwood is also concerned with the politics of representation, that is, to what extent art can be used in the service of political or social power, and how the artist gains power over the artistic object. Her writing, both poetry and fiction, often refers to photographs, paintings and mirrors in relation to these issues.

Atwood focuses on women's problems in western societies, and in particular on the way violence against women continues to be common even in those countries where the goal of gender equality seems to have been reached. For Atwood, women are too often powerless victims, and they have to learn to take control of their own bodies and lives. This struggle is seen in the context of the past (*Alias Grace*, and *The Blind Assassin*), the present (*Lady Oracle*, *Bodily Harm* and *The Robber Bride*), and the future (*The Handmaid's Tale*, *Oryx and Crake*). Men are often the villains in terms of the power they hold over women, and the way the power they hold over women, and the way

they use it. But equally important is each woman's relationship with other women, sometimes mothers, but more often friends, whose assistance or example helps them survive in times of trouble. In this way Atwood's novels do not simply convey one woman's plight, but more often than not they collect many women's lives in the voice of a female narrator.

Reference

1. **Atwood, Margaret** (1997) *In Search of Alias Grace.* University of Ottawa, p. 3.

Selected works:

Poetry: *The Circle Game* (1966); *The Animals in That Country* (1968); *The Journals of Susanna Moodie* (1970); *Procedures for Underground* (1970); *Power Politics* (1971); *You Are Happy* (1974); *Selected Poems 1965–1975* (1976); *Two-Headed Poems* (1978); *True Stories* (1981); *Interlunar* (1984); *Selected Poems II: Poems Selected and New, 1976–1986* (1986); *Morning in the Burned House* (1995); *Eating Fire: Selected Poems, 1965–1995* (1998). **Novels:** *The Edible Woman* (1969); *Surfacing* (1972); *Lady Oracle* (1976); *Life Before Man* (1979); *Bodily Harm* (1981); *The Handmaid's Tale* (1985); *Cat's Eye* (1988); *The Robber Bride* (1993); *Alias Grace* (1996); *The Blind Assassin* (2000); *Oryx and Crake* (2003). **Short Stories:** *Dancing Girls* (1977); *Murder in the Dark; Short Fictions and Prose Poems* (1983); *Bluebeard's Egg* (1983); *Wilderness Tips* (1991); *Good Bones* (1992). **Criticism:** *Survival: A Thematic Guide to Canadian Literature* (1972); *Second Words: Selected Critical Prose* (1982); *Strange Things: The Malevolent North in Canadian Literature* (1995); *Negotiating with the Dead: On Writers and Writing* (2002).

Further reading

Cooke, Nathalie, *Margaret Atwood: A Biography*. ECW Press, 1998.

Cuder, Pilar, *Margaret Atwood, A Beginner's Guide*. Hodder & Stoughton, 2003.

Howells, Coral Ann, *Margaret Atwood*. Macmillan, 1996.

Contributor: Pilar Cuder Domínguez

AUDEN, W. H. (1907–73)

Out of the mirror they stare,
Imperialism's face
And the international wrong.

September 1, 1939

Wystan Hugh Auden, the son of a prominent doctor and a nurse, was sent away from his home in Birmingham to private boarding schools from the age of eight. At the first of these, St. Edmund's in Hindhead, Surrey, he met Christopher Isherwood who was to remain a life-long friend and literary collaborator. Other writers closely associated with Auden are Stephen Spender, Cecil Day-Lewis and Louis MacNeice. They were regarded as the foremost writers of the 1930s, and a poem by Stephen Spender, 'The Pylons', earned the group the nick-name the **Pylon Poets**. Their verses included everyday subjects such as trams, ships and trains, as well as electricity pylons, in contrast to the picturesque landscapes of the **Georgian Poets**, emphasising that the poetic past was dead and buried.

It's farewell to the drawing room's
civilised cry
The professor's sensible whereto and why
The frock-coated diplomat's social
aplomb
Now matters are settled with gas and with
bomb.
[From 'Song For The New Year', 1937]

Under his father's influence Auden had intended to become an engineer, but at Oxford University he started to write, and changed his course of study to English. His first poems were printed by Stephen Spender on a hand press in 1928, and were imitative of **W. B. Yeats** who was regarded as the greatest poet of the time.

Auden is credited with bringing a naturalness to the language of poetry, though he did include some Classical references and obscure vocabulary in his writing. His themes turned on social and political issues, avoiding what he considered to be the comfy verses of the popular bourgeois writers. Indeed, he came to regard his own early poems as **Marxist** and altered or cut them in later editions of his works, considering them as more polemical than poetic.

Comrades who when the sirens roar
From office shop and factory pour
'Neath evening sky;
By cops directed to the fug
Of talkie-houses for a drug
Or down canals to find a hug
Until you die:
[From 'A Communist to Others', 1933]

At Gresham's School in Norfolk, which he attended from 1920 to 1925 before going to Oxford, he had come across the verse of George Crabbe (1754–1832) which described the harsh reality of village life, as opposed to the traditional **Romantic** view of countryside. Auden was influenced by the grittiness of Crabbe, the directness of William Blake, the urban poems of working class London written by W. E. Henley, and the strangely individualistic poetry of **Gerard Manley Hopkins**. He was also influenced by the War Poets who had brought war and death to poetry in an **anti-heroic** manner.

In 1930, when Auden's first professional work appeared, Europe was changing politically. A dozen years after the end of the First World War, the continent that had seen itself as master of the world in 1900 was dogged by Depression and the rise of both Communism and Fascism. The old world of privilege, from which the young group of writers around Auden came, was under threat.

Auden visited Berlin in 1928, and was joined there by Isherwood, who stayed on until 1934 and observed and wrote on the closing years of the Weimar Republic. From 1930 to 1935 Auden worked as a schoolteacher in Scotland and Northumberland. In this period he brought out his second volume of poetry which acknowledged the work of Bertolt Brecht and Kurt Weill, whose *Threepenny Opera* (*Die Dreigroschenoper* – a work adapted from *The Beggar's Opera* of John Gay, 1685–1732) he had seen performed in Berlin.

He visited Iceland, Spain and China in the later 1930s, and wrote accounts of his travels as well as poems. His interest in Marxism was waning and after the Spanish Civil War he turned increasingly towards Christianity, or, more exactly in the United States, to

Episcopalianism, which is close to the Church of England.

His visit to China followed the Japanese sack of Nanking in which tens of thousands of the city's inhabitants were slaughtered. He saw the world as filled with places of evil and looked for a refuge. In 1939, just before the outbreak of the Second World War, he and Isherwood moved to America, where Auden subsequently took US citizenship. He often recounted one of the Immigration Officer's questions on his arrival in New York: 'Can you write?'

Auden and Isherwood were condemned by British writers such as **Evelyn Waugh** and **Anthony Powell** for desertion and for their blatant homosexuality, Waugh referring to them as 'Parsnip and Pimpernell' in *Put Out More Flags* (1942). Although in 1935 Auden married Erika Mann, daughter of the German writer Thomas Mann, it was a marriage of convenience which allowed her to obtain a British passport and escape from Nazi Germany. Chester Kallman (1921–75) became Auden's male partner in the United States and was with Auden when he died in Austria in 1973.

In New York, Auden heard the British ultimatum to Germany, following the invasion of Poland, in response to which he wrote the poem 'September 1, 1939'.

Accurate scholarship can
Unearth the whole offence
From Luther until now
That has driven a culture mad,
Find what occurred at Linz,
What huge imago made
A psychopathic god:
I and the public know
What all schoolchildren learn,
Those to whom evil is done
Do evil in return.

This is the Auden of uneven lines and irregular metre, who likes to end a stanza with a well-turned rhyme, and make almost casual references to history and culture which assume an echo sounding in the mind of an equally educated reader. Here Auden is writing in the manner of a grand European poet for whom the present is constantly referenced to the past. The poetry displays a gift of understanding and clarification of thought; but it tends towards clever comment by a man to whom

ideas and words came easily and whose conversation often expended itself in mockery among like-minded companions.

The poem 'September 1, 1939', may not have found an immediate echo among New Yorkers, because the 'Old World' of Europe was remote, but it was remembered after 11 September 2001.

Into this neutral air
Where blind skyscrapers use
Their full height to proclaim
The strength of Collective Man,
Each language pours its vain
Competitive excuse:
But who can live for long
In an euphoric dream;
Out of the mirror they stare,
Imperialism's face
And the international wrong.

This is not the only poem of foreboding which Auden wrote in New York. The words 'Out of the mirror' are echoed in 'The Sea and the Mirror: A Verse Commentary on The Tempest', written in September 1943, in which Auden gives dramatic monologues to Shakespeare's characters. When Alonso speaks to Ferdinand of how he will ascend the throne of Naples majestically, he ends with a caution more ancient than Christian: beware good fortune, for the Gods visit Hubris with Nemesis.

Remember when
Your climate seems a permanent home
For marvellous creatures and great men,
What griefs and convulsions startled
Rome,
Ecbatana, Babylon.

Auden continued to write for another 30 years and was awarded a Pulitzer Prize in 1948. **Seamus Heaney** has commented on a falling off of style, but **Dylan Thomas** wrote 'I think he is a wide and deep poet and that his first narrow angles of pedantry and careful obscurity are worn almost all away.' Together with Kallman, in 1951, Auden wrote a libretto for Stravinsky's *Rake's Progress*, based on the series of drawings by Hogarth, and it was hard to tell which bit was Kallman and which Auden.

Auden spent a short time as a researcher with the US forces in Europe after the Second

World War, then lectured in the United States, renting an Italian villa in Ischia every summer, and returned to England only when appointed Professor of Poetry at Oxford from 1956 to 1961; after which he was made a Fellow of Christ Church. At Oxford he attracted curiosity by holding afternoon chats in a tea shop where students might approach and ask questions – though never a question about the meaning of an Auden poem. The old Oxford atmosphere of the 1920s and 1930s had vanished with the war and Auden was beginning to appear a relic of a bygone age. He bought a house in Kirchstetten in Austria where he lived for part of each year along with Chester Kallman until his death at the age of 66.

Auden was concerned with the question of whether or not poetry had a use, and believed that poetry can be a form of defence against delusion – even if that defence holds that the only certainty is doubt. He criticised the views of W. B. Yeats in 'In Memory of W. B. Yeats', declaring that 'poetry makes nothing happen', but the implication is that poetry *should* have an effect on readers and society in the hands of a powerful poet. Moreover, Auden was convinced that his poetry had a readership in the sense of an audience that was waiting for him to write, not one he had to please; a readership equal to his talent.

In 'Music Is International' he wrote that poetry, like music, is:

not to be confused
With anything really important
Like feeding strays or looking pleased
when caught
By a bore or a hideola.

Music without words is beyond language and so international. Language is little more than mere sound when the meaning is incomprehensible, a point demonstrated by his invented word 'hideola' which is hideous-old-man cropped to a feminine Spanish ending. It appears to be a joke at the reader's expense.

Auden himself disowned some of his own poems later in life. Writing in the introduction to *Poetry of the Thirties*,[1] Robin Skelton says:

W. H. Auden has been monumentally generous in allowing me to use early texts of five poems of which he now

disapproves. These poems are 'Sir, No Man's Enemy', 'A Communist to Others', 'To a Writer on his Birthday', 'Spain', and 'September 1, 1939.' I have agreed to make it absolutely clear that 'Mr W. H. Auden considers these five poems to be trash which he is ashamed to have written.'

Critical arguments differ over whether Auden was a good poet, or even a great poet. Certainly he had influence. Certainly he was much read and admired by his contemporaries, and even his detractors would, no doubt, have answered the Immigration Officer's question 'Can he write?' in the affirmative.

Reference

1. **Skelton, Robin** (1964) *Poetry of the Thirties.* Penguin Books.

Selected works:

Paid On Both Sides (1928); *Poems* (1930); *The Orators prose and verse* (1932); *The Dance of Death* (1933); *Look, Stranger! in America: On This Island* (1936); *The Dog Beneath the Skin or Where is Francis?* with Christopher Isherwood (1935); *The Ascent of F.6* (1936) with Christopher Isherwood; *Spain* (1937); *Letters from Iceland* with Louis MacNiece (1937); *On the Frontier* (1938); *Journey to a War,* with Christopher Isherwood (1939); *Another Time* (1940); *The Double Man* (1941); *The Quest* (1941); *For the Time Being* (1944); *The Sea and the Mirror* (1944); *Collected Poetry* (1945); *The Age of Anxiety: A Baroque Eclogue* (1947); *Collected Shorter Poems 1930–1944* (1950); *Enchaféd Flood* (1950); *The Rake's Progress* with Chester Kallman, music by Igor Stravinsky (1951); *Nones* (1952); *The Shield of Achilles* (1955); *The Old Man's Road* (1956); *Selected Poetry* (1956); *Homage to Clio* (1960); *Elegy for Young Lovers* with Chester Kallman, music by Hans Werner Henze (1961); *The Dyer's Hand* (1962); *Selected Essays* (1964); *Collected Shorter Poems 1927–1957* (1966); *The Bassarids* with Chester Kallman, music by Hans Werner Henze (1966); *Collected Longer Poems* (1968); *City without Walls* (1969); *Academic Graffiti* (1971); *Epistle to a Godson* (1972); *Forewords and Afterwords* (1973); *Thank You, Fog: Last Poems* (1974); *Selected Poems* (1979); *Collected Poems* (1991).

Further reading

Davenport-Hines, Richard, *Auden*. London: Heinemann, 1995.

Fuller, John, *W. H. Auden: A Commentary*. London: Faber & Faber, 1998.

Contributor: Stephen Colbourn

BAINBRIDGE, BERYL (1934–)

Harriet said: 'No you don't, you keep walking.' I wanted to turn round and look back at the dark house but she tugged at my arm fiercely. We walked over the fields hand in hand as if we were little girls.

Harriet Said

Beryl Bainbridge has published 17 novels, numerous short stories, plays and works of non-fiction including travel writing and journalism. Many of her works have won literary awards, and her services to literature were recognised when she was made a Dame of the British Empire in 2000.

Born in Liverpool to parents who struggled to preserve a veneer of gentility despite bankruptcy, Bainbridge has made an art out of exploring dysfunctional family life through black humour and **Gothic** imagery. Her reliance on the Gothic can also be related to her interest in Catholic rituals, and her conversion to Catholicism in 1952. Her depictions of a run-down Britain after the war, where there were still shortages, and taking a long bath was a luxury, could be read alongside those of Stevie Smith, **Philip Larkin** and Alan Bennett. She has been seen as different from other contemporary women writers such as **Margaret Atwood** and **Angela Carter** in that her novels do not usually present overtly **feminist** gender or sexual debates, possibly because gender and class debates are intertwined in her work. Yet like Atwood and Carter, Bainbridge is sceptical about hetero-sexual romance and the nuclear family. As for literary predecessors, Bainbridge has been influenced by writers such as the Brontës, Charles Dickens, Robert Louis Stevenson and **D. H. Lawrence**.

Although much of Bainbridge's early work is set in or around Liverpool, her settings extend to Wales, in *Another Part of the Wood* (1968), London, in *The Bottle Factory Outing* (1974), and even Moscow, in *Winter Garden* (1980). Most of these novels depict a sour-sweet world where tragedy is never far off but is kept at bay by humour and grotesque portrayals of everyday life. The sinister aspect of this early fiction could be related to her wartime experiences, including being marched to the cinema with other school-children shortly after the war to be shown footage of Nazi concentration camps. These elements are still present, albeit in a different way, in her later novels, particularly in troubled characters such as Captain Scott in *The Birthday Boys* (1991), young Myrtle in *Master Georgie* (1998), and Queeney in *According to Queeney* (2001).

Random or unexplained murders, and other violent acts, frequently surprise the reader of Bainbridge's fiction. In *Harriet Said* (1972) two teenage girls murder a woman after seducing her husband. *The Dressmaker* (1973) ends with the death of the protagonist's boyfriend, a young American soldier, at the hands of her aunt, who then proceeds to hide the body. In *The Bottle Factory Outing*, a murder turns an innocent workers' day out into a sombre yet farcical symbol of their directionless lives. *Injury Time* (1997) which won a Whitbread Prize, starts as a dinner party thrown by Edward and his mistress which turns nasty when hosts and guests are taken hostage in the house. Bainbridge's claim that she writes mostly autobiographically should be treated carefully in the light of such macabre plots.

Bainbridge has always been concerned with representation and story-telling, issues central to the **postmodern** period. *An Awfully Big Adventure* (1989) which draws on her short spell as an actress in the early 1950s, tells the story of Stella, a teenager who works for a theatre company, falls in love with the director, and has an affair with one of the actors. This simple story is given psychological depth by the expressionistic characterisation of Stella, who is always looking for and rejecting love. As the novel progresses, Bainbridge transforms Stella from a sulky teenager to a tragic figure. This transformation occurs in parallel with the intertwining of mysterious messages to her missing mother, whom Stella believes to be the speaking clock, and is further complicated by intertextual allusions to J. M. Barrie's *Peter Pan* (1911) which the company is staging. Barrie's influence can also be seen in *The Birthday Boys*.

As early as 1978 Bainbridge was experimenting with the idea of fictionalising history, in *Young Adolf*, a revealing exercise in reinventing historical characters within a fictional framework. The farce of young Adolf Hitler arriving in Liverpool with artistic ambitions, a lazy disposition and the dangerous opinions that turned him into a fascist, has raised a few eyebrows. Many of the details found in *Young Adolf*, such as the fact that Hitler lived in a homeless hostel between 1910 and 1913, can be documented. The novel, however, does not make any claims to historical authenticity and concentrates instead on class and gender struggles in Liverpool.

In 1991, with *The Birthday Boys*, Bainbridge turned her full attention to the historical novel. Not only is Scott's Antarctic expedition well-documented, it is very much alive in the popular imagination. By rewriting the story of the five explorers, Bainbridge entered the realm of the respectable historical fiction writer while questioning it at the same time. *The Birthday Boys* uses multiple narrators with slightly different accounts of events to create a historical novel which, although accurately researched, does not rely on the authenticity of its representation of history. Instead, it uses historical sources to tackle the subject of the construction of myths.

Bainbridge questions other popular representations of people and events, writing about famous figures from the past, such as Dr Johnson in *According to Queeney*, collectivities, such as the passengers of the Titanic in *Everyman for Himself* (1996), or famous historical events, such as the Crimean War in *Master Georgie*. In *Everyman for Himself*, when we think of heroism in the face of death, she tells us about upper-class snobbery. In *Master Georgie* the Crimean War, well-known for episodes such as the charge of the Light Brigade and the actions of Florence Nightingale, turns into

a futile quest for masculinity and heroism in the context of a fierce critique of Victorian family structures and representations of war. In *According to Queeney*, what has been acclaimed as a portrayal of Samuel Johnson in Georgian London is also a study of memory and the biographer's role.

Bainbridge is at her best when she departs from detailed accounts and refashions her material. This applies to all her novels, including semi-autobiographical and historical works. *According to Queeney*, for example, is weighed down with details about Dr Johnson and Mrs Thrale's household. The brief, interspersed letters that the adult Queeney writes to a would-be biographer, insisting on keeping her memories private, are the most interesting aspect of the novel, interacting with the main narrative but also standing in their own right.

Selected works:

Another Part of the Wood (1968); *Harriet Said* (1972); *The Dressmaker* (1973); *The Bottle Factory Outing* (1974); *Sweet William* (1975); *A Quiet Life* (1976); *Injury Time* (1977); *Young Adolf* (1978); *Winter Garden* (1980); *English Journey or the Road to Milton Keynes* (1984); *Mum and Mr Armitage* (1985); *Watson's Apology* (1985); *Filthy Lucre* (1986; juvenilia); *An Awfully Big Adventure* (1989); *The Birthday Boys* (1991); *Something Happened Yesterday* (1993); *Collected Stories* (1994); *Everyman for Himself* (1996); *Master Georgie* (1998); *According to Queeney* (2001).

Further reading

Lassner, Phillis (1994) '"Between the Gaps": Sex, Class and Anarchy in the British Comic Novel of World War II'. In: G. Finney (ed.) *Look Who's Laughing. Gender and Comedy*, Amsterdam, Reading and Langhorne (PEN): Gordon and Breach, 205–19.

Sánchez-Arce, Ana María (2001) 'The Prop They Need: Undressing and the Politics of War in Beryl Bainbridge's *Master Georgie*'. In A. Usandizaga and A. Monnickendam (eds) *Dressing Up for War. Transformations of Gender and Genre in the Discourses and Literature of War*, Amsterdam and New York: Rodopi, 93–110.

Wennö, Elizabeth (1993) *Ironic Formula in the*

Novels of Beryl Bainbridge. Goteborg: Acta Universitatis Gothoburgensis.

Contributor: Ana María Sánchez-Arce

BALDWIN, JAMES (1924–87)

You save yourself. If you have any sense at all and if you're lucky enough, you save yourself.

Photo credit: © Bettmann/CORBIS

James Arthur Baldwin grew up in a poor household in Harlem, New York, the illegitimate son of a domestic maid, never knowing his real father. Between the ages of 14 and 16 he occasionally preached at a local revivalist church. He also began writing as a teenager, and eventually became one of the most significant American novelists and essayists of the 1950s and 1960s. His works tackle the issues of the rights of African-Americans, and the struggle for personal identity, drawing upon his own experience of being black and homosexual. He lived in Europe for several years, completing his best-known novel, *Go Tell It on the Mountain*, in Paris in 1953.

Like most courageous revolutionary thinkers, Baldwin has both enjoyed acclaim and endured scorn. During the politically-charged 1950s and 1960s in America he was an uncompromising advocate of civil rights, and a visionary leader for a country tearing itself apart with racial strife. He was recognised as one of the most important leaders of the debate on race, discussing the issue at various times with such people as Martin Luther King, Jr, Elijah Muhammad, Medgar Evers and Robert Kennedy. At the same time, because of his constant struggle to **deconstruct** definitions (socially-imposed categories), and his unwillingness to let himself be defined, he was called by some an 'Uncle Tom', and a great 'white writer' – ironic evidence of the very things he spent his life fighting against.

Baldwin's central literary concerns, like his politics, were ahead of his time, exploring issues of racial, national and sexual '**otherness**', and anticipating post-**postmodern** issues: After the system has been deconstructed, what are we left with? How do we define our identities when the old definitions have become invalid? Is identity self-determined or institutionally constructed? Baldwin's novels, plays, essays and speeches answered these questions. He specifically addresses the challenge of constructing a true, authentic identity within almost inescapable definitions of 'otherness', definitions imposed by society, by members of our own race and gender, and even by ourselves. Baldwin maintained that these definitions cannot be escaped, but they can be overcome through turning inward to find self-worth, allowing opposites to merge, and discovering nurturing community contexts.

Baldwin examined the problem of what happens when one's sense of identity is founded on a dichotomy between the demands of two social groups, when the groups are both incompatible, and inadequate in themselves. One such dichotomy was that between the 'Church' and the 'Street', and a scene early in his first novel, *Go Tell It on the Mountain*, shows the inadequacy of both. John, Baldwin's partially autobiographical protagonist, comes home to find that his brother Roy has almost been blinded in a gang fight. Their father, a preacher, immediately blames their mother's sinfulness for Roy's rebellious nature, and slaps her to the ground. John is left disgusted with both Roy (the street) and his father (the church).

The problem of constructing an identity within the confines of street and church was almost insurmountable, especially for a small, gay, black, American man like Baldwin. He specifically attacked the ways in which both the church and the street demanded escape and irresponsibility. In *The Fire Next Time* (1963), he writes about the damaging principles ingrained in their congregations by hypocritical Christian churches:

> The principles were Blindness, Loneliness, and Terror, the first principle necessarily and actively cultivated in order to deny the two others.[1]

At the same time, in the street, heroin is seen as the solution to every problem. So what's to be done when the dichotomy of influences breaks down, when the two choices for defining an identity overlap and neither is desirable? Baldwin makes it clear that mere escape is not the answer. In *Go Tell It on the Mountain*, John's father, Gabriel, attempts to escape Southern racism, only to discover that the situation is little better in the North. Baldwin himself tried to escape American racism by moving to Europe, and discovered that racism knows no borders.

Baldwin's answers are not those provided by society, but those discovered through individual introspection, community support and willingness to deal with the past. In *Go Tell It on the Mountain* the central vehicle for exploring this theme is blues music. In stark contrast to the defeatism and loneliness of the church and the street, which require people to give themselves over to either a corrupted, patriarchal hierarchy, or a needle, the blues encourages musicians to look inward for help. This, for Baldwin, is the critical point; whereas he sees the church and the street as venues for escapism, he considers the blues an honest way to come to terms with life. For Baldwin, truth could only be found individually. He said,

> You save yourself. If you have any sense at all and if you're lucky enough, you save yourself.[2]

But Baldwin also understood the importance of community, of knowing you're not alone in your troubles. In blues and jazz, the musician is allowed self-exploration, but within the supportive environment of the group. According to Baldwin, in order to be 'Saved' in the church context, one must abandon the discovery of the self, while, in contrast, although the blues does require a group mentality, it also encourages individual freedom of exploration. In his essay 'To Be an American', Baldwin explains how the blues helped him construct his own identity and overcome the overwhelming definitions of race:

> It was Bessie Smith through her tone and her cadence, who helped me to dig back to the way I myself must have spoke when I was a pickaninny, and to remember the things I had heard and seen and felt . . . She helped to reconcile me to being a 'nigger'.[3]

References

1. **James Baldwin** (1963) *The Fire Next Time*. New York: The Dial Press, p. 45.

2. **James Baldwin** (1973) *A Dialogue: James Baldwin and Nikki Giovanni*. New York: J. P. Lippincott, p. 41.

3. **James Baldwin** (1998) 'The Discovery of What It Means To Be an American', *James Baldwin: Collected Essays*. Ed. Toni Morrison, New York: Library of America, p. 138.

Selected works:

Fiction: *Go Tell It on the Mountain* (1953); *Giovanni's Room* (1956); *Another Country*, (1962); *Going to Meet the Man* (1965); *Tell Me How Long the Train's Been Gone* (1968); *If Beale Street Could Talk* (1974); *Just Above My Head* (1979). **Plays:** *The Amen Corner* (produced 1955) (1965); *Blues for Mr. Charlie* (produced 1964) (1964); *One Day, When I Was Lost: A Scenario Based on 'The Autobiography of Malcolm X'* (1972); *A Deed from the King of Spain* (produced 1974). **Non-fiction:** *Notes of a Native Son* (1955); *Nobody Knows My Name: More Notes of a Native Son* (1961); *The Fire Next Time* (1963); *Nothing Personal*, with Richard Avedon (1964); *A Rap on Race*, with Margaret Mead (1971); *No Name in the Street* (1971); *A Dialogue: James Baldwin and Nikki Giovanni* (1973); *The Devil Finds Work: An Essay* (1976); *The Evidence of Things Not Seen* (1985); *The Price of the Ticket* (1985); *Conversations with James Baldwin* (1989). **Other:** *The Inheritance* (screenplay) (1973); *Little Man, Little Man* (children's book) (1975).

Further reading

Kinnamon, Keneth (ed.) *James Baldwin*. Englewood Cliffs, N.J.: Prentice-Hall, 1974.

Miller, D. Quentin (ed.) *Re-viewing James Baldwin: Things not Seen*. Philadelphia: Temple University Press, 2000.

Contributor: Kristina Gashler

BECKETT, SAMUEL (1906–89)

VLADIMIR: We have to come back tomorrow.
ESTRAGON: What for?
VLADIMIR: To wait for Godot.
ESTRAGON: Ah! (Silence.) He didn't come?
VLADIMIR: No.

                              Waiting for Godot

Irish novelist and playwright Samuel Beckett, best known for his play, *Waiting for Godot*

(1952) won the Nobel Prize for Literature in 1969. A leading figure in the **Theatre of the Absurd**, and a major influence on British playwrights such as **Harold Pinter** and **Tom Stoppard**, he showed characters struggling to survive in an empty and meaningless universe. Writing in both English and French, he was concerned to pare language down to its minimum. His world view was uncompromisingly bleak, but he drew extensively on the forms and styles of comedy, both the verbal comedy of music hall routines, and the visual comedy of silent movie comedians such as Buster Keaton and Charlie Chaplin.

Samuel Barclay Beckett was born in Dublin into a prosperous Protestant family. He was educated at the Portora Royal School, and Trinity College, Dublin, where he specialised in French and Italian. After gaining his BA in 1927 he worked as a teacher in Belfast and lecturer at the École Normale Supérieure in Paris. In Paris he became acquainted with **James Joyce**, who was working on *Finnegan's Wake*. In 1931 Beckett returned to Dublin, received his M.A., taught briefly at Trinity College, then left to travel around Europe doing odd jobs and writing. From 1933 to 1936 he lived in London, but in 1937 he finally settled in Paris.

As a poet Beckett made his debut in 1930 with *Whoroscope*, a 98-line poem accompanied by 17 footnotes. In this dramatic monologue, the protagonist, Rene Descartes, waits for his morning omelette while meditating on obscure theological mysteries, the passage of time, and the approach of death. A critical work, *Proust*, was published in 1931, followed by *More Pricks Than Kicks*, a series of connected stories set in Dublin, in 1934. Beckett's career as a novelist began in 1938 with *Murphy*, which depicted the protagonist's inner struggle between his desire for his prostitute-mistress and his wish to escape from suffering by withdrawing into a purely mental existence. The conflict is resolved when he is atomised by a gas explosion.

When the Second World War broke out Beckett joined the French Resistance network. Sought by the Nazis, he fled with Suzanne Dechevaux-Dumesnil, his longstanding companion whom he was to marry in 1961, to Southern France, where they remained in hiding in the village of Roussillon for two and half years. Beckett worked as a farm labourer and wrote *Watt* (1953) which was the last of his novels written originally in English.

After the war Beckett worked briefly with the Irish Red Cross in Paris. Between 1946 and 1949 he produced the major prose narrative trilogy, *Molloy, Malone Meurt* and *L'Innomable*, (*Molloy, Malone Dies, The Unnameable*) which appeared in the early 1950s. The novels were written in French and subsequently translated into English with substantial changes. These books reflected Beckett's bitter realisation that there is no escape from illusion, or from the Cartesian compulsion to think and try to solve insoluble problems.

Having seen how Joyce was using the **stream of consciousness** technique to give expression to subjective thought-processes, Beckett developed the idea in his own way, using it to search for the underlying truth of man's nature, having his narrators explore the paradoxical experience of 'self', in which the self, while experiencing existence subjectively, is also able to reflect on its own experience. In contrast to Joyce's relentless exploration of language and style, Beckett waged a lifelong war on words, trying to yield the silence that underlines them.

En Attendant Godot (*Waiting for Godot*) was first performed in Paris in 1953, and quickly earned Beckett world-wide fame. The play, one of the most influential dramatic works of the twentieth century, is a tragic farce presenting an **existentialist** vision of the meaninglessness of human existence. Vladimir and Estragon, who call each other Didi and Gogo, meet near a bare tree on a country road to await the arrival of Godot. To pass the time they try to recall their past, tell jokes, and speculate about Godot. Pozzo, a bourgeois tyrant, and Lucky, his servant, appear briefly. A boy brings word that Godot will not come that day but will surely come the next. In Act II they are still waiting, and Godot sends another message. At the end of each Act they consider hanging themselves, then declare their intention to leave, but have no energy to move. The nihilistic message is delivered in clipped dialogue which is sometimes poetic, but more often comic, being reminiscent of music-hall comedy. The play's debt to comedy, even farce, is exemplified in the closing scene where Estragon's trousers fall down when, searching for a means of hanging himself, he removes the cord he has been using as a belt.

After *Waiting for Godot* Beckett wrote *Fin De Partie* (*Endgame*) (1957) and a series of stage plays and brief pieces for the radio. *Endgame* developed further one of Beckett's central themes, men in mutual dependence. Hamm and Clov occupy a room with Nagg and Nell, Hamm's parents, who live in dustbins. The blind and tyrannical Hamm, apparently unable to move from his armchair, is dependent on his servant Clov, who although determined to leave and become independent of Hamm, never actually does so. One possible approach to this play is to see the two 'characters' as aspects of one man's mind, and to see the set, with two windows in a bare wall, as the inside of a skull.

In *Krapp's Last Tape* (1959) Beckett returned to his native language. The play depicts a disgruntled old man sitting alone in his room. At night he listens to tape recordings from various periods of his past.

Just as Beckett's prose style became increasingly economical and unadorned, so did his plays. *Happy Days* (1961) is almost a monologue, delivered by the protagonist Winnie as she is progressively buried until only her head is visible. The striking image was taken a stage further in *Not I* (1973) in which only a speaking mouth is visible. Beckett also explored the possibilities of the medium of radio, as in his radio plays *All That Fall* and *Embers* (both 1959), television, as seen in his many plays for TV, such as *Eh Joe!* (1967), and film, in *Film* (1967).

Beckett continued his practice of presenting his nihilistic message through bizarrely humorous symbolic images in his last full-length novel, *Comment C'est* (*How It Is*) (1961). The protagonist crawls across the mud dragging a sack of canned food behind him. He overtakes another crawler whom he tortures into speech, then is left alone waiting to be overtaken himself by another crawler who will torture him in turn.

Beckett continued writing until his death, producing works for radio and television, as well as plays, such as *Catastrophe* (1984) which was written for the Czech playwright, poet, and political dissident, Vaclav Havel. Beckett lived on the Rue St Jacques and maintained his usual silence even when his 80th birthday was celebrated in Paris and New York. He revealed something of his aims in writing in this comment he made at the age of 76:

With diminished concentration, loss of memory, obscured intelligence . . . the more chance there is for saying something closest to what one really is. Even though everything seems inexpressible, there remains the need to express. A child needs to make a sand castle even though it makes no sense. In old age, with only a few grains of sand, one has the greatest possibility.[1]

Reference

1. **Plimpton, George** (ed.), *Playwrights at Work.* Harvill, 2000.

Selected works:

Whoroscope (1930); *Proust* (1931); *More Pricks Than Kicks* (1934); *Murphy* (1938); *Molloy* (1950); *Malone Meurt* (*Malone Dies*) (1951); *L'innommable* (*The Unnamable*) (1952); *En Attendant Godot* (*Waiting For Godot*) (1952); *Watt* (1953); *Fin De Partie* (*Endgame*) (1957); *Acte Sans Paroles* (1958); *Krapp's Last Tape* (1959); *All That Fall* (1959); *Embers* (1959); *Happy Days* (1961); *Comment C'est* (*How It Is*) (1961); *Play* (1964); *Imagination Morte Imaginez* (1965); *Film* (1967); *Va Et Vient* (*Come And Go*) (1967); *No Knife* (1967); *Eh Joe!* (1967); *Breath* (1970); *Premier Amour* (1970); *Séjour* (1970); *Not I* (1973); *Still* (1974); *Mercier Et Camier* (1974); *All Strange Away* (1976); *Ghost Trio* (1976); *That Time* (1976); *. . . But The Clouds . . .* (1977); *Mirlitonnades* (1978); *Company* (1979); *Nohow On* (1981); *Rockaby* (1982); *Ohio Impromptu* (1982); *A Piece Of Monologue* (1982); *Mal Vu Mal Dit* (*Ill Seen Ill Said*) (1982); *Worstward Ho* (1983); *What Where* (1983); *Quad* (1984); *Catastrophe* (1984); Teleplays (1988); *Le Monde Et Le Pantalon* (1989); *Stirring Still* (1989).

Further reading

Esslin, Martin, *The Theatre of the Absurd.* Penguin, 1968.

This entry is based on an article by Petri Liukkonen originally published on 'Books and Writers' at www.kirjasto.sci.fi

Contributors: Petri Liukkonen,
                                        Ian Mackean

BELLOW, SAUL (1915–)

I am an American, Chicago born –
Chicago, that somber city – and go at
things as I have taught myself, free-style,
and will make record in my own way
     The Adventures of Augie March

American writer Saul Bellow was awarded the 1976 Nobel Prize for literature, the judges praising 'the human understanding and subtle analysis of contemporary culture that are combined in his work'.[1] This award, his Pulitzer Prize of the same year, and the numerous other awards he has received throughout his prolific career, underline his distinctive position in American twentieth-century literature.

Born in Lachine, Quebec, the son of Russian-Jewish immigrant parents, Bellow grew up in the Jewish ghetto of Montreal, until his family moved to Chicago when he was nine years old. He attended the University of Chicago, receiving his bachelor's degree in anthropology and sociology in 1937. He taught at a teacher training college in Chicago from 1938 to 1942, and served in the merchant marines during the Second World War. He spent the next 15 years teaching at the Universities of New York and Princeton, and travelling to Paris and Rome on a Guggenheim Fellowship. He returned to Chicago in 1962 and since then he has been lecturing at the University of Chicago. Bellow has been married five times, his current wife being Janis Freedman who, in 2001, edited the volume *Saul Bellow: Collected Stories*.

Bellow's first novel, *Dangling Man* (1944), written in the form of a journal, shows the protagonist's estrangement from reality, and gradual retreat into solitude, while awaiting induction into the army. In *The Victim* (1947) Bellow used the journal form again, presenting a psychological study of the protagonist, Asa Leventhal, alone in New York, being unexpectedly confronted by a man from his past – Kirby Albee, a Gentile. In these two novels Bellow explores the consequences that alienation from society has on his characters' sense of self, while at the same time they are brought up against forces larger than themselves. Showing his protagonists' moral dilemmas against naturalistic settings

contributes to the disquieting tone of the narratives.

In 1953 Bellow received critical acclaim, as well as his first National Book Award, with the publication of *The Adventures of Augie March*, a first-person picaresque novel recording the formative experiences of a young Jew from Chicago. This successful novel was followed by *Seize the Day* (1956), a short but fascinating novel which presents a single day in the life of Tommy Wilhelm. The narrative voice alternates between third-person descriptions of the New York settings and Wilhelm's monologues, allowing the reader to see the events of the particular day on which the novel is set juxtaposed with important events in Wilhelm's past, seen through flashbacks.

In 1959 Bellow published *Henderson the Rain King*, in which the main character, Gene Henderson, narrates, in a sentimental but comical manner, the story of his trip to Africa and his encounters with African tribal people and traditions.

In *Herzog* (1964), often considered his greatest novel, Bellow presents another study of an individual at odds with the world. Moses Herzog, a professor and intellectual, inwardly fights against his cultural heritage, which he holds responsible for civilization's problems. Partly prompted by his own marital difficulties, he starts to write imaginary letters to friends, and living and dead public figures, about issues that haunt him.

In *Mr Sammler's Planet* (1970) Bellow's narrative tone gets bleaker as the character's fragmented and suppressed memories from the Second World War are gradually forced to the surface of his consciousness, being triggered by contemporary events. The book's only weakness arises from its lengthy internal monologues which seem to blur the character's voice with that of the author.

With *Humboldt's Gift* (1975) Bellow won his first Pulitzer Prize. This novel examines Charlie Citrine's acquaintance with the poet Von Humboldt Fleisher, showing the beneficial effect the latter, as an artist, has on Citrine while a life-crisis forces him into agonized soul-searching.

The Dean's December (1982) presents the reader with a dual perspective. Through the protagonist's consciousness the reader is confronted with a double-tier narrative concerned with the character's current experiences in Cold War Bucharest, and retrospective reflections on life in Chicago. In this way, Bellow succeeds dexterously in illuminating both the character's inner world, and the surface reality of his daily existence.

As well as further novels, such as *More Die of Heartbreak* (1987) and *Ravelstein* (2000), Bellow has written a number of plays, travel books, and academic publications. His short stories have appeared in *Mosby's Memoirs and Other Stories* (1968), *Him with His Foot in His Mouth and Other Short Stories* (1984), *Something to Remember Me By* (1993) and *Saul Bellow: Collected Stories* (2001).

Bellow's characters are no more, and no less, than ordinary people experiencing and overcoming anguish as they meet the ethical challenges of everyday life. Bellow writes his psychologically penetrating novels in the faith that the reader

> will open his heart and mind to a writer who . . . has experienced the same privations; who knows where the sore spots are; who has discerned the power of the need to come back to the level of one's true human destiny.[2]

References

1. **Baym, Nina** (ed.), *The Norton Anthology of American Literature*, Sixth Edition. W. W. Norton & Company, 2003, p. 2093.

2. **Bellow, Janis** (ed.), *Saul Bellow: Collected Stories*. Viking, 2001, p. 442.

Selected works:

Fiction: *Dangling Man* (1944); *The Victim* (1947); *The Adventures of Augie March* (1953); *Seize the Day* (1956); *Henderson the Rain King* (1959); *Herzog* (1964); *Mr Sammler's Planet* (1970); *Humboldt's Gift* (1975); *The Dean's December* (1982); *More Die of Heartbreak* (1987); *Ravelstein* (2000). **Collections of shorter work:** *Mosby's Memoirs and Other Stories* (1968); *Him with His Foot in His Mouth and Other Short Stories* (1984); *Something to Remember Me By* (1993); *Saul Bellow: Collected Stories* (2001).

Further reading

Bach, Gerhard and Cronin, Gloria L. (eds), *Small Planets: Saul Bellow and the art of Short Fiction*. Michigan State University Press, 2000.

Bach, Gerhard (ed.), *The Critical Response to Saul Bellow*. Greenwood Press, 1995.

Contributor: Tatiani Rapatzikou

BISHOP, ELIZABETH (1911–79)

It takes an infinite number of things coming together, forgotten, or almost forgotten, books, last night's dream, experiences past and present – to make a poem. The settings, or descriptions, of my poems are invariably just plain facts – or as close to the facts as I can write them.[1]

Photo: credit: © Bettmann/CORBIS

Marginalised by literary historians for most of her career, Elizabeth Bishop's work now seems central to an understanding of the main shifts and tensions in twentieth-century poetry. She learnt metre from Marianne Moore, Spanish from Pablo Neruda, and verse forms from **Dylan Thomas**. And like the best students, she then passed on these lessons to younger poets such as Thom Gunn, James Merrill and Anne Stevenson. On a grand scale, she is one of the few writers to link the **Modern** to the **Postmodern**, **Surrealism** to **Abstract Expressionism**. On a smaller scale, she connects us to an old man sitting beside the shoreline ('At the Fishhouses'), some sleepy travellers on a bus ('The Moose'), and even a stray dog trying to evade capture ('Pink Dog'). For such a long life, Bishop published very little – just a hundred poems and fifteen or so stories – yet without her writing we would all feel disorientated.

Bishop is a notoriously difficult writer to place. Truant from any one school or movement, her poems and stories constantly experiment with different registers, tones and voices. At every point in her career, she went her own way. In the 1940s, she was one of the first poets to write sympathetically about America's black and Cuban communities. In the 1950s, she investigated the ethics of tourism and travel in a series of poems on modern and historical Brazil, many of which anticipate the concerns of **postcolonial** writers and thinkers nowadays. In the 1960s and 1970s, she developed a way of addressing autobiographical material distinct from the **Confessional** movement's emphasis on anguish and self-pity. This is perhaps why she continues to be admired and praised by so many different types of poet. She kept a sceptical eye on every important artistic tradition, accepting and rejecting whichever elements she saw fit. While most poets are a combination of two or three formative traditions, Bishop drew on as much as she could read, continually moving between different centuries, languages and tones – from a **Romantic** tribute to nature ('A Cold Spring') at the beginning of a book to a love poem about washing somebody's hair at the end ('The Shampoo'), from a Metaphysical lyric ('The Weed') on one page to an ode to a petrol station on the other ('Filling Station').

All this travelling within language has a source in Bishop's life. As various critics have stated, the act of travel seems to conceal a profound sense of homelessness, pointing back to her own status as a virtual orphan from the age of five. Born in Worcester, Massachusetts, in 1911, she lost her father to Bright's disease when she was only eight months old, and her mother to mental illness soon afterwards. In 1915 she went to stay with her maternal grandparents in Great Village, Nova Scotia, where her mother also stayed between breakdowns. The autobiographical story, 'In the Village' (1953), recreates two of her most haunting memories from this time, that of her mother's scream, and of the 'beautiful pure sound' of the blacksmith's anvil which balances it. Poems such as 'Manners', 'Sestina' and 'First Death in Nova Scotia', also revisit these childhood experiences. She lived for a further two years in Great Village, attending Primer Class there, before being suddenly taken to live in New England, this time with her paternal grandparents. She developed asthma and eczema as a result of this removal. Later on, she also attributed her alcoholism and loneliness to the displacements and traumas of these first seven years.

Bishop's imaginative preoccupation with the idea of home was her main inheritance from childhood. Her poems, as Adrienne Rich[2] once recognised, are full of outsiders for whom the idea of home is precisely that –

only an idea. These include the old hermit in 'Chemin de Fer', left to fend for himself by the side of his 'little pond'; the 'specklike boy and girl' in 'Squatter's Children', waiting for the rain to wash away their 'specklike house'; and the gardener in 'Manuelzinho', forced to sniff and shiver, 'hat in hand', for even a shot of penicillin. While her poems avoid direct political statement, she continues to keep account of the practical consequences of historical events for individual people. She saw 'A Miracle for Breakfast' as a 'Depression poem', 'Songs for a Colored Singer' as 'a prophesy, or prayer, that justice will eventually triumph for the Negro in the USA', and 'From Trollope's Journal' as 'an anti-Eisenhower poem'. We could add to this list her attack on militarism in 'Roosters', her sideways swipe at Cold War politics in 'View of the Capitol from the Library of Congress', and her undermining of American journalism in '12 O'Clock News'.

A few months before graduating from Vassar, Bishop met Marianne Moore for the first time on a bench outside the reading room of the New York Public Library (see Bishop's memoir, 'Efforts of Affection'). The two poets enjoyed a generous friendship, encouraging each other's writing in spite of the odd disagreement, most famously over the subject matter of Bishop's 'Roosters', a poem Moore and her mother wanted to rename, 'The Cock'. North & South, Bishop's first book of poems, was published in 1946. It took its perfectionist author more than a decade to complete, a pattern repeated with each of her subsequent collections. She was in Nova Scotia on the day North & South was published, returning south by bus to Boston, the journey that would later become the setting for one of her greatest poems, 'The Moose'. The following year, Randall Jarrell introduced her to Robert Lowell, who became a lifelong friend. 'I loved him at first sight', she later admitted, 'my shyness vanished and we started talking at once.' The critical success of North & South, together with the influential backing of Jarrell, Lowell and Moore, led to a Guggenheim Fellowship in 1947 and an appointment as Consultant in Poetry in 1950. She was also awarded a Pulitzer Prize in 1956, a National Book Award in 1970 and the Neustadt Prize for Literature in 1976.

In 1951 Bishop visited South America, where an allergy to a cashew nut caused her to fall ill. Bedridden at the home of her hostess, Lota de Macedo Soares, a Brazilian architect and heiress whom she had first met ten years earlier, she was overwhelmed by the care she received and, at Lota's invitation, decided to stay. The two women fell in love. Bishop's asthma and drinking seemed to come under control and she began to write fluently again, after several years of stuttering activity. Her prose masterpiece, 'In the Village', was completed in 1953 and her second collection of poems, *A Cold Spring* followed in 1955. She kept in touch by letter with Lowell and Moore, while at the same time corresponding with new friends such as **Flannery O'Connor** and May Swenson. She translated *The Diary of "Helena Morley"* by Alice Brant in 1955, and was co-editor and co-translator of *An Anthology of Brazilian Poetry* with Emanuel Brasil in 1972. In the early 1960s, Lota was invited to take charge of constructing a public park in Rio. Lota became continually anxious about financing the project in the wake of various political crises and relations between the two women became strained. In the meantime, Bishop bought and began restoring a colonial house in Ouro Prêto in 1965, and the year afterwards accepted her first teaching job in Seattle. *Questions of Travel*, her third collection of poems, appeared in 1965. In 1967 Lota committed suicide in New York on the first night of a trip to see Bishop. Numbed by guilt for not preventing her death, Bishop delayed returning to Brazil for several weeks. In her papers, she left drafts for an elegiac poem about Lota, although she was never able to finish it. Cryptic expressions of grief such as 'Crusoe in England' and 'Five Flights Up' were all she could manage.

After Lota's death, Bishop drifted between San Francisco, Ouro Prêto and New England. In 1970 she began teaching at Harvard. Her fear of losing her partner at the time, Alice Methfessel, prompted the magnificent villanelle, 'One Art'. In 1974 she moved into an apartment overlooking Lewis Wharf in Boston. She kept a ship's log beside the window, thinking it 'curious' that ships from Nova Scotia must have docked there, perhaps even her great-grandfather's. Her last book of poems, *Geography III* (1976), revisits Nova Scotia too, particularly 'In the Waiting Room', 'Poem' and 'The Moose'. In the last decade of her life, Bishop became friends with **Seamus**

Heaney, Helen Vendler, Octavio Paz and others, academics and writers who kept her reputation buoyant in the immediate aftermath of her death in 1979.

Reference

1. **Bishop, Elizabeth**, Letter to Jerome Mazzaro, 1978.

2. **Rich, Adrienne**, 'The Eye of the Outsider: Elizabeth Bishop's Complete Poems', in *Blood, Bread, and Poetry: Selected Prose, 1979–1985.* Virago Press, 1987, pp. 124–135.

Selected works:

North & South (1946); *A Cold Spring* (1955); *The Diary of "Helena Morley"* (1957); *Brazil* (1962); *Questions of Travel* (1965); *Geography III* (1976); *Complete Poems: 1927–1979* (1983); *The Collected Prose* (1984); *One Art: Selected Letters* (1994); *Conversations with Elizabeth Bishop* (1996); *Exchanging Hats: Paintings* (1996).

Further reading

Ellis, Jonathan, *Art and Memory in the Work of Elizabeth Bishop.* Ashgate Press, 2005.

Goldensohn, Lorrie, *Elizabeth Bishop: The Biography of a Poetry.* Columbia University Press, 1991.

Contributor: Jonathan Ellis

BUKOWSKI, CHARLES (1920–94)

I arrived in New Orleans in the rain at 5 o'clock in the morning. I sat around in the bus station for a while but the people depressed me so I took my suitcase and went out in the rain and began walking. I didn't know where the rooming houses were, where the poor section was.

Opening of Factotum

Although he is known mainly for three of his novels, *Post Office* (1971), *Factotum* (1975) and *Ham on Rye* (1982), Charles Bukowski's earliest publications were poems, his first collection, *Flower, Fist and Bestial Wail*, appearing in 1960. For most of his life he worked in low-paid, menial jobs, writing (and drinking) in his leisure time before his publisher, John Martin, funded his full-time writing.

Bukowski was born in Andernach, Germany, to an American serviceman and a German mother, but they moved to the United States before his third birthday. Bukowski's father passed his social aspirations, and his sense of personal failure, on to his son, and the detrimental effect of this relationship forms the basis of *Ham on Rye*, the most obviously autobiographical of his novels. It also helped shape the individualist myth that he used as a psychological veil, hiding behind his hard-drinking, hard man image to disguise his sense of vulnerability – he was excused military service in the Second World War on grounds of his 'extreme sensitivity'.

Raised by a bullying autocrat of a father, and a mother who deferred to her husband's word, Bukowski became withdrawn as a child. It became more difficult to fit in with his peers the more he was excluded from their company on his father's whim. In high school he was an eternal outsider, and this was exacerbated by an outbreak of acne which affected his whole body. His face bore the scars for the rest of his life. Rejected by his young peers (especially, in his eyes, the girls) and brutalised by his father, Bukowski became the embodiment of the loner who was to become the basis of much of his fiction.

First his poems, and later his fiction, were based on a combination of these formative experiences and his observations on his life as a poorly-paid manual worker. The most enduring influence on his writing was his 11-year stint at the United States Post Office, and it is the physically debilitating, demeaning nature of this type of labour, and the exploitative character of work relations, that forms the core of much of his work. Combined with his distinctly problematical relationship with, and attitudes towards, women, his rejection of the work ethic signifies a particular social and psychological underpinning of his writing.

Although Bukowski had no socialist, or any other leftist, agenda, his fiction is a specifically working-class fiction that has as one central theme; the exploitation of the workers by the management classes. Influenced primarily by the novels of John Fante and Knut Hamsun, the dark anti-humanism of Louis Ferdinand Céline, and the work of Henry Miller, Bukowski examines the restricted opportunities and the emotional isolation of the individual through his fictional alter ego, Henry Chinaski.

In Chinaski he constructs a persona who represents the antithesis of the mid-twentieth-century mainstream American values of work and social mobility. Indeed, as the first five words of *Post Office* indicate, his whole experience of the Post Office took place because of his mistaken notion that it would be easy money: 'It began as a mistake.' Flying in the face of the centrality of Calvinist salvation through hard work to American social politics, Chinaski seeks liberation from the tyranny of the workplace. Forced to work in order to survive, he combines periods of exhausting hard work with small personal acts of defiance, such as slacking, undermining supervisors and absenteeism.

Bukowski is often termed a **Beat Writer**. He does share some of the characteristics of the Beat Writers, but he does not come close to their spiritual agenda, their experimentation with drugs or their quest for 'alternative' lifestyles. In *Post Office*, as in much of his work, he is self-isolated from society and takes refuge in alcohol and casual sex. Unlike the Beats, though, this is not a repudiation of mainstream sexual politics. Rather, it is symptomatic of Chinaski's fear of rejection. His inability to connect in a meaningful way with women manifests itself in his abhorrence of intimacy.

Factotum precedes *Post Office* chronologically and recalls Chinaski's itinerant years. Moving from city to city, menial job to menial job and casual affair to casual affair, he hones his nihilist-individualist credentials in his flight from suburban conformity. Taking his lead from Hamsun, he describes Chinaski's attempts to combine low-status manual labour with his writing ambitions. The poverty of existence and the hardship of work combine to undermine his aspirations, culminating in the **deconstruction** of another popular cultural ideal: 'The myth of the starving artist was a hoax.' [*Factotum*].

Chinaski's actions are an attempt to live with dignity without compromising himself to the dictates of wage labour. Each small act of defiance becomes a personal-political stance against prevailing social conditions. An almost complete absence of union activity in his work points to an abiding individualism; collectivism is equal to connection to Chinaski, something he continually strives to avoid. Delusions of absolute self-sufficiency are linked to his exaggerated masculine persona. These attitudes serve to create distance from other people, whom he learned to distrust in his childhood. Much of this is written in a self-deprecatory manner. Bukowski does not lose sight of Chinaski's more ridiculous behaviour, and a wry humour permeates the novels.

In *Ham on Rye* we move further back in time to Chinaski's formative years. The most striking aspect of the novel is the overwhelming figure of Chinaski senior, both physically and psychologically. While the two earlier novels focus on Chinaski junior's problematic interaction with the adult world, here Bukowski deals with the experiences of childhood and youth which helped form his private, individualist worldview. His father is beset by social anxiety, and during the Depression is seen to leave home every morning and return every evening from a job he does not have. Taking out his frustration on his son, he sows the seeds of dissent and a lifelong revulsion towards conformity to suburban expectations in the young boy.

In *Ham on Rye* we also see the beginning of a life that is marked by an inability to form close attachments. Chinaski's mother's refusal to protect him from his father's brutality, his failure to attract girls as he approaches sexual maturity, and his macho persona combine to distance him from women as much as his open aggression distances him from men. Despised by many **feminists** for his alleged misogyny (something he always refuted), Bukowski continues to antagonise many readers.

Forced to leave the Post Office due to persistent absenteeism, Bukowski was promised $100 a month for life by his publisher, John Martin, on condition that he continued to produce poems, short stories and novels. This he did, and was so prolific that the quality of his output varies widely. Towards the end of his life he had achieved a certain notoriety, but also a comfortable lifestyle that included a paid-for house in a relatively affluent neighbourhood, and an expensive car – a lifestyle

contrasting markedly with that of his fictional alter ego. He died of leukaemia in March 1994, aged 73.

Selected works:

Novels: *Post Office* (1971); *Factotum* (1975); *Ham on Rye* (1982); *Hollywood* (1989). **Poetry:** *Burning in Water, Drowning in Flame: Selected Poems 1955–1973* (1974); *The Roominghouse Madrigals: Early Selected Poems 1946–1966* (1988); *Septuagenarian Stew: Stories and Poems* (1990).

Further reading

Harrison, Russell, *Against the American Dream: Essays on Charles Bukowski*. Black Sparrow Press, 1998.

Sounes, Howard, *Charles Bukowski: Locked in the Arms of a Crazy Life*. Rebel Inc., 1998.

Smith, Jules, *Art, Survival and So Forth: The Poetry of Charles Bukowski*. Wrecking Ball Press, 2000.

Contributor: Gary Blohm

CAREY, PETER (1943–)

I lost my own father at 12 years of age and know what it is to be raised on lies and silences my dear daughter you are presently too young to understand a word I write but this history is for you and will contain no single lie may I burn in Hell if I speak false.
True History of the Kelly Gang

Photo credit: © Reuters/CORBIS

Peter Carey is one of the few authors to have won the Booker Prize twice, having won it in 1988 for *Oscar and Lucinda*, and in 2001 for *True History of the Kelly Gang*. These two novels, being set in the nineteenth century, illustrate Carey's interest in the historical novel form, which he refashions through his **postmodern** sensibility, bringing to it an awareness of an irredeemably lost innocence.

Carey was born in Bacchus Marsh, Victoria, Australia. He enrolled to study chemistry at Monash University, but dropped out after a year, realising that his vocation lay elsewhere. Between 1962 and 1967 he worked for advertising agencies in Melbourne. In the late 1960s he travelled through Europe and the Middle East, and worked in advertising in London. He returned to Australia in 1970, to work in advertising in Melbourne and Sydney while writing most of the stories published in the volumes *The Fat Man in History* (1974) and *War Crimes* (1979). His first published novel was *Bliss* (1981), which is based on a theme of '**hippies** versus capitalism', questioning given ideas of normality through a mixture of **realism** and fantasy.

Bliss was followed by *Illywhacker* (1985), a postmodern retelling of his grandfather's experiences delivering the first mail around Australia. The book's title comes from an Australian colloquialism for *con artist*, and its main topic is lying, as announced from the very beginning by Herbert Badgery, the 139-year-old 'Illywhacker'. The novel shows the history of twentieth-century Australia, but, in the true spirit of postmodernist playful treatment of 'reality', the history is presented through a rich interplay of truth and lies, with the narrator himself even questioning the truth of his own stories.

Carey has lived in various parts of Australia, including Bellingen, which made a strong impact on him, and provided some of the inspiration for *Oscar and Lucinda*, a mock-Victorian historical novel, set mainly in nineteenth-century Australia. It combines a lucid critique of bigotry with the beautiful (but impossible) love story of Oscar Hopkins and Lucinda Leplastrier. After quarrelling with his father over their different religious views, the young Anglican reverend Oscar – who believes the ultimate proof of God's existence has been revealed to him through gambling – is driven by his vice to Australia. On the ship he meets Lucinda, an orphaned heiress and an obsessive gambler herself. She owns a glass factory, and their community of thought and feeling – not very obvious

otherwise – finds a metaphorical projection in the glass cathedral they build together. Lucinda bets her inheritance that Oscar cannot deliver his church to his remote missionary post. Oscar's foolish attempt to transport the church down the river Bellingen fails, and the church sinks.

The novel is informed by a postmodern outlook, which encompasses the awareness of the world's fragmentariness, chaos theory, and the French philosopher Blaise Pascal's idea that faith is a form of gambling. This idea faithfully mirrors Carey's attitude to fiction writing in general: as Bruce Woodcock observes, 'If faith was a gamble for Pascal, writing seems to be an incessant gamble for Peter Carey, which is perhaps why he is such a constantly exciting writer' (Woodcock p. 15). Carey's work, remarkable for its fluidity of shape, focus and theme, has an element of risk-taking about it. While interested in revisiting traditional forms, he constantly takes risks by turning them on their heads and filling them up with contemporary content. This ever-present questioning attitude, combined with an awareness of the human condition, has earned him a wide readership. *Oscar and Lucinda* was filmed in 1997 by Gillian Armstrong, and starred Ralph Fiennes and Cate Blanchett.

In the late 1980s Carey took up residence in New York City, where he and his family still live. He teaches creative writing part-time at New York University. In New York, he completed much of *The Tax Inspector* (1991) and wrote *The Unusual Life of Tristan Smith* (1994) and *Jack Maggs* (1997). *Jack Maggs* somewhat prefigures *True History of the Kelly Gang* in that it is also a convict story, indulging in the delights of Victorian melodrama blended with a pervading sense of history and elements of the Australian tradition of convict literature. The novel stages an engaging story of identity reinvention – Maggs reminding the reader of Magwitch from Dickens's *Great Expectations* – against the background of the guilt-haunted past of colonial England.

True History of the Kelly Gang (2001) presents a colourful portrait of the famous Irish-Australian outlaw and 'martyr' Ned Kelly, who was hanged for murder, but transformed by legend into one of the big names of Australian nationalism. Receiving the award,

Carey said that he was indebted to his wife, and to **Ian McEwan**, one of the rival nominees, promising to buy him an expensive meal. In the novel Carey adopts the language of late nineteenth-century rural Australians, using among his sources the outlaw's one surviving letter. Carey takes the reader from Ned's childhood, through his teenage years in and out of prison, his horse thefts and bank hold-ups, and finally to his years as a leader of a rebel band of farmers, fighting against a corrupt system.

In 2001 Carey published *A Wildly Distorted Account*, a travel book of his 30-day visit to Sydney. *My Life as a Fake* (2003) was inspired by Australia's most famous literary hoax, the 'Ern Malley Scandal' of 1944, in which a literary editor was persuaded to publish a collection of fake **'Modernist'** poems which two anti-modernist poets had put together in a few hours and offered under the pseudonym Ern Malley. The hoax humiliated the editor and a number of modernist poets, and sent the two joking poets into exile.

Like Ned Kelly, Carey is a declared anti-conventionalist: not only did he abandon university studies, but years later, having won the Commonwealth Writers' Prize for *Jack Maggs* in 1998, he became famous in the British press for refusing to meet the queen on the occasion.

Selected works:

The Fat Man in History (1974); *War Crimes* (1979); *Bliss* (1981); *Illywhacker* (1985); *Oscar and Lucinda* (1988); *Exotic Pleasures* (1990); *The Tax Inspector* (1991); *The Unusual Life of Tristan Smith* (1994); *Collected Stories* (1994); *A Letter to Our Son* (1994); *The Big Bazoohley* (1995); *Jack Maggs* (1997); *True History of the Kelly Gang* (2001); *A Wildly Distorted Account* (2001); *My Life as a Fake* (2003); **Screenplay:** *Until the End of the World* (1992), dir. by Wim Wenders.

Further reading

Woodcock, Bruce, *Peter Carey*. Manchester and New York: Manchester University Press, 2003.

Contributor: Maria-Sabina Draga Alexandru

CARTER, ANGELA (1940–92)

All books, even cookery books and car-maintenance manuals consist of narratives. Narrative is written in language but it is composed, if you follow me, in time. All writers are inventing a kind of imitation time . . . A good writer can make you believe time stands still.[1]

Angela Olive Carter (née Stalker), novelist, poet, and writer of short stories, children's fiction and non-fiction, was born in Eastbourne, England, but moved to live with her grandmother in Yorkshire during the Second World War. In 1959 she began work as a journalist for the *Croydon Advertiser*, then from 1962 to 1965 studied English at the University of Bristol. She visited and lived in Japan from 1969 to 1972, and in the 1970s and 1980s taught at various universities in the USA, Australia and England. She taught Creative Writing at the University of East Anglia, where **Kazuo Ishiguro** was one of her students.

Carter's work is considered to be at the forefront of late twentieth-century writing, and is accepted as part of the British canon in that it is studied at the highest levels in educational establishments. Both her fiction and non-fiction were influenced by **feminism**, and she, in turn, has become an important figure in second- and third-wave feminist thinking. Her work has not always been readily accepted, but her critics and admirers are generally united by the understanding that it maintains an ambiguity that avoids political dogmatism. She is a problematic writer in that she is difficult to categorise, and is regarded as both imaginative and subversive, her work being interpreted as provocative from various political positions.

Carter's fiction is characterised by her use of **magic realism**, and her interest in gender politics. Female sexuality and eroticism are key themes, and her stories frequently include **Gothic** fantasy, **surrealism** and the rewriting of fairy tales. Carter also makes references to high and popular culture, in a **postmodernist** manner which collapses the hierarchical distinction.

Her first publications appeared in 1966; a

volume of poetry, *Unicorn*, and a novel, *Shadow Dance*. *The Magic Toyshop* (1967), perhaps her best-known novel, was awarded the John Llewellyn Rhys Memorial Prize, and adapted for film in 1986. The novel, a fantasy with **Freudian** undertones, is representative of Carter's early use of magic realist techniques, and of her ambiguous representations of females as victims in patriarchal society.

Several Perceptions (1968) won the Somerset Maugham Award and was followed in 1969 by *Heroes and Villains*, a novel concerned with a post-apocalyptic world. *Love* (1970) is the third of 'the Bristol trilogy', following *Shadow Dance* and *Several Perceptions*.[2]

The Passion of New Eve (1977) uses a post-apocalypse landscape as a background, and explores themes drawing on sexual politics. Sexuality and gender are regarded as constructions – the character Evelyn being told that he is to be the new Eve – and maternal love is presented as a disturbing, ambivalent power. Multiple **intertexts**, from *The Bible* and Greek mythology for example, give depth to the themes and the writing style.

In the non-fiction work *The Sadeian Woman: An Exercise in Cultural History* (1979), Carter explores feminist concerns and the workings of patriarchy, from a perspective which is now seen as typical of her double-edged reasoning. Lorna Sage, in her introduction to *Flesh and the Mirror: Essays on the Art of Angela Carter* (1994), comments on the complexity of *The Sadeian Woman*:

> In the de Sade book she sets out to track down and discredit the lure and prestige of suffering. So her feminist book is also aimed against a certain sisterhood.[3]

Carter adapted two stories from her second collection, *The Bloody Chamber and Other Stories* (1979), as a screenplay for the acclaimed but controversial film *The Company of Wolves* (1984), directed by Neil Jordan. This story is a revision of the *Little Red Riding Hood* fairy tale, with the heroine's sexuality as an overt focus of attention. Carter's interest in fairy tales was demonstrated earlier in her translation of Perrault's tales, entitled *The Fairy Tales of Charles Perrault* (1977).

Nights at the Circus (1984) offers a playful account of the debate on constructed gender.

The character Walser, a journalist, investigates whether the story of Fevvers, a music hall and circus trapeze artist, allegedly half-woman and half-bird, is fact or fiction. Carter's last novel, *Wise Children* (1991), also uses public entertainment as a theme, and draws on Shakespeare, the music hall, film and television for a lively tale about the exploits of twins Dora and Nora Chance. The novel is poignant in its examination of families and parentage, and the inevitability of ageing – although in the story the inevitability is challenged.

Since Carter's death in 1992 there have been posthumous publications such as the selection of critical essays, *Expletives Deleted* (1992), and a short story collection, *American Ghosts and Other World Wonders* (1993). Interest in Carter's writing has continued to increase, and she is valued for her knowledge, originality and irreverence. In *Expletives Deleted* Carter's own words reflect a contradiction which is apparent in her novels and non-fiction:

> I am known in my circle as notoriously foul-mouthed. It's a familiar paradox – the soft-spoken middle-aged English gentlewoman who swears like a trooper when roused.[4]

References

1. **Carter, Angela** (1992) *Expletives Deleted: Selected Writings*. London: Virago, p. 2. (Hereafter referred to as *Expletives Deleted*.)

2. 'The Bristol trilogy' categorisation is used by Marc O'Day in '"Mutability is Having a Field Day": The Sixties Aura of Angela Carter's Bristol Trilogy'. *Flesh and the Mirror: Essays on the Art of Angela Carter*. Ed. Lorna Sage, London: Virago, 1994.

3. **Sage, Lorna** (1994) Introduction. *Flesh and the Mirror: Essays on the Art of Angela Carter*. Ed. Lorna Sage, London: Virago, p. 12.

4. *Expletives Deleted*. p. 1.

Selected works:
Unicorn (1966); *Shadow Dance* (1966); *The Magic Toyshop* (1967); *Several Perceptions* (1968); *Heroes and Villains* (1969); *Love* (1970); *The Infernal Desire Machines of Doctor Hoffman* (1972); *Fireworks: Nine Profane Pieces*

(1974); *The Passion of New Eve* (1977); *The Fairy Tales of Charles Perrault* (1977); *The Sadeian Woman: An Exercise in Cultural History* (1979); *The Bloody Chamber and Other Stories* (1979); *Nothing Sacred: Selected Writings* (1982); *Nights at the Circus* (1984); *Black Venus* (1985); *The Virago Book of Fairy Tales* (compiled: 1990, Vol 2, 1992); *Wise Children* (1991); *Expletives Deleted* (1992); *American Ghosts and Other World Wonders* (1993); *Burning Your Boats* (1995); *Shaking a Leg* (1997).

Contributor: Julie Ellam

CARVER, RAYMOND (1938–88)

But at that moment the young man was thinking of the cork still resting near the toe of his shoe. To retrieve it he would have to bend over, still gripping the vase. He would do this. He leaned over. Without looking down, he reached out and closed it in his hand.
                    Concluding lines of 'Errand'

Raymond Carver was born in Clatskanie, Oregon, where his father worked in a sawmill, his mother as a waitress. The family moved to Yakima, in Washington State, where Carver attended high school, then worked in a sawmill and in other menial jobs. He married at the age of 19 and after having two children in 18 months, struggled to support his family and to complete his education. Although he later became a successful writer, a significant part of his work reflects the struggle for existence of blue-collar workers circumscribed by dead-end jobs, dysfunctional families and, most damagingly, the problems with alcohol that he experienced himself.

As a writer of short stories, Carver's minimalism, with its flattened elliptical style and spare realism, links him with the tradition of Ernest Hemingway, but without the machismo or the exotic tourist agenda. Carver's characters have to endure what the American economy deals out to them: he once said that he explored 'the dark side of Reagan's America'.[1] The term 'Carver Country' has been coined to denote not only the urban malls, diners and bars straggling on the edge of the landscape that are deliberately not made evocative in his stories, but also the seepage of menace and blight that leaks from the early fiction. 'Are These Actual Miles?',[2] in his first collection, *Will You Please Be Quiet, Please?* (1976), is the story of a couple close to bankruptcy having to sell their convertible, the symbol of their extravagance, to prevent it from being forfeited. The wife makes herself glamorous in order to persuade a car dealer to buy it. The husband waits at home drinking, and the wife returns, drunk, at dawn with a cheque. It is characteristic of Carver's omissions that nothing is given of the wife's experience apart from her eruption into hatred, screaming 'Bankrupt!' as she collapses into the marital bed. This is the American Dream gone sour, the roller coaster from surfeit to deprivation, in which spiritual vacancy is expressed through minimal detail, a grim realism that embeds the characters into their no-hope scenarios.

Yet Carver's characters want love, as one of his greatest stories, 'What We Talk About When We Talk About Love', the title story of the collection of the same name (1981), makes evident. Two couples, Mel and Terri, and Nick and Laura, are spending an evening together. The narrator, Nick, observes, through the stories the other couple tell, the unravelling of their relationship. Mel's story, about the devotion of an old couple who, as a doctor, he had treated after a near fatal accident, and his wife Terri's story, about the abusive 'real' love of her first husband, create an unspoken backwash of dissatisfaction in relation to their own marriage. Yet nothing is explicitly stated: Carver works through the device of stories within stories that intersect and become charged with collateral significance, so that the characters become immobilised in their own condition; sitting, drinking, 'not one of us moving, not even when the room went dark'.

Carver wrote poetry throughout his adult life, and his *Collected Poems* (1996) was published posthumously. His poetry is more openly autobiographical than his fiction, a kind of anecdotal journal of his hopes, his decline into alcoholism, and, from 1977 when he quit drinking, an expression of his recovery, as seen in the poem 'Gravy'. He felt he had been given extra time. The poem 'Hummingbird' is a tender love letter to his new partner, the writer, Tess Gallagher.

Carver and Gallagher taught at Syracuse University, New York, in the early 1980s, spending their summers near Port Angeles, Washington. The countryside, especially rivers and his love of fishing, becomes more part of 'Carver Country' in the last ten years of his life: in 'Where Water Comes Together with Other Water' he gives thanks for the renewal of the creative energy that his drinking had almost destroyed.

The last two collections published in Carver's lifetime show how effectively he used what he felt was a second life. The title story of the collection, *Cathedral* (1983), is based on an incident that happened when a blind friend of Gallagher's visited them. The narrator of the story is a husband who is uncomfortable and suspicious when his wife's blind friend visits, a man whom she has known for a long time who is at ease and intimate with her. During the evening the narrator's hostility abates and when a TV programme about cathedrals is switched on, the blind man places his hands over the narrator's as he attempts to draw one. Thus they discover the form of the building together, an act of intimacy and recognition. Robert Altman's film *Short Cuts* (1993) was based on 'A Small Good Thing' from this collection and eight other earlier stories that are cross-cut to create a mosaic of random occurrences, 'of things that just happen to people and cause their lives to take a turn'.[3]

Elephant (1988) shows Carver developing the amplitude of stories like 'Cathedral'. The esteem of, and friendships with, writers such as Tobias Wolf and Richard Ford contributed to his confidence. As editor of a collection of American short stories, he said that he looked for 'the ambition of enlarging our view of ourselves and the world'[4] and such a quality is evident in these stories, which are unlike the pared-down style of his earlier work. He was reading widely in European and American writing, past and present, and the story 'Blackbird Pie' is an ironic critique of the ways in which a man (a pedantic historian) tries to be a historian of his failed marriage, but finally admits to himself:

It could be said, for instance, that to take a wife is to take a history. And if that's so, then I understand I'm outside history now – like horses and fog. Or you could say that my history has left me. Or that I'm having to go on *without history*.

Still pedantic, yet desolate, the historian apprehends his human isolation. The concluding story of the collection, 'Errand', is about the death of Chekhov. Carver remembered a passage in Troyat's biography[5] in which the doctor attending Chekhov, realising that death was imminent, ordered a bottle of champagne for him. Reading this Carver felt he had 'been launched into a short story of my own then and there . . . The only thing that was clear to me was that I thought I saw an opportunity to pay homage . . . to Chekhov, the writer, who has meant so much to me for such a long time'.[6] Carver's story focuses on the young bellman, dishevelled and tired, who brings the champagne in the middle of the night unaware of the significance of the occasion. The young man remains concerned with trivial details the next morning when, clean shaven and smart, he is given a vase of flowers to carry to the morticians. Waiting for further instruction, he becomes preoccupied with the untidiness of the champagne cork that is lying at his feet. It is in these commonplace elements, signifying celebration and tribute, that the larger concerns of the story find an objective expression: through the marginal, consequence is delivered. When Carver died of cancer at the age of 50 obituaries acknowledged him as the 'American Chekhov'.

References

1.   Interview with Kasia Boddy, 'A Conversation', *London Review of Books*, 15 September 1988, p. 16.

2. This is the revised title. It was originally titled 'What Is It? on first publication in *Will You Please Be Quiet, Please?*.

3. **Altman, Robert** (1993) 'Introduction: Collaborating with Carver', *Raymond Carver: Short Cuts*, p. 7.

4. **Carver and Juncos, Tom** (eds) (1987) Introduction to *American Short Story Masterpieces*, p. ix.

5. **Troyat, Henri** (1986) *Chekhov*, trans. M. H. Hein, pp. 330–335.

6. *No Heroics Please: Uncollected Writings*, 1991, pp. 123–124.

Selected works:

Will You Please Be Quiet, Please? (1976); *Furious Seasons* (1977); *What We Talk About When We Talk About Love* (1981); *Cathedral* (1983); *Fires: Essays, Poems, Stories* (1985); *Elephant* (1988); *Where I'm Calling From: The Selected Stories* (1988); *No Heroics Please: Uncollected Writings* (1991); *Short Cuts* introd. Robert Altman (1993); *All of Us: The Collected Poems* (1996); *Call If You Need Me: The Uncollected Fiction and Prose* (2000).

Further reading

Campbell, Ewing, *Raymond Carver: A Study of the Short Fiction*. Twayne, 1992.

Bethea, Arthur F., *Technique and Sensibility in the Fiction and Poetry of Raymond Carver*. Routledge, 2002.

Contributor: Pat Righelato

CATHER, WILLA (1873–1947)

The history of every country begins in the heart of a man or a woman.

from *O Pioneers!*

Willa Cather incorporated elements of both modernism and realism in her much-loved stories of the American West and the immigrant pioneers who settled that untamed land. Her novels deal with distinctly American issues, particularly as experienced by immigrant families trying to bridge the gap between their old and new ways of life. Other important themes are the plight of the artist in the age of industrialism and progress, and the alienation of the young as they come face to face with an increasingly complex and unforgiving world. In 1922 Cather was awarded a Pulitzer Prize for *One of Ours*, despite the fact that it is generally considered one of the least remarkable of her works. In 1932 the American novelist William Faulkner listed her as one of the five best living writers, along with Ernest Hemingway, Thomas Mann, John Dos Passos and himself.

Willa Sibert Cather was born in Back Creek Valley, a small farming community near the Blue Ridge Mountains in Virginia, the first of the seven children of Charles Fetigue Cather and his wife Mary Virginia Boak. In 1883 the family moved west to Webster County, Nebraska, in the frontier land which would provide the background for the majority of Cather's novels. The young Cather discovered that native-born Americans were in the minority in this new territory, but she made friends among the vast numbers of immigrants from Bohemia, Denmark, Germany and Russia, who made a deep impression on her and later became the models for many of her fictional characters.

After graduating from Red Cloud High School in 1890 Cather attended the University of Nebraska at Lincoln, where she was active in journalism and wrote a weekly drama column, which she called 'The Passing Show', for the *Nebraska State Journal*. After university she worked for several years as an editor, book critic and teacher. She worked for *McClure's Magazine* in New York, which published the works of such authors as Rudyard Kipling, Robert Louis Stevenson and Thomas Hardy. In 1902 she had saved up enough money for a long-anticipated trip to Europe accompanied by her friend Isabelle McClung. While abroad the young women visited the poet A. E. Housman, whom Cather greatly admired. Exposure to the world beyond Nebraska strengthened her feeling for the immigrants among whom she had grown up, as she was now visiting their countries of origin. At the same time she obtained a new perspective on, and greater understanding of, her own homeland, from having seen the world.

Cather admired the language and style of fellow American author Henry James (1843–1916), whose influence is seen in her early short story collection *The Troll Garden* (1905). Following in James's footsteps, she focused on narratives of character, in which plot is secondary to character development. Traces of the influence of Walt Whitman (1819–92) are also apparent in Cather's fiction, particularly his emphasis on the theme of nation-building. Cather and Whitman both celebrated the ordinary men and women whose lives generally went unsung.

Believing that the novel as a genre had been 'over-furnished' for some time, Cather departed from the fashion of such realist contemporaries as Sinclair Lewis (1885–1951) and Theodore Dreiser (1871–1945) in favour of a starker style similar to that seen in the work of Stephen Crane (1871–1900) and the early work of Nathaniel Hawthorne (1804–64). She wrote novels characterised by elegantly spare prose, raw prairie settings and strong female protagonists, becoming in the process a pioneer of American fiction.

O Pioneers! (1913), the first of her novels to make use of her Nebraska memories, established Cather's national reputation as a novelist. The title is a reference to a poem by Walt Whitman entitled 'Pioneers! O Pioneers!' from *Leaves of Grass* (1855). Alexandra Bergson, the heroine, owns her own land, chooses whom she will marry and is a clear predecessor to the even more fiercely alive, irrepressible Ántonia.

My Ántonia (1918), considered by many to be her masterpiece, represents Cather's unique blend of fiction and autobiography at its best. She based the character of Ántonia on Annie Sadilek, a young Bohemian hired girl she knew in Red Cloud. In this novel she employed a new narrative device to establish the **viewpoint**. Instead of narrating as an omniscient author she used the character of Jim Burden to relate Ántonia's story. In this way she gave greater scope to the narrative, adding complexity by allowing the reader to see Ántonia from Jim's point of view as she came in and out of his life over the space of many years. The device is reflected in the novel's title, it being Burden who, at the end, affixes 'my' to his account of his childhood friend.

In many ways Ántonia is the most ordinary and unremarkable of Cather's characters. The daughter of poor Bohemian immigrants, she is forced at an early age to work the land, then goes into service as a hired girl for an unappreciative family in town. Eventually she takes an equally unremarkable husband and settles down to a life of obscurity. Despite these inauspicious circumstances, Ántonia surpasses all other Cather heroines in her unquenchable zest for life and her ability to transcend the many obstacles life throws in her way. At the end of Jim's narrative she remains as firm and everlasting as the Nebraska soil beneath her feet, her spirit undimmed and her life worthy of memorial through the novel.

In the acclaimed *Death Comes for the Archbishop* (1927) Cather weaves together the influence of the Roman Catholic Church in the American Southwest, and the history of the Native American tribes in New Mexico. More than any other this novel represents Cather distancing herself from the modern world by delving into a past more remote than her own childhood. Willa Cather died in New York City on 24 April 1947, and is buried in New Hampshire.

Selected works:

April Twilights (1903); *The Troll Garden* (1905); *The Life of Mary Baker G. Eddy and the History of Christian Science* (1909); *Alexander's Bridge* (1912); *O Pioneers!* (1913); *My Autobiography* (1914); *The Song of the Lark* (1915); *My Ántonia* (1918); *Youth and the Bright Medusa* (1920); *One of Ours* (1922); *A Lost Lady* (1923); *The Professor's House* (1925); *My Mortal Enemy* (1926); *Death Comes for the Archbishop* (1927); *Shadows on the Rock* (1931); *Obscure Destinies* (1932); *Lucy Grayheart* (1935); *Not Under Forty* (1936); *Sapphira and the Slave Girl* (1940).

Further reading

Woodress, James P., *Willa Cather: A Literary Life*. University of Nebraska Press, 1987.

Contributor: Angela M. Thompson

COETZEE, J. M. (1940–)

One gets used to things getting harder; one ceases to be surprised that what used to be as hard as hard can be grows harder yet.

Disgrace

Photo credit: © PA Photos-EPA

John Michael Coetzee, winner of the 2003 Nobel Prize for literature, was also the first author to win the Booker Prize twice: in 1983 for *Life and Times of Michael K.* and in 1999 for *Disgrace*. Both novels, although very different, show Coetzee's interest in exploring the common ground between the personal and the political, and the devastating effects the bigger social picture can have on individual lives.

Coetzee is a South African author, and English is not his first language (although it was his mother's language). In this respect he has something in common with the British author of Polish origin Joseph Conrad, and the American author of Russian origin, **Vladimir Nabokov**. Like them, he became a master of style in an acquired language. His decision to write in English rather than Afrikaans came partly through education, and partly through his awareness that English, with its rich literary history and wide usage, opens doors to thematic interculturalism. Also, like **Samuel Beckett**, about whom he has written, Coetzee pursues a style which is anything but ostentatious, displaying an almost cold sobriety which, however, strengthens his portrayal of human drama.

Coetzee's novels frequently establish dialogues with various historical ages and territories. In *Waiting for the Barbarians* (1980), the imaginary setting and time, filtering reality through allegory, clearly allude to the racist South Africa of which he has first-hand experience, and which is the main focus of his writing. Similarly, although the setting of *Life and Times of Michael K.* (1983) is unspecified, the novel tells the story of a group of characters living at the time of the fall of the apartheid regime. For the young gardener Michael K., who takes his mother back home through a country devastated by war, her death on the journey is a more overwhelming tragedy than the brutal macrocosm in which he lives could ever be. Tragedy, however, whether on a large scale or small, whether personal or social, must be lived through with dignity; this is a theme Coetzee pursues repeatedly, particularly in *Disgrace* (1999).

Coetzee's novels are replete with complex **intertextual** allusions, and an omnipresent **metafictional** commentary which won't let us forget that he is also a professor of literature. In *Foe* (1987) and *The Master of Petersburg* (1994), he establishes stylistic dialogues with Defoe and Dostoevsky, his favourite authors, on whose work he draws heavily. Historical allusion is used on the level of form as well as content, as Coetzee reads the contemporary human condition through **postmodern** stylistic pastiche.

Disgrace, Coetzee's most famous novel, and the most powerful on apartheid, dispenses with the refined erudition of earlier novels and presents difficult issues, such as cross-racial and intra-racial relations, through the personal experience of the characters. The blurred distinction between the conflicts to which such issues give rise reinforces the awareness that there is no way to exclude historical and political forces from the private lives of individuals. *Disgrace* is a novel about how collective and individual dramas interpenetrate to the point of complete overlap, and about how to raise the issue of the moral responsibility of the whites in South Africa. Coetzee discusses the issue of racial difference as a variety of human difference in general.

In *Disgrace*, before facing the shock of his daughter Lucy's rape by three black men, Professor David Lurie has himself committed a comparable moral transgression. The action which triggers his dismissal from the Cape Town Technical University, his affair with a student, makes him guilty not only of a loss of a sense of reality, an attempt to conflate real life and the work of **Romantic** poets which he teaches and writes about, but also of taking advantage of his privileged position as a professor.

Having lost his university job, Lurie finds refuge with his daughter, at her farm in Salem, Eastern Cape. In this forsaken place he discovers new meanings to existence, as he contemplates the similarities between human destiny and that of the dogs which, at the vet clinic, Lucy's best friend Bev Shaw puts to sleep when they can no longer be saved.

The quiet banality of Eastern Cape routine seems to follow a rule of accepting life as it comes, undisturbed by too much questioning. Questioning, however, becomes imperative when the farm is attacked and Lucy is raped and made pregnant. From this moment on, the ways in which the white lesbian woman's life is changed becomes the main focus of the novel. From a loose story of the affairs of a literature professor, the theme becomes a psychological study of the responsibility of the whites in South Africa. Lucy's decision to keep the baby – the living outcome of her trauma – is a statement of the need to assume such responsibility. Her wish to be a good mother is a metaphor for her faith in the possibility of turning evil into good, conflict into love, death into life.

Coetzee's intention in *Disgrace* was not to write a political manifesto, but to portray a real life experience which, even if atypical, presents an optimistic view of the future of a country long divided by conflict. It can be read as an alternative way to express the damage done, by prejudice, to people's lives. Happiness may come from the satisfaction of being able to put an end to suffering, as Bev Shaw does for the dogs. But apart from death, Coetzee seems to say, there are few absolute truths.

Elizabeth Costello (2004) seems to mark a return to the intellectual sophistication of Coetzee's earlier work, and a setting aside of his commitment to the South African arena. With its biographical and philosophical overtones the novel challenges its own status as a novel, by breaking through the boundaries of the genre with bursts of complex intellectual discourse. There are many similarities between the heroine and her author: a reluctance to accept literary celebrity and its world of false self-appraisal, and a fear of prejudice, of fixed beliefs that will not lend themselves to change. A plea for thinking and open-mindedness, this novel is, ultimately, faithful to Coetzee's overriding credo that prejudice is the most serious danger humanity has to face.

Selected works:

Fiction: *Dusklands* (1974); *In the Heart of the Country: A Novel* (1977); *Waiting for the Barbarians* (1980); *Life and Times of Michael K.* (1983); *Foe* (1987); *Age of Iron* (1990); *The Master of Petersburg* (1994); *Disgrace* (1999); *Elizabeth Costello* (2004). **Non-fiction:** *White Writing: On the Culture of Letters* (1988); *Doubling the Point: Essays and Interviews* (1992); *Giving Offense: Essays on Censorship* (1996).

Further reading

Kossew, Sue (ed.) *Critical Essays on J. M. Coetzee.* New York and London: Prentice Hall International, 1998.

Contributor: Maria-Sabina Draga Alexandru

DOVE, RITA (1952–)

She wants to hear wine pouring.
She wants to taste change.
She wants pride to roar through the
kitchen.

from Thomas and Beulah

Rita Dove, as an African-American writer and American Poet Laureate from 1993 to 1995, has brought the history and experience of black Americans into the mainstream of American poetry. Her grandparents were part of the movement, in the early twentieth century, of black workers from the impoverished farms of the South to the industrial Northern cities of the United States, a movement known as the 'great migration'. They came to Akron, Ohio, met and married and raised a family. In her Pulitzer Prize-winning poem, *Thomas and Beulah* (1986), Dove draws on their experience, representing it as a search for the American dream of a better life. *Thomas and Beulah* is a long poem divided in two sections each with a sequence of short lyrics, 'Mandolin' from Thomas's perspective; 'Canary in Bloom' from the point of view of his wife, Beulah. Dove said that she wanted to 'string moments as beads on a necklace'[1] so that the lyrics do not form a continuous narrative, but are made up of selected sensory details and compressions of time, in language incorporating blues, gospel and folk idioms. Dove's concern is not only to recover family history; the poem is also an expression of her interest in what she has called the 'underside of history', the 'ordinary citizens and unsung heroes'[2] that history textbooks ignore.

If *Thomas and Beulah* was Dove's return to family origins, it is also important to note that her work has, from the beginning, been markedly international. She has always refused to be confined by a racially marked poetic identity. She published her first significant volume of poetry, *The Yellow House on the Corner* (1980), at the age of 28 after periods of living as a student in Germany. It juxtaposes

American preoccupations with explorations of European history and culture. Thus there are poems such as 'The Bird Frau' which expresses the disorientated anxieties and anticipations of a half-starved German mother in wartime, and 'Robert Schumann, Or: Musical Genius Begins with Affliction', a comic celebration of the composer, an early example of her continuing interest in music, both as subject and as formal inspiration. The bold historical range of this volume is matched by a sense of travel as a stimulus to, and metaphor for, the transforming powers of the imagination: the volume title, *The Yellow House on the Corner*, signifies how the imagination transforms and colours the ordinary. The sense of a poet capable of formal economy and lyric flight is evident in 'Geometry', a poem that has been much anthologised, which explores the analogy between working out a theorem and writing a poem: whereas a theorem is proven, the metaphorical imagination expands 'to some point true and unproven'.

Dove's next volume, *Museum* (1983), studies the past through its representations, the artefacts and works of art that are left for the modern tourist to examine. This is not always comfortable as the poet discovers in confronting a portrait in a German museum, entitled 'Agosta the Winged Man and Rasha the Black Dove', in which it is evident that a black woman like herself, and coincidentally with her own name, was routinely exhibited as a freak in 1920s Berlin. The precise and complex visual layout of Dove's poem of the same title seeks to recover the ordinary lives of the deformed white man and the young black woman in the portrait. Another poem in which Dove takes on issues of race, this time with notable comic poise, is 'The Sailor in Africa', a poem on colonialist enterprise in pursuit of the slave trade, based on a Viennese card game. The volume concludes with 'Parsley', in which the poet dramatises the consciousness of Trujillo, the murderous dictator of the Dominican Republic. This is all controversial territory for the imagination; it shows Dove's grace and toughness of spirit that she undertakes such explorations.

The volume *Grace Notes* (1989), a title suggestive of musical embellishment, is also indicative of the poet's **feminist** intent to note the conditions and possibilities for black American women 50 years on from the subject of the opening poem, 'Summit Beach, 1921', whose date and location signify an important moment in the history of racial segregation. There are a number of autobiographical poems about motherhood as well as others in a more **symbolist** and mythic mode such as 'Medusa' and 'Mississippi'.

Dove is married to the German writer, Fred Viebahn, and they have a daughter, Aviva. Myth and the vulnerabilities of modern motherhood are the subjects of the volume *Mother Love* (1995), a sonnet sequence based on the myth of Demeter and her daughter, Persephone, and composed, as Dove said in her introduction to the volume, 'in homage and as counterpart to Rilke's *Sonnets to Orpheus*'. The sequence sustains a parallel between the contemporary and the classical: Demeter, the earth-goddess grief-stricken at her daughter's abduction, is also the modern American mother whose daughter has left home. The abductor is both Hades, god of the underworld, and a louche middle-aged Parisian artist who opportunistically seduces a modern American girl studying abroad. The title poem, 'Mother Love', is ironically feminist in its critique of gender roles. The success of the volume is in combining a contemporary cutting-edge with a mythic universal mode.

On the Bus with Rosa Parks (1999) foregrounds the part played by ordinary black women in the struggle for civil rights in America, most notably, in the poem 'Rosa'; Dove celebrates Rosa Parks's historic refusal to move to the back of a segregated bus in Montgomery, Alabama, in 1955. Central to the volume is 'Lady Freedom Among Us', written during Dove's period as Poet Laureate to commemorate the return of the Statue of Freedom to the Capitol dome in Washington. The touch of black phrasing, the pun on US in the title, indicates a confidence in ethnic diversity as the norm 'among us'. The poem speaks directly to the American people, imperatively, individually:

don't lower your eyes
or stare straight ahead to where
you think you ought to be going

Genuinely populist, as with other poems in this volume, this poem reflects Dove's mission as Poet Laureate to extend the audience for poetry. The bus, in the volume title, is a symbol not only of civil rights, but also of the life journey westwards, individual and collective, the short span that humanity is allowed. Writing on the eve of the new millennium, Dove also, more sombrely, reflects upon history. The poem, 'Revenant', revisits old sites of freedom and punishment beginning with an image of freedom, the palomino horse associated with American Indians, but then moves to a public execution. The 'black hood of the condemned' signifies a collective human failure. The angel watching the scene turns away. The range of Dove's poetry, from the colloquial and accessible to the highly wrought symbolism of this poem, is an impressive achievement.

Dove has also published a play, *The Darker Face of the Earth*, a version of the Oedipus myth set in a slave plantation in the American South. Its performance at the Cottesloe auditorium in London in 1999 gave an opportunity for young black actors to appear at the National Theatre. She has also published a volume of short stories, *Fifth Sunday* (1985), a novel, *Through the Ivory Gate* (1992) and *The Poet's World* (1995), autobiographical essays and lectures given during her period as Poet Laureate. Dove is currently a Professor at the University of Virginia in Charlottesville.

References

1. **Taleb-Khyar, Mohammed B**. (1991) 'An Interview with Maryse Condé and Rita Dove', *Callaloo*, 14. 2, p. 345.

2. **Ingersoll, Earl G., Kitchen, Judith and Rubin, Stan Sanvel** (eds) (1989) '"The Underside of the Story": A Conversation with Rita Dove', *The Post-Confessionals*. London and Toronto: Associated University Presses, p. 164.

Selected works:

The Yellow House on the Corner (1980); *Museum* (1983); *Fifth Sunday* (1985); *Thomas and Beulah* (1986); *Grace Notes* (1989); *Through the Ivory Gate* (1992); *The Darker Face of the Earth* (1994); *Mother Love* (1995); *The Poet's World* (1995); *On the Bus with Rosa Parks* (1999).

Further reading

Steffen, Therese, *Crossing Color: Transcultural Space and Place in Rita Dove's Poetry, Fiction, and Drama*. Oxford University Press, 2001.

Contributor: Pat Righelato

ELIOT, T. S. (1888–1965)

Let us go then, you and I,
When the evening is spread out against the sky
Like a patient etherised upon a table;
'The Love Song of J. Alfred Prufrock'

Thomas Stearns Eliot, winner of the 1948 Nobel Prize for Literature, was one of the most influential literary figures of the early twentieth century. The period was a melting pot for literary innovations and revolutions, with many of the century's most important writers, such as **W. B. Yeats**, **James Joyce**, **Virginia Woolf** and **D. H. Lawrence**, making an impact, but Eliot holds a special place for the comprehensiveness of his vision and complexity of his outlook. His scholarship was exceptional, and as well as poetry he produced plays, children's fiction and influential literary criticism.

Eliot was born in St Louis, Missouri, the youngest of seven children. His father, Henry, was a businessman, and his mother, Charlotte, a poet. He attended Smith Academy in St Louis, and went on to Milton, Massachusetts, and then Harvard in 1906, where he received his B.A. in 1909. At Harvard he was influenced by the philosopher George Santayana, and the critic Irving Babbitt, the latter being responsible for Eliot's anti-**Romantic** attitude, a stance reinforced by the writings of F. H. Bradley and T. E. Hulme. Eliot spent 1910 and 1911 in France, attending Henri Bergson's lectures on philosophy at the Sorbonne, and studying poetry with Alain-Fournier. His training in European literature and Eastern and Western philosophy could have led to an illustrious career at Harvard, but that was not to be.

His travels and studies interrupted by the First World War, Eliot moved to England in 1915. He spent time in Paris, but never returned to Harvard to complete his PhD. He taught himself Buddhism and Sanskrit, and studied under George Ivanovitch Gurdjieff, who established 'The Institute for the Harmonious Development of Man', first in Russia and later in France. Eliot taught French and Latin for a year at Highgate Junior School in London, then took a post with Lloyds Bank.

Eliot became acquainted with **Ezra Pound**, who encouraged him to write, the result being 'The Love Song of J. Alfred Prufrock', which was published in the Chicago magazine *Poetry* in 1915. Prufrock, the perfect gentleman, is tormented by the meaningless gentility, conventionality and socialising by which he is surrounded, and by his inability to express his anguish. Uncertain of his own identity, he feels he has heard something *other*, but is unable to respond. The fragmented form of the poem reflects his fragmented and anxious state of mind. From a technical point of view the poem was revolutionary, and the extraordinary imagery, such as a quiet evening being likened to a patient etherised on a table, was shocking, but caught the public's attention. Pound introduced Eliot to Harriet Weaver, who published *Prufrock and Other Observations* in 1917; an event which could be taken as the beginning of the **Modernist** revolution in poetry.

In 1915 Eliot married the ballet-dancer Vivienne Haigh-Wood, but the marriage was not a success. His wife was much more vivacious than he was and very temperamental. She suffered from mood swings and was eventually diagnosed as hysterical and confined to a mental institution.

In 1919 *Ara Vos Prec* (entitled *Poems* in the United States) was published, containing the poem 'Gerontion', a contemplative interior monologue in blank verse – another revolution in itself. In the same year Eliot published the influential essay 'Tradition and the Individual Talent', in which he presented the doctrine of impersonality in poetry. This was followed by the collections of essays, *The Sacred Wood* (1920), *The Use of Poetry and the Use of Criticism* (1933) and *The Classics and the Man of Letters* (1942). In 'Hamlet and His Problems' in *The Sacred Wood*, he further developed his theory of impersonality, and coined the term

'objective correlative'. In 'The Metaphysical Poets' and 'Andrew Marvell', published in *Selected Essays, 1917–32* (1932) he re-assessed the seventeenth-century Metaphysical poets, praising the intricate harmony of intellect and passion found in their work. He also used the famous phrase 'dissociation of sensibility', which, like many of the ideas expressed in his criticism, seems to suggest an approach helpful in the appreciation of his own poetry. These influential writings changed the face of literary criticism.

From 1917 to 1919 Eliot was assistant editor of *The Egoist* and in 1922 he founded *Criterion*, a quarterly review which closed only with the beginning of the Second World War. Three years later he joined the publishing house Faber and Gwyer, which later became Faber and Faber.

In 1922 Eliot suffered a breakdown, and during his stay at a sanatorium in Lausanne he composed 'The Waste Land' (1922). The poem attracted adverse reactions from conservative quarters, and praise from younger poets. Among the critics were E. E. Cummings, who regarded Eliot as arrogant and pedantic, and Stephen Spender, who commented that there was a 'certain cultivated heartlessness' about the poem. Nevertheless, the poem became a symbol of the disillusionment of the post-First World War generation, and Eliot's conversational style made him an icon, a model for generations of poets to come.

With Pound's guidance Eliot abridged 'The Waste Land' to about half its original length, and divided it into five parts, each consisting of a series of dramatic monologues. It is a carefully crafted chorus of voices, with delicately mingled cultural and historical references. Material was drawn from sources such as the Grail legend, the story of the Fisher King, Frazer's *Golden Bough*, and Dante's *Divine Comedy*, and the final words are in Sanskrit. This reliance on allusion to cosmopolitan mythology, and the liberal use of foreign words, were the aspects most strongly criticised. These elements can alienate the reader, but one's focus should be on the poem's presentation of the predicament of man searching for salvation, rather than on the scholarly references. Eliot had already shown himself to be a fine craftsman, and in this poem he proved himself to be a metrical magician. The five sections are structured on a system of fragmented discontinuity, reflecting the discordant experience of modern secular man. Eliot himself said in 'Tradition and the Individual Talent' that he was striving to attack the very concept of the unity of soul.

Eliot published three short prose works reflecting his interest in socio-theology: *Thoughts After Lambeth* (1931), *The Idea of a Christian Society* (1939) and *Notes Towards the Definition of Culture* (1948). He converted to Anglicanism in 1927, as well as adopting British citizenship. His focus had not yet shifted entirely to religion, but in place of his earlier suspicion of all organised religion he turned to an examination of the concepts of divinity and humanity.

During this period Eliot published poems such as 'The Hollow Men', 'Ash-Wednesday' and *Four Quartets*, all of them ripe with problems of allusion and linguistics. 'Ash Wednesday' is particularly interesting as it was the first long poem written after his conversion. This poem addresses religion in a way that no other poem had previously, expressing the pain of accepting religion at the cost of one's disbelief. The poem was not well received, its apparently secular outlook being interpreted as an expression of disillusionment.

Four Quartets led to Eliot being awarded the Nobel Prize, and Eliot himself regarded it as his masterpiece. The four poems, 'Burnt Norton' (1936), 'East Coker' (1940), 'The Dry Salvages' (1942) and 'Little Gidding' (1942) are carefully crafted, starting from geography and leading into the exploration of such themes as theology, history and humanity. The four were written separately, but when brought together assumed a harmonious structure, being united by the theme of 'the past'. This work was universally accepted, even those who were not in sympathy with the Christian message being impressed by the thematic and technical mastery.

Eliot's religious searching and slowly-emerging convictions found expression in his plays, from *Sweeney Agonistes* (published 1926, performed 1934) to *The Elder Statesman* (published 1958, performed 1959). He wrote his plays in blank verse in an attempt to re-introduce verse drama to the stage, but not all of them can be ranked with his best poetry.

Murder in the Cathedral (1935) is perhaps the most significant, dealing with a deeply religious experience which is attained through doubt and temptation. Influenced by the seventeenth-century preacher Lancelot Andrews, it is based on the death of St Thomas à Becket. The play resulted in Eliot being appointed to the committee in charge of a new English translation of the Bible. *The Family Reunion* (1939), in which Eliot used dialogue closer to natural speech, did not win the popularity of *Murder in the Cathedral*, the audience finding it difficult to accept the classical story of Orestes adapted to a modern domestic setting and given a heavy dose of psychological realism.

Eliot's wife Vivienne died in a mental institution in 1947. In 1948 he wrote his influential piece of social criticism *Notes Towards the Definition of Culture*, and in 1957 he married his secretary, Valerie Fletcher, and lived with her happily until his death.

During the last years of his life Eliot's views were shaped by Anglo-Catholic Christianity, his belief being that culture is rooted in religion. He did not believe in a so-called progressive mobility of culture, but in regeneration of tradition; tradition not in the sense of following age-old rigid laws, but preserving only those elements which are timeless, and can contribute to the future. He believed that a poet writing in English could accept any tradition, from Homer to his own time, irrespective of language. He maintained that contemporary western culture was a mass of confusion; the decay of religion being the principal problem. In his quest for meaning he found consolation in Anglicanism, but some have doubts about his conversion, which seems to have been more a matter of will than of faith. There is a line of thought that claims that Eliot was more desperate than pious, and grabbed the only rope that was thrown to him. Even his friends, such as Virginia Woolf, shared this view. Although his reliance on religion may seem out of place for a modern writer, his focus on the individual makes him truly modern.

Eliot's fame has not been without blemish; he has been accused of racism, and of supporting Fascism. One particular poem, 'Burbank with a Baedeker: Bleistan with a Cigar', has been the focus of controversy as it contains a suggestion of anti-Semitism, a suggestion which will permanently tarnish his image.

When Eliot died in 1965 he was cremated and, in accordance with his wishes, his ashes were taken to St Michael's Church in East Coker, his ancestral village.

Further reading

Ackroyd, Peter, *T. S. Eliot: A Life*. Simon and Schuster, 1984.

Eliot, Thomas Stearns, *Christianity and Culture: The Idea of a Christian Society and Notes Towards the Definition of Culture*. Harcourt Brace Jovanovich, 1968.

Eliot, Thomas Stearns, *The Frontiers of Culture*. Lecture, Minnesota: University of Minnesota Press, 1956.

Gardner, Helen, *The Art of T. S. Eliot*. Faber and Faber, 1980.

Jain, Manju, *A Critical Reading of the Selected Poems of T. S. Eliot*. Oxford University Press, 2002.

Kenner, Hugh, *The Invisible Poet*. Harcourt, 1969.

Matthiesen, Francis Otto, *The Achievement of T. S. Eliot: An Essay on the Nature of Poetry*. Oxford University Press, 1958.

Moody, A. David (ed.) *The Cambridge Companion to T. S. Eliot*. Cambridge University Press, 1994.

Raffel, Burton, *T. S. Eliot*. Continuum, 1991.

Spender, Stephen, *T. S. Eliot and the Writers of the Thirties*. University of Calcutta, 1990, Prof. Mohinimohan Bhattacharya Memorial Lecture.

Selected works:

Poetry: *Prufrock and Other Observations* (1917); *Ara Vos Prec* (American title: *Poems*) (1919); *The Waste Land* (1922); *Four Quartets* (1943), consisting of: 'Burnt Norton' (1936), 'East Coker' (1940), 'The Dry Salvages' (1942) and 'Little Gidding' (1942). **Prose:** *The Sacred Wood* (1920); *Dante* (1929); *Thoughts After Lambeth* (1931); *Selected Essays, 1917–32* (1932); *The Use of Poetry and the Use of Criticism* (1933); *The Idea of a Christian Society* (1939); *The Classics and the Man of Letters* (1942); *Notes Towards the Definition of Culture* (1948). **Plays:** *Sweeney Agonistes* (1926); *Murder in the Cathedral* (1935); *The Family Reunion* (1939); *The Cocktail Party* (1950); *The Confidential Clerk* (1953); *The Elder Statesman* (1958). **For Children:** *Old Possum's Book of Practical Cats* (1939).

Contributor: Siddartha Biswas

EMECHETA, BUCHI (1944–)

So as Britain was emerging from war once more victorious, and claiming to have stopped the slavery she had helped to spread in all her black colonies, Ojebeta, now a woman of thirty-five, was changing masters.

The Slave Girl

Buchi Emecheta was born in Nigeria's capital, Lagos, but her parents were from the smaller town of Ibuza, and an awareness of the differences between city life and traditional village life is reflected in many of her novels, particularly those set in Nigeria. *The Joys of Motherhood* (1979), for example, one of her most celebrated novels, tells the story of Nnu Ego, who marries and moves to the city with her new husband, makes countless sacrifices for her children and yet dies alone. The novel depicts the shock suffered by the generation which bore the brunt of the transition to a more modern lifestyle, trapped in old beliefs but surrounded by a changing society.

The Slave Girl (1977), which won Emecheta an award for Best Black Writer in the World, also deals with the contrast between village and city life, and the effects of colonialism, with Christianity playing a major role in what is basically a fictionalisation of the life of Emecheta's grandmother. The story of Ojebeta, the slave girl, is an extreme example of the lives of women in a patriarchal society, while also standing for the slavery of a whole continent under colonial rule. When Ojebeta's parents die in an influenza epidemic, the seven-year-old girl is sold by her brother to a distant relative. Her slavery, Emecheta makes clear, is a version of the domestic slavery to which even free women are subjected. The novel is a witty and provocative presentation of the interaction between four different levels of slavery, colonial, religious, indigenous African and the domestic slavery of marriage.

In her depiction of village life in a choral style Emecheta's work resembles that of **Chinua Achebe**, but unlike Achebe she concentrates on the experiences of women. This places her, despite her protestations, in the **feminist/womanist** tradition alongside writers such as Ama Ata Aidoo and **Angela Carter**. She could also be associated with a number of migrant writers who have written about London, including **Jean Rhys** and Sam Selvon.

Emecheta attended several schools in Lagos, and in her autobiography, *Head Above Water* (1986), records being introduced to writers such as Jane Austen, Lord Byron and Charles Dickens. The list of her literary influences, however, would not be complete without including the strong influence of an oral tradition, which can be seen in her deceptively simple prose-style, and in the cumulative effect of her novels as a whole. When taken together, the novels work as a complex series of tales that offer individual perspectives, while at the same time including the reader in the history of an imaginary people. This overall integrity arises from the fact that many of the novels are autobiographically based, and therefore deal with similar concerns. Additionally, Emecheta's degree in sociology (London University, 1974) has helped her to provide her fiction, which is invariably presented in the third person, with nuanced social observations.

The autobiographical novels *In the Ditch* (1972) and *Second-Class Citizen* (1974) fictionalise Emecheta's arrival in Britain, her struggles against prejudice and an abusive husband, separation from him, and the attempt to rebuild a life while living in a council estate. She married at 16, and had five children within the next six years. In 1962 she joined her husband in London but separated from him four years later. One of the factors which made her leave her husband was his burning of the manuscript of her first novel, an earlier, more idealised version of a couple's life that would later become *The Bride Price* (1976). At the age of 22 she had to fend for

herself and her five children while studying and writing *In the Ditch*, her first published novel, which dissects the harsh life of single mothers living on benefit in a state of virtual classlessness. Although published after *In the Ditch*, *Second-Class Citizen* precedes it chronologically and follows the same main character through life with her husband, showing the hostile attitude of white Britons, immigrants from other parts of the Empire, and Nigerian men.

The depiction of difficulties faced by immigrants is also a theme of *Gwendolen* (1989, published as *The Family* in the USA) and *Kehinde* (1994). *Kehinde* is particularly well crafted. The narrative follows the eponymous character's struggle to come to terms with her husband's desertion and his return to Nigeria, first by following him and becoming entangled in extended family politics, which include her husband's second wife and his sisters, and finally by returning to England. Like many immigrants, Kehinde and her husband believe that returning to Nigeria will be akin to going back to a paradisiacal place where they can be happy ever after. This dream of a welcoming homeland is exploded in the novel, a theme which resonates with the notion of 'imaginary homelands' put forward by **Salman Rushdie**.[1] Kehinde's freedom from social bonds (for instance, she realises that being married is not all there is in a woman's life) comes at a high cost, for she must leave her children behind and start anew in London.

The illusion of the 'homeland' is further explored in *The New Tribe* (2000), the first of her novels to feature a male protagonist; Chester is abandoned at birth and brought up by Reverend Arlington and his wife. His feelings of alienation result in a fruitless quest for an imaginary African kingdom of which he is the rightful prince. The 'tribe' he is looking for, however, is not to be found in his origins, but in a future multicultural society, which is perhaps the 'new tribe' to which the title alludes.

Emecheta's heroines experience conflicts while trying to build an identity across different cultural discourses. The conflicts are based on those experienced by Emecheta herself, such as cultural estrangement arising from postcoloniality, race, gender and class issues, and migration to England. Readers often feel unnerved by her work because of its seemingly self-contradictory nature. Hers is not a body of writing that relies on one particular political stance or defends a specific community, as can be seen in her ambiguous relation to feminism, which she rejects as a Western European practice despite sharing many of its tenets. For this reason some critics have seen her writing as inconsistent. She has also been accused of displaying a Eurocentric condescension towards her native Africa. Her Africanness has, it is argued, been diluted and she has 'gone native' in reverse.

Emecheta has been careful not to fall into the trap of the immigrant who looks at her country's affairs from a distance, and she can be seen as a new kind of syncretic, postcolonial writer, whose identity refuses to be resolved in favour of either of its elements, the 'African' or the 'Western'.

References

1. **Rushdie, Salman** (1991) *Imaginary Homelands: Essays And Criticism, 1981–91.* Penguin.

Selected works:

In the Ditch (1972); *Second-Class Citizen* (1974); *The Bride Price* (1976); *The Slave Girl* (1977); *The Joys of Motherhood* (1979); *Double Yoke* (1982); *Destination Biafra* (1982); *The Rape of Shavi* (1983); *Head Above Water* (1986); *Gwendolen* (1989); *Kehinde* (1994); *The New Tribe* (2000).

Further reading

Fishburn, Katherine, *Reading Buchi Emecheta: Cross-cultural Conversations.* Westport, CT: Greenwood Press, 1995.

Sougou, Omar, *Writing Across Cultures: Gender Politics and Difference in the Fiction of Buchi Emecheta.* Amsterdam, Netherlands: Rodopi, 2002.

Umeh, Marie (ed.) *Emerging Perspectives on Buchi Emecheta.* Trenton, NJ and Asmara, Eritrea: Africa World Press, 1996.

Contributor: Ana María Sánchez-Arce

FAULKNER, WILLIAM (1897–1962)

Beginning with Sartoris I discovered that my own little postage stamp of native soil was worth writing about and that I would never live long enough to exhaust it.[1]

William Faulkner was born William Cuthbert Falkner (as his name was then spelt) in New Albany, Mississippi, into a well-established entrepreneurial family which moved to Oxford, Mississippi when he was about five years old. Faulkner emerged as a budding poetic talent while in high school, writing in a style derivative of Robert Burns, Swinburne and A. E. Housman. He left high school before graduating, and by the time he published his first novel in 1926, he had worked as a clerk with the Winchester Repeating Arms Company (where his name was first spelt 'Faulkner', by mistake), tried unsuccessfully (because of his height) to be admitted to the United States Air Force, trained as a cadet in the Canadian Royal Air Force, worked as a bookstore assistant, been scoutmaster of the Oxford Boy Scouts, and postmaster of the University of Mississippi post office. Although he had never completed school, in 1919 he enrolled in the University of Mississippi under a special provision for war veterans, but dropped out in 1920 before taking his degree.

In 1924, with the help of his friend and literary mentor Phil Stone, Faulkner published a volume of poetry *The Marble Faun.* His first novel, *Soldiers' Pay*, was written in the following year and published in 1926. Based partially on his brief experience in the RAF, it was about the homecoming of a fatally wounded aviator.

After a brief tour of Europe and the publication of a second novel, *Mosquitoes* (1927), Faulkner decided to write more about his native region and to use the local lore and family tales that he had absorbed during his childhood and adolescence. He fictionalised the region under the invented name 'Yoknapatawpha County', drawing on both regional geography and his family history, particularly his great-grandfather's military exploits. The first novel to explore this setting was *Sartoris* (1929), and from then on few of his works were set outside Yoknapatawpha. In an interview given in 1956 he said,

> Beginning with *Sartoris* I discovered that my own little postage stamp of native soil was worth writing about and that I would never live long enough to exhaust it, and by sublimating the actual into apocryphal I would have complete liberty to use whatever talent I might have to its absolute top.[2]

Faulkner's next novel, *The Sound and the Fury* (1929), shows the emergence of themes that would recur throughout his fiction. Through the account of the slow decline of a prominent family, the novel explores the decadence of the American South after the Civil War, and the slow dissolution of traditional values and authority. The technical innovation displayed in the novel shows the influence of **Modernist** writers (Faulkner was a great admirer of **James Joyce**). The four parts of the novel are narrated by three brothers, and an idiot who has a weak grasp of the concept of time. This allows Faulkner to employ a range of styles, and freely move the narrative back and forth between past and present.

Faulkner had written another novel, *Sanctuary*, earlier in 1929, but had to wait until 1931 before it was published in a heavily revised form, because of its controversial subject matter. Dealing with the abduction and rape of a young woman, *Sanctuary* attempts to portray the sordidness and violence which he saw as features of the South's moral degeneration. His professed reason for writing it was to make money, and indeed *Sanctuary* remained his best-selling book for a long time, for reasons that are debatable.

The technical experimentation of *The Sound and the Fury* was taken farther in *As I Lay Dying* (1930), a *tour de force* which Faulkner claimed to have written 'in six weeks, without changing a word'. The novel deals with the death of a matriarch in a poor Southern family, and her wish to be buried in Jefferson, 'a hard day's ride away' to the north. The narrative consists of the '**streams of consciousness**' of 15 characters, organised into 59 chapters,

describing the death and the family's subsequent journey with the body.

In 1930 Faulkner bought Rowan Oak, an old house in Oxford, which was to be his home for the rest of his life. He also started to publish short stories in magazines such as *Saturday Evening Post, Forum* and *American Mercury*. Finding it difficult to make a living from novels, he became increasingly dependent on publishing short stories to make ends meet.

Faulkner seems to have wanted to write a novel called *Dark House*, and his manuscripts bear evidence that he started writing it at least twice. The first attempt introduced the theme of racial difference, which gained prominence in his later works. Through the depiction of Joe Christmas, an orphan of uncertain racial origin, Lena Grove, a pregnant girl who is on a quest to find her child's father, and other marginalised characters of Yoknapatawpha, Faulkner produced a tightly structured tale which was published in 1932 as *Light in August*.

The second manuscript which Faulkner originally called *Dark House* became an enormously complex and self-conscious narrative in which four principal narrators (one of them being Quentin Compson who is also one of the narrators in *The Sound and the Fury*) try to put together pieces of evidence in their reconstruction of the mystery behind the life and death of the demonic Thomas Sutpen, killed more than 40 years earlier. The novel, finally called *Absalom, Absalom!* (1936), can be read as addressing problems of textuality and reading strategy, an exploration of how meaning is created through interpretation.

Starting in 1932, Faulkner wrote for the screen for movie companies such as Metro-Goldwyn-Mayer, 20th Century Fox and Warner Brothers. He wrote, among other things, the screenplays for **Ernest Hemingway**'s *To Have and Have Not* and Raymond Chandler's *The Big Sleep*, and collaborated with Jean Renoir on the latter's *The Southerner*. Though mostly poorly paid, Faulkner was obliged to return to Hollywood on several occasions, to ward off financial crisis.

The publication of *Go Down, Moses* in 1942 is sometimes regarded as marking the end of Faulkner's so-called 'great decade' of writing. Faulkner insisted that *Go Down, Moses* was a novel, although it consisted of several short stories, many of them previously published, involving diverse characters spanning a century in the history of Yoknapatawpha County. At the centre of the book is the story 'The Bear', arguably Faulkner's best-known short work. His later works are generally considered to be weak, although Faulkner himself regarded *A Fable* (1954), an intricate symbolic narrative about a reincarnation of Christ during a French soldiers' mutiny in the trenches of the First World War, that took him more than ten years to complete, to be his masterpiece. Along with *Pylon* (1935) and *The Wild Palms* (1939), it was also one of the few mature works by him that did not have Yoknapatawpha County as their setting.

Among his later works is the so-called 'Snopes Trilogy', consisting of *The Hamlet* (1940), *The Town* (1957) and *The Mansion* (1959). The trilogy portrays the ruthless rise to power of a new 'redneck' middle class in the South, embodied in the character of the avaricious and ambitious Flem Snopes, which had little regard for tradition. *Requiem for a Nun* (1951), a semi-dramatic sequel to *Sanctuary* written in collaboration with Joan Williams, earned the distinction of being adapted for the stage by Albert Camus in 1956.

Faulkner was awarded the 1949 Nobel Prize for Literature, and became an increasingly public figure, being chosen by the US State Department as a cultural ambassador and asked to undertake goodwill tours abroad. As well as several other awards and medals, Faulkner received the Pulitzer Prize for Literature twice, in 1955 for *A Fable*, and posthumously in 1963 for his last novel *The Reivers* (1962). He also received the Legion d'Honneur, France's highest civil award, in 1951.

The stress of incessant travel and unending engagements took a toll on Faulkner's health, and this, combined with his drinking problem, saw him hospitalised several times in the late 1950s. In 1962 he suffered two riding accidents while pursuing, in spite of a failing body, his favourite sport of fox-hunting. He died of heart failure on 6 July 1962, leaving behind him a corpus of 19 novels, more than 80 short stories, a few volumes of poetry and several essays.

References

1. **Merriwether, James and Millgate, Michael** (1968) *Lion in the Garden*. University of Nebraska Press.

2. Ibid.

Selected works:

The Marble Faun (1924); *Soldiers' Pay* (1926); *Mosquitoes* (1927); *Sartoris* (1929); *The Sound and the Fury* (1929); *As I Lay Dying* (1930); *Sanctuary* (1931); *Light In August* (1932); *Pylon* (1935); *Absalom Absalom!* (1936); *The Unvanquished* (1938); *The Wild Palms* (1939); *The Hamlet* (1940); *Go Down, Moses* (1942); *Intruder in the Dust* (1948); *Knight's Gambit* (1949); *Collected Stories* (1950); *Requiem For a Nun* (1951); *A Fable* (1954); *The Town* (1957); *The Mansion* (1959); *The Reivers* (1962); *Essays Speeches and Public Letters* (1966); *Flags in the Dust* (1973); *The Marionettes* (1975); *Mayday* (1977).

Further reading

Brooks, Cleanth, *William Faulkner: The Yoknapatawpha Country*. Yale University Press, 1977.

Millgate, Michael, *The Achievement of William Faulkner*. University of Nebraska Press, 1978.

Contributor: Tathagata Banerjee

FITZGERALD, F. SCOTT (1896–1940)

Gatsby, pale as death, with his hands plunged like weights in his coat pockets, was standing in a puddle of water glaring tragically into my eyes.

The Great Gatsby

Photo credit: © Rex Features

Francis Scott Key Fitzgerald, American short story writer and novelist, is best known for his depiction of the 'Jazz Age' of the 1920s. His own reckless, excessive lifestyle came to symbolise the 'Roaring Twenties', characterised first by glitter and glamour, then by the decadence and destruction of self-indulgence, which he depicted in his novels and short stories. Fitzgerald was both a leading participant in the life he described, and an objective observer. Though not generally recognised as a gifted writer during his lifetime, he, along with **Ernest Hemingway** and **William Faulkner**, is now known in critical circles as one of the 'Big Three' American authors of the first half of the twentieth century. The American classic *The Great Gatsby* is the best known and most popular of Fitzgerald's works. Written in 1925, it is a criticism of the moral emptiness and corruption of wealthy American society during the Jazz Age.

Fitzgerald was born in St Paul, Minnesota, the only child of Catholic parents. His father, Edward, from Maryland, had aristocratic ties to the Old South, and was a distant relative of the author of the 'Star Spangled Banner'. His mother, Mary (Mollie) McQuillan, was the daughter of a wealthy Irish immigrant. When Edward failed at furniture manufacturing in St Paul, the family moved to upstate New York. When he lost his job the family returned to St Paul and lived on Mollie's inheritance. Edward's aristocratic aspirations and social values were to become one of the dominant influences in Fitzgerald's life, and as a youth he fantasised he was of royal lineage.

At St Paul Academy, when he was 13, Fitzgerald's first writing, a detective story, was printed in the school paper. He next attended Newman School, a Catholic prep school in New Jersey, but his youthful desire for personal distinction and achievement, and lack of athletic ability, made him unpopular at school. More interested in prestige than academics, his social ambitions were realised when he was accepted as a member of the Princeton Class of 1917.

At Princeton Fitzgerald became a prominent literary figure, writing scripts and lyrics for the Princeton Triangle Club musicals, and contributing to literary magazines. In his pursuit of campus glory he neglected his studies until, after being put on academic probation, he was forced to withdraw from school. He returned to Princeton the following year, where he found he had lost his coveted positions; he never graduated.

With the outbreak of the First World War Fitzgerald signed up for officers' training, and entered the United States army as a second lieutenant. In the army he continued to pursue his literary aspirations. Convinced he would not live through the war if he saw combat, he hurriedly wrote his first novel, *The Romantic Egotist*. The rejection letter from Charles Scribner's Sons praised the novel's originality and encouraged him to revise his work.

While stationed at Camp Sheridan, Fitzgerald fell in love with Zelda Sayre, the daughter of an Alabama Supreme Court judge. Unaware of the family's history of mental instability, he found the 18-year-old belle mesmerising and the romance intensified on the hoped-for success of his novel.

After the war Fitzgerald was sent overseas and on his discharge from the army he went to New York City, determined to achieve success and win Zelda. Unwilling to live on his meagre advertising salary, Zelda broke off their engagement and Fitzgerald returned to St Paul to rewrite his novel for a second time. When *This Side of Paradise* was published in 1920, the 24-year-old Fitzgerald became famous overnight and the couple married. Sudden prosperity gave them the opportunity to play roles in wealthy society. Known as the prince and princess of their generation, the extravagant couple drank excessively and partied relentlessly. Their public frolicking landed them in the gossip columns as they tried to outdo each other's zany antics. Fitzgerald tore off his shirt in a theatre, Zelda rode on the hood of a taxi, and they both jumped into public fountains.

The Fitzgeralds' daughter, Frances, nicknamed Scottie, was born in 1921, but their freewheeling lifestyle continued to include frequent episodes of inebriation. Living in Great Neck, on Long Island's north shore, the couple cavorted and partied, their outrageous behaviour including driving their car into a pond. In 1920 *This Side of Paradise* captured the post-war disillusionment of Fitzgerald's generation and revealed the new morality of the young.

The Beautiful and Damned (1921) chronicled the decline of a beautiful and privileged couple into degeneration and damnation, foreshadowing the Fitzgeralds' own downward drift. Fearing a similar end, they escaped the chaos by moving to the French Riviera in 1924. Shortly after their arrival, Fitzgerald finished his most famous novel, *The Great Gatsby* (1925). In France the couple became part of a group of American expatriates, which included Ernest Hemingway and Gerald and Sara Murphy. Fitzgerald described their society in his last completed novel, *Tender is the Night* (1934).

During the next decade, decline replaced dazzle. Zelda began to dance obsessively in a vain attempt to become a first-rate ballerina and Fitzgerald drank too much. Zelda suffered the first of three devastating mental breakdowns in 1930 and never fully recovered, spending most of her remaining years as a hospital resident or outpatient. The couple returned to America in 1931.

Tender is the Night (1934), Fitzgerald's most ambitious novel, examines the deterioration of a brilliant American psychiatrist who marries one of his wealthy patients. Through fictional alter egos, the book portrays Zelda's breakdown and Fitzgerald's decline.

By 1936 Fitzgerald's own health was fading. He smoked heavily and drank excessively. He described his spiritual and physical collapse in frank detail in a long essay, *The Crack-Up* (1936). Although deeply in debt, he insisted on the best and most expensive care for Zelda and a private education for Scottie.

In 1937 Fitzgerald moved to Hollywood to work as a screenwriter for Metro-Goldwyn-Mayer. Sheila Graham, a famous gossip columnist, became his mistress. His Hollywood experience inspired *The Last Tycoon* (1941), with its hero, Monroe Stahr, based on the producer Irving Thalberg. The novel was Fitzgerald's last attempt to depict his vision of the American Dream and a character who could realise it. He died in 1940, aged 44, of a heart attack, with his novel only half finished. His brief life is a tragic, eloquent symbol of the allure and calamity of self-indulgence. Zelda Fitzgerald died in 1948 in Ashville, North Carolina, in a fire at Highland Hospital.

Fitzgerald wrote with a poetic, vibrant, witty, yet clear style. His image as an irresponsible writer resulted from his reputation as a drinker, but he revised painstakingly. His chief themes were aspiration, success, love and loss, his story collections reflecting both the glittering promise and vulgarity of the Jazz Age. He died believing himself a failure, but interest in his work revived after 1945. By 1960 he had achieved lasting literary importance and a secure place among American writers.

Selected works:
This Side of Paradise (1920); *Flappers and Philosophers* (1920); *The Beautiful and the Damned* (1921); *Tales of the Jazz Age* (1922); *The Great Gatsby* (1925); *All the Sad Young Men* (1926); *Tender is the Night* (1934); *Taps at Reveille* (1935); *The Crack-Up* (1936); *The Last Tycoon* (1941). Fitzgerald wrote 160 short stories, many of them for *The Saturday Evening Post*.

Further reading

Bruccoli, Matthew Joseph and Smith, Scottie Fitzgerald, *Some Sort of Epic Grandeur: The Life of F. Scott Fitzgerald* (2nd ed.). Columbia, SC: University of South Carolina Press, 2002.

Meyers, Jeffrey, *Scott Fitzgerald: A Biography*. New York: HarperCollins, 2000.

Contributor: Karen C. Holt

FITZGERALD, PENELOPE (1916–2000)
Novels arise out of the shortcomings of history.[1]

Penelope Mary Fitzgerald was born in Lincoln, England in 1916 and educated at Wycombe Abbey and Somerville College, Oxford. Her father, E. V. Knox, was the editor of *Punch*. Her writing career began comparatively late in life, in her 60s, but despite this she published nine novels and three biographies before her death in 2000. The biographies, *Edward Burne-Jones* (1975), *The Knox Brothers* (1977) (which draws on the history of Fitzgerald's father and his three brothers) and *Charlotte Mew and her Friends* (1984) are evidence of Fitzgerald's interest in researching others' lives. This biographical methodology infiltrates her novels as they too are generally rich in detailed, contextualised descriptions of the environments her characters inhabit.

Fitzgerald is at present little known in the public arena, but her work is highly regarded by the literary establishment and has achieved national and international recognition. With *Offshore* (1979), her third novel, she was awarded the Booker Prize, and three other novels, *The Bookshop* (1978), *The Beginning of Spring* (1988) and *The Gate of Angels* (1990) were also short-listed. *The Blue Flower* (1995) won the American National Book Critics' Circle fiction award in 1997, beating the works of notable rivals such as Don DeLillo and Philip Roth.

Before her first publication in 1975 (*Edward Burne-Jones*) Fitzgerald had several forms of employment, including being an assistant at the BBC during the Second World War, teaching at the Italia Conti stage school and working in a bookshop. Some of these experiences re-appear in fictionalised form in her early novels, for example in *At Freddie's* (1982), which uses the setting of a West End children's stage school to humorous effect. One instance of Fitzgerald's wit, which is often balanced with pathos, is apparent in the characterisation of the minor figure Ernest Valentine, who teaches the Peter Pan classes and who had been previously, for many years, the understudy for the part of Nana the dog.

Fitzgerald's first novel, *The Golden Child* (1977), a murder mystery, is thought to have been written, at least in part, to help entertain her husband, Desmond, with whom she had run the literary journal *World Review*, through his last illness.

The Blue Flower offers a fictionalised biography of Fritz von Hardenberg, a late eighteenth-century German **Romantic** poet who became famous under the pen-name Novalis. It is apparent that Fitzgerald has researched her subject matter thoroughly, the novel exemplifying her understated style that is rich in detailing the apparently mundane. There is a meticulousness to this novel which is observable in her other works and has become a trademark of her writing style.

Fitzgerald's novels can be typified by an economy of style which allows for grace and humour. They are relatively short works, which tend to simultaneously satirise and respect their characters, as is seen in her treatment of Novalis. Irony is often used to effect a distance from pompousness and it is this stylistic feature that has drawn comparisons between her writing and Jane Austen's. The resemblance to Austen is limited, however, as Fitzgerald's novels are also distinctly her own. Her skill in drawing on experience and historical detail gives depth to her work and her use of distancing humour avoids the risk of her being categorised as simply a writer of historical fiction.

Another characteristic of Fitzgerald's novels is the depiction of a certain type of male character, as mentioned by Harriet Harvey Wood in an obituary of Fitzgerald: 'Throughout Fitzgerald's novels, there are certain recurring themes, the most striking of which is the single-minded and blinkered innocent (usually male), whose tunnel vision causes disaster to those around. There is an example in almost every book, the most satisfying perhaps being Fritz von Hardenberg, Novalis in *The Blue Flower*.[2] Fitzgerald's presentation of Novalis is designed to expose his humanity and frailty. We see this in the episode where his love for Sophie, whom he calls 'my Philosophy', is intentionally deflated by Novalis's brother, who labels her stupid and claims that she has a double chin.

The theme of innocence is also explored in an earlier work, *Innocence* (1986), set in mid-twentieth-century Italy. Once more, the apparently knowledgeable male, Doctor Rossi, is shown to be lacking in perception. But Fitzgerald's penchant for both irony and kindness ensures that these naïve characters are never deflated too much.

Since Fitzgerald's death, there have been two posthumous publications and the reception of these works reiterates the extent to which she is appreciated critically. *A Means of Escape* (2000) is a collection of short stories that offer distilled views of the worlds that she explored in her novels. In 2003, *A House of Air: Selected Writings by Penelope Fitzgerald* was published. Michèle Roberts, reviewing this collection, describes Fitzgerald as having a 'fine, compassionate mind'.[3] These words are fitting for an author whose novels may appear to be light but are, on closer inspection, careful studies of character and place.

References

1. Quoted by Fitzgerald in the epigraph to *The Blue Flower*. It is taken from Fritz von Hardenberg's *Fragmente und Studien*.

2. *The Guardian* 3 May 2000.

3. *The Independent on Sunday* 16 November 2003.

Selected works:
Edward Burne-Jones (1975); *The Golden Child*

(1977); *The Knox Brothers* (1977); *The Bookshop* (1978); *Offshore* (1979); *Human Voices* (1980); *At Freddie's* (1982); *Charlotte Mew and her Friends* (1984); *Innocence* (1986); *The Beginning of Spring* (1988); *The Gate of Angels* (1990); *The Blue Flower* (1995); *A Means of Escape* (2000); *A House of Air: Selected Writings by Penelope Fitzgerald* (2003).

Contributor: Julie Ellam

FORSTER, E. M. (1879–1970)

Clear out, you fellows, double quick, I say. We may hate one another, but we hate you most . . . we shall get rid of you, yes, we shall drive every blasted Englishman into the sea, and then . . . you and I shall be friends.

A Passage to India

Photo credit: © Hulton-Deutsch Collection/CORBIS

E. M. Forster wrote the majority of his well-known books before the First World War and although he became a member of the **Bloomsbury Group**, gave up writing novels altogether after the publication of *A Passage to India* in 1924, confining his literary output to critical works, travel writing, biography and short stories. The novel *Maurice* appeared posthumously in 1971, having been published under the supervision of Christopher Isherwood. It was begun after Forster completed *Howard's End* in 1910 and went through several drafts. It was influenced by the writer Edward Carpenter, a socialist and open homosexual, and had a homosexual theme, but Forster considered its subject matter too indelicate for publication in his own lifetime.

Forster's literary career began in Edwardian times. He was writing at the same time as **John Galsworthy**, Joseph Conrad, Thomas Hardy and Henry James, though Hardy had turned from prose to poetry at the close of the previous century and James was near the end of his productive life, publishing *The Ambassadors* in 1903 and *The Golden Bowl* in 1904. Overshadowing all of them in popular fame at that time was Rudyard Kipling, whose

novel *Kim* (1902) earned him the Nobel Prize for Literature.

Kim is considered to be Kipling's best book, while *A Passage to India* is often considered to be Forster's best. Both novels are set in India and mark the shift in attitude between Victorianism and what we perceive as Modernity. Kipling was in the rear guard defending Empire, while Forster was in the vanguard of anti-imperialism. Forster's friend Lytton Strachey (1880–1932) mocked the great and the good of the late nineteenth century in *Eminent Victorians* (1918) and Forster supported the Indian independence movement.

Edward Morgan Forster – who preferred his friends to call him Morgan – was the son of an architect. His father died in 1881 when Forster was less than two years old, after which he was brought up by his mother and her sisters. A legacy from a great-aunt made him financially independent at the age of 21 and allowed him to travel and write.

After attending King's College, Cambridge, 1897–1901, where he was elected to the intellectual society known as The Apostles, he visited Italy and Greece. Then, for a short time, he worked as a private tutor in Germany.

The period 1905–10 saw the appearance of four novels: *Where Angels Fear to Tread* (1905), *The Longest Journey* (1907), *A Room With a View* (1908) and *Howard's End* (1910). In these novels he developed the theme of what might nowadays be called cross-cultural communication. Forster's characters are restless and unfulfilled because they are trapped by their mode of life or shackled by an insular conservatism. He made a distinction between tourists and travellers in that a traveller is prepared to come into close contact with other cultures, linguistically and emotionally, while a tourist merely observes.

Forster visited India for the first time in 1912–13 together with Syed Ross Masood who employed him as a tutor. During the First World War he served in the Red Cross and was stationed in Alexandria, Egypt, from 1915. Here he met the Greek poet Constantine Cavafy and had a homosexual affair with an Egyptian tram driver. In 1921–22 Forster returned to India where he acted as private secretary to the Maharajah of Dewas, this period giving him the material for *A Passage to India*.

The title of the novel is taken from Walt Whitman, who wrote on the opening of the Suez Canal in 1869 that it heralded the meeting of East and West. The story concerns the visit of Adela Quested to Chandrapore in the company of Mrs Moore. They accept an invitation from Dr Aziz, the local British surgeon's assistant, to visit the mysterious Marabar Caves. During this visit Adela undergoes something akin to a mystical experience while listening to the echo of the caves. Mrs Moore almost faints and believes she has gone mad for a moment. Adela feels she has been sexually assaulted and Aziz is consequently arrested for rape, yet at the trial, Adela withdraws all charges and Aziz is freed. Exactly what happened in the Marabar Caves remains a mystery.

The philosopher G. E. Moore (1852–1933), a leading figure in the Bloomsbury Group, influenced Forster's view on the importance of personal relationships to the extent that Forster later claimed that, should he be faced with the choice between betraying his country and betraying his friend, he hoped he would have the guts to betray his country (*Two Cheers for Democracy*, 1951). Perhaps the well-known quote from *Howard's End*, 'only connect', is also intended to stress the importance of personal relationships, as well as the importance of making a genuine connection with the culture in which one lives – something which Adela in *A Passage to India* is unable to do.

Forster was concerned to address issues such as oppression, prejudice, intolerance and misunderstanding wherever he found them, including in the culture of India under British rule. But **V. S. Naipaul**, the Nobel Prize winner of Indian descent born in Trinidad, claimed that Forster knew little of India beyond a few middle-class Indians and the garden boys whom he wished to seduce.

Although he gave up writing novels after *A Passage to India*, Forster continued to produce essays and stories and was involved in P.E.N. – the international association of Poets, Playwrights, Editors, Essayists and Novelists – over which **John Galsworthy** presided. He also served as the first chairman of the National Council for Civil Liberties and campaigned against the suppression of Radclyff Hall's novel of lesbian love *The Well of Loneliness* in 1928. Over 30 years later he appeared for the defence in the *Lady Chatterley's Lover* trial of 1960.[1]

In the early 1930s the Bloomsbury Group came under attack from the critic F. R. Leavis, writing in the Cambridge literary magazine *Scrutiny*. Leavis accused the Bloomsbury set of being dilettante and ivory tower artists, after which they lost fashionable appeal, though interest in them re-emerged in the 1960s. Forster indeed belonged to a rarefied group of intellectuals whose pursuits and lifestyles were made possible by private incomes and this was at a time of economic depression when the spectres of Communism and Fascism were stalking Europe and unemployment provoked hunger marches.

In 1946 King's College offered Forster an honorary fellowship and residence in hall. He lived in his Cambridge rooms for the rest of his life, dying at the age of 91.

Reference

1. *Lady Chatterley's Lover:* a novel written by D. H. Lawrence in 1926 and privately published in 1928 which caused a sensational trial for obscenity because of its explicit sexual context.

Selected works:
Where Angels Fear to Tread (1905); *The Longest Journey* (1907); *A Room with a View* (1908); *Howard's End* (1910); *The Celestial Omnibus* (1914); *The Story of the Siren* (1920); *Alexandria* (1922); *Pharaos and Pharillon* (1923); *A Passage to India* (1924); *Anonymity, an Enquiry* (1925); *Aspects of the Novel* (1927); *The Eternal Moment and Other Stories* (1928); *Abinger Harvest* (1936); *What I Believe* (1939); *Reading as Usual* (1939); *England's Pleasant Land* (1940); *Nordic Twilight* (1940); *Collected Short Stories* (1948); *Two Cheers for Democracy* (1951); *The Hill of Devi* (1953); *Marianne Thornton* (1956); *Maurice* (1970); *The Life to Come* (1972); *Commonplace Book* (1979); *Selected Letters* (1983–1985) in 2 volumes; *The Uncollected Egyptian Essays* (1988).

Further reading

Furbank, P. N., *E. M. Forster: a Life* (The authorised biography). Abacus, 1988.

Contributors: Stephen Colbourn,
                                            Ian Mackean

FOWLES, JOHN (1926–)

That's why I never believed in God. I think we are just insects, we live a bit and then die and that's the lot. There's no mercy in things. There's not even a Great Beyond. There's nothing.

The Collector

John Robert Fowles was born into a lower-middle-class home in Leigh-on-Sea, Essex. He has said that his upbringing was conformist and conventional and that he has sought to escape from it all his life. The characters in his novels are often unconventional, following paths that set them against society, sometimes successfully, but more often with unintended and unfortunate consequences. Best known for *The French Lieutenant's Woman* (1969), Fowles is widely recognised as an important figure in the development of the novel, his handling of the form having done much to advance the art of fiction writing.

Fowles was educated at Bedford School, briefly at Edinburgh University and, after a spell of compulsory military service, went to New College, Oxford, where he read Modern Languages. He became interested in **existentialism** as exemplified in the writings of Albert Camus and Jean-Paul Sartre, and found their emphasis on the importance of the individual will particularly appealing. After taking his degree in 1950 he taught overseas for several years, first in France, where he met the woman who was to become his wife, and then on the Greek island of Spetsai. He was writing at this time, but was dissatisfied with the results and did not approach a publisher.

Towards the end of 1960, when Fowles was teaching in England, he completed the first draft of *The Collector* in four weeks. He revised it over the next two years and it was finally published in 1963. The novel quickly became a best-seller and Fowles was at last able to achieve his ambition of becoming a full-time writer.

The narrative of *The Collector* is presented in the first person, alternating between the **viewpoints** of the two protagonists. The novel deals with the obsessive desire for possession and misunderstandings between people of different classes. In the story, a young working-class clerk and butterfly collector, Freddie Clegg, wins a lottery. His financial independence and collector's instinct lead him to buy a house and devote his time to trying to win a girl with whom he is obsessed, Miranda, a middle-class art student.

Freddie kidnaps Miranda and keeps her captive. They achieve a limited amount of communication, but Miranda cannot live without liberty and, like the butterflies Freddie captures for his collection, she dies. Freddie buries her and at the end of the book has already chosen his next victim.

In the naming of his characters Fowles makes reference to Shakespeare's last play, *The Tempest*. 'Miranda' is the name of Prospero's daughter in the play and the Miranda of *The Collector* gives Freddie the nickname 'Caliban', the name of a monster-like, sub-human character.

The Collector, with its mixture of **realism** and fantasy, and its exploration of the consequences of absolute power in the hands of an obsessive, looks forward to Fowles's second, more ambitious novel, *The Magus* (1966), which also has references to *The Tempest*. In *The Magus* a young Englishman, Nicholas Urfe, takes a teaching job on the Greek island of Phraxos to escape from a failed love affair. From this realistic beginning, Urfe finds himself entrapped in a mythical world of fantasy and illusion, created by the Prospero-like figure of the Greek 'magus' or magician, Conchis. The story progresses with a magical, sometimes nightmarish, intensity, Urfe's unnerving experiences unfolding as a pageant created for his edification.

In his manipulation of the confusion between illusion and reality Fowles makes *The Magus*, on one level, a novel about fiction itself. He was one of the first British writers to use **magic realism**, which was not then part of the English novelist's stock-in-trade, and the meaning of the novel was often missed by contemporary critics. The meaning lies in the way Urfe gains self-knowledge by confronting hitherto unexplored complexities of his own character, which are presented in **Jungian** terms, and reassessing the history of his century, including the coming to power of the Nazis.

Fowles used his wide knowledge of Victorian novels to write a pastiche of one in *The French Lieutenant's Woman* (1969), while at the same time **deconstructing** the traditional form. In the story, Sarah Woodruff, one of the protagonists, is an enigmatic figure, believed to be pining for a French soldier who is thought to have been her seducer. Fowles contrasts Sarah with his more conventional heroine, Ernestina Freeman, engaged to marry the amateur palaeontologist Charles Smithson. With a touch of literary irony, the three meet on the Cobb at Lyme Regis, where Jane Austen set the climactic episode of her novel *Persuasion*.

The novel is set in 1867, exactly 100 years before Fowles wrote it, and is concerned with the juxtaposition of past and present. The exactness of the historical detail, in descriptions of such items as clothes and houses, highlights the differences between the Victorian era and our own, as a background to the examination of the contrast between Victorian social mores and our own. By setting the novel in that period, and referring to Smithson's interest in fossils, Fowles also emphasised the split that had divided science and religion at that time.

In *The French Lieutenant's Woman* Fowles deconstructs the traditional elements of the novel, such as the steady development of character, the chronological progress of the storyline and the overall authority of the storyteller. Fowles introduces himself into the novel, commenting directly on the actions and views of his characters and, rejecting the neat conclusion found in most Victorian novels, offers two endings, the reader being free to choose the one deemed most appropriate. The novelist is aware, self-conscious and makes us aware of the fictional nature of all fiction, however 'true to life' it may appear to be.

Fowles's experimental **postmodern** form of narrative, which has been called **metafiction** – a fiction about fiction – has antecedent in the English tradition of novel writing. In *Tristram Shandy* Laurence Sterne (1713–68) addresses his readers directly about his characters and the development of the plot, and at least one Victorian novel, Charlotte Brontë's *Villette,* has an ambiguous ending.

In *The Ebony Tower* (1974), a volume of short stories, Fowles pursued the idea of metafiction even further when in the story 'The Enigma' he made the characters know themselves to be fictional.

In the story 'The Ebony Tower', which owed its inspiration to 'Eliduc', a twelfth-century story by Marie de France, Fowles explores the life of an artist, William Breasley. Breasley has become a recluse, railing against both the art establishment and the abstractions of modern art. David Williams, an English art critic, comes to France to interview Breasley, becomes entangled with two young art students, Anne and Diana, with whom he lives, and, like Urfe in *The Magus*, finds himself caught up in a bewildering mixture of illusion and reality.

Fowles's later works include *Daniel Martin* (1977), a complex novel covering three decades in the life of the eponymous protagonist, *Mantissa* (1982), a fable about a novelist and his muse, and *A Maggot* (1985), an eighteenth-century mystery story which combines science fiction and history and is written in the same layered style as *The Magus*.

In *The Aristos* (1964), a work of non-fiction, Fowles discussed his philosophical ideas which are the basic tenets of his fiction. He has also written several books about Lyme Regis and served as honorary curator of Lyme Regis Museum. Other works include poetry, reviews, short stories and essays.

The Collector, The Magus and *The French Lieutenant's Woman* were all made into films, the screenplay for *The French Lieutenant's Woman* being written by **Harold Pinter**. *The Ebony Tower* was made into a film for TV, with Laurence Olivier as the ageing and irascible artist.

Selected works:

Fiction: *The Collector* (1963); *The Magus* (1966); *The French Lieutenant's Woman* (1969); *The Ebony Tower* (1974); *Daniel Martin* (1977); *Mantissa* (1982); *A Maggot* (1985). **Non-fiction:** *The Aristos* (1964); *A Brief History of Lyme* (1981); *Wormholes* (1998).

Further reading

Conradi, Peter J., *John Fowles*. Routledge, 1982.

Contributors: Margaret Tarner, Ian Mackean

FROST, ROBERT (1874–1963)

*My long two-pointed ladder's sticking
through a tree
Toward heaven still,
And there's a barrel that I didn't fill
Beside it, and there may be two or three
Apples I didn't pick upon some bough.
But I am done with apple-picking now.*

After Apple-Picking

Robert Lee Frost was one of the most popular and highly honoured American poets of the twentieth century. His volumes of poetry have received praise from critics and academics on both sides of the Atlantic and have earned him four Pulitzer Prizes.

Born in 1874 in San Francisco, where he spent the first 11 years of his life, Frost moved with his mother and sister, after his father's death, to their native New England. They settled in Lawrence, Massachusetts, where Frost attended high school, graduating as valedictorian in 1891. The honour was shared with Elinor Miriam White, whom he married in 1895. During the years before their marriage, they both attended college, but Frost had to leave Dartmouth College to return to Lawrence to support his family. His time was divided between school teaching and various other jobs. In 1894, his first poem 'My Butterfly: An Elegy' was accepted for publication by *The Independent*, a New York magazine, earning him $15.

Frost and his wife worked as teachers until 1897, when Frost was accepted at Harvard College as a special student. There he intended to follow a three-year programme, but was prevented from completing it by family problems and poor health. In 1900 he settled with his wife and two children on a farm in Derry, New Hampshire. The years there were productive, resulting in most of the poems that appeared in *A Boy's Will* (1913), *North of Boston* (1914) and *Mountain Interval* (1916).

The beauty of Frost's poetry is in its distinctive natural imagery, which, through the cadences of the sentence structures, expresses the anguish of the individual in the struggle to comprehend the world at large. His poems follow the American **Romantic** tradition, while also searching for a new poetic discourse, which, according to Frost, could be achieved through new sound patterns and dramatic natural images.

Always in need of money, Frost took up a teaching post at Pinkerton Academy in 1906, which he held for five years. In 1912, seeking a radical change of scene, he sold the Derry farm and moved with his wife and four children to Britain. Initially, they stayed in London, then settled in Beaconsfield, Buckinghamshire.

Within a few months of his arrival, David Nutt, a London-based publisher, accepted *A Boy's Will* for publication. In the meantime, Frost became acquainted with the poet F. S. Flint, who introduced him to **Ezra Pound**. In 1914 he published *North of Boston*, which contained poems which were lengthier than his early poems and written largely in monologue form, exploring the inner life of the ordinary people who inhabited the New England countryside. The success of his publications, together with favourable reviews from Pound, established Frost's reputation in London literary circles. He was befriended by the **Georgian Poets** Wilfred Gibson and Lascelles Abercrombie, and the poet and essayist Edward Thomas. The latter attributed the success of Frost's verse to the simplicity of its diction and imagery, which differentiated it from the ambiguous and complex poetry of other **Modernist** poets. Frost's regionalism, highlighted by the New England themes that his poems explored, ensured his popularity in America. As a result, Henry Holt in New York City agreed to publish his collections and continued to do so throughout Frost's poetic career.

In 1915 Britain's involvement in the First World War forced Frost to return to the US where he settled on a farm he bought in New Hampshire. Throughout the 1920s he published the poetic collections which established him as an eminent poet in his home country: *Mountain Interval* (1916), *New Hampshire* (1923) and *The West-Running Brook* (1928). The lyrics in these collections became very popular, some of the best known being 'Birches', 'The Road Not Taken', 'An Old Man's Winter Night', 'Fire and Ice' and 'Stopping by Woods on a Snowy Evening'. In these poems, continuing the explorations of traditional forms and natural images that he had employed *North of Boston*, Frost focused on the description of natural scenes and events, and on recording the experiences of country people through dramatic monologues which imitated their language patterns.

A year after the publication of *New Hampshire*, Frost was awarded his first Pulitzer Prize, soon to be followed by two more on the publication of *Collected Poems* (1930) and *A Further Range* (1936). Unfortunately, his life was then overshadowed by a series of family tragedies: the death of his favourite daughter in 1934, the death of his wife in 1938, and the suicide of his son in 1940. Frost's bitterness and despair were distilled in *A Witness Tree* (1942), which won him a fourth Pulitzer Prize and remains one of his most powerful volumes. Poems such as 'The Silken Tent', 'I Could Give All to Time', 'Never Again Would Birds' Songs Be the Same' are darker and wilder in tone, while maintaining metrical formality and thematic coherence.

In *A Masque of Reason* (1945) and *A Masque of Mercy* (1947), Frost explores the relationship between man and God through the use of biblical characters in a series of dramatic poems written in blank verse. In 1947 he published *A Steeple Bush*, which was not one of his best poetic collections, although it contained the important poem 'Directive'. However, this year was marked by another personal blow: his daughter Irma, who suffered from a mental disorder, was committed to a mental hospital. His last volume of poetry, *In the Clearing*, was published in 1962 when he was 88 years old.

Selected works:

A Boy's Will (1913); *North of Boston* (1914); *Mountain Interval* (1916); *New Hampshire* (1923); *The West-Running Brook* (1928); *A Witness Tree* (1942); *A Masque of Reason* (1945); *A Masque of Mercy* (1947). **Collected Poems: Prose & Plays**, eds. Richard Poirier and Mark Richardson (New York, 1995); *Interviews with Robert Frost*, ed. E. C. Lathem (London, 1966); *Selected Letters of Robert Frost*, ed. Lawrance Thompson (New York, 1964; London, 1965).

Further reading

Faggen, Robert (ed.) *The Cambridge Companion to Robert Frost*. Cambridge University Press, 2001.

Frattali, Steven, *Person, Place and World: A Late Modern Reading of Robert Frost*. English Literary Studies, University of Victoria, 2002.

Contributor: Tatiani Rapatzikou

GALSWORTHY, JOHN (1867–1933)

He would be setting up as a man of property next, with a place in the country.
                    The Man of Property

John Galsworthy was among the most popular writers of the early twentieth century. His work dealt in a **realist** manner with social issues of his day, particularly issues of class conflicts and class loyalties. His main focus was on the upper-middle classes, but he also looked sympathetically at the lives of the socially and economically disadvantaged. He was awarded the Nobel Prize for Literature in 1932 and is chiefly remembered today for his novel sequence *The Forsyte Saga* (1901–28).

The Galsworthys were an old and prosperous family and John attended Harrow School, then New College Oxford, a pattern customary to the upper-middle class of that time. John's father was a successful lawyer who intended his son to follow him in the legal profession. John was called to the bar in 1890, by which time he had begun to write. He published four works of fiction at his own expense, under the pseudonym John Sinjohn, the first being a volume of short stories, *From the Four Winds* (1897).

He had taken a voyage to the South Seas in 1893, in part to study maritime law. The Polish mate onboard the ship was a would-be writer and the two became life-long friends. Galsworthy wrote of this meeting

The first mate is a Pole called Conrad,
and is a capital chap though queer to look
at; he is a man of travel and experience in
many parts of the world, and has a fund of
yarns on which I draw freely.

He helped to support Joseph Conrad (Józef Teodor Konrad Korzeniowski) while the former Polish seaman was establishing himself as a writer. Galsworthy inherited his father's money in 1904 and married the woman with whom he had lived in secret for ten years. He volunteered for military service in the First World War but was rejected because of poor eyesight.

During his lifetime, Galsworthy gave away half of his income in support of social causes and reforms, which should be balanced against the criticisms of **D. H. Lawrence** and **Virginia Woolf** that he was a member of the same upper class which, hypocritically, his writings attacked. Galsworthy also refused a knighthood in 1917 on the grounds that writers should not accept titles and he presided over the international writers' association **P.E.N.** founded in 1921 by Catherine Dawson Scott.

Galsworthy's plays are largely forgotten, though they were considered important in the years before the First World War as examples of high-minded and socially committed literature which attempted to address problems of class and justice. Like George Bernard Shaw, under whose influence he was writing, he was a realist, but from a modern standpoint his presentation of social issues was too formulaic, and his characters too lacking in psychological depth, for his dramatic work to have retained appeal beyond its era.

His first play, *The Silver Box* (1906), is a social drama which depicts two families, one rich and one poor, and their inequality before the law. *Strife* (1909) is a balanced study of labour relations at a time of industrial unrest. *Justice* (1910) attempted a realistic portrayal of life in prison and made such an impact on contemporary audiences that it influenced the Home Secretary, Winston Churchill, in his programme of prison reform. *The Skin Game* (1920) examines a conflict between a manufacturer and an aristocrat and was filmed by the young British director Alfred Hitchcock in 1932. *Loyalties* (1922) dealt with anti-Semitism during the early growth of the British Fascist movement and was later adapted for television. *Escape* (1926) was a little more free-flowing and adventurous in structure than his earlier plays and has been filmed twice. It tells the story of how an ordinary man meets a prostitute and accidentally kills a policeman.

He is sent to prison and escapes, meeting various low-life characters before giving himself up.

Above all, Galsworthy is remembered for the series of novels collectively known, after 1922, as *The Forsyte Saga*, which enjoyed great popular success as a BBC TV production in 1967, and has since been shown again. The Forsyte family appeared first in *Man of Devon* (1901), then in *The Man of Property* (1906), *In Chancery* (1920), *Awakening* (1920) and *To Let* (1921). The Forsytes are nouveau riche and acquisitive, Soames Forsyte being a lawyer who regards his wife Irene as a form of property. Through the novels, Galsworthy implies that the quest for wealth alone is morally repugnant. The family saga continued in *The White Monkey* (1924), *The Silver Spoon* (1926) and *Swan Song* (1928), published together in *A Modern Comedy* (1929).

Selected works:

From the Four Winds, as John Sinjohn (1897); *Jocelyn*, as John Sinjohn (1898); *Villa Rubein*, as John Sinjohn (1900); *A Man Of Devon*, as John Sinjohn (1901); *The Island Pharisees* (1904); *The Silver Box* (1906); *The Country House* (1907); *A Commentary* (1908); *Fraternity* (1909); *The Silver Box* (1906); *A Justification For The Censorship Of Plays* (1909); *Strife* (1909); *Fraternity* (1909); *Joy* (1909); *Justice* (1910); *A Motley* (1910); *The Spirit Of Punishment* (1910); *Horses In Mines* (1910); *The Patrician* (1911); *The Little Dream* (1911); *The Pigeon* (1912); *The Eldest Son* (1912); *Moods, Songs, And Doggerels* (1912); *For Love Of Beasts* (1912); *The Inn Of Tranquillity* (1912); *The Dark Flower* (1913); *The Fugitive* (1913); *The Mob* (1914); *The Freelands* (1915); *The Little Man* (1915); *A Sheaf* (1916); *Beyond* (1917); *Five Tales* (1918); *A Saint's Progress* (1919); *The Foundations* (1920); *In Chancery* (1920); *Awakening* (1920); *A Family Man* (1922); *Loyalties* (1922); *Windows* (1922); *Captures* (1923); *Abracadabra* (1924); *The Forest* (1924); *Old English* (1924); *The Show* (1925); *Escape* (1926); *Verses New And Old* (1926); *Castles In Spain* (1927); *A Modern Comedy* (1924–28); *Exiled* (1929); *The Roof* (1929); *Two Essays On Conrad* (1930); *The Creation Of Character In Literature* (1931); *Maid In Waiting* (1931); *Forty Poems* (1932); *Flowering Wilderness* (1932); *Over The River* (1933); *Autobiographical Letters Of Galsworthy: A Correspondence With Frank Harris* (1933).

Further reading

Marrot, Harold V., *The Life and Letters of John Galsworthy* (Scribner Reprint Editions). Augustus M. Kelley, 1973.

Frechet, Alec, *John Galsworthy: A Reassessment.* Palgrave Macmillan, 1982.

Gindin, James, *John Galsworthy's Life and Art: An Alien's Fortress.* Palgrave Macmillan, 1987.

Contributors: Stephen Colbourn,
                                Ian Mackean

GINSBERG, ALLEN (1926–97)

I saw the best minds of my generation destroyed by madness, starving hysterical naked, dragging themselves through the negro streets at dawn looking for an angry fix, angelheaded hipsters burning for the ancient heavenly connection to the starry dynamo in the machinery of night.

'Howl'

Louis Ginsberg was a published poet, a high school teacher and a moderate Jewish Socialist. His wife, Naomi, was a radical Communist and irrepressible nudist who went tragically insane in early adulthood. Somewhere between the two in temperament was the Ginsbergs' second son, Irwin Allen, born on 3 June 1926.

A shy and complicated child growing up in Paterson, New Jersey, Ginsberg's home life was dominated by his mother's bizarre and frightening episodes. Severely paranoid, she often trusted him when she was convinced the rest of the family and the world was plotting against her. As the sensitive boy tried to understand what was happening around him, he also had to struggle to comprehend what was happening inside him because he was consumed by lust for other boys his age.

He discovered the poetry of Walt Whitman (the original Beatnik) in high school, but despite his interest in poetry he followed his father's advice and began planning a career as a labour lawyer. This was what he had in mind when he began his freshman year at Columbia University, but he fell in with a crowd of wild souls there, including fellow students Lucien Carr and **Jack Kerouac** and non-student friends William S. Burroughs and Neal Cassady. These delinquent young philosophers were obsessed in equal measure with drugs, crime, sex and literature. Ginsberg, the youngest and most innocent member of the circle, helped them develop their literary interests, while they helped him in turn by utterly shattering his bookish naïvety.

Ginsberg's new crowd was based at Columbia, but they did not encourage him in his studies and he was eventually suspended for various small offences. He began consorting with Times Square junkies and thieves (mostly friends of Burroughs), experimenting with Benzedrine and marijuana, and cruising gay bars in Greenwich Village, all the time believing himself and his friends to be working towards some kind of uncertain great poetic vision, which he and Kerouac called the New Vision. He began a passionate (for him, anyway) sexual affair with the reluctant Neal Cassady, whom he visited in Denver and San Francisco, helping to set in motion the cross-country trend that would soon inspire Kerouac's *On The Road* adventures. The joyful craziness of his city friends somehow became a symbolic counterpoint for Ginsberg to the real craziness of his mother, whose condition continued to worsen until she was hospitalised for life and finally lobotomised. Some might deal with insanity in the family by becoming exaggeratedly normal, but Ginsberg went in the opposite direction – knowing himself to be basically sane, he embraced bizarreness as a style of life, as if seeking to find the edge over which his mother had fallen. Reading William Blake in a Harlem apartment one summer day in 1948, the 26-year-old Ginsberg had a tremendous mad vision in which Blake came to him in person. This, he felt, was the great moment of his life, and he joyfully told his family and friends that he had found God.

Ginsberg changed his lifestyle when the criminal activities of several of his friends (such as Burroughs and Herbert Huncke) resulted in his arrest and imprisonment. He entered a 'straight' phase, renouncing Burroughs, immersing himself in psychoanalytic treatment and even, in an attempt to convert to heterosexuality, dating a woman named Helen Parker. He took a job as a marketing researcher, during which time, in an office in the Empire State Building, he helped develop an advertising campaign for Ipana toothpaste.

But this phase did not last long and his life changed again after he met a kindred spirit, Carl Solomon, in the waiting room of a psychiatric hospital. He introduced himself to the important New Jersey poet William Carlos Williams, whose epic visionary poem about the town of Paterson had impressed Ginsberg greatly. Bearing a letter of introduction from the poet Williams, Ginsberg travelled to San Francisco and met Kenneth Rexroth, leader of an emerging vibrant and youthful local poetry movement, of which Ginsberg became a part almost instantly.

At the age of 29, Ginsberg had written much poetry but published almost none. He worked hard to promote the works of Kerouac and Burroughs to publishers, neglecting to promote his own. Even so, he was the first Beat writer to gain popular notice when he delivered a thundering performance of his poem 'Howl' at the now-legendary Six Gallery poetry reading in October 1955. This great poem, conveniently publicised by a bungled obscenity charge that made Ginsberg, for some, a symbol of sexual depravity (as homosexuality was then perceived), was the great expression of Beat defiance, just as Kerouac's *On The Road*, published two years later, would be the great expression of Beat yearnings.

Ginsberg followed 'Howl' with other important new poems, such as 'Sunflower Sutra'. Now at a critical stage in his career, he was somehow able to avoid the 'fame burnout' that would soon engulf Kerouac. According to Bruce Cook in his book *The Beat Generation*, Ginsberg even mellowed considerably during this period, after travelling the world, discovering Buddhism and falling in love with Peter Orlovsky, who would remain a constant companion (though their relationship was not monogamous) for 30 years. Perhaps most importantly, he exorcised some internal demons by writing 'Kaddish', a brilliant and surprising poem about his mother's insanity and death.

Ginsberg's celebrity continued to grow as the 'Beat' concept evolved from an idea into a movement and then into a cliché. In the early 1960s he threw himself into the hippie scene. He and Timothy Leary worked together to publicise Leary's new discovery, the psychedelic drug LSD, and Ginsberg attempted to turn on every famous cultural figure in his address book, including Willem De Kooning, Franz Kline, Dizzy Gillespie, Thelonius Monk, Robert Lowell and Jack Kerouac (whose cranky response sent Timothy Leary on his first bad trip).

As a famous American poet, Ginsberg was able to gain audiences with important political figures all over the world and during the 1960s he took advantage of this repeatedly. He antagonised one important official after another, causing furores in India, getting kicked out of Cuba and Prague, and continually annoying America's right wing. He was a familiar bushy-bearded figure at protests against the Vietnam War and his willingness to state his controversial views in public was an important factor in the development of the revolutionary state of mind that America developed during the 1960s.

Ginsberg participated in the Acid Test Festivals organised by Ken Kesey in San Francisco and helped Kesey break the ice between the San Francisco hippies and the antagonistic Hell's Angels. In the summer of 1965 Ginsberg made a seminal trip to London with several other Beat figures. Their reading at the Royal Albert Hall signalled the beginning of the London underground scene, based at the UFO Club, from which bands such as Pink Floyd and the Soft Machine would emerge. He also visited Liverpool, where he made a big impression on the Liverpool Poets, who were also developing poetry as live performance.

Bob Dylan often cited Ginsberg as one of the few literary figures he could stand. Ginsberg can be seen standing in the alley in the background of Dylan's 1965 *Subterranean Homesick Blues* video and would later play a part in Dylan's 1977 film *Renaldo and Clara*. Ginsberg, Gary Snyder and Michael McClure led the crowd in chanting 'OM' at the San Francisco Be-In in 1967, and Ginsberg, Burroughs, Jean Genet and Terry Southern were key figures at the Chicago Democratic Convention antiwar protests in 1968. One of the few radical events of the 1960s that Ginsberg was *not* a part of was the Stonewall gay uprising, though he did show up at the site the next day to offer his support.

In 1970 Ginsberg met the controversial Tibetan guru Chogyam Trungpa Rinpoche and later accepted him as his personal guru.

He and poet Anne Waldman joined to create a poetry school, the Jack Kerouac School of Disembodied Poetics, at Trungpa's Naropa Institute in Boulder, Colorado.

In the early 1980s, Ginsberg even joined the punk rock movement, appearing on the Clash's *Combat Rock* album and performing with them on stage.

Ginsberg never moved away from his humble apartment in the poetry-rich streets of New York City's Lower East Side and was frequently seen at local readings and multicultural gatherings, either on a stage or in the crowd. He carried on an active social schedule until his death on 5 April 1997.

Seeing Ginsberg perform was always a magical experience. He was truly and simply a free soul on stage, clinking little finger cymbals and barking weirdly melodic chants, with an impish smile behind his greying beard and thick glasses.

Selected works:

Howl and Other Poems (1956); *Siesta In Xbalba and Return To The States* (1956); *Kaddish and Other Poems* (1961); *Empty Mirror* (1961); *The Yage Letters* (with William Burroughs) (1963); *The Change* (1963); *Reality Sandwiches* (1963); *A Strange New Cottage In Berkley* (1963); *Kral Majales* (1965); *Mystery In The Universe* (Ed. E. Lucie-Smith) (1965); *Wichita Vortex Sutra* (1966); *Tv Baby Poems* (1967); *Ankor Wat* (1968); *Message Ii* (1968); *Airplane Dreams* (1968); *Planet News* (1968); *Scrap Leaves, Hasty Scribbles* (1968); *Wasles – A Visitation* (1968); *Don't Go Away Mad* (1968); *The Moments Return* (1970); *Indian Journals* (1970); *Notes After An Evening With William Carlos Williams* (1970); *Declaration of Independence For Dr Timothy Leary* (1971); *Improvised Poetics* (1972); *The Fall of America* (1972); *Kaddish* (1972); *The Gates of Wrath* (1972); *Iron Horse* (1972); *New Year Blues* (1972); *Open Head* (1972); *The Fall of America: Poems of These States* (1973); *Allen Verbatim* (1974); *The Vision of The Great Remember* (1974); *Chicago Trial Testimony of Allen Ginsberg* (1975); *First Blues* (1975); *Sad Dust Glories* (1975); *To Eberhart From Ginsberg* (1976); *As Ever: The Collected Correspondence of Allen Ginsberg and Neal Cassady* (Ed. B. Gifford) (1977); *Journals* (1977); *All Over The Place* (1978); *Composed On The Tongue* (1980); *Straight Hearts Delight* (1980); *Plutonium Ode* (1982); *Collected Poems* (1984); *Many Loves* (1984); *Old Love Story* (1984); *White Shroud* (1986); *The Hydrogen Jukebox* (1990); *Kaddish For Naomi Ginsberg 1894–1956* (1992); *Cosmopolitan Greetings* (1994); *Mind Writing Slogans* (1994); *The Works of Allen Ginsberg 1941–1994* (1995); *Selected Poems: 1947–1995* (1996); *Illuminated Poems* (with Eric Drooker, Illustrator) (1996); *Death and Fame: Poems 1993–1997* (Allen Ginsberg et al.) (1999).

Further reading

Cook, Bruce, *The Beat Generation*. Scribner, 1971.

This is an edited revision of an article by Levi Asher, which was originally published on 'Literary Kicks' at www.litkicks.com

GOLDING, SIR WILLIAM (1911–93)

Fancy thinking the Beast was something you could hunt and kill! You knew, didn't you? I'm part of you?

Lord of the Flies

Photo credit: © Bettmann/CORBIS

Sir William Golding published his first novel, *The Lord of the Flies*, in 1954, at the age of 44, but continued his career as a school teacher until he was 50, when the success of his novels allowed him to take up writing full-time. As well as several novels he published poems, essays and a play. He received the Booker Prize in 1980, the Nobel Prize for Literature in 1983 and a knighthood in 1988.

Golding grew up in Cornwall. His father, a schoolmaster, wanted him to study natural science, but Golding had an inclination towards literature. From Marlborough Grammar School he went to Brasenose College, Oxford, where he published his first work, *Poems* (1934). He initially read physics, but switched to English literature, beginning with a study of Anglo-Saxon which, together with his scientific training, lent him a clear and rational prose style that many readers find appealing.

After university he attempted to live as an actor-writer, but the need to earn a living led him to take up a teaching post at Bishop Wordsworth School in Salisbury. His teaching career was interrupted by the war and he volunteered to join the Royal Navy in 1940. He witnessed the sinking of the Bismarck in May that year and on 6 June 1944, as a lieutenant, commanded a rocket ship off the coast of Normandy. He returned to teaching when he was demobilised in 1945.

The Second World War left Golding doubtful about the state of European civilisation and the prospects for human progress. The immediate onset of the Cold War, bringing fears of the destruction of humanity by nuclear weapons, hardly made him feel more optimistic. He has a reputation for painting a grim picture of the human condition, although he claimed in his Nobel acceptance speech that he was not a pessimistic writer. Rather, he said, he was acutely aware that history, and by extension literature, is written by survivors, and the ethical question that troubled him most was whether survival is its own justification.

The manuscript of *The Lord of the Flies* was rejected by many publishers, yet on the novel's publication it gained rapid success and **E. M. Forster** named it Book of the Year. It was fresh and highly readable in its day and has outlived other works of the mid-1950s. The novel is allegorical, telling the story of a group of well-bred boys who, when stranded on an island, quickly lapse into barbarism. The strong subdue the weak and their conflicts lead to the deaths of two of them. Out of the darkness of their minds they conjure an image of Beëlzebub, Lord of the Flies, and worship him in the form of the severed head of a boar they have captured and slaughtered. Meanwhile, the adult world has been devastated by nuclear war and no help comes until the very end.

The novel is, in part, Golding's riposte to *The Coral Island* (1857) by Robert Michael Ballantyne (1825–94). Ballantyne's novel, also about boys marooned on an island, was based on the conviction that human beings had innate virtues which would sustain their humanity even in isolation from society. In contrast, Golding's work shows his characters reverting to a more primitive state, suggesting that this would be a natural outcome in the absence of civilised models and rules. He implies that there are no innate moral constraints on human behaviour and that men behave in a civilised fashion only through fear of punitive consequences.

The themes of fall, guilt, corruptibility and the depravity of human nature run through Golding's subsequent novels, and in a clear reference to *Paradise Lost*, the title of one of them, *Darkness Visible* (1979), is taken from Milton's depiction of Hell.

The darkness of Golding's subject matter can be contrasted with the lucidity of his prose. He showed men as behaving irrationally, but capable of reason, and believed that man's best hope for the future lay in the exercise of his reasoning faculty in communication with others. In consequence, there is little by way of experimentation in Golding's prose and he deliberately imitated an eighteenth-century style in his later books *Rites of Passage* (1980), *Close Quarters* (1987) and *Fire Down Below* (1989). In part this befitted the period in which the novels were set, the early 1800s, but it also served to illustrate his point that writing in a clear and interesting manner is a difficult enough task in itself, without attempting the avant-garde postures of **Modernist** writers. He wished to speak directly to his readers rather than impress them with his cleverness and learning.

Golding regarded science fiction and historical novels as legitimate forms of literature and his second book, *The Inheritors* (1955), is effectively a work of science fiction, the story being a challenge to H. G. Wells's optimistic view of human progress. The novel shows the destruction of Neanderthal man by the more aggressive Cro-Magnon breed of Homo Sapiens, in what would now be called genocide or ethnic cleansing.

Pincher Martin (1956) describes a naval officer adrift after his ship has been torpedoed. *Free Fall* (1959) concerns the reflections of an artist in 1950s England. *The Spire* (1964) tells the story of how a medieval dean instigates the erection of a cathedral spire, supposedly to the glory of God, but bringing all manner of human corruption in its wake.

Golding was not a prolific writer but aimed for quality rather than quantity. Living quietly in Cornwall he was regarded as a mildly eccentric and reclusive literary figure, noted for his shabby clothes and long hair. The award of the Booker Prize in 1980 for *Rites of Passage*, which portrays a voyage on a sailing ship to Australia during the early years of British colonisation, returned Golding to public attention.

At the time of his death in Cornwall at the age of 82, Golding was working on *The Double Tongue*, set in Greece under the Roman Empire. It retells the life of Pythia, last priestess of the Oracle at Delphi, and is an exposition of the author's theme that that which is worthy of preservation is not necessarily that which endures.

Selected works:

Poems (1934); *Lord of the Flies* (1954); *The Inheritors* (1955); *Pincher Martin* (1956); *The Brass Butterfly* (1958); *Free Fall* (1959); *The Anglo-Saxon* (1962); *The Spire* (1964); *The Hot Gates* (1965); *The Pyramid* (1967); *The Scorpion God* (1971); *Darkness Visible* (1979); *Rites Of Passage* (1980); *A Moving Target* (1982); *The Paper Men* (1984); *An Egyptian Journal* (1985); *Close Quarters* (1987); *Fire Down Below* (1989); *The Double Tongue* (draft) (1995).

Further reading

Crawford, Paul, *Politics and History in William Golding: The World Turned Upside Down.* University of Missouri Press, 2002.

Contributors: Stephen Colbourn,
                       Ian Mackean

GREENE, GRAHAM (1904–91)

O God, You've done enough, You've robbed me of enough, I'm too tired and old to learn to love, leave me alone for ever.
                       The End of the Affair

Henry Graham Greene was the son of a public school headmaster; his father, an intellectual with a poor academic record, had intended to practise law but instead became a master at Berkhamsted School, where he stayed until his retirement. He and his family lived on the premises, his sons attending classes at the school.

Greene was firmly a member of the upper class which he claimed, later, to reject. His mother was a cousin of the writer Robert Louis Stevenson (1850–94). His uncle was a founder of British Naval Intelligence, working with Admiral Hall in Room 40, the forerunner of MI5, during the First World War. His older brother served in the navy, spying against Japanese shipping and eventually becoming Permanent Under-secretary at the Admiralty, and his sister worked for the Secret Intelligence Service during the Second World War.

The first manifest rejection of his background came at the age of 15, when he ran away from school and attempted to commit suicide. For a time he was placed under psychiatric care, where his therapist encouraged him to write as an outlet for his emotions. Greene later declared himself a Communist and then converted to Catholicism. He maintained friendships with raffish characters such as Noel Coward, Ian Fleming and Kim Philby, and went out of his way to meet anti-American figures such as Ho Chi Minh and Fidel Castro. He was also familiar with South American dictators, such as Manuel Noriega and Omar Torrijos, about whom he wrote *Getting to Know the General* (1985).

Much of Greene's life was spent abroad, visiting the world's trouble spots and playing the part of an unorthodox but progressive and sympathetic writer in self-imposed exile. Yet Evelyn Waugh, a fellow convert to Catholicism, assured friends that Greene was really on the side of the establishment, 'one of us'.

Greene graduated from Balliol College, Oxford, in 1925. During his time there his first published works appeared in university magazines and in 1925 he brought out a volume of poetry, *Babbling April*. After university he took a number of short-lived jobs, including one as a copy editor in Nottingham, then moved to London to work for *The Times*.

In 1926 he was received into the Catholic Church and the following year he married Vivien Dayrell-Browning, who had encouraged his conversion. Their marriage, however, did not last and after a series of affairs he married his second wife, Dorothy Glover, a costume designer. Eventually he separated from her too, although they did not divorce.

Determined to make his living as a writer Greene gave up his job with *The Times* and contributed articles and reviews of books and films to *The Spectator* and to *Night and Day*, which he edited. His first novel, *The Man Within*, was published in 1929. Years later he entered a competition run by *The Spectator*, in which the brief was to write 'in the style of Graham Greene' – his entry was unplaced.

At the start of his literary career Greene attempted to write in the manner of his favourite authors, Joseph Conrad, Ford Madox Ford and Henry James, but with little success. The first of his books to gain attention was *Stamboul Train* (1932). Greene made a distinction between his serious novels and what he called 'entertainments', and *Stamboul Train* was an 'entertainment', deliberately written to make money. The book, which contains a parody of the writer J. B. Priestley in the character of Quin Savory, is a thriller set onboard the Orient Express, which ran from Paris to Istanbul.

Several highly successful novels followed: *England Made Me* (1935), *A Gun For Sale* (1936), *Brighton Rock* (1938), *The Confidential Agent* (1939) and *The Power and the Glory* (1940). Royalties from these novels, and films made from them, allowed Greene to travel and, after the Second World War, to live abroad. But his journeys were not always made in comfort and style, as seen for example in *Journey Without Maps* (1936), which describes a difficult and dangerous trek through Liberia. During the war he was sent to Sierra Leone by the British SIS (Secret Intelligence Service, also known as MI6) and found that the job allowed him ample time for writing. His supervisor at MI6 was Kim Philby, who became infamous when he defected to Moscow in 1963.

Greene had gained international fame by the time he published *The End of the Affair* (1951), which centres around a deeply religious notion – a silent vow. The book was inspired by Greene's affair with Catherine Walston, wife of a rich industrialist and mother of five children, particularly by his fear that the affair would end (although in fact it continued for another ten years). The book describes how Sarah Miles has an illicit affair with a popular novelist Maurice Bendrix, who is wounded in an air raid. Sarah makes a solemn vow to God that, if Bendrix is allowed to live, she will end the affair, even though she loves him. Bendrix recovers and Sarah leaves, without telling him why. They never meet again and the novel recounts Maurice's attempt to reconstruct the events after Sarah dies of pneumonia.

But, successful as he was, Greene was not without critics. **George Orwell** reviewed *Brideshead Revisited* by **Evelyn Waugh** and

Greene's *The Heart of the Matter* and disliked the Catholic content of both. In particular he criticised Greene's posture as a sanctified sinner and his presentation of hell as a kind of exclusive night-club reserved for Catholics. Greene's answer was that he saw Catholicism not as a creed for the triumphant but as a refuge for the desperate.

Greene took a trip to Asia after the French defeat at Dien Bien Phu in 1954 had led to the partition of Vietnam. His stay in Saigon (Ho Chi Minh City) gave him material for *The Quiet American* (1955), which accurately predicted further American involvement in South-East Asia. He next visited Cuba, and Latin America provided the setting for a number of his novels: *Our Man in Havana* (1958), *The Comedians* (1966) and *The Honorary Consul* (1973).

One of Greene's best-selling books was *The Human Factor* (1978), which returned to the subject of spies and treachery. The main character appears to resemble Kim Philby in many respects, although Greene denied that Philby was the model. He sent a copy to Philby in Moscow and visited his old friend, who was never able to return to the country he betrayed, in the late 1980s. Philby died a year before the collapse of the Soviet Union, so he never saw the end of the regime to which he had devoted himself.

Greene's last years were spent in France and Switzerland. He became involved in a controversy over corrupt politics in Nice, which inspired *J'Accuse – The Dark Side of Nice* (1982), and wrote an account of his friendship with the Panamanian dictator, Torrijos, after the latter's death in a plane crash.

In 1978 Greene gave a map to the biographer Professor Norman Sherry, showing all the places in the world he had visited. Sherry set off to visit them himself, which took him 20 years, and began work on a biography of Greene which the author himself approved. A rival volume by Michael Shelden caused a literary storm when it emphasised the darker side of Greene's life and character, calling him a pathological liar, a callous womaniser and a bumbling political rabble-rouser. In a public debate in London, Norman Sherry, to the accompaniment of supportive jeers from the audience, accused Michael Shelden of writing a book which contained a thousand errors.

The first volume of Sherry's official biography, *The Life of Graham Greene: 1904–1938*, appeared a year before Greene's death at Vevey in Switzerland, where he had been living with Yvonne Cloetta, his last companion.

Selected works:

Babbling April (1925); *The Man Within* (1929); *The Name of Action* (1930); *Rumour at Nightfall* (1931); *Stamboul Train* (1932); *It's a Battlefield* (1934); *England Made Me* (1935); *Journey Without Maps* (1936); *A Gun For Sale* (1936); *Brighton Rock* (1938); *The Lawless Roads* (1939); *The Confidential Agent* (1939); *The New Britain*, a screenplay (1940); *The Power and the Glory* (1940); *The Ministry of Fear* (1943); *The Little Train* (1946); *The Heart of the Matter* (1948); *The Fallen Idol*, a screenplay (1948); *The Third Man*, a screenplay (1948); *After Two Years* (with Catherine Walston) (1949); *The Lost Childhood* (1951); *For Christmas* (1951); *The End of the Affair* (1951); *The Living Room*, a play (1953); *Twenty-One Stories* (1954); *The Quiet American* (1955); *Loser Takes All* (1955); *Saint Joan*, film script (1957); *The Potting Shed*, a play (1957); *Our Man in Havana* (1958); *The Comedians* (1966); *Victorian Detective Fiction* (1966); *Collected Essays* (1969); *Travels With My Aunt* (1969); *A Sort of Life* (1971); *The Virtue of Disloyalty* (1972); *The Pleasure Dome* (1972); *The Honorary Consul* (1973); *Lord Rochester's Monkey* (1974); *The Human Factor* (1978); *Dr. Fisher of Geneva or The Bomb Party* (1980); *Ways of Escape* (1980); *Monsignor Quixote* (1982); *J'Accuse – The Dark Side of Nice* (1982); *Yes and No* (1983); *A Quick Look Behind* (1983); *Getting to Know the General* (1985); *The Tenth Man* (1985); *Graham Greene Country* (1986); *The Captain and the Enemy* (1988); *Why the Epigraph?* (1989); *Yours, Etc.* (1989); *The Last Word* (1990); *The Destructors* (1990); *Reflections* (1991); *A World of My Own* (1992); *The End of the Party* (1993).

Further reading

Shelden, Michael, *Graham Greene: The Enemy Within*. Random House, 1995.

Sherry, Norman, *The Life of Graham Greene: 1939–1955*. Penguin Books, 1996.

Contributors: Stephen Colbourn,
                         Ian Mackean

HEANEY, SEAMUS (1939–)

So hope for a great sea-change
On the far side of revenge.
Believe that a further shore
Is reachable from here.
Believe in miracles
And cures and healing wells.
                         The Cure at Troy

Seamus Heaney was born in 1939 in County Derry, Northern Ireland. His father was a farmer and his mother came from a family of mill workers. He was brought up, the eldest of a family of nine children, on the family farm, observing the rhythms and minutiae of country life and listening to cadences ranging from the local accent of his family to the resonant tones of BBC radio announcers, developing a sensitivity to language on which he drew when he started writing poetry. While Northern Ireland was predominantly Protestant, Heaney's family was Catholic, and he grew up aware of the discriminations against those of his religion, which were later to reach political breaking point and to prove a catalyst to his work.

Heaney was one of the many from modest backgrounds who, thanks to the 1947 Education Act, were able to extend their education beyond the legal minimum. At the age of 12 he won a scholarship to St Columb's College, Derry, which he attended as a boarder. From 1957 to 1961 he studied English Literature at Queen's University, Belfast, graduating with a first, and then went on to teachers' training college. He began work as a teacher in 1962 at St Thomas's Intermediate School and has continued to combine writing with teaching in schools, education colleges and universities, including Queen's University Belfast, the University of California, Berkeley, Harvard and Oxford.

Heaney's first volume of poetry, *Death of a Naturalist*, was published in 1966. One of the best-known poems from this collection is 'Digging', which tells of the poet sitting in an upstairs room (metaphorically higher, that is, better educated), watching his father digging potato drills. The poem is emblematic of Heaney's work, illustrating his preoccupation with his roots and his respect for the natural world of the farming community and the labour of his ancestors. It also reveals his concern with the fact that, by obtaining an education, he has broken his family line and will from now on have to 'dig' with his pen.

In elevating details of the everyday rural world to the realms of poetry Heaney was influenced by Irish poet Patrick Kavanagh and American poet Robert Frost, and his finding solace in recalling past events harks back to Wordsworth's 'Tintern Abbey'. He continues to draw on nature and his farming background. 'Churning Day', for example, describes in painstaking, almost voluptuous detail how butter was made by hand, while 'Thatcher' illustrates the disappearing art of thatching cottage roofs. In the volume *Field Work* (1979) we see descriptions of animals in poems such as 'Badgers', while in *Station Island* (1984) he recalls how sloe gin is made, and in *Seeing Things* (1991) he remembers his favourite farm implement in 'The Pitchfork'.

The language of *Digging* and *Blackberry-Picking*, both from his first collection, gives us a hint of Heaney's linguistic influences, notably that of his contemporary, Ted Hughes. Like Hughes he employs onomatopoeia, in lines such as, 'Once I carried him milk in a bottle / Corked sloppily with paper', where 'corked sloppily' suggests the milk moving unsteadily in the bottle, or when he describes the 'squelch and slap' of wet peat being dug. He makes use of alliteration, as in 'spade sinks into gravelly ground', 'nicking and slicing neatly', 'the curt cuts of an edge' or 'fresh berries in the byre', and assonance, as in 'The cold smell of potato mould'.

Individual words have an exquisite fascination for Heaney, be they place names such as *Broagh* (a name that was anglicised from its original Gaelic, suggesting in itself a kind of linguistic colonialism), which seem to him to encapsulate their history in their etymology and their geography in their sound, or the luscious babble of the gale forecast that opens poem VII of the 'Glanmore Sonnets'. He uses words like a craftsman, like the blacksmith in 'The Forge' to 'expend himself in shape and music'. Sometimes two carefully selected words juxtaposed can have an almost breathtaking power, as when he refers to the atrocities of the political situation as 'neighbourly murders'.

As Heaney set out on his working life, married and began to bring up a family, the escalating political unrest in Northern Ireland inevitably became subject matter for his poetry. In early poems images such as the 'squat pen . . . snug as a gun', 'obscene threats', 'mud grenades' and a description of good grain as 'hard as shot', suggest an inner awareness of stress and subdued violence. But it is in *Wintering Out* (1972) and *North* (1975) that Heaney really begins to face 'the troubles'. The late 1960s and early 1970s were turbulent years in Northern Irish history, with civil rights protesters being strongly opposed and internment without trial being introduced into the Province.

In 1969 came the publication of P. V. Glob's *The Bog People*, another source of inspiration to Heaney. The book concerns Iron Age people who were sacrificed to the 'Earth Mother' to ensure a good harvest, whose bodies were found preserved under the peat of Jutland. Heaney was fascinated by the way the earth was able to file away its history and saw connections between pagan Jutland and Celtic Ireland and between the sacrificial rites of the Iron Age and events in contemporary Ireland. In 'The Tolland Man' (from *Wintering Out*) he also saw the bog people as holding the seeds for human regeneration after a season of unspeakable violence.

North contains other bog poems, such as 'Punishment', where Heaney describes a woman who was drowned for adultery. 'My poor scapegoat' he calls her and says that he almost loves her but is aware he 'would have cast, I know, the stones of silence'. He goes on to describe women who were tarred and feathered for colluding with British soldiers, concluding that while he felt 'civilised outrage', he could also understand the 'exact and tribal, intimate revenge'. The poem seems to sum up Heaney's ambivalent attitude to 'the troubles'. Like most in Northern Ireland, his life was changed by the violence – his cousin was killed, a barman he knew was killed by a bomb, a mild-mannered school friend was interned for political murder. But he was also aware, on the one hand, of a poet's ability to recount what he sees while being unable to offer solutions and on the other that certain political factions expected partisan reactions from him. He felt he risked being 'appropriated by the bombs' and was determined not to become 'a feeder off battlefields'.[1]

Although *North* enjoyed public acclaim and won the W. H. Smith Award and the Duff Cooper Prize, Heaney himself came under attack during this period for having moved with his family to Glanmore in the Republic of Ireland in 1972, nine months after the Bloody Sunday incident, and for refusing to take sides or suggest a cure for the sociopolitical malady from which Northern Ireland suffered.

In 'Exposure' (from *North*) and 'The Flight Path' (from *The Spirit Level*), Heaney captures the natural cadence of everyday speech. 'How did I end up like this?' he asks in the former; 'When, for fuck's sake are you going to write / Something for us?' a politically-active acquaintance asks him in the latter. The language in these poems is direct and brutal and the lines short and deceptively simple, as if reflecting the desolation of the political situation. At other times he uses poets of the past as inspiration to help him come to terms with what he sees. Dante's influence can often be seen, particularly in *Field Work* and *Seeing Things*. In 'The Strand at Lough Beg', for example, the poet cleans the face of his murdered cousin, just as Virgil cleans that of Dante in the *Divine Comedy*.

In 1990 Heaney wrote his own version of Sophocles's *Philoctetes*, entitled 'The Cure at Troy'. In the closing verses we see a new sense of hope, due partly to improvements in the political climate and partly perhaps to his finding that his struggles with the ageless stories of the classics were helping him find a new personal optimism. The poem ends with some of Heaney's most quoted lines:

So hope for a great sea-change
On the far side of revenge.
Believe that a further shore
Is reachable from here.
Believe in miracles
And cures and healing wells.

As Andrew Murphy has written, what characterises Heaney's political poems is 'a deep sense of honest striving towards some kind of meaningful encounter with the history and politics of his native country'. Heaney ranks, Murphy continues, 'as one of a handful of writers who have genuinely struggled to bring their work into some kind of fruitful relationship with the contemporary situation and its historical antecedents'. It was perhaps this 'honest striving' and 'genuine struggle' that led to Heaney being awarded the Nobel Prize for Literature in 1995.

In *The Spirit Level*, published the following year, 'Mycenae Lookout' retells Aeschylus's story of Agamemnon. The poem is a complex recreation of a circle of violence and revenge that ends with a suggestion of hope and fragile peace. This collection, with its tentative optimism, came out just after the first round of cease-fires in Northern Ireland.

Heaney has drawn on numerous other sources. In his Nobel Prize speech he spoke of his love of the classics of English literature, such as Keats, and his early works owe much, in their passionate language, to **Gerard Manley Hopkins**. He also admires a number of contemporary East European poets, the ancient poetry of Ireland and Nordic legends. In 1972 he published *Sweeny Astray*, a translation of the medieval Irish poem *Buile Suibhne*, and he later turned to translation again, publishing his acclaimed version of *Beowulf* in 2000 and adding the Whitbread Poetry Award to his already long list of accolades.

Reference

1. Nightwaves. 16 September 1998 BBC Radio 4. www.bbc.co.uk/bbcfour/audiointerviews/profilepages/heaneys1.shtml

Selected works:

Death of a Naturalist (1966); *Door into the Dark* (1969); *Wintering Out* (1972); *North* (1975); *Field Work* (1979); *Preoccupations*, collected essays (1980); *Selected Poems 1965–1975* (1980); *The Rattle Bag* – an anthology, joint edited with Ted Hughes (1982); Translation of *Buile Suibhne, Sweeny Astray*, published Ireland (1983), UK (1984); *Station Island* (1984); *The Haw Lantern* (1987); *The Government of the Tongue*, collected essays (1988); *New Selected Poems* (1990); *Seeing Things* (1991); *The Redress of Poetry*, an essay (1995); *The Spirit Level* (1996); *Opened Ground: Poems 1966–1996* (1998); *Beowulf*, a translation (2000).

Further reading

Corcoran, Neil, *A Students' Guide to Seamus Heaney*. Faber and Faber, 1986.

Morrison, Blake, *Seamus Heaney*. Routledge, 1982.

Murphy, Andrew, *Seamus Heaney,* a volume in the *Writers and their Work Series* (2nd ed.). Tavistock, Devon, 2000. Includes a concise but illuminating *Brief Sketch of Irish History* in the Appendix.

Vendler, Helen, *Seamus Heaney*. London: HarperCollins, 1998.

Contributor: Amanda Thursfield

HEMINGWAY, ERNEST (1899–1961)

A man can be destroyed but not defeated.
Old Man and the Sea

Photo credit: © Bettmann/CORBIS

Ernest Miller Hemingway, Nobel and Pulitzer Prize-winning author, is recognised for his concise and concentrated prose. He stripped language of inessentials, his experience as a journalist having contributed to his objective and honest writing style, free of embellishment and sentimentality. His short, simple sentences, composed primarily of nouns and verbs and free from emotional rhetoric, relied on repetition, rhythm and understatement for effect. The most widely imitated prose style in the twentieth century, Hemingway's succinct telegraphic style exerted a commanding influence on American and British fiction.

Hemingway was born in Oak Park, Illinois, to Clarence Edmonds Hemingway, a physician, and Grace Hall Hemingway, a professional singer and music teacher. He enjoyed a happy childhood, the family spending every summer on Walloon Lake in Michigan, where his father, an ardent outdoorsman, taught him to hunt and fish. In school he played football, sang in the choir, played the cello and wrote for the school paper. After graduating from high school he became a reporter for the *Kansas City Star.* It was from the *Star*'s stylebook that he adopted his artistic credo and he remained faithful to it throughout his literary career: 'Use short sentences. Use short first paragraphs. Use vigorous English. Be positive, not negative. Eliminate every superfluous word.'

Hemingway was rejected for military service in the First World War because of a defective eye. To get to the front, he volunteered as an ambulance driver for the American Red Cross. He was sent to Italy, where he was wounded in a major assault. At the age of 18 he met the first great love of his life, Agnes von Kurowsky, a 26-year-old nurse. Agnes broke his heart, but years later surfaced as Catherine Barkley, the heroine of *A Farewell to Arms* (1929).

After the War Hemingway moved to Toronto, wrote short stories and married 29-year-old Elizabeth Hadley Richardson, eight years his senior. With letters of introduction from novelist Sherwood Anderson to influential American writers living in Paris, **Ezra Pound** and Gertrude Stein, the young couple used Hadley's inheritance to sail to France. In Paris, as a foreign correspondent for the *Toronto Star*, Hemingway mingled with other writers, including **F. Scott Fitzgerald** and **James Joyce**, and in 1925 saw his first work published, *In Our Time*, a collection of short stories. Hemingway's first great success came when Fitzgerald wrote to Max Perkins, editor of Charles Scribner's Sons, recommending he sign Hemingway to the publishing house. Scribner's published *The Sun Also Rises* (1926), a story of American expatriates in France and Spain, members of the post-war 'lost generation', a phrase made famous by Hemingway when he attributed it to Stein in one of the epigraphs to the book.

Hemingway and Hadley had one son. After they divorced Hemingway married Pauline Pfeiffer in 1927 and two more sons were born in 1928 and 1931. In 1928 Hemingway's father committed suicide. Hemingway remained in Paris but travelled widely and became known not only for the intense masculinity of his writing but for his adventurous lifestyle. His travels in pursuit of bullfighting, hunting, fishing and skiing formed the background for his writing.

After 1930, Hemingway's health declined rapidly, partly due to drinking and accidents, but he still managed to make four trips to Spain as a correspondent during the Civil War. After leaving Spain in 1940 he divorced Pfeiffer and married Martha Gellhorn and moved from Key West to Havana, Cuba, where he would live for the next 20 years.

During the Second World War Hemingway went to London as a journalist. He flew missions with the Royal Air Force and crossed the Channel on D-Day, 4 June 1944. He saw action in Normandy and the Battle of the Bulge and was present at the liberation of Paris. He was now an international celebrity, famous for his adventurous lifestyle and macho image, and his once-solitary hunting and fishing expeditions escalated to widely publicised African safaris and big game hunting. After the war he returned to Cuba, but continued to travel. His marriage to Martha ended in 1945 and he married Mary Welsh, his fourth and final wife.

In addition to his novels Hemingway authored numerous short stories, some of the most famous being 'A Clean, Well-Lighted Place', 'The Short Happy Life of Frances Macomber' and 'The Snows of Kilimanjaro'. Fascinated by war and sport, Hemingway wrote on universal themes of courage, honour, love, suffering, endurance and death, many of his stories being based on his own experiences. His war experiences in Italy, and his love for Agnes von Kurowsky, were the basis for *A Farewell to Arms* (1929) and the war in Spain provided the background for what some consider his finest work, *For Whom the Bell Tolls* (1940).

In 1953 Hemingway was awarded the Pulitzer Prize for fiction for *Old Man and the Sea* (1952), the greatest of his later works. Written in Hemingway's characteristic economical style, *Old Man and the Sea* is the heroic story of an old Cuban fisherman's long struggle with a giant marlin. The old man exhibits what had become known as 'the Hemingway code', which means conducting oneself with courage, honour and dignity. Rising to a challenge and behaving well in a losing battle was to show grace under pressure, considered a victory even in defeat. The book contributed to Hemingway's winning the Nobel Prize for Literature in 1954.

In 1960 Fidel Castro drove Hemingway from Cuba and he and Mary settled in Ketchum, Idaho. Hemingway's many injuries and illnesses contributed to depression and anxiety and he received electroshock treatments at the Mayo Clinic. Two days after his return from his second stay at the Mayo, on 2 July 1961, he took his life with a shotgun. He was buried at Ketchum, Idaho, and a stone pedestal, with a bust of Hemingway, was erected in his memory on the road to Sun Valley. The monument bears a plaque inscribed with lines Hemingway wrote in 1939 for his friend Gene Van Guilder:

Best of all he loved the fall
The yellow leaves on the cottonwoods
Leaves floating on the trout streams
And above the hills
The high blue windless skies
Now he will be part of them forever.

Selected works:

In Our Time: Stories (1925); *The Torrents of Spring* (1926); *The Sun Also Rises* (1926); *Men Without Women* (1927); *A Farewell to Arms* (1929); *Winner Take Nothing* (1933); *To Have and Have Not* (1937); *The Fifth Column and the First Forty-Nine Stories* (1938); *For Whom the Bell Tolls* (1940); *Across the River and into the Trees* (1950); *Old Man and the Sea* (1952); *Islands in the Stream* (1970); *The Garden of Eden* (1986); *The Nick Adams Stories* (1972); *The Complete Short Stories of Ernest Hemingway* (1987); *Short Stories: Plays: The Fifth Column* (1938). **Non-fiction:** *Death in the Afternoon* (1932); *The Green Hills of Africa* (1935); *A Moveable Feast* (1964).

Further reading

Baker, Carlos, *Ernest Hemingway: A Life Story*. New York: Scribner's, 1969.

Meyers, Jeffrey, *Hemingway: A Biography*. New York: Da Capo, 1985.

Contributor: Karen C. Holt

HOPKINS, GERARD MANLEY (1844–89)

I caught this morning morning's minion,
kingdom of daylight's dauphin, dapple-
dawn-dawn falcon.

The Windhover

Although Gerard Manley Hopkins lived and wrote in the nineteenth century, his work did not enter the canon of English literature until 1918, when a volume of his poetry was published by the then Poet Laureate, Robert Bridges. Once it appeared, Hopkins's poetry became a major influence on twentieth-century English poetry and his innovative approach to language can be seen as prefiguring the experimentation with language as a medium in the works of many Modernist writers.

Hopkins was a brilliant scholar at Balliol College, Oxford, who became a Jesuit priest. He was also an amateur musician, writing atonal music, and kept a journal which he illustrated with drawings from nature. In his journal he records some of the terms he coined for concepts he was trying to express in his poetry and which he expanded upon in the Preface to the first edition of his poems. W. H. Gardner explains the two main terms as follows:

As a name for that 'individually-distinctive' form (made up of various sense-data) which constitutes the rich and revealing 'one-ness' of the natural object, he coined the word *inscape*; and for that energy of being by which all things are upheld, for that natural (but ultimately supernatural) stress which determines an *inscape* and keeps it in being – for that he coined the name *instress*.[1]

With the exception of a few Latin verses, Hopkins did not write his poetry for publication. Instead, he sent his works to his life-long friend Robert Bridges (1844–1930) and Coventry Patmore (1823–96) and burned his own copies.

His verse was so unusual that it was considered inept in the nineteenth century, almost a product of language disorder or mental disturbance, but its highly individual and personal approach, and innovative use of language,

struck a chord with, and inspired, poets of the Modern era.

Hopkins was innovative not only in the way he selected and combined words for their sensual and musical qualities but also in the way he broke up the traditional metre of poetry, using unpredictable rhythms as part of his technique of 'sprung rhythm', which he also explained in his Preface. In sprung rhythm the conventional regular rhythms of poetry are mixed with the rhythms of speech, varying the number of syllables and intervals between stresses in each line.

The effect of Hopkins's poetry is cumulative and impressionistic and often defies an answer to 'what does it mean?' but begs the questions 'what does it imply, or feel like, or how does it accord with memory?' It is the poetry of dreamscape and inner life and its purpose, to Hopkins, was deeply religious and akin to prayer. He attempted to go beyond language to convey what words cannot say. He could never have accepted Ludwig Wittgenstein's dictum that 'Whereof one cannot speak, thereof must one be silent'; on the contrary, he strove to give voice to the ineffable.

One now-famous poem, 'The Wreck of the Deutschland', which he submitted for publication in a Catholic journal, demonstrates how he strained at the limits of language. The poem was rejected, which disheartened the highly sensitive Hopkins who could hardly bear to show his works to others for fear that he would not be understood, or worse, would be ridiculed.

'The Wreck of the Deutschland', an odd and convoluted work, is a meditation on man and God, and shows Hopkins attempting a new form of expression to energise the art of poetry. He used everyday idiom, employed Anglo-Saxon words and assonance, internal rhyme, alliteration and a complex rhythmic and linguistic scheme that came to him from his study of Welsh poetry:

Thou mastering me
God! giver of breath and bread;
World's strand, sway of the sea;
    Lord of living and dead;
Thou hast bound bones and veins in me,
fastened me flesh,
And after it almost unmade, what with
dread,
    Thy doing: and dost thou touch me
    afresh?
Over again I feel thy finger and find thee.

More typical of Hopkins are the sonnets that he wrote in 1877, such as *God's Grandeur, The Lantern out of Doors* and *The Windhover*, his most celebrated poem, describing the flight of a falcon:

I caught this morning morning's minion,
kingdom of daylight's dauphin,
dapple-dawn-drawn falcon, in his riding
Of the rolling level underneath him
steady air, and striding
High there, how he rung upon the rein of
a wimpling wing
In his ecstasy!

Hopkins's final 'dark sonnets' owe something, in their approach to their religious subject matter, to the Metaphysical poets John Donne and George Herbert. The poems constitute a record of an acute spiritual crisis and the verse is simpler in style.

I wake and feel the fell of dark, not day.
What hours, O what black hours we have
spent
This night! what sights you, heart, saw;
ways you went!
And more must, in yet longer light's
delay.

The powerful expression of spiritual pain is seen again in:

No worst, there is none. Pitched pastpitch
of grief,
More pangs will, schooled at forepangs,
wilder wring.
Comforter, where, where is your
comforting?
Mary, mother of us, where is your relief?
My cries heave, herds-long; huddle in a
main, a chief
Woe, world-sorrow; on an age-old anvil
wince and sing
Then lull, then leave off. Fury had
shrieked 'No lingering!
Let me be fell: force I must be brief'.

There are direct echoes of these language forms in *Finnegan's Wake* by **James Joyce**, and **Dylan Thomas** attempted to imitate the word-music and striking collocations. The critic Walford Davis identifies the influence of Hopkins not only in the poetry of Dylan

Thomas, who was an enormous influence on later poets, but also in the work of **W. H. Auden** (insofar as he could consciously write a Hopkinsian pastiche) and in the works of W. R. Rodgers and William Empson, in that they were influenced by Hopkins's ability to give weight and density to lines of verse.[2] Hopkins was also a direct influence on Ivor Gurney and **Seamus Heaney**, and a favourite of the influential American poet **Elizabeth Bishop**.

Hopkins's style is seen at its simplest and most direct in such a poem as 'Heaven Haven' in which a nun contemplates taking the veil:

I have desired to go
Where springs not fail,
To fields where flies no sharp and sided
    hail
And a few lilies blow.

And I have asked to be
Where no storms come,
Where the green swell is in the havens
    dumb,
And out of the swing of the sea.

References

1. **Gardner, W. H.** (1953) *Gerard Manley Hopkins: a selection of his poems and prose.* Penguin.

2. **Davies, Walford** (ed.) (1974) *Dylan Thomas, Selected Poems.* Dent.

Contributors: Stephen Colbourn,
                                 Ian Mackean

HOUSMAN, A. E. (1859–1936)
Into my heart an air that kills
From yon sad country blows;
What are those blue remembered hills,
What spires, what farms are those?
                    'A Shropshire Lad'

Alfred Edward Housman might be considered a late-Victorian rather than modern writer because his most famous collection of verse, *A Shropshire Lad*, appeared in 1896. However, the work did not gain popularity until the First World War, since when it has been one of the best-selling volumes of poetry in English ever published, and Housman's other major works appeared in the modern period: *Last Poems*

(1922), *The Name and Nature of Poetry* (1932) and *More Poems* (1936).

Housman was a scholarly and reclusive man. Although a brilliant academic, he failed his final examinations at Oxford in 1881 while in emotional turmoil over his homosexual love for fellow student Moses Jackson. He was employed by day in the Patents Office from 1882 to 1892 and in the evenings he worked on emending Latin texts in the British Museum until he was offered a professorship at University College London. After the publication of *A Shropshire Lad* he regarded himself as an academic, not a poet, and published only one other volume of poetry, *Last Poems* (1922), which he completed on hearing the news that Moses Jackson was fatally ill with tuberculosis in Canada.

By this time he had become Professor of Latin at Cambridge University where he continued to teach until a few months before his death. During this time he wrote *The Name and Nature of Poetry*, a highly regarded analysis of the nature of poetic inspiration. His brother Laurence was a well-known illustrator, writer, critic and dramatist, one of whose plays, *Bethlehem* (1902), was banned as blasphemous. Alfred also wrote verses which he never published for fear that they might be considered irreligious. These, such as 'If in that Syrian garden, ages slain', appeared posthumously in *More Poems* (1936).

The hugely popular lyrical poems of *A Shropshire Lad* deal evocatively with the English countryside and its seasons, and with love, regret and the effect of passing time. Their tone is often romantically elegiac, even morose, and the collection includes some highly memorable verses such as:

Into my heart an air that kills
From yon sad country blows;
What are those blue remembered hills,
What spires, what farms are those?

Housman had a reputation for acerbic literary criticism and one might imagine that he subjected his own poetry to the same glaring scrutiny as the Latin texts he studied because he achieved an epigrammatic compression of style which reflected his Classical studies.

These, in the day when heaven was falling,

The hour when Earth's foundations fled,
Followed their mercenary calling
And took their wages and are dead.

Their shoulders held the sky suspended;
They stood, and Earth's foundations stay;
What God abandoned, these defended,
And saved the sum of things for pay.
[Epitaph on an Army of Mercenaries]

Perhaps Housman's repressed homosexuality, which would have been unspeakable in his own time, contributed to the intensity of his poetry. The theme of unrequited or thwarted male love runs through his works.

Crossing alone the nighted ferry
With one coin for fee,
Whom, on the wharf of Lethe waiting,
Count you to find? Not me.

The brisk fond lackey to fetch and carry,
The true sick-hearted slave,
Expect him not in the just city
And free land of the grave.
[From *More Poems*]

One other work of Housman to gain notoriety among scholars was an uncharacteristic book of Classical erotica, *Praefanda* (1931), available only in Latin. Another work, *De Amicita*, was deposited in a vault for 25 years and not read until 1960. It revealed Housman's love for a Venetian gondolier named Andrea whom he met in 1900.

Several of Housman's verses were set to music, including 'On Wenlock Edge', for which Vaughan Williams wrote a score.

Housman's ashes are buried in St Laurence's Church, Ludlow. There is a Blue Plaque on the house at 17 North Road, London, N6 where he lived from 1886 to 1905 and where he wrote *A Shropshire Lad*.

Selected works:

A Shropshire Lad (1896); *Last Poems* (1922); *The Name and Nature of Poetry* (1932); *More Poems* (1936); *Collected Poems* (1940).

Further reading

Birch, J. Roy (ed.) and Parker, Agnes Miller (illustrator) *A. E. Housman, Poet and Scholar*. Housman Society, 1996.

Graves, Richard Perceval, *A. E. Housman: The Scholar-Poet*. Routledge, 1979.

Holden, Alan W. and Birch, J. Roy (eds) *A. E. Housman: A reassessment*. Macmillan, 1999.

Contributors: Stephen Colbourn,
                             Ian Mackean

HUGHES, LANGSTON (1902–67) – AMERICAN

I am the darker brother.
They send me to eat in the kitchen
When company comes,
But I laugh,
And eat well,
And grow strong.

I, too, sing America

Langston Hughes was the first African-American to have a successful career based solely on writing. He aimed to change society through his work and was influential in promoting the inclusion of African-American culture and traditions in American literature. Having grown up in an era of discriminatory laws and public lynchings, he sought to break down barriers of prejudice through poetry, stories and plays that explored African-American life, with all its inequality, humour, hope and hopelessness. An important figure in the **Harlem Renaissance**, his writings are steeped in the sounds of lower-class black society, both its music and its dialect. Published in white journals from an early point in his career, his writings forged new paths for black writers and won several prestigious national and international awards. He was the first black American member of the international writers' organization, **P.E.N.**, and the second black member of the National Institute of Arts and Letters.

Hughes was born in 1902, the only child of James Nathaniel and Carrie Mercer Langston Hughes. His parents split up when he was five years old, after which he was passed back and forth between his unstable mother, his strict and severe grandmother, some generous family friends and, later in his adolescence, his controlling father. He spent most of his childhood in poverty and was usually isolated from other children. Because of this, he developed a last-

ing appreciation of literature and the theatre and began to write poetry at a young age. At high school, a teacher introduced him to the poetry of Carl Sandburg and Walt Whitman and the influence of both poets is evident in his early works. When he was only 19, while living with his father in Mexico, he began to have work published, first in a black children's magazine and then in the Harlem-based *Crisis* magazine, which later published more of his poetry and arranged his first poetry readings.

These first publications served the valuable purpose of convincing James Hughes to send Langston to college, despite his wish that Langston should become a mining engineer and make a respectable living. Langston attended New York's Columbia University for a year, then dropped out to write and travel. He worked aboard ships bound for Africa and Holland and lived for nearly a year in Paris, where his writing took on the sound and rhythm of the jazz he heard every night in the club where he worked washing dishes. His poetry continued to be published in magazines in the United States and when he returned from abroad he found his reputation as a poet had grown considerably in his absence.

A few months after his return to America Hughes's poem 'The Weary Blues' won first prize in a poetry contest sponsored by *Opportunity* magazine and soon his first book was published, a collection of poems also entitled *The Weary Blues*, which was innovative in its incorporation of blues lyrics into poetry.

Hughes then began college for the second time, this time studying at the all-black Lincoln University in Pennsylvania. His second book, *Fine Clothes to the Jew* (1927), was published during his sophomore year, but was poorly received. However, his next book, the autobiographical *Not Without Laughter* (1930), went on to win the Harmon Gold Award for distinguished black literature in 1931. After a trip to Cuba and Haiti on the prize money, Hughes resolved to dedicate himself to writing and began a poetry-reading and lecture tour through the southern states. Although he sometimes met with hostile and prejudiced reactions, he felt that this was a way that his poetry could make a difference in the lives of ordinary people and continued to give live poetry readings throughout the rest of his career.

In 1932 Hughes was hired to make a movie in Soviet Russia and although the movie failed in pre-production he stayed for a year, travelling throughout Central Asia to fulfil writing assignments for the Russian magazine *Izvestia*. He was initially attracted by the ideals of social and economic equality espoused by the Soviet Union and wrote impassioned poetry on the subject, but later he became disillusioned by the repressive nature of the Soviet regime. In 1953 he was investigated by Senator Joseph McCarthy's Sub-Committee as a result of the poetry he wrote at this time and while he was not found guilty of treason, his reputation and career were damaged by the trial.

On returning from Russia Hughes was awarded a Guggenheim Fellowship, which allowed him to focus on his writing without financial worries, although most of this money eventually went to support his stepbrother and his sick mother. In 1936 Hughes began to have plays performed by black theatre groups.

In 1937 Hughes travelled to Madrid as a correspondent in the Spanish Civil War. He came into close contact with the fighting and was shot in the arm by a sniper. His writing during this time went under the heading of 'Letters from Spain'. Upon his return to the USA in 1938 he founded the Harlem Suitcase Theatre, the first of three black theatres he established between 1938 and 1942.

During the Second World War Hughes became involved in raising money and encouraging support for the war effort, utilising his writing talents to do so. In 1942 he began writing 'Simple' stories for his column in the *Chicago Defender*. These stories, based around the character Jesse B. Simple, strove to catch the complexity and resilience of black people. Hughes continued to use Simple in his writings for the next 25 years.

In 1947 Hughes settled permanently in Harlem and wrote prolifically, as well as editing many anthologies of African-American writing, until his death in 1967.

Selected works:

The Weary Blues (1926); *Fine Clothes to the Jew* (1927); *Not Without Laughter* (1930); *Dear Lovely Death* (1931); *The Dream Keeper and Other Poems* (1932); *The Ways of White Folks* (1934); *The Big Sea* (1940); *Shakespeare in Harlem* (1942); *Fields of Wonder* (1947); *One-Way Ticket* (1949); *Simple Speaks his Mind* (1950); *Montage of a Dream Deferred* (1951); *Laughing to Keep from Crying* (1952); *The First Book of the Negroes* (1959); *Simple Takes a Wife* (1953); *Famous American Negroes* (1954); *The First Book of Rhythms* (1954); *Famous Negro Music Makers* (1955); *The Sweet Flypaper of Life* (1955); *The First Book of Jazz* (1955); *The First Book of the West Indies* (1956); *I Wonder as I Wander: An Autobiographical Journey* (1956); *A Pictorial History of the Negro in America* (1956); *Simple Stakes a Claim* (1957); *Famous Negro Heroes of America* (1958); *Selected Poems of Langston Hughes* (1959); *Tambourines to Glory: A Novel* (1959); *First Book of Africa* (1960); *Ask Your Mama: 12 Moods for Jazz* (1961); *The Best of Simple* (1961); *Fight for Freedom: The Story of the NAACP* (1962); *Something in Common and Other Stories* (1963); *Five Plays by Langston Hughes* (1963); *Simple's Uncle Sam* (1965); *The Panther and the Lash* (1967); *Black Magic: A Pictorial History of the Negro in American Entertainment* (1967); *Collected Poems* (1994). **Anthologies edited by Hughes:** *The Poetry of the Negro 1746-1949* (1949); *The Langston Hughes Reader* (1958); *The Book of Negro Folklore* (1958); *An African Treasury* (1960); *Poems from Black Africa* (1963); *New Negro Poets: USA* (1964); *The Book of Negro Humor* (1966); *The Best Short Stories by Negro Writers* (1967).

Further reading

Jemie, Onwuchekwa, *Langston Hughes: An Introduction to the Poetry*. New York, 1973.

Rampersad, Arnold, *The Life of Langston Hughes*. Vol. I, 1902–1941, I, Too, Sing America. Vol. 2, 1941–1967, I Dream a World. New York, 1986–1988.

Contributor: Victoria J. Essary

HUGHES, TED (1930–98)

I imagine this midnight moment's forest:
Something else is alive
Beside the clock's loneliness
And this blank page where my fingers
move.

                                The Thought-Fox

Ted Hughes was one of the most highly acclaimed British poets of the twentieth century. He wrote poetry and prose for both adults and children, translated verse and plays, and collected and edited the work of other writers. He received an OBE in 1977, was Poet Laureate from 1984 until his death and received the Order of Merit in 1998. He received many literary prizes, including The Whitbread Book of the Year two years running, for *Tales from Ovid* in 1997 and *Birthday Letters* in 1998. He was an intense, imaginative writer, known for his stern, direct style and his depiction of the elemental forces of nature and animal life. Among other influences his writing drew upon his Yorkshire background, his parents' experiences, Shakespeare and his interests in mythology, shamanism and the occult.

Edward James Hughes was born in Mytholmroyd, a town surrounded by the unforgiving, bleak landscape of the Yorkshire moors. In childhood he learned to hunt game and developed a profound knowledge of, and respect for, nature. His father, who had fought at Gallipoli, told stories of his experiences during the First World War, and his mother talked of seeing ghosts. All these experiences fed into his work, as seen for example in the collection of short stories, *Difficulties of a Bridegroom* (1995), which includes 'The Rain Horse' (originally published in *Wodwo*, 1967), a story of a man chased by a horse on a stormy moor, 'The Wound', about an injured soldier's demon-filled hallucinations, and 'The Deadfall', in which a ghost helps to free a fox cub caught in a trap.

Hughes started writing comic verse at the age of 11 and had poetry published in the school magazine. In 1948 he won an Open Exhibition to Pembroke College, Cambridge, but did not go up until 1951 as he was required to do National Service between 1949 and 1951. During National Service, stationed in Yorkshire, he spent much of his spare time reading Shakespeare and was later to write a criticism of Shakespeare's work, *Shakespeare and the Goddess of Complete Being* (1992). He occasionally included Shakespearean references in his poems, and in 'Setebos' from *Birthday Letters* (1998) he compares himself and his wife with Ferdinand and Miranda from *The Tempest*.

At Cambridge Hughes found that studying English literature restricted his writing style, so he switched to archaeology and anthropology. He read the poetry of primitive societies and became interested in their folklore. After university he wrote under various pseudonyms while working as a rose gardener, night watchman, zoo attendant and school teacher. In 1956, with a group of friends, he launched a poetry magazine, *The St Botolph's Review*. The magazine ran for only one issue, but at its inauguration party he met the talented but troubled American writer **Sylvia Plath**, who was attending Cambridge on a Fulbright Scholarship, and they married later that year. Soon after, Plath entered some of Hughes's poems for a poetry competition; he won. As a result, 1957 saw the publication of *The Hawk in the Rain*, a collection which demonstrated that Hughes did not shy away from the less attractive aspects of nature: apes adore their fleas and the jaguar is on a short, fierce fuse. It also contains some of his best-known early poems such as 'The Thought Fox' and the title poem, 'Hawk in the Rain'.

Once Plath had finished her Masters Degree, the couple travelled to the USA, where Hughes wrote many of the poems which appeared in *Lupercal* (1960), a volume which consolidated his reputation as a nature poet who was unafraid of the more violent aspects of the natural world. In the collection the pike is described as a malevolent killer, thrushes use a deadly eye to stab at prey, and even the water lily has horror nudging her root.

In 1959 they moved to England and in 1960 their daughter, Frieda Rebecca, was born. Needing extra income Hughes wrote for various magazines and newspapers and did radio shows for the BBC. In 1961 he published a book of children's verse, *Meet My Folks!* The unconventional family in the story includes an octopus grandmother and an aunt who turns into a witch.

In January 1962 their second child, Nicholas Farrar, was born, but soon afterwards the marriage broke down. Plath suffered mood swings and fits of jealousy. Hughes met Assia Wevill and the couple had an affair; their daughter, Shura, was born in 1965. In 1962, the year in which he and Thom Gunn published *Selected Poems*, Hughes moved to London. Tragically, in 1963 Sylvia Plath committed suicide. Although this was

Plath's second suicide attempt, the first having occurred before she met Hughes, some blamed Hughes for her death. Hughes was deeply affected by the loss and wrote no new adult poetry for about three years. He concentrated on children's books, such as *How the Whale Became* (1963), a series of children's Aesop-like fables, *The Earth-Owl and Other Moon People* (1963) and *Nessie the Mannerless Monster* (1964). He also wrote radio plays for children including *The Coming of the Kings* (1964), *The Tiger's Bones* (1965) and *Beauty and the Beast* (1965).

By 1966 Hughes had started writing for adults again and was working on the poems which would appear in *Wodwo* and *Crow*. The poems in *Wodwo* (1967) combine Hughes's interests in mythology and nature. The title was borrowed from the name of a troll-like character in the fourteenth-century poem *Sir Gawain and the Green Knight*.

In 1968, Hughes wrote *The Iron Man*, his most famous children's story, which was adapted into a film, *The Iron Giant* (1999), which uses the character created by Hughes but in a different setting. In both stories a huge metal man arrives mysteriously on earth. In *The Iron Man* the giant saves the world from a dragon-like creature the size of Australia. *The Iron Giant* is set in Cold War America and the arrival of the giant sparks fears of a Soviet attack. The giant saves a town from destruction when a nuclear missile is launched.

Another tragedy beset Hughes in 1969 when Assia Wevill killed herself and their daughter. A year later Hughes married his second wife, Carol Orchard, and the family settled in Devon. In 1970, Hughes wrote *Poetry in the Making* in which he argued that there is no single or ideal form of poetry. In 1971 he developed the language 'Orghast' which was a form of wordless communication aimed at freeing actors from the boundaries of language.

In the collection *Crow* (1972) Hughes presented a new, nihilistic mythology. In the USA in 1958 he and Plath had been friendly with sculptor and graphic artist Leonard Baskin, who sculpted crows and suggested that Hughes write about them. This subject, together with Hughes's interest in the supernatural and mythology, led to the creation of the character Crow. In Hughes's Crow legend

God has a nightmare and feels a hand at his throat. At the same time Man has come up from earth to ask God to take back mankind. God is outraged and challenges the nightmare hand to do better. Crow is born. A series of Crow poems followed which contain a fatherly but fallible God and the amoral Crow who is partly drawn from Native American literature.

In the mid-1970s Hughes retreated from public life and worked on his father-in-law's farm. Many of his works were published during this time, including *Gaudete* (1977) and *Cave Birds* (1979), presenting further combinations of nature and mythology.

In *Shakespeare and the Goddess of Complete Being* (1992) Hughes proposed the theory that the myths established in the poems *Venus and Adonis* and *The Rape of Lucrece* formed the basis for many of Shakespeare's later plays. *Tales from Ovid* was published in 1997 and in 1998, *Birthday Letters*, which soon became one of his best-known collections. The poems address his relationship with Sylvia Plath from their first meeting until after her death. The poems are a personal tribute to Plath and show the strength of their relationship as well as its tempestuous nature.

Selected works:

Poetry: *The Hawk in the Rain* (1957); *Lupercal* (1960); *Selected Poems*, with Thom Gunn (1962); *Recklings* (1967); *Wodwo* (1967); *Crow* (1972); *Gaudete* (1977); *Cave Birds* (1979); *Shakespeare and the Goddess of Complete Being* (1992); *Birthday Letters* (1998). **Verses and Stories for Children:** *Meet my Folks!* (1961); *How the Whale Became* (1963); *The Earth-Owl and Other Moon People* (1963); *Nessie the Mannerless Monster* (1964); *The Coming of the Kings* (1964); *The Tiger's Bones* (1965); *Beauty and the Beast* (1965); *The Iron Man* (1968). **Prose:** *Poetry in the Making* (1970); *Shakespeare and the Goddess of Complete Being* (1992); *Difficulties of a Bridegroom* (1995).

Further reading

Feinstein, Elaine, *Ted Hughes: The Life of a Poet*. W. W. Norton, 2003.

Contributor: Sarah Jones

HUXLEY, ALDOUS (1894–1963)

Onward Nazi soldiers, onward Christian soldiers, onward Marxists and Muslims, onward every chosen People, every Crusader and Holy War-maker. Onward into misery, into all wickedness, into death!

Island

Aldous Huxley wrote 'novels of ideas', in which little attempt was made to give psychological depth to characters and dialogue was a pretext for intellectual discussion. From its beginnings in social satire his fiction became increasingly serious and didactic, but its cleverness and clear prose style earned him a wide readership, and *Brave New World* (1932) in particular continues to enjoy popularity. Huxley revised *Brave New World* in the 1950s, in the light of the global threat of nuclear weapons, and its reference to anthrax bombs and other weapons of mass destruction ensures that it is as relevant today as it was in the 1960s. Huxley was involved in campaigning against nuclear weapons in the 1960s and became associated with the **hippie** movement, particularly in America, through his involvement with Eastern religion and his experimentation with drugs.

Huxley was born into a family of prominent academics. His grandfather, T. H. (Thomas Henry) Huxley, was a lecturer and public speaker, well known for promoting scientific ideas, particularly Charles Darwin's Theory of Evolution. Aldous's father, Leonard, was a writer and his brother Julian became a noted biologist and author.

Educated at Eton and Oxford, Huxley was an able scholar, though his studies were interrupted at the age of 16 by an eye disorder which left him blind for several months and partially sighted in one eye for the rest of his life. He learned Braille and graduated from Balliol College in 1915. Most of his contemporaries were called up during the First World War, but Aldous, being unfit for military service, worked in the War Office. After the war he taught at Eton for a short while, after which he became an editor of *The Athenaeum,* a literary and artistic journal published by John Middleton Murry.

Huxley attended Lady Ottoline Morrell's literary salon at Garsington Manor near Oxford where, along with his friend **D. H. Lawrence**, he met members of the **Bloomsbury Group**. Like **T. S. Eliot**, Huxley became a fringe member of the Bloomsbury set and Garsington provided material for his first novel, *Crome Yellow* (1920), a witty piece of social criticism which gained him a reputation as a fashionable literary figure.

In the 1920s Huxley lived mainly in Italy, then in 1930 moved to a village outside Toulon in south-eastern France, where he began work on *Brave New World*. The title of this novel is an ironic reference to a line in Shakespeare's *The Tempest,* in which Miranda declares, "*O, brave new world that hath such people in it*" on seeing a young man, Ferdinand, for the first time.

Brave New World is a **dystopia**, which in Greek means a 'bad place' or the opposite of **Utopia** which means either a good place or no place at all. It was inspired by Huxley's response to the rapid social changes occurring in the wake of industrialism, in particular his perception of the mass-production methods used in the manufacture of cars by Henry Ford in America. The action takes place in the year 632 AF (After Ford). Children are produced on a conveyor belt and predesignated for their roles in life, from Alpha Plus, the leadership rank, to Epsilon Minus, the semi-moronic mechanicals. Everyone is obliged to be happy all the time; sex is for pleasure, not for reproduction, the cinema has become 'the feelies', offering total virtual reality, and a euphoria-inducing drug, 'soma', is widely available. Trouble only comes when a savage from a primitive reservation intrudes, bringing twentieth-century doubts and unhappiness into the highly controlled society.

In creating his dystopian world Huxley was inspired by *We* (1924), a book by the Russian writer Zamyatin (1889–1937) which was suppressed in the Soviet Union and published abroad. **George Orwell** also read the book and was influenced by it when writing *Nineteen Eighty-four.* Zamyatin depicts a workers' paradise in which life is regulated under the guidance of a wise 'Benefactor' and no one is allowed to be idle, bored or unhappy. This vision, which appealed to Huxley and Orwell, was the opposite of the progressive utopian socialism proclaimed by H. G. Wells and George Bernard Shaw. Wells had recently revised his *Outline of History,* completed *The Science of* Life (1931), which he co-wrote with Julian Huxley, and was working on *The Shape of Things to Come. Brave New World* was Huxley's riposte to Wells and his brother.

Huxley was deeply committed to pacifism and feared the outbreak of another war in Europe. In 1937 he moved to California and worked for several years as a Hollywood script writer, producing screen plays for *Madame Curie* (1938), *Pride and Prejudice* (1940) and *Jane Eyre* (1944). In this period he came increasingly under the influence of Indian religion and lived with a guru figure, Gerald Heard. Christopher Isherwood joined them in 1939 and co-wrote *Jacob's Hands* with Huxley. Through Isherwood, Huxley met the Swami Prabhavananda, with whom he translated the Indian classic *Bhagavad-Gita* as *The Song of God* (1944).

In 1952 Huxley published *The Devils of Loudun,* which describes religious mania in a seventeenth-century nunnery. The book was adapted as a play, by John Whiting (1917–63), which in turn was the basis for Ken Russell's film *The Devils* (1971).

Believing that his eyesight was about to fail completely, Huxley began experimenting with the mind-altering drug mescaline and described his experiences in *The Doors of Perception* (1954), the title being taken from the late-eighteenth-century poet William Blake. He also brought out *Brave New World Revisited* in 1958, as an update of the original.

Huxley's last work was the utopian novel *Island* (1962), in which he looked back over the Second World War and other horrors of the twentieth century. The book reads rather like a series of dramatic monologues or public lectures in which he attempts to encapsulate his experience and learning and all that he had loathed in his lifetime. While working on this book in 1961, Huxley's house outside Los Angeles was destroyed by a bush fire. He regarded the loss as a liberation from material possessions, as well as a trial of faith. Huxley died in Los Angeles in 1963, on the same day that President John F. Kennedy was assassinated in Dallas.

Selected works:

The Burning Wheel (1916); *The Defeat Of Youth* (1918); *Limbo* (1920); *Crome Yellow* (1921);

Antic Hay (1923); *On The Margin* (1923); *Along The Road* (1925); *Those Barren Leaves* (1925); *Jesting Pilate* (1926); *Essays New And Old* (1926); *Proper Studies* (1927); *Point Counter Point* (1928); *Do What You Will* (1929); *Holy Face, And Other Essays* (1929); *Brief Candles* (1930); *The World Of Light* (1931); *Music At Night* (1931); *Brave New World* (1932); *Beyond The Mexique Bay* (1934); *Eyeless In Gaza* (1936); *An Encyclopaedia Of Pacifism* (1937 – edited); *After Many A Summer Dies The Swan* (1939); *Ape And Essence* (1948); *The Perennial Philosophy* (1948); *Gioconda Smile* (1948); *Themes And Variations* (1950); *The Devils Of Loudun* (1952); *The Doors of Perception* (1954); *Adonis and The Alphabet* (1956); *Collected Short Stories* (1957); *Brave New World Revisited* (1958); *Collected Essays* (1959); *On Art And Artist* (1960); *Island* (1962); *Literature and Science* (1963).

Further reading

Baker, Robert S. and Sexton, James (eds) *Aldous Huxley.* Ivan R. Dee, Inc, 2000.

Contributors: Stephen Colbourn,
                                    Ian Mackean

ISHIGURO, KAZUO (1954–)

You realise soon enough when a wound is not going to heal. The music, even when I was a conductor, I knew that's all it was, just a consolation. It helped for a while. I liked the feeling, pressing the wound, it fascinated me. A good wound, it can do that, it fascinates. It looks a little different every day.

The Unconsoled

Kazuo Ishiguro seems an easy writer to categorise. All his novels are written as first-person narratives with **unreliable narrators** and most of them deal with post-Second World War societies, either Japanese or

English. Ishiguro's themes include the unreliability of memory, **existential** concerns in relation to feelings of guilt, intergenerational familial relationships and a deep reflection on art forms and their function in society.

Ishiguro's first two novels have been called his 'Japanese' novels because they are set mostly in Japan. *A Pale View of Hills* (1982) is narrated by Etsuko, an elderly Japanese woman who married an Englishman and lives in England. Etsuko reminisces about post-war Nagasaki – Ishiguro's birthplace – recounting some of her memories to her English daughter Niki after the suicide of her eldest daughter, Keiko. Gradually, Etsuko's memories about a neighbour and her daughter blend with Etsuko's own life and her feelings of guilt over Keiko's death. Reflecting its title, the novel offers the reader a 'pale view' of Etsuko's past. We are not told whether this is because she cannot bear to remember or because some of what she 'remembers' is imaginative invention.

An Artist of the Floating World (1986) follows a similar pattern. The narrator is a painter who reassesses his artistic achievements and his support for the Japanese nationalistic movement that led to Japan's involvement in the Second World War, with its subsequent tragic consequences. Masuji Ono worries that his past may be preventing the marriage of his younger daughter because good families may not want to be associated with him. He feels guilty about his past, in particular about his denunciation of a former pupil, and his own inflated ego. By the end, we are not sure whether Ono was as influential as he believes he was or whether he is just an old man convinced of his self-importance. The novel is also a beautiful treatise on painting and, by extension, writing and the different options open to artists, such as whether to pursue **aestheticism** or political involvement.

The fact that Ishiguro was born in Japan and has a conveniently 'exotic' name was used to market his early novels, but has also pigeonholed him as a '**postcolonial**' writer – a farcical categorisation since Japan has never been part of the Empire. Besides, Ishiguro left Japan with his family in 1960 at the age of five, speaks only rudimentary Japanese and was brought up and schooled in England. His books have been read as being Japanese and compared to those of Japanese writers such as Masuji Ibuse, Yasunari Kawabata and Junichiro Tanizaki, but they owe more to writers such as Chekhov, Dostoevsky and Kafka. In the Anglophone tradition, Ishiguro has parodied P. G. Wodehouse and genres such as detective fiction of the 1930s, while declaring his admiration for American writers such as **Raymond Carver**, Richard Ford, **Ernest Hemingway** and Henry James. He has also pointed to Charlotte Brontë and Charles Dickens as major influences. In addition, his writing has been informed by his MA in Creative Writing from the University of East Anglia, where he was taught by Malcolm Bradbury and **Angela Carter**, and he shares a concern with expanding the scope of British literature with fellow writers Timothy Mo and **Salman Rushdie**, although his approach differs from theirs.

After the 'Japanese' phase, Ishiguro wrote his most popular novel, the best-selling *The Remains of the Day* (1989), which won the Booker Prize and was adapted for the screen. The novel is set in post-Second World War England and follows the trip which Stevens, an old-fashioned butler, takes in his new American boss's car to visit a former housekeeper. This relatively straightforward plot is beautifully chiselled into a journey of self-awareness by Stevens's first-person narrative. Stevens, like all of Ishiguro's narrators to date, is unreliable not only because he hides things from the reader but also because he deceives himself. He hides behind his professionalism to avoid having to take decisions and make moral judgements. He lives his whole life trying to become the perfect butler and not letting anything or anyone interfere with his job. This is shown to be a fallacy since, in pursuit of this impossible perfection, he lets all his chances for love and happiness slip away. Besides, he has doubts about his actions (or lack of action) in the light of his previous employer's appeasement policy and fascist sympathies. The more the reader becomes accustomed to Stevens's elaborate, somewhat old-fashioned vocabulary and overcomplicated sentence structures, the easier it becomes to unravel the layers of self-deception. In keeping with Ishiguro's passion for film and the remarkably cinematic style of his prose, he makes ample use of Stevens's reminiscences, which work as flash-backs.

The Remains of the Day has attracted a great deal of critical attention. To some reviewers it is the most 'Japanese' of Ishiguro's books. This, however, is misguided and rather parochial, for Ishiguro is fascinated with a certain type of behaviour which is not privy to any particular nationality. What English critics identify as Japanese is perceived by the rest of the world as quintessentially English. Ishiguro has also been criticised for turning away from his ethnic background and having white protagonists in all his books from *The Remains of the Day* on. A minority of critics mistakenly deplore the fact that he does not write about immigrant experience in Britain, forgetting the fact that Etsuko is an immigrant and Niki, though half-Japanese, is English.

Ishiguro's fourth novel, *The Unconsoled* (1995), provoked a mixed critical response. Most reviewers declared it a failure, but a few thought it a masterpiece. The book is narrated by Ryder, a 'renowned pianist' who is in a central European city to give a concert which never takes place. Ryder, however, is not a 'normal' unreliable narrator. He appears not to have a structured memory and never finishes what he sets out to do, distracted by polite requests that he is unable – or unwilling – to refuse. Other characters float in and out of his narrative as if they were ghosts of his past or aspects of his former or future selves. Ryder's troubled past, vacuous present and possible future are thus hinted at in a novel that also addresses its own function in a **metanarrative** way, as discussions on music echo literary debates about **Modernism** and **postmodernism**. *The Unconsoled* pushes narrative conventions and characterisation to the limits and could perhaps be seen as standing in relation to contemporary literature as *Finnegan's Wake* does to Modernism.

When We Were Orphans (2000) seems to be a belated transitional novel between the mainstream phase and the imaginative and technical experimentation of *The Unconsoled*. The title indicates the novel's concern with family relations and the past, but in this novel we are taken as far back as the 1930s and, geographically, to England and Shanghai. The main character, Christopher Banks, narrates retrospectively and makes a series of assertions about himself and his past that become less and less believable as we go on. The last third of the novel, except for the final section, becomes the mapping of a disintegrating mind. Stylistically the novel is a compromise between the more accessible novels readers are accustomed to and the ground-breaking technique of *The Unconsoled*. Ishiguro cunningly lures readers into feeling safe, only to lead them into unfamiliar territory when least expected. This is both the strength of this novel and its weakness.

Ishiguro's novels are narrative masterpieces which transform the genres they tackle. They seem historically 'true' without being historical. They invite us to sympathise with their characters while seeing through their masks. Above all, they provide a floating, imaginative world which is nevertheless very much grounded in universal human concerns.

Selected works:

A Pale View of Hills (1982); *An Artist of the Floating World* (1986); *The Remains of the Day* (1989); *The Unconsoled* (1995); *When We Were Orphans* (2000).

Further reading

Lewis, Barry, *Kazuo Ishiguro*. Manchester University Press, 2000.

Petri, Mike, *Narratives of Memory and Identity. The Novels of Kazuo Ishiguro*. Peter Lang, 1999.

Shaffer, Brian W., *Understanding Kazuo Ishiguro*. The University of South Carolina Press, 1998.

Contributor: Ana María Sánchez-Arce

JOYCE, JAMES (1882–1941)

I will not serve that in which I no longer believe, whether it call itself my home, my fatherland, or my Church: and I will try to express myself in some mode of life or art as freely as I can, using for my defence the only arms I allow myself to use – silence, exile, and cunning.

A Portrait of the Artist as a Young Man

Photo credit: © Hulton-Deutsch Collection/CORBIS

James Joyce, one of the best-known and most influential novelists of the twentieth century, was a prominent contributor to the **Modernist** movement. He showed remarkable artistry in his use of language, adapting his style to suit his purpose of going beyond traditional **realism** to explore the subjective reality of his characters. Although he did not invent the **stream of consciousness** technique, he developed its use as a means of presenting the inner workings of characters' minds in his novel *Ulysses*, and in the extraordinary *Finnegan's Wake* he took it a stage further by using it to explore the unconscious mind through the dreams of a sleeping protagonist.

James Augustine Aloysius Joyce was born in Dublin and educated at Jesuit schools and University College, where he took an interest in the plays of Henryk Ibsen – even learning Norwegian in order to understand them better. His first publication was a study of Ibsen's play *When We Dead Awaken* which was accepted by a literary review in 1900, and his own play, *Exiles* (1918), showed the influence of Ibsen.

His novels and short stories are set in Dublin, but Joyce lived outside Ireland for most of his life and regarded himself as a European. He left Ireland in 1902 and returned to Dublin only for short spells. After working in Paris he came home to visit his dying mother then set off again in 1904 together with Nora Barnacle, a chambermaid, whom he eventually married. They lived precariously

in Pola and Trieste, which at the time was part of Austria-Hungary but is now in Italy, and had a son and a daughter. Most of the time Joyce was poverty-stricken and made ends meet by working as a teacher, journalist and translator.

Joyce's first volume of poetry, *Chamber Music*, was published in 1907. The 36 poems owed something to the style of Elizabethan lyricists and in keeping with his sensitivity to the musicality of language, which is apparent in all of his writing, Joyce wrote them with the intention that they should be sung.

Dubliners, a collection of short stories, was published in 1914. In the 15 connected stories Joyce captured what he felt to be significant and revealing moments in the lives of Dublin people, one of the important themes being moral paralysis.

In Trieste, Joyce reworked an early autobiographical story *Stephen Hero*, written in 1904–06, and turned it into *A Portrait of the Artist as a Young Man*, which was published, with the help of **Ezra Pound**, in the USA in 1916. A fictionalised autobiography, it concerns the education and intellectual development of Stephen Dedalus (who reappears in *Ulysses*). Stephen's education is deeply Catholic. He contemplates becoming a Jesuit and entering a seminary but is troubled by sensual desires. One powerful passage in the book is a priest's depiction of hell during a religious retreat, which causes Stephen to experience agonies of guilt and fear.

The material from *Stephen Hero* was used mainly in the final chapter of *A Portrait of the Artist as a Young Man*, the preceding four chapters presenting stages in Stephen's development from infancy to young manhood. In keeping with Joyce's liking for embedding layers of meaning in his work, many of the images, words and names in the novel have symbolic significance, making points about the church and the Irish mentality, which would not be apparent to the casual reader. At key points in the story Stephen experiences 'epiphanies' (moments of heightened awareness and insight) which help him decide on his course of action. At the end of the novel Stephen rejects the claims of nationality and religion. He adopts the ambition of becoming an artist and leaves Ireland for Paris in order to live more freely and fully.

When the soul of a man is born in this country there are nets flung at it to hold it back from flight. You talk to me of nationality, language, religion. I shall try to fly by those nets . . . I will not serve that in which I no longer believe, whether it call itself my home, my fatherland, or my Church: and I will try to express myself in some mode of life or art as freely as I can, using for my defence the only arms I allow myself to use – silence, exile, and cunning.

The First World War disrupted Joyce's life in Trieste, which lay on the border between two belligerent powers. When Italy claimed the city, Joyce moved to Zurich in neutral Switzerland. Here he worked on the first draft of *Ulysses*, a part of which he wrote as a stream of consciousness – a technique influenced by the French writer Edouard Dujardin (1861–1949), and used by the English novelists Dorothy Richardson and **Virginia Woolf**. The aim of the stream of consciousness technique is to reproduce as accurately as possible the moment-to-moment flow of an individual's thoughts.

Other exiles had come to Zurich, including the Russian revolutionary Vladimir Ilych Ulyanov, known as Lenin, and the Rumanian poet Tristan Tzara. Together with a group of like-minded exiles, Tzara opened a café, The Cabaret Voltaire, in 1916, which became known as the birthplace of **Dadaism**. Lenin was a regular visitor and Joyce met him there, a meeting which provided **Tom Stoppard** with the theme for his play *Travesties* (1974), the three protagonists of which are Tzara, Lenin and Joyce.

Joyce was at ease in this polyglot environment, speaking German, Italian and French and picking up some Russian, Turkish and Arabic. He was a cosmopolitan exile and a lifelong student. The language of *Finnegan's Wake* reflects this multicultural aspect of Joyce's mind, with its welter of linguistic associations creating an effect like a vast pun or puzzle or cipher.

Ulysses is his most famous work, *Finnegan's Wake* is his most intriguing and impenetrable. Joyce had trouble finding a publisher for both books. Leonard Woolf accepted *Ulysses* for publication in London but printers refused to set the type because the Molly Bloom soliloquy was considered obscene. Joyce managed to publish the work in Paris in February 1922 through *Shakespeare & Co.*, the famous English bookshop owned by Sylvia Beach. Copies were burned by the US Customs and the book was condemned at the seventh Communist International of 1935 as inimical to Socialist Realism. East and West abominated Joyce who could not be labelled as Capitalist, Communist or Fascist but merely as a writer of obscene books.

Ulysses is set in Dublin and the action takes place on 16 June 1904, a date celebrated as 'Bloomsday' by Joyce enthusiasts. It describes the day as spent by Leopold Bloom and his wife, Molly, and Stephen Dedalus. Bloom works for a Dublin newspaper, Dedalus is a young intellectual whose thoughts are carried away by abstruse philosophy and Molly Bloom is a bored housewife. Incidents in the novel correspond to incidents in Homer's *Odyssey* and the principal characters can be seen as modern counterparts of Ulysses, Telemachus and Penelope. Joyce uses an extensive variety of literary styles and includes all manner of learned quotations and esoteric allusions, yet these are less remote than those incorporated into *Finnegan's Wake*.

At the end of the First World War Joyce moved to Paris and began *Finnegan's Wake* in 1923. The first section appeared in Ford Madox Ford's *Transatlantic Review* the following year entitled *Work In Progress*, but the final part of the book was not completed until 1938 and the first proof copy was given to Joyce on his 57th birthday in 1939. By this time Joyce could no longer see clearly enough to correct the proofs himself. The words were read aloud to him.

In *Finnegan's Wake* Joyce pushed his experimentation with language and with burying hidden layers of significance within his writing, even further, to the extent that to many the novel is incomprehensible. Literary critics and ordinary readers alike struggle to unravel the nuances of meaning in this extraordinarily ambitious work, but whether comprehensible or not, few could deny the musicality of the language or the sense of joy with which Joyce has imbued it.

War caused Joyce to move yet again – back to Switzerland. Germany invaded France in May 1940 and he returned to Zurich where he died eight months later, on 13 January 1941.

Selected works:

Chamber Music (1907); *Gas from a Burner* (1912); *Dubliners* (1914); *A Portrait of the Artist as a Young Man* (1916); *Exiles* (1918); *Ulysses* (1922); *Poems Penyeach* (1927); *Collected Poems* (1936); *Finnegan's Wake* (1939).

Further reading

Anderson, Chester G., *James Joyce and His World*. Thames and Hudson, 1967.

Contributors: Stephen Colbourn,
                                       Ian Mackean

KEROUAC, JACK (1922–69)

Somewhere along the line I knew there'd be girls, visions, everything; somewhere along the line the pearl would be handed to me.
On the Road

Jack Kerouac was born Jean-Louis Kerouac, of French-Canadian descent, on 12 March 1922 in working-class Lowell, Massachusetts. He spoke a local dialect of French, called *Joual*, before he learned English. The youngest of three children, he was heartbroken when his older brother Gerard died of rheumatic fever at the age of nine.

He was an intense and serious child, devoted to Memere (his mother) and constantly forming important friendships with other boys, as he would continue to do throughout his life. He was driven to create stories from a young age, inspired first by the mysterious radio show *The Shadow* and later by the fervid novels of Thomas Wolfe, the writer after whom he would model himself.

Lowell had once thrived as the centre of New England's textile industry, but by the time of Kerouac's birth it had begun to sink into poverty. Kerouac's father, a printer and well-known local businessman, began to suffer financial difficulties and started gambling in the hope of restoring prosperity to the household. Young Jack hoped to save the family himself by winning a football scholarship to college and entering the insurance business. He was a star on his high school team and won some miraculous victories, securing himself a scholarship to Columbia University in New York. His parents followed him there, settling in Ozone Park, Queens.

Things went wrong at Columbia. Kerouac fought with the football coach, who refused to let him play. His father lost his business and sank rapidly into alcoholic helplessness and Kerouac, disillusioned and confused, dropped out of university, bitterly disappointing the father who had so recently disappointed him. He tried and failed to fit in with the military (the Second World War had begun) and ended up sailing with the Merchant Marine. When he wasn't sailing, he was hanging around New York with a crowd his parents did not approve of: depraved young Columbia students **Allen Ginsberg** and Lucien Carr, a strange but brilliant older downtown friend named William S. Burroughs and a joyful street cowboy from Denver named Neal Cassady.

Kerouac had already begun writing a novel, stylistically reminiscent of Thomas Wolfe, about the torments he was suffering as he tried to balance his wild city life with his old-world family values. His friends loved the manuscript and Ginsberg asked his Columbia professors to help find a publisher for it. It would become Kerouac's first and most conventional novel, *The Town and the City* (1950), which earned him respect and some recognition as a writer, although it did not make him famous.

It would be a long time before he would be published again. He had taken some cross-country trips with Neal Cassady while working on his novel and in his attempt to write about these trips he had begun experimenting with freer forms of writing, partly inspired by the unpretentious, spontaneous prose he found in Neal Cassady's letters. He decided to write about his cross-country trips exactly as they had happened, without pausing to edit, fictionalise or even think. He presented the resulting manuscript to his editor on a single unbroken roll of paper, but the editor did not share his enthusiasm and the relationship was broken. Kerouac would suffer seven years of rejection before *On The Road* would be published.

He spent the early 1950s writing one unpublished novel after another, carrying them around in a rucksack as he roamed back and forth across the country. He followed Ginsberg and Cassady to Berkeley and San Francisco, where he became close friends with the young Zen poet Gary Snyder. He sought enlightenment through the Buddhist religion and tried to follow Snyder's lead in communing with nature. His novel *The Dharma Bums* (1958) describes a joyous mountain climbing trip he and Snyder went on in Yosemite in 1955 and captures the tentative, sometimes comic steps he and his friends were taking towards spiritual realisation.

His fellow starving writers were beginning to attract fame as the **Beat Generation**, a label Kerouac had invented years earlier during a conversation with fellow novelist John Clellon Holmes. Ginsberg and Snyder became underground celebrities in 1955 after the Six Gallery poetry reading in San Francisco. Since they and many of their friends regularly referred to Kerouac as the most talented writer among them, publishers began to express interest in the forlorn, unwanted manuscripts he carried in his rucksack wherever he went. *On The Road* was finally published in 1957 and when it became a tremendous popular success Kerouac did not know how to react. Embittered by years of rejection, he was suddenly expected to snap to and play the part of Young Beat Icon for the public. He was older and sadder than everyone expected him to be and probably far more intelligent as well. Literary critics, objecting to the Beat 'fad', refused to take Kerouac seriously as a writer and began to ridicule his work, hurting him tremendously. Certainly the Beat Generation was a fad, Kerouac knew, but his own writing was not.

Kerouac's sudden celebrity was probably the worst thing that could have happened to him because his moral and spiritual decline in the next few years was shocking. Trying to live up to the wild image he'd presented in *On The Road*, he developed a severe drinking habit that dimmed his natural brightness and aged him prematurely. His Buddhism failed him, or he failed it. He could not resist a drinking binge and his friends began viewing him as needy and unstable. He published many books during these years, but most had been written earlier, during the early 1950s when he could not find a publisher. He kept busy, appearing on TV shows, writing magazine articles and recording three spoken-word albums, but his momentum as a serious writer had been disrupted.

Like Kurt Cobain, another counter-culture celebrity who seemed to be truly (as opposed to fashionably) miserable, Kerouac expressed his unhappiness nakedly in his art and was not taken seriously. In 1961 he tried to break his drinking habit and rediscover his writing talents with a solitary nature retreat in Bixby Canyon, Big Sur. But he was unnerved by the vast natural landscape and returned to San Francisco to drink himself into oblivion. He was cracking up and he laid out the entire chilling experience in his last great novel, *Big Sur* (1962).

Defeated and lonesome, he left California to live with his mother in Long Island and would not stray from her for the rest of his life. He would continue to publish and remained mentally alert and aware (though always drunk). But his works after *Big Sur* displayed a disconnected soul, a human being sadly lost in his own curmudgeonly illusions. Despite the 'beatnik' stereotype, Kerouac was a political conservative, especially when under the influence of his Catholic mother. As the beatniks of the 1950s began to yield their spotlight to the **hippies** of the 1960s, Kerouac took pleasure in standing against everything the hippies stood for. He supported the Vietnam War and became friendly with the conservative editor, William F. Buckley.

Living with his mother in Northport, Long Island, Kerouac stayed in his house most of the time and carried on a lifelong game of 'baseball' with a deck of playing cards. His drink of choice was a jug of the kind of cheap, sweet wine, Tokay or Thunderbird, usually preferred by winos. He became increasingly devoted to Catholicism, but his unusual Buddhist-tinged brand of Catholicism would hardly have met with the approval of the Pope.

Through his first 40 years Kerouac had failed to sustain a long-term romantic relationship with a woman, though he fell in love many times. He'd married twice, to Edie Parker and Joan Haverty, but both marriages had ended within months. In the mid-1960s he married again, but this time to a maternal and older childhood acquaintance from small-town Lowell, Stella Sampas, whom he hoped would help around the house as his mother entered old age.

He moved back to Lowell with Stella and his mother and then moved again with them to St Petersburg, Florida. His health destroyed by drinking, he died at home on 21 October 1969. He was 47 years old.

Selected works:

The Town and The City (1950); *On The Road* (1957); *The Dharma Bums* (1958); *The Subterraneans* (1958); *The Floating World* (1959); *Mexico City Blues* (1959); *Maggie Cassady* (1959); *Doctor Sax* (1959); *The Scripture of The Golden Eternity* (1960); *Lonesome Traveller* (1960); *Tristessa* (1960); *Pull My Daisy* (1961); *Book of Dreams* (1961); *Big Sur* (1962); *Visions of Gerald* (1963); *Desolation Angels* (1965); *Satori In Paris* (1966); *Vanity of Duloutz* (1968); *Pic* (1971); *Scattered Poems* (1971); *Visions of Cody* (1972); *Heaven* (1977).

Further reading

Charters, Ann, *Kerouac.* St Martins Press, 1987.

This is an edited revision of an article by Levi Asher, which was first published on 'Literary Kicks' at www.litkicks.com

KESEY, KEN (1935–2001)

One flew east, one flew west,
One flew over the cuckoo's nest
                    Children's folk rhyme

Ken Kesey made his reputation as the author of the novel *One Flew Over the Cuckoo's Nest* (1962) and as a hero of American countercul-ture, having played a significant role in bring-ing about the change from the **Beat Generation** to the **hippie** movement.

Kesey was born in La Junta, Colorado, the son of a dairy farmer. When he was still a child his parents moved to Oregon, on the west coast of America, the region in which he spent most of the rest of his life. He studied at the University of Oregon, graduating in 1957. After winning a scholarship to Stanford University he moved to Palo Alto on San Francisco Bay, where he lived a bohemian life and attended a creative writing course taught by the eminent novelist Wallace Stegner.

While at Stanford he became involved in a government-sponsored programme investigat-ing the effects of 'psychomimetic' drugs such as LSD. He became fascinated by the effects of the drug and later became well known for promoting its use. The experiments took place at a Veterans' Hospital in Menlo Park, California, where Kesey also took a part-time job as an orderly on a psychiatric ward. While working there he experienced hallucinations of an Indian sweeping the floor and incorpo-rated this figure, as Chief Bromden, into *One Flew Over the Cuckoo's Nest*, the novel he had begun at Stanford. He had felt that the story, about patients in a psychiatric hospital, needed cohesion and using Chief Bromden as the narrator helped weave the threads together.

Bromden is a schizophrenic and Kesey used some of his own drug-induced hallucina-tions as the source for Bromden's delusions. By incorporating drug experiences into his lit-erature Kesey was following in the footsteps of writers such as Thomas De Quincy, with his *Confessions of an English Opium-Eater* (1821) and **Aldous Huxley** with *The Doors of Perception* (1954).

Bromden, a tall half-American-Indian, believed by the staff and inmates to be deaf and dumb, recounts the story of the power struggle between the patients and the all-pow-erful 'Combine' – his term for hidden agents of social control which force people into con-formity. The story focuses on the effects on hospital routine of the arrival of a new patient, Randle McMurphy, who challenges authority, particularly Nurse Ratched, or 'Big-Nurse' as the patients call her, who is in charge of the ward and with her inhuman mechanical atti-tudes embodies Bromden's concept of the 'Combine'. McMurphy has a catalytic effect on the other inmates, inspiring them to assert their individuality and aspire to freedom, but with mixed results. Some are liberated, while others commit suicide, particularly when McMurphy himself succumbs to institu-tional pressure. McMurphy is eventually lobotomised and Bromden kills the zombie-like body, devoid of individuality, which is all that remains of him, and escapes to freedom.

The underlying theme of the novel is that human qualities such as individuality, free-dom of choice, sexuality and humour are sup-pressed in clandestine ways by the authorities and the individual has to struggle to overcome this oppression, assert his individuality and achieve freedom. The story is allegorical, in that while it is shown in the context of a men-tal hospital, it can be extended to apply to society as a whole and in this way it had great appeal to the counterculture of the 1960s.

Kesey demonstrates how the delusions of

schizophrenics can in fact have significant meaning. Bromden's notion that there are hidden machines controlling everything is an accurate, if metaphorical, representation of how the patients on the ward have their movements, actions and thoughts controlled by the regime of the hospital and the medication they are given. His delusion that the ward is periodically saturated with fog is an accurate representation of the confusion and lack of insight which characterises the thinking of both the patients, whose minds are kept under the fog of medication, and the hospital staff. Through vignettes from the life stories of some of the inmates Kesey implies that serious mental disorders such as schizophrenia can arise as a result of emotional maltreatment in childhood and can be not only perpetuated but also aggravated by the type of mental institution he is portraying. In these ways Kesey's views on mental illness are in tune with those presented by the prominent but controversial Scottish psychiatrist R. D. Laing, particularly in his books *The Divided Self* (1960) and *Sanity, Madness and the Family* (1964), and by others in the 'anti-psychiatry' movement which came to the fore in the 1960s.

The novel was made into an Oscar-winning film in 1975, with Jack Nicholson playing the lead role of McMurphy. Kesey did not approve of the film, however, because Chief Bromden's role as narrator had been removed.

In 1964 Kesey published his second novel, *Sometimes a Great Notion*, a story set in a logging community, focusing on the rivalry between two brothers, one a union official, trying to force the other into conformity. This book was also reworked into a film, attracting such Hollywood stars as Henry Fonda and Paul Newman. But although it received good reviews, the novel failed to achieve the cult status of *One Flew Over the Cuckoo's Nest*.

In the summer of 1964 Kesey and a group of friends, including the Beat Generation hero Neal Cassady, who featured in *On the Road* (1957) by **Jack Kerouac**, began a journey across the USA which was catalytic in starting the hippie movement which swept across America and Europe. They travelled in an old school bus which was painted in psychedelic designs and called themselves The Merry Pranksters, with Kesey, dressed in a jester's outfit, as the chief prankster. They gave parties known as 'Acid Tests', at which participants drank LSD-laced soft drinks, listened to music and watched light shows. They urged young people to throw off the restrictions of society and believed the use of LSD would have a liberating effect on the world. The pranksters kept a film record of their journey, which was also written about in Tom Wolfe's best-selling *The Electric Kool-Aid Acid Test* (1968).

When LSD was made illegal the pranksters sought refuge in Mexico. The authorities caught up with Kesey, however, when he returned to the USA to do a performance entitled 'Acid Test Graduation' and he was arrested for possession of marijuana and spent a few months in a Californian prison. When released he bought a farm in Pleasant Hill, Oregon.

A series of articles and essays followed, some of which were published in the collection *Demon Box* (1986), and Kesey also published a number of books for children. In 1993 he published his third novel, *Sailor Song*, a futuristic story set in Alaska, which tells of a world rife with life-threatening diseases and atmospheric and nuclear pollution. In the last years of his life he occasionally gave live performances, including a show in which he read one of his children's stories to the accompaniment of The New York Philharmonic Orchestra. On these occasions he revived his role as a showman, wearing an outfit befitting his life as a Merry Prankster.

Selected works:

One Flew Over the Cuckoo's Nest (1962); *Sometimes a Great Notion* (1964); *The Last Whole Earth Catalog* (contributor) (1971); *Kesey's Garage Sale* (Compiler and contributor) (1973); *Demon Box* (1986); *The Further Inquiry* (with R. Bevirt) (1990); *Caverns* (written under the pseudonym O. U. Levon with creative writing students) (1990); *Little Tricker The Squirrel Meets Big Double The Bear* (1990); *The Sea Lion: A Story of the Sea Cliff People* (1991); *Sailor Song* (1993); *Last Go Round* (with Ken Babbs) (1995); *Kesey* (with Michael Strelow) (1997); *Kesey's Jailbook* (2003).

Further reading

Tanner, Stephen L., *Ken Kesey (Twayne's United States Authors Series)*. Gale Group, 1990.

Contributors: Helen Soteriou, Ian Mackean

LAHIRI, JHUMPA (1967–)

There are times I am bewildered by each mile I have traveled, each meal I have eaten, each person I have known, each room in which I have slept. As ordinary as it all appears, there are times when it is beyond my imagination.

The Third and Final Continent

Jhumpa Lahiri was the first woman of South-Asian origin to win a Pulitzer Prize for Fiction. Her accomplishment was even more striking in that she was only 32 years old when she won the award, in 2000, for her debut collection of short stories, *The Interpreter of Maladies*. The collection of nine stories, which has been translated into over 25 languages, deals with universal themes such as love, fidelity, tradition and alienation. She is at her most profound, however, when dealing with the experience of emigration and adjustment, using the fragile relationships of her characters as a catalyst for exploring assimilation and cultural differences. Many of the stories are set in America, but India remains a constant presence throughout the collection. Lahiri's ability to write authentically in both gender voices is remarkable, as is her ability to convey a profound understanding of the various shades of human sadness.

Like many of her characters, Lahiri grew up between cultures. Born in London, England, to Bengali parents, she moved to Rhode Island while very young and grew up in America, taking frequent holidays in Calcutta. In America, her father worked as a librarian and her mother as a teacher. As a second-generation immigrant, Lahiri has said, 'It's hard to have parents who consider another place "home" – even after living abroad for 30 years, India is home for them.'[1] As a child she was conscious that she looked different, and often felt like an outsider. Writing allowed her to observe and make sense of activities without actually having to participate in them. In the company of her friends, Lahiri spent many recesses writing ten-page 'novels'.

Lahiri received a B.A. in English Literature from Barnard College, then attended Boston University, where she gained M.A.s in English, Creative Writing and Comparative Literature and the Arts, and a Ph.D. in Renaissance Studies. Lahiri felt, however, that she was not meant to be a scholar and that pursuing degrees was something she did out of a sense of duty and practicality. She wrote stories while at university and the year she finished her dissertation she was also awarded a fellowship of the Fine Arts Work Center in Provincetown. Within seven months she had found an agent, sold a book and the first of three stories was published in the *New Yorker*. Lahiri was awarded a Guggenheim Fellowship in 2002.

The story 'Interpreter of Maladies', from the collection of the same name, was selected for the O'Henry Award for best American short story. The other eight stories also reflect the title in that each deals with external manifestations of internal maladies. In dealing with love and marriage, the stories raise questions such as 'what creates intimacy?' and 'what creates division and separation?' In a sense, the reader becomes the interpreter of the characters' maladies. The stories also convey echoes of the violent partitioning of India, as themes of separation and destruction are played out in various ways. The heritage of **postcolonialism** manifests itself too, with characters being forced to choose between assimilation and isolation.

The Namesake (2003), Lahiri's debut novel, continues the pattern established by *Interpreter of Maladies*. The story follows the lives of the Gangulis, an Indian family living in America, exploring the consequences of emigration through the experience of characters who exist simultaneously within two cultures. In this novel Lahiri also looks at the tension that often exists between different generations within one family and the breakdown in cultural traditions. The crux of the novel focuses on the identity quest of Gogol Ganguli, a son born in America to Indian parents and named after his father's favourite Russian author. In many ways the life of the main character echoes Lahiri's own experience as a child born to emigrant parents.

The *New York Times* praised Lahiri as a

'writer of uncommon elegance and poise.'[2] According to Lahiri, many writers have influenced her writing style, including Virginia Woolf, William Trevor, James Joyce, Anton Chekhov and Mavis Gallant. She says that *Midnight's Children* by Salman Rushdie is the best book she has ever read. Lahiri lives in New York City with her husband and son.

References

1. An interview with Jhumpa Lahiri by Vibhuti Patel, Newsweek International, 9/20/99.

2. **Kakutani, Michiko**. Reviewing *Interpreter of Maladies* in the New York Times, 8/23/99.

Selected works:

The Interpreter of Maladies (2000); *The Namesake* (2003).

Contributor: Katie Richie

LARKIN, PHILIP (1922–85)

Rather than words comes the thought of high windows:
The sun-comprehending glass,
And beyond it, the deep blue air, that shows
Nothing, and nowhere, and is endless.
                          High Windows

Philip Larkin's reputation as possibly the most important English poet of the second half of the twentieth century rests upon three slim volumes, in which he established the familiar Larkin persona: the ironic, detached observer of everyday life, self-denying and self-deprecating, casting a cold eye upon post-war England and his own bleakly perceived life. Larkin wrote about the chasm, as he saw it, separating human hopes from chill reality, the unhappiness and frustration and lack of real choice offered by life – and the terror of death at the end of it all.

He was, however, also a celebrant of a more ordered and settled past, as well as of all that he saw as best in both nature and humanity. Even the darkest of his poems can be leavened by sardonic wit and humour. He dealt unflinchingly with sentiments that many read-

ers recognised and understood, even if they were not able to confront and articulate them as he could. He was also a memorable phrases-maker. His poems tend to lodge in the reader's mind, leaving resonances long after their initial reading.

For the most part, Larkin rejected the entire Modernist project in literature. He wrote in traditional rhyme and metre throughout his career – with occasional forays into free verse – developing a style interweaving often colloquial and demotic language with traditional verse forms. He believed,

'that every poem must be its own freshly created universe, and therefore [I] have no belief in "tradition" or a common myth kitty or casual allusions in poems to other poems or poets'.[1]

This is surely a barely concealed attack on T. S. Eliot and the views he expressed in *Tradition and the Individual Talent*.

The persona seen in Larkin's poems and the poet himself are hard to separate and Larkin's rare public statements and interviews reinforced this impression, most memorably when he declared: 'Deprivation is for me is what daffodils were for Wordsworth.'[2] But a biography by Andrew Motion, and various memoirs that have appeared since Larkin's death, depict a sometimes different personality from the 'Hermit of Hull' image he assiduously cultivated during his lifetime.

Larkin's early years were spent in Coventry where his father was City Treasurer. Educated at the local grammar school, Larkin began writing poetry in his mid-teens. An early example, 'Summer Nocturne', although derivatively sub-Keatsian, already shows a firm grasp of poetic technique and structure, which was to remain a hallmark of his verse.

In 1940 Larkin went to St John's College, Oxford, to read English, where he met his lifelong friend Kingsley Amis. Graduating in 1943, and to his immense relief being unfit for military service, Larkin drifted into a job as a public librarian in Wellington. By this time he had published a handful of poems in *Poetry from Oxford in Wartime* (1944), alongside other nascent poets such as John Heath-Stubbs and Christopher Middleton.

In 1945, Larkin's first volume of poetry, *The North Ship*, was published. This can be seen as something of a false start: heavily influenced by **W. H. Auden**, **Dylan Thomas** and above all **W. B. Yeats**, the collection proved to be uncharacteristic of the later, mature Larkin. However, the title poem, in ballad form, anticipates the themes of isolation and death which figure prominently in subsequent work. After 1945, Larkin fell under the more temperamentally congenial influence of Thomas Hardy, with whom he stands in a more direct line of 'English' descent than with a Modernist such as Yeats. Indeed, he noted in 1966: 'A year or so later . . . the Celtic fever abated and the patient [was] sleeping soundly.'[3] When Larkin edited *The Oxford Book of Twentieth Century Verse* in 1973, he included a more generous selection from Hardy than from Yeats.

At this period in his life, Larkin saw himself primarily as a novelist: 'I wanted to "be a novelist" in a way I never wanted to "be a poet".'[4] In his novels *Jill* (1946) and *A Girl in Winter* (1947) the protagonists are outsiders: in *Jill*, John Kemp, newly arrived at Oxford University, lonely and with a stammer (partially based on Larkin himself), and in *A Girl in Winter*, Katherine, a young European girl living in exile in war-time England. Both characters attempt to deal with loneliness and isolation by retreating into a fantasy world and for both this strategy turns out badly. Larkin attempted a third and a fourth novel, but was never able to complete another work of fiction, a matter of 'great grief'[5] to him.

After *The North Ship* Larkin tried unsuccessfully to publish a further collection, *In the Grip of the Light*, and after working at Leicester University Library in the late 1940s – a period which coincided with his father's death and when his poetic muse virtually abandoned him – he moved in 1950 to a post at Queen's University Library in Belfast. This marked the end of a fallow period as a poet and the emergence of his authentic poetic voice, as exemplified in 'At Grass', written in January 1950, a poem demonstrating Larkin's apparently effortless phrase-making, describing the lives of retired race horses, who

Have slipped their names, and stand at
ease,
Or gallop for what must be joy

In 1951, *XX Poems* was published privately. It received little acclaim, although several poems were to be praised when they appeared in his next important collection. *The Less Deceived* (1955) announced the arrival of a new, distinctive poetic voice. Coinciding, again, with a change in Larkin's professional life – he became librarian of Hull University, a post he held until his death – it also appeared shortly after the identification of a new, if unofficial grouping in English poetry. Dubbed '**The Movement**' in an anonymously penned article in *The Spectator* in 1954, the writer suggested that some younger poets (including Kingsley Amis, Elizabeth Jennings and D. J. Enright, as well as Larkin) were 'bored by the despair of the Forties, not much interested in suffering and extremely impatient of poetic sensibility' and were also 'sceptical, robust, ironic'. Anthologies along these lines appeared in 1955 and 1956, the latter including poems by Larkin.

Several poems appeared in *The Less Deceived* which were to become central to the Larkin canon. Perhaps the most celebrated was 'Church Going', with the agnostic persona coming to terms with religion and Christianity, and speculating upon future possible uses for churches in a post-Christian world. 'Toads' interrogates the whole notion of the work ethic, with its marvellous metaphor of the toad as work itself:

Why should I let the toad *work*
Squat on my life?

The ironic, anti**romantic** Larkin persona is perhaps most vividly depicted in 'I Remember, I Remember', with its humorous description of the place 'where my childhood was unspent', debunking the convention of colourfully remembered childhood memories, as portrayed in poems such as Dylan Thomas's 'Fern Hill'.

Never a prolific poet, Larkin's next volume, *The Whitsun Weddings*, did not appear until nearly a decade later, in 1964. This collection, considered by many to be his best, not only consolidated Larkin's position as possibly the major poet of the mid-twentieth century but also was instrumental in his being awarded the Queen's Medal for Poetry in 1965.

The title poem vividly describes a series of wedding parties which the poet witnesses from the safety and isolation of his seat in a train bound for London. The landscape through which they travel is powerfully evoked in a poem written in a strong, conventional meter, with a driving rhythm replicating the rhythm of the train:

All afternoon, through the tall heat that slept
For miles inland,
A slow stopping curve southwards we kept.

The depiction of the wedding couples and their families, with the girls

In parodies of fashion . . .
The fathers with broad belts under their suits . . .
. . . mothers loud and fat

is both very visual and painfully accurate. As the train nears London, the tone of the poem deepens, with the poet becoming aware of the religious significance of what he has observed, as well as the new possibilities which are being created that day by the weddings.

Larkin's belief in a settled, ordered past is described in 'MCMIV', which captures the quality of English life that changed for ever with the coming of the First World War in that year. In this poem the details are evocative:

dark-clothed children at play
Called after kings and queens

The sense of history and tradition is also adumbrated in 'An Arundel Tomb' which ends somewhat optimistically for a Larkin poem, 'What will survive of us is love'.

In 'Dockery and Son' Larkin explores the notion that by not willing something to happen, we are in fact making choices in our lives. This is one of his most moving and autobiographical poems, in which he lays bare his determination not to have children when, comparing himself to Dockery, he muses:

Why did he think adding meant increase?
To me it was dilution

He also contemplates the inevitability of death as, 'the only end of age'.

In the year *The Whitsun Weddings* was published, Larkin made his only full appear-ance before television cameras in a 'Monitor' programme shot in Hull, with his friend John Betjeman.

Between 1961 and 1971, Larkin was the jazz record reviewer for the *Daily Telegraph*, later noting: 'Few things have given me more pleasure in life than listening to jazz.'[6] In 1970 his assembled reviews were collected into book form as *All What Jazz?*. In his introduction, Larkin sets out his antiModernist credentials, which applied as much to music, with his rejection of Charlie Parker and John Coltrane, as they had done to all the other arts.

Larkin's fourth and final collection, *High Windows*, appeared in 1974. This collection shows an increasing use of demotic and even profane language, especially in the title poem, and the much quoted 'This Be the Verse', with its depiction of parental blame for one's own defects and shortcomings:

Man hands on misery to man.
It deepens like a coastal shelf.
Get out as early as you can
And don't have any kids yourself.

There are also poems of great beauty and tenderness such as 'The Trees' and the highly uncharacteristic 'The Explosion'. The volume contains 'Going, Going', which expresses Larkin's regret at the encroaching urbanisation of the English countryside and can be seen as an early example of an environmental or 'green' poem, as well as the ironically titled 'Annus Mirabilis', which precisely locates the year 1963 as the moment of sexual liberation for an entire generation:

Between the end of the *Chatterley* ban
And the Beatles' first LP

The same theme is explored in the title poem with its coarse statement about the kind of sexual freedom brought about by contraception and the sweeping away of sexual and religious hypocrisies.

In his final decade, Larkin completed only a handful of poems. However, one last important poem, 'Aubade', was written and published in the *Times Literary Supplement* in 1977, around the time that his mother died at the age of 91. In this poem, Larkin's previously barely concealed terror of death and extinction is finally given full vent. He does not seek consolation, for he believes he can find no consolation in religion:

> That vast moth-eaten musical brocade
> Created to pretend we never die

Nor does he offer any resolution to the terror of death. Indeed, the other conventional support in the face of death, courage, is dismissed for:

> . . . Being brave
> Lets nobody off the grave
> Death is no different whined at than
> withstood.

The poem is one of Larkin's most heartfelt and personal and is all the more poignant for being one of his last.

Larkin's final book was *Required Writing* (1983), a collection of essays, reviews and interviews. These show him to have been an acute literary critic with a wide range of sympathies and a generous, if at times acerbic, wit and humour. The interviews are revealing and are the closest Larkin ever came to autobiographical statements. The book won the W. H. Smith Award in 1984.

Larkin became ill with throat cancer in the summer of 1985 and died at the end of that year, shortly after being made a Companion of Honour.

References

1 **Larkin, Philip** (1983) *Required Writing*, p. 79.

2 Ibid. p. 47.

3 Ibid. p. 30.

4 Ibid. p. 63.

5 **Larkin, Philip** (2001) *Further Requirements*, p. 32.

6 *Required Writing*, p. 285.

Selected works:

Poetry: *The North Ship* (1945); *The Less Deceived* (1955); *The Whitsun Weddings* (1964); *High Windows* (1974); *Collected Poems*, Ed. Anthony Thwaite (1988). **Novels:** *Jill* (1946); *A Girl in Winter* (1947). **Prose:** *All What Jazz?* (1970); *Required Writing* (1983); *Selected Letters*, Ed. Anthony Thwaite (1992); *Further Requirements*, Ed. Anthony Thwaite (2001). **As Editor:** *The Oxford Book of Twentieth Century English Verse* (1973).

Further reading

Brownjohn, Alan, *Philip Larkin*. Longman's for the British Council, 1975.

Chambers, Harry, *An Enormous Yes: In Memoriam Philip Larkin 1922–1985*. Peterloo Poets, 1986.

Day, Roger, *Philip Larkin*. Open University Press, 1987.

Lerner, Laurence, *Philip Larkin*. Northcote House, 1997.

Motion, Andrew, *Philip Larkin: a Biography*. Faber and Faber, 1993.

Timms, David, *Philip Larkin*. Oliver and Boyd, 1973.

Contributor: Michael King

LAWRENCE, D. H. (1885–1930)

It was like a circle where life turned back on itself, and got no farther. She bore him, loved him, kept him, and his love turned back into her, so that he could not be free to go forward with his own life, really love another woman.

Sons and Lovers

David Herbert Lawrence is remembered as a pioneer of sexual and psychological description and his reputation as a writer and the notoriety of his books cannot be clearly separated. Like Thomas Hardy, he saw the last of rural England disappearing before the final onslaught of industrialisation and felt that mechanisation of the world also implied a corroding of human relationships. In fact Lawrence believed most people are only half alive most of the time. His attempt at an honest description of human sexual relations was condemned as pornography by some, and two of his books were suppressed for indecency. A more serious criticism of his works came from Bertrand Russell, a one-time friend with whom Lawrence quarrelled, that the apparent cult of 'man-alive' and 'blood-consciousness' propounded in the sub-text of the books, together with the over-use of certain words, were an expression of racism or fascism that could be connected, ultimately, to the extermination camp at Auschwitz.

Unlike so many of his famous contemporaries, Lawrence did not come from a background of privilege and money. He was born the fourth child of an illiterate coal miner and grew up in poverty, being obliged to leave school and work as a factory clerk at the age of 15. In spite of these disadvantages he gained a place at Nottingham University and became a schoolteacher in Croydon, where he worked from 1908 to 1911. During this period he wrote his first novel, *The White Peacock* (1911), and contributed poetry to Ford Madox Ford's literary periodical *English Review*.

The death of his mother, to whom he was very attached, in 1910 provided material for his third novel, *Sons and Lovers* (1913), which established his reputation as a writer. The book, which is largely autobiographical, shows the sensitive Paul Morel to be attracted to his mother and afraid of his brutal and drunken father.

Completion of his second novel, *The Trespasser* (1912), was delayed by illness. Lawrence was unhealthy throughout his life and was aware of his constitutional weakness – his puny skin-and-bone frame – and his lack of physical attractiveness. Yet his personality and talents were engaging enough to bring him to the attention of many famous names including Bertrand Russell, Lady Ottoline Morrell, John Middleton Murry, **Katherine Mansfield** and a writer with whom he never argued – unlike so many others – **Aldous Huxley**.

Lawrence gave up teaching in 1911 and attempted to support himself by writing. In 1912 he met Frieda Weekley, the wife of a Nottingham professor and mother of three children, whom he eventually married. They ran off to Bavaria where they were sheltered by Frieda's relatives, members of the aristocratic von Richthofen family. (Frieda's cousin Manfred became the famous First World War flying ace.) The local people, however, regarded Lawrence with suspicion. Political and military tension was mounting between Britain and Germany and Lawrence was thought to be an English spy. Ironically this situation

recurred in 1917 when he and Frieda were suspected of being German spies in Cornwall. Lawrence was a pacifist as well as being unfit for military service during the war. Conscientious objectors such as Bertrand Russell were imprisoned for their beliefs; the Lawrences were merely harassed by officials and rural busybodies.

Lawrence and Frieda returned to London and married in 1914. They were not allowed a passport to leave the country after the outbreak of the First World War and settled in Cornwall where they lived precariously while Lawrence worked on his next novel.

The Rainbow (1915) introduces the Brangwen family, who are representatives of the older agricultural way of life and reappear in the sequel, *Women in Love* (1920). Although Edward Garnett strongly recommended *The Rainbow* to his publishing partner William Heinemann, the work was rejected and William Heinemann refused to accept or look at any further works by Lawrence. The book was suppressed shortly after its eventual publication on the grounds of obscenity. In 1978, however, it was prescribed as a set book for study in UK schools.

Lawrence was forced to leave Cornwall in 1917 after local people claimed they had seen Frieda signal to German submarines by waving her scarf on the cliff tops. He and Frieda spent the remainder of the war in London, then emigrated in 1919, vowing never to return.

In *Women in Love* Gerald Crich, the son of a mine owner, represents the cold mechanical world that the author loathed. There is a void in Crich's life that cannot be filled even by the love of a woman, Gudrun Brangwen. Although attracted to the intellectual school inspector Birkin, who is the lover of Gudrun's sister Ursula, Gerald's incapacity for real human love leads to his death, which takes place in the Alpine snows.

The Lawrences went to Italy in 1919, then to France, Ceylon, Australia, Mexico and, finally, the United States where they settled on a ranch at Taos in New Mexico in 1926. An American socialite gave them the property in return for the original manuscript of *Sons and Lovers*.

During their travels Lawrence completed *Aaron's Rod* (1922), *Kangaroo* (1923) and *The Plumed Serpent* (1926). At Taos Lawrence was again overcome by illness, which was diagnosed as tuberculosis. He began work on his most notorious novel, *Lady Chatterley's Lover*, in 1926. It was printed privately in Italy in 1928 but banned in the USA and the UK for over 30 years. Knowing that he did not have long to live, Lawrence made one last journey to France in 1930 and died in Venice in the company of Frieda and Aldous Huxley, at the age of 45. His and Frieda's graves lie beside one another in the grounds of their New Mexico ranch.

Critics invariably claim that *Lady Chatterley's Lover* is far from the best of Lawrence's novels, although it is the one that ensured his notoriety. It describes how Constance Chatterley, the aristocratic wife of a rich mine owner, takes a lover – a game keeper called Oliver Mellors – because her husband is impotent. Mellors' speech is written in Nottinghamshire country dialect and is hard to follow, though the censors concentrated on certain words which even when printed in reverse cipher as *kcuf* and *tnuc* were deemed highly offensive.

In 1960, 30 years after Lawrence's death, the unexpurgated edition of *Lady Chatterley's Lover* was brought out by Penguin Books and caused a sensational trial. Luminaries such as E. M. Forster and Richard Hoggart appeared for the defence and the prosecution made a comment which is more memorable than anything in the novella itself. Asked of an all-male jury *'Is this a book you would wish your wife or your servants to read?'*, the question appeared so absurdly anachronistic in 1960 that it was greeted with jeers from the public gallery. The book became freely available and provided a model for much 1960s' erotically charged fiction.

Selected works:

The White Peacock (1911); *The Trespasser* (1912); *Sons and Lovers* (1913); *Love Poems and Others* (1913); *The Prussian Officer and Other Stories* (1914); *The Rainbow* (1915); *Twilight In Italy* (1916); *Look! We have come through* (1917); *New Poems* (1918); *Women In Love* (1920); *The Lost Girl* (1920); *Sea and Sardinia* (1921); *Aaron's Rod* (1922); *England, My England* (1922); *The Ladybird* (1923); *Kangaroo* (1923); *The Plumed Serpent* (1926); *Mornings In Mexico* (1927); *Lady Chatterley's Lover* (1928); *The Woman Who Rode Away* (1928); *Pansies* (1929); *The Escaped Cock* (1929); *Nettles* (1930); *The Virgin and The Gipsy* (1930); *Love Among The Haystacks* (1930).

Further reading

Leavis, F. R., *D. H. Lawrence: Novelist.* Chatto and Windus, 1975.

Contributor: Stephen Colbourn

LEE, HARPER (1926–)

Mockingbirds don't do one thing but make music for us to enjoy. They don't eat up people's gardens, don't nest in corncribs, they don't do one thing but sing their hearts out for us. That's why it's a sin to kill a mockingbird.

To Kill a Mockingbird

Harper Lee's first and only novel, *To Kill a Mockingbird* (1960), won a Pulitzer Prize in 1961 and went on to become an international best-seller, being translated into 40 languages. The story, set in a small Alabama town, deals with the subject of race relations in the southern states, being the story of a white lawyer who defends a black man against a charge of rape. Lee's background, subject matter and style place her in the tradition of American writers associated with the South, including Mark Twain (1835–1910), William Faulkner (1897–1962), Tennessee Williams (1911–83), Carson McCullers (1917–67) and Flannery O'Connor (1925–64).

Nelle Harper Lee was born in Monroeville, Alabama, to Amasa Coleman Lee, a lawyer who had also served as a state senator, and Frances Cunningham Finch Lee. Truman Capote, who lived next door during the summers, was a childhood friend. She attended public schools and then went on to Huntington College in 1944–45 and studied law at the University of Alabama from 1945 to 1949. She spent a year in England as an Oxford exchange student, but before graduating she moved to New York to pursue a career in writing.

In 1957 Lee submitted several essays and stories to the J. B. Lippincott Company and was encouraged to develop one of the stories, which two-and-a-half years later emerged as

To Kill a Mockingbird. The novel, published at a time when civil rights was a growing issue in the USA, is set in the small town of Maycomb, Alabama during the 1930s. The narrator is a remarkably astute and intelligent young girl (a narrative voice which some critics find unconvincing) nicknamed Scout. When her father, Atticus Finch, a respected lawyer, defends Tom Robinson, an African-American wrongly accused of raping a white girl, Scout and her brother, Jem, learn powerful lessons about prejudice, morality and justice.

Finch knows, when he takes on the case, that there is little or no chance of truth prevailing over prejudice and that he and his family will incur the hostility of the community, but he is determined to defend the innocent (the mockingbird is a symbol of innocence) and to stand up for individual rights, equality and the law:

> There is one way in this country in which all men are created equal – there is one human institution that makes a pauper the equal of a Rockefeller, the stupid man the equal of an Einstein, and the ignorant man the equal of any college president. That institution, gentlemen, is a court. It can be the Supreme Court of the United States or the humblest J.P. court in the land . . . our courts are the great levelers, and in our courts all men are created equal.

The small town in which the novel is set is similar to the one in which Lee grew up and although Lee has never confirmed this, many speculate that the characters were based on real people. As a child she was aware of the 1931 'Scottsboro Trials' of nine black men accused of raping two white women. The widely publicised trials were extremely controversial, many suspecting that the accusations were false and motivated by racial prejudice. The trial in the novel has parallels with the Scottsboro case and the lawyer, Atticus Finch, as well as probably being modelled on Lee's father, has many similarities to the Scottsboro judge. In 1959 Lee went with Truman Capote to Holcombe, Kansas, as a research assistant for his book *In Cold Blood*, about a multiple murder committed by two youths, an experience which also fed into her idea of the novel, and her law studies influenced her clear, suc-

cinct style of writing. The drama of the book is intensified, and the depiction of good and evil accentuated, by the use of **Gothic** elements, such as a mad dog, a Halloween party and several deaths.

In 1962 *To Kill a Mockingbird* was made into a film, with Gregory Peck as Atticus Finch, which won three Oscars. In 1997, presenting Lee with an honorary doctorate from Spring Hill College in Mobile, Alabama, Professor Margaret Davis stated that Lee was honoured for her 'lyrical elegance, her portrayal of human strength and wisdom'. Lee has written nothing substantial since *To Kill a Mockingbird* and avoids publicity.

Further reading

Bloom, Harold (ed.), *Harper Lee's To Kill a Mockingbird*. New York, 1996.

Contributor: Holly Hancey

LESSING, DORIS (1919–)

People say it all began in the '60s; I think it began in the '50s. The thing was, there were no rules. There were no rules at all. In the past, everybody knew what the rules were. You could break them or keep them. But not to have any rules at all . . . [1]

Doris Lessing was born Doris May Taylor in Persia (now Iran) to British parents who had met during the First World War when her father was nursed by Emily Maude McVeagh after losing a leg in the fighting. After the war the Taylors moved to Kermanshah and later Tehran, where Taylor worked as a bank clerk. In 1925, having visited the Empire Exhibition while on leave in London, Taylor decided to become a maize farmer in Southern Rhodesia, now Zimbabwe, where he hoped to make his fortune. The move was not a success for her father, but Lessing enjoyed her childhood in the African bush.

By the time Lessing entered her teens she had become disillusioned with colonial attitudes. The divisions between white and black disgusted her and she reacted against her early education and her parents and their constricting and stultifying lives by dropping out of school at 14 and leaving home a year later. She had, however, educated herself through reading, having sought to escape from the restraints of her home life by imaginatively entering the worlds of Dickens and Kipling and, later, Tolstoy and Dostoevsky.

Lessing escaped one trap only to fall into another – marriage at 19; followed by motherhood. She felt impelled to leave the unhappy marriage a few years later; she had become committed to **Marxist** ideology and later married the Communist activist, Gottfried Lessing, by whom she had a son. This marriage broke down too and in the post-war years Lessing became disillusioned with the Communist Party.

In 1949 Lessing arrived in England, with her young son from her second marriage and the manuscript of her first novel, *The Grass is Singing*. The novel, which drew on her African background, was a success and launched Lessing on her career as a professional writer. It is the story of the relationship between Mary Turner, a white farmer's wife stifled by the tensions of her life, and her black servant, Moses. The relationship cannot possibly flourish and Moses eventually kills Mary. But more disturbing than the murder itself is the attitude of the white colonialists to it.

In London in the 1950s Lessing brought up her son alone, just managing to support them both by her writing. This was a turbulent London where many adopted left-wing views, while newly arriving black immigrants were seen by many as second-class citizens. In this period she wrote the sequence of novels known collectively as the *Children of Violence* series about the troubled, defiant and idealistic Martha Quest. These works, which constitute a **Bildungsroman**, were largely autobiographical, drawing on Lessing's experiences in Africa and London.

In 1962 Lessing published *The Golden Notebook*, the novel which made her reputation and is still probably her most widely read book. The name of the heroine, Anna Wulf, is significant, indicating Lessing's acknowledged debt to **Virginia Woolf** and her views on the eclectic and unreliable nature of memory. Wulf is a novelist in crisis, keeping notebooks of various colours which signify the different strands of her life: black for the revolutionary struggle in Africa, red for the Communist and Socialist movements, yellow for erotic love (a Lawrentian theme seen from the woman's viewpoint) and blue for psychotic experience. While attempting to write a novel entitled 'Free Women', Wulf has to deal with the domestic and political issues which faced women in the 1960s. While on one hand striving towards a synthesis, on the other Lessing was sure that the raw unfinished quality of life was what mattered (*Blue Notebook*, p. 237). The amalgam of the notebooks is *The Golden Notebook* itself.

As always with Lessing, the struggle of the character to come to terms with her inner self is set against the wider canvas of contemporary society. Like Lessing herself, Anna Wulf was trying to break free from the feminine stereotypes of the previous generation. Lessing's bold account of the often angry and aggressive women of the 1960s, striving to live with the freedom men took for granted, made her, against her will, an icon of the **feminist** movement.

Several of Lessing's later books deal with the future, as though she had exhausted her patience with the past and present. In *Memoirs of a Survivor* (1974) she deals with a bleak future in a ruined London, portraying the breakdown of society in a degenerating city. The novel stresses the need for hope, love and personal commitment and ends with the troubled protagonists accepting a way out of this collapsed world into another order of reality altogether.

Lessing entered a world of inner-space fiction of a spiritual kind in her series of science-fiction novels known collectively as *Canopus in Argos: Archives* (1979–83). These novels draw on her interest in Sufi mysticism as expressed by Idris Shah. According to this doctrine consciousness must and does evolve, but only when people seek their individual liberty by linking their own fate with that of the society in which they live.

With *The Good Terrorist* (1985) Lessing reverted to a contemporary theme and a **realist** style, telling a story of the bitter anger of the disillusioned young, set in the revolutionary worlds of the squat and the commune.

Under My Skin, the first volume of Lessing's autobiography, was published in 1995 and the second, *Walking in the Shade*, two years later. In a *Guardian* report in August 2001 she wrote that she had decided not to write a third volume because she did not want to offend eminent people by reminding them of their silliness.

In 2001 she published the novel *The Sweetest Dream*, in which she describes the life of a mother in the 1960s coping with the bitterness of the middle-aged and the selfishness of the young. A book of four short novels, *The Grandmothers*, was published in 2003.

Through her writing Lessing distances herself from her own experiences, transmuting them, through fiction, into a general philosophical reality concerning the individual and his/her place in society. Like her heroines, she is always moving on to the next problem, the next challenge. Throughout her long career she has not been afraid to change her views or perhaps the views that people had attributed to her. Her passionate integrity and far-reaching vision made her a seminal figure in the development of twentieth-century literature.

Lessing has won many literary awards and was appointed a Companion of Honour in 1999, having previously refused an offer of becoming a Dame of the British Empire on the grounds that there was no British Empire.

Reference

1. **Lessing, Doris** (1997) Interview with 'Salon', 11 November.

www.salon.com/books/feature/1997/11/cov _si_11lessing.html

Selected works:

The Grass is Singing (1950); *Children of Violence, 1952–1969* – Comprising of: *Martha Quest* (1952); *A Proper Marriage* (1954), *A Ripple from the Storm* (1958); *Landlocked* (1965); *The Four Gated City* (1969); *The Golden Notebook* (1962); *The Memoirs of a Survivor* (1974); *Canopus in Argos: Archives* (1979–83); *The Good Terrorist* (1985); *The Fifth Child* (1988); *The Sweetest Dream* (2001); *The Grandmothers* (2003).

This is a small selection from Lessing's vast output, which also includes a libretto for an opera by Philip Glass, based on a volume of her science fiction, books about her later visits to Africa, and several books about cats. She has also written essays and reviews and given many interviews.

Further reading

Bradbury, Malcolm, *The Modern British Novel*. Secker and Warburg, 1993.

Contributor: Margaret Tarner

LOWRY, MALCOLM (1909–57)

I think I know a good deal about physical suffering, but this is worst of all, to feel your soul dying. I wonder if it is because tonight my soul has really died that I feel at the moment something like peace?

Under the Volcano

Although Malcolm Clarence Lowry was an alcoholic throughout his adult life and suffered from mental disorders which led to spells in mental hospitals, he earned himself a place in the canon of great modern writers with his novel *Under the Volcano* (1947), which is regarded by many as one of the outstanding novels of the twentieth century.

Lowry was born into a wealthy family in Birkenhead, Cheshire, a town dominated by docks, flour mills and ships, which had expanded rapidly in the nineteenth century, along with Liverpool, its larger neighbour across the Mersey. From his father, a cotton broker with holdings in Egyptian and American plantations, Lowry received a small financial allowance, on which he lived in near-poverty for the rest of his life.

Lowry almost went blind at the age of nine from a disorder of the corneas and did not recover his sight until after an operation four years later. He was frustrated and rebellious at his private school and at the age of 17 ran away to sea, working as a deckhand on a ship bound for Hong Kong and Yokohama. His grandfather had been a Norwegian master mariner and Lowry claimed he had the sea in his blood and travel in his blood.

Lowry's early literary influences were adventure writers, such as Joseph Conrad and Jack London, and like Conrad he drew upon his experience of life at sea in his first novel, *Ultramarine* (1933). *Ultramarine* also owed a debt to *Blue Voyage* (1927) by his friend Conrad Aiken and to *The Ship Sails On* (1924), a novel by Nordahl Grieg, whom he had met in Norway.

Lowry went to Cambridge University in 1929 and graduated with first class honours in English Literature. He lived in Paris for a time, then travelled with Aiken to Spain, where he met Jan Gabrial, an American writer, who became his first wife. After visiting the United States, where he socialised on the fringes of the Hollywood film world, Lowry moved with his wife to Mexico. The idea for *Under The Volcano*, already in his mind, was strengthened by their stay in Cuernavaca, south of Mexico City, and by the sight of Popocatépetl, the snow-capped and smoking volcanic mountain which provides the symbolic backdrop for the novel.

Lowry, who had been a heavy drinker since his schooldays, was a confirmed alcoholic by this time and the first draft of *Under The Volcano* was almost lost when he left it in a bar. His wife had to retrieve it by going round the bars of Cuernavaca asking for the Englishman's writing. This brought Lowry to the attention of the Mexican police, who believed he was a spy making reports to Spain, and Lowry was thrown into jail in Oaxaca. His wife managed to get him back to Los Angeles, at which point she left him and sought a divorce.

Lowry then met the novelist Margerie Bonner, who was to become his second wife. They moved to Canada in 1939 and lived in a shack on an inlet of Vancouver harbour. This was where he worked on *Under The Volcano*, though he also spent periods wandering the streets of Vancouver begging for beer money. He even wrote to the Governor-General of Canada, John Buchan, whose adventure novels he had admired as a schoolboy, appealing to him to help support a fellow writer. Buchan sent $50, which Lowry promptly gambled on a horse and lost.

Under The Volcano was written and rewritten between 1936 and 1947. The first version was ready in 1940 and placed with a literary agent, Harold Matson, but after 12 publishers had refused the work, Matson recommended that he rewrite it. The Lowrys' house burned down in 1944 with the loss of most papers and possessions, though the redraft of *Under The Volcano* survived. Lowry rebuilt the clapboard shack the following year, in spite of objections from the local authority, which tried to evict the Lowrys as undesirables. In 1987 the same

authority constructed 'Lowry Park' on the site and restored the house, named 'Wicket Gate', on the water's edge where Lowry, a passionate swimmer, would dive into the bay directly from his porch. Lowry is now often labelled as a Canadian writer.

In *Under The Volcano* Lowry used the material of his life to create a work in which readers and critics find a representation of the suffering and isolation of modern man. The story is set in Quauhnahuac, Mexico, and the protagonist, Geoffrey Firmin, is an alcoholic ex-British Consul. As in *Ulysses* by **James Joyce**, the main action describes the lives of several interconnected characters on one day, in this case the last day of Firmin's life. The other main characters are his ex-wife Yvonne who hopes to revive their relationship and his half-brother, Hugh. Geoffrey is estranged from them, having cut himself off from human contact and become lost in a hell of his own making, driven by his need for alcohol. Through drink and peyote he tries to escape from the inhumanity of the modern world – with civil war raging in Spain and the Second World War looming – and his sense of guilt and failure.

Like James Joyce and **Virginia Woolf**, Lowry uses the **stream of consciousness** technique to explore the inner workings of his characters' minds. He also employs abundant literary references and layers of symbolism, not least in the ominous looming volcanoes themselves and the Mexican festival of the 'Day of the Dead', against which the action is set.

After innumerable revisions, often with Margerie Lowry's help, the novel was accepted for publication by Jonathan Cape. Its appearance in 1947 was not greeted with great critical acclaim, but the book attracted growing interest and popularity in the two decades following Lowry's death. For a time appreciated only as a cult novel, *Under The Volcano* is now regarded as a **Modern** classic. With the discovery of the 1940 manuscript sent to the literary agent Matson, two versions of the book have now been published.

Lowry's last ten years were dogged by ill-health and periods of hospitalisation, and on 27 June 1957, intoxicated by a mixture of drink and drugs, he died in a cheap boarding house in Ripe, Sussex. An inquest returned a verdict of death by misadventure.

His posthumously published *Lunar Caustic* (1958) draws on his periods in psychiatric hospitals and among his other posthumous works were *Hear Us O Lord In Heaven Thy Dwelling Place* (1961), which won a Canadian Governor-General's Award, and *Selected Poems* (1962).

Selected works:

Ultramarine (1933); *In Ballast To The White Sea* (1936); *Under The Volcano* (1947); *Lunar Caustic* (1958); *Hear Us O Lord In Heaven Thy Dwelling Place* (1961); *Selected Poems* (1962); *Selected Letters* (1965); *Dark As The Grave Wherein My Friend Is Laid* (1968); *October Ferry To Gabriola* (1970); *The Collected Poetry Of Malcolm Lowry* (1992); *Sursum Corda! The Collected Letters Of Malcolm Lowry, Volume 1, 1926–1946* (1995).

Further reading

Asals, Frederick and Tieseen, Paul (eds) *A Darkness That Murmured: Essays on Malcolm Lowry and the Twentieth Century.* University of Toronto Press Inc, 2000.

Contributors: Stephen Colbourn,
                       Ian Mackean

MANSFIELD, KATHERINE (1888–1923)

To be alive and to be a 'writer' is enough . . . There is nothing like it!
Katherine Mansfield, 30 May 1917

Photo credit: © Bettmann/CORBIS

Mansfield was only 34 when she died in 1923 and her early death, coupled with the details of her tempestuous life, have resulted in the critical assessment of her writing being overshadowed by her biography. Yet when Virginia Woolf heard of Mansfield's death,

she wrote, 'I was jealous of her writing. The only writing I have ever been jealous of' (Stead, p. 20).

Mansfield revolutionised the short story, devising a subversive poetic narrative which conveys the immediacy of the moment, the uncertainty of perceptions and the multiple nature of personality. Thematically, 'her best fiction radically questions the forms and ideas that bind women, and men as well, into inauthentic lives' (Fullbrook, p. 8). A major influence was symbolism, particularly Oscar Wilde's theory of the mask, for Mansfield refuted all ideas of the stable ego. The attempts of Imagism and Post-Impressionism to convey events and emotions as they are *felt*, also inform Mansfield's technique. Her tales are generally non-linear, driven by symbol rather than plot, and lack conventional closure. She erases the omniscient narrator, using a free indirect style to present a character's consciousness, and her characters often experience special moments of insight or 'epiphanies'.

Born Kathleen Mansfield Beauchamp in Wellington, New Zealand, she was the third of five children born to the successful merchant banker Harold Beauchamp and Annie Dyer Beauchamp. In 1903 her father took the family to England, enrolling the eldest girls at Queen's College, Harley Street. Mansfield revelled in the culture and freedom of London, but in 1906, reluctantly, the girls had to return home, where Mansfield read incessantly, particularly Wilde and Arthur Symons.

By 1908 Mansfield had convinced her parents that a writer must live in London, but on returning, she became pregnant by Garnet Trowell, a cello player from Wellington. Precipitously, Mansfield married a singing teacher, George Bowden, but left him almost immediately. Her mother sailed to England, took Mansfield to the German spa of Bad Wörishofen, and returned to New Zealand – to disinherit her daughter. Mansfield suffered a miscarriage, but stayed on to write the stories that formed *In a German Pension* (1911).

Back in London in 1910, Mansfield's German stories were published in *New Age*. They examine traditional gender, class and racial stereotypes, providing a 'biting caricature of brutality, mutual exploitation and moral blindness' (Fullbrook, p. 53). The stories are robust comedies of manners, with the narrator's abrupt comments satirising all absurdities, while tales such as 'At Lehman's' and 'Frau Brechenmacher Attends a Wedding' provide visceral accounts of women's unrecorded lives. Mansfield later resisted the republication of *In a German Pension*, feeling it gauche and cynical and being wary of encouraging anti-German sentiment.

Between 1912 and 1913, Mansfield's stories, such as 'The Woman at the Store', appeared in *Rhythm*, a journal edited by John Middleton Murry. The two soon became lovers and remained together until her death. An unproductive period followed for Mansfield, until her brother Leslie – in England in 1915, training to be an officer – catalysed her story, 'The Wind Blows', which captures incandescent moments from their New Zealand youth. Leslie's death in a grenade accident devastated Mansfield, but precipitated her masterpiece, *Prelude* (1918), which secured her reputation.

The 12 seemingly discontinuous sections of *Prelude* are carefully organised and associated movements of interwoven imagery. The non-intrusive narrator conveys the **viewpoints** of the characters, revealing their conscious and unconscious perceptions without explanation or description. Specific symbols are associated with certain characters. The grandmother's crescent moon brooch with its five owls, and her lamp carrying, symbolise her wise, nurturing creativeness. The men in *Prelude* are unintentional destroyers, with Stanley always eating – even consuming Linda with his love. Linda fears all things that grow and overwhelm her – hating childbirth and childrearing, she considers Stanley's passion a bondage. Kezia is the one character who may achieve an authentic life. She is creative and evades male control, refusing to acknowledge Moses's power. Overall, the story is a multiple *Prelude*, with Kezia on the threshold of life, while Mansfield's finest work was beginning to flower.

A medical consultation in December 1917 confirmed that Mansfield had tuberculosis (Stead, p. 87) and precipitated constant searches for cures and Mediterranean retreats. By 1918, in the South of France and aware that she was dying, the quality of her work changed, with 'Je ne parle pas Français' one of her most technically innovative stories. The tale presents a single perspective which distances the reader from the narrator – the writer, pimp and gigolo, Raoul Duquette – who epitomises the corruption that Mansfield opposed.

'Bliss' (1918) charts the inauthentic life of a superficially sophisticated woman, Bertha Young. Mansfield's symbolism and immediately felt impressions – as the narrator merges with Bertha's perceptions – expose hypocrisy and provide a new means of writing about female desire. Bertha searches for fulfilment but misreads the symbols and the reader experiences *with her* the epiphanic realisation that her life is an emotional and ethical vacuum.

Mansfield married Richard Murry in May 1918, having finally divorced Bowden. Back in the Mediterranean by 1920, stories multiplied and 'The Stranger', 'Life of Ma Parker', 'The Daughters of the Late Colonel' and 'Miss Brill' followed. Writing to Richard Murry in 1921, Mansfield stressed the importance of 'craft': 'In Miss Brill I chose not only the length of every sentence, but even the sound of every sentence' (O'Sullivan 1989, p. 195). Miss Brill's inner monologue has no external description and unsuspecting readers may accept the character's perceptions and ignore the clues that reveal her poor, empty, isolated life, until Miss Brill's false epiphany of music, joy and community is shattered.

In 1921 Mansfield celebrated New Zealand and family love in *At the Bay*, an impressionistic companion piece to *Prelude*, similarly composed of 12 passages linked by imagery. The controlling structure is the passage of a single day, with the lyrical pastoral of the dawn reflecting Mansfield's description of New Zealand as 'dipped back into the dark blue sea during the night' (Stead, p. 85). The story is concerned with love, accepting mortality and loving life – thus the grandmother makes Kezia laugh, while revealing that both of them will die. The most affirmative parts are Linda's joy in her baby son and Beryl's strength in refusing corrupt advances. Mansfield's final stories from 1921 to 1922, such as 'The Doll's House', 'The Garden Party', 'The Fly' and 'The Canary', explore empathy and, increasingly, death and its effects on the living.

By October 1922, after further, extreme treatments, Mansfield decided that her final need was for spiritual well-being and she entered George Gurdjieff's Institute at Fontainebleu, where she died of a pulmonary haemorrhage in January 1923.

Mansfield left all her papers to Murry in her will, requesting that he 'publish as little as possible and tear up and burn as much as possible' (Stead, p. 10). Instead, Murry published many posthumous collections and created a sanctified Mansfield persona from her letters and journals. However, feminist criticism has restored Mansfield's writing to its central position in Modernist literature, while *The Collected Letters* and *The Katherine Mansfield Notebooks* have finally released Mansfield's life and art from Murry's myth.

Selected works:

In a German Pension (1911); *Prelude* (1918); *Je ne parle pas français* (1920); *Bliss and Other Stories* (1920); *The Garden Party and Other Stories* (1922); *The Doves' Nest and Other Stories* (1923); *Poems* (1924); *Something Childish and Other Stories* (1924); *The Aloe* (1930); *The Complete Stories of Katherine Mansfield*, Golden Press (1974).

Further reading

Alpers, Anthony, *The Life of Katherine Mansfield*. Cape, 1980.

Fullbrook, Kate, *Katherine Mansfield*. Harvester, 1986.

O'Sullivan, V. (ed.) *Katherine Mansfield: Selected Letters*. Clarendon, 1989.

O'Sullivan, V. and Margaret Scott (eds) *The Collected Letters of Katherine Mansfield*. Clarendon, 1984–96.

Scott, Margaret (ed.) *The Katherine Mansfield Notebooks*. NZ: Lincoln UP, 1997.

Stead, C. K., *Katherine Mansfield: Letters and Journals*. Penguin, 1977.

Tomalin, Claire, *Katherine Mansfield: A Secret Life*. Penguin, 1988.

Contributor: Carole Jones

MCCARTHY, CORMAC (1933–)

When they came south of Grant County Boyd was not much more than a baby and the newly formed county they'd named Hidalgo was itself little older than the child. In the country they'd quit lay the bones of a sister and the bones of his maternal grandmother. The new county was rich and wild. You could ride clear to Mexico and not strike a crossfence.

The Crossing

Although Cormac McCarthy is now regarded as one of the most important US writers, he laboured in virtual obscurity for the better part of his career. His dark and often violent early works were critically lauded but publicly ignored. Nevertheless, beginning with the publication of his first novel, *The Orchard Keeper*, in 1965, McCarthy began to create a niche for himself in the landscape of American literature that would be uniquely his own.

Charles McCarthy (he would later change his first name to Cormac, the Gaelic equivalent of Charles) was born in Rhode Island in 1933 and moved to Tennessee when he was four years old. He grew up outside Knoxville, where he attended a Catholic high school. McCarthy's father was an attorney and the family lived a comfortable life that bore no ostensible resemblance to the lives of the characters in his books. After graduating from high school in 1951, he enrolled at the University of Tennessee, where he majored in liberal arts. He took a hiatus from his studies in 1953 to join the US Air Force and it was during this time that he developed an interest in literature. While stationed in Alaska he spent most of his free time reading voraciously, familiarising himself with some of the authors whose influence he was later to acknowledge: Fyodor Dostoevsky, Herman Melville, William Faulkner and Flannery O'Connor.

After serving in the Air Force for four years, McCarthy returned to his university studies and began writing seriously. He showed considerable promise, publishing two short stories in the university literary magazine and winning a university prize for creative writing. He decided to devote himself to his writing full-time, so he withdrew from university and moved to Chicago, where he laboured on his first novel while working part-time as a car mechanic.

In 1965 McCarthy published *The Orchard Keeper*. Set in rural Tennessee, it tells the haunting story of a boy who forms a relationship with the man who, unbeknownst to the boy, killed the boy's father. This first work, which received praise from reviewers and critics, evidences some of his stylistic trademarks: a recondite vocabulary reminiscent of Faulkner, minimal punctuation and spare, objective prose.

McCarthy's next two novels, *Outer Dark* (1968) and *Child of God* (1973), about an incestuous relationship and a necrophiliac respectively, dealt with dark and disturbing subject matter that deterred a popular audience but nonetheless impressed critics, many of whom compared him favourably to Faulkner. McCarthy was developing a reputation as a writer's writer – a writer greatly admired by other writers and critics but virtually unread by the general public. *Child of God* was followed by *Suttree* (1979), a novel whose protagonist, the eponymous Cornelius Suttree, abandons an upper-class lifestyle to wander the slums of Knoxville. This large, sprawling work brought even more critical attention to McCarthy, who was subsequently awarded the prestigious McArthur Fellowship. Collectively, these first four novels are often referred to as the Appalachian (or Southern) novels because of both their location and the Southern sensibilities which imbue them.

McCarthy's next book, *Blood Meridian, or the Evening Redness of the West* (1986), marks a division in his work. It constitutes the first of what have come to be known as his Western novels, for by the time of its publication he had moved to El Paso, Texas, where his changed venue resulted in a corresponding change in subject matter. From *Blood Meridian* on, his novels take place in the US southwest and deal with Western themes. *Blood Meridian* is considered by many to be McCarthy's greatest and most important work. A revisionist history of the American south-west of the 1840s, *Blood Meridian* tells the terrifying story of a 14-year-old runaway boy, referred to only as 'the kid', who falls in with the Glanton gang, a collection of outlaws and Indian scalpers who contract themselves out to Mexican governors along the US/Mexican border. The novel is a harrowing exploration of the violence that attended the westward expansion of the USA. In this novel McCarthy subverts the myth of Indian victimisation, for in McCarthy's telling of the story the victims of violence and the perpetrators of violence are one and the same; while Glanton's gang hunt, slaughter and scalp Indians, the Indians are shown to be equally capable of horrendous acts of unprovoked violence.

In 1992 McCarthy published *All the Pretty Horses*, the first novel in his 'border trilogy' and the first to bring him to popular attention. While his previous works were too dark, disturbing and literate for popular tastes, *All the Pretty Horses* gained widespread acceptance. The novel is the coming-of-age story of John Grady Cole, a teenage boy who leaves his Texas home and travels to northern Mexico in search of adventure and a mythic, vanishing, cowboy lifestyle. For the first time, McCarthy presents a heroic protagonist, while his moral stance is clearer than in his previous works, and he even includes a love story. Yet despite these elements which give the novel its popular appeal, *All the Pretty Horses* retains many of the trademarks of McCarthy's best work: lyrical prose, evocative landscape descriptions, idiosyncratic style and complex treatment of deep themes and philosophy. For this achievement McCarthy was awarded, among other honours, the National Book Award for fiction.

McCarthy followed *All the Pretty Horses* with *The Crossing* (1994) and *Cities of the Plain* (1998), the other two instalments of the border trilogy. *The Crossing* introduces Billy Parham, a teenage boy living in New Mexico before and during the Second World War. Parham takes a number of perilous and heartbreaking journeys across the Mexican border and back. *Cities of the Plains* unites the two protagonists of *All the Pretty Horses* and *The Crossing* in a dark and apocalyptic tale that reinforces the themes of the previous two books. The border trilogy stands as one of McCarthy's greatest achievements, a testament to his power as a writer.

Selected works:

The Orchard Keeper (1965); *Outer Dark* (1968); *Child of God* (1973); *Suttree* (1979); *Blood*

Meridian (1986); *All the Pretty Horses* (1992); *The Crossing* (1994); *Cities of the Plain* (1998).

Further reading

Arnold, Edwin T. and Luce, Dianne C., *A Cormac McCarthy Companion. The Border Trilogy.* University Press of Mississippi, 2001.

Contributor: Mark Mills

M^cEWAN, IAN (1948–)

It was not at all clear to me now why we had put her in the trunk in the first place . . . Nor could I think whether what we had done was an ordinary thing to do
            From *The Cement Garden*

Ian Russell McEwan was born in Aldershot in southern England, but spent much of his childhood abroad where his father, an army officer, was posted. He studied English and French at the University of Sussex from 1967 to 1970, then went on to do an MA at the University of East Anglia, being one of the first graduates of the prestigious creative writing department run by Angus Wilson and Malcolm Bradbury. One of the best-known names in contemporary British literature, he is a proven versatile writer with novels, short stories, screenplays, children's fiction and an oratorio (*Or Shall We Die?* performed in 1983) to his credit. His novel *The Child in Time* (1987) won a Whitbread Prize. *Amsterdam* (1998) won a Booker Prize, for which *The Comfort of Strangers* (1981) and *Atonement* (2001) were also short-listed.

An overview of his work shows a development from the overtly macabre earlier short stories and novels to a more detailed concentration on the psychological impact of cruelty and lies, as seen for example in *Atonement.* While a transition is evident, there has always been an interest in the nature of brutality in contemporary Western society and a prevailing **postmodern** approach to his material.

McEwan's first book, *First Love, Last Rites* (1975), a collection of short stories which won

a Somerset Maugham Award, was followed in 1978 by another collection, *In Between the Sheets.* Both are representative of his early style in their uncompromising focus on adolescent sexuality, violence against the body and taboos such as incest. There is a willingness to disturb the reader, although he claims that this is not a deliberate aim:

> It turns out that what I have written is unsettling, but I don't sit down to think about what will unsettle people next.[1]

The Cement Garden (1978), which was released as a film in 1993, continues this embrace of uneasiness in a story of four children who survive the death of their parents without help from external authorities. They progressively isolate themselves from the outside world and sibling incest, which is latent throughout the story, is acted out at the novel's climax.

In 1979 a proposed television production of 'Solid Geometry', a story from *First Love, Last Rites*, was halted by the BBC for perceived obscenity. McEwan's script was later published in *The Imitation Game: Three Plays for Television* (1981), which also included the eponymous *The Imitation Game* (1980) and *Jack Flea's Birthday Celebration* (1976). *Solid Geometry* has since been adapted by the actor Dennis Lawson and was screened on Channel 4 in 2002. McEwan also wrote the script for *The Ploughman's Lunch* (1983), which won an *Evening Standard* award for the best screenplay.

McEwan's second novel, *The Comfort of Strangers*, was adapted for film by **Harold Pinter** in 1991. Set in Venice, this novel is concerned with the complexity of violence in sexual relationships, as shown in the story of a couple, Colin and Mary, who, as tourists, become entangled in a power struggle with another couple, Robert and Caroline. Sado-masochism and the implication that the victims are complicit in their abuse is a major theme.

The Child in Time is concerned with slippages of time and the nature of masculinity. *The Innocent* (1990), set in post-Second World War Berlin, examines innocence and guilt against a backdrop of the Cold War. *Black Dogs* (1992) similarly draws on the scars left by war on Europe, the eponymous black dogs being a motif for a constant threat from the past. The fall of the Berlin Wall and the death of idealism colour this fiction too, and Kiernan

Ryan notes how the novel understands the menace of absence:

> In *Black Dogs* McEwan squares up to the fact that nothing can fill the abyss into which this novel peers. All we have is the fleeting respite of the stories we tell ourselves, the fictions we concoct to feed our hunger for sense. McEwan's omnivorous art of unease prowls on.[2]

In *Enduring Love* (1997), an incident with a hot air balloon and the repercussions of surviving a tragedy are central narrative concerns. Guilt and selfishness are investigated through the impact of a single unexpected event on ordinary lives, a device also used in *Black Dogs* and *Atonement*.

Amsterdam begins with the funeral of Molly Lane and an introduction to her former lovers. As with earlier McEwan works, this novel offers a study of male rivalry and a consideration of amorality. Blackmail, revenge and euthanasia are the forces that drive the narrative to a disturbing conclusion.

Atonement marks a notable change in McEwan's writing. There is a return to an interest in the darker aspects of childhood and adolescence, but the novel is wider in scope in that it spans the second half of the twentieth century with more confidence. The narrator, Briony, is a writer and the novel is her act of atonement for the sin of lying. The protagonist being a writer results in a dimension of **metafiction** entering the narrative. Briony reflects, 'The problem these fifty-nine years has been this: how can a novelist achieve atonement when, with her absolute power of deciding outcomes, she is also God?' (p. 317). The irony of the author being as powerful as the Almighty is revealed through the story Briony (and McEwan) tells. Through its self-consciousness about writing, the novel explores the **postmodern** issue of how language can shape reality and create new versions of events. The fiction Briony finally creates is her invention of her sister's romantic happy ending.

References

1. **McEwan, Ian**, quoted in Haffenden, John. *Novelists in Interview*. London: Methuen, 1985, p. 169.

2. **Ryan, Kiernan** (1994) *Ian McEwan*. Plymouth: Northgate House, p. 68.

Selected works:

First Love, Last Rites (1975); *In Between the Sheets* (1978); *The Cement Garden* (1978); *The Imitation Game: Three Plays for Television* (1981); *The Comfort of Strangers* (1981); *The Ploughman's Lunch* (1983); *The Child in Time* (1987); *The Innocent* (1990); *Black Dogs* (1992); *Enduring Love* (1997); *Amsterdam* (1998); *Atonement* (2001).

Contributor: Julie Ellam

MILLER, ARTHUR (1915–)

The man who makes an appearance in the business world, the man who creates a personal interest, is the man who gets ahead. Be liked and you will never want.
The Death of a Salesman

Arthur Miller gained international fame in 1949 with his play *The Death of a Salesman*, which won a New York Drama Critics' Circle Award and a Pulitzer Prize. His importance as a major American playwright was confirmed by *The Crucible* (1953) and he remains one of America's foremost dramatists, writing plays which, combining social awareness with compassion, examine the values of American society.

Miller was born into a Jewish immigrant family in a small Brooklyn house which is taken to be the model for the Loman home in *The Death of a Salesman*. The Depression was the ruin of his father's clothing business, forcing him to close down his shop, and this virtually overnight reversal in their fortunes had a lasting effect on Miller. In spite of his poverty-stricken, non-intellectual upbringing, Miller decided, after reading Dostoevsky's *The Brothers Karamazov* at the age of 17, to become a writer.

In 1934 he went to the University of Michigan to study journalism, supporting himself by working in a warehouse. There, along with **Tennessee Williams**, he won awards for playwriting. He graduated in 1938 and returned to New York. When the

Second World War broke out in 1939 he was spared military service because of a football injury. He joined the Federal Theatre Project, and Cavalcade of America, which were later to become the media giants CBS (Columbia Broadcasting System) and NBC (National Broadcasting Company) respectively.

In 1940 Miller married Mary Slatterey and they later had two children. In 1944 his first play, *The Man Who Had All the Luck*, appeared on Broadway but ran for only four nights. The same year he visited army camps to collect material for his screenplay for *The Story of G.I. Joe*. The film was released in 1945, but his first real success came in 1947 with *All My Sons*. This play, a condemnation of profiteering during the war, won him a New York Drama Critics' Circle Award. The protagonist, Chris Keller, who is determined to dredge up a past that holds painful truths, introduces us to a prototypical Miller character: the idealist who pays too highly for his inability to compromise.

With *The Death of a Salesman* Miller's reputation spread worldwide. One of the outstanding achievements of this play lay in the originality of the staging, through which Miller created a theatrical correlative for Willy Loman's tortured mind. The action had to move easily between the past and the present. The realistic texture of Willy's environment was crucial, but so were the distortions created by his memory, the fragments of the past through which he sifted with increasing desperation. The result was a form of **realism** combined with expressionism, which dramatised individual psychology in the context of social change.

In *The Death of a Salesman* two largely incompatible dreams exist side by side. We see parts of the American emotional landscape in Willy's lost elms, the scene in which he tries to plant seeds, Biff's desire to work in the open without his shirt, and the picture of Willy's father working around the country in a horse-drawn wagon, images which represent archetypal ideals of the American heart. But these ideals are denied in the world of salesmanship and the success myth, leaving Willy trapped in a world in which he is a stranger. The play has the sounds and rhythms and cycles of dream, and we sympathise with Willy, being moved by his unattainable dream of purity, knowledge and power.

The aspect of the 'American dream' with which Willy grapples, the success myth, according to which virtue was supposed to bring wealth, was strongly influenced by Benjamin Franklin, and Willy's brother Ben (the name may not be coincidental) is an embodiment of Franklin's vision. Willy's quest for the 'secret of success' lies at the core of the play and he is representative of a large segment of American society. For Miller, the salesman is a personification of the success myth, which he subverts by making Willy's story one of suffering caused by the pressure of the myth, and of failure. In place of a young, determined hero, we find an exhausted old salesman who has failed to cope with, let alone overcome, each successive challenge. Even his sons fail after trying to live by their father's ideals. The dream never becomes real and turns out to be a lie, a disappointment, a delusion. Having passed on these flawed ideals to his sons, Willy dies still under his delusions, never learning what it is apparent he should learn: that while the shadowy figure of Ben, the outgoing man of action who travels into the unknown and wins riches, establishes the general truth that any man can succeed, Willy cannot accept Ben's methods.

Miller does offer positive values in the play. He stresses family solidarity centring around the wife and mother. Linda Loman holds the family together, although at the same time, through her silence and her support, she unwittingly sustains the myth. She believes in the rules established by the advocates of 'self-making'. As an alternative to the success myth Willy imagines a return to a non-competitive agrarian or trade-oriented society. Some critics argue that in this respect the play merely romanticises the post-Depression rural-agrarian dream, while denying that lifestyle to Willy, and that it therefore does not present a definitive comment on the business-success ideal. According to this view the play is not convincing in its presentation of the system as the villain; the fault lies with Willy, rather than with society, so he is not a tragic hero but an ineffectual man who arouses pity but not admiration.

In 1950 the McCarthy witch-hunt caught up with Miller and he was subjected to scrutiny by the Congressional Committee whose purpose was to investigate 'Communist influence in the arts'. Miller channelled his experience of this era into *The Crucible* (1953). The first Broadway production was not successful, but eventually it almost equalled *The Death of a Salesman* in fame and popularity. The play is set in late seventeenth-century Salem and the events are largely historical. In 1692 a series of trials took place in which 13 men and women were accused of witchcraft and hanged, and a man named Giles Corey was crushed to death because he refused to confess. Hundreds of people were accused and jailed and in this historical narrative Miller saw an exact parallel to the McCarthy era. The same 'witch-hunt' mentality, misrepresentation of facts, people imprisoned on the basis of mere suspicion and a general mistrust among even closely knit people pertained to both situations.

Miller's next two plays, *A Memory of Two Mondays* and *A View from the Bridge*, both produced in 1955, were concerned primarily with incest, jealousy and betrayal. Then in 1956, while John Osborne was presenting *Look Back in Anger* on the other side of the Atlantic, Miller was called before the House Committee on Un-American Activities. The reason for this hearing was that he had attended writers' meetings organised by the Communist Party, supported a Peace Conference in New York and given his signature in support of many appeals. As he refused to name his compatriots he was held in contempt of the Congress. In June 1957 **John Steinbeck** wrote:

> The Congress has the right to do nearly anything conceivable. It has only to define a situation or an action as a 'clear and present danger' . . . We have seen and been revolted by the Soviet Union's encouragement of spying and telling, children reporting their parents, wives informing on their husbands. In Hitler's Germany, it was considered patriotic to report your friends and relations to the authorities. And we in America have felt safe from and superior to these things. But are we so safe or superior? . . . There is a clear and present danger here, not to Arthur Miller, but to our changing and evolving way of life.[1]

Two years later the contempt order was revoked by the courts following Miller's appeal.

Miller's five-year marriage with Marilyn Monroe, whom he married after her divorce from Joe DiMaggio, began in 1956. He wrote little during that period and by the time he published *The Misfits* (1961) their marriage was already breaking down. According to many commentators Maggie from his 1964 play *After the Fall* was based on Monroe, though Miller denied this.

In 1965 Miller was elected president of the international literary organisation **P.E.N.** He has written many plays since and won many awards, including seven Tony Awards, two Drama Critics' Circle Awards, the John F. Kennedy Lifetime Achievement Award and the Dorothy and Lillian Gish prize. He holds honorary doctorate degrees from the Universities of Oxford and Harvard.

Miller's autobiography, *Timebends: A Life,* was published in 1987. This book contained his insights on his creative genius and accounts of his childhood in Harlem, his academic years, his showdown with the House Committee on Un-American Activities and his marriages. It also includes details of his interactions with Elia Kazan, **Tennessee Williams**, **Saul Bellow** and political leaders such as Ronald Reagan, John F. Kennedy and Mikhail Gorbachev.

Reference

1. *Esquire,* June 1957. Quoted on web page by William Scott Simkins, The University of Southern Mississippi. http://ocean.otr.usm.edu/~wsimkins/trial.html

Selected works:

Honors At Dawn (1936); *No Villain / They Too Arise* (1937); *The Pussycat and The Expert Plumber who was a Man* (1941); *William Ireland's Confession* (1941); *The Man Who Had All The Luck* (1944); *That They May Win* (1944); *Situation Normal* (1944); *Grandpa And The Statue* (1945); *The Story of G.I. Joe* (1945); *FOCUS* (1945); *The Guardsman* (1947); *Three Men on a Horse* (1947); *All My Sons* (1947); *Death of a Salesman* (1949); *An Enemy of the People* (Adaptation of Ibsen's play) (1950); *The Crucible* (1953); *A View from the Bridge* (1955); *A*

Memory of Two Mondays (1955); *The Misfits* (1961); *Jane's Blanket* (1963); *After The Fall* (1964); *The Incident at Vichy* (1964); *The Price* (1967); *The Archbishop's Ceiling* (1977); *Two-Way Mirror* (consisting of 'Elegy for a Lady' and 'Some Kind of Love Story') (1982–84); *The Ride Down Mount Morgan* (1991); *The Last Yankee* (1993); *The Broken Glass* (1993); *Mr. Peter's Connections* (1998); *Resurrection Blues* (2002).

Further reading

Bhatia, S. K., *Arthur Miller: Social Drama as Tragedy*. Prometheus Books, 1985.

Bloom, Harold (ed.) *Arthur Miller*. DeCapo Press, 2003.

Sing, Pramila, *Arthur Miller and His Plays*. H. K. Publishers, 1990.

Contributor: Siddartha Biswas

MISTRY, ROHINTON (1952–)

You have to maintain a fine balance between hope and despair.

                                  A Fine Balance

Northrop Frye's formulation, 'Where is here?',[1] remains peculiarly pertinent to any analysis of the work of the Indian-Canadian author Rohinton Mistry. In Canada, Mistry's work represents only one strand of the complex Indian diaspora. Born and educated as a Parsee, however, Mistry belongs to a cultural and religious group that fled from Persia to India in 900 CE* but which has never been fully accepted. Thus Mistry was already alienated – part of a much older diaspora within India – and his work captures perfectly the displacement and loss of 'not belonging'.

Born in Bombay (now Mumbai) in July 1952, Mistry, like most middle-class Indian boys, attended an English-Christian mission-ary school, yet fully absorbed his Indian-Parsee culture. He is no longer a practising Parsee, but his faith enthralled him, especial-ly the injunction to choose good over evil – a major theme in his work.

The prophet Zoroaster founded the Parsee religion in the sixth century BCE*.

Fleeing Persia in order to escape persecu-tion, the Parsees were allowed to settle in India and practise their faith, on condition that they adopted local traditions and did not proselytise. They have contributed enor-mously to Indian society, although their pref-erential treatment by the British aroused prejudice and Parsee status has declined fur-ther with the growth of Hindu nationalism, while numbers have decreased due to assimi-lation and emigration.

In 1974 Mistry graduated from the University of Bombay with a BA in Mathematics and Economics. By 1975 he had followed his girlfriend, Freny Elavia, and emigrated to Toronto, where they married, and Mistry became a bank clerk. Finding his work unrewarding, he attended the University of Toronto, part-time, studying English and Philosophy, and it was here that he began to write short stories. By the time he graduated in 1984, 'One Sunday' had won first prize in the 1983 Canadian Hart House Literary Contest, with 'Auspicious Occasions' winning the following year.

Tales from Firozsha Baag (1987/1992) is a collection of short stories concerning the Parsee families who live in a run-down apart-ment block in 1970s Bombay. The 11 tales interconnect in a style reminiscent of **Alice Munro**, with characters weaving in and out of each other's stories. Time passes and people change, yet the discursiveness of Mistry's storytelling disrupts linearity. His style is simple and conventional, but with superb dialogue that reproduces perfectly the idioms and rhythms of Parsee-Indian. Zoroastrianism and family love are the main unifying themes of the stories, as youngsters rebel against a faith which limits their per-sonal freedom, while parents fear the changes that erode both status and belief. This conflict between tradition, personal freedom and wider social change is present throughout Mistry's work and the issues on which he focuses in limited communities reflect the problems of a larger world.

Such A Long Journey (1991), Mistry's first novel, won the 1991 Governor General's Literary Award for fiction, the 1992 Commonwealth Writers' Prize, the Giller Prize for Canadian fiction, and was shortlisted for the 1991 Booker Prize. Again, middle-class Parsee families are examined, but *Such a Long Journey* is set in 1971 during the India-Pakistan war and the interweaving of political crises with the ever-increasing turmoil of the hero's personal life conveys both the decay of all India and the increasing mass of the people, with the Parsee community as an insecure minority.

Gustad Noble is a Parsee bank clerk, happily married, with three children. He is an ordinary man, decent, loyal and always trying to choose 'good', yet his son's disobedience precipitates Gustad's bizarre act of loyalty for his old friend, Major Bilimoria. This homely Parsee tale then spirals into a world of **post-colonial** corruption, for the Bilimoria plot is based on a genuine extortion racket – the Nagarwal case – which involved Indira Gandhi. This exposure of corruption is Mistry's insider/outsider review, as he laments the loss of post-independence idealism, although his political attacks lack subtlety. The wall outside Gustad's apartment symbolises Parsee denial of the changing reality of India. When the wall and its gods are destroyed, however, the artist Malak's complete acceptance signals that creativity and life will go on and Gustad is able to acknowledge a life beyond. Mistry celebrates Gustad's humanity and empathy and, in keeping with the novel's title and epigraphs, suggests that such individual journeys are essential.

A Fine Balance (1995) is Mistry's masterpiece, yet its chilling epigraph predicts unremitting tragedy. The novel won the 1995 Giller Prize, the *Los Angeles Times* Award for fiction, the Commonwealth Writers' Prize for best book, and was shortlisted for the 1996 Booker Prize. With its multiple plots and moral symbolism, *A Fine Balance* has been likened to a nineteenth-century novel, but Mistry's digressive plotting disrupts linearity, while his documentary **realism** presents an India of **postmodern** despair.

Set in 1975 Bombay, *A Fine Balance* follows the intertwined lives of four of India's 'dispossessed' and the impact of Indira Gandhi's state of emergency. Three separate stories converge. Dina Dalal, a courageous Parsee widow, attempts to survive economically by employing two Hindu tailors. Ishvar and his nephew, Omprakash, are members of the Chamaar caste and were originally tanners –

contaminated untouchables. The story of the two tailors proceeds through cycles of horror while structurally their tale refocuses the novel onto a wider Indian perspective. Maneck Kohlah, a young student from the north, lodges with Dina; he feels rejected by his parents' desperate concern to secure his professional future. All four characters, in trying to break the restraints of sex, caste and heritage, help each other in a personal world where selflessness and integrity abound.

Mistry's main theme is India's self-destruction, with Western materialism, caste oppression, social injustice and Indira Gandhi all being criticised, although Mistry's polemics detract from his study of human behaviour. By contrast, when describing the many horrors experienced, Mistry's cool, flat narrative maintains a balance that largely avoids melodrama, sentiment and voyeurism, with the very lack of rhetoric promoting the reader's involvement. The oppression of women is also foregrounded in an understated way.

The accounts of despair and misery are unremitting, so that readers feel condemned to a predetermined doom, with tragedy becoming almost banal. The love, integrity and empathy of the main characters save the novel – and nearly eclipse despair – but still, 'good' does not triumph. In *A Fine Balance*, Mistry is asking why these wonderful, individual lives lack the power to defeat evil. He provides no answers, but he does surprise his readers into questions.

Family Matters (2002) is set in 1990s Bombay and after the wide canvas of *A Fine Balance*, returns to apartment-based Parsee life. As the punning title suggests, the novel examines mundane family life, while also insisting that families are deeply and universally important. The novel won the prestigious Kiriyama Pacific Rim Book Prize in 2002 and was shortlisted for the James Tait Black Memorial Prize and the Mann Booker Prize.

Family Matters concerns Nariman Vakeel, a 79-year-old Parsee widower suffering from Parkinson's disease, who lives with his middle-aged stepchildren, Jal and Coomy Contractor. Coomy forces her stepsister, Roxana, to care for Nariman in the tiny apartment where she lives with her husband Yezad and two sons. The novel charts how Roxana's family is slowly undermined – financially, emotionally and morally – by this burden of caring and by the political and economic changes of the time.

Mistry's complex interweaving of histories and examination of the constant slippage between personal and public demonstrate that no one event leads to tragedy, but that its causes are myriad and complex. Further, he does not present his characters as determined, but by mapping the restricted choices available, he demonstrates that none is a free agent; thus, by following her ethics and caring for her father, Roxana unwittingly precipitates the corruption of both her husband and son.

Mistry's overall presentation of, and care for, individuals is unsurpassed, with affection and humour abounding. His main concerns are always the universals – love, care and duty – but also an examination of the contradictions and ambiguities which result whenever these are extended to family, community, nation, faith and beyond. Mistry's exploration of these complexities – in *Family Matters* and throughout his work – demonstrates that tidy closures and happy endings are not always possible, but questions must always be asked and hope should never give way to despair. (* CE = AD, BCE = BC)

Reference

1. **Frye, Northrop**. From: 'Conclusion' to *A Literary History of Canada*, reproduced in *The Bush Garden: Essays on the Canadian Imagination*, Toronto: Anansi, 1971, p. 220.

Selected works:

Tales from Firozsha Baag (Penguin, 1987; Faber and Faber, 1992); *Such a Long Journey* (1991); *A Fine Balance* (1995); *Family Matters* (2002).

Further reading

Dodiya, Jaydipsinh (ed.) *The Fiction of Rohinton Mistry: Critical Studies.* Sangam Books, 1998.

Contributor: Carole Jones

MORRISON, TONI (1931–)

An artist . . . is not a solitary person who has no responsibility to the community. [Writing] is a totally communal experience where I would feel unhappy if there was no controversy or no debate.[1]

From an interview with
Christina Davis, 1986

Toni Morrison's novels about dysfunction and reconstruction in the experience of African-Americans have received both critical recognition and commercial success. Acclaimed in both the academic and popular spheres, her powerful and intimate stories focus on essential human issues such as love, family, identity and community. She wants her writing to speak to readers: 'If anything I do in the way of writing novels (or whatever I write) isn't about the village or the community or about you, then it is not about anything.'[1]

Morrison was awarded the Nobel Prize for Literature in 1993, becoming the first black woman ever to claim that honour. According to the Nobel press release, she is an author 'who, in novels characterized by visionary force and poetic import, gives life to an essential aspect of American reality'. The essential reality of which Morrison writes resonates with Americans, especially African-Americans. Five years before Morrison received the Nobel Prize, 48 prominent African-American writers, including Maya Angelou, Alice Walker and John Wideman, signed a letter to the editor of the *New York Times* praising Morrison for advancing 'the moral and artistic standards by which we must measure the daring and the love of our national imagination and our collective intelligence as a people'. In addition to gaining this high praise from her fellow authors, Morrison's novel *Beloved* won several awards in 1988, including the Pulitzer Prize. These awards served to solidify Morrison's place in the American canon and consolidated the acclaim she had received for *Song of Solomon* in 1977, which won the National Book Critics' Circle Award and the American Academy and Institute of Arts and Letters Award, and for *Sula* in 1975 which gained a National Book Award nomination and the

Ohioana Book Award. Such acclaim is impressive for someone who never intended to become a writer.

Chloe Anthony Wofford (she legally changed her name to Toni in college) was born in 1931 in Lorain, Ohio, to George and Ramah (Willis) Wofford. She married Harold Morrison in 1958, but after having two children, they divorced. Morrison obtained degrees from Howard and Cornell Universities, writing her thesis on suicide in the writings of **William Faulkner** and **Virginia Woolf**. She then taught English at Texas Southern University and Howard University, before moving to New York in 1965 to become the senior editor for Random House. It wasn't until after establishing her editing career that Morrison began to write seriously. Her first book, *The Bluest Eye*, was published in 1970 when she was nearly 40.

The Bluest Eye, and many of Morrison's other novels, proved her unique in the depiction of relationships between blacks. Much contemporary literature deals with conflicts between blacks and whites; Morrison, on the other hand, suggests that interracial tension cannot be dealt with until the problems within the black family and the immediate community are understood. *The Bluest Eye* is the story of 11-year-old Pecola Breedlove, who is shunned by her mother and raped by her father. Because of the way her mother dotes on the white children she cares for, Pecola believes that having blue eyes will solve her problems and eventually goes mad wishing she had them. *Sula* (1973) is about two black women who must negotiate their friendship in the face of community disapproval, illicit affairs, rebellion and foul play. *Song of Solomon* (1977) follows Milkman Dead's journey to discover his family history, which is riddled with pain and mistreatment. In all of these story lines, issues of identity and the place of African-Americans within their community supercede interracial issues.

Through her stories of collective racial problems Morrison works to reconstruct history and promote compassion by focusing on identity and experience. The trilogy that comprises *Beloved* (1987), *Jazz* (1992) and *Paradise* (1998) traces the history of African-Americans from their roots in Africa, through the experience of slavery, to the pains of the post-slavery era and the struggle to find a place in American society. This reconstruction of history is also an exploration of the position of black women. Motherhood, for example, is a strong theme for Morrison. Whether it be Eva Peace in *Sula*, who places her leg on a railroad track to collect the insurance for her family, or Sethe in *Beloved*, who tries to kill her children to prevent them from being raised as slaves, Morrison portrays black motherhood as traumatic and painful. Along with these negative female experiences, however, Morrison writes of the power of love and the hope associated with compassion. *Beloved*'s Paul D and Sethe approach a healthy relationship, as do Violet and Joe in *Jazz*. The nuns in *Paradise*, who accept and love the misfits of the nearby community, temporarily create a place of healing and growth, a place that is destroyed only when the town's citizens refuse to extend that same love.

The universally important content of Morrison's novels is made rich by her lyrical style, critics often commenting on the poetic prose, vivid dialogue and resonant images that characterise her elegant writing. Her novels capture the speech and song of her heritage and invite oral readings. Her fluid dialogue shows Morrison's compassion for her characters and the power of language to reveal truth.

In 2004, Morrison was the Robert F. Goheen Professor of the Humanities at Princeton University, where she continues to teach and to write. Her widely acclaimed work provides insight into what it's like to be a woman, to be black, to be American, to be loved or not loved, to be part of a family and to be part of a community.

Reference

Morrison, Toni (1984) 'Rootedness: The Ancestor as Foundation' in *Black Woman Writers (1950–1980)*, ed. Mari Evans. Doubleday.

Selected works:
The Bluest Eye (1970); *Sula* (1973); *Song of Solomon* (1977); *Tar Baby* (1981); *Dreaming Emmett* (play) (1981); *Beloved* (1987); *Jazz* (1992); *Playing in the Dark: Whiteness and the Literary Imagination* (1992); *Paradise* (1998); *Love* (2003).

Further reading

Furman, Jan, *Toni Morrison's Fiction (Understanding Contemporary American Literature)*. University of South Carolina Press, 1999.

Contributor: Amy Glauser Bankhead

MUNRO, ALICE (1931–)

People's lives, in Jubilee as elsewhere, were dull, simple, amazing, and unfathomable – deep caves paved with kitchen linoleum.

From Lives of Girls and Women

Canadian author Alice Munro is considered one of the finest ever writers of short stories. Her tales map the social geography of ordinary, unheroic protagonists, while exploring Canadian rural small-town existence and urban and suburban lifescapes. Simultaneously, she reveals the dark chasms that underlie ordinary lives. Exploring this paradox between the surface of life and the shadow-world beneath is a major part of her fictional terrain, together with a **postmodernist** questioning of language and its ability to convey meaning.

Born Alice Ann Laidlaw, in Wingham, south-west Ontario, Munro's father, Robert, raised silver foxes before becoming a turkey farmer, while her mother, Anne Chamney Laidlaw, was a former teacher. When Munro was ten, her mother was diagnosed with Parkinson's disease; the ensuing period of struggle is explored fictionally in 'The Peace of Utrecht' in the volume *Dance of the Happy Shades* (1968). Written in 1959, this tale was a major turning point, for working through the slow, gradual loss of her mother catalysed the reflectiveness that is a hallmark of Munro's work.

Growing up in a rural community, Munro experienced alienation through not being a practical, hands-on person. Like Del Jordan, in *Lives of Girls and Women* (1971), Munro tried to conceal her intelligence and difference, but failed. Her daughter Sheila confirms this, describing how Munro lacked Del's dating experiences because the boys considered her odd (Munro, 2001, p. 13).

Composing stories became Munro's escape, yet writing was considered useless. Despite her success, Wingham is still unhappy with the attention that Munro's work attracts.

In 1949 Munro won a scholarship to the University of Western Ontario. The scholarship ended after only two years and she married James Armstrong Munro in 1951. It was a pragmatic decision, but her daughter confirms that Munro always wanted both roles: sexuality, marriage, children *and* a career (Munro, p. 12). They had three daughters and lived in Vancouver, before running a bookstore in Victoria. Munro refers to this period as her double life – snatching writing time while the children slept – and it was a long, yet vital apprenticeship before her first collection, *Dance of the Happy Shades* (1968), was published. In 1973 she and James separated, divorcing in 1976. Munro remet the geographer Gerry Fremlin and they married in 1976. She now divides her life between Clinton, Ontario and Comox, British Columbia.

Munro's work has won many prizes, including three Governor General's Awards. *Friend of My Youth* (1990) won the Ontario Trillium Book Award and the Commonwealth Writers' Prize, while *The Love of a Good Woman* (1998) won The Giller Prize and the 1999 National Book Critics' Circle fiction prize. *Hateship, Friendship, Courtship, Loveship, Marriage* (2001) won the 2002 Annual Canadian 'Writers' Craft Award'. Despite such accolades, some critics still dismiss Munro as a regional or provincial writer. She acknowledges that some cannot accept a literature that is geographically limited, yet insists that the emotions and experiences she explores are not limited. Writers of the American South, such as Eudora Welty, Carson McCullers, **Flannery O'Connor** and **Katherine Anne Porter**, were major influences on Munro, partly because they wrote about provincial issues.

Some critics also dismiss Munro because she writes only short stories, yet her texts challenge the conventions of the novel *and* short story forms. Her tales are extremely discursive, with many incidents and apparent irrelevancies and more characters than conventional short stories. Stories may take six or more months to evolve, passing through several drafts, and during this process she creates her characters so completely that she can suggest an entire life in a page – as well as the rooms or landscapes where her characters move – using condensed poetic language to convey history and personality. This is Munro's super-realism, a tremendous, **postmodern** artifice, which creates a seeming reality. In the essay 'What is Real?' (Metcalf and Struthers, p. 331–334) Munro attempts to explain what short stories are to her and how she writes them. Crucially, a story is not linear: 'It's more like a house. Everybody knows what a house does, how it encloses space and makes connections between one enclosed space and another and presents what is outside in a new way. This is the nearest I can come to explaining what a story does for me, and what I want my stories to do for other people.'

Munro charts lives from childhood through adolescence to maturity and death. Early works, such as *Dance of the Happy Shades* and *Lives of Girls and Women*, are shown from predominantly a child's or adolescent's perspective, with much first-person narration. Discursiveness, and the multiple snapshot effect of the protagonist Del Jordan's episodic life, result in past and present being collapsed to indicate growth. Many tales touch on **feminist** themes, examining the sexual conditioning that relegates women to inauthentic lives, as when the narrator in 'Boys and Girls' has the epiphanic realisation that she *is* only a girl, while 'The Office' charts how the narrator is not accorded the right to work undisturbed because she is only a woman. Repeatedly, Munro excavates such subtle but awkward and embarrassing situations.

Lives of Girls and Women is one of Munro's most powerful works and was originally planned as a novel. Del Jordan explores, survives and manages to reject objectification and the romantic fantasy trap. She wants men to love her, but she also wants to think of the universe when she looks at the moon. The narrative perspective modulates from a child's to a woman's, while being complemented by the adult narrator's insight, as Del explores different writings, situations and realities in each section, comparing them to her life and sense of self. The whole text is a retrospective, a 'Portrait of the Girl

becoming an Artist *and* a Woman'.

In her next few collections, Munro adopted more mature female narrative voices – intelligent narrators who question the expectations and demands that society places on them, just because they are women. The tales in *Something I've Been Meaning to Tell You* (1974) are more aggressive and darker, moving into the realm of marriage, divorce and middle-aged disillusionment, but concentrating on the effects of time and memory. In 'Material' the narrator reluctantly admires her ex-husband's story-version of a shared memory, while still insisting that no matter how stylishly and movingly he rememories the past, it is 'not enough'. In *Who Do You Think You Are?* (1978) Rose is the narrator-protagonist whose indirect third-person presents her different lives – all enacted while she searches for an identity. Rose is trapped between reality and romantic fantasy, a situation Munro often explores, while subverting both sides.

The Moons of Jupiter (1983) and *The Progress of Love* (1986) continue these themes, while exploring the problems of middle-aged women who have to accept diminishing physical attractiveness. There is, however, a change in method, for everything is spread over a larger frame of time and space, with 'Moons of Jupiter', setting this cosmic tone, while the female genealogies of the 'Chaddeleys and Flemings' rewrite the discredited 'his-stories' that men have traditionally told. Many of the stories in *Friend of My Youth* (1990) are concerned with looking back and rewriting memories and histories. The title story, dedicated to Munro's mother, shows how we rewrite things to suit our changing frames of reference. Both the narrator and her mother change Flora's story, while the narrator attempts to redream a mother with whom she can cope. As Munro has become increasingly aware of the artifice of writing, so her stories draw attention to their fictionality – in both 'Meneseteung' and 'Friend of My Youth', the narrators point up the construction of their tale.

In *Open Secrets* (1994) Munro extends the short story form further and aims to challenge readers. 'It's pointless to go on if you don't take risks' (*Meanjin* 1995, pp. 222–233). There is an increased displacement, with time and memory not in sequence and far more spatial and temporal gaps. In 'Carried Away', Louisa encounters all the possible future realities that were available to her, yet there is no resolution. *The Love of a Good Woman* and *Hateship, Friendship, Courtship, Loveship, Marriage* tell tales of older adult life. There is more illness and death, yet the tales are not pessimistic, for there is a strong celebration of the lives that once were.

Munro's writing, while not overtly political, is a powerful defamiliarising force. Her work, while not an easy read, is formally entrancing, promoting both deep enjoyment and serious questioning. As Munro says: 'As long as the stories disturb people or point to the ways they should be dissatisfied with the status quo, then I assume I've done my job' (*Meanjin*).

Selected works:

Dance of the Happy Shades (1968); *Lives of Girls and Women* (1971); *Something I've Been Meaning to Tell You* (1974); *The Beggar Maid (*Canada – *Who Do You Think You Are?)* (1978); *The Moons of Jupiter* (1983); *The Progress of Love* (1986); *Friend of My Youth* (1990); *Open Secrets* (1994); *Selected Stories* (1996); *The Love of a Good Woman* (1998); *Hateship, Friendship, Courtship, Loveship, Marriage* (2001); *No Love Lost: Selected Stories* (2003).

Further reading

Cox, Ailsa, *Alice Munro* (Writers and their Work Series). Northcote House Publishers, 2004.

Howells, Coral Ann, *Alice Munro*. Manchester University Press, 1998.

Meanjin – interview, Vol. 54/2, 1995.

Metcalf, John and Struthers, J. R. (eds) *How Stories Mean*. The Porcupine Quill, 1993.

Munro, Sheila. *Lives of Mothers and Daughters: Growing Up With Alice Munro*. McClelland & Stewart, 2001.

The New Yorker. On-line interview, 2002.

Rasporich, B. J., *Dance of the Sexes: Art and Gender in the Fiction of Alice Munro*. University of Alberta Press, 1990.

Contributor: Carole Jones

MURDOCH, DAME IRIS (1919–99)

All artists dream of a silence which they must enter, as some creatures return to the sea to spawn.

The Black Prince

Jean Iris Murdoch was born in 1919, in Dublin, Eire, of Protestant Anglo-Irish parents. She was an only child and from an early age peopled her world with characters from her imagination, about whom she began to write from the age of nine. By the time she died in 1999 she had produced many highly regarded works of literature and philosophy.

When Murdoch was six, her parents moved to London, although the family's holidays were spent in Ireland. She was educated at Badminton School and Somerville College, Oxford, where she read Classics – her knowledge of the myths of the Classical World later helping to shape her novels and their characters. She quickly found her place in the new world of Oxford; she was a brilliant scholar and became involved in politics and amateur dramatics. She was popular and made many friends, most of whom remained close for the rest of her life. Some were European scholars who had escaped Hitler's Germany, others would become important in the worlds of art and politics.

After leaving Oxford, Murdoch became a civil servant in the Treasury and lived in London. During this period she was a profuse letter-writer, but longed to give her ideas artistic shape by writing novels. Later she worked for the United Nations, first in London and then in Brussels and Austria. She won a place at Vassar, New York State, in 1947, but was unable to go to America because she had previously been a member of the Communist Party. Instead, she went to Cambridge where she just missed hearing Wittgenstein's lecture, though she did meet him twice. In 1948, she returned to Oxford as philosophy tutor at St Anne's and was associated with teaching there for the next 15 years. Oxford was then the centre of the philosophical world and Murdoch taught moral and political philosophy to students of PPE (Politics, Philosophy and Economics) and Classics.

In these early Oxford years Murdoch had several love affairs, notably with the Czech poet Franz Steiner and later his friend Elias Canetti who was much older than herself. When she married, however, in 1956, it was to the critic and novelist John Bayley. It was not an entirely conventional marriage, but it lasted.

Bayley and Murdoch bought an old farmhouse in the village of Steeple Aston, 14 miles from Oxford, and lived there until 1985, when they returned to Oxford. The house was cold and damp and always untidy, but there was a heated pool in a greenhouse where they both loved to swim. In 1997, two years after publishing her last novel, *Jackson's Dilemma*, Murdoch was diagnosed with Alzheimer's disease and the last years of her life saw her decline into what Bayley called 'a very nice three-year-old'. He continued to look after her until her death in February 1999. At Murdoch's request, there was no funeral and no memorial service.

Murdoch is remembered as a novelist of great substance and distinction, but her first book, *Sartre, Romantic Rationalist* (1953), was a work of philosophy on the French Existentialist Jean-Paul Sartre, whom she had met in Paris. Sartre was an early influence on Murdoch, but she later considered him 'dangerous' because he diminished the individual's inner life and its ability to love 'the other'.

Under The Net (1954), Murdoch's first novel, has an Existentialist hero, Jake Donaghue, an Irish Londoner and struggling writer, whose mentor is Hugo Belfounder, a character based on a pupil of Wittgenstein's. The novel is the first of six Murdoch wrote in the first-person, with a male narrator. As in most of her novels, some of the characters are based on people she knew. She was at once hailed as a writer with a brilliant talent and a flair for fast-paced comedy.

The Bell (1958), Murdoch's fourth novel, is one of her most successful. It concerns an Anglican religious community based on one known to her. The community members are seeking to hang a replacement bell in an abbey tower. In spite of tragic events, including the loss of the bell, the novel is also a comedy and most of the characters survive and even find an inner strength. Like *The Time of The Angels* (1966), *The Bell* has a partly, but not exclusively, religious theme. Anything that influenced the human personality interested and fascinated Murdoch.

Her interest in psychoanalytical theories of the unconscious is apparent in *A Severed Head* (1961), one of Murdoch's own favourites. The novel deals with the theories of Jung and Freud, particularly Jung's theory of archetypes and Freud's ideas about male sexuality and the fear of castration. The book was adapted into a successful play and later a film.

Murdoch was also deeply concerned with the Irish problems of her own time and set her novel *The Red and the Green* (1965) on the eve of the Easter Rising of 1916. As always, the story and characters are strong and well defined. Characters in Murdoch's later novels sometimes take on the power and significance of mythical beings, but even so, they are often based on her friends, as was the case in *The Time of The Angels* (1966) and *The Black Prince* (1973).

Philosophical questions of good and evil occur in many of the novels but are not always resolved. Readers of a Murdoch novel are encouraged to give their own answers to the moral questions she poses. Complexities of plot challenge the reader too, and one is always forced to engage with Murdoch's own intellect when reading her fiction. Her inventiveness overflowed with wit, however, and all her books have scenes of comedy or even farce.

Murdoch always planned her novels carefully before she started writing, but she did not find the writing process easy. She wrote and rewrote until she was satisfied, then having reached that stage, she would never allow a word to be changed. She was a writer fully in command of her material and her books were widely acclaimed in her own lifetime. *The Sacred and Profound Love Machine* won the Whitbread Prize in 1974 and she was awarded the Booker Prize for her 19th novel, *The Sea, the Sea* (1978). She was given a CBE in 1976 and a DBE in 1987.

To Murdoch, the novel was the tool of

truth and a guide to moral behaviour. Her lasting achievement is that her novels, though firmly in the mainstream of English literary narrative, have continued to be read and enjoyed and, by their powerful example, to exert an influence on later novelists.

Selected works:

Sartre (1953); *Under The Net* (1954); *The Flight From The Enchanter* (1956); *The Sandcastle* (1957); *The Bell* (1958); *A Severed Head* (1961); *The Unofficial Rose* (1962); *The Unicorn* (1963); *The Italian Girl* (1964); *The Red and the Green* (1965); *The Time of the Angels* (1966); *Under The Net* (1966); *The Sovereignty Of Good And Other Concepts* (1967); *The Nice And The Good* (1968); *Bruno's Dream* (1969); *The Sovereignty Of Good* (1970); *A Fairly Honourable Defeat* (1970); *An Accidental Man* (1971); *The Servants And The Snow* (1973); *The Black Prince* (1973); *The Sacred And Profane Love Machine* (1974); *A Word Child* (1975); *Henry And Cato* (1976); *The Fire And The Sun: Why Plato Banished The Artist* (1977); *The Sea, The Sea* (1978); *A Year Of Birds* (1978); *Art And Eros* (1980); *Nuns And Soldiers* (1980); *Reynolds Stone* (1981); *The Philosopher's Pupil* (1983); *The Good Apprentice* (1985); *Acastos: Two Platonic Dialogues* (1986); *The Book And The Brotherhood* (1987); *Above The Gods* (1987); *The Black Prince* (1989); *The Message To The Planet* (1989); *The Existentialist Political Myth* (1989); *Metaphysics As A Guide To Morals* (1992); *The Green Knight* (1993); *Jackson's Dilemma* (1995); *Existentialists And Mystics. Writings On Philosophy and Literature* (1997, Ed. Peter Conradi).

Further reading

Byatt, A. S., *Degrees of Freedom: The Early Novels of Iris Murdoch*. Vintage, 1994.

Conradi, Peter J., *Iris Murdoch: a Life: The Authorized Biography*. HarperCollins, 2002.

Conradi, Peter J., *Iris Murdoch: the Saint and the Artist (Studies in Twentieth-century Literature)*. Palgrave Macmillan, 1988.

Contributors: Margaret Tarner, Ian Mackean

NABOKOV, VLADIMIR (1899–1977)

I am thinking of aurochs and angels, the secret of durable pigments, prophetic sonnets, the refuge of art. And this is the only immortality you and I may share, my Lolita.[1]

Russian-born American novelist Vladimir Nabokov, best known for his controversial novel *Lolita* (1955), was awarded the American National Medal for Literature in 1973. Throughout his literary career critics have acclaimed his magnificent command of English – which for him was a second language – his resourceful narrative skill and his inventive experimentation with the novel form.

Vladimir Vladimirovich Nabokov was born in St Petersburg, Russia, the eldest son of an eminent and wealthy family. His father, a member of the Russian Constituent Assembly, moved the family to exile in 1919 following the Bolshevik Revolution (1917) and just before the White Army's defeat in the Crimea in 1920. The family first moved to London and then to Berlin, where Nabokov rejoined them in 1922 after the completion of his studies in modern languages at Trinity College, Cambridge.

Nabokov spent the period between 1923 and 1940 in Berlin and Paris, marrying his partner, Vera Slonim, in 1925. During these years he published a number of poems, short stories and novels in Russian under the pseudonym of V. Sirin, establishing a reputation as a leading Russian *émigré* writer. Works from this period include *Korol, Dama, Valet* (1928), published in English as *King, Queen, Knave* (1968); *Zashchita Luzhina* (1930), translated into English as *The Defence* (1964); *Soglyadatai* (1930), whose English title is *The Eye* (1966); *Kamera Obskura* (1932–33), published in English as *Laughter in the Dark* (1963); *Priglashenie na Kazn* (1938), which in English reads as *Invitation to a Beheading* (1959); and

Dar (1937–38), published in America as *The Gift* (1963).

In 1940 Nabokov emigrated to America with his wife and their son Dimitri and settled in Boston. He took a post as a lecturer in Russian Literature at Wellesley College, where he taught from 1941 to 1948, and later became Professor of Russian Literature at Cornell University, where he remained until his retirement from teaching in 1959. He became an American citizen in 1945.

In 1941 Nabokov published his first novel in English, *The Real Life of Sebastian Knight*, which, through a fictitious but plausible biography, deals with issues of identity. Its narrator is a young Russian in Paris. Through the writing of a biography, he attempts to reconstruct the life and trace the origins of his half-brother, Sebastian Knight, an uprooted Russian writer. The novel explores Knight's narrative techniques and his struggle to bridge the semiotic and intellectual gap between his native and adopted languages. His second novel, *Bend Sinister* (1947), tells the story of a politically uncommitted professor who tries to retain his integrity in a totalitarian state. The theme is overtly political, but the book's strength is in its ingenious wordplay and concealed puns.

In his first memoir, *Conclusive Evidence* (1951), Nabokov attempted to outline his life in Russia before the revolution. A revised and expanded edition was published in 1966 as *Speak, Memory: An Autobiography Revisited*. The book offers a sketch, rather than an accurate account, of his family history and perceptive insights into his major works, such as *Lolita*, *Pnin* and *The Gift*.

Worldwide success came in 1958 with the publication of *Lolita*, a novel which centres around literature professor Humbert Humbert's obsession with the 12-year-old nymphet Lolita – who symbolises fleeting eroticism and desire – and their journey across America. Although this novel was initially regarded as scandalous because of its paedophiliac subject matter, its remarkable sensibility and evocative style exemplify Nabokov's descriptive skill and playfulness in a language that was never his own. The complex fictional realities he constructs through language are continually challenged by the intense yearnings and personality twinnings of his characters, which subtly highlight the intertwining of 'reality' and language itself.

Nabokov comments on his personal engagement with language in his essay 'On a Book Entitled Lolita' (1956):[2]

> My private tragedy, which cannot, and should not, be anybody's concern, is that I had to abandon my natural idiom, my untrammelled, rich, and infinitely docile Russian tongue for a second-rate brand of English, devoid of any of those apparatuses – the baffling mirror, the black velvet backdrop, the implied associations and traditions – which the native illusionist, frac-tails flying, can magically use to transcend the heritage in his own way.

While also working on a translation of Aleksandr Pushkin's novel in verse *Eugene Onegin*, which appeared in 1964 in four volumes, Nabokov published three more novels. *Pnin* (1957) tells the story of a professor of Russian in an American college who is trying to deliver a lecture in a language he cannot master. *Pale Fire* (1962) is a labyrinthine narrative comprising a number of intersecting imaginative and seemingly factual narratives, exemplifying Nabokov's wit and mastery when constructing narrative landscapes. The novel is a satirical fantasy whose subject is an unfinished poem of 999 lines of heroic couplets composed by John Shade under the instruction of Charles Kinbote. The plot is further complicated when Kinbote, after killing Shade, steals the manuscript and sets out to produce his own elaborate commentary. In 1969 Nabokov published the philosophical novel *Ada, or Ardor: A Family Chronicle*. The story is set in an imaginary country and deals with a long incestuous love affair, which metaphorically applies to the art of novel writing itself. The novel contains an appendix provided by the author under the anagrammatic pseudonym Vivian Darkbloom.

Nabokov's short stories were published in two collections, *Dozen* (1958) and *Quartet* (1966). The text of his novella *The Enchanter*, which was thought to be lost for 30 years, was rediscovered and published in 1987. Its narrative, revolving around the theme of male infatuation, appears to be linked with *Lolita*.

Nabokov died in Montreux in Switzerland in 1977. His son Dimitri undertook the translation of most of his father's Russian works into English.

Selected works:

The Real Life of Sebastian Knight (1941); *Bend Sinister* (1947); *Conclusive Evidence* (1951); *Lolita* (France, 1955; USA, 1958); *Pnin* (1957); *Dozen* (1958); *Invitation to a Beheading* (Russia, 1938; USA, 1959); *Pale Fire* (1962); *The Gift* (Russia, 1937; USA, 1963); *Laughter in the Dark* (Germany, 1932; Britain, 1963); *The Defence* (Germany, 1930; USA, 1964); *The Eye* (Russia, 1930; Britain, 1966); *Quartet* (1966); *Speak, Memory* (1966); *King, Queen, Knave* (Russia, 1928; Britain, 1968); *Ada, or Ardor: A Family Chronicle* (1969); *The Enchanter* (1987).

References

1. Nabokov, Vladimir (1995) *Lolita* [1959]. Harmondsworth: Penguin Books (closing lines).

2. Ibid. pp. 316–317.

Further reading

Connolly, Julian W. (ed.) *Nabokov and His Fiction: New Perspectives.* Cambridge University Press, 1999.

Shrayer, Maxim, *The World of Nabokov's Stories.* University of Texas Press, 2000.

Contributor: Tatiani Rapatzikou

NAIPAUL, SIR V. S. (1932–)

Home was hardly a place I could return to. Home was something in my head. It was something I had lost.

A Bend in the River

Vidiadhar Surajprasad Naipaul, winner of the 2001 Nobel Prize for Literature, was born in Chaguanas, a small town in Trinidad. His grandfather, an Indian Brahmin, had emigrated to Trinidad to work on a plantation as an indentured labourer. His father, Seepersad Naipaul, was a journalist and a correspondent for the *Trinidad Guardian* and his literary aspirations were mirrored in his son. In 1938 the family moved to Port-of-Spain,

the capital of Trinidad, where Naipaul attended Queen's Royal College until, at the age of 18, he received a scholarship to University College, Oxford. There he met his future wife, Patricia Hale, whom he married in 1966. After graduation he started work as a freelance journalist and began to write novels. He worked as a broadcaster for the BBC's *Caribbean Voices* from 1954 to 1956, and reviewed fiction for *The New Statesman* from 1957 to 1961. He was knighted in 1989.

Naipaul's first novel, *The Mystic Masseur* (1957), was awarded the *Mail on Sunday*/John Llewellyn Rhys Prize in 1958 and filmed with a screenplay by Caryl Phillips in 2001. The novel describes changes in Trinidadian society through the life of the protagonist, Ganesh Ramsumair. Starting his career as a masseur, then becoming a mystic, and eventually receiving a knighthood from the British government, he earns respect in both Eastern and Western cultures. He is also representative of an Indian in the Caribbean in that he learns about Western culture through books, and becomes more conscious of his inner Eastern culture as he becomes involved in Western capitalistic society. The novel's portrayal of the ambivalence of Indian immigrants to the West Indies, caught between West and East, is characteristic of Naipaul's early work.

In 1958 Naipaul published *The Suffrage of Elvira* and in 1959, *Miguel Street*, both presenting satirical views of life in the Caribbean. *Miguel Street,* a collection of short stories which won a Somerset Maugham Award, presents lively sketches of the inhabitants of Miguel Street, such as Bogart, whose name is taken from the film *Casablanca*, and B. Wordsworth, who sells his poetry. The story is narrated by a boy who grows up in the street and, as did Naipaul, goes abroad to study.

In 1961 Naipaul published *A House for Mr Biswas*, considered by many to be his masterpiece. It tells the tragicomic story of Mohun Biswas, an Indian immigrant to Trinidad. After struggling at various jobs, Biswas manages to become a journalist, although his real ambition is to be a novelist. He marries the daughter of the rich Tulsi family, but the marriage brings him into conflict with Indian immigrant society. He wishes to be free of the intricate family relationships and wants his own house. For him, the house symbolises his independence and the assertion of his own identity. He dies soon after the realisation of his dream.

Since arriving to take his place at Oxford, Naipaul has continued to live in England, but has travelled extensively and published travel writing. In 1962, *The Middle Passage*, his first non-fiction work, was published, after a journey to the Caribbean, funded by a grant from the Trinidad government. It describes his first revisiting of the West Indies and its examination of racial conflicts caused some hostile reactions, some black West Indians labelling him as 'racist'.

In the 1960s and 1970s Naipaul travelled in India, South America, Africa, Iran, Pakistan, Malaysia and the USA, his experiences being crystallised in works such as *In a Free State* (1971), *India. A Wounded Civilization* (1977), *A Bend in the River* (1979) and *Among the Believers: An Islamic Journey* (1981). *In a Free State*, structured as a prologue, three stories and an epilogue, depicts the lives of individuals living in turmoil after decolonisation. The first story, 'Out of Many', describes the plight of an Indian who arrives in Washington from Bombay. The second, 'Tell Me Who to Kill', depicts the struggle of a Caribbean immigrant in London. The third, 'A Free State', is about a couple who live in a newly independent state in Africa and demonstrates Naipaul's critical view of a 'Third World' state where freedom is guaranteed but society is in chaos.

From the 1960s to the 1980s Naipaul focused mainly on non-fiction, but among his few fictional works, *The Enigma of Arrival* (1987) has emerged as one of his finest books. Its narrator is indistinguishable from the author, describing Naipaul's experience of studying in London, living in Wiltshire, his neighbours and the landscape around Salisbury. It reveals how he freed himself from the memory of Trinidad and came to find his true self by identifying with English culture. It is an examination of the narrator's cultural roots, while also being a story of change and death.

Further non-fictional works followed, such as *India: A Million Mutinies Now* (1990), *Beyond Belief: Islamic Excursions* (1998) and *Letters Between Father and Son* (1999). He also wrote an autobiographical novel, *A Way in the World* (1994), which depicts a fictional history of colonialism, presenting stories from the time of Sir Walter Raleigh to the nineteenth-century revolutionary Francisco Miranda.

In *Reading and Writing* (2000) Naipaul continued in the intimate semi-autobiographical mode. The book comprises two autobiographical essays, 'Reading and Writing' and 'The Writer and India'. 'Reading and Writing' tells of how he started as a writer and found the themes which were important to him. He remembers his determination to be a writer at the age of 11, even though he was not good at composition. With his father's help, he came to know the pleasure of reading Shakespeare, Dickens, Conrad and Maugham. But the joy was dampened by the reality of his ethnic roots and his life in the Asian society of the Caribbean. 'The Writer and India' describes the inertia and chaos in India and also reveals his views on literature and his literary roots.

Selected works:

The Mystic Masseur (1957); *The Suffrage of Elvira* (1958); *Miguel Street* (1959); *A House for Mr Biswas* (1961); *The Middle Passage* (1962); *Mr Stone and the Knights Companion* (1963); *An Area of Darkness* (1964); *The Mimic Men* (1967); *A Flag on the Island* (1967); *The Loss of El Dorado* (1969); *In a Free State* (1971); *The Overcrowded Barracoon* (1972); *Guerrillas* (1975); *India: A Wounded Civilisation* (1977); *A Bend in the River* (1979); *The Return of Eva Peron with the Killings in Trinidad* (1980); *Among the Believers: An Islamic Journey* (1981); *Finding the Centre* (1984); *The Enigma of Arrival* (1987); *A Turn in the South* (1989); *India: A Million Mutinies Now* (1990); *Beyond Belief* (1998); *Reading and Writing* (2000); *Half a Life* (2001); *Magic Seeds* (2004).

Further reading

Khan, Akhtar Jamal, *V. S. Naipaul: a critical study*. New Delhi: Creative Books, 1998.

King, Bruce, *V. S. Naipaul*. Basingstoke: Macmillan, 1993.

Levy, Judith, *V. S. Naipaul: displacement and autobiography*. New York: Garland, 1995.

Contributors: Midori Saito, Ian Mackean

**NARAYAN, R. K.
(1906–2001)**

*This education has
reduced us to a nation of
morons; we were strangers
to our own culture and camp followers of
another culture, feeding on leavings and
garbage . . . What about our own roots?*
                                    The English Teacher

Photo credit: © PA Photos-EPA

Rasipuram Krishnaswami Narayan was one of
India's most accomplished and best-known
writers in English. He was born in Madras, on
the eastern coast of South India, the son of a
school headmaster. After completing his education he worked briefly as a teacher before
devoting his time to writing. His first novel,
Swami and Friends, was published in 1935, and
like most of Narayan's stories is set in a fictitious southern Indian town called Malgudi.
Many novels and volumes of short stories followed, and he also published modernised
versions of two classics of Indian literature, *The
Ramayana* (1972) and *The Mahabharata* (1978).

Narayan's output straddles the period
before and after Indian independence.
India's colonial status under the British cannot be said to have been a major theme in his
writing, but it is a theme which is relevant to
one of his finest and best-known novels, *The
English Teacher*, which was published in
1945, two years before India was granted
independence.

The title, *The English Teacher,* is pertinent,
indicating the role in Indian culture which
Krishnan, the central character, has when the
story opens – a role which, at the end of the
novel, he decides to reject. We first see him
teaching English literature, passing on the
culture of the British colonisers to a new generation, in the same place where he was
taught it himself. During the course of the
novel he drifts away from this regimented
transmission of a foreign culture and eventually resigns from his post, starts a new job at a
nursery school and learns to communicate
psychically with his dead wife. In the final
chapter, as he composes his resignation letter,
we see how much he has come to resent the
system of which he had been a part:

This education has reduced us to a nation
of morons; we were strangers to our own
culture and camp followers of another
culture, feeding on leavings and garbage
. . . What about our own roots? (Ch. 8,
pp. 467–468)

Krishnan's change comes about as a result of
his responses to a series of challenging circumstances which arise once he begins to
take steps away from the cloistered environment of his school, and in the course of his
emotional and intellectual journey a number
of themes seem to be being worked out, these
being his progress, from predictability to
unpredictability; the academic world to the
real world of life and death; adulthood to
childhood; and a Western outlook to an
Eastern outlook.

Krishnan is roused from his predictable
life by the news that his wife and child, both of
whom are to be sources of spontaneity and
unpredictability throughout the novel, are
coming to join him. He has to move out of his
lodgings at the school and find a house for
them and this marks the first step of what
becomes a journey into the real world of
ordinary people leading ordinary lives.

Susila, his wife, brings unpredictability
into his life at every turn, but he does not
adjust to this new influence without a
struggle, as is seen in the episode where she
gets rid of his predictably unpredictable alarm
clock. He had kept the clock, which was liable
to set off its alarm at arbitrary times of day and
night, on his desk for years, although he
stifled it with a literary tome whenever it
sounded its alarm. He seems to have cher-
ished it for its unpredictability, even though
that unpredictability was inappropriate and
ineffective, and when his wife disposes of it
this causes a row which drags on for several
days. The jarring episode marks his transition
from a world dominated by predictability to a
world dominated by unpredictability, and
from that point on he has to start living day
to day on the understanding that there is a
limit to what can be achieved through any
system which is ordered, predictable and
knowable.

The turning point of the plot arises from
Susila's unpredictability, when while visiting a
prospective new house, she goes for a walk on
her own, gets stuck in a contaminated lavatory

and contracts typhoid. The futility of clinging to the belief that life can be predictable is further illustrated by two central, and symmetrical, predictions which occupy prominent places in the novel. The first is the doctor's assertion that typhoid 'is the one fever which goes strictly by its own rules. It follows a time-table' (Ch. 3, p. 366) and that Susila will be well in a few weeks. But in spite of his further assurances that her attack is 'absolutely normal course. No complications. A perfect typhoid run' (Ch. 3, p. 369), Susila dies. The second is the headmaster's belief in a prediction made by an astrologer, 'who can see past present and future as one, and give everything its true value' (Ch. 7, p. 450) that he (the headmaster) will die on a given date. But although the headmaster has previously found that his 'life has gone precisely as he predicted' (Ch. 7, p. 450), when the appointed day arrives, he lives.

The scientifically based prediction of life is thwarted by death and the mystical prediction of death is thwarted by life. The implication is that any view of life, whether deriving from modern Western science or ancient Eastern mysticism, which disregards the unknowable is hopelessly inadequate.

While these events fail to provide Krishnan with anything rational to believe in, they do bring him face to face with the reality of life and death, and confronting the realities of life without retreating into the safe cerebral world of literature and philosophy is an important component of his journey. In an outburst with one of his students Krishnan says of literature:

Don't worry so much about these things – they are trash, we are obliged to go through and pretend we like them, but all the time the problem of living and dying is crushing us. (Ch. 7, p. 438)

In coming to terms with the death of his wife, literature and philosophy are no use to him. They are illusions, and the journey he is on involves leaving illusions behind.

Living without illusions seemed to be the greatest task for me in life now . . . humanity, nurtured in illusions from beginning to end! The twists and turns of fate would cease to shock us if we knew, and expected nothing more than, the barest truths and facts of life. (Ch. 4, p. 387)

Krishnan calls the truth he has to come to terms with 'the law of life'.

The law of life can't be avoided. The law comes into operation the moment we detach ourselves from our mother's womb. All struggle and misery in life is due to our attempt to arrest this law or get away from it (Ch. 7, p. 465)

Children are very much in evidence throughout *The English Teacher* and his daughter, Leela, and the children at her nursery school become guides for Krishnan on his journey. The young children are important because they are spontaneous and natural; they have not yet had their creative energy stifled by the educational system.

The headmaster of Leela's school is a champion of childhood, having devoted his life to children since receiving the prediction that he would die, and believes children are 'angels' (Ch. 6, p. 434), 'the real gods on earth' (Ch. 6, p. 423) and employs what he calls 'The Leave Alone System' in his school.

The Leave Alone System, which will make them wholesome human beings, and also help us, those who work along with them, to work off the curse of adulthood. (Ch. 6, p. 436)

Krishnan is drawn towards the headmaster's views, which are reinforced by his wife's psychic communication that children are more in tune with the psychic side of life than adults, and at the climax of the novel he decides to work with the headmaster in his nursery school.

Another component of Krishnan's journey is that he encounters the coexistence of Western and native cultural attitudes and the attitudes of Indians of younger and older generations. When Susila is ill she is treated both by a doctor who practises Western scientific medicine and by a Swamiji who uses mystical methods of healing. The Swamiji is summoned by Susila's mother who believes the 'Evil Eye' (Ch. 3, p. 372) has fallen on her daughter, and it is notable that Krishnan feels 'ashamed' (Ch. 3, p. 373) when the doctor finds the Swamiji in the house, showing that he is alienated from, and embarrassed by, the native culture of the older generation of his own country.

Other references to the juxtaposition of British and native cultures arise in the novel. The street where the headmaster lives, with its poor sanitation, where 'unkempt and wild-looking children rolled about in the dust' (Ch. 6, p. 431), is named Anderson Street and Anderson may have been 'some gentleman of the East India Company's days!' (Ch. 6, p. 431).

The final stage of Krishnan's journey takes him further from the outlook inherited from the British and towards native Indian spiritual practices. To reach his goal of 'a harmonious existence' (Ch. 8, p. 467) he takes up his deceased wife's psychically communicated challenge to develop his mind sufficiently to communicate with her psychically. Although initially he had been bemused by his wife's devotional practices, mocking her with 'Oh! Becoming a yogi!' (Ch. 2, p. 325), he now relies on her to guide him, from the afterlife, in his 'self-development'.

This self-development consists of Zen-like meditation in which, for a certain amount of time each day, he empties his mind. His motive is to reach closer psychic communication with his wife, but he also experiences a general improvement in his state of mind.

> It was a perpetual excitement, ever promising some new riches in the realm of experience and understanding . . . There was a real cheerfulness growing within me, memory hurt less. (Ch. 7, p. 457)

Compare this to the boredom and spiritual deadness he had come to find in Western literature and philosophy and we see how he has found something truly enriching in his native culture. The simple message of 'belief' which his wife offers as the key to his progress also shows how inadequate the Western approach, with its 'classifying, labelling, departmentalising' (Ch. 8, p. 468), was for his real needs:

> 'Belief, belief.' Above reason, scepticism,

and even immediate failures, I clung to it. (Ch. 7, p. 457)

Having thrown off the cultural inheritance from the West and decided to 'withdraw from the adult world and adult work into the world of children' (Ch. 8, p. 472), Krishnan is free to take a further step in his traditional Indian self-development and reach a state in which 'one's mind became clean and bare and a mere chamber of fragrance' (Ch. 8, p. 473). He finally learns to experience at the psychic level and when his wife appears before him he reaches

> a moment of rare, immutable joy – a moment for which one feels grateful to Life and Death. (Ch. 8, p. 474)

Krishnan's outcry at the time of his resignation, 'What about our own roots?', could apply to all of us as adults, alienated from our roots in childhood, to modern Indians, alienated from their native cultural roots, and to humanity as a whole, in that we have become rational human beings, alienated from our roots in the unknown.

Reference

Quotes taken from Narayan, R. K., *The English Teacher*, in *A Malgudi Omnibus*. London: Vintage, Random House, 1999. (*The English Teacher* was first published in England by Eyre and Spottiswoode, 1945.)

Selected works:
Swami and Friends (1935); *The Bachelor of Arts* (1937); *The Dark Room* (1938); *The English Teacher* (1945); *Mr. Sampath: The Printer of Malgudi* (1949); *The Financial Expert* (1952); *Waiting for the Mahatma* (1955); *The Guide* (1958); *The Vendor of Sweets* (1967); *The Ramayana* (1972); *My Days* (1973); *The Painter of Signs* (1977); *The Mahabharata* (1978); *Malgudi Days* (1982); *My Dateless Diary: An American Journey* (1988).

Further reading

Kain, Geoffrey R., *R. K. Narayan*. Michigan State University Press, 1993.

Contributor: Ian Mackean

O

O'CONNOR, FLANNERY (1925–64)

I see from the standpoint of Christian orthodoxy. This means that for me the meaning of life is centered in our Redemption by Christ and that what I see in the world I see in relation to that. I don't think that this is a position that can be taken halfway or one that is particularly easy in these times to make transparent in fiction.[1]

Flannery O'Connor's fiction centres around grotesque and violent people who suddenly confront grace. She creates bizarre characters and circumstances to illustrate her theme of redemption, showing that even those who seem unworthy can experience moments of revelation. Being variously classified as a Southern **Gothic** and a Christian humanist writer, O'Connor combines her Southern heritage with her deeply religious background to create fiction that is satiric, enigmatic and memorable. To explain her shocking stories she once wrote that 'to the hard of hearing you shout and for the almost blind you draw large and startling figures'.[2] Her large and startling figures illustrate traditional religious topics in unique and challenging ways.

O'Connor's work won much critical acclaim during and after her life. She received many fellowships including the *Kenyon Review* fellowship, the National Institute of Arts and Letters grant and the Ford Foundation grant. Her writing was awarded the O. Henry Award for Short Fiction six times, and her *Collected Short Stories* won the National Book Award in 1972, eight years after her death.

Mary Flannery O'Connor was born in Savannah, Georgia, in 1925, to Edward Francis and Regina (Cline) O'Connor and as an only child was doted on by her parents. The juxtaposition of her Catholic family with her Baptist environment shaped the religious position that coloured all her fiction. She attended Georgia State College for Women, where she excelled as a cartoonist for the school paper. She began to publish fiction shortly after entering college and later attended the Iowa Writers' Workshop. After a few years of living in Connecticut, then writing in New York's Yaddo artists' colony, she became very ill with lupus, the disease that killed her father when she was 16, and returned to Georgia where she was cared for by her mother for the rest of her life. During her final years, she corresponded with many writers, including Richard Stern, John Hawkes, **Katherine Ann Porter** and Caroline Gordon. She was an avid reader of literature and religious philosophy, enjoying authors such as Henry James and the Jesuit theologian and paleontologist, Teilhard de Chardin. She continued to publish and speak publicly until her death in 1964.

The bizarre people in O'Connor's first novel, *Wise Blood* (1952), exemplify the kinds of character she created throughout her career. Hazel Motes, the son of a preacher, spends his time avoiding Jesus and preaching the Church Without Christ. He ends up killing a hired prophet, blinding himself with lime and using various forms of self-punishment until he is killed by a police officer. Enoch Emery is an 18-year-old boy who listens to his 'wise blood' that tells him to steal a museum exhibit, a shrunken man, in order to offer it to Hazel Motes as the new Jesus for the Church Without Christ. He eventually steals a gorilla costume and roams the streets wearing it. Asa Hawks is an evangelist of the Free Church of Christ who pretends to blind himself in a show of piety. He encourages Hazel Motes to take advantage of his daughter so that he can abandon her to Motes. Such characters are social misfits, yet through their diverse experiences O'Connor addresses issues of doubt and faith and the spiritual question of individual calling.

Because O'Connor was so adamant that her work was primarily religious, and because her fiction addresses the spiritual questions of Modernity, critics continually explore the religious themes of her work. In contrast to the contrived literary Christ figures that characterised professedly religious fiction of the time, O'Connor's characters are misanthropes, criminals and hypocrites, jaded and often violent. She explores holiness by delving into the profane and the demonic, the current of her stories always pushing towards a stark realisation of the need for redemption. She raises questions of belief and **existentialism** which have caused critics to compare her to such authors as Fyodor Dostoyevsky, Herman Melville, Albert Camus, Franz Kafka and **William Faulkner** – authors who attempt to find eternal significance within extreme experiences of the human psyche.

The short stories 'Good Country People' and 'A Good Man is Hard to Find', published in the collection *A Good Man is Hard to Find* (1957), have attracted much critical attention. 'Good Country People' is the story of Hulga, an educated, atheistic woman who has her wooden leg stolen by a Bible salesman when she attempts to seduce him. The ridiculousness of the situation satirises the worldwide spiritual crippling resulting from philosophical pursuits that do not account for faith. The story ends when the Bible salesman, who turns out to be a scam artist who travels the country stealing false appendages, tells Hulga, 'You ain't so smart. I been believing in nothing ever since I was born!' O'Connor here exposes the way both a PhD in philosophy and a life of selling Bibles can lead to loss of faith. And yet there is a sense in which Hulga finds grace, in that having been stripped of her physical crutch, she is left to face her spiritual handicap.

'A Good Man is Hard to Find' has a similar moment of grace when a selfish, smug, nagging grandmother runs into a psychopathic killer called The Misfit. In the face of death, she suddenly becomes pious and kind. She also begins to question the Christianity to which she has subscribed all her life. When The Misfit asserts that Jesus had 'thrown everything off balance' by raising the dead, the grandmother fearfully says, 'Maybe He didn't raise the dead.' This essential question of Christianity is something she has never thought about until the moment of her death. Her religion was a prideful, cultural construct. But she too receives a moment of grace articulated by The Misfit himself: 'She would have been a good woman if [there] had been somebody there to shoot her every minute of her life.' Through the many misfits in her stories, O'Connor brings to light both the futility of uncritical religious subscription and the redemptive power of a genuine recognition of humanity's need for grace.

References

1. **O'Connor, Flannery** (1969) *Mystery and Manners: Occasional Prose.* Edited by Sally Fitzgerald and Robert Fitzgerald. Farrar, Straus.

2. Ibid.

Selected works:

Wise Blood, novel (1952); *A Good Man is Hard to Find,* collection of stories containing 'A Good Man is Hard to Find', 'The River', 'The Life You Save May Be Your Own', A Stroke of Good Fortune', 'A Temple of the Holy Ghost', 'The Artificial Nigger', 'A Circle in the Fire', 'A Late Encounter with the Enemy', 'Good Country People' and 'The Displaced Person' (1957); *The Violent Bear It Away,* novel (1960); *Everything That Rises Must Converge,* collection of stories containing 'Everything That Rises Must Converge', 'Greenleaf', 'A View of the Woods', 'The Enduring Chill', 'The Comforts of Home', 'The Lame Shall Enter First', 'Revelation', 'Parker's Back' and 'Judgment Day' (1965); *Mystery and Manners: Occasional Prose* (1969); *The Habit of Being: Letters* (1979).

Further reading

Cash, Jean W., *Flannery O'Connor.* University of Tennessee Press, 2002.

Contributor: Amy Glauser Bankhead

ORWELL, GEORGE (1903–50)

The Ministry of Truth – Minitrue, in Newspeak – was startlingly different from any other object in sight. It was an enormous pyramidal structure of glittering white concrete, soaring up, terrace after terrace, 300 metres into the air. From where Winston stood it was just possible to read, picked out on its white face in elegant lettering, the three slogans of the Party:

WAR IS PEACE
FREEDOM IS SLAVERY
IGNORANCE IS STRENGTH
                      Nineteen Eighty-four

Photo credit: © Rex Everitt Archive

Few writers have been so straightforward yet so controversial as Eric Arthur Blair, who took the pen-name George Orwell in order not to embarrass his parents on the publication of *Down and Out in Paris and London* (1933). Orwell was a great thinker, whose writing has influenced our understanding of twentieth-century politics. He was outspoken in his opinions, sometimes to the point of rudeness, yet those who knew him considered him to be a genteel man. His use of English is impeccable in its transparency, with the result that his writings are a pleasure to read.

Orwell was straightforward yet controversial in that he held firm to his belief in the value of individuality and humanity, even when his views brought him into conflict with those on the political left or right. He refused to adapt his views to fit political doctrines and although generally socialist in outlook he never joined a political party; to have done so he would have considered restraining, and he was not to be restrained. He preferred to offer his readers the truth as he saw it, even though most of his early writing was rejected because of publishers' reservations about its political content. For example, **T. S. Eliot** rejected *Animal Farm* in 1944 when Orwell offered it to Faber and Faber.

Orwell was born in the Indian city of Motahari in 1903, the son of Richard and Ida Mabel Blair, both civil servants. After an undistinguished academic career in England, he joined the Indian Civil Police in Burma, during which time he acquired an aversion to colonialism, which he expressed in *Burmese Days* (1934) and in essays such as 'Shooting an Elephant' and 'A Hanging'.

Returning to Europe in 1927 Orwell went to Paris, initially intending to make his living as a teacher and a writer. Instead he voluntarily spent 18 months struggling at subsistence level in the streets, observing the appalling circumstances of the poor and destitute. He wrote about this experience in the first of his books to be published, the autobiographical *Down and Out in Paris and London*.

Orwell's book *Homage To Catalonia* (1938) drew on his experience in Spain in 1937, where he reported on the Spanish Civil War and was shot in the neck while fighting against the Fascists. It was during this period that he saw through the pettiness of totalitarian regimes. Orwell was a communist in the literal sense of the word. To him Communism should involve the commune of man, each bearing his own burden, the sharing of

responsibilities and the fair distribution of wealth. He expressed this in the political satire *Animal Farm* (1945), which was misunderstood by both the Capitalist and Communist worlds, being acclaimed in America and forbidden in the Soviet Union.

Some of Orwell's books, such as *Burmese Days* and *The Road to Wigan Pier* (1937) – about unemployment in the north of England at the height of the economic depression – and *Animal Farm*, were not accepted wholeheartedly by the literary establishment. As a result his writing did not make him financially independent; he still had to work to pay his bills. His best-known novel, *Nineteen Eighty-four* (1949), could have brought him a degree of wealth, but by then he was too ill with tuberculosis to enjoy the financial gain and he died shortly after its publication, at the age of 46.

In 1949, the year 1984 was sufficiently remote for Orwell to project onto it his fears for the continued existence of free man in a free society. *Nineteen Eighty-four* shows his **dystopian** vision of a world in which propaganda has come to dominate man's thought and permeate every aspect of his life to the extent that free will has become subordinate to the dictates of the state.

The central character, Winston Smith, tries to keep himself aloof from the oppressive control of the state, determined to retain his individuality rather than conform to the behaviour expected of a model citizen. He wishes to have a place of his own in which he can be himself, unobserved by Big Brother's ever-alert watchdogs, and he sustains his sense of individuality by keeping a diary.

Whether or not 'Big Brother' exists in reality is beside the point; he exists as an idea in the mind of the authorities and the people, a symbol of repression to Winston and an object of love and reverence to those who have adapted to the state's notion of what is acceptable. The citizen of Airstrip One (Britain) must love Big Brother and if he doesn't, he is doomed.

The novel can be seen as a thriller in which the good guy suffers the fate of the bad guy; a world turned upside down. As does the bad guy in most thrillers, Winston believes himself to be successful for a while. He embarks upon a forbidden relationship with Julia, who has rebellious attitudes similar to his own, and believes that they can become part of the resistance movement, having contacted its leader, O'Brien.

His hopes are dashed when he is betrayed by this very O'Brien whom he thought to be his ally. Then follow some of the most horrific torture scenes ever described in prose fiction, ending in the ultimate betrayal. Winston's mind and body are broken and he wishes that the thing he fears most should be done to Julia. He now loves Big Brother, and he doesn't just say so in order to be rid of his torturers; at the moment he utters the words 'I love Big Brother', he means what he says. The state has won and he is now 'normal'. When he meets Julia again, all human passion has evaporated and the only conversation that takes place is bland, devoid of feeling and meaningless.

In many ways the story draws on Europe as it was just before and after the Second World War, when the political convictions held by opposing groups, each claiming to hold the ultimate truth, were as stifling as the dictates of Big Brother. In Europe the dividing lines between political and religious factions are less rigid today, but there is still division and propaganda is still a powerful influence on human action. In some regions of the world an individual's refusal to give in to what his society wants him to be will bring about his isolation and downfall.

Orwell was acutely aware of the power of propaganda to manipulate a society. Not only had he gained knowledge of the workings of Hitler's Nazi Germany and Stalin's Soviet Russia in his time as a journalist, but he had also seen propaganda at work when he fought in Spain and when he had been a BBC propagandist, broadcasting messages to wartime Germany imploring the German troops to surrender.

Orwell was an acute observer of his time and a sage in that he accurately saw the weakness of man and his willingness to believe anything that reinforces his preconceived ideas. His plea was for people to stop being led by those in charge and to start thinking for themselves. He expressed this notion most clearly in the behaviour of the sheep in *Animal Farm* and the proles in *Nineteen Eighty-four*. The sheep declare themselves guilty of dissatisfaction even though they have no notion of the implications of doing so and are actually quite

innocent; the mindless proles are a weapon in the hands of the state.

Orwell was conscious of his limitations as a novelist and some critics argue that *Nineteen Eighty-four* can hardly be termed a novel because a novel ought to offer more in the way of characterisation, with the action and the setting being subordinate to character development. In Orwell's writings the message is paramount and the characters are there to drive that message home. His 'novels' are novels of ideas – elaborate and brilliantly conceived political expositions. In this respect he can be seen as continuing the long tradition of prose fiction used as a vehicle for social criticism, the satirical and science-fiction elements of his work even having something in common with Jonathan Swift's fantastic satire *Gulliver's Travels* (1726).

Another criticism is that *Nineteen Eighty-four* is incomplete because Orwell needed an appendix to explain terms such as 'Newspeak' and 'Doublethink', while a competent fiction writer should incorporate all relevant information into the narrative itself. On the other hand it can be argued that the appendix is not really necessary and that its presence adds a certain pseudo-authority to the fictitious world.

Orwell was the chronicler of a confused society, caught between two world wars. He depicted the wrongs of colonialism, Stalin's communism and authoritarianism in all its manifestations. He feared the power of the few, whether placed in their position by the workers or by privilege of class, and he did not write from the safe lodgings of the pampered bohemian whose writings, albeit well meant, were not based on actual experience, but wrote from his own experiences, taking risks and never giving in.

Selected works:

Down And Out In Paris and London (1933); *Burmese Days* (1934); *A Clergyman's Daughter* (1935); *Keep The Aspidistra Flying* (1936); *The Road to Wigan Pier* (1937); *Homage to Catalonia* (1938); *Coming Up For Air* (1939); *Inside The Whale And Other Essays* (1940); *The Lion And The Unicorn* (1941); *Animal Farm* (1945); *Critical Essays* (1946); *James Burnham And The Managerial Evolution* (1946); *The English People* (1947); *Nineteen Eighty-four* (1949); *Shooting An Elephant* (1950); *England Your England and*

Other Essays / Such Were The Joys (1953); *A Collection Of Essays* (1954); *The Orwell Reader* (1956); *Selected Essays* (1957); *Selected Writings* (1958); *Collected Essays* (1961); *Decline of the English Murder and Other Essays* (1965); *Orwell: The War Broadcasts* (1985); *The Complete Works Of George Orwell* (1998).

Further reading

Hitchens, Christopher, *Orwell's Victory*. Penguin, 2003.

Meyers, Valerie, *George Orwell* (Modern Novelists Series). Palgrave Macmillan, 1991.

Meyers, Jeffrey (ed.) *George Orwell* (Critical Heritage Series). Routledge, 1975.

Contributors: Bram de Bruin, Ian Mackean

PINTER, HAROLD (1930–)

There can be no hard distinction between what is real and what is unreal, nor between what is true and what is false. A thing is not necessarily either true or false; it can be both true and false.[1]

Harold Pinter, playwright, director, actor, poet and political activist, made his reputation as a central figure in the generation of dramatists who began writing plays in the era when British drama had been revolutionised by John Osborne's *Look Back in Anger* (1956). He came from a Jewish family in East London and grew up at a time when London was witnessing fascist demonstrations. He studied briefly at the Royal Academy of Dramatic Art and acted in a repertory company as a young man. His first play, *The Room*, was written and produced in 1957. In addition to his work for the theatre, he has written works for radio and television and several screenplays, based on such novels as Marcel Proust's *A la Recherche du Temps Perdu* and *The French Lieutenant's Woman* by **John Fowles**. He also adapted his own play, *Betrayal*, for the screen.

With his outstanding success in the late 1950s, Pinter was frequently associated with the **social realism** of the **Angry Young Men**. Plays such as *The Room* (1957), *The Birthday Party* (1958) and *The Caretaker* (1960), with their realistic setting and naturalistic dialogue, seemed part of this movement – but only at first glance. In fact the plays display only a surface realism and Pinter claimed that although what goes on in his plays is 'realistic', what he is doing is not 'realism'.[2] His work did not have the dimension of social criticism found in Osborne's *Look Back in Anger*, and unlike playwrights of the Realist tradition, he does not take a recognisable political stand. In fact he breaks down social realism by not identifying character with the environment.

Pinter's early plays bewildered the audiences and were regarded as obscure. The ambiguity of *The Room*, *The Birthday Party* and *The Caretaker* led critics to identify him with the **Theatre of the Absurd**. Martin Esslin, for example, lists Pinter as a follower of Eugene Ionesco and **Samuel Beckett** in his influential study, *The Theatre of the Absurd* (1961). The definition given by Ionesco, 'Absurd is that which has no purpose, or goal, or objective',[3] seemed applicable to Pinter's plays. The label, however, became increasingly difficult to justify. His later plays, such as *The Homecoming* (1965) and *No Man's Land* (1975), with their recognisable social contexts, could not be categorised as Absurd. Pinter moved on from the Absurdism of the 1950s, but his name was still linked with that of Beckett because of the ambiguity of his plays and his insistence on not being explicit.

Another dramatist with whom Pinter is often compared is Anton Chekhov. The plot lines of both dramatists are very simple, the emphasis being on dialogue rather than action. The plays of both dramatists are elusive, difficult to analyse, and they both use comedy to elicit compassion for the plight of characters. In *The Caretaker*, for example, Davies, the tramp, wearing the jacket of a sophisticated gentleman is hilarious. However, the jacket symbolises all that Davies is denied, such as status, friendship, love and security. His comic affectation induces laughter, which is soon replaced with compassion. Comedy is more than mere laughter for Pinter; he uses it to bring out the conflict between surface appearances and deeper feelings.

Pinter's dramatic world is set in contemporary society and his setting is typically a room (suggestive, perhaps, of a refuge, a prison cell or a trap) with ordinary occupants in everyday situations. Beneath this surface realism, however, there is a vague but very real sense of characters' fears, unease, guilt, foreboding and secrets which they are afraid of disclosing. The plays mirror the anxious states of mind of the characters and the stratagems they use to deal with their predicaments.

The seemingly safe environment of the room in a Pinter play is usually disturbed by menacing outsiders who appear unexpectedly. Those in the room are trapped, endangered and have no way out. Pinter has said that this pattern represents what has been happening repeatedly in history. The sudden appearance of the two interrogators in *The Birthday Party*, for example, reflects the psychological environment of a police state. In his early works Pinter avoided specific political references, showing instead the roots of tyranny in the everyday lives of ordinary people. His later plays, however, are more overtly political. *One for the Road* (1984) openly depicts state terrorism. A man is tortured, physically and mentally, after being arrested by soldiers who vandalise his home, rape his wife and kill his son. The directness of this play forces the audience to contemplate the possibility that the fate of the characters could be their own.

Pinter's usual cast is rarely more than three to five characters, linked in unstable relationships. Each tries to dominate, control, exploit, subjugate or victimise the others, either alone or in alliance with another, with the alliances continually shifting. In *Old Times* (1970), for example, a husband tries to disrupt his wife's relationship with a woman from her past, but ends up being the rejected, outcast one.

In some plays, such as *Landscape, Silence* (both 1969), *Old Times* (1970) and *No Man's Land* (1975) Pinter dwells more on the relationship between past and present, in situations where it is difficult, if not impossible, for characters to verify their pasts. Past experiences are distorted and shared experiences are interpreted differently. These later plays deal more extensively with the themes of time, memory and self-reflection, which were latent in the early plays.

One element of Pinter's originality was to depict the chaotic and incoherent speech of ordinary people in a way that no other British dramatist had done before. His characters do not speak in complete grammatical sentences, the connection between sentences seems illogical, and characters do not seem to listen to, or understand, each other.

GUS. What time is he getting in touch?
BEN. What's the matter with you? It could be any time. Any time.
GUS. Well, I was going to ask you something.
BEN. What?
GUS. Have you noticed the time it takes the tank to fill?
BEN. What tank?
GUS. In the lavatory.
[The Dumb Waiter]

In these ways Pinter's use of language imitated ordinary conversation, another similarity to Chekhov, who was the first European playwright to use dialogue with such realism.

Pinter's dialogue also often shows the influence of the quick-fire repartee of the music-hall comedy sketch.

LULU. (*rising*). Come out and get a bit of air. You depress me, looking like that.
STANLEY. Air? Oh, I don't know about that.
LULU. It's lovely out. And I've got a few sandwiches.
STANLEY. What sort of sandwiches?
LULU. Cheese.
STANLEY. I'm a big eater, you know.
LULU. That's all right. I'm not hungry.
[The Birthday Party]

But dialogue in Pinter's plays is far from being casual or inconsequential. As often as not it is a form of psychological warfare.[4] His characters do not aim to understand or be understood. Language is used to threaten, dominate or evade confrontation. It is also used to find comfort in one's isolation, as in *Landscape* and *Silence*. Pinter does not believe people are unable to communicate, but that they evade communication in an attempt to keep themselves to themselves, to resist 'being known'.

Pinter became famous for the technique of pauses and silences. At other times a torrent of language pours out, in which case under what is said something unsaid is hidden. Both stratagems are a smokescreen for what a character thinks or feels but does not say.

In his later plays Pinter foregrounds the idea of the powerful versus the speechless. In *Mountain Language* (1988) two wives, whose husbands have disappeared, are inarticulate because speech is banned by the authorities. Those in power do all the speaking.

Pinter is a political activist in his private life but not a propagandist in his plays. He does not believe that the stage can change the world. However, he feels a moral commitment to present the world as he observes it.

References

1. **Pinter, Harold** (1981) 'Writing for the Theatre', *Plays: One*. London: Methuen, p. 11.

2. **Pinter, Harold** (1996) 'Writing for Myself', *Plays: Two*. London: Faber, p. ix.

3. **Esslin, Martin** (1973) 'The Theatre of the Absurd', *Existentialist Philosophy*. James A. Gould and Willis H. Truitt (eds) California: Dickinson Pub. Co. Inc, p. 305.

4. **Mackean, Ian** (2001) *Winners and Losers in the plays of Harold Pinter*. www.english-literature.org/essays/pinter.html

Selected works:

The Room (1957); *The Birthday Party* (1958); *The Dumb Waiter* (1959); *The Caretaker* (1960); *A Slight Ache* (1961); *The Homecoming* (1965); *Silence* (1969); *Old Times* (1970); *No Man's Land* (1975); *Betrayal* (1978); *A Kind of Alaska* (1982); *One for the Road* (1984); *Mountain Language* (1988); *Celebration* (1999); *Remembrance of Things Past* (2000).

Further reading

Billington, Michael, *The Life and Work of Harold Pinter*. London: Faber and Faber, 1996.

Knowles, Ronald, *The Birthday Party and The Caretaker: Text and Performance*. Macmillan Education, 1988.

Contributor: Ünal Norman

PLATH, SYLVIA (1932–63)

O sister, mother, wife,
Sweet Lethe is my life
I am never, never, never, coming home!
                                    Amnesia

In February 1963, Sylvia Plath was found dead in her London flat after her suicide. In the following decades she gained a reputation as one of the most important American female poets. In her well-crafted verse, the reader discovers an array of intense emotions, ranging from love, hatred and fury to hopelessness and a sense of betrayal. Her posthumous collection, *Ariel* (1965), consists of a series of 40 poems, some of the best known being 'Daddy', 'Lady Lazarus', 'Words', 'Cut' and 'Ariel', all written in less than two months, during October and November 1962. The poetic self that emerges from these poems is overflowing with dynamic energy, seeking to address the inner turmoil, mental breakdowns and uncertainties of a troubled female voice, while at the same time being aware of the problems of the world at large.

Born in Boston, Massachusetts, in 1932, Plath was the elder child of Otto and Aurelia Schoeber Plath. Her father's death, when he was eight, from gangrene, due to diabetes, was a critical event during her childhood years, as was her mother's subsequent struggle to support her two young children.

Plath started writing at an early age with the encouragement of her mother. In the 1950s she studied at Smith College, in Massachusetts, on a scholarship and graduated *summa cum laude* (with the highest distinction) in English. She then won a Fullbright grant to Cambridge University, where she received her MA in 1957. There she met the English poet **Ted Hughes** whom she married the same year. They initially lived in Massachusetts where she taught poetry at Smith College and then moved to Boston. At Boston University she attended poetry seminars offered by Robert Lowell, where she was influenced by his style of poetry which became known as **confessional poetry**. The focus of this approach to poetry was on the correlation between the poet's personal and often painful experiences and the socio-historical problems of contemporary society. The literary critic and poet Al Alvarez, who knew both Lowell and Plath, talks about the extreme state of 'psychosis'[1] that the work of the poets cultivates. However, in the case of Plath, the torment of the self, or its 'psychosis', is not disassociated from the tensions of the external world. Plath once observed: 'I cannot sympathize with those cries from the heart that are informed by nothing except a needle of a knife . . . I believe that one should control and manipulate experiences, even the most terrifying.'[2]

Initially, Plath's marriage seemed a happy one. Her first poetic collection, *The Colossus* (1960), was published by Heinemann just after her move to London with her husband. In this volume, inspired by the poetry of Theodore Roethke, she is interested in the transformations of the self and recontextualisation of experience as moulded by poetic language. The imagery of death and rebirth that informs the background of these poems reveals her yearning for regeneration, both artistically and emotionally.

Plath and Hughes's first child, Frieda, was born in 1960, and their second, Nicholas, in 1962. The couple moved from London to Devon where Plath managed to complete her partly autobiographical novel *The Bell Jar* (1963), which was published just before her death under the pseudonym Victoria Lucas. This book deals with the stereotyped roles women were expected to fulfil in the 1950s and the tension they experienced being torn between social expectations and personal ambition. The novel helped to make Plath an enduring icon of feminism, a reputation which was reinforced with the publication of *Ariel*. *The Bell Jar* is rooted in Plath's experiences as guest editor of a young women's magazine, *Mademoiselle*, in 1953 and her breakdown and suicide attempt during her years in college. These events are fictionalised in the form of her female protagonist's descent into depression, attempted suicide and electroshock treatment.

In 1962, Plath's marriage to Hughes was seriously shaken up when she found out that he was having an extramarital affair. While still in Devon, she wrote most of the poems that would later appear in the *Ariel* collection. In December 1962, she moved to London with her two young children during one of the worst winters of the century in Britain. Her broken marriage and difficult living conditions added to her depression but fortified her poetic genius. She wrote fervently and passionately, energised by her personally intense but painful experiences, her love for her children and her distinctive vision of the natural world.

Hughes was responsible for the selection and publication of the poems included in *Ariel*. Plath had carefully arranged the poems in a sequence, which Hughes decided to alter by omitting some of her belligerent poems from 1962 and including others that she had designated for a different collection. Despite the changes, *Ariel* is considered to be Plath's best work. Although death or suicide feature in her poems as the only way out, Plath's mastery of poetic diction, rhythm and sound, along with her extraordinary creative energy, resulted in powerful poetry which reaches beyond her difficult personal circumstances to speak to the heart and sentiments of every reader.

References

1. **Holbrook, David** (1991) 'Robert Lowell, Theodore Roethke, and Sylvia Plath', *The New Pelican Guide to English Literature: American Literature. Volume 9*. Ed. Boris Ford. London: Penguin Books, p. 534.

2. **Orr, Peter** (ed.) *The Poet Speaks: Interviews with Contemporary Poets*. London: Routledge and Kegan Paul, 1966. stinf www.informatik. uni-leipzig.de/~beckmann/plath/orrinter view.html (12.02.04)

Selected works:

The Colossus and Other Poems (Britain, 1960; USA, 1962); *Ariel* (1965); *Crossing the Water* (Britain, 1971; USA, 1972); *Winter Trees* (Britain, 1971; USA, 1972); *The Bell Jar* (Britain, 1963; USA, 1971); *Johnny Panic and the Bible of Dreams: Short Stories, Prose, and Diary Excerpts* (1979); *The Journals of Sylvia Plath* (1982).

Further reading

Axelrod, Steven, *Sylvia Plath: The Wound and the Cure of Words*. The Johns Hopkins University Press, 1990.

Wisker, Gina, *Sylvia Plath: A Beginner's Guide.* Hodder & Stoughton, 2001.

Contributor: Tatiani Rapatzikou

PORTER, KATHERINE ANNE (1890–1980)

My fiction is reportage, only I do something to it. I arrange it and it is fiction but it happened.

Porter in Givner, p. 23

The stories of Katherine Anne Porter, the Texan-born writer and journalist, received critical acclaim, with *Collected Stories* (1965) winning a Pulitzer Prize, while her novel, *Ship of Fools* (1962), achieved popular success. Although seldom read now, Porter influenced generations of writers, from Eudora Welty to Tillie Olsen, and her writing deserves greater consideration.

Callie Russell Porter was born in Indian Creek, Texas, the fourth child of Harrison Boone Porter and Mary Alice Jones Porter. When her mother died in 1892, the family moved to Kyle, Hays County, to live with Harrison's mother. They were very poor and this was a deeply unhappy period, not at all the genteel Southern girlhood that Porter later implied.

Despite Porter's fantasies of convent school and elopement, she married John Koontz, in 1905 – the first of four marriages – in order to escape hardship. By the time of her divorce in 1915, she had educated herself and was writing short stories. Porter worked as a journalist in Fort Worth and Denver, nearly dying in the 1918 Denver influenza epidemic, as fictionalised in her story 'Pale Rider, Pale Horse'. Once in New York, Porter continued to write and in 1920 a magazine sent her to war-ravaged Mexico. This experience provided excellent story material and Carl Van Doren published her first tale, 'Maria Concepcion' (1922), in *Century Magazine*.

Porter wrote her stories in order to examine human behaviour and trace the reasons for man's moral and intellectual failure. Theme and content were paramount and she was often annoyed when praised as a stylist (Givner, p. 137). Her constant moral theme is 'the dangerous apathy of the apparently innocent' (Givner, p. 205).

In 1930, Harcourt & Brace published her first collection, *Flowering Judas*. In 'Theft', Porter achieves a tension between the surface story of an exploited woman and the latent moral story – which blames the woman's indifference for her exploitation. 'Flowering Judas', the story that established Porter's reputation, contains a web of moral paradoxes within an evocative and heavily symbolic narrative. By not rejecting the revolutionary leader Braggioni, and by following her instructions unquestioningly, Porter suggests that Laura, a revolutionary sympathiser, is innocently guilty of evil.

In 1931, Porter received a Guggenheim Fellowship, which funded her first trip to Europe and her voyage from Veracruz, on the SS *Werra*, informs her novel *Ship of Fools*. In Berlin, Porter witnessed Hitler's rise to power, which she later used in her story, 'The Leaning Tower'.

Back in the United States in 1936, Porter wrote the three short novels that form *Pale Horse, Pale Rider* – the pinnacle of her writing career. In 'Noon Wine' she investigates responsibility and guilt, with the readers and characters, especially Mr Thompson, being challenged to make moral judgements. The scene between Hatch, the bounty hunter, and Mr Thompson is superb, with the narrator's free indirect style conveying the growing menace of Hatch and Thompson's confusion and fear.

'Old Mortality' introduces a genteel Southern world, which Porter **deconstructs**, rereading the legends and myths of a family's history. Two sisters, Miranda and Maria, enjoy the tales, yet rebel against their obvious inconsistencies. Later, they discover that 'romantic' Uncle Gabriel is a drunken gambler and realise the damage done by the idealised myths of Aunt Amy. Finally, Cousin Eva rereads the past to Miranda, who is shocked by Eva's vilifying version of Amy. Miranda rejects the family and their destructive tales, separating from them in order to know the truth about herself. Yet this is not a new myth of certainty, for Miranda acknowledges that her quest is undertaken 'in her hopefulness her ignorance'. In such stories Porter demystifies and rejects 'the Southern family romance' (Manning, p. 7), yet she continued to romanticise her own life.

Miranda reappears in 'Pale Rider, Pale Horse'. Having rejected her family's stories, she now creates her own, as both a journalist and an independent woman. The narrative moves confidently between Miranda's dreams and thoughts, which symbolically anticipate her illness and her battles as a woman journalist. It also introduces the tentative beginnings of her romance with Adam, the Texan officer, who nurses Miranda before dying himself. Most impressive is Porter's **stream of consciousness** representation of Miranda's fever.

The Leaning Tower and Other Stories (1944) is an uneven collection, with 'The Old Order' sequence featuring Miranda again. Although the stories stand alone, when read together they coalesce to form hazy snapshots of her background. This is Porter's most impressionistic work, with histories told as a wandering through time, while the narrative variously focuses on different characters, leaving the reader to put the images together.

'The Holiday' is the finest story in the collection. The first-person narrator gradually unfolds the complex minds of seemingly simple people and undercuts romantic notions of pastoral idylls. Images of hard work narrow to a revelation about Ottilie, the disabled servant. The narrator succumbs to anger and romanticism, misreading Ottilie's grief. Yet Ottilie's tears become laughter at being alive and Porter depicts her joy, and the narrator's humiliated confusion, with pathos and tenderness.

A Ford Foundation Award in 1959 prompted intense writing and after a 20-year gestation, Porter's novel, *Ship of Fools*, finally appeared on All Fools' Day, 1962, to mixed reviews. It is an account of a voyage from Mexico to Germany during Hitler's rise to power. There is an episodic introduction to the characters, with the narrative **point of view** constantly switching between them. The novel's main failing is that Porter's simplistic idea of characters as villainous, virtuous or apathetic does not permit any discernible development or movement. The critic Theodore Solotaroff considered them all predictable caricatures (Warren, p. 139) and as little virtue is depicted in any character, many critics find the novel misanthropic. Others consider it anti-Semitic and racist, with Porter's representation of Herr Lowenthal,

the Jewish salesman, lacking any sympathy or understanding. Nevertheless, the novel was a great popular success.

In 1965, *The Collected Stories of Katherine Anne Porter* appeared, winning both the National Book Award and the Pulitzer Prize. In addition, the University of Maryland library created the 'Katherine Anne Porter Room' which holds her manuscripts and papers. Sadly, Porter became increasingly difficult and confused in her final years and died in a Maryland nursing home on 18 September 1980.

Selected works:

Flowering Judas (1930); *Flowering Judas and Other Stories* (1935); *Pale Horse, Pale Rider* (1939); *The Leaning Tower and Other Stories* (1944); *The Days Before* (1952); *Ship of Fools* (1962); *Collected Stories* (1965); *Collected Essays and Occasional Writings* (1970).

Further reading

Givner, Joan, *Katherine Anne Porter: A Life*. Simon & Schuster, 1982 (revised 1991).

Manning, Carol S., *The Female Tradition in Southern Literature*. University of Illinois Press, 1993.

Warren, Robert, Penn (ed.) *Katherine Anne Porter: A Collection of Critical Essays*. Prentice-Hall, 1979.

Contributor: Carole Jones

POUND, EZRA (1885–1972)

The apparition of these faces in the crowd; Petals on a wet, black bough.
In a Station of the Metro

Ezra Weston Loomis Pound was a critical essayist and translator who fervently pursued the revitalisation of American poetry, was an important influence on **T. S. Eliot** and many other poets, and was one of the most controversial of American **Modernist** poets.

Pound was born in Hailey, Idaho, and educated at the University of Pennsylvania and Hamilton College in New York State. His aim, even as an adolescent, was to become a poet. During his undergraduate years, from 1901 to 1905, he was acquainted with Hilda Doolittle (H. D.) and William Carlos Williams, who were also to become important American poets. Together they discussed the possibility of regenerating the poetry of their country, at a time when European poetry had already started leaving Victorianism behind under the influence of French **Symbolism** in the 1890s. Williams believed that America should explore the dynamics of its own speech, but Pound looked for inspiration beyond his homeland. As a graduate student at the University of Pennsylvania he focused on the study of French, Italian, Old English and Latin. After receiving his MA in 1906 he took up a teaching fellowship with Wabash College in Indiana, then moved to Europe in 1908, spending a few months in Venice before finally settling in London.

While in Venice, he published his first volume of poetry, *A Lume Spento* (1908), which is characterised by mythical allusions, organic imagery and dramatic monologues, and shows the influence of Dante Gabriel Rossetti, Robert Browning, Ernest Dowson and Algernon Charles Swinburne. He moved to London in September of that year and got in touch with **W. B. Yeats**, whom he had initially met in the States in 1903. He was introduced to London's literary circles and exposed to the radical artistic movements in vogue at the time. He met British and Irish writers as well as expatriate American poets, all seeking to revolutionise poetry. Pound embraced the experimental attitudes and literary techniques of the two seemingly distinct literary worlds – the British and the American – as he sought to establish his own poetic style.

Influenced by Ford Madox Ford and T. E. Hulme, Pound began to see the role of the poet as an adventurer and no longer as a spiritual aesthete or public orator. His poetry was moving in a new direction and in 1912 he launched the **Imagist** movement. This literary event was announced in Harriet Monroe's *Poetry: A Magazine of Verse* in Chicago, through which Pound promoted the work of fellow imagists as well as that of T. S. Eliot and **Robert Frost**. The essential principles of this new kind of poetry were the direct and concrete presentation of visual images, the avoidance of embellished

language patterns and the composition of poetry in the sequence of a musical phrase rather than following rigid verse forms. An anthology of imagist poetry, *Des Imagistes*, was published in 1914 including poems by H. D., Richard Aldington, Amy Lowell, William Carlos Williams and **James Joyce** as well as Pound himself.

Pound's succinct poem 'In a Station of the Metro', with its condensed, haiku-like but dynamic, visual imagery and its modern railway station setting, is indicative of his transition from Imagism to **Vorticism**, an artistic movement which attempted to address the modern industrial world through art. According to the movement's leader, the writer and artist Wyndham Lewis, Vorticism regarded images as 'a radiant node or cluster . . . into which ideas are constantly rushing'.[1] Pound put this idea into practice in 1915 when he started working on one of his most important poetic endeavours, *The Cantos*.

Although Pound always favoured the different and the new, he adhered to the tradition of the long poem when he came to compose his *Cantos*. Comprising a number of separate poems, the cantos varied in length and in the ways they combined the poet's meditations with **intertextual** quotations from older texts and in other languages. This poetic composition subverts the tradition of the epic since it is not characterised by linear narrative but by the amalgamation of disparate poems united by the poetic imagination. Pound produced 117 cantos whose stylistic intricacies and challenging composition still intrigue readers and critics alike.

Pound's London period was also marked by two other major poems, 'Homage to Sextus Propertius' (1919) and 'Hugh Selwyn Mauberley' (1920), which expressed his disappointment and disillusionment after the First World War. In the former poem, utilising the persona of Propertius, Pound indirectly addresses the intelligentsia of London during the Great War and, by flouting conventional word order, attempts to articulate human sorrow and pain. What some Latinists mistook as bad translation proved to be a complex but well-crafted poetic form. 'Hugh Selwyn Mauberley', being more satirical and ironic in its tone, expresses Pound's disillusionment with a civilisation in ruins, governed by

Capitalism and false values.

Wishing to understand the reasons behind the cultural and social upheaval of the First World War, Pound turned to the 'social credit' theories of the social economist Major Clifford Hugh Douglas, who held Capitalism responsible for the destruction of human creativity, regarding it as the source of all evil. As a result, Pound's political beliefs fused with his poetry as he recorded his search for a society in which art would be protected from monetary concerns.

In 1920, Pound and his wife, Dorothy Shakespear, whom he married in 1914, left London for Paris. There he worked with Eliot on the first draft of 'The Waste Land' and then in 1924 moved to Italy, where they settled in Rapallo. In 1930 he published *A Draft of XXX Cantos*, in which he revealed the repetitive patterns that govern history by revisiting a selection of historical events. Shortly after this he became attracted to the Italian fascist dictator Benito Mussolini, seeing him as a strong leader and social reformer. During the Second World War Pound openly supported Fascism and his anti-Semitism and provocative radio broadcasts to America led to his arrest in 1945. He was held at a Disciplinary Training Centre near Pisa, then taken to the USA to be tried for treason. The trial never took place, on the grounds of insanity, and Pound was consequently hospitalised from 1946 to 1958 in St Elizabeth's Hospital in Washington DC.

The Pisan Cantos, which Pound had started writing while detained in Pisa, were completed at St Elizabeth's in 1946 and published in 1948. In these personal and retrospective poems he revisits his past and reveals his suffering, as well as his concern about the world around him. There was much controversy when in 1948 this poetic collection received the Bollingen Prize for poetry awarded by the Library of Congress.

On his release, Pound returned to Italy and died in Venice at the age of 87. Although his poetic achievements were overshadowed by his political notoriety, he unquestionably contributed to the revitalisation of American poetry. Through his poems, the American identity emerges as all-encompassing, extending beyond its history and culture by delving into the mythological past of other civilisations.

Reference

1. **Ruland, Richard and Bradbury, Malcolm** (eds). *From Puritanism to Postmodernism*. Penguin, 1992, p. 262.

Selected works:

A Lume Spento (1908); *A Quinzaine For This Yule* (1908); *Exultations* (1909); *Personae* (1909); *Provencal* (1910); *The Spirit Of Romance* (1910); *Canzoni* (1911); *Ripostes* (1912); *Personae & Exultations* (1913); *Lustra* (1916); *Noh, Or Accomplishment: A Study Of The Classical Stage Of Japan* (1916) – with Ernest Fenollosa; Gaudier-Brzeska (1916); *Pavannes And Divagations* (1918); *Quia Pauper Amavi* (1919); *The Fourth Canto* (1919); *Umbra* (1920); *Hugh Selwyn Mauberley* (1920); *Instigations* (1921); *Indiscretions* (1923); *Antheil And The Treatise Of Harmony* (1924); *A Draft Of XVI Cantos* (1925); *A Draft Of The Cantos XVII–XXVII* (1928); *Ta Hio* (1928); *Imaginary Letters* (1930); *A Draft Of XXX Cantos* (1930); *How To Read* (1931); *Prolegomena I* (1932); *ABC Of Economics* (1933); *ABC Of Reading* (1934); *Make It New* (1934); *Eleven New Cantos XXXI–XLI* (1934); *Homage To Sextus Propertius* (1934) – original pub. 1919; *Jefferson And/Or Mussolini* (1935); *Social Credit* (1935); *Polite Essays* (1937); *The Fifth Decade Of Cantos* (1938); *Guide To Kulchur* (1938); *What Is Money For?* (1939); *Cantos LII–LXXI* (1940); *Carta Da Vista* (1942); *L'America, Roosevelt E Le Cause Della Guerra Presente* (1944); *Oro E Lavoro* (1944); *Orientamenti* (1944); *'If this be treason…'* (1948); *The Pisan Cantos* (1948); *The Cantos Of Ezra Pound* (1949); *Seventy Cantos* (1950); *Patria Mia* (1950); *Confucian Analects* (1951); *The Letters Of Ezra Pound 1907–1941* (1950); *Literary Essays* (1954).

Pound also published a large number of translations. His letters have appeared in several collections.

Further reading

Cookson, William, *A Guide to the Cantos of Ezra Pound*. Anvil Press Poetry, 2001.

Nadel, Ira (ed.) *The Cambridge Companion to Ezra Pound*. Cambridge University Press, 1999.

Contributor: Tatiani Rapatzikou

POWELL, ANTHONY
(1905–2000)

I found myself in the Wallace Collection, standing in front of Nicolas Poussin's picture A Dance to the Music of Time. *An almost hypnotic spell seems cast by this masterpiece on the beholder. I knew all at once that Poussin had expressed at least one important aspect of what the novel must be.*

To Keep the Ball Rolling: Faces in My
Time, 1980

Anthony Dymoke Powell, novelist and critic, was one of the generation of gifted English writers who attended Oxford University in the 1920s. His contemporaries included **Evelyn Waugh**, **Graham Greene**, John Betjeman and Cyril Connelly, and even among these illustrious names, Powell's shines. Born in Westminster, London, Powell had attended Eton school before reading History at Balliol College, Oxford.

In 1926 Powell joined the publishing firm Duckworth's, eventually becoming an editor. In 1931 Duckworth published his first novel, *Afternoon Men*, a sophisticated comedy in a similar vein to Evelyn Waugh's *Vile Bodies* (1930). In 1934, Powell married Lady Violet Pakenham, daughter of the Earl of Longford. Two years later he went to Hollywood to work as a scriptwriter for Warner Brothers and while in America met **F. Scott Fitzgerald**, and travelled to Mexico. The following year he returned to England and became a full-time writer. He was commissioned into the army at the beginning of the Second World War and served until 1945.

By the beginning of the war Powell had already published five novels, following *Afternoon Men* with *Venusburg* (1932), *From a View to a Death* (1933), *Agents and Patients* (1936) and *What's Become of Waring?* (1939). His sharp characterisation, humour and witty observation of the social scene ensured that his novels would retain their strong appeal.

Powell is best known for his 12-volume masterpiece of English life and manners, *A Dance to the Music of Time*, which **Kingsley Amis** described as 'the most important effort in fiction since the war'. The story covers the decline of the English aristocracy seen through the eyes of Nicholas Jenkins, a survivor, and ironic observer, of the class war. Powell leads us through the crisis-strewn inter-war years, the Second World War and into the post-war world. He drew upon his own experiences – of Eton, Oxford, the army, publishing, bohemian life in London's Fitzrovia and the changing England of the late 1960s and 1970s.

The series takes its name from Nicholas Poussin's seventeenth-century painting of the same title, in which the classical figures of the four Seasons perform a stately, unending dance to the music of Time's lyre. In these books, Powell created hundreds of characters, some of whom live through seven decades of the century, developing and changing in unexpected ways. The story is told by the almost-neutral observer, Nicholas Jenkins, who is, perhaps more than he realises, influenced by the people he meets, loses touch with and meets again, often to find them strangely changed.

Powell's lifelike characters are boldly drawn, without ever lapsing into caricature, three of the most memorable being Kenneth Widmerpool, the uncouth schoolboy who becomes an arrogant soldier and then a blustering politician, forcing himself onwards by sheer effort of the will that eventually deserts him and leaves him destroyed; Jean Templer, the sulky schoolgirl who becomes Jenkins's mistress, deceives him, then becomes the aloof wife of a South American dictator; and Charles Stringham, the elegant, witty Etonian who becomes an alcoholic and meets his death in the war through the machinations of his old school enemy, Widmerpool.

Powell's characters seem at once bizarre and entirely believable, and were considered so lifelike that he was often pressed to reveal their 'true' identities. He maintained that fictional characters are a 'mixture' and wrote in an article for the *Sunday Telegraph* magazine (25 September 1997):

People won't believe that you are capable of inventing characters. All right, a couple of people might occur to you but to make it work you have to invent a 'third person' to pull it all together.

Later, however, Powell confirmed that he had used certain real people as models for his characters.

However wide his canvas, Powell is always in control of his characters and the development of his story. His concern for structure can be illustrated by the way in which the chronicle opens and closes. The first book, *A Question of Upbringing*, opens with a description of workmen gathered round a bucket of burning coke, amidst gently falling snow. The last, *Hearing Secret Harmonies*, ends with a few flakes of snow falling on another workman's bucket, and then the drifting smoke of the bonfire in the mists of Nicholas Jenkins's own garden where 'even the formal measure of the Seasons seemed suspended in the wintry silence'.

Powell was also a literary critic and at various times he was on the literary staff of the *Times Literary Supplement*, *Punch* and the *Daily Telegraph*. His first volume of memoirs, *Infants of the Spring*, was published in 1976 and three other volumes were to follow. His last novel, *The Fisher King*, was published in 1986 and his *Journals 1982–1986* in 1995. His interest in genealogy led to his being elected Vice-President of the Society of Genealogists in 1997.

Powell was a reserved man who shunned publicity, which is perhaps the reason why he refused a knighthood in 1973, though he was made a CBE in 1956 and a Companion of Honour in 1988.

A character in Nancy Mitford's *The Pursuit of Love* laments that she belonged to a 'lost generation': 'I am sure in history the two world wars will count as one war and that we shall be squashed out of it altogether.' It is thanks to Anthony Powell's chronicle of that time that the 'lost generation' is still remembered and at least partially understood.

Selected works:

The 12 volumes of *A Dance to the Music of Time* are: *A Question of Upbringing* (1951); *A Buyer's Market* (1952); *The Acceptance World* (1955); *At Lady Molly's* (1957); *Casanova's Chinese Restaurant* (1960); *The Kindly Ones* (1962); *The Valley of Bones* (1964); *The Soldier's Art* (1966); *The Military Philosophers* (1968); *Books Do Furnish a Room* (1971); *Temporary Kings* (1973); *Hearing Secret Harmonies* (1975).

Further reading

Brennan, Neil, *Anthony Powell*. Twayne New York, 1974 (revised 1995).

Tucker, James, *The Novels of Anthony Powell*. Macmillan, 1976.

Contributors: Margaret Tarner, Ian Mackean

RHYS, JEAN (1890–1979)

I would never be part of anything. I would never really belong anywhere, and I knew it, and all my life would be the same, trying to belong, and failing. Always something goes wrong. I am a stranger and I always will be, and after all I didn't really care.

Smile Please: An Unfinished Autobiography

Jean Rhys became a major literary figure with the publication of her novel *Wide Sargasso Sea* in 1966 and in the year before her death she was awarded a CBE. She had returned to the literary scene in 1956, after a radio broadcast of an adaptation of *Good Morning, Midnight*, having previously dropped out of literary life for over 20 years. But in the 1930s she had already achieved moderate recognition with a volume of short stories and four novels which drew on her bohemian existence in Europe in the 1920s and 1930s. Being a Creole woman of West Indian origin Rhys felt she never really belonged to either the white or black communities, or to either the West Indies or Europe, and the sense of rootlessness features strongly in her autobiographically based writing.

Rhys was born Ella Gwendolyn Rees Williams in Dominica, a small Caribbean island, to a Welsh Father, Dr William Rees Williams, and a Creole mother who was the daughter of a Scottish-born plantation owner and a West Indian woman. In 1907, at the age of 16, Rhys was sent to study in England. She lived under her aunt's care and attended the

Perse School in Cambridge and the Royal Academy of Dramatic Arts in London, where she began training as an actress. Her training was cut short when her father died, but instead of returning to the Caribbean as her mother and aunt intended, she remained in London and found work as a chorus girl. She also had the first of a number of troubled relationships with men, with Lancelot Grey Hugh Smith, a man from an upper-class family which disapproved of his association with a chorus girl. He ended the relationship, but continued to send her money for several years afterwards. The experience formed the basis of her novel *Voyage in the Dark* (1934).

In 1919 Rhys married the Dutchman Jean Lenglet and moved with him to Holland, then to Paris. The couple had a son, who died in infancy, and a daughter, Maryvonne. They moved to Vienna, then to Budapest, while Lenglet was working for a disarmament Commission and when, in 1922, he misappropriated his employer's funds they fled back to Paris.

While delivering some articles written by Lenglet to the offices of the *Continental Daily Mail*, Rhys met Mrs Adam, who introduced her to Ford Madox Ford, editor of *The English Review*. Ford encouraged her to write and introduced her to literary circles. In 1924 Lenglet was arrested and jailed for his financial crime, and Rhys, with no means of financial support, took up residence with Ford and his partner Stella Bowen and became Ford's mistress. In 1927 *The Left Bank and Other Stories*, about life in Paris in the 1920s, was published with a preface by Ford introducing Rhys as an exotic writer from the West Indies.

The affair with Ford ended acrimoniously. Rhys wrote about it in *Postures* (1928) and Ford retaliated with his novel *When the Wicked Man* (1931). Other accounts of the affair appeared in Lenglet's novel *Sous les Verrous* (1932) and Bowen's book *Drawn from Life* (1941).

In *Postures* (entitled *Quartet* and published in 1929, in the USA) the protagonist Marya Zelli, having been a chorus girl in England, marries a Pole, Stephan, and moves to Paris. When Stephan is arrested and jailed, leaving her with no money, Marya turns to her friend Miss De Solla for help. De Solla introduces her to the Heidlers and Marya moves in with them. The couple seem to have an under-standing that Marya will become Mr Heidler's mistress, and although she is initially revolted by him, she eventually does so. The *ménage à trois* continues until Marya's husband is freed from prison. Marya, paralysed by loneliness and guilt, is unable to cope with the emotional pressure and loses both men. In Marya – poor, rootless, insecure, victimised and drawn into unstable relationships – we find the first embodiment of the Rhys heroine.

The year 1931 saw the publication of *After Leaving Mr Mackenzie*, a novel set in Paris in the late 1920s. The protagonist, Julia Martin, has been surviving on money sent by her ex-lover, Mr Mackenzie. When the funds are suddenly cut off she travels to London. She meets her mother and sister, but they cannot help her and she realises that love affairs, and drink, have taken their toll on her. She returns to Paris, has one final meeting with Mr Mackenzie and is left facing an insecure future.

Having divorced Lenglet in 1933, Rhys returned to England and it is there, in London in 1914, that her next novel, *Voyage in the Dark* (1934), is set. The novel, drawing on her affair with Lancelot Grey Hugh Smith, tells the story of Anna Morgan, a 19-year-old chorus girl who has come to England from Dominica. Throughout the story Anna's warm memories of her childhood in the West Indies are contrasted with the cold atmosphere of England. She meets Walter Jeffries, who seduces her and offers her a room. She moves in with him, but he eventually tires of her and rejects her. Numbed by misery Anna drifts towards prostitution and the novel ends with her having an abortion.

The year 1934 marked an upturn in Rhys's life. *Voyage in the Dark* was a success, and she married Leslie Tilden-Smith, an editor who gave her help and support in her writing. In 1936 the couple travelled to the Caribbean, visiting Martinique, St Lucia and Dominica, and in 1939, with Tilden-Smith's help, *Good Morning, Midnight* was published. The novel tells the story of Sasha Janses who revisits Paris in 1937. The city brings back bitter memories of failed love affairs and she sets about drinking herself to death. She becomes involved with a gigolo who, deceived by her fur coat into thinking she is wealthy, approaches her. Their relationship becomes nightmarish as she plans to take revenge on him for all the harm men have done to her, while he also harbours revengeful feelings towards her. The novel is a powerful exploration of the theme of women's mistrust of men and men's misunderstanding of women.

After publishing *Good Morning, Midnight* Rhys disappeared from the literary scene and her five books went out of print. Although her work had achieved some critical success, it was ahead of its time and had not earned the recognition it gained later. She dropped out of literary life to such an extent that some of her acquaintances thought she had died. In fact she spent much of the period of the Second World War living in a cottage in Devon.

When Tilden-Smith died in 1945 Rhys met his cousin, Max Hamer, a solicitor and the executor of her late husband's will. They were married in 1947, but they had financial difficulties and Rhys started drinking excessively. In 1948 she was arrested for assaulting her neighbours and the police. She was sent to Holloway Prison Hospital for psychiatric evaluation and released on probation after a week. Hamer, also a heavy drinker, was arrested and imprisoned for misappropriating his firm's money.

Rhys returned to the public arena after being contacted twice, through advertisements in the press seeking information about her whereabouts, by the actress Selma Vas Dias who wanted to adapt her work for radio. In 1956 *Good Morning, Midnight* was broadcast by the BBC and she started to write and publish short stories again. In the same year, she signed a contract with Deutsch for *Wide Sargasso Sea*, which came out 1966, won the W. H. Smith Award and the Heinemann Award, and is considered her masterpiece.

Wide Sargasso Sea, set in the West Indies in the 1840s, is an imagined prequel to Charlotte Brontë's *Jane Eyre*, telling the story of Bertha (renamed Antoinette in Rhys's novel), the mad wife of Mr Rochester. The narrative is split between Rochester's and Antoinette's **points of view**, thus giving Antoinette a voice which she did not have in Brontë's story.

The story begins with an account of Antoinette's childhood in the West Indies, in the nineteenth century, as the daughter of former slave owners – a childhood similar to Rhys's own. The plantation on which Antoinette grows up is in decline, her father having died. As a poor white Creole she has

no social status, her family being shunned by both the white and black communities. Annette's mother remarries, but the recently liberated slaves burn the plantation, her brother dies in the fire and her mother becomes insane.

Rochester arrives in the West Indies, expected to marry a rich heiress of the plantation. Antoinette rejects him at first, but they are eventually married. They are happy for a while, but their cultural differences soon become apparent. Rochester receives a letter from Antoinette's half-brother, Daniel Cosway, telling him about Antoinette's mother's insanity and that her madness is hereditary, and becomes emotionally distant. Antoinette, sensing that he no longer loves her, asks her servant, Christophine, to work voodoo on him. Rochester discovers what she has done and, outraged, sleeps with their maid Amelie before taking Antoinette back to England. Antoinette is devastated and descends into madness.

Being a response to a canonical text and exploring themes of racial, political and sexual oppression, the novel has received a lot of attention in the context of **feminist** and **postcolonial** criticism.

Max Hamer died in 1966 and Rhys, despite her old age, continued to write. In 1968 *Tigers Are Better Looking*, a collection of short stories, was published; in 1975, *My Day*, a collection of three autobiographical pieces appeared in *Vogue*; and in 1976 another collection of stories, *Sleep It Off, Lady*, was published. *Smile Please: An Unfinished Autobiography* was published posthumously.

Selected works:

The Left Bank and Other Stories (1927); *Postures* (1928) (published in the USA as *Quartet* in 1929); *After Leaving Mr. Mackenzie* (1931); *Voyage in the Dark* (1934); *Good Morning, Midnight* (1939); *Wide Sargasso Sea* (1966); *Tigers Are Better Looking* (1968); *My Day* (published in *Vogue*, 1975); *Sleep It Off, Lady* (1976); *Smile Please: An Unfinished Autobiography* (1979).

Further reading

Angier, Carole, *Jean Rhys: Life and Work*. Boston: Little Brown and Company, 1990.

Frickey, Pierrette (ed.) *Critical Perspectives on*

Jean Rhys. Washington, D.C.: Three Continents Press, 1990.

Savory, Elaine, *Jean Rhys.* Cambridge: Cambridge University Press, 1999.

Contributors: Midori Saito, Ian Mackean

ROY, ARUNDHATI (1961–)

Big God howled like a hot wind, and demanded obeisance. Then Small God (cosy and contained, private and limited) came away cauterized, laughing numbly at his own temerity . . . Worse Things had happened. In the country that she came from, poised forever between the terror of war and the horror of peace, Worse Things kept happening. So Small God laughed a hollow laugh, and skipped away cheerfully.

The God of Small Things

Photo credit: © Camera Press – Findlay Kember

Arundhati Roy is best known for her novel *The God of Small Things*, which won the Booker Prize in 1997. She was the first non-expatriate Indian author and the first Indian woman to win the prize, and the year she won it coincided with the 50th anniversary of India's independence from Britain. Admired for her challenging novel and for raising the profile of Indian woman writers, Roy is also a highly controversial figure, particularly in her native India.

Roy was born in Bengal and grew up in Aymanam, a district in the state of Kerala, on the south-west coast of India. Her mother, a Syrian Christian who married and then divorced a Bengali Hindu, ran a successful school which Roy attended as a child and was a prominent social activist. Roy was raised without a *tharawaad* lineage (an extended family structure in which the main power is held by the oldest male member), which meant she grew up free from the conditioning and restraints imposed upon girls in conventional middle-class Indian families.

At the age of 16 Roy left home and went to study at the Delhi School of Architecture, but her main interest was writing and in the 1980s she wrote the script for the film *In Which Annie Gives it to Those Ones*, in which she also starred. She also wrote the script for, and starred in, the film *Electric Moon* (1992), directed by Pradip Kishen, whom she later married. She wrote TV drama scripts, but changed the course of her career after being subject to a court case concerning her article *The Great Indian Rape Trick*, in which she claimed that the Indian outlaw and hero of the oppressed, Phoolan Devi, had been exploited by the film *Bandit Queen* (1994) by Shekhar Kapur.

She spent the next few years concentrating on her novel, completing *The God of Small Things* in 1997. Set against a background of political turbulence in the region of Kottayam, in Kerala, the novel is presented largely from the **point of view** of children, showing the loss of childhood innocence, while exploring such issues as hypocrisy, single-parent families, mixed-caste relationships and forbidden and unrequited love. It tells the story of twins Estappen and Rahel, and their mother, Ammu, a Syrian Christian who has returned to her parental home after divorcing an abusive alcoholic Hindu man. She returns to Mammachi, her blind mother, founder of the family pickle factory, and stays with her twin children and Baby Kochamma, Mammachi's sister-in-law, who converted to the Roman-Catholic faith in an unsuccessful attempt to win the priest's love. Ammu's brother, Chacko, later joins them to run the family's factory as a capitalist enterprise, even though he is a self-proclaimed communist.

The narrative moves backward in time to events that took place 23 years earlier, in 1969, beginning with Rahel returning to her family home and her brother Estappen, in the hope that memories recollected from a distance will heal their emotional wounds. The unfolding plot centres around the visit, and subsequent death by drowning, of the twins' half-English cousin, a nine-year-old girl named Sophie Mol, the daughter of Uncle Chacko, who divorced the girl's English mother Margaret Kochamma. The climax of the story reveals that the tragedy of Sophie Mol's death coincided with Ammu's love affair with Velutha, the family's carpenter, a Dalit (a member of the Hindu caste formerly known as 'untouchables'). The consequences of these intertwined events are dire. Ammu is banished from her home, dying miserably and alone at the age of 31; Estappen is traumatised by his mother's departure and feels so guilty about her death that he stops speaking; and Rahel is expelled from school for 'unwomanly' behaviour and marries an American, whom she has left to return to India.

The novel was hugely successful, but while winning acclaim in England it caused controversy in India, attracting angry criticism from Kerala's leftists for its caricature of Kerala communist E. M. Namboodiripad. It also attracted a lawsuit on the grounds of obscenity, coupled with demands that the final chapter be removed because of its sexual content. The chapter antagonised Indian sensibility by portraying both an incestuous relationship and a sexual relationship between a Christian woman and a Dalit. Roy attributed the hostile reactions primarily to the book's explicit treatment of the role of Dalits.

Roy settled in New Delhi and was the winner of the Lannan Foundation Prize for Cultural Freedom in 2002. In keeping with her lifelong interest in social issues, she has immersed herself in causes such as the antinuclear movement and Narmada Bachao Andolan, an organisation which campaigns against the building of dams. She has written a large number of political essays and participated in events around the world, making passionate speeches. Her political activism has resulted in her being prosecuted and taken to court several times.

Roy sees herself as taking a stance of antiglobalisation, which she defines as a mutant variety of colonialism, remote controlled and digitally operated. Two of her major essays, 'The End of Imagination', about India's nuclear bomb, and 'The Greater Common Good', about the Narmada Dam, were published in her book *The Cost of Living* (1999).

Her collection of essays, *Power Politics* (2001), deals with the politics of writing and the human and environmental costs of development, such as the threat of nuclear war, the privatisation of India's power supply by Enron and the construction of dams. The expanded edition of the book also includes her essays 'The Algebra of Infinite Justice' and 'War is Peace', about violence against innocent people in Afghanistan.

In a further collection of essays, *War Talk*, published in 2003, she discusses general issues such as democracy and dissent, racism and empire, and war and peace, as well as more specific issues concerning violence against Muslims in Gujarat and the US war on Iraq.

Selected works:

In Which Annie Gives It To Those Ones – film script (1988); *Electric Moon* – film script (1992); *The God of Small Things* – novel (1997); *The Cost of Living* – essays (1999); *Power Politics* – essays (2001); *War Talk* – essays (2003).

Further reading

Dhawan, R. K., *Arundhati Roy – the Novelist Extraordinary*. Sangam Books, 1999.

Contributor: Antonia Navarro-Tejero

RUSHDIE, SALMAN (1947–)

I must work faster than Scheherazade, if I am to end up meaning – yes, meaning – something.

Midnight's Children

Salman Rushdie gained international recognition with his second novel, *Midnight's Children* (1980), which won the 1981 Booker Prize and is still regarded by many critics as his best work. This success did a great deal to raise public awareness of Indian literature in English and of postcolonial literature in general.

In 1989 Rushdie gained less welcome worldwide attention as a result of the extreme reaction of Muslim fundamentalists to his novel *The Satanic Verses* (1988), which included an allegedly blasphemous rewriting of the life of the prophet Mohammed. He became the subject of a *fatwa* issued by the leader of Iranian Shia Muslims, Ayatollah Khomeini, which condemned him to death and called on every Muslim to try to the best of his ability to execute the sentence.

Rushdie was born in Bombay in 1947, the year India gained independence from Britain and was partitioned from Pakistan – two events which he incorporated in a quasi-autobiographical manner in *Midnight's Children*. The protagonist Saleem Sinai's narrative, delivered to Padma in an inverted *Arabian Nights*-like dialogue, with the male character telling stories to a female listener who is in love with him, takes shape as the author's body breaks apart under the impact of various catastrophes, reflecting the upheavals in the 'body' of his homeland. Storytelling for survival, one of the novel's themes, is a theme frequently found in postcolonial writing, in which a need is felt to rewrite history from a more authentic point of view than the traditional imperialist one. The theme is combined with a perpetual negotiation between good and bad forces, symbolised by the two main characters, Saleem and Shiva. The two heroes, swapped at birth by Mary Pereira, Saleem's symbolic mother and future *ayah* (nursemaid), exchange social class and family background in a way that highlights the different social strata of Indian society.

One of the characteristic features of Rushdie's work is his use of **magic realism**, though he uses a form different from that used by its South American originators, such as Alejo Carpentier, Carlos Fuentes and Gabriel García Márquez. Magic realism, which recreates the real in a way that derives from **Surrealism**'s deconstruction of the world into its component parts, and reconstruction according to the will of the artist, produces a hierarchical reversal of the real and the imaginary, which works in *Midnight's Children* to connect the protagonist's individual destiny and the destiny of his nation. It is also the code through which the act of storytelling works. Telling his story as a means of survival, like Scheherazade, a character with whom the history-rewriting fiction of postcolonial authors has frequently been associated, Saleem Sinai's narrative traces the history of the first thousand Indian children born after midnight on 15 August 1947 – the moment India became independent. As in Scheherazade's case, the meaning of Saleem's story depends on his ability to tell it. Saleem's story is also full of references to Indian mythology, including the myth of Purusha, a Hindu god who created the universe out of the parts of his own body. As Saleem is dying, his disintegrating body gradually turns into the story he tells and survives through it. With Rushdie, therefore, magic realism is a means of negotiating a perception of history, implicitly connected to the timeless art of storytelling, and an ironical **postmodern metafictional** comment on it.

Shame (1983) **deconstructs** the Muslim world of Pakistan to such an extent that, in many ways, the novel is more critical of the Islamic faith than *The Satanic Verses*. Perhaps the highly encoded, metaphorical and allegorical nature of its narrative protected it from the criticism which otherwise might have been directed against it. Though lacking the solid architecture of *Midnight's Children*, which remains structurally unique among Rushdie's works, *Shame* is very effective in its analysis of the concept of shame. This concept, expressed by the Hindi/Punjabi/Urdu word *sharam*, which the novel opposes to the Western concept of honour, underlies the whole novel. Sufiya Zinobia, the idiot daughter of the Hyder clan, allegorically embodies a shame which is, in fact, that of a whole nation and which is presented as being the moving force behind the post-independence history of Pakistan.

In 1998 the Iranian authorities announced that they would no longer seek to enforce the death-sentence *fatwa* and Rushdie, who had been living in hiding for almost ten years, emigrated to America. His 'American' novels, *The Ground Beneath Her Feet* (1999) and *Fury* (2001), transfer the critical, sometimes even sarcastic discourse once directed against India, then Britain, onto America. In *The Ground Beneath Her Feet*, the story of Vina Apsara and Ormus Cama rewrites the history of American rock and roll music, the story revolving around two fictional Indian-born singers and omitting any reference to real historical figures such as Elvis Presley. In Rushdie's imaginary America, Vina and Ormus develop in two parallel worlds: the world of music (whose influence is so intense that it influences the narrative structure) and the world of myth, namely the tragic story of Orpheus and Eurydice. Vina, like Eurydice, is swallowed by the mercilessly shaking ground which won't give her back to the man who loves her desperately. Made known to a wider audience by the rock group U2's song 'The Ground Beneath Her Feet', which emphasised the Biblical undertones of the title, the novel is also widely debated among critics, whose opinions differ as to its quality. However, the novel is, at the very least, a fascinating page-turner, its suggestion of an alternative to history captivating the reader with its irresistible magic.

Fury, in contrast, is a novel that seems to take itself much more seriously. While the subject of *The Ground Beneath Her Feet* could be seen as the defeating of death through mentally constructed survival strategies such as music and myth, *Fury* demonstrates almost the opposite. It is a concrete example of how language, overused to express destructive feelings, such as revolt, and the rejection of traditional values, and of established systems of order, even of love, finally turns against its own creator. In terms of the theory put forward by J. L. Austin[1] of the capacity of language to either describe realities (**constative**) or trigger them into being (**performative**), Rushdie's use of language in *Fury* is a demonstration of its potential for **performativity**. Indeed, the capacity of language to create realities is so radical that, in the end, the character Professor Malik Solanka, in his total rejection of conventions, manages to destroy everything which he has felt to be a limitation on his freedom and ends up, irrespective of his intentions, with nothing to return to.

The book captivates its readers from its very first pages with a strikingly vivid picture of New York. The multicultural city appears with its patchwork of identities, the result of layer upon layer of migration, which creates its cultural specificity. New York is also seen as a place of identities that are no longer migrant but nomadic, unfixed in space, in perpetual movement. It is such a nomadic construction of identity that actually characterises all of Rushdie's protagonists and, up to a point, reflects his own migration from Bombay to London and then New York.

In addition to his sarcastic antifundamentalist criticism, Rushdie is a strikingly innovating, daring, often iconoclastic writer in many ways. As one of the most original postmodern authors, he experiments with form, content and narrative voice as part of his project to rewrite postcolonial history. His manipulation of fictional forms, moreover, projects his image as that of a subversive migrant writer, whose main project in the world of literature seems to be to criticise all established authorities. Thus, even nowadays, when Rushdie is part of the canon of British literature, his subversive status is still relevant.

Reference

1. Austin, J. L. (1976) *How to Do Things with Words*: The William James Lectures Delivered in Harvard University in 1955 (Oxford Paperbacks). (First published 1962.)

Selected works:
Grimus (1975); *Midnight's Children* (1980); *Shame* (1983); *The Jaguar Smile: A Nicaraguan Journey* (1987); *The Satanic Verses* (1988); *Haroun and the Sea of Stories* (1990); *Imaginary Homelands: Essays and Criticism 1981–1991* (1991); *East, West* (1994); *The Moor's Last Sigh* (1995); *The Ground Beneath Her Feet* (1999); *Fury* (2001); *Step Across This Line: Collected Non-Fiction 1992–2002* (2002).

Further reading

Appignanesi, Lisa and Maitland, Sarah (eds) *The Rushdie File*. Syracuse: Syracuse University Press, 1990.

Fletcher, M. D., *Reading Rushdie: Perspectives on the Fiction of Salman Rushdie*. Amsterdam and Atlanta: Rodopi, 1994.

Contributor: Maria-Sabina Draga Alexandru

S

SALINGER, J. D. (1919–)

If you really want to hear about it, the first thing you'll probably want to know is where I was born, and what my lousy childhood was like, and how my parents were occupied and all before they had me, and all that David Copperfield kind of crap, but I don't feel like going into it, if you want to know the truth.

Opening of The Catcher in the Rye

Photo credit: © Bettmann/CORBIS

Considered by many to be a major American author of the twentieth century, J. D. Salinger's reputation stands on his single novel, *The Catcher in the Rye* (1951), and four volumes of short stories.

Jerome David Salinger was born in New York in 1919, to a Jewish father and Irish Catholic mother. He had a strained relationship with his father, particularly after rejecting the offer to enter the family's meat-and-cheese business. He attended Valley Forge Military Academy, Ursinus College, and New York University, but was not particularly diligent in his studies. When the Second World War broke out in Europe, Salinger was recruited into the infantry. He was involved in the invasion of Normandy, many of his wartime comrades later testifying to his bravery in action. The horrifying experiences of war, however, cured him of his youthful love for the military and his revised opinion of war later found expression in the short story 'For Esmé – With Love and Squalor' (1950).

During and after the war, Salinger's short stories began to be published in magazines such as *Story, The Saturday Evening Post, Esquire* and *The New Yorker.* In 1948 his story 'A Perfect Day for Bananafish' won critical acclaim and introduced the character Seymour Glass, of the Glass family which was to play a major role in his later fiction. In 1951 he published *The Catcher in the Rye,* which attracted instant attention and earned high praise. The cult status his work still enjoys is due mainly to this book. Salinger continued to publish in magazines and anthologies until the mid-1960s, since when he has published little, though he is reputed to have continued writing. Salinger prefers to avoid public attention, remaining in isolation in his home in New Hampshire, where he lives with his third wife.

The Catcher in the Rye is the story of Holden Caulfield, a 16-year-old boy growing up in Manhattan, showing the stress and anxiety he experiences as, facing expulsion from preparatory school, he stands on the threshold of adulthood. The narrative consists of Holden's intense and deeply personal monologue, the language, complete with contemporary slang and profanities typical of a disillusioned teenager, having a natural colloquial tone. Holden's main quest in life is for authenticity in ideals, people and relationships, which he mostly fails to find. His world is infested with 'phonies' – his term for people who do not measure up to his stringent private standards of sincerity and honesty. There are only two people he can, or ever could, fully trust – his younger sister and his brother, who died some years earlier. The novel's title derives from Holden's misquote from a

Robert Burns poem, when he explains to his sister that he sees himself, metaphorically, as guarding the edge of a cliff to save the children playing in the rye fields from plummeting over the edge. Being a powerful expression of teenage angst and a lively portrait of American society seen through the eyes of a young person, *The Catcher in the Rye* is often compared to Mark Twain's *The Adventures of Huckleberry Finn* (1885).

Many of Salinger's short stories involve the Glass family of New York. Some are narrated by Buddy Glass while others are about his brother Seymour who is, in Buddy's estimate, one of the few 'non-expendable' poets of America. Seymour's death, in 'A Perfect Day for Bananafish', begins the Glass family saga which links tales scattered through Salinger's volumes of short stories: *Nine Stories* (1953), *Franny and Zooey* (1961), *Raise High the Roofbeam, Carpenters and Seymour: an Introduction* (1963). Like *The Catcher in the Rye,* the stories show exceptionally powerful characterisation and subtlety of observation.

There is something in Salinger's prose style that encourages mimicry. There have been numerous attempts to imitate the language of *The Catcher in the Rye,* even hostile reviewers and critics sometimes trying to emulate Holden's speech. Salinger is sometimes accused of 'overcharacterising' his characters and is not unaware of this, as revealed in his statement: 'There is a real-enough danger, I suppose, that sooner or later I'll bog down, perhaps disappear entirely, in my own methods, locutions, and mannerisms'.[1] Salinger's later style moved somewhat away from narrative and became more introspective and self-conscious, as John Updike observed in an influential review of *Franny and Zooey* in 1961.[2]

Salinger's life seems to attract as much attention as his works. The fact that he has been a recluse since the mid-1960s has been the subject of a surprising amount of public curiosity and conjecture. Societies and fan clubs have been formed whose main purpose seems to be to discover and circulate trivia about Salinger. His marriages and extramarital affairs, his adoption of Zen Buddhist philosophy, his habit of writing while sitting in a lotus position on a car seat that he moved into a special brick bunker detached from the main house, his hostility towards reporters and other visitors – such snippets of information have gone into the creation of his public image. Ian Hamilton, in his biography, has virtually accused Salinger of stage-managing his persona by finely timing his rare public appearances and deliberately provoking controversy. Though Salinger has not published since 1965, he testified in a court of law in 1986 that he continues to write.

References

1. **Updike, John** (1961) *Anxious Days For The Glass Family.*
www.morrill.org/books/updikeonsalinger.
shtml (accessed 2.3.04)

2. Ibid.

Selected works:

The Catcher in the Rye (1951); *Nine Stories* (1953); *Franny and Zooey* (1961); *Raise High the Roof Beam, Carpenters and Seymour: An Introduction* (1963).

Further reading

Bloom, Harold (ed.) *Salinger: Modern Critical Views.* Chelsea House Publishers, 1992.

Hamilton, Ian, *In Search of J. D. Salinger.* Heinemann, 1988.

Marsden, Malcolm (ed.) *A Catcher Casebook.* Scott, Foresman, 1963.

Contributor: Tathagata Banerjee

SHIELDS, CAROL (1935–2003)

A room of one's own. Good old Virginia.
She had her head screwed on right.
                    Happenstance: The Wife's Story

Born in Oak Park, Illinois, in 1935, but resident in Canada from 1957 until her death in 2003, Carol Shields is largely regarded as a Canadian writer – and one of the foremost of the late twentieth century. A poet, a playwright, a biographer, a short-story writer and an essayist as well as a novelist, it is for her nine novels that Shields is most acclaimed. Her numerous literary awards include the Canadian Governor General's Award for fiction (1993) and the Pulitzer Prize (1995), both for *The Stone Diaries* (which was also short-listed for the Booker Prize), and the Orange Prize (1998) for *Larry's Party.* Shields was Professor of English at the University of Manitoba and Chancellor of the University of Winnipeg, and received eight honorary doctorates from North American universities.

Set variously in her adopted homeland and her birthplace, Shields's narratives frequently address questions of national cultures and geographies, depicting Canadians and Americans as foreigners to one another in many respects. In pursuing this theme she is perhaps alluding playfully to an irony which attaches to Furlong Eberhardt's national identity (in *Small Ceremonies*, 1976) but which could equally be applied to her own: the irony that a novelist 'who is said to embody the ethos of the [Canadian] nation, is an American!'.

Shields's novels, being largely character-driven and revolving around family and romantic relationships, have widely been regarded as domestic **realist** fictions akin to those by contemporary North American women writers such as Anne Tyler and Alison Lurie, exploring both satirically and compassionately the dynamics that determine the shape of family and sexual lives. The individual search for fulfilment is a pervasive theme, with a special focus on the tensions between home and work, or service and self-expression, experienced by women. However, Shields's abiding interest in the limitations of language and narrative, and in the difficulty of knowing – let alone representing – the other or the self, has generated a view of her work as belonging to a more **postmodern** school. This reading is supported by her frequent mixing of genres and experimentation with unconventional forms. *Swann* (1987), for instance, ends with a section in the style of a film script, while the complex structure of *The Stone Diaries* (1993) invites an understanding of the individual subject as a postmodern construct.

Many of Shields's lasting preoccupations were present from the start, in *Small Ceremonies,* which recounts biographer Judith Gill's difficult personal encounter with issues of intellectual ownership and theft. Judith herself is accustomed to constructing narratives out of the raw material of her subjects' lives, having found that writing a biography of Susanna Moodie entailed 'setting out to exhume her, searching, prying into the small seams, counting stitches . . . invading an area of existence where I've no real rights'. She is nevertheless outraged when her friend Furlong Eberhardt, a commercially successful novelist, 'steals' a plot from notes she once made towards a novel of her own, which she eventually abandoned. The fact that she in turn 'borrowed' the storyline from an English academic whose house she and her husband once rented, and that this man subsequently publishes a first novel revolving around a thinly disguised depiction of her and her family, subtly complicates questions of legitimate and illegitimate literary use.

In *Swann* (1987) Shields returns to related territory, examining the use made by four individuals (a scholar, a biographer, a neighbour and a publisher) of the work, personal life and few surviving possessions of a rural Canadian poet brutally murdered by her husband. On one level a **feminist** manifesto decrying the domestic enslavement and suppression of women like Mary Swann, and urging the recovery and appreciation of their voices, this novel also perceptively – and often comically – exposes the self-serving motives and dishonest actions of some of the poet's most devoted followers.

The title of *Small Ceremonies* alludes to the symbolic significance Shields identifies in the minor private rituals (such as eating high tea on a Sunday) by means of which people give order and meaning to their daily lives. In *Happenstance: The Wife's Story* (2003; first published as *A Fairly Conventional Woman* in 1982), the value of habit and continuity is eloquently described: 'Every morning Brenda wakes up, slips into her belted robe, and glides – *glides* – down the wide oak stairs . . . The descent down the broad, uncarpeted stairs has something of ceremony about it, it has gone on so long.' For Brenda, shape and structure can still more significantly be found in the quintessentially North American craft of quilt-making, through which she finds private satisfaction and public recognition, when one of her quilts receives special mention at a National Handicrafts Exhibition, as well as a measure of economic independence. One of her quilts sells for $600 and Brenda's friend Hap Lewis sees this as a 'milestone': 'When you get your own tax form. You've made it, kiddo.'

Celebrating women's creativity and promoting a reappraisal of traditional crafts as fully fledged arts, *Happenstance* again adopts a feminist stance. Rebelling against a common experience of being 'expected to do [their] stuff between loads of wash', the predominantly female handicrafts practitioners ally themselves with a renowned literary forebear, **Virginia Woolf**, in demanding more time and space in which to pursue their creative agenda: 'A room of one's own. Good old Virginia. She had her head screwed on right.'

Sometimes criticised for an excessively feminine perspective and for appealing to an almost exclusively female audience, Shields perhaps runs the risk in *Happenstance* (1980) of associating what Elaine Showalter[1] calls a 'Female Aesthetic' too closely with the home. A stereotypically gendered model of intellectual male and instinctual, natural, anti-intellectual female does seem to emerge: Brenda is 'thankful no one asked her anymore what such-and-such a quilt was "about". She wouldn't have known', while her husband Jack, a historian, scrutinises her quilt-in-progress, determined to articulate its meaning, which slips into his head like 'a silverfish, in and out, too quick to grasp'.

Elsewhere in Shields's fiction, however, male characters experience the rewards and the 'rhapsody' of working with their hands. In *Larry's Party* (1997), which employs a consistently male central consciousness, men find fulfilment through clock-making and upholstering, while Larry himself works first as a florist and later as a landscape designer specialising in hedge mazes. His occupation involves many of the same skills of patterning and patient nurturing as the 'feminine' folk-art of quilting and becomes a metaphor for a truly creative, rather than reductively analytical, mode of making meaning. It is Larry's second wife, Beth Prior, who is the official intellectual in this story. She is an academic whose work on the lives of early female saints introduces a theme of female virtue which Shields developed in her last novel, *Unless* (2002).

In *Unless*, translator and novelist Reta Winters is anguished and uncomprehending at her daughter Nora's decision to drop out of university, leave her boyfriend and spend her days begging on a Toronto street corner while displaying a placard bearing the word 'goodness'. Reta eventually interprets Nora's behaviour as a passive protest against the sidelined and powerless position of women in wider society and herself takes up arms, in the form of her pen, against patriarchal discrimination. *Unless* combines passages of explicit feminist argument with gentler, more reflective sections in which Reta takes stock of the frail foundations of her previous happiness: a stable home life, joyful motherhood, a loving sexual partnership, enjoyable work, good and long-lasting friendships – all of which recur as trademark themes in Shields's oeuvre.

In *The Stone Diaries* (1993), the inventory made by Daisy Goodwill Flett at the end of an unfulfilled life lists all the things she has *not* done, including, most pitifully, being addressed with the words 'I love you'. This absence places Daisy beyond the saving realm of human cherishing described in Shields's most popular comic romance, *The Republic of Love* (1992): 'Almost everyone gets a chance to say it – I love you. And to hear it said to them. Love is, after all, a republic'. Unlike Daisy's dispiriting chronicle of misfortunes, Reta's life history up until the crisis with Nora is largely positive, and it is the very vulnerability of human happiness to sudden destruction that makes *Unless* – a novel written during Shields's terminal illness – a dark and unsettling book.

Taking refuge in a night shelter for the homeless, Nora enacts what is identified in *Small Ceremonies* as the Canadian 'national theme': 'shelter from the storm of life.' Not only physical spaces – the houses to which Shields's fiction pays so much attention – but work, love, friendship, memories and favourite items of clothing are all represented as offering places of safety in an unpredictable world.

In *Larry's Party*, which sustains a particular focus on the power of words, even language is invested with the capacity to comfort and protect: by continuing to use vocabulary such as 'cooker' and 'petrol' exported from their native Lancashire, Larry's expatriate parents 'have . . . improvised for themselves a crude shelter in an alien land'.

Reference

1. **Showalter, Elaine** (1994) *Sister's Choice: Tradition and Change in American Women's Writing*. Oxford University Press, p. 146.

Selected works:

Novels: *Small Ceremonies* (1976); *The Box Garden* (1977); *Happenstance* (1980); *A Fairly Conventional Woman* (1982); *Swann: A Mystery* (1987); *The Republic of Love* (1992); *The Stone Diaries* (1993); *Larry's Party* (1997); *Unless* (2002). **Poetry:** *Others: Poems* (1972); *Intersect: Poems* (1974); *Coming to Canada* (1992). **Short stories:** *Various Miracles* (1985); *The Orange Fish* (1989); *Dressing Up for the Carnival* (2000). **Plays:** *Departures and Arrivals* (1990); *Thirteen Hands* (1993). **Non-fiction:** *Susanna Moodie: Voice and Vision* (1977).

Further reading

Eden, E. and Goertz, D. (eds) *Carol Shields, Narrative Hunger, and the Possibilities of Fiction.* University of Toronto Press, 2003.

Special issues of journals devoted to Shields: *Room of One's Own* 13.1/2 (1989) and *Prairie Fire* 16.1 (Spring 1995).

Contributor: Alison Kelly

SILLITOE, ALAN (1928–)

There's bound to be trouble in store for me every day of my life, because trouble it's always been and always will be.
Saturday Night and Sunday Morning

Alan Sillitoe was one of the most prominent British novelists of the 1960s and is remembered as one of the group known as the **Angry Young Men**, although his best-known novel, *Saturday Night and Sunday Morning* (1958), was published a little too late for him to have been at the forefront of the movement – *Hurry On Down* by John Wain having been published in 1953, *Lucky Jim* by **Kingsley Amis** in 1954 and *Look Back in Anger* by John Osborne having been performed in 1956.

In Britain of the 1950s and 1960s harsh **realism** such as Sillitoe's was the predominant style in literature, being used by prominent writers of the era such as Arnold Wesker, John Braine, Keith Waterhouse, Stan Barstow, Shelagh Delaney and Nell Dunn. These writers may not have reached a working-class readership – people like Arthur Seaton of *Saturday Night and Sunday Morning* would not have spent their Saturday nights or Sunday mornings reading novels – but many of their works were filmed and thus reached a wide audience.

The son of an illiterate factory worker who became unemployed in the Depression of the 1930s, Sillitoe spent his early life in poverty and was largely self-educated after leaving school at the age of 14. After working in factories for six years he joined the RAF and served in Malaya, but was invalided out at the age of 21 with tuberculosis, and began to write during his subsequent months in hospital. He also read widely, being particularly impressed by such classics as Plutarch's *Lives*, Gibbon's *History of the Decline and Fall of the Roman Empire* and Carlyle's *French Revolution*.[1]

He then spent seven years abroad, in France and Spain, living with Ruth Fainlight, an American poet, scraping a living and recovering his health in warmer climates. He read American writers such as Norman Mailer, William Styron, Carson McCullers and **J. D. Salinger**, as well as the first novels of John Braine, **Kingsley Amis** and John Wain.[2] He visited Robert Graves on the island of Mallorca in 1956 and Graves encouraged him to write realistically about his experience of life in Nottingham, a suggestion which bore fruit in the highly successful *Saturday Night and Sunday Morning*. He married Ruth Fainlight in 1959 when she obtained a divorce from her first husband, and he had the prospect of some money coming in from books and film rights.

Like **D. H. Lawrence** before him and the later **Liverpool Poets**, Sillitoe wrote from a provincial standpoint which was distant from, and a challenge to, London, the middle classes and the literary establishment. His early novels were more firmly rooted in the working-class milieu than were most of the other works of Angry Young Men, and had an underlying political intent, highlighting the situation of the working classes in a modern industrial society.

In *Saturday Night and Sunday Morning* Sillitoe presents Arthur Seaton as a victim of a society which promotes escapism and consumerism through the propaganda of advertising, while at the same time demanding conformity to the class roles of workers and administrators. An **antihero**, Seaton is dissatisfied with his lot as a factory worker and like Jimmy Porter of *Look Back in Anger*, is brimming with resentment and defiance, feeling himself to be subject to the established order in which power is wielded by the upper and middle classes. On Saturday nights he indulges in excessive drinking and riotous behaviour, then experiences a period of calm and reflection on Sunday mornings before returning to the factory and a working week of mindless boredom. Seaton expresses his rebellious spirit by antagonising the established order in any way he can and the story ends at a point where he has some prospect of improving his life, through promotion and marriage. The novel earned respect on its publication, admired for its dialogue and social realism, and became a best-seller when the film, which Sillitoe adapted for the screen himself, was released in 1960.

Sillitoe's other well-known work is 'The Loneliness of the Long-Distance Runner', a short story published in a volume of the same name in 1959 and filmed in 1962. The anti-heroic protagonist, Smith, is a thief detained in borstal. The governor of the institution hopes that Smith will win a cross-country race and that the achievement will motivate his rehabilitation into society. Smith enjoys long-distance running because while running he is alone, with no one to tell him what to do, free to think for himself and reflect upon his life. His thoughts are dominated by his view of society as divided into the 'In-laws', those who own property and wield power, such as the borstal governor, and those, such as himself, who do not, the 'Out-laws'.

While running the race he reflects on the fact that if he wins it will not only give the governor a chance to claim credit for having 'rehabilitated' him but also entrap him (Smith) in the system of competition and reward imposed by the establishment. In an act of anarchic defiance, he stops running, sacrificing his chance to win, affirming that he will not join or support the class that represents authority and ownership. In society's terms he has spoiled his chance for 'success', but in his own terms he has triumphed by being true to his beliefs and acting upon his own values. Smith's attitude foreshadows the 'drop-out' trend of the later 1960s.

The protagonist of Sillitoe's novel *Key to the Door* (1961) is Brian Seaton, the brother of Arthur of *Saturday Night and Sunday Morning*. The novel deals with Brian's experience of the Depression and army service in Malaya and, like Sillitoe's other novels, shows the character's rejection of the attitudes and goals imposed upon him by the establishment.

In 1963 Sillitoe visited the Soviet Union for a month to see how a classless society operated, and gave an account of it in *Road to Volgograd* the following year. The rigours of his early life were depicted in the autobiographical *Life Without Armour* (1995). In *Birthday* (2001) the characters from *Saturday Night and Sunday Morning* meet again in old age. Sillitoe has also published poetry and a series of children's stories about a cat named Marmalade Jim.

References

1. **Sillitoe, Alan** (2002) *On Books and Reading*, from *Reading the Decades*. Open University. www.open2.net/readingthedecades/expert_opinion/expert_sillitoe.htm

2. Ibid.

Selected works:

Without Beer or Bread (1957); *Saturday Night and Sunday Morning* (1958); *The Loneliness of the Long-Distance Runner* (1959); *The Rats, and Other Poems* (1960); *The General* (1960); *Key To The Door* (1961); *The Ragman's Daughter* (1963); *A Falling Out of Love, and Other Poems* (1964); *Road To Volgograd* (1965); *The Death of William Poster* (1965); *A Tree On Fire* (1967); *The City Adventures of Marmalade Jim* (1967); *Love In The Environs of Voronezh* (1968); *Guzman, Go Home* (1968); *Shaman and Other Poems* (1968); *A Start In Life* (1970); *This Foreign Field* (1970); *Travels In Nihilon* (1971); *Poems* (1971); *Shaman and Other Poems* (1973); *Men, Women, and Children* (1973); *Barbarians* (1974); *Storm* (1974); *The Flame of Life* (1974); *Raw Material* (1974); *The Widower's Son* (1976); *Pit Strike* (1977); *Big John and The Stars* (1977); *Three Plays* (1978); *The Incredible Fencing Fleas* (1978); *The Storyteller* (1979); *Snow On The North Side of Lucifer* (1979); *Marmalade Jim At The Farm* (1980); *The Second Chance and Other*

Stories (1981); *Her Victory* (1982); *Sun Before Departure* (1982); *The Lost Flying Boat* (1983); *Down From The Hill* (1984); *Marmalade Jim and The Fox* (1984); *Life Goes On* (1985); *Tides and Stone Walls* (1986); *Every Day of The Week* (1987); *Three Poems* (1988); *Out of The Whirlpool* (1988); *The Open Door* (1989); *Lost Loves* (1990); *Leonard's War* (1991); *Collected Poems* (1993); *Snowstop* (1993); *Collected Stories* (1995); *Life Without Armour* (1995); *Alligator Playground* (1997); *The Broken Chariot* (1998); *Leading The Blind: A Century of Guide Book Travel 1815–1914* (1999); *Birthday* (2001).

Further reading

Hanson, Gillian Mary, *Understanding Alan Sillitoe* (Understanding Contemporary British Literature). University of South Carolina Press, 1998.

Contributors: Ian Mackean,
                                   Stephen Colbourn

STEINBECK, JOHN (1902–68)

We was farm people till the debt. And then – them people. They done somepin to us. Ever' time they come seemed like they was a-whippin' me – all of us.

The Grapes of Wrath

Photo credit: © Bettmann/CORBIS

John Ernst Steinbeck gained a reputation for writing about the plight of the ordinary working man and the dispossessed, particularly during the Great Depression of the 1930s. He wrote novels, short stories, plays, screenplays and articles and is best known for his novel *The Grapes of Wrath* (1939) which earned him the Pulitzer Prize for fiction in 1940. He was awarded the Nobel Prize for literature in 1962.

Steinbeck was born in Salinas, California; his father was County Treasurer and his mother a teacher. He attended Stanford University, studying marine biology. He never took his degree, but his appreciation of biological processes to do with survival fed into the themes of his writing. He later collaborated with biologist Edward F. Rickett in researching and writing about marine life in the Gulf of California, their co-authored book *The Sea of Cortez* being published in 1941.

Steinbeck began writing at Stanford, where some of his poems and short stories were published in university magazines. After leaving university he worked briefly as a reporter in New York, then returned to California to pursue his writing while supporting himself with a series of casual jobs, including some agricultural work, which provided first-hand contact with the types of people he depicted in his stories.

His early novels, *Cup of Gold* (1929), *The Pastures of Heaven* (1932), *To a God Unknown* (1933), were not successful in either commercial or critical terms. *Tortilla Flat* (1935), a humorous picaresque tale about Mexican-Americans, which parallels their lives with tales of King Arthur and his Knights of the Round Table, brought more recognition, but his first major success came with the publication of the novella *Of Mice and Men* in 1937. The story tells the ultimately tragic tale of two migrant workers who fail to realise their dreams, and deals with themes – particularly the inability of the poor to change their lives after becoming trapped in circumstances beyond their control – which were realised more fully in *The Grapes of Wrath*.

In 1937, fearing that his growing literary success might distance him from the lives of ordinary people, and in preparation for writing *The Grapes of Wrath*, Steinbeck joined a group of migrant workers travelling from Oklahoma to California and lived with them in a government camp. These agricultural labourers had had to leave their Oklahoma farms because the land had become unworkable as a result of the severe drought which led to the region becoming known as the 'Dust Bowl'. It was the time of the Depression and California could not support the influx of migrants, many of whom starved to death.

The Grapes of Wrath, whose title is taken from the 'Battle Hymn of the American Republic', written in 1861, is largely documentary in style, following the journey of one family, the Joads, to California. The novel has a strong political message and caused controversy by being critical of government policies which contributed to the fate of people like the Joads. In

telling the story Steinbeck raises themes which were central to his work, such as the struggles of the poor, man's inhumanity to man, the destructive effects of selfishness and the saving power of the family.

During the Second World War Steinbeck served as a reporter for the *New York Tribune* and was based in Britain and the Mediterranean. He wrote anti-Nazi propaganda, including a wartime story called 'The Moon is Down' (1943).

His concern with the social hardship of ordinary people continued after the war, resulting in such novels as *Cannery Row* (1945), which is sometimes seen as idealising the life of the lower classes, and *East of Eden* (1952), which updated the biblical story of Cain and Abel.

A number of Steinbeck's books were made into films, including *The Grapes of Wrath*, which was directed by John Ford in 1940 and starred Henry Fonda as Tom Joad. *East of Eden* was filmed in 1955, directed by Elia Kazan, and starred James Dean. Steinbeck himself wrote screenplays, including one based on his own short story *The Red Pony* (1948), *The Forgotten Village* (1949) and *Viva Zapata!* (1952), directed by Elia Kazan.

Steinbeck's concern for the injustices suffered by the less privileged in society places him in a tradition of American socially concerned writing, represented for example by Harriet Beecher Stowe with *Uncle Tom's Cabin* (1851–52), Upton Sinclair with his novel *The Jungle* (1906) and John Dos Passos with his trilogy *USA* (1930–36). Steinbeck sought to expose the oppression of the working man, not just in terms of employer/employee relations but also the conflicts between ordinary people themselves, who often exploited one another for relatively little gain. Steinbeck offers no vision of Utopia, but does stress the positive values of endurance, companionship, acts of kindness and the supportive nature of the family.

Steinbeck's approach to his subject matter displays a humanist view of society, emphasising the huge external forces that bear down on his characters and their struggles for survival. The conflict between people's expectations and changes in society, in particular from a pastoral world to a more industrialised one, underpins his work. He displays a belief in human progress and champions the notion that people can stake out an intellectual or moral claim in their lives, despite the evident hardships many suffer. Steinbeck was not only a social critic and a chronicler of the Depression era, he was also a great storyteller.

One of the most popular works of his later period was *Travels with Charley* (1962), in which he recounted his travels around America with his pet poodle. His final work, *The Acts of King Arthur and his Noble Knights*, a modern update of the Arthurian legend, on which he had worked in England, was published posthumously in 1976.

Selected works:

Cup of Gold (1929); *The Pastures of Heaven* (1932); *To a God Unknown* (1933); *Tortilla Flat* (1935); *In Dubious Battle* (1936); *Saint Katy the Virgin* (1936); *Nothing so Monstrous* (1936); *Of Mice and Men* (1937); *The Red Pony* (1937); *The Blood is Strong* (1938); *The Long Walley* (1938); *The Grapes of Wrath* (1939); *A Letter to the Friends of Democracy* (1940); *The Sea of Cortez* (1941, with Edward F. Rickett); *The Forgotten Village* (1941); *Bombs Away* (1942); *The Moon is Down* (1942); *How Edith McGillicuddy met R.L.S.* (1943); *Steinbeck* (1943, ed. Pascal Covici); *Cannery Row* (1945); *The Wayward Bus* (1947); *The Pearl* (1947); *A Russian Journal* (1948); *Burning Bright* (1950); *East of Eden* (1952); *Short Novels* (1953); *Sweet Thursday* (1954); *The Short Reign of Pippin IV* (1957); *The Crapshooter* (1957); *Once there was War* (1958); *The Winter of Discontent* (1961); *Travels with Charley* (1962); *Journal of a Novel* (1969); *Steinbeck: a Life in Letters – 1902–1968* (1975); *The Acts of King Arthur and his Noble Knights* (1976).

Further reading

Parini, Jay, *John Steinbeck: A Biography*. Minerva, 1995.

Timmerman, John, *John Steinbeck's Fiction: The Aesthetics of the Road Taken*. University of Oklahoma Press, 1991.

Contributors: Gareth Vaughan, Ian Mackean

STEVENS, WALLACE (1879–1955)

He rode over Connecticut
In a glass coach.
Once a fear pierced him,
In that he mistook
The shadow of his equipage
For blackbirds.
            'Thirteen Ways of Looking at a
                              Blackbird'

As a **romantic modernist**, Wallace Stevens, one of the main influences behind the New York School in American poetry, is the poet who imbues nature with the imagination's light, as he is also the poet as artificer of a world distinct from nature, conscious of its own making. The combination is exotic, yet austere, generating evocative poem titles such as 'Thirteen Ways of Looking at a Blackbird', 'The Emperor of Ice-Cream', 'The Idea of Order at Key West' and 'Le Monocle de Mon Oncle'. The considerable output of Collected Poems (1954), however, came from a man who qualified as a lawyer, married and worked all his life for an insurance company in Hartford, Connecticut, rising to a senior position. Poetry, for Stevens, was always a spare-time activity: the substantial body of work was carved out of the spaces that he could make in a taxing professional career. Temperamentally, he needed financial security in order to cultivate the pleasures of the imagination.

Harmonium, Stevens's first volume of poetry, appeared in 1923. It is poetry of the senses, of music (as the title suggests), colour, mood, clowning around, yet it is witty, as suggested by 'Peter Quince at the Clavier', a poem in sonata form, in which one of Shakespeare's rustics is at the instrument, or in 'Sea Surface Full of Clouds', a magical confection of colour and sound. Poems such as 'Fabliau of Florida' and 'Nomad Exquisite' respond to the sensuality and fecundity of the Florida Keys that became a favourite holiday place for Stevens. *Harmonium* is a volume of fantastic vocabulary, most notably in 'The Comedian as the Letter C', a comic poem in which the consciousness of the modern poet, seeking a language, gorges itself on gaudy phrases such as 'pampean dits' and 'felicity in cantilene': this is the poet producing 'poems of plums'. Yet there is also the 'The Snow Man', which advocates a wintry bareness of language, and 'The Paltry Nude Starts on a Spring Voyage', which proclaims an American mode of modernity stripped of the past, an energy that is future-directed, hungry for success. However, the most moving poem in the volume, 'Sunday Morning', is a meditation upon loss, upon the modern condition in which humanity, 'unsponsored' by God, is exiled from paradise. In this predicament, the imagination must trace its own patterns in nature; there is no divine order. Stevens's affinity with Keats is apparent in the closing image of transience:

At evening casual flocks of pigeons make
Ambiguous undulations as they sink,
Downward to darkness, on extended
wings.

Stevens, in one of his rare lectures, said that 'the great poems of heaven and hell have been written and the great poem of the earth remains to be written',[1] yet his own 'Sunday Morning' is a 'great poem of the earth', an evocation of the wilderness as our potential Eden.

Harmonium was an extraordinary achievement, yet it did not sell well and did not receive the acclaim of **T. S. Eliot**'s 'The Waste Land', the great **Modernist** landmark poem published a year earlier in 1922. Stevens wrote little for six years after the publication of *Harmonium*. His daughter, Holly, was born in 1924 and during the downturn of the American economy in the Depression, he concentrated on his business career to ensure stability for his family.

Ideas of Order, published in 1935, signalled Stevens's return to poetry writing. In the signature poem of the volume, 'The Idea of Order at Key West', the female singer in the opening is the 'artificer' of a world, yet the poet constantly asks if the other world of nature, the 'tragic-gestured sea', is made meaningful in her song. This questioning, yet assertion of the imagination's value in relation to reality, the natural world in which we exist, preoccupied Stevens throughout his artistic career.

In 'The Man with the Blue Guitar', from the volume of that title (1937), blue represents the imagination's power to transform reality. Throughout his work, Stevens developed a symbolic mythology of colour and a theatre of exotic characters that were an escape from what he called the 'poverty'[2] of the world without imagination. As a modernist he knew that this world was a fictive artifice, as a romantic he hued it with nature's colours. But for all Stevens's attachment to the gaudy, there is an underlying sadness in his sense that humanity is part of but apart from nature:

From this the poem springs: that we live
in a place
That is not our own and, much more, not
ourselves[3]

It is paradoxical that a poet who expresses so poignantly our human isolation in the natural world is also the great poet of the American landscape, climate, season and region. In the volumes *Parts of a World* (1942), *Transport to Summer* (1947) and *The Auroras of Autumn* (1950), the poems about the imagination's weather are also the poems of light and air and atmosphere. In the long poems of his maturity, Stevens distilled both poetic wisdom and a kind of summation of the senses, of our existence in the physical world. In 'Credences of Summer' the mind lays aside its troubles and finds a point in which the characters in the theatre of summer are 'Complete in a completed scene, speaking / Their parts in a youthful happiness'. Stevens also found, as he grew older, that at times the poet could indeed read from the book of life: in 'Large Red Man Reading', the listeners are 'ghosts' whose 'spended hearts' take on colour and shape as the poetic lines 'spoke the feeling for them, which was what they had lacked'.

Stevens's final volume, *The Rock* (1954), included poems in which his life-long meditations upon imagination and reality reached a fitting finale. In 'Final Soliloquy of the Interior Paramour' he acknowledges that there may be 'small reason' why we think the 'world imagined is the ultimate good', yet it is our human 'dwelling' that 'lights the dark'. In 'Not Ideas about the Thing but the Thing Itself' (the poem that he chose to conclude *The Collected Poems of Wallace Stevens*) he expresses the coming into being of a poem as the thing itself. The world of poetry and the world of nature in which poems are composed seem somehow more at ease with each other in these poems of old age such as 'The Planet on the Table' in which the poet, playfully represented as Ariel, Prospero's spirit, finds in his own 'planet' (the volume of poems on the table) some 'affluence' in the words 'Of the planet of which they were part'.

Stevens's later poems are plainer in diction, more abstract and expository than the early music of *Harmonium*; they have acquired authority and *gravitas*. However, there is, as before, a mesmeric cadence, a belief in the 'supreme fiction'[4] of the imagination, and an enigmatic dazzle of import that teasingly withholds meaning yet beckons the reader to 'behold' the world created by poetry, the world that Stevens, to quote the last word of 'Final Soliloquy', felt was 'enough'.

References

1. 'The Imagination as Value', *The Necessary Angel: Essays on Reality and the Imagination*, 1951, p. 142.

2. 'The Ordinary Women', *Collected Poems*, 1954, p. 12.

3. 'Notes Toward a Supreme Fiction', *Collected Poems*, 1954, p. 383.

4. 'A High-Toned Old Christian Woman', *Collected Poems*, 1954, p. 59.

Selected works:

Harmonium (1923, revised edition, 1931; reprinted 2001); *Ideas of Order* (1935); *The Man with the Blue Guitar* (1937); *Parts of a World* (1942); *Transport to Summer* (1947); *The Auroras of Autumn* (1950); *The Necessary Angel: Essays on Reality and the Imagination* (1951); *Selected Poems* (1953); *Collected Poems* (1954); *The Rock* (1954); *Opus Posthumous* (1957, revised 1989); *The Palm at the End of the Mind: Selected Poems and a Play* (1971).

Further reading

Bloom, Harold, *Wallace Stevens: The Poems of our Climate*. Ithaca, New York: Cornell University Press, 1977.

Vendler, Helen, *On Extended Wings: Wallace Stevens' Longer Poems*. Cambridge, Massachusetts: Harvard University Press, 1969.

Contributor: Pat Righelato

STOPPARD, SIR TOM (1937–)

You don't understand the humiliation of it – to be tricked out of the single assumption which makes our existence viable – that somebody is watching.

Rosencrantz and Guildenstern are Dead

Tom Stoppard was born in Czechoslovakia, the son of a company physician. His family moved to Singapore when he was two years old, to escape the Nazis. Then in 1941 his mother took him and his brother to live in India just prior to the Japanese invasion of Singapore, in which his father, who had stayed on, was killed. In India his mother married a British officer, Kenneth Stoppard, and in 1946 the family moved to England, where, after leaving school at the age of 17, Stoppard began work as a journalist and drama critic.

He began writing plays in 1960 and achieved fame with *Rosencrantz and Guildenstern are Dead,* which was performed at the Edinburgh Festival in 1966 and the National Theatre in 1967. His next major play, *Jumpers* (1972), was also extremely successful. Both plays show Stoppard's genius for exploring philosophical concepts in a dazzlingly witty way, not only through dialogue but also through an inventive use of the medium of the theatre. Many more plays, screenplays and a novel followed and Stoppard was awarded a knighthood in 1977.

The types of issue his plays explore has evolved during his career. Having been primarily concerned with philosophical themes in his early works he took on political and human rights issues with *Every Good Boy Deserves Favour* (1977), a drama with music by André Previn, and a TV play *Professional Foul* (1977). These and subsequent works such as *Dogg's Hamlet* and *Cahoot's Macbeth* (1979) were highly critical of the suppression of human rights exercised by the regimes of Eastern Europe of the era.

In *Arcadia* (1993) Stoppard returned to an examination of contemporary philosophical issues, particularly chaos theory, and in 1998 he won high public acclaim once again when, along with his co-writer Marc Norman, he won an Oscar for the best original screenplay for the film *Shakespeare in Love*.

Rosencrantz and Guildenstern are Dead is probably Stoppard's best-known and most frequently studied play and is one of the most original and inventive plays of British post-war theatre. Beneath the verbal and visual wit lies a concern with serious philosophical and moral issues, in particular to do with the opposition between determinism and free will, and reality and illusion, and it is part of Stoppard's genius that he manipulates the medium of the theatre itself to mirror the intellectual themes.

The play is structured around the idea that Rosencrantz and Guildenstern's predicament of being minor characters from *Hamlet*, trapped within the plot of Shakespeare's play, is equated with Man trapped in a deterministic universe. Thus the play functions throughout on two levels and occasionally on three when the play draws attention to itself as a play, in relation to us, the audience. Stoppard has used Rosencrantz and Guildenstern exactly as Shakespeare created them – that is, as undeveloped, flat characters, with minimal and ineffectual roles, largely ignorant of the events into which they have been drawn, and whose deaths pass almost unnoticed – and transposed them into a twentieth-century idiom by equating them with **antiheroes** of the **Theatre of the Absurd**. In fact the play owes a clear debt to *Waiting for Godot*, by **Samuel Beckett**, with Rosencrantz and Guildenstern resembling Vladimir and Estragon, waiting, without knowing what they are waiting for, in an incomprehensible, perhaps meaningless universe, in which death is the only certainty. The appearance of The Players also mirrors, structurally, the appearance of Pozzo and Lucky in *Waiting for Godot*.

The theme of fate versus free will is introduced in the opening scene: Rosencrantz and Guildenstern are tossing coins, and the coins have come up heads 92 times in a row. The act of tossing a coin is an act of free will and the result apparently depends on chance, but in the long run it seems that the attempt to influence the future by an individual act of free will is futile because the outcome has been predetermined. Thus we have an image in which free will and determinism co-exist, with free will operating in the short term and determinism

in the long term. This duality is demonstrated again later when, in a scene which is reported but not actually shown in *Hamlet*, Rosencrantz and Guildenstern are on a boat bound for England.

> Guil: Where we went wrong was getting on a boat. We can move, of course, change direction, rattle about, but our movement is contained within a larger one that carries us along, as inexorably as the wind and current. (Act 3)

Free will and determinism are both present in their world, but whichever way they look at it, they cannot escape their imminent deaths.

The inevitability of death is also the pivot around which Stoppard builds his exploration of the reality versus illusion dichotomy. Rosencrantz tries to comprehend death as a reality but is unable to battle through the illusions thrown up by the mind in the face of the unknown.

> Ros: It's silly to be depressed by it. I mean one thinks of it like being alive in a box, one keeps forgetting to take into account the fact that one is dead. (Act 2)

When a troupe of actors, The Players – specialists in illusion – arrive, the whole relationship between illusion and reality is thrown into doubt.

> Guil: You die so many times: how can you expect them to believe in your death?
> Player: On the contrary, it's the only kind they do believe. They're conditioned to it. I had an actor once who was condemned to hang for stealing a sheep . . . I got permission to have him hanged in the middle of a play . . . and you wouldn't believe it, he just wasn't convincing. It was impossible to suspend one's disbelief. (Act 2)

The suggestion is that we cannot believe in reality even when we see it and are all too eager to believe in illusions. The Player proves his point later when Guildenstern stabs him and he falls to the ground and 'dies'. Guildenstern is taken in by the Player's act, thinking he has killed him, until the Player revives and says:

'For a moment you thought I'd – cheated.'
(Act 2)

'Cheated' by substituting reality for the illusion, implying that we can never be absolutely sure whether something we perceive is reality or an illusion, a theme which occurs repeatedly in Stoppard's work and is exemplified by *After Magritte* (1970), the thesis of which might be paraphrased as what we 'know' depends upon how we choose to interpret what we think we see.

Guildenstern tries again to comprehend the reality of death:

It's just a man failing to reappear, that's all – now you see him, now you don't. That's the only thing that's real: here one minute and gone the next and never coming back. (Act 2)

Stoppard gives this idea dramatic expression when Act 3 opens in pitch darkness. The audience, staring at blackness, wonders whether the actors will reappear. Later, in the scene in the boat bound for England, the medium of the theatre is again used to add a layer of meaning to the action. Rosencrantz considers suicide, raising the question of whether in this way he can exercise his free will to escape his predetermined fate. He moves to the edge of the stage:

Ros: I wish I was dead. (considers the drop).
I could jump over the side. That would put a spoke in their wheel.
Guil: Unless they're counting on it.
Ros: I shall remain on board. That'll put a spoke in their wheel. (Act 3)

Three levels of meaning fuse at this point: 1) A man is considering an escape from his fate. 2) Shakespeare's character is contemplating an escape from *Hamlet*. 3) An actor is considering an escape from the play we are watching. The bid to assert free will fails on all three levels.

As well as these philosophical themes, Stoppard is exploring a moral theme in the play: the moral and spiritual desolation of a civilisation without God. The loss of meaning to life in the absence of God is suggested in this speech by the Player:

You don't understand the humiliation of it – to be tricked out of the single

assumption which makes our existence viable – that somebody is watching . . . We pledged out identities, secure in the conventions of our trade; that someone would be watching. And then, gradually, no one was. (Act 2)

The view that modern man is adrift in a meaningless universe without God is in keeping with the Absurdist view of man with which Stoppard is working, but Stoppard goes further and says something about the moral decline which follows the adoption of a philosophical position which denies the existence of God. The Players are supposed to be taking culture to the king's court, but they are 'a comic pornographer and a rabble of prostitutes' (Act 1) and their plays are obscene performances in which, for a price, the audience can participate. That this particular situation can be extended to modern society as a whole is suggested by the frequent repetition of the phrase 'the times being what they are' and reinforced by Guildenstern's comment 'the very air stinks' (Act 1), a joking reference to Hamlet's line, 'Something is rotten in the state of Denmark' (Hamlet 1.iv.90).

The emptiness and uncertainty of modern times are also conveyed by the contrasting languages and dramatic styles used in the play. The intermittent appearance of scenes from *Hamlet* reminds us of times when religious and moral values were accepted as absolutes, every line of Shakespeare's dialogue conveying a confidence, purpose and eloquence which is in marked contrast to the clipped, artless dialogue of Rosencrantz and Guildenstern, in which words often fail them altogether. The picture of contemporary life Stoppard is suggesting is one in which the disappearance of religious faith, along with the moral standards and purpose which it conferred on life, leaves Man in a state of moral desolation, unsure of his identity.

Selected works:

Plays for the stage: *A Walk on the Water* (1960); *The Gamblers* (1965); *Rosencrantz and Guildenstern are Dead* (1966); *The Real Inspector Hound* (1968); *Enter a Free Man* (1968); *After Magritte* (1970); *Dogg's Our Pet* (1971); *Jumpers* (1972); *Travesties* (1974); *Dirty Linen and New-Found-Land* (1976); *Every Good Boy Deserves Favour* (1977); *Night and Day* (1978); *Dogg's Hamlet* (1979); *Cahoot's Macbeth* (1979); *The Real Thing* (1982); *Hapgood* (1988); *Arcadia*

(1993); *Indian Ink* (1995); *The Invention of Love* (1997). **Plays for radio:** *The Dissolution of Dominic Boot* (1964); *"M" is for Moon Among Other Things* (1964); *If You're Glad I'll be Frank* (1966); *Albert's Bridge* (1967); *Where Are They Now?* (1970); *Artist Descending a Staircase* (1972); *The Dog It Was That Died* (1982); *In the Native State* (1991). **Plays for TV:** *A Walk on the Water* (1963); *A Separate Peace* (1966); *Teeth* (1967); *Another Moon Called Earth* (1967); *Neutral Ground* (1968); *The Engagement* (1970); *Professional Foul* (1977); *Squaring the Circle: Poland 1980–81* (1984); *The Dog It Was That Died* (1988). **Screenplays:** *The Romantic Englishwoman* (1975); *Despair* (1978); *The Human Factor* (1980); *Brazil* (1985); *Empire of the Sun* (1987); *The Russia House* (1990); *Rosencrantz and Guildenstern are Dead* (1990); *Billy Bathgate* (1991); *Shakespeare in Love* (1988). **Novel:** *Lord Malquist and Mr. Moon* (1966).

Further reading

Bigsby, C. W. E., *Tom Stoppard* (Writers and Their Work). Northcote House, 1996.

Hayman, Ronald, *Tom Stoppard: Contemporary Playwright*. Heinemann Educational Secondary Division, 1982.

Contributor: Ian Mackean

THOMAS, DYLAN (1914–53)

The force that through the green fuse drives the flower
Drives my green age; that blasts the roots of trees
Is my destroyer
        The force that through the Green
                Fuse Drives the Flower

Dylan Marlais Thomas is one of the most celebrated poets of the twentieth century and also one of the most controversial, supporters and detractors having strong feel-ings regarding both the merits of his poetry and his qualities as a man. He gained a reputation for wildness, drunkenness, womanising and borrowing money. The reputation undoubtedly had some truth behind it, but was exaggerated by those to whom the romantic image of a wild bohemian poet appealed and has been disputed by people with whom he lived and worked. His daughter Aeronwy observed that no one ever wants to hear about the Thomas she knew, who enjoyed domestic routines, drank in moderation, worked diligently and was devoted to his parents. Similarly, those who worked with him at the BBC emphasise that he was known for being reliable, professional, sober and conscientious.[1]

The story of Thomas's death after a night's drinking in a bar in Manhattan, as told by John Malcolm Brinnin in *Dylan Thomas in America* (1965), may also be a distorted version of the truth. He apparently boasted to his American girlfriend, Liz Reitell, that he had drunk 18 straight whiskies (the equivalent of 18 British 'doubles'), but the story cannot be corroborated and it is also probable that a doctor had, unwisely, given him various drugs, including an injection of morphine.[2]

Thomas grew up in a suburb of Swansea in South Wales and wrote profusely even in childhood. His father, a school teacher, was by all accounts an ill-humoured man but an enthusiastic and inspiring teacher of English literature. Thomas paid little attention to school subjects other than English, at which he excelled, and had no desire to go to university. He was determined to be a poet and he found his gift early, being only 19 when one of his best-known poems, 'And Death Shall Have no Dominion', was published in 1933.

Thomas did not speak Welsh, his father having discouraged him from learning it in the belief that it would impede his progress, but the tone of his poetry shows that he had absorbed the lyrical style of Welsh preachers, a style which probably also influenced his father, who read Shakespeare to him from an early age. Thomas claimed not to be religious, but his poems, in which biblical imagery occasionally appears, often convey a sense of awe and he said in the introduction to his *Collected Poems* of 1952 that he wrote 'for the love of man and in praise of God'.

Thomas's first volume of poetry, *18 Poems*, was published in 1934 and he continued to publish poetry through the 1930s. Had he been faced with serving in the Second World War he would have been a conscientious objector, but he was found unfit for active service and worked as a documentary film script writer. The poems he wrote in the period leading up to and during the war, particularly those included in *Deaths and Entrances* (1946), gained him the attention of the literary establishment. The volume contained some of his best-known poems, such as 'Fern Hill', 'A Refusal to Mourn the Death, by Fire, of a Child in London' and 'Poem in October'. Where his earlier poetry had often been obscure and difficult, to the extent that some critics had seen little more in it than experiments with words, he was now writing poems which conveyed an accessible meaning and rapidly becoming the foremost poet of the 1940s.

Thomas's work was striking and new, appealing to the emotions and conveying a tone of almost religious wonder; a distinct break from the emotional restraint and religious intent of the later **T. S. Eliot** and the politically orientated poetry of **W. H. Auden** and his followers. His poems had the quality of song and celebration, liberating poetry from the baggage of political and intellectual concerns.

Thomas's technique, influenced by **Gerard Manley Hopkins**, makes use of startling juxtapositions of words and images.

It was my thirtieth year to heaven
Woke to my hearing from harbour and
neighbour wood
And the mussel pooled and the heron
Priested shore
The morning beckon
[From 'Poem in October']

Thomas deals with elemental themes, such as birth, growth, sensuality, the passing of time and decay, conveying a sense of how individual life is connected to natural processes. With his striking use of words and his concern with childhood, and with the mystical power of nature, his work can sometimes seem like an amalgam of Gerard Manley Hopkins and William Wordsworth. Many of his poems are untitled, indicating that he was not prepared to give the reader a preconceived idea through which to approach them, but wanted them to experience them in the reading.

In 1937, when Thomas was living in London and a well-known figure on the literary scene, he married Caitlin Macnamara, with whom he had a daughter and two sons. Being always short of money they moved from place to place, often depending on the hospitality of others. In 1949 they settled in a cottage, 'The Boat House', at Laugharne, on the south coast of Wales, which was purchased for them by Margaret Taylor, the wife of the historian A. J. P. Taylor.

Thomas became particularly well known to the British public as a regular broadcaster for the BBC. He enjoyed performing for the microphone and gained the status of a media star. He had a striking, resonant voice, which made his live readings immensely popular, and one can perhaps best appreciate the power of his poems by listening to recordings. His mastery of the medium of radio is particularly apparent in his well-known radio play *Under Milk Wood*, first performed in America in 1953 and published posthumously in 1954. The play, like the stories of *Portrait of the Artist as a Young Dog* (1940), show his humour and his ability to present a community of characters, while his poems always convey personal individual experience.

His American tours between 1950 and 1953 were hugely popular, drawing large audiences and elevating him to celebrity status. But having earned the reputation of being wild and drunken he felt under pressure to live up to it and the constant round of performances and partying took a toll on his health.

Thomas directly inspired several contemporary poets, such as George Barker and W. S. Graham, who went under the name **New Romantics**, and Henry Treece and J. F. Hendry, who adopted the name **New Apocalypse**, but their work is generally considered by critics to be poor and their prominence was short-lived, being taken over by the more sober and restrained poets of **The Movement**, such as **Philip Larkin** and **Kingsley Amis**.

Thomas also inspired artists in the field of pop music. Bob Dylan, whose real name is Robert Zimmerman, was inspired to use the name 'Dylan' out of respect for Thomas, and Thomas's face appears among the images of influential people on the **pop art** cover of The Beatles' *Sergeant Pepper's Lonely Hearts Club Band* LP of 1967.

As Nigel Williams observed,[3] Thomas's wild, uncontrollable streak may have been due to part of his personality never having matured from childhood, but on the other side of the coin, his ability to retain a connection to his childhood joy, awe and fascination with the world, and with words, may also have lain at the heart of his poetic inspiration.

References

1. **Williams, Nigel** (presenter) (2003) *Arena. Dylan Thomas: From the Grave to the Cradle.* BBC2, broadcast 22 November.

2. Ibid.

3. Ibid.

Selected works:
Eighteen Poems (1934); *Twenty-Five Poems* (1935); *The Map Of Love* (1939); *The World I Breathe* (1939); *Portrait Of The Artist As A Young Dog* (1940); *New Poems* (1943); *Deaths And Entrances* (1946); *Selected Writings* (1946); *Twenty-Six Poems* (1950); *Collected Poems* (1952); *In Country Sleep* (1952); *The Doctor And The Devils* (1953). **Posthumous publications:** *Quite Early One Morning* (radio essays) (1954); *Under Milk Wood* (1954); *A Prospect Of The Sea* (1955); *A Child's Christmas In Wales* (1955); *Adventures In The Skin Trade* (1955); *Letters To Vernon Watkins* (1957); *The Beach Of Falesá* (1963); *Miscellany* (1963); *The Colour Of Saying* (1963); *Selected Letters* (1963); *The Notebooks Of Dylan Thomas 1930–34* (1968); *Dylan Thomas: The Complete Screenplays* (1995); *The Love Letters Of Dylan Thomas* (2002).

Further reading

Lycett, Andrew, *Dylan Thomas: A New Life.* Weidenfeld & Nicholson, 2003.

Contributor: Ian Mackean

Derek Alton Walcott, winner of the 1992 Nobel Prize for literature, is the best-known West Indian poet and dramatist writing in English today. He has lived most of his life in Trinidad and his work deals with the conflict between West Indian and European culture, the struggle from slavery to independence, and his predicament as a nomad between cultures. His poems are characterised by allusions to the English poetic tradition and a symbolism that is at once personal and Caribbean. He has written both in standard English and West Indian dialect and has called himself 'a mulatto of style'.

Walcott was born in Castries, in St Lucia, an isolated Caribbean island. His father, Warwick, was a civil servant and amateur painter, who died when Walcott was very young. His mother, Alix, a teacher, born in Dutch St Maarten, was very well read and taught her children to love poetry. Walcott was educated at St Mary's College, Castries, then received a scholarship to the University of the West Indies in Kingston, Jamaica, where he studied French, Latin and Spanish. In 1950 he founded the St Lucia Arts Guild and his first play, *Henri Christopher*, was performed in the same year. He moved to Trinidad in 1953, studied theatre in New York from 1958 to 1959, with the help of a Rockefeller Foundation Fellowship, and travelled in the USA and Europe in the 1960s.

Walcott taught at schools on several Caribbean islands and wrote features for the Kingston journal *Public Opinion*, and features and drama criticism for *The Trinidad Guardian*.

He moved to America in 1981 to live in Boston, Massachusetts, while teaching at the Universities of Boston and Harvard. His marriage to Fay Moston, a secretary, broke up after a few years. His second wife, Margaret Maillard, was an almoner in a hospital. In 1976, after divorcing Margaret, he married Norline Metivier; the marriage also ended in divorce.

Walcott made his debut as a poet at the age of 18 with *25 Poems* (1948), which was privately printed and gained widespread recognition with *In A Green Night* (1962), which manifested his primary aim of creating a literature truthful to the complexity of West Indian life. In 'The Schooner Flight' from *The Star-Apple Kingdom* (1979), the Odyssean figure of Shabine expresses Walcott's sense of uncertainty about his identity, arising from his mixed African and European ancestry.

> I'm just a red nigger who love the sea,
> I had a sound colonial education,
> I have Dutch, nigger and English in me,
> and either I'm nobody, or I'm a nation.

In *The Fortunate Traveller* (1981) and *Midsummer* (1984) Walcott explored his situation as a black writer in America, estranged from his Caribbean homeland. In an interview he spoke of 'an isolation in the sense that, as West Indian writers, whether we live in London or the West Indies, we are both cut off from and are a part of a tradition', and the titles of such books as *Castaway* (1965) and *The Gulf* (1969) refer to his feelings of artistic isolation and alienation.

Walcott's most ambitious work to date is the epic poem *Omeros* (1990), which takes its title from the Greek word for 'Homer' and recasts the dramas of Homer's *Iliad* and *Odyssey* in a Caribbean setting. The work consists of 192 songs and the central characters are two fishermen, Achilles and Philocrete. Among its subjects are contemporary Caribbean life and the sufferings of exile.

From 1959 to 1976 Walcott was the director of the Little Carib Theatre (later the Trinidad Theatre Workshop) and he has written a large number of plays for stage and radio. His plays examining postcolonial issues owe much to Creole folk tradition and history. They combine story-telling, singing, dancing and the rhythms of calypso with richly metaphorical speech which mingles verse and prose. *Dream of Monkey Mountain* (1967), considered to be his most impressive play, was commissioned originally by the Royal Shakespeare Company but produced finally in the USA. The play's central character is Makak, a charcoal burner, and the action explores the nature of West Indian identity through a series of dreams concerning Caribbean, African and European history.

Walcott has also collaborated on several musicals with Galt McDermott, best known as producer and co-writer of the hippie musical *Hair*. The Basement Theatre, under Walcott's direction, participated in Canada's Centennial Celebrations in 1967, being the first West Indian drama company to perform outside the region. 'Walcott's 1993 play *The Odyssey*, like *Omeros*, uses the work of Homer as a foundation on which to construct an exploration of West Indian history and contemporary life'.

Walcott's autobiographical works include the poem 'Another Life' (1973), inspired by James Joyce's self-examination in *Portrait of the Artist as a Young Man*. *Tiepolo's Hound* (2000) deals with the Caribbean-born painter Camille Pissarro and Walcott himself, the poem being accompanied by reproductions of Walcott's paintings.

Walcott's success has inspired many aspiring Caribbean writers. West Indian poet David Dabydeen said of Walcott's winning the Nobel Prize: 'When he won the Nobel Prize in 1992 we all won the Nobel Prize. The symbolism of this on the 500th anniversary of Columbus's arrival in the region was immense. There is enormous local pride. There is a fish cake named after him in St Lucia, Columbus Square is now Walcott Square, and he carries all this with a great deal of humility.'[1]

Selected works:

Poetry: *25 Poems* (1948); *Epitaph for the Young* (1949); *Poems* (1951); *In a Green Night: Poems 1948–60* (1962); *Selected Poems* (1964); *The Castaway and other Poems* (1965); *The Gulf and other Poems* (1969); *Another Life* (1973); *Sea Grapes* (1976); *The Star-Apple Kingdom* (1979); *Selected Poetry* (1981); *The Fortunate Traveller* (1981); *Midsummer* (1984); *Collected Poems 1948--84* (1986); *The Arkansas Testament* (1987); *Omeros* (1990); *Poems 1965–1980* (1993); *Bounty* (1997); *Tiepolo's Hound* (2000). **Plays:** *Cry for a Leader* (1950); *Henri Christophe* (1950); *Robin and Andrea* (1950); *Senza Alcun Sospetto* (1950); *The Price of Mercy* (1951); *Three Assassins* (1951); *Harry Oernier* (1952); *The*

Charlatan (1954); *Crossroads* (1954); *The Sea at Dauphin* (1954); *The Golden Lions* (1956); *The Wine of the County* (1956); *Ti-Jean and his Brothers* (1957); *Drums and Colours* (1958); *Jourmard* (1959); *Malcochan* (1959); *Batai* (1965); *Dream on Monkey Mountain* (1967); *Franklin* (1969); *In a Fine Castle* (1970); *The Joker of Seville* (With G. McDermott) (1974); *Remembrance* (1977); *The Snow Queen* (1977); *Pantomime* (1978); *Marie Leveau* (With G. McDermott) (1979); *The Isle is Full of Noises* (1982); *Beef, No Chicken* (1985); *The Odyssey* (1993). **Non-fiction:** *What The Twilight Says* (1998).

Reference

1. **Dabydeen, David** (2000) quoted in Wroe, Nicholas, *Derek Walcott The Laureate of St Lucia.* The London Guardian Sunday Express 17 September, pp. 50, 51, 53, 54. www.nalis.gov.tti/Biography/bio_Derek Walcott-2-NobelLaureate.htm (accessed 25.6.04)

Further reading

Breslin, Paul, *Nobody's Nation: Reading Derek Walcott.* University of Chicago Press, 2002.

Thieme, John, *Derek Walcott (Contemporary World Writers).* Manchester University Press, 1999.

This entry is based on an article by Petri Liukkonen originally published on 'Books and Writers' at www.kirjasto.sci.fi

Contributors: Petri Liukkonen, Ian Mackean

WAUGH, EVELYN (1903–66)

Particularly against books the Home Secretary is. If we can't stamp out literature in the country, we can at least stop it being brought in from outside.

Vile Bodies

Photo credit: © Bettmann/CORBIS

Evelyn Arthur St John Waugh's reputation as a prose stylist is due to the elegance and wit of his early novels, which remain highly readable,

though his general fame may be credited to cinema and TV versions of his works. In 1981 a critically acclaimed 13-part ITV adaptation of *Brideshead Revisited* drew popular attention to the novel, *The Loved One* and *Decline and Fall* were filmed in 1965, *The Sword of Honour* was adapted for TV in 1967 and a film of *Vile Bodies*, directed by Stephen Fry and renamed *Bright Young Things*, appeared in 2003.

Waugh attended Hertford College, Oxford, in the 1920s, by which time his brother Alec, who had been expelled from his public school for homosexuality, had already gained notoriety as a writer with his novel *The Loom of Youth* (1917). Evelyn attempted to imitate the sexual undertones of his brother's successful book in *Decline and Fall* (1928), in which a student, Paul Pennyfeather, is expelled from Oxford and becomes a private school-master. An aristocratic mother of one of his pupils then employs him in her business. The woman keeps an American Negro lover (very risqué for 1928) and her business turns out to be a prostitution racket. When Pennyfeather is arrested in the lady's service for procuring female 'entertainers' and sending them to South America, his lady sponsor arranges with the Home Secretary for him to be certified dead in a prison hospital, after which he returns to Oxford in the guise of his cousin.

The book, which was based, loosely, on Waugh's experience of working as a school-master at Arnold House in North Wales, was considered immoral and flippant, but it gained attention and earned him a name. He attached himself to the fringe of smart society in London and fell in love with Diana Guinness, one of the Mitford sisters, who was to marry the British fascist leader Oswald Mosley, while her sister Unity admired and supported Adolf Hitler. Waugh later married Evelyn Gardner but divorced within two years. His second wife was Laura Herbert, by whom he had six children, though he was believed to be a homosexual. In 1930 he became a Roman Catholic.

Vile Bodies (1930) depicts a world of sex and snobbish society and achieved success, as did most of Waugh's books, despite criticism from **Virginia Woolf** that it lacked **realism**. Waugh, however, lived beyond his income and was always short of money. He accepted an offer of free passage from a shipping company to write travel articles, with appropriate mention of his sponsor, and visited Europe and Africa. He wrote *Black Mischief* (1932) following the coronation of the Emperor Haile Selassie in Abyssinia.

Waugh's travels also provided material for *Scoop* (1938), set in a fictitious African country called Ishmaeliah. The novel lampoons foreign correspondents and their invention of news, and, like *Decline and Fall*, shows a naïve man discovering the tricks and turns of the real world. The unfortunate William Boot is mistaken by the managing editor of *The Daily Beast* for a travel writer, John Boot:

'He's supposed to have a particularly high class style: "*Feather-footed through the plashy fen passes the questing vole*" . . . would that be it?'
'Yes,' said the Managing Editor. 'That must be good style.'

Boot of *The Beast* is sent to cover an African civil war where he learns the trade of reportage.

Waugh enlisted for military service during the Second World War and in 1944 was parachuted into Yugoslavia along with Randolph Churchill, son of the Prime Minister. While recovering from an injury he wrote *Brideshead Revisited*, depicting members of an upper-class family who live in a vast country house. Its subtitle is *The Sacred and Profane Memories of Captain Charles Ryder*, and the Catholic theme prompted George Orwell to write:

Analyse 'Brideshead Revisited'. (Note faults due to being written in first person.) Studiously detached attitude. Not puritanical. Priests not superhuman . . . But. Last scene, where the unconscious man makes the sign of the Cross. Note that after all the veneer is bound to crack sooner or later. One cannot really be Catholic and grown-up.

Conclude. Waugh is about as good a novelist as one can be (i.e. as novelists go today) while holding untenable opinions.[1]

A Hollywood studio wished to make a film based on the novel and invited Waugh to California in 1947. Waugh refused to accept

proposed changes to the storyline and the film project was abandoned, but he used this trip to create a satire on Californian funeral customs in *The Loved One* (1948).

Waugh wrote *Put Out More Flags* while serving in the military in 1942. In this work he satirised W. H. Auden and Christopher Isherwood for avoiding military service and emigrating to the USA, calling them 'Parsnip and Pimpernell'. His trilogy of novels about military life was reissued in 1965 as *The Sword of Honour*, the original titles being *Men at Arms* (1952), *Officers and Gentlemen* (1955) and *Unconditional Surrender* (1961). Two other well-known works of these later years were *Helena* (1950), in which he credits a British woman from Colchester as being mother of Constantine, the first Christian Emperor of Rome, and *The Ordeal of Gilbert Pinfold* (1957), a painful description of Waugh's nervous breakdown.

Waugh became increasingly eccentric towards the end of his life. He affected the manners of an eighteenth-century country squire and was notoriously rude. He also claimed to be going deaf and used an exaggeratedly large ear trumpet rather than a hearing aid. He died of heart failure in 1966, soon after hearing mass on Easter Sunday.

Reference

1. George Orwell, quoted in Hitchens, Christopher, 'The Permanent Adolescent. His vices made Evelyn Waugh a king of comedy and of tragedy'. *The Atlantic Monthly*, May 2003.

Selected works:

Decline and Fall (1928); *Vile Bodies* (1930); *Labels* (1930); *Remote People* (1930); *Black Mischief* (1932); *A Handful of Dust* (1934); *Ninety-two Days* (1934); *Edmund Campion* (1935); *Waugh in Abyssinia* (1936); *Mr. Loveday's Little Outing and other sad stories* (1936); *Scoop* (1938); *Robbery Under Law* (1939); *Put Out More Flags* (1942); *Work Suspended* (1942); *Brideshead Revisited* (1945); *When the Going was Good* (1946); *The Loved One* (1948); *Helena* (1950); *Men at Arms* (1952); *Love Among the Ruins* (1953); *Officers and Gentlemen* (1955); *The Ordeal of Gilbert Pinfold* (1957); *The Life of the Right Reverend Ronald Knox* (1959); *Unconditional Surrender* (1961); *A Tourist in Africa* (1960); *Basil Seal Rides Again*

(1963); *A Little Learning* (1964); *The Diaries of Evelyn Waugh* (1976); *A Little Order – A Selection From His Journalism* (1977); *The letters of Evelyn Waugh* (1980); *The essays, articles and reviews of Evelyn Waugh* (1984); *Mr. Wu and Mrs. Stitch: the letters of Evelyn Waugh and Lady Diana Cooper* (1991); *The letters of Nancy Mitford and Evelyn Waugh* (1997).

Further reading

Patey, Douglas Lane, *The Life of Evelyn Waugh: A Critical Biography*. Blackwell, 2001.

Sykes, Christopher, *Evelyn Waugh: A Biography*. Little Brown, 1975.

Contributors: Stephen Colbourn,
                                 Ian Mackean

WEST, NATHANAEL (1903–40)

Had he gone on, there would have unfolded . . . the finest prose talent of our age.

William Carlos Williams[1]

An observer of 'the secret inner life of masses',[2] Nathanael West sought to expose the reality of the American Dream and its detrimental effects on individuals and society. A black humorist and social critic, West profaned the sacred, lampooned the aesthetic and dramatised and marginalised the grotesque, effectively underscoring in surreal detail the predominant but unperceived fruits of American life: perversion, corruption, despair and violence. Though West was marginally successful during his short-lived career, his resentment towards, and denigration of, the societal effects of the illusory American myth resonate among readers in a **postmodern** era faced with similar disillusionment.

Nathanael West was born Nathan Weinstein to Max and Anna Wallenstein Weinstein, German Jews who emigrated from Lithuania to New York. An indifferent student, he left high school before graduation, mainly to spite his parents, who anxiously encouraged his assimilation into American culture, but gained admittance into Tufts College with an altered high-school transcript. When asked to withdraw from Tufts on the basis of his poor academic performance,

he used the transcript of another Nathan Weinstein to transfer to Brown University.

Despite his lack of commitment to institutionalised learning, West demonstrated sustained interest in art, literature and theatre. He was well read in Greek and Roman classics, European literature including the Russian **realists**, and British and American **Modernist** writers. Rejecting the American traditions of **realism**, West found inspiration from French authors such as Breton, Cocteau, Proust and Flaubert, as well as **Symbolist** poets such as Charles Baudelaire and Arthur Rimbaud. By the time he graduated from Brown in 1924, West had decided to become a writer. Prior to sailing for Paris, where he planned to write his first novel, he officially changed his name.

After his visit to Paris, West returned to New York and worked in a hotel, where he finished drafting his first novel. *The Dream Life of Balso Snell* (1931) found its origins in West's experiences in Paris, as well as in short **surrealist** sketches he had written while at college. The novel, set inside the Trojan Horse, follows Balso, a poet/sceptic figure, as he travels through the major events of Western civilisation in search of meaning and identity. The experimental comic novella, replete with scatological images, anti-Catholicism, anti-Semitism and misogyny, satirises the perversion of art and its estrangement from society in mass culture. Though recommended by William Carlos Williams for publication, *The Dream Life of Balso Snell* sold poorly and gained little public or critical attention for West.

At this time, West began co-editing, with Williams, the magazine *Contact: An American Quarterly*, in which he published material he would later use in his second novel. Described as a tragic farce, *Miss Lonelyhearts* (1933) is a story of a lovelorn columnist who promulgates the Christian ideals of love and compassion, which he himself has failed to experience, to his miserable readers. Miss Lonelyhearts' despondent condition is aggravated by his editor's destructive cynical and antireligious antagonism. The novel supplants the hopeful ideal of love, leading to order and peace, with self-interest, leading to disorder and violence. West's artful portrayal of suffering humanity evokes in the reader the conflicting sensations of pity and disdain. Despite receiving critical attention, *Miss Lonelyhearts* sold poorly.

West's third novel, *A Cool Million* (1934), is

an assault on the American myth embodied in the Horatio Algers 'rags-to-riches' narratives, which West grew up reading thanks to his father's encouragement. The novel, a satirical fable, follows the young Lemuel Pitkin who, motivated by clichéd capitalistic goals, leaves his hometown to make a fortune in order to prevent the foreclosure of his mother's house. However, Lem's moments of opportunity lead to his misfortunes as he falls victim to the forces of a chaotic, corrupt and violent society which ultimately dismantles and destroys him. Dubbed a burlesque comedy, *A Cool Million* received negative reviews and, like West's previous novels, sold poorly.

Shortly after the publication of *A Cool Million*, West moved to California and began writing screenplays for financial gain. His experiences in Hollywood provided material for his fourth and final novel, *The Day of the Locust* (1939). The novel follows the story of Tod Hackett, a recent Yale graduate and aspiring painter, as he begins working as a set and costume designer in Hollywood. In the process of pursuing 17-year-old Faye Greener, an amoral, would-be actress, Tod encounters, and becomes one of, the Hollywood grotesques who inhabit the fringes of the movie industry. The novel, which portrays the artificiality and surreal atmosphere of Hollywood, culminates in an apocalyptic riot scene which represents Tod's unfinished painting, 'The Burning of Los Angeles'. Many critics consider *The Day of the Locust*, along with *The Last Tycoon* (1941) by **F. Scott Fitzgerald**, to be one of the best novels written about the emptiness and illusory nature of Hollywood. Yet, despite good reviews, West's final novel failed to sell well.

On 22 December 1940, West and his wife, Eileen McKenney West, were returning from a hunting trip to Mexico when West, preoccupied with the news of his friend and colleague F. Scott Fitzgerald's death the previous day, failed to yield to a stop sign and collided with another vehicle. Neither West nor his wife survived the accident.

West associated with many prominent American writers, including **William Faulkner**, with whom he hunted; William Carlos Williams, co-editor of *Contact* magazine; S. J. Perelman, who married West's sister Laura; and F. Scott Fitzgerald. Though West's novels failed to gain sustained critical attention, fol-lowing the publication of his *Complete Works* (1957), his influence grew significantly, extending to younger novelists such as James Purdy, Joseph Heller, Thomas Pychon, John Hawkes and **Flannery O'Connor**. Relentlessly sardonic and oddly prophetic, West's literature offers 'permanent and true explorations into the Siberia of the human spirit'.[3]

References

1. Quoted in Martin, p. 12.

2. **Isaac Rosenfeld**, quoted in Martin, p. 164.

3. Martin, p. 10.

Selected works:
The Dream Life of Balso Snell (1931); *Miss Lonelyhearts* (1933); *A Cool Million: The Dismantling of Lemuel Pitkin* (1934); *The Day of the Locust* (1939); *The Complete Works* (1957).

Further reading

Martin, Jay, *Nathanael West: The Art of His Life*. New York: Farrar, Straus and Giroux, 1970.

——. *American Writers in Paris, 1920–1939*. *Dictionary of Literary Biography*, Vol. 4. Detroit: Gale Research Company, 1981.

Walden, Daniel, *Dictionary of Literary Biography*, Vols. 9, 28. Detroit: Gale Research Company, 1981.

Contributor: David Stock

WEST, DAME REBECCA (1892–1983)

An artist . . . is goaded into creation by his need to resolve some important conflict, to find out where the truth lies among divergent opinions on a vital issue.

West, in Glendinning, p. 24

Dame Rebecca West is not easily categorised as a writer, having been a novelist, journalist, biographer, essayist, travel writer and **feminist**. In 1907, aged only 14, her first publication, a letter in support of women's enfranchisement, appeared in the *Scotsman* newspaper.

She was born Cicily Isabel Fairfield in London in 1892, the third daughter of Charles Fairfield and Isabella Campbell Mackenzie Fairfield. Her father, who was descended from Anglo-Irish nobility, was a journalist and a brilliant writer; however, he was careless with his family's welfare, being an inveterate gambler and womaniser. He left the family in 1901 and Isabella took the girls to Edinburgh. West's sisters, Letitia and Winifred, were her lifelong friends, despite many disagreements.

West attended the George Watson Ladies' College in Edinburgh, before returning to London in 1910 to attend the Academy of Dramatic Art. She soon began writing for the feminist journal the *Freewoman*, as well as the *New Statesman*, *The English Review* and the *Clarion*, adopting the pen-name 'Rebecca West', the name of the strong-minded heroine of Ibsen's *Rosmersholm*. She was acclaimed as a brilliantly acerbic and versatile, socialist-feminist writer. Bernard Shaw said of her: 'Rebecca can handle a pen as brilliantly as ever I could, and much more savagely' (Marcus, p. x).

In 1911 West reviewed H. G. Wells's novel *Marriage* in such a lively and irreverent manner that Wells was intrigued and they met in 1912. By 1913 they were lovers and their son, Anthony Panther West, was born in August 1914.

West's reputation for critical work was growing. Her book *Henry James* appeared in 1916 and by 1921 her 'Notes on Novelists' series began in the *New Statesman*, becoming her major claim to pre-eminence. Her essays on literature, art and science for the *New York Herald Tribune* were collected and published as *The Strange Necessity* (1928).

Her relationship with Wells was finally severed in 1923. She had several other relationships, most notably with Lord Beaverbrook, but in 1930 married the banker Henry Maxwell Andrews and finally experienced a sense of 'belonging' and being loved.

Throughout this period, the reputation of her novels was always eclipsed by her journalism, yet West had been producing fiction steadily. In *The Return of the Soldier* (1918), Chris Baldry suffers from amnesia caused by shell-shock. He barely recognises his cousin Jenny, does not know his wife Kitty at all, and is in love with his former sweetheart, Margaret Allington, who is now a provincial matron. Jenny, the first-person narrator, holds the novel

in check, for she conveys all extremes of emotion, without succumbing to them. Chris Baldry is a stock English male, but all three women love him and their emotions create the tension of the novel. The resolution of his condition, and thus the novel, by the use of a simple psychoanalytic ploy now seems trite. Nevertheless, the central debate remains critical: is the greatest expression of love to leave Chris in the past, where he is happy, or, rather than allowing him to live a falsehood, must he be returned to the present, even though this will mean a return to the front?

West's second novel, *The Judge* (1922), is an ambitious and startlingly feminist work, which explores the trials of the lively, intelligent and resourceful Ellen Melville, a working-class suffragette, and her involvement with Richard Yaverland and his mother Marion. Central to the novel is a debate about unmarried mothers. The 'Judge' of the title is not a patriarch but a mother, for West's epigraph reads: 'Every mother is a judge who sentences her children for the sins of the fathers.' While this may have been the case with Richard's mother, a child of Ellen's will flourish without adverse judgement.

Harriet Hume: A London Fantasy (1929) is an underrated humorous fantasy – and a bizarre departure for West – with the two characters, Harriet and Arnold Condorex, as spiritual poles of femaleness and maleness. The Wall Street Crash of 1929 and the general air of fear and decline in the late 1920s and early 1930s fuelled West's subsequent works, *The Harsh Voice: Four Short Novels* (1935) and *The Thinking Reed* (1936).

The Fountain Overflows (1957) is undoubtedly West's finest work of fiction and her most autobiographical, particularly in its portrait of Piers Aubrey as a brilliant but improvident man. Music is the central and extended metaphor that guides the work, communicating all that is required for moral, spiritual, aesthetic, mental and even physical aspiration and achievement. Rose Aubrey, the first-person narrator, is recounting turn-of-the-century events from the vantage point of 50 years on, but West's narrative control, dialogue and description render the events immediate for the reader and inform the precise socio-historical background of this rich emotional saga of eccentric family life. West began two sequels, *This Real Night* (1984) and *Cousin Rosamund*

(1985). Neither was completed, but their posthumous publication is a boon to any reader in mourning at the end of *The Fountain Overflows*.

West's final published novel, *The Birds Fall Down* (1966), is a work of intrigue set among expatriate Russians before the Revolution. Laura Rowan innocently helps to foil a plot against her Tsarist grandfather in the face of danger to both herself and her family. West considers the nature of treason, terrorism and corrupt governments, suggests the far-reaching consequences for world history, and demonstrates the profound effect on a child of its first realisation of the capacity for evil and deceit in adults.

Of West's many other works of fiction, *The Sunflower*, written in the mid-1920s, was published posthumously in 1986, and an early and incomplete work, *The Sentinel*, was published in 2002.

By the late 1930s West was recognised as one of the most distinguished political journalists of the time. *Black Lamb and Grey Falcon: A Journey Through Yugoslavia* (1939/1941) is based on her travels in Yugoslavia and her growing interest in its politics, history and geography. It is her most distinguished and original work, with perceptive insights into the growth and origins of nationalist feelings. Writing on the cusp of war, West saw in Yugoslavia the truth of all wars, that those who hate or who are obsessed are always willing to martyr the innocent, while the innocent are always willing to be killed. She oversimplifies history and was not unprejudiced in her accounts of Germany and Islam, but her work still stands as an introduction to the region's history as perceived by the West.

Another of West's seminal works, *The Meaning of Treason* (1949), originated when the *New Yorker* commissioned her to report on the trial of William Joyce (Lord Haw-Haw) in 1945. Other prosecutions for treason were pending and in following them West became interested in attitudes to treason. She reported on the Nuremburg trials, her reports being published in *A Train of Powder* (1955), and as the Cold War developed broadened her subject matter to investigate scientific and diplomatic treason, including the cases of Ward, Philby, Maclean and Burgess.

West was made a Dame in 1959. She died, aged 90, in March 1983. She always believed that the writer has a duty to society and needs

to rouse and involve the reader in debate – and West never fails to rouse her readers.

Selected works:

Fiction: *The Return of the Soldier* (1918); *The Judge* (1922); *Harriet Hume: A London Fantasy* (1929); *The Harsh Voice: Four Short Novels* (1935); *The Thinking Reed* (1936); *The Fountain Overflows* (1957); *The Birds Fall Down* (1966); *This Real Night* (1984); *Cousin Rosamund* (1985); *Sunflower* (1986); *The Only Poet* (1992); *The Sentinel* (2002). **Criticism:** *Henry James* (1916); *The Strange Necessity: Essays and Reviews* (1928); *Black Lamb and Grey Falcon: The Record of A Journey Through Yugoslavia* (1939, revised 1941); *The Meaning of Treason* (1949) revised as *The New Meaning of Treason* (1964); *The Court and the Castle: A Study of the Interactions of Religious and Political Ideas in Imaginative Literature* (1958); *Rebecca West: A Celebration*, Macmillan (1977).

Further reading

Glendinning, Victoria, *Rebecca West: A Life*. Weidenfeld and Nicolson, 1987.

Marcus, Jane (ed.) *The Young Rebecca: Writings of Rebecca West 1911–17*. Macmillan Press, 1982.

Orel, Harold, *The Literary Achievement of Rebecca West*. Macmillan, 1986.

Wolfe, Peter, *Rebecca West, Artist and Thinker*. Southern Illinois Press, 1971.

West's papers are held at Yale and Tulsa.

Contributor: Carole Jones

WILLIAMS, TENNESSEE (1911–83)

I'm trying to catch the true quality of experience in a group of people, that cloudy, flickering, evanescent – fiercely charged! – interplay of live human beings in the thundercloud of a common crisis.
                    Cat on a Hot Tin Roof

Thomas Lanier Williams was born in Columbus, Missouri, the grandson of an Episcopal clergyman and the son of a travelling salesman. Later the family moved to St Louis, but he could not settle down to city life and he chose the name 'Tennessee' to celebrate the Deep South where most of his plays are set. In 1938 he entered the University of Iowa and in 1940 he received a Rockefeller Fellowship for *Battle of Angels*, later rewritten as *Orpheus Descending* (1957), the first of the many plays, stories and poems Williams was to publish. Williams was awarded Pulitzer Prizes in 1948 and 1955.

Williams did not attempt to reproduce everyday reality on the stage but was thoroughly theatrical in his approach. When he envisaged a play he saw not only his characters in his plot but also his actors in his stage-set, under his lights and with a background soundtrack of his devising. In conversation with J. Devlin[1] Williams said he was 'creating imaginary worlds into which I can retreat from the real world because I've never made any kind of adjustment to the real world'. The same might be said of his characters, many of whom have their own imaginary worlds.

Much of Williams's work has its roots in the stresses of his early family life; for example the fact that he had a physically disabled sister is reflected in his first critical and commercial success, *The Glass Menagerie* (1945), which many consider his best play. Amanda Wingfield lives with her son Tom and her disabled daughter Laura in a setting described by Williams, who characteristically asked for a fire escape as part of the stage set, as 'one of those vast hive-like conglomerations of cellular living units that flower as warty growths in overcrowded urban centres'. Tom is a writer, who has returned in memory to his family, Amanda lives on memories of the past and Laura retreats from the real world into her imagination (through her collection of glass animals) to find safety and contentment. Tom and Amanda persuade a 'gentleman caller' to come to the house to meet Laura and in the scene between the two Laura is gradually brought out of herself. She is made to laugh and dance and they even kiss – before he tells her that he is to marry someone else.

Williams's control of dialogue is crucial to *The Glass Menagerie*, the four characters' words being carefully orchestrated: the nostalgic chatter of Amanda, the halting hesitation and final silence of Laura, the smooth, confident clichés of the 'gentleman caller' and the fluent speeches of Tom the narrator who, significantly, has the playwright's first name. The play ends at the only moment of real communication. Amanda, we're told, finds 'dignity and tragic beauty' as her silly chatter is finally silenced, while Laura merely smiles.

A Streetcar Named Desire (1947) is much tougher and more violent than *The Glass Menagerie*. Indeed violence, especially sexual violence, became increasingly prominent in Williams's work as his career progressed, being particularly apparent in the pederasty and cannibalism of *Suddenly Last Summer* (1958). With reference to this violence Williams wrote: 'I prefer tenderness but brutality seems to make better copy.'[2] On another occasion, however, he said that the violence was the result of his fear of the world and that his plays were 'defiant aggressions', which gave him a cathartic release.

In *A Streetcar Named Desire* Blanche Dubois arrives in New Orleans to stay with her sister Stella and Stella's husband Stanley, and the whole play is concerned with the contrast between Blanche and Stanley. Blanche has the vulnerability of Laura Wingfield and like her mother, hangs on to memories of being a Southern belle. Stanley is violently physical and as enraged by Blanche's affectations as she is shocked and fascinated by his physicality. There is almost a flirtation as well as an antipathy between them and the tension leads eventually to rape.

At the end of the play, and much against her sister's wishes, a doctor and a matron from a state institution come to take Blanche away, in a scene in which the theatricality of Williams's vision is clear and masterly:

The 'Varsouviana' [A Mexican tune] is playing distantly.

Blanche rushes into the bedroom. Lurid reflections appear on the walls in odd, sinuous shapes. The 'Varsouviana' is filtered into weird distortion, accompanied by the cries and noises of the jungle.

Matron: Hello, Blanche.

The greeting is echoed and re-echoed by other mysterious voices behind the walls, as if reverberated through a canyon of rock.

As they take her away, Blanche holds tight to the doctor's arm and says. 'Whoever you are – I have always depended on the kindness of strangers.'

Summer and Smoke (1948) has similarities with *The Glass Menagerie*, but the symbolism which was so delicately handled in *The Glass Menagerie* seems too heavy-handed and *Summer and Smoke* never enjoyed the same success. *The Rose Tattoo* (1951) carries this heavy use of symbols even further, to the extent that it seems almost to take over the play. In *Camino Real* (1953) this is exactly what happens: symbols and theatrical effects swamp the whole plot, which is based on rather a puzzling hotchpotch of good and bad.

Williams gave up symbolism in *Cat on a Hot Tin Roof* (1955), which although in many ways a highly successful and perhaps truthful play, could be said to be flawed by being too complex, with too many disparate, incompletely developed themes. As well as the issue of Brick's relationship with Maggie, the 'cat', there is the issue of his alcoholism and Big Daddy's cancer, and at the end, of the family greedily fighting over the estate.

In Act II of the play Williams writes:

> The bird that I hope to catch in the net of this play is not the solution of one man's psychological problem. I'm trying to catch the true quality of experience in a group of people, that cloudy, flickering, evanescent – fiercely charged! – interplay of live human beings in the thundercloud of a common crisis.

'Fiercely charged' certainly defines the play and 'flickering' suggests its underdevelopment.

Williams's later plays are not considered as successful as the earlier ones. *Orpheus Descending* (1957) is brilliantly written but dramatically flawed. *Suddenly Last Summer* is beautifully written and has the brightest imagery but, as has been noted above, is extremely violent. *Sweet Bird of Youth* (1959), a drama on the theme of youth's transience, is rather melodramatic.

Drugs and alcohol played a large part in the final years of Tennessee Williams's life and by the late 1970s other playwrights were claiming the attention of the American public. But the gentle poetic symbolism of *The Glass Menagerie*, the powerful and complete theatricality of *A Streetcar Named Desire,* and the sheer honesty and power of *Cat on a Hot Tin Roof* have earned Williams a lasting place in the history of American theatre.

References

1. **Devlin, Albert J.** (1986) *Conversations with Tennessee Williams.* University Press of Mississippi.

2. **Lumley, Fredrick** (1972) *New Trends in 20th Century Drama: A Survey Since Ibsen and Shaw.* Barrie & Jenkins.

Selected works:

American Blues (1939); *The Glass Menagerie* (1945); *A Streetcar Named Desire* (1947); *One Arm And Other Stories* (1948); *Summer And Smoke* (1948); *The Roman Spring of Mrs. Stone* (1950); *The Rose Tattoo* (1951); *Camino Real* (1953); *Hard Candy, A Book of Stories* (1954); *Cat on a Hot Tin Roof* (1955); *In the Winter of Cities* (1956); *Baby Doll* (1956); *Orpheus Descending* (1957); *Suddenly Last Summer* (1958); *Sweet Bird of Youth* (1959); *A Period of Adjustment* (1960); *The Night of the Iguana* (1962); *The Milk Train Does Not Stop Here Any More* (1962); *The Eccentricities of a Nightingale* (1964); *Slapstick Tragedy* (1966); *The Knightly Quest* (1967); *Kingdom of Earth (The Seven Descents of Myrtle)* (1967); *In The Bar of a Tokyo Hotel* (1969); *Dragon Country* (1970); *Small Craft Warnings* (1973); *Out Cry* (1973); *Eight Mortal Ladies Possessed* (1974); *Flee, Flee This Bad Hotel* (1974); *Moise and The World of Reason* (1975); *Memoirs* (1975); *The Red Devil Battery Sign* (1976); *This Is (An Entertainment)* (1976); *Androgyne, Mon Amour* (1977); *Vieux Carré* (1978); *Where I Live: Selected Essays* (1978); *A Lovely Sunday For Creve Coeur* (1978); *Clothes for a Summer Hotel* (1980); *Will Mr. Merriweather Return From Memphis?* (1981); *Something Cloudy, Something Clear* (1981); *The Bag People* (1982); *27 Wagons Full of Cotton and Other Short Plays* (1982); *It Happened the Day the Sun Rose* (1982); *A House Not Meant To Stand* (1982); *Collected Stories* (1985); *Five O'clock Angel* (1990).

Further reading

Bigsby, C. W. E., *Modern American Drama 1945–1990.* Cambridge University Press, 1990.

Bloom, Harold (ed.) *Tennessee Williams (Bloom's Major Dramatists)*. Chelsea House Publishers, 2000.

Gascoigne, Bamber, *Twentieth Century Drama*. Hutchinson, 1967.

Spoto, Donald, *The Kindness of Strangers: The Life of Tennessee Williams*. Bodley Head, 1985.

Contributor: Hugh Croydon

WINTERSON, JEANETTE (1959–)

The books are the best of me. When people ask me why I write I tell them it's what I'm for. It really is as simple as that.[1]

Jeanette Winterson was born in Manchester, England, and was adopted and raised in nearby Accrington by working-class, Pentecostal parents. She went on to read English at Oxford University after supporting herself while studying for A-levels. To date she has written novels, a collection of short stories, a children's book, essays, and has adapted work for film and television. In addition, Winterson has written articles for various newspapers, including a column for the *Guardian*. She has also constructed her own web site, http://jeanettewinterson.com, which came about partly as a reaction against Simon Hogarth's attempt to register her and other authors' names for his own use.

With *Oranges Are Not the Only Fruit* (1985), Winterson won the Whitbread Award for first novel. In many ways this work is semi-autobiographical because its narrator, Jeanette, is similarly adopted and raised by evangelically inspired parents. The novel focuses particularly on the influence of the narrator's mother. This is also a lesbian **Bildungsroman**, tracing the development of the narrator from early childhood to late adolescence. Jeanette's love for her mother, God and girlfriend Melanie is told with wry humour and with the assistance of layered fairy tales. **Realism** is adapted and inverted to accommodate Jeanette's version of events. It is structured by chapters named chronologically after the first eight books of the Old Testament, which has the effect of blending in, but also self-

consciously highlighting, the effect of the power of narrative on the development of Jeanette. Winterson's interest in love, sexuality and story-telling continue to be dominant themes in her work up to and including *Lighthousekeeping* (2004). **Feminist** critics warmed to this first novel and, although her work has not always been well received, it now has a wide readership and is studied in schools and universities. Public interest in *Oranges Are Not the Only Fruit* was heightened in January 1990 when BBC2 screened Winterson's three-part dramatised version to an average audience of almost six million viewers.

Her second novel, *Boating for Beginners*, was also published in 1985. Described on her web site as 'a comic book with pictures', this novel tends to be overlooked by Winterson and critical readers of her work. The third novel, *The Passion* (1987), a historical-cum-fantasy novel, which uses elements of **magic realism** and is set around the time of the Napoleonic Wars, is taken more seriously. Its two narrators, Henri and Villanelle, share the narrative as the setting shifts between France, Moscow and Venice.

In 1989 *Sexing the Cherry* was published and, like *The Passion*, has two main narrators, Jordan and Dog Woman, who relate another tale that incorporates historical detail with fantastical elements. As with *Oranges Are Not the Only Fruit*, a narrator (Jordan) is an adopted child. *Sexing the Cherry* is set in the seventeenth century and the 'present' day, shifting its two narrators across time in a style that takes both a diachronic and a synchronic perspective.

Written on the Body (1992) and *Art and Lies* (1994) continue to explore the themes of love and the power of language, which were evident in earlier works. In these novels, however, Winterson is increasingly experimenting with formal techniques. In *Written on the Body*, the narrator is unnamed and the gender is disguised. In *Art and Lies* there is a further move from realist techniques as Winterson focuses on style, in a manner comparable to **Virginia Woolf** in *The Waves*.

Winterson's admiration of Woolf is made explicit in *Art Objects* (1995) and also makes evident her debt (and homage) to **Modernism**. This book of essays is useful for any Winterson scholar as it gives a perspective on her views on art and the art of writing. Here, she also specifically denotes the influence of various authors on her writing, such as **T. S. Eliot**, Gertrude Stein and Woolf.

A concern with love and adultery is foregrounded in Winterson's next novel, *Gut Symmetries* (1997), where a love triangle between one man and two women, Jove, Alice and Stella, culminates in the ousting of the third party – Jove. This thematic use of adultery is another recurring feature in Winterson's work, specifically seen in *Written on the Body* and *The Powerbook* (2000). *The Powerbook* also concentrates on the love between two women and uses the internet and e-mails to drive the narrative. Dramatised by Winterson in 2002 and part of the 'Transformations' season for the National Theatre, it demonstrates Winterson's versatility as a writer of both novels and of adaptations of her own work.

The connection across Winterson's oeuvre lies in her willingness to employ **postmodern** techniques, as in the self-reflexive allusions to writing and literature and in the blurring of distinction between truth and lies. This destabilisation of certainty is, interestingly, often balanced by a more traditional regard for a faith in love. *Lighthousekeeping*, the latest novel, continues this stylised view with an orphaned narrator (Silver) who is apprenticed to the blind lighthouse keeper, Pew (who is also a master story-teller). Art and science are other thematic concerns and Robert Louis Stevenson and Darwin are invoked as means to challenge the illusory realist certainties of self and time.

Reference

1. **Winterson, Jeanette**.
www.jeanettewinterson.com

Selected works:

Oranges Are Not the Only Fruit (1985); *Boating for Beginners* (1985); *The Passion* (1987); *Sexing the Cherry* (1989); *Written on the Body* (1992); *Art and Lies* (1994); *Art Objects: Essays on Ecstasy and Effrontery* (1995); *Gut Symmetries* (1997); *The World and Other Places* (short stories) (1998); *The Powerbook* (2000); *The King of Capri* (book for children) (2003); *Lighthousekeeping* (2004).

Further reading

Bengston, Helene, Børch, Marianne and Maagaard, Cindie (eds) *Sponsored by Demons: The Art of Jeanette Winterson*. Denmark: Scholars' Press, 1999.

Grice, Helena and Woods, Tim (eds) *'I'm Telling You Stories': Jeanette Winterson and the Politics of Reading*. Amsterdam: Rodopi, 1998.

Contributor: Julie Ellam

WOOLF, VIRGINIA (1882–1941)

Life is . . . a luminous halo, a semi-transparent envelope surrounding us from the beginning of consciousness to the end . . . Is it not the task of the novelist to convey this varying, this unknown and uncircumscribed spirit, whatever aberration or complexity it may display with as little mixture of the alien and external as possible?

Modern Fiction

Like most women of her time, Virginia Woolf received no formal education. From her earliest years, however, she was surrounded by books and she spent her teens reading in her father's library. She thus acquainted herself with the most important works of world literature and developed a love for them which provided a firm basis for her writing.

Woolf has been a great influence on later women novelists, many of whom have declared themselves as **feminists**. But her influence transcends gender and should be judged accordingly. Like Coleridge, she believed in the androgynous nature of the writer and her novels exhibit both feminine sensitivity and masculine rigour.

Woolf, born Virginia Stephen, one of the four children of Sir Leslie and Julia Stephen, was brought up in a large, gloomy house at 22 Hyde Park Gate, London. The Stephen family was eccentric but close-knit, and Woolf was deeply affected by the deaths of her mother (when she was 13) and of her brother Thoby (when she was 24), who died aged 26. Her mother's death triggered Woolf's first breakdown and although family relationships were a source of inspiration to her, they were also to prove intensely traumatic, contributing to further breakdowns until her eventual suicide in 1941.

In 1905 Woolf wrote her first review for *The Times Literary Supplement* and continued to write for the paper for most of her life. She published her first novel, *The Voyage Out*, in 1915, having begun the first draft several years earlier, before her marriage to Leonard Woolf in 1912. Like all her novels, it was written and rewritten with the most intense scrutiny of every detail. *The Voyage Out* is a young woman's novel, but Woolf was even then intellectually mature, with a sophisticated view of the world she wished to portray – a world filtered through her imagination. As her niece Angelica Garnett wrote several decades later, 'We do not read such a book for its resemblance to our own lives, but for its power to discriminate.'[1]

At the time Woolf began writing fiction, novelists such as John Galsworthy and Arnold Bennett were writing from their own masculine viewpoints. Their narrative style was linear and realist and their stance objective. They were solidly Victorian and Edwardian, and they presented the lives of their characters with clear and unambiguous definition. Using the omniscient author technique, they tell us what their characters are thinking, and the characters are not, as it were, allowed to think and speak for themselves. Woolf, in contrast, allows characters their autonomy. She lets their thoughts wander and weave uncertainly among the great and small events of their lives, without understanding their ultimate significance. Woolf never attempts to build her characters in realistic time, but shows them against the changing background of the trivia of their daily lives. The action may take place over one day, as in *Mrs Dalloway* (1925), or over a long period, as in *To the Lighthouse* (1927) and *The Years* (1937).

Many of Woolf's central characters are women, but women seen in the context of a male-dominated society. In *Mrs Dalloway*, the first novel of the writer's maturity, Woolf deals with the trivia of one woman's life as inchoate impressions and memories flow through her mind. In *The Years* objects such as a hat, a chair or a brush take on importance as they are observed at different times by the characters and thus, indirectly, through the microscopic lens of Woolf's own vision. *The Years* gives us a picture of the changing lives of middle-class women from 1880 to the post-First World War period, through which Woolf herself lived. In *Orlando* (1928) the eponymous hero/heroine breaks through the bounds of gender by becoming alternately male and female, while English history unrolls century by century.

As a woman, Woolf felt that she had more barriers to overcome than her masculine counterparts, a view she states clearly in *A Room of One's Own* (1929). Her contention was that women writers start at a distinct disadvantage owing to the circumstances of their lives. This book, which was later to become a feminist bible – something that Woolf would not perhaps have anticipated – is the most important of her non-fiction works.

Woolf's personal vision was greatly influenced by the members of her family. In writing *To the Lighthouse*, for example, she worked through the difficulties that had been present in her relationship with her sternly Victorian father and paid homage to the selfless life of her mother. The character of the young man in *Jacob's Room* (1922) is based on her brother. So although Woolf, with her stream of consciousness style of narrative, has sometimes been accused of losing touch with real life, her novels are in fact firmly based on historical reality, a reality described in exquisite detail.

Woolf desperately wanted to be a fine writer and she wanted her writing to change the world she lived in. The praise and judgement of her family and close friends were very important to her. She was a compulsive writer, penning long, detailed letters to everyone she knew, as well as personal diaries which give us a fascinating insight into the many facets of her intricate personality.

Woolf fought against mental health problems all her life. It was probably only the unswerving support of her husband that enabled her to write as much as she did. Unfortunately, her mental breakdowns were precipitated both by the intensity of her literary efforts and by the exhaustion that always followed publication.

Woolf was always keenly aware of the changes taking place in her own times. The events of the two wars she lived through tormented her, as did the deaths among her family and friends, eventually leading to her taking her own life. Woolf expresses her attitude to war in *Three Guineas* (1938) and it is clear that her despair with the way in which contemporary events were changing her world played a part in her suicide.

The development of British and European literature in her own time was another of her concerns. The Hogarth Press, founded and managed by Woolf and her husband Leonard, published the novels and poems of many of the most important and forward-looking contemporary writers in English. Woolf's links with her artist sister, Vanessa Bell, brought her into contact with the visual arts and enabled her to write a biography of Roger Fry, the influential art critic.

Wolf was fully aware that she was an innovator. From the beginning of her literary journey she formulated her own ideas about the **Modern**, poetic novel. She searched for a new form to be made from the fragments of the old, but shaken into new patterns, transformed by an awareness of contemporary poetic sensibility. Her aim was to fashion the English novel into an art form, self-conscious perhaps, but also clinically composed. **E. M. Forster** wrote: 'She is always stretching out from her enchanted tree and snatching bits of the flux of daily life as it floats past, and out of these bits she builds novels.'[2] As early as 1919 she wrote in her essay *Modern Fiction* this definition of the way in which she was seeking to write:

Life is . . . a luminous halo, a semi-transparent envelope surrounding us from the beginning of consciousness to the end . . . Is it not the task of the novelist to convey this varying, this unknown and uncircumscribed spirit, whatever aberration or complexity it may

display with as little mixture of the alien and external as possible?

She was not the only writer to attempt a new kind of novel, but she was one of the first to articulate her aims, which helped to earn her a prominent place in contemporary literary circles. She also benefited by being an important member of the forward-looking **Bloomsbury Group**, the members of which developed their often startling ideas through close and well-reasoned argument.

In the decades following the Second World War, Woolf's work was valued less and she was thought of as a writer whose time had passed. But in the 1960s, as her biographer, Hermione Lee, says, 'Woolf began to be transformed into a heroine, an icon and a myth, for a wider and wider circle of readers'. Lee considers Wolf to be of both historical and contemporary importance, her ideas about issues such as **Modernism** and feminism making her seem 'both near and far'.

References

1. **Garnett, Angelica** (1992) Introduction to *The Voyage Out*, Definitive edition 1989, quoted in the Vintage edition.

2. Quoted in **Bradbury, Malcolm** (1994) *The Modern British Novel*. Penguin, Chapter 3, pp. 180–181.

Selected works:
Novels: *The Voyage Out* (1915); *Night and Day* (1919); *Jacob's Room* (1922); *Mrs Dalloway* (1925); *To the Lighthouse* (1927); *Orlando* (1928); *The Waves* (1931); *Flush* (1933); *The Years* (1937). **Essays:** *A Room of One's Own* (1929); *Three Guineas* (1938).

Further reading

Lee, Hermione, *Virginia Woolf*. Random House, 1997.

Marcus, Laura, *Virginia Woolf* (Writers and their Work). Northcote House, 1997.

Contributor: Margaret Tarner

YEATS, W. B. (1865–1939)

Turning and turning in the widening gyre
The falcon cannot hear the falconer;
Things fall apart; the centre cannot hold;
Mere anarchy is loosed upon the world
                                    'The Second Coming'

William Butler Yeats is regarded as not only the most important Irish poet but also one of the most important English language poets of the twentieth century. He was a key figure in the Irish Cultural Revival, his later poems made a significant contribution to Modernism and he was awarded the Nobel Prize for Literature in 1923.

Yeats's life, and his poetry, bridged the late nineteenth and early twentieth centuries. As a youth he studied art in *fin de siècle* London and absorbed the prevailing outlook of aestheticism, which was also expressed in the writing of Oscar Wilde and the painting and poetry of the Pre-Raphaelites. He was also influenced by the French Symbolist poets and developed a lifelong interest in mysticism and the occult, which fed into his poetry, lifting it above the concerns of everyday life.

His early poems, the first being published when he was 20, are characterised by a dreamy romanticism in both their form and content. He was interested in the Gaelic language, song and folklore and used effects borrowed from Gaelic literature in his poems. He wanted to reawaken Ireland to its ancient literature. According to an article written a year before his death, his efforts had a mixed reception. On the one hand,

> these evocations of Celtic beauty, heroism, and strangeness wakened . . . Ireland's ears to the sound of its own voice speaking its own music[1]

while on the other,

political societies and the press turned against his aesthetic purposes. The poems in *The Wind among the Reeds* (1899) were termed "affected," "un-Irish," "esoteric," "pagan," and "heretical."[2]

Yeats's poetic style underwent a number of transformations as he grew older, becoming leaner and more direct. Unusually for a poet, he wrote his best work late in life, between the ages of 50 and 74. His greatest period is generally said to have begun with the publication of *The Wild Swans at Coole* in 1919, and by the end of his career he was ranked along with Ezra Pound and T. S. Eliot as a foremost Modernist poet.

Yeats's grandfather and great-grandfather were Protestant rectors, but Yeats himself rejected Protestantism because of the materialism with which he felt it to be associated and in London he joined the Theosophical Society, having met its co-founder, Madam Blavatsky. He was also a member of the occult Order of the Golden Dawn. He considered himself to be a visionary, like William Blake, whom he admired, and devised his own mystical view of life, which owed more to paganism and oriental religion than to Christianity, which he set out in *A Vision* (1925, revised 1937).

In *A Vision* he developed his theory of 'gyres', which lies behind the concept of the 'widening gyre' in the opening lines from 'The Second Coming' (quoted above). 'Gyres' were spirals of cyclic time which widened to the point of collapse and in those lines Yeats expressed the idea that world history was spiralling out of control towards the end of an era and that an apocalypse was drawing close. He returned to the theme in 'The Gyres', from *Last Poems*, expressing his view that the approaching end of our civilisation was not necessarily a matter for despair. In fact it was an inevitability about which we could 'laugh in tragic joy', and 'Rejoice!'.

> Hector is dead and there's a light in Troy;
> We that look on but laugh in tragic joy.
>
> . . .
>
> What matter? Out of cavern comes a voice,
> And all it knows is that one word

'Rejoice!'
['The Gyres']

Throughout *Last Poems* Yeats faces the decline of his ageing body, as well as that of civilisation, but finds ample reason to rejoice in response to art, dance, nature and sensual pleasure.

Yeats lived through a turbulent period in Irish history, including the rise and fall of Parnell, the Easter Rising of 1916 and ultimately, in 1922, independence from Britain. He joined the Irish Nationalist cause as a youth and in 1922 became a senator in the Irish Free State. But although he was a 'fiery young Nationalist'[3] and his work was embedded in, and drew upon, the politics of his day, his writing is far from being overtly political. He was opposed to literature being used as a vehicle for political propaganda, feeling that:

The danger to art and literature comes today from the tyranny and persuasions of revolutionary societies and forms of political and religious propaganda.[4]

Yeats said of the dramatist J. M. Synge, whose plays he put on in the Abbey theatre:

He was the man that we needed because he was the only man I have ever known incapable of a political thought or of a humanitarian purpose . . . he was so little a politician that the world merely amused him and touched his pity.[5]

Irish politics was a theme to which Yeats returned frequently, particularly in the middle phase of his career, but he was responding as an individual to the turmoil and violence which was on the one hand tearing his country apart and on the other hand setting it free. In his poem 'Easter 1916' his concern is to commemorate the individuals who suffered and died in the struggle to bring about what he calls 'a terrible beauty' and in his Nobel lecture he drew attention to the 'monstrous savagery' perpetrated on both sides of the conflict.

A trumpery dispute about an acre of land can rouse our people to monstrous savagery, and if in their war with the English auxiliary police they were shown

no mercy they showed none: murder answered murder.[6]

The themes of Yeats's poetry transcend political argument and the Ireland we see in his poems owes as much to the ancient myths and legends which had fascinated him during his visits to his grandparents in Sligo as to the political events of his day. He expressed his nationalism through a passionate desire to revive the Irish literary tradition and worked towards this end by founding clubs and societies, and by setting up an Irish national theatre. He wanted to revive the spirit of the ancient oral tradition of Gaelic folklore and song, to

bring the imagination and speech of the country, all that poetical tradition descended from the middle ages, to the people of the town . . . It seemed as if the ancient world lay all about us with its freedom of imagination, its delight in good stories, in man's force and woman's beauty, and that all we had to do was to make the town think as the country felt; yet we soon discovered that the town could only think town thought.[7]

He felt it important to promote literature through theatrical performances, he says, because

the great mass of our people, accustomed to interminable political speeches, read little.[8]

With the help of Lady Isabella Augusta Gregory, a fellow nationalist who was also interested in Irish traditional folklore and was herself a playwright, he set up the Irish National Theatre Company, which took up residence in the Abbey Theatre in Dublin. The plays they put on brought them into frequent conflicts with the public, the press and the religious establishment. The most notorious was J. M. Synge's *The Playboy of the Western World*, presented in 1904, which initially had to be performed under police protection because it caused riots due to its implication that the rural Irish tend to glamorise lawless thugs, but later became a regular part of the theatre's repertory. In 1923 they produced *The Shadow of a*

Gunman by Sean O'Casey, which drew directly upon the conflict between the Irish and the British and stirred up a lot of Irish feeling.

Yeats's own plays drew on the same sources of inspiration as his poems. He was also fascinated by Japanese *Noh* plays, to which Ezra Pound introduced him while working as his secretary, and was influenced by them in the writing of a number of short plays, such as *At the Hawk's Well* (1916), *Four Plays for Dancers* (1921), *Wheels and Butterflies* (1934) and *The King of the Great Clock Tower* (1935).

Another important source of inspiration in Yeats's life and writing was his unrequited love for the actress and Irish nationalist activist Maude Gonne, who played the leading role in his most successful play *Cathleen ni Houlihan* (1902) and to whom he proposed, only to be rejected. It is generally accepted that it was this love which inspired the passages about love and passion in his poems and plays. He later proposed to her daughter, but was rejected by her too.

Yeats's poems frequently took mystical flight, into regions where it was not easy for the reader to follow, but he also had a 'balancing streak of common sense'[9] and he could bring us down to earth with a bump with stark honest lines such as these:

> I have found nothing half so good
> As my long-planned half solitude,
> Where I can sit up half the night
> With some friend that has the wit
> Not to allow his looks to tell
> When I am unintelligible
> *Fifteen apparitions have I seen;*
> *The worst a coat upon a coat-hanger.*
> ['The Apparitions', from *Last Poems*, 1936–39]

In those lines we see the direct, colloquial, modern voice which influenced later poets of the twentieth century. Yeats's mystical temperament is still present in his reference to 'apparitions', but the worst being 'a coat upon a coat hanger' is surely a reference to the stark reality we all have to face – the fear of death; his coat is there, but he isn't in it. We also see the change Yeats's style and tone had undergone when we compare those lines to the romantic opening lines of his best-known early poem:

> I will arise and go now, and go to
> Innisfree,
> And a small cabin build there, of clay and
> wattles made
> ['The Lake Isle of Innisfree']

He had come a long way from his original stance of 'a romantic exile seeking, away from reality, the landscape of his dreams'.[10]

Yeats's ardent pursuit of the occult and spiritual was idiosyncratic and cannot in itself be said to have been a major influence on the generation of poets to come, but in leaving behind the escapist romanticism of his youth and developing a stronger, leaner, more direct style in response to the changing times, he became a leading figure in Modernist literature and could be said to have opened a door through which later British, Irish and American poets followed.

In Yeats's old age, in 'Under Ben Bulben' (a hill in Sligo, near which he was buried), he addressed future Irish poets:

> Irish poets, learn your trade,
> Sing whatever is well made,
> Scorn the sort now growing up,
> All out of shape from toe to top,
> ['Under Ben Bulben', from *Last Poems*]

References

1. **Bogan, Louise** (1938) 'William Butler Yeats', *The Atlantic Monthly*, May, Vol. 161, No. 5; pp. 637–644. www.theatlantic.com/unbound/poetry/yeats/bogan.htm (Hereafter referred to as 'Bogan').

2. Ibid.

3. Ibid.

4. **Yeats, W. B.**, Nobel Lecture. 15 December 1923. www.nobel.se/literature/laureates/1923/yeats-lecture.html. From *Nobel Lectures, Literature 1901–1967*, Elsevier Publishing Company, Amsterdam.

5. Ibid.

6. Ibid.

7. Ibid.

8. Ibid.

9. Bogan.

10. Ibid.

Selected works:

Poetry: *Crossways* (1889); *The Wanderings of Oisin, and Other Poems* (1889); *The Rose* (1893); *Poems* (1895); *The Wind Among the Reeds* (1899); *The Old Age of Queen Maeve* (1903); *Baile and Aillinn* (1903); *In the Seven Woods* (1904); *The Shadowy Waters* (1906); *The Green Helmet and other poems* (1910); *Poems Written in Discouragement* (1913); *The Two Kings* (1914); *Responsibilities: Poems and a Play* (1914); *The Wild Swans at Coole* (1919); *Michael Robartes and the Dancer* (1921); *Seven Poems and a Fragment* (1922); *The Gift of Harun Al-Rashid* (1923); *The Cat and the Moon and Certain Poems* (1924); *October Blast* (1927); *The Tower* (1928); *The Winding Stair and other Poems* (1929); *Words for Music Perhaps and Other Poems* (1932); *A Full Moon in March* (1935); *New Poems* (1938); *Last Poems* (1939). **Plays:** *The Countess Cathleen* (1892); *The Land of Heart's Desire* (1894); *Cathleen ni Houlihan* (1902); *The Hour Glass* (1903); *The King's Threshold* (1904); *The Pot of Broth* (1904); *On Baile's Strand* (1905); *Deirdre* (1907); *At the Hawk's Well* (1916); *Four Plays for Dancers* (1921); *Wheels and Butterflies* (1934); *The King of the Great Clock Tower* (1935); *The Herne's Egg* (1938). **Prose:** *Fairy and Folk Tales of the Irish Peasantry* (1888); *John Sherman and Dhoya* (1891); *The Celtic Twilight* (1893); *The Secret Rose* (1897); *A Vision* (1925, revised 1937); *Dramatis Personae* (1936); *Autobiographies* (published posthumously in 1955). **As editor:** *The Poems of William Blake* (1893); *The Works of William Blake* (with E. J. Ellis) (1893); *Poems of Spenser* (1906); *The Oxford Book of Modern Verse, 1892–1935* (1936).

Further reading

Ellmann, Richard, *Yeats: The Man and the Masks*. E. P. Dutton, 1979.

Jeffares, A. Norman, *W. B. Yeats: A New Biography*. Continuum Publishing Group, 2001.

Kermode, Frank, *Romantic Image*. University of Chicago Press, 1985.

Contributor: Ian Mackean

Part 2

Major themes in modern literature

Critical studies of modern literature

Modernism and popular literature

'**Modernism**' remains one of the most ambiguous labels devised for the study of literature, art and society as a whole. The problem begins with the root word 'modern', used as both an adjective and a noun to designate a bewilderingly wide array of things and ideas. The online *Oxford English Dictionary* (OED)[1] offers 21 meanings of the word, one of which is 'of the present and recent times as opposed to the remote past'. The question that follows is, what then is 'remote' past? The suffix '-ism' in 'modernism' is no less problematic. Is modern*ism* a cult or a religion, an organised body of thought with clearly laid down principles, like, say, Buddh*ism*, or a political ideology like Marx*ism*? In fact modernism is anything *but* an organised system of ideas or thoughts. Malcolm Bradbury and James Macfarlane, in their landmark collection of essays on the topic, *Modernism: A Guide to European Literature 1890–1930* (Penguin, 1976, reprint 1991), talk of literary Modernism as 'an appallingly explosive fusion' of ideas and styles.

When spelt with a capital 'M', Modernism broadly refers to a period in European and American art, literature, music and architecture at the start of the twentieth century. The term is narrowly applied, especially for the purposes of teaching literature in the academies, to a small but by no means homogeneous cluster of writers such as Joseph Conrad, **W. B. Yeats**, **T. S. Eliot**, **James Joyce**, **Ezra Pound**, **Virginia Woolf** and **D. H. Lawrence**, most of whom reached their literary prime between 1900 and 1939. But in this historical bracketing is cocooned one of the biggest problems with the term Modernism. How can a cultural phenomenon now almost a hundred years old be dubbed modern? Therefore the question *when* was Modernism is as valid as the question *what* is Modernism.

These are some of the dates and events frequently cited in historical evaluations of Modernism.

In 1900 **Sigmund Freud** published *The Interpretation of Dreams*, a book that not only laid the founding principles of psychoanalysis but also led to radically new questions about authorship and criticism in art and literature. Freud's work realigned the focus from a world out there to the worlds locked up in the mind.

The year 1901 marked the beginning of the twentieth century but it was also the year in which Queen Victoria died. The death of Victoria literally and figuratively marked the end of an era whose stolid values were reflected in the arts and literature of her time.

In her seminal essay 'Mr Bennet and Mrs Brown',[2] Virginia Woolf observed, 'In or around 1910, human nature changed.' She was referring to the first Post-Impressionist exhibition curated by Roger Fry at the Grafton Gallery in London that year. While Woolf's comment may have been a loose generalisation, Post-Impressionist art nevertheless broke up planes of consciousness, fragmented perspective, reorganised space in painting and suggested new forms of representation to writers.

It is impossible to establish a direct causal relationship between Post-Impressionist art and the literature of the first quarter of the twentieth century. However, if we consider a representative 'Modernist' poem like T. S. Eliot's *The Waste Land* (1922), with its five disjointed sections, its disorderly pile of sharply drawn but broken images, its narrative limbo and its halting language feverishly flitting between bland descriptions and random utterances, it is possible to see similarities between the poem and paintings such as van Gogh's *Wheatfields with Crows* (1890) and Picasso's *Les Demoiselles d'Avignon* (1907).

In 1914, with the outbreak of the First World War, European nations, and later on America, became entangled in a conflict that rapidly escalated to engulf a large section of the world. For the first time in the history of human conflict the full array of products of large-scale industrial arms manufacture – from mustard gas to battle tanks to aerial bombings – was let loose on frontline soldiers. The sense of doom and grim foreboding that marks much of Modernist literature and art can be traced to this catastrophic event.

These dates and events have their use in mapping the contours of Modernism. But what if we think of a few other dates, not always cited while talking of literary Modernism?

In 1918 the guns were eventually silenced on the Western Front, marking the end of the First World War. However, that year, after decades of vehement campaigning by the 'Suffragettes', women over 30 years of age were allowed to vote for the first time in the British Parliamentary elections, an event as crucial to an assessment of Modernism as any other. The following year Ernst Rutherford split the atom and the idea of the Modern arrived with a bang. In 1913, the Indian poet **Rabindranath Tagore** won the Nobel prize for literature for his slim volume of poems in English, *Gitanjali*. The colonies started rewriting the script of the Empire.

In the winter of 1932–33, the English cricket captain Douglas Jardine applied his infamous 'leg theory' mercilessly to help his team to win the Ashes 4–1. But the resulting controversy threatened to sever diplomatic ties between Australia and England and was thus as significant a turning point in the process of the decline of the British Empire as the Jalianwalla Bagh massacre in Punjab on 13 April 1919. England, after 1932, lost its high moral ground and the Empire was no longer on a mission to civilise the savage races. Now that the gloves were off, the Empire revealed itself as an instrument of looting and plunder, in which the end justified the means. So, as Douglas Jardine won the Ashes, England began to lose its Empire, an event as 'Modern' as, say, the splitting of the atom or the death of Queen Victoria.

The consideration of such non-literary, non-cultural events as the splitting of the atom, the triumph of the suffragettes and the Bodyline Series in cricket draws attention to the danger of trying to pin Modernism to specific historical events, approaching it with a set of preconceived ideas, or even trying to restrict it merely to the world of arts and letters. Modernity, perhaps more than any other cultural movement, resists such a limitation. The implementation of the Education Acts in the 1870s in England, which made education compulsory and literacy almost universal, the invention of cinema by the Lumiere brothers in 1895, the first powered flight by the Wright brothers in 1903, Henry Ford's innovation of the moving assembly line leading to the first mass-produced car, the Ford Model T in 1909 – these are arguably as central to the idea of Modernism as the publication of James Joyce's *Ulysses* or Eliot's *The Waste Land*.

The Modernist period was marked by rapid changes in every sphere of society and its politics, changes which sparked furious debates.[3] The newspapers and journals of the day were replete with issues that still concern us today – urban housing and space, public health and hygiene, transportation, diet, immigration, ethnic relations. These debates show why Modernity is seen as a period of cultural churning and, therefore, crisis. The fact that some of these issues are still prominent is one reason why Modernism *is* still relevant and continues to be called Modernism, conveying that sense of *immediacy*, of *here* and *now*.

A characteristic common to the 'representative' literature of Modernism – the authors and works most often taught in schools, colleges and universities – is its perceived 'difficulty' or 'inaccessibility'. The works of writers such as Joyce, Pound, Eliot and Woolf can hardly be called thumping good reads. Their writing is marked by stylistic complexities that are deliberate and wilful and tend to shut the reader out from the text rather than invite him or her in. 'Persons attempting to find a plot in [this narrative] will be shot,' wrote Mark Twain at the start of *The Adventures of Huckleberry Finn*. Twain's 'notice' to his readers could serve as a caveat to readers of Joyce's *A Portrait of the Artist as a Young Man* (1916) or Woolf's *To the Lighthouse* (1927).

One reason why this body of writing appears perversely difficult is that it was meant to be so. The break with tradition was sharp and abrupt, as Modernist writers appeared to rally around Pound's cry 'Make it new'. Michael Levenson offers an explanation of why elitism and exclusivity appear to be the hallmarks of literary Modernism:

Because [Modernism's] leading voices eagerly assumed not only the burden of making new artefacts, but also the responsibility of offering new justifications, the misunderstandings of Modernism began at the start, began with the ambition of writers and artists to set the terms by which they would be understood, where this often meant setting the terms by which others would not qualify for understanding. The circle of initiates was closed not only against the unwashed public, but also against rival artists who were excluded from the emerging narrative of Modernism triumphant.[4]

The rise of English studies as an academic discipline, serious enough to be taught at universities, and the codification of the 'Eng. Lit. Crit. Canon' are also complicit in Modernism's notorious complexity. In 1917 Cambridge University became the first institution of higher learning to offer a course in contemporary literature in English. Dons trained in history, moral sciences and the classics, such as I. A. Richards and F. R. Leavis at Cambridge, the founding fathers of English studies there, and John Churton Collins who lobbied for the same at his alma mater Oxford but was overlooked for a chair, cast their long shadow on the staple diet of Modernist 'classics' that have conditioned the response of generations of readers.[5] Thus the 'emerging narrative of Modernism triumphant' is only half the tale, a half that excludes 'rival artists' in a strategy which echoes the machinations of the canonised works of Modernism.

A more inclusive narrative of Modernism has to acknowledge the distinction between 'High' and 'Low' Modernism, even if the purpose is to challenge the binary split into 'high' and 'low'. The notion of 'high' and 'low' in literature is itself a product of the intellectual ferment of the first quarter of the twentieth century. The *OED* dates the word 'highbrow', meaning an intellectual elite, back to 1908, attributing frequent usage of the word to Arnold Bennett and D. H. Lawrence.[6]

In the field of fiction written between 1900 and 1938 we can identify one of the sharpest, most definitive contradictions of Modernist literature: High Modernism's oppositional status vis-à-vis popular writing.

One of the outcomes of the near universal literacy resulting from the Education Acts was that the neo-literates created a huge demand for printed matter. The rise in the sheer number of literate people resulted in the exponential growth of, first, newspapers and then, popular fiction. Alfred Harmsworth, later Lord Northcliffe, established the *Daily Mirror*, the 'first daily newspaper for gentlewomen' and staffed exclusively by women, in 1903. Renamed the *Daily Illustrated Mirror*, with photographs dominating the text, the paper became, by 1914, the first daily in the world to sell 1 million copies on a weekday. However, the weekly papers, like *Pearson's Weekly* and *The News of The World*, had reached the magic mark of 1 million earlier, in 1897 and 1910 respectively.[7]

The advertising spiel of the *Daily Mail*, another paper from the Northcliffe stable, was 'The Busy Man's Paper'. That paper drew the battle lines between what we now distinguish as the opinionated broadsheets and the frenzied tabloids. John Carey insightfully comments on the way the *Daily Mail* and everything it represented 'created an alternative culture' and 'bypassed the intellectual and made him redundant'. More importantly, Carey observes, 'it took over the function of providing the public with fiction, thus dispensing with *the need for novelists*'.[8]

Though not yet technically tabloids in format, papers from Lord Northcliffe's stable, the *Daily Mail* and the *Mirror*, were well on their way to becoming tabloids as far as their content was concerned. The tabloid as we know it today was the innovation of one of the pioneers of newspaper design and layout, Arthur Christiansen, who in 1933 revamped the *Daily Express*, introducing screaming headlines and sensational reporting in short, snappy sentences. By 1939, the *Daily Express* sold 2.5 million copies a day. Contrast this with *The Times*'s circulation figure in 1848 of only 30,000.[9]

The emergence of popular fiction was another direct consequence of mass literacy, aided to a great extent by the technology which enabled the production of cheaper paper and cheaper imprints. The nature of literary output changed in a significant and irreversible way. The term 'popular literature' itself was coined in the first quarter of the twentieth century, the need for a new term giving us a good idea of how significant the divide between serious and light literature became in that period.

It is important to distinguish 'popular' literature from the 'best-seller'. *The Bible* has been a consistent best-seller since the advent of printing in the fifteenth century, but by no means can it be considered as an example of popular literature. What constitutes popular reading matter is an issue of debate, but there was a significant overlap between newspapers and popular literature at the start of the twentieth century, in form as well as content. The numerous journals of the day, for instance *The Strand Magazine* or *Tit Bits*, serialised tales of romance, adventure and crime. *The Strand Magazine* published Arthur Conan Doyle's Sherlock Holmes stories. In 1906, the *Daily Mail* brought out in serial form William Le Queux's alarmist novel *The Invasion of 1910*, a fictional account of a German offensive on Britain.

Edgar Wallace was the grand Mogul of this mass-market fiction. His *Four Just Men*, written in 1905, is regarded as one of the landmarks of the hardboiled political thriller. Its pared-down language and racy narrative imitates the diction and style of the *Daily Mail*, the paper that employed him at the time. In the 1920s his publishers put out the dubious claim that Wallace was the author of a quarter of all the books published in Britain at that time. John Buchan's *Thirty Nine Steps*, published in book form in 1915, was first serialised by *Blackwood's Magazine* from July 1914.[10]

These tales of high adventure, hushed romance and breathtaking intrigue, set against the gigantic and exotic map of the Empire, offer a clue as to why Joseph Conrad's *Heart of Darkness,* also published by *Blackwood's Magazine*,[11] was published in three parts before being published as a book. The format of published fiction changed and the price plummeted. By 1900 the ponderous three-volume novel of the Victorian era, prohibitively priced at half a guinea a volume, had been replaced by the single-volume novel costing a more affordable six shillings. The mass-circulation magazines owed much to their Victorian predecessors, which had published the work of such writers as Charles Dickens and Wilkie Collins, but differed markedly in both quality and quantity.

The following extract from the *Daily Express*, the first tabloid, published in early October 1922, shows how transferable and interchangeable the language of popular fiction and sensational news reports became:

> The flickering light of a match revealed to a doctor a dead man huddled against a wall in Belgrave Road, Ilford, at half-past twelve yesterday morning. It did not reveal the fourteen wounds in the man's back and throat or the trail of blood for nearly twenty yards along the pavement.[12]

Not everyone was pleased with the consequences of mass literacy. Following on from George Bernard Shaw and Thomas Hardy in the late nineteenth century, the keepers of Britain's cultural distinction, the intellectuals, ranted and raved in the 1930s about this production line of literature and its wholesale prices. Prominent among these critics of popular and democratic literature were Leavis, through his journal *The Scrutiny*, Eliot, as an editor of the *Criterion*, and Pound and Joyce, who explicitly equated the output of this literature factory and newspaper machine with bodily filth and human excreta, Pound in his *Cantos* and Joyce in *Ulysses*.[13]

Curiously, these elite critics themselves were not immune from the effects of popular culture. Leavis's Ph.D. thesis was entitled 'The Relationship of Journalism to Literature Studied in the Rise of and Earlier Development of the Press in England'.[14] The title of Eliot's play *Murder in the Cathedral* could well have been the title of an Agatha Christie novel. The presence of newspapers and news headlines is pervasive in *Ulysses*. Consider, also, the titles of Conrad's novels and tales: *The Secret Agent*, 'The Secret Sharer', *Heart of Darkness*. They all point to a market of mass consumption to which he and his publishers were quite prepared to pander. In her essay 'Mr Bennet and Mrs Brown' (mentioned earlier), Virginia Woolf cannot resist a pot-shot at the modern Georgian cook who intrudes into the drawing room in the morning to borrow the *Daily Herald*.

The world of printed matter in the Modernist period was thus carved out into two warring factions: one camped in the newspaper offices of Fleet Street and the other amidst the dreaming spires of the universities.

The products of popular culture – newspapers, magazines and cheap novels – found an outlet where their consumption was guaranteed: the train compartment and railway stations. While the railways were a Victorian invention, mass commuter travel is a distinctly modern phenomenon. Not only did commuter travel provide the perfect opportunity to read newspapers and penny dreadfuls, the rapidly expanding railway network could now carry newspapers and fiction as soon as they were published to all corners of Britain.

In Oscar Wilde's play *The Importance of Being Earnest*, Gwendolen says: 'I always travel with my diary. One should always have something *sensational* to read on the train.' Gwendolen might well have been talking about the *Daily Mail*, the *Mirror* or the *Express*, or the fictions of Marie Corelli, author of *Sorrows of Satan*. Published in 1895, by 1910 Corelli's book was in its 55th edition. W. H. Smith opened its first retail outlet in Euston Station in 1858 and the publishing trade, even to this day, is geared to entertain and amuse on modes of mass transportation, the aeroplane and the train.[15] Considering the latest 'tabloids' in the market, the compact versions of *The Times* and the *Independent*, a slew of women's magazines designed to fit into handbags and the television advertisements that promote these products, it is probably safe to say that we continue to conduct our daily lives under the spell of the modern.

References

1. **OED Online:** dictionary.oed.com accessed on 6 April 2004, 18:54 BST.

2. Printed originally as 'Character in Fiction' in *The Criterion* 11, 8 (July 1924) and then revised and reprinted as 'Mr Bennet and Mrs Brown' in a pamphlet by the Hogarth Press the same year. Source: Peter Faulkner (ed.) (1986). *A Modernist Reader: Modernism in England 1910–1930*. London: B. T. Batsford.

3. Michael Levenson suggests, 'Social *modernization* [...] was always a challenge to a cultural Modernism.' Michael Levenson, *Cambridge Companion to Modernism*, Cambridge: Cambridge University Press, 1999, p. 2. Author's emphasis.

4. Ibid, p. 2.

5. For the emergence of English studies and literary criticism as an academic discipline, see Chris Baldick, *The Social Mission of English Criticism 1848–1932*, Oxford: Clarendon Press, 1983.

6. **OED Online:** dictionary.oed.com accessed on 8 April 2004, 19:22 BST.

7. **Clive Bloom** (ed.) (1993) *Literature and Culture in Britain, Volume One: 1900–1929*, London: Longman.

8. **John Carey** (1992) *The Intellectuals and the Masses: Pride and Prejudice among Literary Intelligentsia, 1880–1939.* London and Boston: Faber and Faber, p. 7.

9. **Matthew Engel** (1996) *Tickle the Public: One Hundred Years of the Popular Press.* London: Victor Gollancz, p. 21.

10. www.spartacus.schoolnet.co.uk/Jbuchan.htm accessed on 22 January 2004, 18:29 BST.

11. www.victorianweb.org/authors/conrad/pva46.html accessed on 22 January 2004, 18:39 BST.

12. 'British Newspapers in Early Twentieth Century' in *Literature and Culture in Britain 1900–1929.* Clive Bloom (ed.), London: Longman, 1993, p. 129.

13. In a memorable episode in Book II of *Ulysses* Leopold Bloom wipes himself after defecating with sheets torn from Titbits. James Joyce, *Ulysses*, Paris: Shakespeare and Company, 1922. Reprint London: Penguin Twentieth-Century Classics Annotated Students Edition, 1992. Ed. Declan Kiberd, p. 85.

14. **Stefan Collini** (1998) 'The Critic as Journalist: Leavis after Scrutiny' in *Grub Street and Ivory Tower: Literary Journalism and Literary Scholarship from Fielding to the Internet.* Jeremy Treglown and Bridget Bennett (eds), Oxford: Clarendon, p. 158.

15. For a fascinating account on railways and modernity see Ian Carter, *Railways and Culture in Britain: The Epitome of Modernity.* Manchester and New York: Manchester University Press, 2001.

Further reading

Bradshaw, David (ed.) *A Concise Companion to Modernism.* Oxford: Blackwell, 2003.

Childs, Peter, *Modernism.* New Critical Idiom Series, London: Routledge, 2000.

Poplawski, Paul (ed.) *Encyclopedia of Literary Modernism.* Westport, CT, USA; London: Greenwood Press, 2003.

Contributor   Debanjan Chakrabarti

The language of modern literature in English

An investigation into the language of modern literature in English is in many ways an investigation of the **Modernist** movement itself. While all canonical literature is to some extent self-conscious about its language, the exploration and playful objectifying of linguistic resources is a characteristic of many of the most admired works of the modern, and **postmodern**, periods. It has been said that the modern movement comprised a shift from meaning perceived *through* language to meaning found *in* language, that the form came to be treated as the art, rather than merely the vehicle of art. The shift developed further in the second half of the twentieth century, when we find the emergence of the postmodern view that form, particularly language, is meaning itself.

A concern with language was already apparent in the work of some pre-modern writers such as the nineteenth-century poet **Gerard Manley Hopkins** (1844–89) and novelist and poet Thomas Hardy (1840–1928), whose writing spanned the nineteenth and twentieth centuries. From early in the twentieth century we find attempts at linguistic democratisation and truthfulness in the use of dialect in the work of Thomas Hardy, Wilfred Owen (1893–1918), Hugh MacDiarmid (1892–1978) and **D. H. Lawrence** (1885–1930). Even the long, difficult sentences of late Henry James (1843–1916) may be seen as foreshadowing modern styles that draw attention to themselves and resist being treated as transparent media of story or meaning.

More radical experiments in language were demonstrated by **Virginia Woolf** (1882–1941) in using words as the Impressionist painter used the brush (*To the Lighthouse*, 1927)[1] or as the Greek choruses chanted (*The Waves*, 1931), Lawrence's expressionist use of repetitions (especially in *The Rainbow*, 1915), the fragmented, multi-voiced poems of **T. S. Eliot** (1888–1965) and from **James Joyce** (1882–1941) the formulations and re-formulations of written language, culminating in *Finnegan's Wake* (1939). These early modern writers pushed the frontiers of English literary language further than ever before.

Within this experimentation, however, the language remains in many ways familiar. Unlike the plastic arts, the book and theatre businesses rely on sales, so published experiments in literary prose tend to be restricted to those in which the context together with a little effort from the reader will suffice to decode unfamiliar forms. (Although disheartened readers of *Finnegan's Wake* may disagree with 'a little'.) Joyce aside, it is usually in poetry, which has always been allowed to demand more work from its readers, that we find the most extreme examples of deviation from conventional literary language. Drama, which does not give its audience the luxury of a re-reading, and in which the visual conventions of the written word are hidden, necessarily tends to be less linguistically adventurous than fiction.

The areas of literary language to have exhibited experiment and change are syntax, which has always been open to manipulation in poetry but is now also treated with freedom in prose, and vocabulary, which remains the richest area of invention. The appearance of modern writings is often quite different from that of earlier texts because many of the linguistic experiments affect typography. Occasionally the typographical details are important to the meaning of the work.

Incomplete utterances are a frequently occurring form of ungrammatical sentence. In prose they mostly happen where there is interruption by another character's utterance, or some other event. This is common in plays, where unfinished or interrupted sentences are usually attempts to represent the ungrammaticality of everyday speech. In novels, meandering or incomplete sentences can also be used to indicate the wandering language of thought. Thus Virginia Woolf, with her **stream of consciousness** technique, shows interactions between thought, spoken or unspoken, and the outside world through interrupted syntax, as in the following passage from *Between the Acts* (1941):

'Where we know not, where we go not, neither know nor care,' she hummed.
'Flying, rushing through the ambient, incandescent, summer silent . . .'
The rhyme was 'air'. She put down her brush. She took up the telephone.
'Three, four, eight, Pyecombe,' she said.
'Mrs Oliver speaking . . . What fish have you this morning? Cod? Halibut? Sole? Plaice?'
'There to lose what binds us here,' she murmured. 'Soles. Filleted. In time for lunch please,' she said aloud. 'With a feather, a blue feather . . . flying mounting through the air . . . to lose what binds us here.'

The chopped effect of a sequence of incomplete sentences may indicate a sequence of short attention spans, as in Stephen Dedalus's silent reading of a letter to a newspaper in Joyce's *Ulysses*:

May I trespass on your valuable space. That doctrine of *laissez faire* which so often in our history. Our cattle trade. The way of all our old industries. Liverpool ring with jock-eyed the Galway harbour scheme. European conflagration. Grain supplies through the narrow waters of the channel. The pluterperfect imperturbability of the department of agriculture. Pardoned a classical allusion. Cassandra. By a woman who was no better than she should be. To come to the point at issue.

Runs of short sentences, sometimes incomplete, can also be found in the works of **Samuel Beckett** (1906–89). Again they indicate inner experience, representing the narrator's frame of mind:

Live and invent. I have tried. I must have tried. Invent. It is not the word.
Neither is live. No matter. I have tried.
(*Malone Dies*)

Experiments in syntax can involve the exploitation of ambiguity rather than infringement of grammar. To take an example from Hopkins, the sentence 'why wouldst thou rude on me/Thy wring-world right foot rock?' ('Carrion Comfort', 1918) is not necessarily ungrammatical. It is difficult because of the ambiguous grammatical status of the words *rude* and *rock*, the first being familiar as an adjective but here occupying the position of a main verb, the second being either verb or noun. Hesitation and diffi-culty are increased by the mental effort involved in trying to understand the unusual images. In the end, the sentence resists clear paraphrase because of insurmountable ambiguity, appropriate to a poem in which the tackling of extreme difficulty is a theme.

Other instances of what appear to be ungrammatical passages may be expressions of unconventional types of discourse. An example is provided by the early diary pas-sages in *Nineteen Eighty-four* (1949) by George Orwell, where a lack of explicit dis-course connections, punctuation and capitalisation is indicative of the character's mental stress and his unfamiliarity with even the idea of expressing his thoughts:

> theyll shoot me i dont care theyll shoot me in the back of the neck i dont care
> down with big brother they always shoot you in the back of the neck I don't care
> down with big brother

Perhaps the most consistent use of this kind of narration is found in the interior mono-logues of Beckett. It is above all his use of language that creates the world of an alien-ated narrating mind in *Trilogy* (1959).[2] Here various features, such as sudden jumps from one subject to another, present the appearance of a pathologically solipsistic nar-rator, who is nevertheless extremely verbal. A distorted perception of reality is indicat-ed by distortions of conventional text presentation: very short and very long sentences are found, along with lists and concatenated, unconventionally set-out reported speech. Beckett's very short sentences are often perfectly grammatically formed; it is the fact that they are written as separate sentences rather than connected into longer utterances that gives them a jerky, disconnected feel. The excessively long sentences, such as the last sentence in *The Unnameable* (1959), which goes on for three-and-a-half pages, break down grammatically as strings of shorter sentences connected by commas. Paragraphs and chapters are also unconventional, with the first chapter of *Molloy* (1955) compris-ing a single, 84-page-long paragraph and the whole story having only two chapters. *Malone Dies* (1956) and *The Unnameable* have no chapter divisions at all.

In poetry it is not often that the internal structure of a sentence is broken and a truly ungrammatical construction presented, although unusual structures can be found, as in the following examples:

> And you, my father, . . .
> Curse, bless, me now with your fierce tears, I pray

These lines from 'Do Not Go Gentle into That Good Night' (1951) by Dylan Thomas require a conjunction between 'curse' and 'bless' to be strictly grammatical, and the comma after 'bless' disallows a default reading in which the speaker's initial demand, 'curse', is replaced by a request for a blessing. Instead both the curse and the bless-ing seem to be demanded equally by the speaker, the whole poem being an expres-sion of the contradictions inherent in his grief.

In 'MCMXIV' (1960) by Philip Larkin, his three stanzas of listed images followed by one stanza of brief commentary has no main verb or grammatical predicate.[3] In

'Ambulances' (1964), he uses the dissolution of sentence structure to enact the dissolution of life's structures as described in the poem:

> . . . Far
> From the exchange of love to lie
> Unreachable inside a room
> The traffic parts to let go by
> Brings closer what is left to come,
> And dulls to distance all we are.

A number of descriptive poems by **Ted Hughes** owe their force in part to the omission of main verbs, especially in the opening lines, as in 'Pike' (1959):

> Pike, three inches long, perfect
> Pike in all parts, green tigering the gold.
> Killers from the egg: the malevolent aged grin.

On occasion what seems to be an omitted opening main verb in a Hughes poem is found at the end of the sentence, as in 'An Otter' (1960), and what may seem to be an omitted subject may in fact be present as the title, as in 'The Retired Colonel' (1960) and 'River' (1983).

Vocabulary is the area of most frequent linguistic innovation, the modern period abounding in examples of writers who made up new words, used words unconventionally or included words not previously found in literature. Among poetic neologisers Hopkins and Dylan Thomas are most famous for their original compounds, such as 'Worlds of wanwood leafmeal lie' (Hopkins, 'Spring and Fall', 1918) and functional conversions, such as 'rivers of the windfall light' (Thomas, 'Fern Hill', 1946). The early poetry of Edith Sitwell (1887–1964) and Joyce's *Finnegan's Wake* contain so many blends and coinages that many readers find them impossible to read, let alone to understand. Although a prose work, the linguistic innovations and difficulties of *Finnegan's Wake* place it in a category of its own, closer to poetry than to other prose writings. Some of Joyce's blendings involve mixtures of languages, a practice also found in the blending of Standard English with words, parts of words and the rhythms of Indian speech in *Midnight's Children* (1981) and *The Moor's Last Sigh* (1995) by **Salman Rushdie**.

Although mostly written in conventional prose, Orwell's *Nineteen Eighty-four* is one of the few novels to present a new language, 'Newspeak', required by the regime described in the novel. Fragments of Newspeak are inserted as illustrations of the world within the narrative:

> reporting bb dayorder doubleplusungood refs unpersons rewrite fullwise upsub antefiling

Another disturbing work of fiction that includes made-up words is Anthony Burgess's *A Clockwork Orange* (1962). The novel is narrated through the perceptions and idiom of a teenage gangster, whose language is stylistically self-conscious (he frequently comments on his own and other people's speech) and peppered with neologisms whose origins are explained in the following passage:

> 'These grahzny sodding vesches that come out of my Gulliver and my plot,' I said, 'that's what it is.'
> 'Quaint,' said Dr Brodsky, like smiling, 'the dialect of the tribe. Do you know anything of its provenance, Branom?'
> 'Odd bits of old rhyming slang,' said Dr Branom, who did not look quite so much like a friend any more. 'A bit of gipsy talk, too. But most of the roots are Slav.'

Closely connected with lexical innovation is the mixing of voices and languages within a single text. The sustained use of multiple narrators and, especially, multiple **viewpoints** in novels is a frequently found device. In poetry one of the best-known examples of this must be Eliot's 'The Waste Land' (1921), which starts with a classical Greek epigram and ends with a Sanskrit utterance. The cast of voices found in this poem includes speakers of different languages and the languages of different social classes and historical periods.

Virginia Woolf's *The Waves* (1931) is presented through the perceptions and voices of six characters. There is also an anonymous voice which identifies the other voices (e.g. 'said Susan', 'said Rhoda') and provides the intermittent descriptions of nature that divide the work into something approximating chapters. The characters also comment on their own actions in a way that can be seen as a transposition into the novel of the role of the chorus in classical drama. The overall effect is an unusual combination of stylistic self-consciousness and intimacy. In some ways this novel might be seen as an opposite of 'The Waste Land'. True to their titles, whereas there is almost hypnotic regularity in the parallelisms of *The Waves*, readers of 'The Waste Land' search for regularities of theme and image in order to build up a sense of meaning.

Plurality of narratives is a favourite device of **Doris Lessing** (1919–) and **John Fowles** (1926–). An ingenious use of multiple narration was produced by Lessing in her *Golden Notebook* (1962), where the different narratives are all produced by the same narrator but represent the fragmentation of her existence and personality. She has used multiple narrative on several occasions since, in works as diverse as *Briefing for a Descent into Hell* (1971) and the five-novel sequence the *Canopus in Argos Archives* (1979–83), especially in the first and fifth of this sequence. Fowles's novel *A Maggot* (1985) comprises different narratives relating the same event, as did his first novel, *The Collector* (1963). His *The Magus* (first version 1966), *The Ebony Tower* (1974) and *Daniel Martin* (1977) also contain multiple narratives, but in these novels one narrative is dominant and the others are subsidiary.

This form of multiplicity is found in many recent novels, such as Julian Barnes's *A History of the World in 102 Chapters* (1989) and *Flaubert's Parrot* (1984) which cleverly parrots a great deal of Flaubert. *Possession: A Romance* (1990) by A. S. Byatt possesses many sub-texts and her novel *Babel Tower* (1996) has another novel nestling within.

The use of multiple narratives reflects the modern awareness that different perceptions of reality exist and may be equally valid. Another reflection of this awareness is the introduction into literature of a new range of experiences and realms of existence. This has involved the exploration of voices rarely previously represented in the literary canon. For example there has been an increase in the number of working-class voices and informal registers in literature. This is rooted in, and strengthened by, changes in social and linguistic habits in Britain, where a near-universal literacy pertains, the majority of the population have become able to afford books and people no longer feel it necessary to adopt an upper-class accent as a marker of professional or educational status. Since, in England, a working-class voice is also a regionally placed voice, we find an increase in the amount and varieties of dialect found in literature.

The early modern period saw only a few examples of dialect literature accepted into the canon, such as poems by Thomas Hardy and Hugh MacDiarmid, poems and plays by D. H. Lawrence, and the Irish idiom in *Ulysses*. From the middle of the century drama became more realistic in this respect, with some dramatists, such as **Harold Pinter**, Arnold Wesker and Dylan Thomas (*Under Milk Wood*), writing plays almost entirely in dialect. More recent playwrights of dialect works include Christina Reid (1942–) (Belfast English), Jim Cartwright (1958–) (Lancashire English) and Mike Packer (Tyneside English). Dialect poems have continued to be produced, for example by the Manchester and Liverpool schools, and include Tom Pickard's (1946–) disturbing poem 'Rape',[4] which opens:

canny bord ower there
sharrap man yi think I nowt but tarts

The rise of the **Angry Young Men** and the 'working-class novel' in the 1950s did not see the rise of the dialect novel because these works included dialect passages only in the dialogue of certain characters, as seen for example in *Saturday Night and Sunday Morning* (1958) by **Alan Sillitoe**. By the 1990s, however, novels emerged that were entirely narrated in regionally identifiable voices (especially, it seems, Scottish ones) and disregarded many of the conventions of written Standard English. Examples are *Swing Hammer Swing!* (1992) by Jeff Torrington, *Trainspotting* (1993) by Irvine Welsh, *How Late it Was How Late* (1994) by James Kelman and *Last Orders* (1996) by Graham Swift. Thus by the end of the century dialect was no longer an oddity used only by selected characters.

The changing world perspective and cultural climate have been reflected in the rise and development of **postcolonial** novels. Varieties of English originating in countries where English is spoken as a legacy of colonisation have entered canonical literature. Whether set in the UK or not, the idioms of what have been called 'other Englishes' are more commonly met on the page now than at any time previously. Like British regional dialects, they are mostly first found as occasional words and expressions, different writers including different quantities of 'other' English in their works. *Sour Sweet* (1982) by Timothy Mo (1950–) and *The Famished Road* (1991) by Ben Okri (1959–), for instance, include only very occasional examples, whereas the whole of

Rushdie's *Midnight's Children* is narrated through that idiom. Among the many recent novels enriching the literary language in this way is *White Teeth* (2000) by Zadie Smith, which includes many different 'other' English voices in the multi-racial, multi-cultural setting of North London.

Changes in social attitudes towards homosexuality opened new opportunities for writers to use overtly gay narrators, as in *Earthly Powers* (1980) by Anthony Burgess and *Oranges Are Not The Only Fruit* (1985) by **Jeanette Winterson**. As further examples of new worlds entering literature we may also mention the representations of the internal worlds of the mentally ill (Woolf, particularly in *Mrs Dalloway*, Lessing, especially in *Four-Gated City* (1969) and *Briefing for a Descent into Hell* (1971)); down-and-outs (Orwell, Beckett); criminals (Fowles, *The Collector* (1963), Burgess, *A Clockwork Orange* (1962), Lessing, *The Good Terrorist* (1985)); Neanderthals (Golding, *The Inheritors* (1955)); aliens (Lessing, *Canopus in Argos Archives*); animals (Barnes, *A History of the World in 10½ Chapters*, Richard Adams, *Watership Down* (1972)); and an unborn baby (*Behind the Scenes at the Museum* (1995) by Kate Atkinson).

Alongside linguistic experimentation we may finally note an enjoyment of typographic freedom. The use of different languages has always involved printers in the use of different typefaces and when writers such as Eliot and Joyce write multi-lingual texts this has meant that the texts look different, with patches of italic or Greek typeface among the Roman print. Free verse can involve unconventional spacing on the page, as can other sorts of experimental versification, as seen for example in the works of **Liverpool Poets** Adrian Henri and Roger McGough. Patterned or 'concrete' poetry is also found occasionally, such as Dylan Thomas's 'Now say Nay' and 'Vision and Prayer'. Typographical mixing is involved in textual mixtures, as is evident on skimming through Eliot's 'The Waste Land', Joyce's *Finnegan's Wake*, Beckett's *Trilogy*, Fowles's *A Maggot*, Lessing's *Shikasta* (the first of the *Canopus* series) or Byatt's *Possession*. Among these, *Finnegan's Wake* contains a ballad (including the score), a geometrical figure and a long section set out as a central text with footnotes and glossed in the left margin with lower-case italic notes, a short musical notation and drawings. Novels claiming to have been written in the past may be set in appropriately dated typeface and style, as are some of the texts in *A Maggot*. Some stories may include illustrations within the lines of text, as in Rushdie's *The Moor's Last Sigh*, where a small picture of a man's head appears.

Conclusion

In stories, novels, poems and plays the experiments of the early moderns and their successors have encouraged a view of language as art. This in turn encouraged experiments not only with language but also with form and narrative structure. In fact the whole question of how story and 'reality' are represented has been re-examined. In printed works this has included a freedom from earlier linguistic and typographic conventions that manifests itself in a playfulness not seen in prose since early eighteenth-century parodists such as Swift and Sterne, or in poetry since the Middle English period when the low status of English gave poets a degree of linguistic and representational freedom. A result of these tendencies is that we must be aware of the style of a modern writer, for all writers now have to make a conscious decision about whether or not to join the intensified language game that started in the early twentieth century. There is no such thing as a neutral style; the language of literature has become thoroughly **problematised**.

References

1. All dates of works are dates of first publication.

2. All comments and dates concerning Beckett's works in this paper refer to his English works.

3. This is not an innovation – George Herbert (1593–1633) did the same in his poem 'Prayer'.

4. Raban refers to this poem as 'Shag', but I prefer the title given in *The Faber Book of 20th Century Verse* because it more effectively renders the violence of the piece.

Contributor: Margaret J-M Sonmez

Feminist literature

Rewriting canonical portrayals of women: Margaret Atwood's 'Gertrude Talks Back'

> *I always thought it was a mistake, calling you Hamlet. I mean, what kind of a name is that for a young boy? . . . I wanted to call you George.*
>
> 'Gertrude Talks Back'

In her collection of short stories, *Good Bones* (1992), Margaret Atwood included 'Gertrude Talks Back', a piece which rewrites the famous closet scene in Shakespeare's *Hamlet*. The character of Gertrude, Hamlet's mother, has posed problems of interpretation to readers, critics and performers, past and present, and has been variously or simultaneously appraised as a symbol of female wantonness, the object of Hamlet's Oedipus complex, and an example of female submissiveness to the male principle (Hamlet's as much as Claudius's). Like other revisionist rewritings produced by women writers in the last few decades, Margaret Atwood's short story challenges received concepts of the female and particularly the 'Frailty, thy name is woman' notion that has marked so much canonical literature.

Recent developments in the humanities, usually grouped under the common label of '**poststructuralist** theory', have contributed to making us sensitive to the politics of culture, in general, and of literature, in particular. Much thought has been given in the last few decades to how the literary canon emerges and holds its ground, and to the relations between canonical and non-canonical, between the centre and the margins. **Postcolonial** theorist Edward Said reminds us that the 'power to narrate, or to block other narratives from forming and emerging, is very important to culture and imperialism, and constitutes one of the main connections between them' (p. xiii). Here, as in other respects, the political agendas of **feminism** and postcolonialism overlap; both aim at challenging the canon and at inscribing the experiences of the marginal subject (female and/or postcolonial).

Revisionist rewritings are one of the strategies that can serve that purpose, as have, for example, the many rewritings of such canonical texts as *The Tempest* and *Robinson Crusoe*. As regards Margaret Atwood, critics have paid extensive attention to a recurrent feature of her fiction: her repeated reworking of fairy tales, most importantly the different versions of *Bluebeard's Egg*, a reshaping which culminates in her novel *The*

Robber Bride (1993). We should also note that what is perhaps her most popular novel to date, *The Handmaid's Tale* (1985), thematises the politics of reading and writing or, as Hutcheon has aptly put it, 'the opposition between product and process' (p. 139).

Similar concerns are apparent in the compilation of her short stories under the title *Good Bones* (1992). If the constructions of womanhood and manhood occupy her in 'The Female Body' and 'Making a Man', in other stories, such as 'There Was Once' and 'Unpopular Gals', it is the *literary* construction of womanhood that is foregrounded. Thus, one of these tales ends with 'Let us now praise stupid women,/who have given us Literature' (p. 37). In no other story, however, has Atwood engaged the issue so deeply and strikingly as in 'Gertrude Talks Back'.

If there is any one author who can be said to have persistently influenced cultural representations in the English-speaking world, we would probably agree that it is William Shakespeare. And if one of his works had to stand for the canon of 'English' literature, it would likely be *Hamlet*. Atwood's story then engages the very centre of that canon and through Gertrude she rewrites a canonical text from the very margins of its own discourse.

The author's endeavour, nevertheless, is fraught with problems. Gertrude is, after all, one of Shakespeare's most elusive female characters and one over whom criticism (feminist and otherwise) has long been debated. The most common representation would see her, as Hamlet and the Ghost do, as a lustful, adulterous and incestuous woman. This portrayal has marked not only critical readings but also film versions of the play, as Rebecca Smith pointed out in her account of Olivier's (1948), Kozintsev's (1964) and Richardson's (1969) versions – a list to which Zeffirelli's *Hamlet* (1990) might be added. The keystone for this portrayal is of course the famous closet scene, where 'Olivier's Hamlet brutally hurls Gertrude – the ultimate sexual object – onto her bed, alternating embraces and abuse' (Smith, p. 195).

Feminist criticism of Shakespeare has tried to read the character differently. An early attempt was made in 1957 in the article 'The Character of Hamlet's Mother', in which Carolyn Heilbrun questioned the influential views of Bradley and Dover Wilson among others, and argued that Gertrude was 'intelligent, penetrating and gifted, with a remarkable talent for concise and pithy speech'; she nevertheless had to admit to Gertrude's being also 'passion's slave' (p. 17). Rebecca Smith went further. After thoroughly examining the textual evidence, she concluded that

> . . . the traditional depiction of Gertrude is a false one, because what *her* words and actions actually create is a soft, obedient, dependent, unimaginative woman who is caught miserably between 'two mighty opposites', her 'heart cleft in twain' (III.4.156) by divided loyalties to husband and son. She loves both Claudius and Hamlet, and their conflict leaves her bewildered and unhappy.
> (p. 194)

More recently, but in a similar vein, Adelman has claimed, again after a close textual reading, that what is seen is 'a woman more muddled than actively wicked; even her famous sensuality is less apparent than her conflicted solicitude both for her husband and for her son' (p. 15). Adelman would even suggest that Gertrude's death could be read as a suicide in order to protect her son, on the grounds that 'she shows unusual determination in disobeying Claudius's command not to drink [from the poisoned cup]' (p. 16).

Other studies of the character have attempted to place Gertrude in the wider context of gender representation in Elizabethan and Jacobean drama, by arguing that deviant behaviour in women is consistently associated with and portrayed as sexual waywardness. Thus, Jardine's point that it is 'the male characters who perceive free choice on the part of the female character as an inevitable sign of irrational lust, and as the inevitable prelude to disorder and disaster' (*Still Harping*, p. 72) proves helpful in understanding Shakespeare's handling of the character.

What lies at the bottom of these disparate readings is the ambiguity of the Shakespearean text. Whereas its main sources, twelfth-century Saxo Grammaticus' *Historiae Danicae* and sixteenth-century Belleforest's *Histoires Tragiques*, give a clear account of Gertrude's knowledge of the plot against the elder Hamlet and/or her adultery before his death, these matters are rather obscure in Shakespeare's play. Besides, Gertrude remains relatively inarticulate. Even though she is central to the motivation of others, especially her son, she has few lines for a major character; Gertrude is construed by others rather than by herself:

> Virtually silent on her own behalf . . . [Gertrude's] depth as a protagonist is accumulated out of the responses to her of others. Thus she captures for feminist critics the constructedness of femaleness which has absorbed us for more than a decade.
>
> (Jardine, *Reading*, p. 149)

These ambiguities provide the leverage for Atwood's rewriting of the closet scene (*Hamlet* 3.4). It should be noted, first of all, that Atwood passes over two of the main moments of this scene in Shakespeare's text, the accidental murder of Polonius and the apparition of the Ghost, as not being relevant for her purposes, and she focuses instead on the confrontation between Hamlet and Gertrude. Atwood's story, however, does not present an explicit dialogue between both; it is a one-sided dialogue, Gertrude's voice being the only one we hear/read. Thus Atwood turns the tables and gives Gertrude the articulateness she lacks in the play.

Hamlet's voice may not be heard, but it is nevertheless there. Shakespeare's and Atwood's texts are tied by cross-referential links which are shown even in the very disposition of the latter on the page. The new Gertrude does not produce one continuous speech but rather a number of utterances separated by pauses, thereby announcing that this is in fact an exchange, part of which has been left out. The elided section would correspond to Hamlet's words, that is, to the **intertext** of Shakespeare's play. Moreover, a closer look at the story will lead us to identify each of Gertrude's utterances as both a challenging move and a response to Hamlet's accusations in the intertext, though muted here.

Putting the texts side by side not only serves to reconstruct the whole 'dialogue', i.e. the connections between text and intertext, but also renders clear the very mechanics of Atwood's revisionist rewriting. What is then immediately apparent is that Atwood does not follow Shakespeare's ordering of the scene, but has built her portrayal of Gertrude on a handful of specific moments which have been relocated, hence completely disrupting Hamlet's/Shakespeare's discourse.

'Gertrude Talks Back' opens with a reference to the name of the implied listener, Hamlet, which together with the very title of the story serves the purpose of placing it in its literary context and identifying the intertext for the reader:

> I always thought it was a mistake, calling you Hamlet. I mean, what kind of a
> name is that for a young boy? It was your father's idea. Nothing would do but
> that you had to be called after him. Selfish. The other kids at school used to
> tease the life out of you. The nicknames! And those terrible jokes about pork.
> I wanted to call you George.
> (*Good Bones*, p. 15)

But Atwood's Gertrude's naming of the listener is at the same time a renaming that belittles the figure of Hamlet through a humorous observation ('those terrible jokes about pork') and its recontextualisation in the norm ('I wanted to call you George'). This first move would represent a response to Hamlet's words below and a challenge of their implicit accusation, since by naming Gertrude as 'the Queen, your husband's brother's wife', Hamlet is accusing her of the unspeakable crime of incest:

> GERTRUDE:
> Have you forgot me?
>
> HAMLET:
>   No, by the rood, not so.
> You are the Queen, your husband's brother's wife,
> And, would it were not so, you are my mother.
> (*Hamlet* 3.4. 13–15)

Gertrude's opening words in Atwood are thus characteristic of what will be the three main lines of attack of this revisionist rewriting of the character: a belittling of Hamlet through both humour and recontextualisation in the norm, the dismissal of guilt and, correspondingly, a rejection of his (male) construction of her.

The first of these strategies rests on Gertrude's alternative construction of Hamlet. In Atwood's text he is construed as a youngster who moves awkwardly ('That'll be the third [mirror] you've broken') and a student of unclean habits who lives in a 'slum pigpen' and does not bring laundry home often enough. Even his sombre clothing, so inseparable from the character's psychological portrait, is parodied through his black socks, which now read simply as one of the many fashions young people are tempted into in contemporary society. What's more, Hamlet's very raison d'être in Shakespeare's play, his heart-felt wish to take revenge on Claudius, is deflated in Atwood's version and their antagonism transformed into commonplace friction between a grown-up stepson and a newly acquired stepfather: 'By the way, darling, I wish you wouldn't call your stepdad *the bloat king*. He does have a slight weight problem, and it hurts his feelings' (*Good Bones*, p. 16).

If this new Hamlet has become an unremarkable contemporary young man, he nevertheless retains the faithfulness to 'the law of the Father' that marks him in Shakespeare's play. The belittling of the son also aims at the figure, quite literally in this scene, standing behind him; the father's naming his son makes him an imprint and recreates the same flaw: the masculinist code (the elder Hamlet's 'holier-than-thou principle', in Atwood's rendering below) that constrains women's actions and would particularly control their sexuality. Gertrude clearly implies as much in accepting Hamlet's muted challenge to compare both husbands:

> Look here upon this picture, and on this,
> The counterfeit presentment of two brothers.
> See what a grace was seated on this brow,
> Hyperion's curls, the front of Jove himself,
> An eye like Mars to threaten and command,
> A station like the herald Mercury
> New-lighted on a heaven-kissing hill,
> A combination and a form indeed
> Where every god did seem to set his seal
> To give the world assurance of a man.
> This was your husband. Look you now what follows.
> Here is your husband, like a mildw'd ear
> Blasting his wholesome brother. Have you eyes?
> Could you on this fair mountain leave to feed
> And batten on this moor? Ha, have you eyes?
> (*Hamlet* 3.4. 53–67)

Whereas in Shakespeare's play Gertrude does not challenge the attack, in Atwood's version she vindicates Claudius and disparages the elder Hamlet:

> Yes, I've seen those pictures, thank you very much. I *know* your father was handsomer than Claudius. High brow, aquiline nose and so on, looked great in uniform. But handsome isn't everything, especially in a man, and far be it from me to speak ill of the dead, but I think it's about time I pointed out to you that your Dad wasn't a whole lot of fun. Noble, sure, I grant you. But Claudius, well, he likes a drink now and then. He appreciates a decent meal. He enjoys a laugh, know what I mean? You don't always have to be tiptoeing around because of some holier-than-thou principle or something.
> (*Good Bones*, pp. 15–16)

As a result, in Atwood's story Hamlet's remaining defining trait (like his father's before him) is his prudishness. Gertrude's accusation that he lacks sexual drive challenges his own of giving way to her animal instincts in 3.4. 88–96. This is probably Atwood's trump card, since it validates Gertrude's famous lustful nature through an effective reversal of the very notions of normality/abnormality, thus making Gertrude's acknowledgement of guilt utterly irrelevant:

GERTRUDE:
     O Hamlet, speak no more,
Thou turn'st my eyes into my very soul,
And there I see such black and grained spots
As will not leave their tinct.

HAMLET:
     Nay, but to live
In the rank sweat of an enseamed bed,
Stew'd in corruption, honeying and making love
Over the nasty sty!

GERTRUDE:
     O speak to me no more.
These words like daggers enter my ears.
No more, sweet Hamlet.

The rank sweat of a *what?* My bed is certainly not *enseamed,* whatever that may be. A nasty sty, indeed! . . . Go get yourself someone more down-to-earth. Have a nice roll in the hay. Then you can talk to me about nasty sties.
(*Good Bones,* pp. 16–17)

The canonical interpretation of guilt as being central to Gertrude's behaviour is also explicitly dismissed earlier in the story with the statement 'I am *not* wringing my hands. I am drying my nails', which gives a humorous lie to Hamlet's declared intention of wringing her heart in 3.4. 34–35 ('Leave wringing of your hands. Peace, sit you down/And let me wring your heart'). That explicit denial is a necessary step in order to **deconstruct** the Shakespearean writing of Gertrude as **other**, and therefore it immediately precedes a less obvious rejection of the mirror Hamlet sets up before her:

Come, come, and sit you down, you shall not budge.
You go not till I set you up a glass
Where you may see the inmost part of you.
(*Hamlet* 3.4. 17–19)

Gertrude's scolding, 'Darling, please stop fidgeting with my mirror', in Atwood's rewriting implies that the 'inmost part' of her that he sees and would have her see is not at all *her* inmost part. Her rejection of the male gaze forestalls his unwelcome intrusion, his unwanted meddling in her private affairs. Regarding this issue, it is appropriate to bear in mind that the scene is supposed to take place in Gertrude's closet. According to Jardine, this was the only domestic space over which early modern women exercised total control (*Reading*, p. 151). Atwood's choice of the closet scene, and of each element in it, is therefore no mere coincidence. Instead, her rendering comes to clarify and highlight what in Shakespeare's play is taken for granted, that the closet encodes Gertrude's body. The control she now displays gives her back her agency.

Gertrude also rejects Ophelia as a mirror. Hamlet's mistreatment of Ophelia is commonly understood as being caused by Ophelia's taking on or participating in Gertrude's inherently lustful nature. But Ophelia is erased in Atwood's story; whereas Hamlet is renamed, Ophelia is de-named: she is simply referred to as 'that pasty-faced what's-her-name'. Like Hamlet, she is transformed into the abnormal, the exception rather than the rule, and the margin to Gertrude's centre:

> And let me tell you, everyone sweats at a time like that, as you'd find out very soon if you ever gave it a try. A real girlfriend would do you a heap of good. Not like that pasty-faced what's-her-name, all trussed up like a prize turkey in those touch-me-not corsets of hers. Borderline. Any little shock could push her right over the edge.
>
> (*Good Bones*, p. 17)

When Gertrude utters, earlier, 'Go get yourself someone more down to earth', this can be read as Atwood's rebuke to Hamlet's exclamation to Ophelia in 3.1. 121 ('Get thee to a nunnery'). Nor is Ophelia here an innocent victim; indeed, her tragic end is comically anticipated as resulting from that very abnormality. Once more, Atwood's interpretation of Ophelia makes clear that the Shakespearean character is shaped by patriarchal specularisation (i.e. by the projection of men's desires or fears rather than seeing a woman as she truly is).

But Gertrude is guilty of crime here too. Atwood's Gertrude may not confess to pangs of conscience, but she does own up to the murder of her first husband, the elder Hamlet:

> Oh! You think *what*? You think Claudius murdered your Dad? Well, no wonder you've been so rude to him at the dinner table!
> If I'd known *that*, I could have put you straight in no time flat.
> It wasn't Claudius, darling.
> It was me.
> (*Good Bones*, p. 18)

In that sense, yes, she is guilty. Atwood works on the dark areas of the Shakespearean text in order to re-inscribe her own Gertrude: one that takes responsibility for her actions and that unambiguously asserts her right to choose. What she is claiming for herself is agency; what she re-appropriates is her sexuality. Therefore, her refusal to acknowledge Ophelia as a mirror also implies refusing to be victimised.

It must be noted, however, that Atwood rewrites Gertrude by building on the standard reading of the character. Unlike some feminist critics, she does not vindicate Gertrude by recasting her as a humble, soft, dependent woman (cf. Smith's reading).

On the contrary, she writes a non-canonical revision of the canonical reading of the text. She simply forces us to reconsider the very values that lie at the heart of that reading. In a way, she is asserting Gertrude's right to be lustful and denying Hamlet/Shakespeare the power to pass judgement on her. She has rewritten him/them as other.

Finally, we should bear in mind that Atwood is a Canadian author daring to challenge the very foundation of the English literary canon. She is not only re-inscribing the female subject, she is also writing the postcolonial mind as she dislodges the centre from its throne. 'Gertrude Talks Back' represents not just a dialogue between Gertrude and Hamlet, between Atwood and Shakespeare, but also a dialogue between Canadian literature and English literature, and one where the former (Gertrude/Atwood/Canada) get the upper hand. Atwood's story exemplifies how Canadian culture assimilates and resists.

References

Adelman, Janet (1992) *Suffocating Mothers*. London: Routledge.

Atwood, Margaret (1992) 'Gertrude Talks Back', *Good Bones*. Toronto: Coach House, 1992. pp. 15–18.

Heilbrun, Carolyn G. (1990) *Hamlet's Mother and Other Women*. London: The Women's Press.

——. 'The Character of Hamlet's Mother.' *Hamlet's Mother,* pp. 9–17.

Hutcheon, Linda (1988) *The Canadian Postmodern: A Study of Contemporary English-Canadian Fiction*. Toronto: Oxford University Press.

Jardine, Lisa (1996) *Reading Shakespeare Historically*. London: Routledge.

——. *Still Harping on Daughters: Women and Drama in the Age of Shakespeare*. Brighton: The Harvester Press, 1983.

Lenz, Carolyn, Ruth Swift; Greene, Gayle; Neely, Carol Thomas (eds) (1980) *The Woman's Part: Feminist Criticism of Shakespeare*. Urbana: University of Illinois Press.

Said, Edward (1994) *Culture and Imperialism*. New York: Vintage.

Shakespeare, William (1982) *Hamlet*. The Arden Shakespeare. London: Methuen.

Smith, Rebecca (1980) 'A Heart Cleft in Twain: The Dilemma of Shakespeare's Gertrude.' Lenz, pp. 194–210.

Contributor: An earlier draft of this article was delivered at the 5th International Conference on Canadian Studies by Pilar Cuder Domínguez (Madrid, November 1994). The article was first published on English Literature Essays: www.english-literature.org/essays/

Postcolonial feminist theory: an overview

Postcolonial **feminist** criticism examines how women are represented in colonial and **postcolonial** literature and challenges assumptions which are made about women in both literature and society. Colonialism and patriarchy have been closely entwined historically, but an end to formal empire has not meant an end to the oppression of women in the former colonies. Postcolonial feminists point out the ways in which women continue to be stereotyped and marginalised, ironically sometimes by post-colonial authors who might claim to be challenging a culture of oppression.

Prior to the 1990s, much Black, Hispanic and Asian theory, criticism and creative writing was overlooked by academia in the West. More recently, developments have taken place in feminist literary criticism, some of the best-known authors being Gloria Anzaldúa, Chandra Mohanty, Trinh T. Minh-ha, Gayatri Spivak, Rey Chow, Rosario Castellanos and Cheryl Johnson-Odim. These critics reject earlier feminist approaches which assumed that women shared a common identity based on a shared experience of oppression. They reject the assumption that white middle-class women should be considered the norm, arguing that the concerns of such women are not necessarily those of all women and that differences in the social positions of women produce very different problems and responses, even in relation to the same broad issues.

The groundwork for this new feminist criticism developed over several years through a number of anthologies of the work of ethnic women authors. Carole Boyce Davies and Anne Adams Graves edited *Ngambika: Studies of Women in African Literature* in 1986, in which they created an African feminist criticism. Cherríe Moraga and Gloria Anzaldúa edited *This Bridge Called My Back: Writings by Radical Women of Color* in 1981, in which they claimed, in the second edition, that they had bridged the gap between American women of colour and Third World women. In India, the first collection of critical essays on women poets was *Studies in Contemporary Indo-English Verse* (1984) edited by A. N. Dwivedi.

International feminism

Postcolonial feminist criticism makes a radical contribution to literary studies by drawing together many disciplines, challenging Western ethnocentricity and restoring plural subjectivities to literary history. The idea of a global 'sisterhood' took root in academia in the 1990s, embracing the articulation of many voices to create an inclusive feminism. The aim was to make the writings of postcolonial women visible and intelligible to the West. However, the term 'postcolonial women' has turned out to be as problematic as other phrases related to colonialism. For some theorists the term has led to over-simplification and unthinking assertions of oppression, an approach which is an impediment to a reading beyond obvious questions of 'good' and 'bad'. Other theorists seem to claim that the terms 'racist' and 'sexist' are more or less interchangeable, resulting in a confusion between the image of postcolonial women in the context of feminism and that of the native in the context of colonialism.

Major issues

Modern postcolonial feminist criticism does not simply highlight the works of women from the developing world but allows for multiple approaches drawn from many disciplines. It challenges Western academia by showing that it has tended to treat Third World women as other, denying their subjectivity and imagination. It takes into account changes in the modern world by questioning assumptions about what is 'core' (the norm) and what lies at the periphery (designated as 'other') in a postcolonial world characterised by migration. Postcolonial feminist criticism is necessarily eclectic because Third World writing so often responds to different social, regional and national groups whose aesthetic values are very diverse.

Postcolonial feminism challenges traditional white Western feminism for the latter's association with political liberation movements. Women around the world have very different histories with respect to their postcolonial inheritance, involving such experiences as imperial conquest, slavery, enforced migration and even genocide. Thus, postcolonial feminists have argued for the rewriting of history based on the specific experiences of formerly colonised people and their various strategies for survival.

Black theorists

Black feminist criticism has attacked the misogyny of early Black Studies and misrepresentations by white feminist critics. Afro-American feminist criticism began in 1974 with the publication of a special issue of *Black World,* containing essays by June Jordan and Mary Helen Washington, and Alice Walker's 'In Search of Our Mothers' Gardens' (1983) in *Ms* magazine. Here, since the term 'feminism' itself is sometimes challenged by women suspicious of white imperialism, Alice Walker uses the term 'womanist' (meaning a black feminist or feminist of colour). This field of study arose in the wake of the burgeoning visibility of black women writers in the 1960s and 1970s, an influential critical work being Barbara Smith's *Toward a Black Feminist Criticism* (1984), in which she reconstructs the Afro-American literary tradition to include women writers who had previously been excluded.

Bell Hooks, in *Feminist Theory: From Margin to Centre* (2000), pointed out that much feminist theory has emerged from privileged women who live at the centre of dominant societies, whose perspectives on reality rarely include genuine knowledge of the lives of women and men who live in the margin. As a consequence, feminist theory has lacked the broad analysis that could encompass a variety of human experiences. Barbara Smith and bell hooks agree on the idea that the involvement of women of colour, both within and outside the United States, has accounted for the broadening definitions of feminism to incorporate race and class analysis.

In her essay 'The Race for Theory', Barbara Christian claims that feminist theorists seldom take into account the complexity of real life, in which women are of many races and ethnic backgrounds, with different histories and cultures, belonging to different classes with different concerns. She points out that notions such as the *centre* and the *periphery* reveal a tendency to oversimplify reality by organising it according to one principle, and that a feature of ideologies of dominance, such as sexism and racism, is to dehumanise people by stereotyping them, denying them their individuality and complexity. She also points out the dearth of studies of black women authors, claiming that when theory is not rooted in practice it becomes prescriptive and elitist.

Chicana theorists

Feminist writing and criticism in Latin America have been fertile from the 1930s, some of the important theorists being Rosario Castellanos, Victoria Ocampo and Luisa Valenzuela, who address such issues as education, sexual division of labour and the family.

Simultaneously there has been a **Chicana** (American of Latin American origin) movement in Western academia, of which Gloria Anzaldúa has been a prominent exponent. In *This Bridge Called My Back: Writing By Radical Women of Color* (1981), a volume she edited with Cherríe Moraga, many contributors express disillusionment with white feminism. Anzaldúa also edited *Borderlands/La Frontera: the New Mestiza* (1987), an exploration of Chicano history and myths. In *Making Face, Making Soul* (1990), Anzaldúa aims to teach white critics to read in non-stereotypical ways and points out that women of the developing world may confront similar issues, but are very different in approach and style.

Cherríe Moraga and Gloria Anzaldúa's soliciting letter of April 1979 shows the intention behind their anthology:

> We want to express to all women – especially to white middle-class women – the experiences which divide us as feminists; we want to examine incidents of intolerance, prejudice and denial of differences within the feminist movement. We intend to explore the causes and sources of, and solutions to these divisions. We want to create a definition that expands what 'feminist' means to us.

Gloria Anzaldúa discusses the concept of *la mestiza* (mixed race) in her essay *La Conciencia de la Mestiza: Towards a New Consciousness*, arguing that a mixture of races, rather than resulting in an inferior being, provides hybrid progeny, a mutable, more malleable species with a rich gene pool. She goes on to say that *la mestiza* is a product of the transfer of the cultural and spiritual values of one group to another, and that in individuals of mixed race conflicting allegiances can result in states of mental and emotional perplexity.

Asian theorists: the Indian context

The Indian critic Kumari Jayawardena, writing about feminist movements in Asia in the late nineteenth and early twentieth centuries, defines feminism as a movement which encourages equality within the current system and embraces the struggles which have attempted to change the system. Chandra Talpade Mohanty, in her introduction to *Third World Women and the Politics of Feminism* (1991), points out that the political struggle of women in India is a continuation of the fight against racist, colonialist states. These movements arose in the context of the formulation and consolidation of national identities which mobilised anti-imperialist movements during independence struggles, and the remaking of pre-capitalist religious and feudal structures in attempts to 'modernise' Third World societies.

Mohanty argues that Western criticism, both non-feminist and feminist, artificially constructs two entities, the coloniser and the colonised, and that the consequence of this is to suggest that the colonised is allowed only a language permitted, or indeed constructed, by the coloniser. She attacks the principles at work in Western feminist criticism regarding the Third World, particularly the assumption that postcolonial women are a homogenous group regardless of nationality or ethnicity. She also criticises the self-representation of Western women in literature as modern women with some degree of control over their bodies and sexualities, and Western feminists' representation of women in the developing countries as domestic or uneducated victims.

The Indian critic Vasudha Narayanan argues that the terms 'feminism' and 'rights' are alien to Hindu discourse, as both concepts carry a special Western flavour. Madhu Kishwar, the editor of *Manushi*, a journal about Indian women and society, rejects the term 'feminism', arguing that the particular socio-historic context in which the movement arose in the West is specific to that culture and very different to that prevailing in India. She also points out that another factor in the Indian context that makes it different from that of the feminist movement in the West is that many of the catalysing agents to improve the status of women and include them in socio-political and religious movements have been Indian men.

Conclusions: a political base for alliance

Feminist analysis in the 1990s evolved in response to the challenges posed by ethnic and postcolonial studies to white Western feminism. One of the most important points it makes is that 'women' does not comprise a coherent group solely on the basis of gender. The status and roles of women vary according to complex interactions between factors such as ethnicity, class, culture and religion.

Although it is difficult to generalise about postcolonial feminism, we can foreground Third World women as a broad category, within which we can explore the histories and struggles of postcolonial women against colonialism, racism, sexism and economic forces. Chandra Mohanty suggests the concept of an 'imagined community' of postcolonial oppositional struggles. She emphasises the abstract meaning of this concept, which suggests potential alliances and collaborations across divisive boundaries, and the opportunity for a deep commitment to 'sisterhood'. The idea of an imagined community leads us away from traditional notions of postcolonial feminist struggles, suggesting a political rather than biological or cultural basis for alliance.

Not only are postcolonial feminist women challenging ideologies which have belittled the status of women, they are also challenging the prevailing assumption that white Western middle-class woman is the norm. At the same time, they are struggling to eradicate stereotypes which define them as subordinate and pointing out that in spite of the decline of imperialism they are still subject, in many ways, to the pressures of neo-colonialism.

Further reading

Anzaldúa, G. and Moraga, C. (eds) *This Bridge Called My Back: Writings by Radical Women of Color.* Kitchen Table Press, 1981.

Anzaldúa, G. *Borderlands/La Frontera: The New Mestiza.* Aunt Lute Books, 2000.

Anzaldúa, G. *Making Face, Making Soul.* Aunt Lute Books, 1990.

Boyce Davies, Adams, Carole and Graves, Anne (eds) *Ngambika: Studies of Women in African Literature.* Africa World Press, 1986.

Christian, Barbara *Black Feminist Criticism: Perspectives of Black Women Writers.* Teachers College Press, 1992.

Dwivedi, A. N. (ed.) *Studies in Contemporary Indo-English Verse*, Bareilly: Prakash Book Depot, 1984.

hooks, bell *Feminist Theory: From Margin to Centre.* Pluto Press, 2000.

Mohanty, Talpade *Third World Women and the Politics of Feminism.* Indiana University Press, 1991.

Smith, Barbara *Toward a Black Feminist Criticism.* Out & Out Books, 1984.

Contributor: Antonia Navarro-Tejero

Modern drama

A survey of British, Irish and American drama of the twentieth century

At the beginning of the twentieth century, the best of British/Irish theatre was produced by Irish writers. By the 1940s and 1950s, new influences came to bear when European and American dramatists introduced innovatory concepts of what a play might be. British playwrights were quick to take up the challenge and by the end of the century the theatre was flourishing, with dramatists producing plays with the originality and vitality to keep theatre alive and, importantly, to challenge audiences on contemporary issues.

The nineteenth century had seen steady progress in the development of the novel and poetry, but drama had lacked any real innovation until the end of the century, which saw the emergence of a few significant dramatists, such as Oscar Wilde and George Bernard Shaw, both Irishmen. Oscar Wilde (1854–1900) belongs to the nineteenth century but deserves a mention here for the way, perhaps more through his life than through his art, he challenged contemporary moral values, foreshadowing similar challenges in the twentieth century. He made use of fiction, the best-known work being *The Picture of Dorian Gray* (1891), and poetry to express his ideas, but it is as a dramatist that he is best remembered. He wrote light comedies, the most popular and enduring being *The Importance of Being Earnest* (1898). He was much admired for his wit, but eventually his amorality and homosexuality brought about his downfall. He was tried, in two of the most sensational trials of the century, and jailed on a charge of 'corrupting the morals of various young people'. On his release from prison he moved to France, where he died a broken man.

George Bernard Shaw (1856–1950), in contrast to Wilde, was a revolutionary thinker and writer and much less of a public wit. Where Wilde could entertain an audience for hours with impromptu speeches, Shaw would bore an audience to tears after only a few words. But as a writer he was more eloquent and his plays earned him the Nobel Prize for Literature in 1925. Shaw was a moralist, intent on giving a serious, often political point to his social comedies, which were critical of the self-centredness and materialism of London society. Although out of fashion now, at least one of his plays, *Pygmalion*, first produced in London in 1914, has remained in the popular consciousness, even if it is mainly known through Rodgers and Hammerstein's musical *My Fair Lady*. In *Pygmalion*, Professor Higgins and the Eynsford-Hills show the privileges of wealth, while in Eliza we see the poverty of the labouring class and the working out of the idea that, with the right education, a flower girl might be taken for a lady. *Heartbreak House* (1917), a comedy of manners, is critical of the same privileged set, as is *St Joan* (1924), in which after Joan has been abandoned by kings, captains, bishops and lawyers, the soldier concludes that she has as good a right to her notions as they have to theirs. However, forward-looking as his ideas were at the time, Shaw's plays now appear dated in style.

In Ireland the theatre played an important part in the **Irish Cultural Revival**. Having caused one controversy by staging *The Playboy of the Western World* by J. M. Synge in 1904, the Irish National Theatre Company, under the leadership of **W. B. Yeats**, stirred up Irish feeling again by putting on plays by Sean O'Casey (1884–1964), which drew upon the bitter conflicts between the Irish and the British. Like Shaw, O'Casey was born in Dublin, where his plays were performed at the famous Abbey Theatre. The trilogy for which he is best known could hardly be a greater contrast to the plays of Shaw. *The Shadow of a Gunman* (1923), *Juno and the Paycock* (1924) and *The Plough and the Stars* (1926) deal with real events, naturalistically portrayed. They depict not only family tragedy but also the birth of the Irish Free State. The strongest and most beautifully crafted of them is *Juno and the Paycock*. Juno is tough and heroic, like her goddess namesake. Her husband, Boyle, the peacock, is a boastful philanderer with links to Jupiter. His extravagance ruins the family financially, while the Irish Civil War causes tragedy on a grander scale. Their son dies and Juno decides to abandon her husband as her world collapses. The play is full of humour which counterpoints the tragedy and on stage it works powerfully.

The English stage in the wake of Shaw was dominated by social drama. Much of it did not have lasting value and many of the dramatists of the period are better remembered for their fiction. **John Galsworthy** (1867–1933), for example, is much better known for his series of novels *The Forsyte Saga* than he is for his plays. Another well-known playwright of the era was William Somerset Maugham (1874–1965), a cynical observer of his age and its morals. He wrote several plays which were first performed between 1904 and 1933, but, like Galsworthy, he is best remembered today for his novels. A third novelist who wrote for the stage was J. B. Priestley (1894–1984), whose plays were also concerned with moral and social problems.

Some poets added their contribution to social drama, such as the prominent young poet of the 1930s, **W. H. Auden** (1907–73). He wrote the verse for a number of socially and politically challenging plays by his friend, Christopher Isherwood (1904–86). These plays were highly critical of British complacency in the face of Hitler's rise to power in Germany.

Noel Coward (1899–1973) excelled at the comedy of manners, as had Shaw. In *Private Lives* (1929) his two main characters, Amanda and Elyot, are divorced. When they meet again, their old love-hate relationship is resumed. The play is written, as was common at the time, in three acts, with witty dialogue and many comic moments. In its analysis of the married state, it captures both the fun and the joy, the pain and the absurdity. Whenever it is played, it continues to prove immensely popular.

The period between the two world wars was characterised by an urge to experiment, to find new ways of expressing oneself, which can be seen in fiction, drama and poetry as well as in art. This was particularly apparent in Europe where, in the wake of the shock of the First World War, the sense of a break in continuity, the loss of confidence in traditional values and the need to expcriment gave rise to the **Modernist** movements of **Dadaism** and **Surrealism**. These radical innovations, however, did not make a real impact on British drama until the 1950s.

In England the main poet and playwright of the inter-war years was the American **T. S. Eliot** (1888–1965) who had settled in London after having studied at various universities in Europe. He attempted to revive verse drama, with his play *Murder in the Cathedral* (1935). Other writers, such as Christopher Fry (1907–), contributed to this trend. Their aim was to revive an interest in presenting plays following the tradition of Classical drama, medieval Miracle plays, and the work of sixteenth- and seventeenth-century dramatists. Although rarely given professional performances today, the attempt to combine West End theatrical convention with depth of thought in poetic form remains of interest. Eliot wrote further examples of the genre in his three comedies, *The Cocktail Party* (1950), *The Confidential Clerk* (1954) and *The Elder Statesman* (1958). Fry wrote *The Lady's Not for Burning* (1948) and *Venus Observed* (1950), both known as comedies although including in each plot the near death of the main character.

An Inspector Calls, the best-known play by J. B. Priestley (1894–1984), was performed in 1946, as Attlee's Labour government came to power. It is set in 1912, so that social changes can be pinpointed. The play is outwardly a mystery: who is responsible for the death of Eva Smith? But the theme is political: in a society, each member has responsibility for every other member. It seems over-didactic to a twenty-first-century play-goer but it was a play for its time, unashamedly emphasising the relationship between the individual and society.

Until the 1950s the predominant form for drama was 'the well-made play', written chronologically in three acts comprising an introduction in Act I, development in Act II and a conclusion in Act III. Coward and Priestley frequently used this form, as did Terence Rattigan (1911–77), one of the most successful playwrights during the Second World War and post-war years. His plays of middle-class life seem dated now, yet in theme they were 'problem' plays, dealing with many of those issues taken up by the new wave of young dramatists of the 1950s who denigrated Rattigan, chiefly for the perfection of his dramatic style. In Rattigan's *The Deep Blue Sea* (1951) Hester has left her husband for a younger man and is driven to attempt suicide when he no longer loves her.

When *Look Back in Anger* (1956) by John Osborne (1929–94) burst onto the stage at the Royal Court theatre, it was heralded as a real breakthrough, railing against accepted middle-class conventions. It is written in three acts and examines the failing relationship of Jimmy Porter and Alison, who is driven to despair by his treatment of her. The main difference between *The Deep Blue Sea* and *Look Back in Anger* lies not in the plot outline, concerning the complexity of human relations, but in Rattigan's measured emotional restraint compared with Osborne's passionate verbal fireworks. Osborne's style was direct and immediate, and he is credited with having begun the new wave of **realism** in drama which heralded the beginning of an exciting period for British theatre.

The title of Osborne's play gave rise to the name the **Angry Young Men** being applied to a group of authors, mainly novelists, who were highly critical of established morals and conventional society. Many of the plays which followed *Look Back in Anger* dealt with working-class conditions and were jokingly referred to as 'kitchen-sink drama'.

The initial impact of *Waiting for Godot* by **Samuel Beckett** (1906–89) when it reached London in 1955, having been performed first in France in 1953, was neither so instant nor so electrifying as that of Osborne's play, yet it had a great influence on British drama in the later twentieth century. Beckett was an Irishman who lived in France, and his play brought with it the European influence of the **Theatre of the Absurd,** a manifestation of Modernism which drew, among other sources, upon Dadaism and Surrealism. Beckett was also influenced by his experience of life in France under Nazi occupation. The plot of *Waiting for Godot* is minimal and its dialogue is spare. Its humour is drawn from the music hall, comically mocking the theme, which concerns the absurdity of searching for meaning in life. His view of mankind is highly pessimistic. He sees little hope for the future. Beckett wrote novels, short stories and a little poetry, as well as plays for the stage, TV and radio, and was awarded the Nobel Prize for Literature in 1969.

The Irish dramatist Brendan Behan (1923–64) was a political activist and member of the IRA, who spent time in jail as a political prisoner. He began writing while in jail, drawing on his experiences for his plays *The Quare Fellow* (1954), about the hours leading up to an execution, and *The Hostage* (1958), about a British soldier captured by the IRA.

In 1958 one of the few female dramatists of the era, Shelagh Delaney (1939–), won critical acclaim at the age of 19 for her first play, *A Taste of Honey,* which, like *Look Back in Anger,* deals with working-class life in a down-to-earth manner. Set in a bleak northern industrial town it shows a girl's illegitimate pregnancy by her black lover, and her relationship with her mother and a homosexual art student.

The formative influences on **Harold Pinter** (1930–) were the writings of Beckett and the Theatre of the Absurd. *The Caretaker* (1960) was his first London success. Showing the influence of Beckett, the play is limited to a small cast, portraying three dysfunctional characters on the edge of society living constantly in hope, though generally facing a bleak existence. Their attempts at conversation mask their fears and inadequacies, while their silences speak volumes and their frustrations erupt into violence. The humour in the play serves to highlight the pathos of the human situation, in which nothing can be taken as definite. We are left to decide for ourselves who the real 'caretaker' might be: none of the characters fulfils the pun in the title, though each thinks that he does. So tautly and beautifully is the play written that its prose has often been compared to poetry.

The Irish writer Brian Friel (1929–) began his career by publishing short stories in the early 1960s, but became well known as a dramatist, particularly with his play *Philadelphia, Here I Come!* (1964) about an Irishman's response to the prospect of emigrating to the USA. Many of his later plays took up more overtly political themes, concerning the politics of Northern Ireland. *Translations* (1980) looks at British/Irish relations, taking as its starting point British actions in Ireland in the 1830s, when Anglicised place-names were imposed during map-making, showing the assertion of colonial power through the imposition of one language over another.

Joe Orton (1933–67) might be seen as a modern version of Oscar Wilde, to the extent that his comic plays, such as *Entertaining Mr Sloane* (1964) and *Loot* (1965), were outrageously witty, and his homosexuality was his downfall. In Orton's case, however, his plays were subversive black comedies and he was murdered by his homosexual partner.

Edward Bond (1934–) writes bleak plays which use humour to indicate unwarranted optimism on the part of characters who live in societies where violence predominates. Their language is so austere that it has been claimed that the plays lack a poetic dimension, yet the plot of *Saved* (1965) suggests that redemption is possible, even in the midst of despair and even if it is only temporary. The theme is echoed in many of Bond's plays, particularly in *Lear* (1971) and *The Fool* (1976). Bond sees the solution to current problems in a socialist society, and his didacticism and use of extreme violence have not endeared him to theatre-goers.

The early plays of **Tom Stoppard** (1937–) dazzled audiences with their theatricality and intellectual wit. His work is characterised by vitality, humour, witty dialogue and improbable situations, while being based on philosophical thought. Beckett's influence is apparent in his early plays in that both writers explore the meaning of life and the theme of waiting for some undefined event. This is seen in *Rosencrantz and Guildenstern are Dead* (1966) in which minor characters from Shakespeare's *Hamlet* are promoted to the roles of lead players who, like the protagonists in *Waiting for Godot*, must pass their time in pointless triviality. *Travesties* (1974) echoes this situation, yet borders on hilarious farce. Historically, **James Joyce**, Lenin, Tristan Tsara and Henry Carr, the main protagonists of *Travesties*, were all stranded in Zurich in 1917 by the First World War. Stoppard's elaborate plot causes them to meet in ridiculous circumstances, capturing simultaneously both the splendour and the absurdity of the human situation. The language of the play sparkles with witty Wildean epigrams.

In England in the 1970s and 1980s drama which was more overtly political than the works of Pinter, Orton or Stoppard came to the fore, tackling social and economic issues and taking an anti-establishment stance. The leading dramatists of this era were Howard Brenton (1942–) and David Hare (1947–). Hare is known as a left-wing playwright critical of capitalist corruption, but not above trenchant satire at the expense of the Labour party. His plays convey a sense of there being something missing from the life of the second half of the twentieth century. The ironic title, *Plenty* (1978), reflects this theme. The play contrasts a moment of exhilaration felt by a young female courier with the French Resistance during the hardships of the Second World War with her profound disillusionment 20 years later. Her world, now in a time of plenty, has not in fact changed for the better. Like Osborne, Hare sees Britain as trapped in its past and failing in the effort to progress towards a better society.

Alan Ayckbourn (1939–) specialises in farce, satirising the new lower-middle classes. *Absurd Person Singular* (1972) shows him using a device he has made famous and which has been imitated by others: repeated scenes are shown through the eyes of different characters at different times and in different locations. Each couple in the play feels themselves to be superior to the others. None has a sympathetic understanding of their neighbours' problems and all enjoy the discomfort of others. This play caught the selfishness of the new upwardly mobile society, noted also by Caryl Churchill.

Caryl Churchill (1938–) has written 28 plays, many with **feminist** themes, including *Top Girls* (1982). The title and the final act sum up the theme: the rift between women who have chosen home and family and those (often their friends or sisters) who have chosen the career path. Churchill presents us with individual and social issues such as the value of the family unit and the success of women in men's occupations. In Act I, famous women in history and legend exchange views on their careers; in Act II, we see a comedy about the career success of Marlene; in Act III, there is a move to social realism when Marlene visits the sister whose concern has been to make a home for Marlene's daughter, thus enabling her to progress at work. The audience is left to ponder a modern dilemma.

Closer by Patrick Marber (1964–) was praised as the best comedy of 1997 and the play has many hilarious moments. Its main contribution to end-of-the-century drama is two-fold: firstly it exploits the computer, as Dan and Larry write to each other via a chat-room in typical internet style, using increasingly pornographic language – Dan claims to be his friend, Anna, searching for a partner. More significantly, the play captures four lonely people, each looking for love but losing what they most desire. One dies, while the others fail to find a successful closer relationship. Each ends alone in the loneliness of a modern city. The play frankly defines the lot of many young thirty-somethings in the 1990s.

The importance of radio, television and film as media for drama increased during the second half of the twentieth century. Beckett, Pinter and Stoppard all worked in one or more of these media, and the output of some of the most talented dramatists, such as Dennis Potter, Alan Bleasdale and Mike Leigh, was found in television and film.

Dennis Potter (1935–94) preferred to write for TV rather than for the stage and was credited with raising the standards of TV drama. He produced numerous works in the 1960s, coming to the public's attention particularly with the political plays *Stand up, Nigel Barton* and *Vote, Vote, Vote for Nigel Barton*, both in 1965. *Blue Remembered Hills* of 1979 was a powerful drama about childhood and the loss of innocence, unusual in having adult actors playing the parts of children. *Pennies from Heaven* (1978) and *The Singing Detective* (1986) were two of his most popular productions.

Liverpool-born Alan Bleasdale (1946–) began his career writing drama for radio in the 1970s but became famous for his TV series *Boys From the Blackstuff* in the 1980s, about the effects of unemployment among a group of road workers in Liverpool. He has continued to work in the medium of TV, as both a writer and producer.

Mike Leigh (1943–) was born in Salford and began his directing career working in experimental theatre, but became well known through plays for TV which he produced in the 1970s, *Abigail's Party* (1977) being one of his early successes. Much of his subsequent work has been for the cinema, examples being *Life is Sweet* (1991), *Naked* (1993) and *Secrets and Lies* (1996). His work has a highly distinctive quality, achieving new levels of **realism** as a result of his working methods in which the actors begin building their characters on unscripted improvisations.

In the 1990s a number of plays dealt with questions of science. In *Arcadia* (1993),

Tom Stoppard examined chaos theory, while in *Copenhagen* (1998), Michael Frayn (1993–) combined quantum mechanics with an incident from the Second World War, an unsolved mystery and a questioning of the morality of the motives of his two pro-tagonists. In 1941, German nuclear physicist Heisenberg visited Nazi-occupied Copenhagen to meet Bohr, his Danish counterpart. Critics have argued whether the erstwhile colleagues met to compare notes on their research, to enable Heisenberg to spy for the Nazis, or to warn the Allies of Germany's success in nuclear science. Their meeting is shown from three points of view: those of Bohr, his wife and Heisenberg himself. Bohr's thinking is quick and precise, but the three steer round the point, arriving at no conclusion. We are left feeling that even Heisenberg himself was uncertain of his motives. This, ironically, reminds the initiated of his early achievement in introducing the Uncertainty Principle into quantum mechanics.

American drama

Throughout this period of intense activity on the English stage, much had been hap-pening in the theatre in America, but until the 1950s little was known of it in Britain.

In 1939 Eugene O'Neill (1888–1953) had begun his most famous play, *Long Day's Journey into Night*, based on his early life with his family. He asked that it should not be published until 25 years after his death but it was printed in 1953 and acted in London in 1958. It is long and at times repetitive, dealing with man's unrealisable hopes, yet many critics find it compelling and mythical. O'Neill was intent on making his audience feel the inner pain of his characters undertaking their 'long day's jour-ney' towards death. The play struck a chord with American audiences because it denied the authenticity of the American Dream, a theme it has in common with the best-known play by **Arthur Miller** (1915–), *The Death of a Salesman* (1949), originally called 'The Inside of his Head'.

Miller's Willy Loman (the name is suggestive of his depression) is a surprising tragic hero – an ordinary man with no pretensions to greatness of action or of spirit, except in his imagination. The play's construction mirrors Greek tragedy in taking place within 24 hours, using time-slips to fill in the necessary background. At the end Willy commits suicide so that his family can gain from an insurance policy. He lives his life claiming to be a success, yet knowing he has failed as a husband, a father, a friend and a businessman. Miller's intention was to show how American capitalism ruined the Loman family by setting impossible goals and pressuring men to be materially successful.

O'Neill, Miller and **Tennessee Williams** (1911–83) are regarded as the three great American playwrights. Williams was born in the South and his plays are full of pas-sion. Blanche Dubois, the nymphomaniac heroine in *A Streetcar Named Desire* (1945), is one of his supreme creations. In youth she was bright and innocent, but when we meet her in her sister's New Orleans apartment she has been corrupted by life, par-ticularly by her marriage to a homosexual who committed suicide. Outwardly she remains a ladylike figure, but as the play progresses she is shown to be manipulative, and we see the power of sex to destroy her. She is raped by Stanley, her brother-in-law, and as she is taken, a lonely figure, to a mental home, she evokes pathos with her final statement that we must always rely on the kindness of strangers.

Once the work of these three playwrights was known in London, the plays of a younger generation of American writers were more readily accepted. One of these was Edward Albee (1928–), whose writing was influenced by the Theatre of the Absurd, and whose play *Who's Afraid of Virginia Woolf?* (1962) is seen as a metaphor for American society in the 1960s, caught up in illusion and unable to face reality. Martha and George ferociously play out the domestic drama of a failed marriage, but they symbolise a wider social situation. Their final quiet words to each other, monosyllabic and halting, indicate that this is merely a lull in their war of attrition, not a conclusion: they might have come from plays by Beckett or Pinter. In *The Goat, or Who is Sylvia?* (2002), Albee explores the limits of tolerance within a marriage when a woman has to confront the fact that her husband is having an affair with a goat.

Langston Hughes (1902–67), a leading figure in the Harlem Renaissance, played a significant role in promoting African-American drama in the 1930s and 1940s. As well as writing plays he founded theatres, including, in 1938, the Harlem Suitcase Theatre. In 1959 *A Raisin in the Sun* by Lorraine Hansberry (1930–65) was the first play by an African-American woman to be staged on Broadway. The play, which won a New York Drama Critics' Circle Award, looks at the constraints on the lives of a working-class African-American family in Chicago, experiencing the difficulties of living in a society where they are discriminated against by whites. The play also looks at tensions within the black community itself and raises issues to do with marriage and the role of women which would later be taken up by feminist writers. The play is important for its presentation of the issues of its time, but also transcends particular issues by being about the importance of family and home, and the need to maintain hope and meet oppression with defiance.

David Mamet (1947–) deals realistically with the problems of individuals who fail to understand each other. In *Oleanna* (1992) John is a confident university professor whose student, Carol, is unsure of herself and has come to him for advice. By Act II she has reported his conduct during their interview to the tenure committee of the university and their roles are reversed. She has taken remarks he made and added other implications, and John loses his job when Carol accuses him of attempted rape. None of Carol's accusations can be substantiated, yet the sympathy of the committee lies with Carol.

Angels in America, the innovative two-part play by Tony Kushner (1956–), was performed in London in 1992/1993. It deals with many important topics in many different styles, examining America during the 1980s, with homosexuality and AIDS playing a significant part. The subtitle, 'A Gay Fantasia on National Themes', employs the pun wittily. Part One is an analysis of America; Part Two insists that the country must change as radically as the Soviet Union. The play is daring and original in form, content, theme and the sheer dimension of its aims.

The twentieth century saw drama flourish against all the odds, in spite of competition from cinema, radio, television and the internet. Successful new plays have reflected the problems of the day combined with a wider view relating them to the human condition: the passion, the love and the intense suffering and insecurity that make up our lives.

Contributors: Ann Severn, Ian Mackean, Bram de Bruin

Postcolonial literature

An introduction to postcolonial literature

Definition

The term '**postcolonial** literature' is a relatively new addition to the lexicon of literary study and is used to highlight a particular genre of writing. However, this genre is both highly flexible and sometimes difficult to define. Put simply, postcolonial literature can be defined as literature produced by countries that gained independence from colonial rule in the twentieth century. In 1900 the British Empire covered a pink swathe of the globe that included the Indian sub-continent and other parts of Asia, much of Africa, Australasia, Canada, Ireland, many Caribbean islands as well as numerous and scattered smaller possessions. By 2000, the vast majority of the countries in these areas had become independent nations. In this essay, only the countries which were formerly part of the British Empire are considered (there were, of course, other European and non-European empires).

Now, while this definition provides a very good guideline, we must constantly be aware that the history is more complex. Exact times and dates for the imposition, or the removal, of colonial rule are notoriously difficult to pin down. A country is rarely colonised overnight, in one sweeping socio-political movement. Equally, the road to independence is usually long, tortuous and often bloody. The effects of colonial rule on a country's future economic, social and political development may be both far-reaching and long-lasting and may continue in the present. In addition, when considering a postcolonial world we must be mindful that some would argue there is continuing financial and military neo-colonial expansion, taking place both overtly and covertly in our ever-changing, globalised community.

The term 'postcolonial literature' has largely replaced the term 'Commonwealth literature' for political reasons. Commonwealth literature defined and located in terms of geography (and as special areas of literary study within English) various regions from the newly decolonised Empire that had strong bodies of emergent writing. It was challenged by literary critics in the 1980s, who saw it as effacing any serious investigation of the relationship between the colonial past and the postcolonial present in these diverse literatures. (None of this is to suggest that there was not [nor continues to be] an enormous amount of outstanding critical work done under the aegis of Commonwealth literature.) Postcolonial, then, suggests less a socio-geographic entity and more the processes of historical dialogue and intervention. Writers from the formerly colonised countries are not viewed as simply finding a voice of their own but doing so from within a history, where the voices of their peoples were silenced and marginalised by the imposition of colonial rule. It assumes that the process of decolonisation is not a 'once and for all' event and that the danger of focusing on universal themes, as many proponents of Commonwealth literature did, is to miss the historical, geographical and cultural specificities of postcolonial texts in part caused by the nature of Empire.

South Africa is a country that provides an excellent example of the relation of pre- and postcolonial issues. As South Africa grapples with the political, economic and social issues arising from the removal of the Apartheid system, writers constantly reflect upon their own issues and experiences. Athol Fugard is well known for the political and ethical commitment of his earliest plays (*The Island*, 1973; the *Port Elizabeth Plays*, 1974), which provided a critique of the oppressive Apartheid regime. However, Fugard's more recent work has apparently ignored contemporary social issues such as the spread of HIV/AIDS, the problem of structural economic development, poverty and continued violence, choosing to focus on more private and personal issues. *Playland* (1993) and *Sorrows and Rejoicings* (2001) represent a struggle to come to terms with a traumatic, painful past and to explore the difficult process of the post-Apartheid healing of South African society. Apartheid may be dead and gone, but its legacy at a social and psychological level lingers. Similar perspectives inform contemporary novels such as Nadine Gordimer's *Burgher's Daughter* (2000), *Disgrace* (1999) by **J. M. Coetzee** and the work of poets such as Kelwyn Sole, for instance *Mirror and Water Gazing* (2001).

Main geographical areas and writers

The main areas of significant postcolonial Anglophone writing (this means written in English) and some of the best-known writers are as follows:

- **The Caribbean**: Sam Selvon, George Lamming, **V. S. Naipaul**, Grace Nichols, **Derek Walcott**, **Jean Rhys**.
- **South East Asia (India, Pakistan, Bangladesh, Sri Lanka)**: **Rabindranath Tagore**, **R. K. Narayan**, Anita Desai, Ruth Prawer Jhabvala, Nirad C. Chaudhuri, **Salman Rushdie**, Imtiaz Dharker, Henry Louis Vivian Derozio, Michael Madhusudan Dutt, Kaiser Haq, G. M. Muktibodh, Moniza Alvi, **Arundhati Roy**, Romesh Gunesekera.
- **Africa**: **Chinua Achebe**, Wole Soyinka, Ngugi wa Thiong'o, Tsitsi Dangarembga, **Buchi Emecheta**, Mariama Ba, Athol Fugard, Nadine Gordimer, **J. M. Coetzee**, Bessie Head, Chris Van Wyk, Joan Metelerkamp.
- **Australasia**: Patrick White, **Peter Carey**, Janet Frame, Keri Hulme.
- **Canada**: **Margaret Atwood**, **Malcolm Lowry**.
- **Ireland**: A special exception has to be made in the case of Ireland, where its writers may be considered both postcolonial and, in another sense, fundamentally part of the main body of English literature, for example Oscar Wilde, George Bernard Shaw, **W. B. Yeats**, **James Joyce**, **Samuel Beckett**, **Seamus Heaney**.

Interestingly, this would not apply to writers who are part of the Irish language tradition such as Nuala Ní Dhomhnaill.

■ **Diasporic**: In addition, the term postcolonial is often applied to migrant or diasporic writers, such as Rushdie, Romesh Gunesekra and Hanif Kureishi.

Key themes

Tradition or modernity

A central issue for the process of decolonisation has to be its political result: what new structures will replace the socio-political framework of colonial rule? Should there be a return to the past forms of government and culture, or something that resembles the democratic, secular Western institutions that the British themselves had? This is often played out, for the individual inhabitants of these new nations, in terms of a tension between the claims of tradition versus the pull of modernity. In India, Tagore (like Gandhi) was unhappy to embrace uncritically the structures of Western modernity, insofar as he saw this as promoting a mechanistic and materialist world-view, where capitalism would replace spirituality as the motor of Indian society, whatever the advantages of a pluralist, liberal society. Narayan's *The English Teacher* (1945) would appear a novel very much in the mode of Tagore/Gandhi. It shows a hero Krishna who achieves spiritual enlightenment and oneness with his society only when he learns, after his wife Susila's death, to value traditional Hindu spiritual concerns and to see education as predominantly about human growth. In sharp contrast, Naipaul's *A House for Mr Biswas* (1961) shows a hero eager to create himself as a new and individual person, away from the traditional values of a decayed Hindu social order. He wants not just a house away from the overbearing and engulfing Tulsi family, but a modern marriage based on love and equality. Biswas's values are Western and modern. Hearing Achebe's villagers in *Things Fall Apart* (1958) is an important step towards recognising the existence of a displaced and destroyed culture. However, the issue of what this society can teach its modern African counterparts is far more complex and ambiguous. Few African **feminists** would be uncritically happy about endorsing many traditional (male) African values. This debate between tradition and modernity has been made even sharper by the impact of globalisation, where all local cultures are becoming increasingly linked and homogenised, and traditional local cultural values face possible extinction.

Gender and postcolonialism

Recently, the relationship between postcolonial literature and **feminism** and representations of gender has become increasingly important. At one level, women from postcolonial contexts ask whether their separate and distinct voices and agendas have been heard within postcolonial literature. Yet at the same time we must be aware that while postcolonial women may indeed be seen as doubly disempowered compared with their male counterparts, in a different way the women of the British Empire had more power than almost all native males. *The Grass is Singing* (1950) by **Doris Lessing** is a feminist novel insofar as it explores the disintegration of a woman (Mary) in the face of patriarchal social expectations, but she is so terrified of her weakness and vulnerability in front of her African servant Moses that she ends up destroying both of them. Colonial stereotypes of the white woman menaced by supposedly 'primitive' male natives did not end with the demise of the Empire but live on in Western media reports and the popular consciousness, as do reiterated images of the 'passivity' of the native woman in the face of her 'barbaric' men folk.

Beverley Naidoo is a modern African woman writer who highlights the need to listen to the voices of the disenfranchised, whether children or women. Her children's novels such as *No Turning Back* (1995) and *The Other Side of Truth* (2000) suggest that even within a political crisis one should remain mindful of the multiple strands of social oppression. The breakdown of family groups, following the fracturing of a post-colonial society through war or major political change, has a significant impact upon the lives of both women and children. Contemporary South Asian female novelists have begun to challenge the image of South Asian women as long-suffering, self-sacrificing, maternal figures (for example, Sara Suleri with *Meatless Days* (1990) or Anees Jung with *Unveiling India: A Woman's Journey* (1987). Instead, they favour confused characters searching for identity, who explore their role in a society which deliberately marginalises and simultaneously elevates them. In some cases, the dual focus of feminism and the postcolonial might produce the need for a complex double voice, as in Eithne Strong, a poet who wrote in both English and Irish. *Flesh the Greatest Sin* (1982) addresses the subjugation of the self to God and ideas of Irish womanhood as well as the individual's sense of nation. Postcolonial women writers are no more restricted than male writers in terms of the issues they choose to address.

Linguistic issues

Choosing to write in English is not as straightforward as it seems. While it has become one of the world's main second languages, which often means for the writer larger and more varied audiences, it also carries with it the history of British colonisation and often the oppression of native languages. The countries of the Commonwealth use English as a *lingua franca* because of the Empire. Ngugi wa Thiong'o argues in *Decolonising The Mind: The Politics of Language in African Literature* (1986) that writers should always use their mother tongue and must reject English for this very reason. The alternative to this view is a kind of reinvention or expansion of existing Standard English, by which the decolonising writers make it relevant to their own experience and culture. Achebe's use of short, pellucid sentences and translation of Ibo proverbs is one example of the way many postcolonial writers make use of local words and their communities' speech patterns. The use of Creoles (discussed below) by many Caribbean poets is another.

New and traditional forms and genres

Just as writing in English is problematic because it means using the language of Empire, most literary forms (the novel especially, but also genres within poetry and drama) also belong to that colonial past. Some writers have attempted to either rein-vent these forms or to hybridise them with indigenous examples. *Ulysses* by **James Joyce** is a radical reinvention of the novel and has influenced other postcolonial writ-ers such as Rushdie and Carey. Wole Soyinka's *Death and the King's Horseman* (1975) redeploys some of the conventions of traditional African religious drama in a secular context, while poets such as Tagore and Das model their work on traditional South Asian poetic genres, and poets of Caribbean origin, like Grace Nichols and David Dabydeen, recall the oral conventions of the slave songs and stress the **performative** aspects of their work.

Redefinition and cultural decolonisation

Postcolonial writing can serve as both cultural decolonisation of the habits, views and assumptions of British colonialism (subject peoples were seen in stereotyped ways) and as part of the aspirant or newly independent nation's building of its own separate identity. It can thus be both part of the struggle for independence and the creation of a new national identity when that country is freed from Empire. W. B. Yeats is often seen as a template for this process. As a leading figure in the **Irish Cultural Revival** he attempted to define through literature a positive Irish cultural identity that was dif-ferent from that of being British (thus suggesting Ireland was very different from Britain), was continuous with past definitions of Ireland before Britain intervened, and which challenged colonial stereotypes that affirmed the inferiority of the Irish as a people. His play *Cathleen Ni Houlihan* (1902), in this way, is part of the struggle for political independence (Cathleen, as a representation of Ireland, calls on Irish men to free her from those who have stolen her lands). Yet it reflects what was happening in Yeats's poetry and drama on the terrain of cultural identity: his work helped invent/reinvent many of the contemporary representations of Ireland. Writing can thus link self-definition of an author with that of a people or nation.

In South Africa, as we have seen, an attempt has been made to redefine the new national identity as opposed to the old representations existent during Apartheid. Margaret Atwood's *Surfacing* (1972), Janet Frame's *An Angel at My Table* (1990) and Patrick White's *Voss* (1957) all attempt to define what it means to be a Canadian, New Zealander or Australian respectively, as opposed to being British, as part of a broad-er attempt at cultural nation-building among the 'white settler nations'. The indige-nous people living among dominant communities in these nations 'created' during Empire find such self-definition particularly arduous as they are defining themselves against majority communities doing much the same thing. Nevertheless, there is impressive work which has moved beyond the maintenance of tradition alone, from the Aboriginal community in Australia, the 'First Nations' of Canada and the Pacific (Maori) people of New Zealand.

Rereading colonial history and colonial texts

The historical interrogation of colonialism (to perceive how it can be seen as differ-ent from what it claimed to be), as both an ideology and actual material practice, has always been an important theme for postcolonial writers. It was necessary as part of the struggle for independence and is now seen as part of the process of cultural decolonisation. Historical fictions and the use of themes which revisit the past are therefore popular. Examples include Michael Ondaatje's *The English Patient* (1992), Caryl Phillips's *Cambridge* (1991) and Timothy Mo's *An Insular Possession* (1986). Ruth Prawer Jhabvala's *Heat and Dust* (1975) is set partly in the 1970s; it tells of the destructive, scandalous, passionate affair during the 1920s between Olivia, the British wife of a civil servant, and the local Indian ruler, the Nawab. The story is narrated by Olivia's step-granddaughter, who discovers her letters and local memories of the affair when she travels to India in the 1970s.

Sometimes this historical exchange occurs in the form of a rewriting/rereading of the familiar and canonical texts of English literature. Peter Carey's *Jack Maggs* (1997) retells the story of the convict and transportee Magwitch from Charles Dickens's *Great Expectations* (1861), while Jean Rhys's *Wide Sargasso Sea* (1966) renarrates the story of the first Mrs Rochester from Charlotte Brontë's *Jane Eyre* (1874). Texts important to colonial ideology such as Shakespeare's *The Tempest*, Rudyard Kipling's *Kim* (1901) and Daniel Defoe's *Robinson Crusoe* (1719) are often re-inhabited by postcolonial writers in order to analyse and to question colonial ideologies. In J. M. Coetzee's *Foe* (1986) (a retelling of *Robinson Crusoe*), Cruso and Friday are joined by a woman, Susan Barton, who narrates the story, and we are given a strikingly different account of life on the island and its aftermath in England. The myth of the pioneering, religiously 'elect' Crusoe who transforms the wilderness where he is shipwrecked into something approaching civilisation is gone for good. In these cases, such rewritings/rereading represents the engagement of the reader in a productive, critical dialogue with the past through the original literary texts.

The metropolitan, the margins and diasporas

The Empire modelled the relationship between the 'mother country' and the colonies as that of the 'metropolitan' as opposed to the 'margins'. This, too, has been contended by Anglophone postcolonial writers. Often fearing they will be seen as little more than 'local colour' by metropolitan audiences, they have sought to readdress such assumptions in different ways. R. K. Narayan's novels, set in the fictional South Indian village of Malgudi, imply that this is as much the centre of a world of meaning and rich fictional possibilities as London or Oxford. V. S. Naipaul's *Miguel Street* (1959) does the same for Trinidad. Diasporic writers such as Sam Selvon (*The Lonely Londoners*, 1956), Timothy Mo (*Sour Sweet*, 1982) and Hanif Kureishi (*The Buddha of Suburbia*, 1990; *The Black Album*, 1995) show us an immigrant and postcolonial London very different from the metropolitan image in colonial representations.

The diasporic experience of a community in exile is a powerful creative force and many postcolonial writers (like their communities) have travelled to Britain in hope of a better life or to flee persecution in their home countries. Sam Selvon's *Lonely Londoners*, for example, describes the experience of living in another country, but it also creates a new London, a place defined by the immigrant experience: 'normal' British perspectives are shifted and defamiliarised by the use of Creole so that the reader too becomes 'displaced'. This short novel enables the reader to glimpse the pressures and constraints of the West Indian immigrants; they face hardship and prejudice, but their experiences are framed in their own voices rather than those of the dominant British culture in which they have arrived. Selvon allows his character Moses to evolve to owner-occupier of a dilapidated home in *Moses Ascending* (1975) and he eventually returns to the West Indies in *Moses Migrating* (1983), where he finds himself neither British nor West Indian any more. Diasporic writings have in this way questioned traditional notions of Englishness/Britishness, as well as the way in which ethnic communities live out the conflicts and negotiations between dominant and minority communities and between colonial, traditional and multicultural values. Ayub Khan Din's play *East is East* (1996), Zadie Smith's *White Teeth* (2000) and Monica Ali's *Brick Lane* (2003) are all examples of the 'uncanny' position of the diasporic postcolonial writer, simultaneously both British and not British.

Caribbean hybridity

Of the new literatures the Caribbean is an unusual case, as it lacks any indigenous precolonial native tradition to return to. The Caribbean population is composed of different ethnic groups and communities 'transported' there by various empires (slavery and indentured labour) and is culturally fragmented due to having been colonised by several empires (Britain, France, Spain). Here Anglophone writers have also faced a choice between writing in Standard English and the local Creoles (local hybridised languages) of individual islands. Whereas Edward Kamau Brathwaite's poetry uses Creole as a decolonising gesture (he argues it is 'nation language'), Derek Walcott uses Standard English with some Creole inflections. In addition, some would argue we should see postcolonial writing in the Caribbean as 'creolised' in a cultural rather than just a linguistic sense: a product of many cultures rather than just one.

Postcolonial theory/criticism

The approach of postcolonial theory/criticism is associated with the types of literary text and theme discussed above. We might describe it as a way of reading which emphasises the following: a critical interrogation of colonialism in terms of both its presence within English literature and its continuing political and cultural effect upon the world and its literatures; an exploration of how texts written from the decolonised former British empire contest and subvert colonial ideology ('writing back'); an analysis of how the new national literatures represent their own societies, cultures and issues.

Edward Said in *Orientalism* (1978) produced the most celebrated example of such an approach. Said argues that the 'knowledge' of the East created by the West was, in fact, a representation, or in Michel Foucault's phrase a 'discourse', based upon fantasy, assumptions and stereotypes. That is to say, Orientalism was enshrined in a host of institutions and linguistic practices (including literature) which served to 'permit' and legitimise European colonisation of these lands by imposing on the Orient Western ideas about what it was/is, which 'showed' its 'inferior' nature. (Said refers to the Middle East and North Africa, but his theory has been applied to the East in general.) This 'knowledge' included damaging and negative stereotypes: the East was ancient and timeless (needing Western modernisation); irrational, abnormal, magical; degenerate and primitive (a culture requiring restoration and to be civilised); 'feminine' and infantile (needing a patriarchal West to give it firm guidance and protect it from itself). Racial stereotypes accompanied these cultural stereotypes (for example, all Indians had the same characteristics). In addition, this image of the East, insofar as it was the presumed opposite of the West, helped to construct Europe's notion of its own identity. Said's theory has been enormously influential and is often used not only to analyse texts of the colonial period but also to show how postcolonial texts have disputed such Orientalist stereotypes. (It has been criticised, however, as many argue that Orientalist discourse is more fractured, ambivalent and contradictory than he suggests.)

Bill Ashcroft, Gareth Griffiths and Helen Tiffin in *The Empire Writes Back* (1989) produced another influential account of how postcolonial writers position themselves against the linguistic, ideological and representational values of the colonial past (the 'centre'), through disputing the centre's view of their presumed subsidiary and secondary nature. (Jean Rhys's retelling the story of Jane Eyre in *Wide Sargasso Sea* from the point of view of the marginal first Mrs Rochester exemplifies such a challenge.) In effect, they largely imply that all postcolonial literature is a form of textual 'decolonisation' through literary creation, even as it subverts and contends with past values. They argue, for example, that postcolonial writers were creating new 'Englishes' to subvert the dominance of the standard form (as for example in Salman Rushdie's *Midnight's Children* (1981) or the 'creolised' poetry of Edward Kamau Brathwaite). Simultaneously, they might oppose traditional ideological representations of the colonised and their native culture (Chinua Achebe's *Things Fall Apart*, 1958) or retell aspects of the history of colonialism from a deliberately marginal view in a subversive way (Peter Carey's *Oscar and Lucinda*, 1988). (This theory too has some difficulties; it effectively disenfranchises any postcolonial texts that do not primarily address such concerns.)

Lastly, we should recognise two important caveats to the label 'postcolonial writing'. There is a significant danger we can miss or ignore specific national issues and debates that are not ostensibly contesting or subverting a colonial agenda. Chinuah Achebe's fine novel *Anthills of the Savannah* (1987) is a critique of the failure of African political leadership, cognisant that such leaders often blame the West to excuse their own failings. Salman Rushdie's *Midnight's Children* is a novel about India's failure to live up to its political aspirations proclaimed by Nehru at independence. The second caveat is that there are those who argue that the contemporary is a neo-colonial moment, in which American-led capitalism and globalisation is the world power which postcolonial writers must face. Margaret Atwood's *Surfacing* delineates and combats the relationship between American-led capitalism and ecological devastation in Canada, as well as debating Canadian national identity. Postcolonial literature's fate, then, is always to negotiate between local concerns and global ones, to be very much of its own time and place, and in an equally important sense turned towards the larger world and community.

Contributors: Steven Barfield, Ian Foakes

Postmodern literature

An introduction to postmodern literature

The term '**postmodernism**' is applied to many areas of human activity, including art, architecture, literature, film and music, but it is difficult to pinpoint an exact date for the beginning of postmodernism as a movement. The late 1960s and 1970s witnessed various artistic, literary and cultural productions which may be called 'postmodern', but the concept became a subject of academic study and discussion in the 1980s. Postmodernism is still a significant issue of philosophical and theoretical debate, and many of the artistic, literary and cultural productions of our time may be described as 'postmodern'.

Many '-isms' defy simple and exact definitions, and postmodernism is no exception. Unlike many other '-isms', however, postmodernism celebrates the idea of resisting any definition or categorisation because it is in the nature of postmodern thought to reject definitive and comprehensive explanations. In fact a significant component of the postmodern outlook is a high degree of scepticism about the existence of universal truths or ultimate meanings by which human beings could or should live.

In his book *The Postmodern Condition: A Report on Knowledge* (1974), the French philosopher Jean François Lyotard argues that the 'grand narratives' by which the western world has been living since the Enlightenment are no longer valid in the postmodern world. One such 'grand narrative' that has lost credibility is the belief in the power of science and reason to bring about progress and happiness for humankind. This loss of credibility arises from the fact that the twentieth century witnessed not only two world wars, rendered particularly devastating by technology, but also the growth of extremist ideologies leading to various kinds of dictatorship and totalitarianism. Among other 'grand narratives' that have diminished in the twentieth century, one can list religion (e.g. belief in Christianity as a way to make sense of one's life) and ideology (e.g. **Marxism** as a system of government and philosophical outlook).

Modernist authors writing in the first few decades of the twentieth century shared the same scepticism, but with one significant difference: while the Modernists felt a tragic sense of loss and looked for ways of restoring 'meaning' to the way they felt, postmodernists rejoice in the dissolution of those 'grand narratives' which, according to them, dictated one truth, one meaning, one essence – a position which was totally unacceptable to them. Postmodernism, therefore, rejects a single truth and instead promotes a plurality of meanings and the co-existence of a wide variety of 'small' narratives, none of which is inferior or superior to the others.

An interest in the nature of language and the relationship between language and reality is another significant concern of postmodern thought. These issues were taken up by a movement called '**poststructuralism**', which emerged in the late 1960s and 1970s in the work of French thinkers such as Roland Barthes and Jacques Derrida. Poststructuralist theories on language and its relationship with reality, however, are closely associated with postmodern ideas. One of the basic tenets of poststructuralist thought is that language creates and shapes reality. Language, however, is not so stable and reliable a system as we normally assume. It is fraught with uncertainty and indeterminacy, which makes it impossible to arrive at a full, complete meaning unified in itself. If language is the shaper of reality and language itself is unreliable, then it is impossible to talk about the existence of a reality or a meaning that is stable and unchanging. In postmodern thought, therefore, we are always on shaky ground concerning language and reality. This, however, is not something to feel too anxious about. On the contrary, this is an idea which can lead one to explore – in an almost playful manner – how language constructs our understanding of reality and how this reality can be refuted, dissolved or '**deconstructed**' to be replaced by other equally valid 'realities'.

Such an attitude of playfulness is frequently found in postmodern fiction – the genre in which postmodern ideas are reflected most openly. The sense of loss and dismay that pervaded many Modernist works is not found in postmodern novels. The playful attitude of postmodern writers can best be observed in the way they employ literary devices such as parody and pastiche. Quoting from the works of others, putting those quotations in new contexts and using earlier literary forms and conventions with a parodic intent are common practices. This suggests that originality is no longer a significant criterion in the production of literature, and the postmodern outlook does not accept the possibility of creating a totally original work. Literature is marked by '**intertextuality**'. That is to say, each literary text inevitably bears traces of other texts and is dependent on those texts for its existence.

The traditional novel is often designed to create an 'illusion of reality' for the reader. In other words, during the reading process, the reader is temporarily made to forget about the fictional nature of what he is reading. A stable sense of reality is thus created within the world of the novel and language is simply a means to communicate that reality to the reader. It is exactly this sense of security about language and reality that postmodern novelists refuse to create for the reader. Meaning and reality are unstable, and language creates and shapes everything. The postmodern novelist, therefore, often feels the need to break the illusion of reality, which he does by referring to his own writing process and to the fictional nature of what he is describing. The reader is thus made to consider the novel primarily as a literary artefact, a work of art, or a construct of language, and is denied the satisfaction of getting carried away by the illusory reality of the story. *The French Lieutenant's Woman* (1969) by **John Fowles** is a good example. The book is written mostly in a manner similar to a Victorian novel, but in fact it exposes and parodies the conventions of this form. The novel's intrusive narrator breaks the illusion of reality by furnishing his story with a twentieth-century outlook and by stopping the narrative from time to time to comment on the Victorian novel and on his own writing process. He even admits to his inability to know everything about his characters – an attitude which creates confusion in the reader:

> I do not know. This story I am telling is all imagination. These characters I create never existed outside my own mind. If I have pretended until now to know my characters' minds and innermost thoughts, it is because I am writing in . . . a convention universally accepted at the time of my story: that the novelist stands next to God. He may not know all, yet he tries to pretend that he does.[1]

Fiction which breaks the illusion of reality by drawing attention to its own writing process is termed '**metafiction**' or 'self-conscious fiction'. In fact, such strategies can be traced back to the seventeenth and eighteenth centuries, as seen for example in *Don Quixote* (1605) by Cervantes and Lawrence Sterne's *Tristram Shandy* (1760), which describes an attempt by the first-person narrator, Tristram, to write his autobiography. The novel, however, turns out to be a comical manifestation of his inability to do so. Tristram's frequent digressions and interruptions, his practice of addressing the reader directly and his frequent consideration of his own writing process are all techniques which our age has labelled as 'postmodern' or 'metafictional'.

Postmodern fiction reflects its concern with the indeterminacy of meaning and reality in other ways, too. The sense of closure that characterises most traditional novels is often non-existent in postmodern works. *The French Lieutenant's Woman*, for example, provides multiple endings for the story. Similarly, *The Black Prince* (1973) by **Iris Murdoch** ends abruptly and the main story is followed by four different postscripts contradicting the preceding narrative in different ways. The reader is left baffled and confused, not knowing what to believe in or which character to trust.

Postmodern fiction does not leave much room for fully developed characters either. Postmodern characters, as well as themes and forms, are fragmented. Characters may behave inconsistently and the reader is continually prevented from regarding them as stable and unified identities. In-depth psychological accounts are often avoided. Muriel Spark, for instance, is well known for having aloof and distant narrators who do not allow the reader to develop sympathy for the characters. Descriptions of psychological states are reduced to a minimum in her novels and the emphasis is on plot – on events and actions – instead.

The idea of an indeterminate reality also invites a reconsideration of concepts such as 'fact' and 'fiction'. Prior notions of a sharply drawn boundary between the two no longer apply in the postmodern world. It is possible, instead, to regard 'facts' as fictional constructs created by language. Postmodern writers often explore this idea by intermingling 'fact' and 'fiction' in their works. In *The White Hotel* (1981), for example, D. M. Thomas presents his fictional protagonist, Lisa Erdman, as a patient of the famous psychoanalyst, **Sigmund Freud**. A 'real' historical personage is, therefore, situated in a fictional world. Thomas's 'Freud', however, is an 'imagined' one. Neither his letters nor his case study of Lisa Erdman, which make up a significant part of the book, are based on historical 'facts'. The novel therefore constructs a 'fictional' Freud out of the 'real' one, blurring the boundaries between fact and fiction. Juxtaposing realism and fantasy is another way in which *The White Hotel* inquires into the relationship between the real and the fictional. The novel combines the extravagant fantasies of Lisa Erdman with Freud's case study, or with third-person accounts written in a **realist** manner. This kind of writing, which is widely employed by postmodern writers, is termed '**magic realism**'. Among other writers whose works bring together the realistic and the fantastic, one can count **Angela Carter**, **Salman Rushdie** and **Jeanette Winterson**.

Postmodern fiction also dissolves the boundaries between genres, often bringing together diverse forms and styles in a single work. A novel, therefore, may be made up of forms as dissimilar as first-person subjective narrative and journalistic writing. Julian Barnes's novels, for instance, are well known for challenging the boundaries of fiction through their mixture of disparate forms and styles. The eclecticism of postmodern literature is also observed in the way it freely employs popular cultural forms. Writers no longer adhere to previous distinctions between 'high' and 'low' forms in literature and frequently employ genres such as the thriller, the horror story and detective fiction: forms traditionally considered 'inferior', as products of popular culture. A postmodern work, therefore, is often a mosaic of differences in language, form and style. Salman Rushdie's remarks about the language of his fiction nicely sum up this trend in literature:

> [a] kind of rapid transition [from high philosophy to street language] is . . . something that I'm interested in doing, so that a text can include . . . high literature, could include classical references . . . and at the same time be kind of streetwise . . . and have the language that people actually speak to each other in.[2]

The term 'postmodern fiction' is well established, but the same cannot be said of 'postmodern drama' or 'postmodern poetry'. To what extent these two genres embrace postmodernism is an issue of debate, but one can observe postmodern trends in drama and poetry. Some recent plays, for instance, are regarded as examples of 'metadrama' since they break the illusion of reality created on the stage by drawing attention to their theatricality. Parody, pastiche and word-play are common practices, as seen for example in plays by **Tom Stoppard**. Postmodern concerns about language and reality are also reflected in contemporary plays. Caryl Churchill, for example, leads the audience to question the way their 'reality' is constructed by subverting gender stereotypes and upsetting audience expectations through various experimental techniques.

Contemporary poetry often shares similar concerns, too, by exploring the nature of 'reality' and the role played by language in shaping our perceptions. Parody and pastiche are again commonly employed, and elements of popular culture, as well as different dialects and languages, freely enter the realm of poetry. Furthermore, poets often refrain from creating a sense of wholeness and unity for the reader, open-endedness being a preferred quality. These practices are in line with postmodern ideas, and poets such as James Fenton, Craig Raine and Paul Muldoon may be listed among those whose work exhibits such postmodern trends.

References

1. **Fowles, John** (1969) *The French Lieutenant's Woman.* New York: Signet, p. 80.

2. **Reder, Michael** (ed.) (2000) *Conversations with Salman Rushdie.* Jackson: University Press of Mississippi, p. 107.

Contributor: Nil Korkut

Part 3

Regional influences in modern literature

American literature

A survey of modern American poetry and fiction

Poetry

At the dawn of the twentieth century, American poetry was notable for the absence of prominent poets or 'schools' of poetic development. Newly ensconced as the 'good grey bard', Walt Whitman's presence cast a formidable shadow on the American poetry scene, despite his death before the turn of the century, while Emily Dickinson's terse poems – verse which, next to Whitman's, would emerge as arguably the most important contribution to nineteenth-century American poetry – were finally published in posthumous collections in the first decades of the twentieth century. Before 1912, when **Ezra Pound** (1885–1972) and his circle rose to cultural power, the most important American poet was probably Edwin Arlington Robinson (1869–1935), whose poetry evidenced – as can be seen in some of his most anthologised pieces, like 'Miniver Cheevy' and 'Richard Cory' – an early sense of the alienation and irony that would come to characterise later twentieth-century American poetry.

It is difficult to overstate the influence that Pound and his associates exerted on the development of both British and American **Modernist** poetry. Born in Idaho in the American West and schooled in Pennsylvania, Pound moved to London shortly after completing his university studies to begin a 'revolution' in poetry, which he, together with his erstwhile partner Hilda Doolittle (1886–1961), better known by her initials, and friend Richard Aldington, codified in the **Imagist** manifesto of 1912. This manifesto envisioned a poetry focused on the 'direct treatment of the "thing", whether subjective or objective', an economy of word use that would exclude any language 'that does not contribute to the presentation' and a 'rhythm' that followed the 'sequence of the musical phrase' rather than 'the sequence of the metronome'. Though Pound would quickly eclipse the terse extremes of Imagism and another similarly conceived mode of poetry that he called **Vorticism** to move on to larger and longer poetic forms, he and his circle consistently tried to purge poetry of the prolixity, verbosity and hackneyed presentation of morality-in-meter that they detested in the Victorian and Edwardian poetry of previous generations.

Pound's revolution also meant that he would aggressively promote young poets whose work – though not always written lockstep with his early principles of poetry – he admired, both in his role as the poetry editor of magazines like *The Dial* and through his connections with editors back in America. Harriet Monroe (1860–1936), an accomplished poet in her own regard, was editor of the fledgling *Poetry* magazine and willingly published poets that Pound advocated; indeed, 'The Love Song of J. Alfred Prufrock' by T. S. Eliot (1888–1965) appeared in *Poetry* in 1915. Besides Eliot, the poet born in Missouri and educated at Harvard University who, like Pound, relocated to England to perfect his poetic craft, Pound also promoted Robert Frost (1874–1963), Amy Lowell (1874–1925), his longtime friend William Carlos Williams (1883–1963) and H. D. Though Frost and Williams would eventually choose to remain in America and Amy Lowell would take Imagist principles back to Boston to promote such poetry there among more sceptical New England poets (Pound, who quickly tired of Lowell, disparaged her poetry as 'Amygism'), the transatlantic exchange of poetic principles forged by Pound and his friends would create a productive cross-fertilisation of artistic ideas well into mid-century.

T. S. Eliot, first a protégé of Pound and then, increasingly, the dominant figure in both British and American poetry, shook the world of poetry with his publication of 'The Waste Land' in 1922. The poem, which details the ravages of a modern life in London 'wasted' by war, failed communication, lust and lack of authentic spiritual guidance, commanded a new means of reading and understanding poetry. Eliot's poem was erudite, highly allusive to an ancestry of texts seemingly drawn from the entirety of the canon of Western civilisation (and therefore elusive to many readers), and demonstrated a unity of fragmented voices and perceptions that demanded much from readers weaned on Tennyson, Whitman and others. William Carlos Williams famously declared that 'The Waste Land' would set back American poetry 20 years, suggesting that its victory over the emerging modern sensibility was so complete that poets would feel the weight of the poem's accomplishment on their artistic shoulders for decades. He was right.

Eliot became the elder statesman of a generation of formalist poets who pursued a style designed to be appreciated according to the principles of what was called 'The New Criticism', namely, a way of studying literature that privileged the image, the symbol, the paradox, the allusion and other figurative language and saw poetry and fiction as something that could, in an almost scientific manner of study, be understood by a faithful dissection of these parts. In such a formalist aesthetic, the knowledge and study of a particular poet's history, personality and proclivities took a back seat. 'Poetry is not personality, but an escape from personality,' Eliot asserted. Many American poets flourished in the New Critical emphasis on the formal aspects of poetry, among them Marianne Moore (1887–1972), e e cummings (1894–1962), John Crowe Ransom (1888–1974), Allen Tate (1899–1979) and Randall Jarrell (1914–65).

While Pound and Eliot were busy transforming American poetry from afar in their self-imposed European exile, another sort of American poetry emerged. As a result of the Great Migration of African-American workers and their families from an impoverished and racially threatened life in the American South to fill industrial jobs in Northern cities such as Chicago, Detroit, Philadelphia and New York City, a critical mass of black intellectuals, artists, poets and other writers developed in Harlem, an older neighbourhood of New York City's borough of Manhattan. There, writer Alain Locke pronounced a 'New Negro Renaissance', also called the Harlem Renaissance, in which the new affluence of African-American workers led to their acquiring the opportunity and leisure necessary for African-American poetry and prose to flourish. The most notable Harlem Renaissance poet was **Langston Hughes** (1902–67), whose world travels on merchant ships and personal experience of racism throughout the United States led him to write sharp-edged, terse political poetry that sought to revise world history to include what he saw as the noble genealogy of the African.

An immigrant from Jamaica, Claude McKay (1890–1948), also wrote in this mode, as did Countee Cullen (1903–46), James Weldon Johnson (1871–1938) and others who saw in the birth of this new artistic community in Harlem a chance for African-Americans to begin to deal with the complexities of their racial and historical heritage, as well as with the continued racism and other challenges faced by their community. These poets achieved wide acclaim, though often as 'Negro' poets viewed alongside the exoticism of the Harlem jazz scene and the sometimes problematic white consumption of black art forms. When the Great Depression brought an end to the economic stability of the Harlem community and effectively ended the Harlem Renaissance, however, a tradition of African-American poetry had been born, to be reincarnated and retooled by the Black Arts Movement in the 1960s into a new and continued flourishing of African-American poetry.

By mid-century, the dominance of the American poetry scene by formalist, New Critical modes of composition gave rise to a need for new 'revolutions' in poetry, especially by younger poets who wanted to return to the personal and the experimental. Just as at the beginning of the century, these innovators started their work within coteries of like-minded poets. In the 1950s, the group of writers that would be known as the **Beat writers** – most notably, poet and 'spontaneous prose' writer **Jack Kerouac** (1922–69), **Allen Ginsberg** (1926–97) and William Burroughs (1914–77) – met in New York City in and around Columbia University and started a wave of experimentation that again tried to pare down poetry and prose to its bare essentials. This time, though, what was considered 'essential' was the spontaneity, feeling and message that the poetry offered – a window, as it were, to a sense of disaffection with the increasingly capitalist, conservative, suburban dreams of the majority of Americans and the menace of American Cold War politics. Like 'The Waste Land' a little more than 30 years previously. Ginsberg's 'Howl' (1956) shook the poetry world with its wild, seemingly unrestrained Whitmanian rage against the machine of America, as well as with its scatological, profane style that openly invoked homosexuality, drug use and a lifestyle that emphasised bardic nomadism over a suit-and-tie social responsibility.

No less shocking to the mid-century poetry establishment was the turning of Robert Lowell (1917–77), a poet who originally wrote formalist verse, to a poetry soon identified as **Confessional**. Where Eliot and others militated against the overt baring of one's indiscretions, failures, breakdowns and insanities in the poetic form, Lowell's *Life Studies* (1959) embraced it, talking of his mental illness, his marital strife and other personal problems as a way of achieving a new sort of 'honesty' and 'universality' in his poetry. Despite encouragement from other prominent poets, like Lowell's close friend **Elizabeth Bishop** (1911–79), to abandon the form, Lowell instead emerged as the first of many mid-century American poets to embrace the confessional mode of poetry, others being W. D. Snodgrass (1926–), Anne Sexton (1928–74), Sylvia Plath (1932–63) and John Berryman (1914–72).

Other 'schools' of American poetry also emerged mid-century. The New York School of poets, inspired by the intellectual abstraction found in the poetry of Wallace Stevens (1879–1955) as well as by the emergence of surrealism and Abstract Expressionism in the visual arts, sought to use words in a similar way. The New York School included Frank O'Hara (1926–66), Kenneth Koch (1925–) and John Ashbery (1927–), all friends from Harvard whose lives as art critics and connoisseurs in New York City colour their work. Likewise, poets loosely grouped under the aegis of the Black Mountain Poets, among them Charles Olson (1910–70), Robert Creeley (1926–) and Robert Duncan (1919–88), worked with the 'projectivism' of open form and style.

The advent of postmodernism and of poststructuralist thought between the end of the Second World War and the 1960s hippie youth rebellion also gave rise to other ethnic literatures of the United States inspired by the ascension of African-American literature and politics from the Harlem Renaissance and beyond. Latino/a literature, first manifest in the rise of English-language Chicano poetry of writers such as Rodolfo 'Corky' Gonzales and Alurista, and in the Nuyorican (New York Puerto Rican) poets, gathered momentum in the final decades of the century, and Asian-American poets like Li-Young Lee emerged from the California coast and major metropoles of the USA as prominent forces. Similarly, women's poetry, long relegated to a separate or second-class status by male poets and critics, also emerged as a powerful body within American poetry, concurrent with the gathering force of the feminist movement from the 1960s onwards. Adrienne Rich, once the darling of male American formalists, is one of the best examples of the strong voice and important politicisation of this tradition, with her poem 'Diving into the Wreck' chronicling the recovery of a voice long buried that would soon speak out against the male-dominated tradition of American poetry.

Fiction

Whereas many of the innovations in American poetry in the early twentieth century developed because of a new transatlantic community of American poets, American fiction had enjoyed a strong transatlantic tradition from the dawn of the twentieth century that would continue for several decades. Henry James (1843–1916), the New Englander turned 'American in Europe', composed several of his most famous novels in the first decade of the century. One of the most important American expatriate writers, however, was Gertrude Stein (1874–1976), who relocated to Paris in 1903 and quickly developed a salon where young American writers visiting the Continent could nurture their talents, drawn to Paris not only by Stein but by her close association with visual artists, such as Pablo Picasso, whose experimentation with Primitivism, Cubism and other artistic innovations of the early twentieth century offered American writers a chance to escape the political and cultural isolationism prevalent in many parts of the United States. When writers like F. Scott Fitzgerald (1896–1940), Ernest Hemingway (1899–1961) and others were drawn to Europe first by the 'Great War' and then as part of the 'Americans in Paris' phenomenon of the Roaring Twenties, Stein's salon seemed an almost obligatory stop. Europe also offered a more progressive site for many ethnic American writers.

Those American writers who didn't leave for Europe in the first decades of the twentieth century often gravitated towards Chicago, Los Angeles and New York City, where the perception of a more cosmopolitan haven for their sometimes socially challenging art seemed unusually attractive. Indeed, it is difficult to separate the work of writers like Theodore Dreiser (1871–1945), Richard Wright (1908–60) or Nathanael West (1903–40) from the urban landscapes that are integral to their most important novels. Those writers who chose to locate their art in the smaller towns or in rural settings tended increasingly to question the romanticised vision of small-town America; the short story cycle *Winesburg, Ohio,* by Sherwood Anderson (1876–1941), and the treatment of the American South of the fictional Yoknapatawpha County that formed the Nobel Prize-winning work of William Faulkner (1897–1962), bear out this new scepticism about the desirability of rural American life.

Stylistically, American fiction of the twentieth century owes much to the heritage of realist and naturalist texts at the turn of the century. William Dean Howells and Stephen Crane, and certainly Dreiser, were all very popular writers at the beginning of the century, and Fitzgerald's studies of the Jazz Age, the studies of African-American culture by Ralph Ellison (1914–94) and darkly humorous stories of the poor of the American South by Flannery O'Connor (1925–64) all owe significant debts to this tradition. The rise of New Critical, formalist trends in the work and criticism of American poetry in the first half of the century can also be observed in American fiction of the time, especially since the associations between American poets and prose writers in the urban centres of the United States as well as in American universities were significant. In fact, the regularised study of American literature as a separate tradition from British literature in US university English departments is largely a twentieth-century phenomenon. This new university validation for American literature gave American poets and prose writers a growing incentive to think about the academic use (and, occasionally, the appropriation) of their work and the audiences such use could generate. In many ways, the New Journalism of writers like Thomas Wolfe (1900–) and Norman Mailer (1923–) or the 'non-fiction novel' that writers such as Truman Capote (1924–84) popularised blended realist, naturalist and formalist methodologies and again affirmed the sense that American experience could be inherently interesting when adapted to imaginative prose.

The questioning of formalist methodology in the study of literature by postmodern, poststructural approaches to the writing and analysis of literary production in the 1960s led to a revolution in American fiction and what critic Linda Hutcheon has called 'historiographic metafiction' – that is, fiction self-consciously concerned with its use of historical tradition and established patterns of formal technique that break down the then-accepted boundaries between author and reader and 'reality' and 'artifice'. *The Crying of Lot 49* and *Gravity's Rainbow* by the famously reclusive Thomas Pynchon (1937–), as well as *Lost in the Funhouse* by John Barth (1930–), short stories by Donald Barthelme (1931–89), all works which emphasise various indeterminacies of perception, language and literary tradition, date from this period.

Writers like Joseph Heller (1923–99) and Kurt Vonnegut (1922–) proved with their respective novels *Catch-22* and *Slaughterhouse-Five* that historiographic metafiction wasn't just about defeating the 'literature of exhaustion' (to quote John Barth's description of the state of American prose in the 1960s) but about calling into question many of the stable, master narratives of American history, American politics and the very foundations of institutional knowledge in the United States. African-American writers like Ishmael Reed skilfully adopted this mode to address the racialised history and cultural experience of the United States in *Mumbo Jumbo*, as did Chicano writers such as Rudolfo Anaya (1937–) in *Bless Me, Última* and Native American writers like Leslie Marmon Silko in *Ceremony*.

The postmodern questioning of language and its destabilising of all language-based knowledge – in history, art, religion and so forth – led American fiction from the 1980s on to focus on what the American Jewish prose, evidenced in the work of Bernard Malamud (1914–86), Philip Roth (1933–), **Saul Bellow** (1915–) and Isaac Bashevis Singer (1904–), had been doing for decades: namely, to preoccupy itself with fictions of identity-formation and the negotiation of one's own cultural heritage vis-à-vis 'dominant' American culture. The most important American writer of this mode is undoubtedly **Toni Morrison** (1931–), whose revisions and reimaginations of African-American history and cultural experience in novels like *The Bluest Eye* (1970), *Beloved* (1988) and *Jazz* (1992), among other works, have gained international critical recognition. *The Woman Warrior* (1976) by Maxine Hong Kingston (1940–) exemplifies similar imaginative impulses in Asian-American literature of the period, as do novels by Sandra Cisneros, Julia Alvarez and Cristina Garcia in the rising US Latino/a literary tradition. Recently, new fiction writers like **Jhumpa Lahiri** (1967–) and Bharati Muhkerjee have also attested to a growing Indian-American literary presence in American fiction.

It is clear that this emphasis on personal, 'ethnic' experience will continue in this century, especially as such writing is bolstered in the popular media by public figures like Oprah Winfrey (and her now-famous book club, which encourages specific fiction purchases for millions of viewers), film adaptations of these contemporary works and the growing multiculturalism of American demographics in general.

Contributor:　　　　　　　　　　　　　　　　　　　　　　　Trenton Hickman

Modern American poetry – the influence of Elizabeth Bishop

By means of these beginnings, these slight differences, and the appeal . . . of my carefully subdued, reserved manner, I shall attract to myself one intimate friend, whom I shall influence deeply.[1]

American poet **Elizabeth Bishop** (1911–79) was one of the most praised poets of her generation. Yet she was never the most read or respected at the time. **Allen Ginsberg's** *Howl* (1956) and **Sylvia Plath**'s *Ariel* (1965) both sold more copies than any of her collections, while Robert Lowell's *Life Studies* (1959) continues to take the critical plaudits as the key work of poetry for most post-Second World War readers. Lowell was godfather to the **Confessional** poets. His gift was somehow to fuse the radical themes of

Beat writers like William Burroughs and Jack Kerouac with the formal ingenuity of poet-critics like Randall Jarrell and Allen Tate. As a teacher at Harvard in the late 1950s and 1960s, he also acted as an informal mentor to a new generation of younger poets, including Plath and Anne Sexton. Bishop's influence, on the other hand, took time to make itself felt and is still something of a well-kept secret. While each of her four collections of poetry gained recognition from her peers in the form of various fellowships and prizes, this acclaim did not immediately translate into much academic interest or popular success. At the time of her death there was just a single critical book on her work, a short introductory study by the poet Anne Stevenson. Poetry readers knew her, if at all, as the author of the much-anthologised piece 'The Fish' (Bishop called it 'that damned Fish',[2] so sick was she of requests to republish it).

Much has changed since the 1980s. Bishop, rather than Lowell, is the poet new writers usually cut their teeth against. She is a favourite poet of authors as diverse as Thom Gunn and Paul Muldoon, Jorie Graham and Louise Glück, Lavinia Greenlaw and Jo Shapcott. In fact, poets have been instrumental in raising Bishop's profile, as well as providing some of the most acute and intelligent assessments of her work. Adrienne Rich's 1983 review of Bishop's *Complete Poems* is central to this. It was one of the first feminist readings of Bishop's life and art, connecting 'her experience of outsiderhood' with 'the essential outsiderhood of lesbian identity'.[3] While other poets disagreed with this assessment – notably Alicia Ostriker, who characterised Bishop in 1987 as one of those 'poets who would be ladies'[4] – it laid the groundwork for women poets' rereading of Bishop in the 1990s as a more sensual and sexual writer than had previously been thought. The poetry of Deryn Rees-Jones in England, Caítriona O'Reilly in Ireland and Sandra McPherson in America all owe something to Bishop's understated, almost invisible focus on the human body.

Seamus Heaney has also been a prominent advocate of Bishop's poetry, praising her 'ultimate fidelity to the demands and promise of the artistic event'.[5] Other poets have stressed her fascination with science (Jo Shapcott), her interest in Surrealism (Mark Ford and Jamie McKendrick), and again and again, her sense of being an exile. Eavan Boland, for instance, sees in Bishop's 'fishhouses' and 'cold springs' the index of the 'true exile, the inner émigré, who sees them for the first time and may not see them again',[6] while Tom Paulin praises her fondness for 'makeshift, temporary dwellings'[7] which he sets in opposition to the ideological dangers implicit in being rooted in one place. Michael Donaghy makes a similar point in his recognition of Bishop's 'exile' accent, which he celebrates for rejecting the two godparents of American poetry, Walt Whitman's 'yawp' and Emily Dickinson's 'centripetal concision'.[8] It is not for nothing that John Ashbery once called her 'the writer's writer's writer'.[9] She is *the* American poet to make sense to British and Irish writers, the only American poet of the last 50 or so years to be read and liked by almost all of her contemporaries.

The phenomenon of Bishop's rising reputation has been attributed to many causes. Robert Pinsky recently related it to the impersonality of her poetry, suggesting that 'hers was a pure reputation based upon the quality of her work'.[10] Other readers have been more cynical about the process of canon formation. Joseph Epstein, for example, labels Bishop a careerist, blaming her rising star on the flood of biographical information that made her work 'more penetrable and a little less impressive'[11] than it had previously seemed. While Pinsky props Bishop up as a late Modernist, Epstein denigrates her as a watered-down confessional, too shy to own up to her own autobiographical impulses. These two positions are the twin poles around which most scholarly activity now revolves. She has either to be an anti-Romantic like H. D. or Gertrude Stein, or a feminist subversive similar to Adrienne Rich or Sharon Olds. Vernon Shetley's scathing attack on the 'bizarre sentimentality' of this kind of criticism is worth invoking here.[12] He pokes fun at the way in which Bishop has become a 'kind of secular saint'[13] for both types of reader. To the Modernists she is a 'prime weapon to wield against the egotistical sublime, and the baggage of phallocracy, hierarchy, and colonialism that is now assumed to come with it'.[14] To the polemicists her life is considered somehow 'exemplary'.[15] She is *the* 'autobiographer without ego'.[16]

Perhaps poets have often been more willing than academics to embrace and describe this movement of form and focus. Free to steal and borrow across countries, cultures and languages, they do not seem as impelled as others to fit Bishop into a particular tradition or school. Her evasiveness may in fact be the reason behind their attraction to her poetry in the first place. Whatever the case, the sudden rise in Bishop's fortunes has no real precedent. How has she replaced Lowell so quickly in poets' affections? When did she suddenly become such an imitated poet?

The truth of course is that Bishop was always admired among her peer group. Her first book of poems, *North & South* (1946), was ecstatically reviewed by Randall Jarrell, Robert Lowell and Marianne Moore, all of whom were (or would soon become) close friends and regular correspondents. Influence works both ways. The Bishop–Moore relationship, for example, is one of the most keenly debated literary friendships in the twentieth century. Lorrie Goldensohn, Victoria Harrison and others see Moore's role as that of a mentor-mother to Bishop's student-daughter. According to this interpretation, Bishop learnt how to become a poet from Moore, having grown up as a writer in the older poet's shadow. More recent readings have stressed Bishop's independence. They see the infamous quarrel over Moore's editing of Bishop's poem, 'Roosters', as bringing to the surface tensions that had always been present. Some even see Bishop as providing Moore with poetic examples to follow in her later writing. Whatever one borrowed from the other, their friendship clearly nourished each other's ego, providing Moore with the sense that her poems were still being read by a younger generation and Bishop with the reassurance that she could actually write.

Critics and readers often discover forgotten or undervalued poets through the praise and recommendation of their more famous friends. For most of Bishop's life, readers heard of her through Moore. She was admired for coming after Moore, for writing in what critics saw as a continuation of the elder poet's Modernist style. The reverse is now the case, in spite of the recent publication of Moore's *Complete Poems*. Moore is now known as the addressee of Bishop's poem, 'Invitation to Miss Marianne Moore', or as the eccentric subject of her memoir, 'Efforts of Affection'. One can only imagine both poets' feelings of amusement at this state of affairs, conscious as both were of the vagaries of literary taste. Poets, Bishop once wrote, do not have to worry about being 'consistent'. They can borrow and steal from whomsoever they please. The truth about influence in this particular case is surely somewhere in between both versions. Bishop's borrowings were probably less than has been assumed, just as

Moore's were probably greater. If contemporary poets are imitating Bishop now, they are perhaps imitating a little of Moore through her, just as Moore in turn famously appropriated all kinds of other writings. I make this point not to underestimate Moore as a presence in Bishop's poetic life or to undermine Bishop's own influence on contemporary poets today, but to show how fugitive a subject influence remains.

The same ambiguities that characterise the Bishop–Moore relationship are also at work in regard to Bishop and Lowell. Revising the way we think about their relationship revises the way we think about the development of American poetry in general. For many years, the idea of a breakthrough narrative dominated discussion of post-war American poetry. According to the majority of critics, Lowell was *the* main transitional figure in this story. His single collection of poems, *Life Studies*, was credited for bridging various disparate schools and traditions under one banner: the Age of the Confessional (or, as Bishop nicknamed it, the 'School of Anguish'). This type of narrative obviously privileges certain kinds of poetry above others. In terms of Confessional poetics, the life of the poet becomes the main object of attention. Political engagement is preferred to political detachment, sexual frankness to sexual reserve. There is no place in this kind of tradition for poets like Bishop who always made a point of effacing their lives from the work.

Since Lowell's death, the extent to which he himself borrowed and stole from other artists has become more apparent. In the case of *Life Studies* in particular he relied on both the practical advice and writing example of Bishop who was then in Brazil and had just published her autobiographical story, 'In the Village' (1953), and her second collection of poems, *A Cold Spring* (1955). Lowell versified the former as 'The Scream' and was inspired to begin work on autobiographical prose himself. His own childhood memoir, '91 Revere Street', is very different in tone from 'In the Village', though both address the role of childhood memories in forming the artist. 'Skunk Hour', one of the signature poems in *Life Studies*, is also a tribute of sorts to Bishop's poem, 'The Armadillo'. Bishop thus freed Lowell to write autobiographically rather than the other way round. This undermines the idea that Lowell is responsible for a sudden breakthrough in American poetry or even that there was one at all.

This does not mean that Bishop is the secret founder of the Confessional poets or a more autobiographical poet than she looks, but it certainly questions the need to define poetry according to neatly defined categories and schools that the majority of writers revise and sidestep. The grandiloquence of Lowell is obviously no longer fashionable. In the 1960s and 1970s, he straddled American poetry like a Colossus, absorbing and reshaping whatever historical or personal crisis passed his way. Yet there is a less egotistical side to his work that reminds us of Bishop. The same could be said of the way her reputation has shifted. For most of her career, the conversational intimacy of her poems and stories was misunderstood for a lack of intellectual scope. This same voice is now being read for its nuanced take on the ethics of travel and the politics of gender. Yet there remains a trace of egotism to her work that is reminiscent of Lowell. Perhaps we simply need to read poems one by one, noting their debts to other poets as they occur, not as a means to make one writer more important or original that the rest, but to show how each of us passes on knowledge to the future.

There are of course differences between Bishop and Lowell. Whereas the majority of Bishop's poems float free of conventional categories, Lowell's nearly always operate within recognisable boundaries and registers. In the 1940s, he is an ornate, rather precious stylist, in the 1950s a personal chronicler, in the 1960s and 1970s a plunderer of his own and other people's lives. Bishop went through more phases than she probably completed poems. Aside from the debts to Moore and Lowell already noted, she was an avid reader of baroque prose and metaphysical poetry. Her favourite poets were Charles Baudelaire, George Herbert and **Gerard Manley Hopkins**. In her teens and twenties, she went through a **W. H. Auden** phase; in Key West she imitated **Wallace Stevens**, in New York and Washington **Dylan Thomas**; in Brazil she translated poems by Manuel Bandeira, Carlos Drummond de Andrade and Vinícius de Moraes. It is this aspect of Bishop's writing above all that has made her such an influential figure among contemporary poets. There are many different Elizabeth Bishops to imitate. This was the case even before her biography became better known. John Ashbery was an early fan of her writing, praising the Surrealism of her early books. May Swenson, a close friend and another lifelong correspondent, was drawn to the erotic nature of her middle phase. Even **Philip Larkin** had heard of Bishop (though he was a little surprised that she had heard of him).

With relatively few exceptions, our best poets still have time for Bishop and time to write about their readings of her work. She can be heard through their poetry in various registers and voices as her own poems echo with the words of old friends and numerous loved writers from the past. In the words of 'In the Waiting Room', she shows us the 'similarities' that hold 'us all together', the poetic forms and traditions that continue to bring different sorts of poet and reader into the same room, all falling over and into the same book.

References

1. **Bishop, Elizabeth** (1994) 'In Prison', *Collected Prose*. Chatto & Windus, p. 190.

2. **Bishop, Elizabeth** (1996) *One Art: The Selected Letters*. Pimlico, p. 515.

3. **Rich, Adrienne** (1987) 'The Eye of the Outsider: Elizabeth Bishop's Complete Poems, 1927–1979' in *Blood, Bread and Poetry: Selected Prose, 1979–1985*. Virago, p. 127.

4. **Ostriker, Alicia** (1987) *Stealing the Language: The Emergence of Women's Poetry in America*. The Women's Press, p. 54.

5. **Heaney, Seamus** (1988) 'The Government of the Tongue' in *The Government of the Tongue*. Faber and Faber, p. 101.

6. **Boland, Eavan** (1988) 'An Un-Romantic American', *Parnassus: Poetry in Review*, Vol. 14, No. 2, pp. 85–86.

7. **Paulin, Tom** (1990) 'Dwelling Without Roots: Elizabeth Bishop', *Grand Street*, No. 35, Summer, pp. 94–95.

8. **Donaghy, Michael** (2000) 'The Exile's Accent', *Metre* 7/8, Spring/Summer, pp. 182–183.

9. **Ashbery, John** (1977) 'Second Presentation to the Jury', *World Literature Today*, 1, Winter, p. 8.

10. **Pinsky, Robert** (1994) In Gary Fountain and Peter Brazeau (eds), *Remembering Elizabeth Bishop: An Oral Biography*. University of Massachusetts Press, p. 351.

11. **Epstein, Joseph** (1995) 'Elizabeth Bishop: Never a Bridesmaid', *The Hudson Review*, Vol. 48, No. 1, Spring, p. 41.

12. **Shetley, Vernon** (1995) 'On Elizabeth Bishop', *Raritan*, Vol. 14, No. 3, Winter, p. 160.

13. Ibid. p. 161.

14. Ibid. p. 160.

15. Ibid. p. 152.

16. Ibid. p. 161.

Further reading

Anderson, Linda and Shapcott, Jo (eds) *Elizabeth Bishop: Poet of the Periphery*. Bloodaxe Books, 2002.

Diehl, Joanne Feit, *Elizabeth Bishop and Marianne Moore: The Psychodynamics of Creativity*. Princeton University Press, 1993.

Dodd, Elizabeth, *The Veiled Mirror and the Woman Poet: H.D., Louise Bogan, Elizabeth Bishop, and Louise Glück*. University of Missouri Press, 1992.

Goldensohn, Lorrie, *Elizabeth Bishop: The Biography of a Poetry*. University of Columbia Press, 1992.

Harrison, Victoria, *Elizabeth Bishop's Poetics of Intimacy*. Cambridge University Press, 1993.

Kalstone, David, *Becoming a Poet: Elizabeth Bishop with Marianne Moore and Robert Lowell*. Hogarth Press, 1989.

Lowell, Robert, *Collected Poems*. Faber and Faber, 2003.

Moore, Marianne, *The Poems of Marianne Moore*. Faber and Faber, 2003.

Roberts, Neil (ed.) *A Companion to Twentieth-Century Poetry*. Blackwell, 2001.

Travisano, Thomas, 'The Elizabeth Bishop Phenomenon' in Margaret Dickie and Thomas Travisano (eds) *Gendered Modernisms: American Women Poets and their Readers*. University of Pennsylvania Press, 1996, pp. 217–244.

Zona, Kirsten Hotelling, *Marianne Moore, Elizabeth Bishop, and May Swenson: the feminist poetics of self-restraint*. University of Michigan Press, 2002.

Contributor: Jonathan Ellis

Australian literature

'Who am I when I am transported?' Postcolonialism and Peter Carey's *Jack Maggs*

Whereas Great Expectations *is largely the story of Pip's struggle to grasp the true meaning of the concept 'gentleman', the bulk of Carey's reworked narrative is devoted to the convict's attempt to work out his relationship to both his native and adopted lands.*

Bernice M. Murphy

In *Decolonising Fictions*, theorists Diana Brydon and Helen Tiffin claim that **postcolonial** writers create texts that 'write back' against imperial fictions and question values taken for granted by the once dominant Anglocentric discourse of the imperial epicentre. In *Jack Maggs* the process of 'writing back' is well illustrated. As in *Wide Sargasso Sea* by **Jean Rhys**, which 'writes back' to Charlotte Brontë's *Jane Eyre*, the colonial 'other' character from a canonised Victorian novel becomes the principal figure in a modern 'decolonising' text and the peripheral reaches of empire become of central importance.

In *Jack Maggs* (1997) Australian novelist **Peter Carey** reconfigures the plot of Dickens's classic *Great Expectations* so that the marginalised (colonial) convict figure becomes the narrative focus. By filtering the experiences of the exiled convict through a postcolonial lens, Carey creates a text that pays homage to Dickens, yet simultaneously questions the values at the heart of the source text's imperialist discourse.

As Brydon and Tiffin point out, Anglocentrism refuses colonised territories the right to their own identities, assuming instead that they are merely engulfable parts of the imperial centre. Thus, in *Great Expectations*, Australia functioned not as a coherent, cohesive nation, but rather, as an 'off-stage' peripheral location where characters await their return to the 'on-stage' action of the imperial centre, London. Carey tackles this trend head on, by writing a novel that seeks 'non-repressive alternatives to imperialist discourse' (Brydon and Tiffin) and which refuses to privilege the metropolitan centre over the colonial margins.

At the heart of Carey's reconfiguration of imperialist discourse lies the complex relationship between returned convict Jack Maggs – the modern reworking of Magwitch, one of Dickens's most memorable characters – and up-and-coming writer Tobias Oates. Significantly, Oates bears more than a few biographical similarities to

Charles Dickens. For instance, like Dickens, Oates has a feckless, indebted father, an unhappy marriage, a fascination with mesmerism, and a fierce desire to make his name 'not just as the author of comic adventures, but as a novelist who might one day topple Thackeray himself' (Carey, p. 43).

By having Oates, a fictionalised Charles Dickens figure, exist in the same imaginative space as Jack Maggs, Carey is able to explore not only the questions left unanswered by the source text but also the complex relationship between character and creator.

The relationship between Oates, soon to become the Empire's greatest living writer, and Maggs, the marginalised colonial figure, is one that parallels the manner in which the literary potential of the Imperial colonies was mined by Victorian writers. Oates, who fancies himself a 'cartographer of the criminal mind', takes an interest in Maggs not because he feels sympathy for the fugitive's plight but because he sees literary potential in his story.

Under the pretence of easing Jack's painful facial tics, Oates employs mesmerism in order to gain access to the darkest corners of the convict's mind. He even equates his invasion of Maggs's past and mind with his exploration of the seedy streets of London: 'What a puzzle of life exists in the dark little lane ways of this wretch's soul, what stolen gold lies hidden in the vaults between his filthy streets?' (Carey, p. 90).

Oates is simultaneously fascinated and repulsed by Maggs, drawn to the convict by his interest in human nature and the literary potential of the man's life, yet always fearful in his presence. He wants to use Maggs in the same way that the majority of Victorian writers (including Dickens) used the Colonies, as a blank imaginative space, a territory to be filled with fictional representations emanating from the metropolitan centre. The comparison is borne out by Maggs himself who, while writing to his feckless ward Henry Phipps (the counterpart of Dickens's character Pip), states, 'I have left a blank map for you and you have doubtless filled it with your worst imaginings' (Carey, p. 238).

Just as the Colonies typically functioned in the economy of the Victorian novel as a convenient starting and ending point, so too is Maggs's brutal and unhappy life used by Oates as a mere fictional device. Carey provided Maggs with the means to resist imaginative categorisation; when he realises that his trust in Oates has been sorely abused, Maggs explodes in anger at the appropriation of his life story for a sensational novel ('The Death of Maggs') about convict life. But Oates is unable to understand Jack's reaction to the appropriation of his dead fiancée's character and name in the first draft of the novel: 'I write that name Jack, like a stonemason makes the name upon a headstone, so that her memory may live for ever. In all the empire, Jack, you could not have employed a better carver' (Carey, p. 280).

Furthermore, when Oates's life collapses around him with the discovery of his adulterous affair with Lizzie Warriner, he 'heaps up all his blame' on Jack Maggs and creates a brutal fictional counterpart (Carey, p. 326).

Throughout the novel Maggs is identified with the Colony of Australia, often being referred to as 'the Australian', thereby underscoring the fact that his decade in exile has had a far greater effect on his development than his previous existence in England. As with Magwitch, Australia has served both as his prison and as a means of creating a prosperous new life (Litvack, p. 8). Following his pardon from the New South Wales prison gangs, Maggs became so successful that he was able to build a brick mansion, have a street named after him and anonymously raise a poor English boy to gentlemanly status. Like Magwitch, his Dickensian counterpart, Maggs seeks to renew his acquaintance with the 'son' whose ascent in society he has surreptitiously financed. However, whereas *Great Expectations* is largely the story of Pip's struggle to grasp the true meaning of the concept 'gentleman', the bulk of Carey's reworked narrative is devoted to the convict's attempt to work out his relationship to both his native and adopted lands.

Jack's compulsion to return to England despite the threat of arrest and imprisonment, and to justify his dark past, can be seen as an illustration of the question asked by Alan Lawson who, discussing the problem of national identity as a structural problem, defines the ultimate colonial question as, 'Who am I when I am transported?' Lawson's rhetorical question arises from the situation of the individual transported from the imperial centre to a peripheral outpost, 'where the climate, the landscape and the native inhabitants did little to foster any sense of continuity, where the sense of distance, both within and without, was so great that a new definition of self – metaphysical, historical, cultural, linguistic and social – was needed' (Lawson, p. 169).

This need to search for a definition of self is why Maggs, who has not yet formulated a stable identity in Australia, returns to London despite the risk. Jack rejects his Australian family in order to risk all in the search for an arrogant young man who cares nothing for his benefactor but who, nevertheless, represents his naïve idea of an English gentleman.

In *Great Expectations* the convict who returns to metropolitan space from his exile in the Australian Colony is punished with death, despite his rehabilitation, for his transgression of imperial space. Australia therefore functions in that text as a place where transformations of fortune and character are permitted, but from which the transported individual can never return.

Significantly, in Carey's decolonising text, Jack Maggs is allowed to return to the distant continent, happily marry the servant girl Mercy Larkin, prosper in business, live to a ripe old age and father 'five further members of "that race"' (Australians) (Carey, p. 327). However, Jack's happy ending comes about only when he finally accepts that there are alternatives to the repressive imperialist discourse of Britain and ceases to privilege the abusive land of his birth over the adopted land that has given him so much.

Similarly, Peter Carey uses his postcolonial reworking of Dickens's canonised text as an opportunity to explore the complex relationship between the imperial centre, the colonised nation and the writer who fictionalises that relationship, and as a chance to privilege the colony and the colonised individual over the seat of Empire and its citizens.

References

Brydon, Diana and Tiffin, Helen (1992) *Decolonising Fictions*. Aarhus: Dangaroo.

Carey, Peter (1997) *Jack Maggs*. London, Boston: Faber and Faber.

Lawson, Alan (1995) *Who Am I When I Am Transported? The Post-Colonial Studies Reader.* London and New York: Routledge.

Litvack, Leon (1999) *Dickens, Australia and Magwitch, Part 1: the Colonial Context.* Dickensian 95.1, 7–32.

This essay, by Bernice M. Murphy, was originally published on 'The Imperial Archive', a project supervised by Dr Leon Litvack, School of English, Queen's University Belfast at www.qub.ac.uk/en/imperial/imperial.htm

British and Irish literature

A survey of British fiction and poetry of the twentieth century

A radical break from the literary traditions established in the Victorian era took place in the 1920s, with the rise of **Modernism**, bringing with it a type of literature which, with its experimental approaches to form, style and language, would have been unthinkable to nineteenth-century readers and writers. The roots of Modernism were already present at the end of the nineteenth century, showing themselves, for example, in the alienation and uncertainty experienced by Marlow, the central character of *Heart of Darkness* (1902) by Joseph Conrad, in the emphasis on the inner psychological complexity of characters seen in the novels of Henry James, and in the highly individual poems of **Gerard Manley Hopkins**, published posthumously. But it took the shock of the First World War to bring the movement fully into being.

In the first few years of the century there was little in the way of radical change. In Ireland **W. B. Yeats**, who would later become one of the leading lights of Modernism, was playing a leading role in the **Irish Cultural Revival** and shocking audiences with controversial productions at the Abbey Theatre in Dublin, but in England Victorian ideals and values persisted beyond the death of Queen Victoria in 1901 into the Edwardian and Georgian eras.

The British Empire was powerful, its rulers being confident of their right to rule over a quarter of the world's population and, particularly in India, more alert to the threat from Russian expansion than to the possibility of internal revolt – a picture reflected in *Kim* (1901) by Rudyard Kipling. In 1924 King George V proudly demonstrated, at the great Empire Exhibition, that he could send a telegram around the world, passing exclusively through British territory. But the desire of the colonised countries for independence was growing stronger year by year and England's status as a colonial power was about to diminish.

Poetry

From an unremarkable start at the beginning of the century, one can see English poetry gradually gathering new momentum. The tendency runs towards a more democratically accessible sort of verse, i.e. a type of poetry that deals with themes close to the concerns of ordinary people and draws its imagery from our immediate surroundings.

The first quarter of the century saw the rise of the so-called **Georgian Poets**, whose writing coincides roughly with the early years of the reign of George V (1910–36).

These poets wrote lyrical poetry often concerned with nature and largely ignoring social issues. Among the best known are Rupert Brooke, Edmund Blunden, Walter de la Mare and Edward Thomas. John Masefield, Poet Laureate from 1930 to 1967, was writing at the same time, although not usually thought of as a 'Georgian Poet' himself.

The political and human catastrophe of the First World War (1914–18) profoundly shook the complacency about the stability, power and progress of England which had carried over from the Victorian era. Previously held attitudes were undermined as the full horror of the war penetrated the British psyche.

The horrors of war were brought home in the poems of the **War Poets**, the best known being Siegfried Sassoon (1886–1967) and Wilfred Owen (1893–1918). They themselves were soldiers who fought at the front. Sassoon was wounded twice, and Owen returned to the front after having been injured, only to be killed a week before the Armistice of November 1918. They were friends and both thoroughly convinced of the incompetence of those in charge, whom they saw as being responsible for the senseless waste of young lives. (see: *Does it Matter?* by Sassoon and *Anthem for Doomed Youth* by Owen.) The Poet Laureate from 1913 to 1930 was Robert Bridges, best remembered for his long poem *The Testament of Beauty* (1929) and for publishing the influential work of **Gerard Manley Hopkins** (1844–89) in 1918.

By the second decade of the century the great American poet **Ezra Pound** (1885–1972) and his disciple, **T. S. Eliot** (1888–1965), were already at work writing a more intellectual, challenging poetry, showing evidence of wide reading. Their poems were full of references to earlier authors, including the Ancients, as well as to Oriental writers and thinkers. They attempted to avoid an affectedly poetic style and lyrical manner, seeking to write in natural language, incorporating everyday idioms. Pound, along with some American poets living in London, and influenced, as was Yeats, by the French **Symbolist** poets, founded the **Imagist** movement and was later associated with **Vorticism**. With Pound and Eliot and the later poems of Yeats, we see the flowering of Modernism in poetry.

Pound, Eliot and Yeats had a strong influence on the poets of the 1930s. **W. H. Auden** (1907–73), Cecil Day-Lewis (1904–72) (Poet Laureate 1967–72), Stephen Spender (1909–95) and Louis MacNeice (1907–63). But the latter group felt that the urgency of the political situation in Europe made a poetry of obscure academic references and formal experimentation redundant. They introduced political (anti-fascist) subject matter and imagery drawn from the increasingly mechanised world of aeroplanes, factories and electricity power stations. The title of one of Spender's poems, *The Pylons*, earned the group the nickname the **Pylon Poets**. Some of this influence can even be seen in the later work of Yeats.

The year 1934 saw the publication of the first volume of poetry by the fiery Welsh poet, playwright and short story writer **Dylan Thomas** (1914–53). His highly original and individual poetry was characterised by striking imagery and musicality, in which words made their impact through their sound as much as through their meanings. Poems by Thomas were included in an anthology produced by a group of poets who called themselves the **New Apocalypse**. The main poets behind this movement and a similar movement from around the same time, known as the **New Romantics**, were Henry Treece (1911–66), George Granville Barker (1913–91), W. S. Graham

(1918–86), J. F. Hendry (1912–86) and Dorian Cooke, and their aim was to react against the politically orientated realist poetry of the 1930s by drawing inspiration from mythology and the unconscious.

The Poet Laureate from 1972 to 1984 was Sir John Betjeman (1906–84), whose first volume of poetry, *Mount Zion*, was published in 1933. He became well known for his light, often satirical verse which celebrated a nostalgic view of England, and for his writing on English architecture. He was knighted in 1969.

The 1960s saw the rise of the **Liverpool Poets**, Adrian Henri (1932–2000), Roger McGough (1937–) and Brian Patten (1946–) and their popularisation of live poetry readings. Their poetry was influenced by the explosion in pop music which was taking place at the time, much of it, especially that of The Beatles, coming from Liverpool; by **pop art**; and by the mood and attitudes of the 'Swinging Sixties'. Also influenced by the American **Beat poet**, **Allen Ginsberg**, their poetry, being written to be read aloud, was colloquial in style, loose in form, and dealt with the everyday life of ordinary people.

The more dominant and longer-lasting figures in poetry of the mid and later twentieth century, however, had made their mark before the 'Pop' trend set in. They were **Philip Larkin** (1922–85), Thom Gunn (1929–2004) and **Ted Hughes** (1930–98), who was Poet Laureate from 1984 to 1998. In the 1950s Larkin and Gunn were loosely associated with **Kingsley Amis**, D. J. Enright, John Wain and other poets under the name of **The Movement**. The Movement poets were opposed to the free form and emotional tone of poets such as Dylan Thomas and W. S. Graham, and wrote poetry which was intellectual, witty and carefully crafted.

In the later 1950s and 1960s several major poets reacted against the stance taken by The Movement poets and banded together under the name of **The Group**. They were **Ted Hughes**, Peter Porter, George Macbeth, Peter Redgrove and Alan Brownjohn.

A poet who came to prominence in the 1970s and 1980s was Tony Harrison (1937–). One of his main themes is the sense of having become distanced from his Northern working-class roots by his education. Harrison has written verse drama for opera and plays, but is probably best known for his poem 'V', which was televised in 1987.

Among the many poetic voices prominent at the end of the twentieth and beginning of the twenty-first centuries, two of the best known are Irish poet **Seamus Heaney** (1931–), who won the Nobel Prize for Literature in 1995, and the Glasgow-born Carol-Ann Duffy (1955–). Heaney's work draws upon his background in rural Northern Ireland, Irish history and mythology, and the political troubles of Northern Ireland. Duffy's poems offer social criticism, frequently in the form of dramatic monologues which give voice to a wide variety of characters, particularly female characters through the ages.

The novel

At the beginning of the twentieth century the scientific and fantastic novels of H. G. Wells (1866–1946) were highly popular. Wells wrote an early form of science fiction, with visions of space travel and things to come, for example *The Time Machine* (1895) and *The War of the Worlds* (1898). There were social novels, too, dominated by the work of John Galsworthy (1867–1933). His *Forsyte Saga* series (1906–21) depicts the upper-middle-class scene, with a central figure, Soames Forsyte, intent on accumulating material wealth. Wells also wrote social novels, such as *The History of Mr Polly* (1910), which looked at the lives of the lower-middle classes. Arnold Bennett (1867–1931) won great fame with his novels about the people of the Potteries in the North-West Midlands. At this time, however, there was no question of the literary scene being dominated by a school or a movement based on social realism; Rudyard Kipling (1865–1936) was enjoying great popularity with his stories and poems about India, his novel *Kim*, and his animal fables and books for children, such as *The Jungle Book*.

The American novelist Henry James (1843–1916), who lived a large part of his life in England, and whose novels frequently explored the theme of the differences between European and American culture, had produced many of his novels before the turn of the century, but three of the greatest appeared in the early twentieth century: *The Wings of the Dove* (1902), *The Ambassadors* (1903) and *The Golden Bowl* (1904).

One of the most significant English novelists of the twentieth century was D. H. Lawrence (1885–1930), a miner's son, who began by writing about the society of his birthplace in Nottinghamshire, but, influenced by his reading of Freud, moved on to delving into the heart and soul of Man, and other topics, political, social and sexual in his major novels such as *Sons and Lovers* (1913), *The Rainbow* (1915) and *Women in Love* (1921).

At around the same time novels were being published by a very different writer, Aldous Huxley (1894–1963), who was from a famous family of intellectuals. He wrote amusing but biting social satires, such as *Crome Yellow* (1921) and *Antic Hay* (1923). His best-known novel is *Brave New World* (1932), which may be termed a Dystopia, i.e. the opposite of a Utopia, because it describes a future society as it should not be. In *Brave New World Revisited* (1958) he showed that many of his prophecies had come true, and in *Island* (1962) he looked at a potentially Utopian society in the South Seas. In a sense *Brave New World* foreshadows the publication of a later novel, by George Orwell (1903–50), *Nineteen Eighty-four* (1949), a depressing depiction of an all-powerful state and the negation of individuality.

The second decade of the twentieth century saw the emergence of a new way of writing, known as stream of consciousness, with the works of the Irish author James Joyce (1882–1941), the twentieth century's greatest innovator in literature, and Virginia Woolf (1882–1941), the most prominent literary figure in what was known as The Bloomsbury Group. Their aim was to show what was going on inside people's minds, instead of focusing on outward behaviour and external reality. Such prose was perceived as more difficult to comprehend and was not very widely read outside intellectual circles. Its influence, however, has been enormous and can be seen in much of the literature which followed. While Pound, Eliot and Yeats represent the flowering of Modernism in poetry, Joyce and Woolf represent its full emergence in the novel. Joyce's novel *Ulysses* (1922) is frequently cited as the greatest novel of the twentieth century, and his *Finnegan's Wake* (1939) is sometimes said to mark the height, and end, of Modernism. **E. M. Forster** (1879–1970), best known for *A Passage to India* (1924), was acquainted with Virginia Woolf and loosely associated with The Bloomsbury Group.

William Golding (1911–93) published his best-known novel, *Lord of the Flies*, in 1954. It presents a pessimistic view of human nature through the story of a group of schoolboys whose attempts at social organisation, after being stranded on a desert island, descend into anarchy and violence. Golding was awarded the Nobel Prize for Literature in 1983 and was knighted in 1988.

Up to 1953 literature continued to be thought of as 'sensitive' writing of a refined and intellectual nature, but a change of direction took place with the advent in the early 1950s of the **Angry Young Men**, a movement which took place in both fiction and drama. One of the first was John Wain (1925–44) with his novel *Hurry On Down* (1953), about a graduate who finds the classical training he received at university useless in the outside world, so that he slides down the career ladder into increasingly mundane jobs. This humorous novel, and others in the same vein, represented an attack on the unworldly intellectualism and protected existence of socially privileged people such as those who formed The Bloomsbury Group. The attack came from down-to-earth young men, associated not so much with the traditional universities, the ancient seats of learning such as Oxford and Cambridge, but with the new 'red-brick' universities of industrial cities such as Liverpool and Manchester. The 'red-brick' university environment was the setting of *Lucky Jim* (1954), the best-known novel by **Kingsley Amis**.

A clear trend had been marked by the large number of novels by young men from the industrial North of England. Of these, **Alan Sillitoe** (1928–) is notable, with his novel *Saturday Night and Sunday Morning* (1958) and short story *The Loneliness of the Long-Distance Runner* (1959), as are Stan Barstow (1928–) with *A Kind of Loving* (1960) and John Braine (1922–86) with his *Room at the Top* (1962). Of all who go by the label of Angry Young Men, Sillitoe is the angriest. The message 'Down with the ruling classes' can be heard clearly in his novels. The type of hero, or **anti-hero**, he creates is the sort of person who is honest to himself, or at least tries to be, but whose gorge rises at the thought of having to conform to the expectations of the establishment.

The late 1950s saw the publication of three novels by Colin MacInnes (1914–73), known as 'The London Trilogy': *City of Spades* (1957), *Absolute Beginners* (1959) and *Mr Love and Justice* (1960). These novels look at London in the late 1950s, particularly the working-class youth culture and its interaction with the culture of West Indian immigrants.

Not all the writers of the era were men or working-class, however. Important women writers included intellectuals such as Dublin-born **Iris Murdoch** (1919–99) and **Doris Lessing** (1919–) born in Iran and raised in South Africa. Murdoch was a philosophy lecturer as well as a novelist, and philosophical, religious and ethical themes run through her novels. Lessing takes a radical **feminist** stance in many of her novels, and has also written poetry, short stories and travel works.

Another woman writer who achieved moderate fame in the 1960s was Nell Dunn (1936–). Her collection of short stories, *Up the Junction* (1963) and novel *Poor Cow*

(1967) both dealt with the harsh lives of working-class London women and, like many of the novels of the Angry Young Men, were both filmed.

Angus Wilson (1913–91) and Malcolm Bradbury (1932–2000) were two of the best-known British writers of the post-war era. They both wrote satirical novels and explored a variety of narrative techniques. They are also known for having set up a creative writing course at the University of East Anglia. Ian McEwan (1948–) attended Wilson and Bradbury's course and made his debut on the literary scene in the 1970s with two books of short stories, *First Love Last Rights* (1975) and *In Between the Sheets* (1978), and his first novel – *The Cement Garden* (1978). These early works displayed an interest in macabre and perverse themes – *The Cement Garden*, for example, describing the moral decline of a group of children who live alone after burying the corpse of their mother in the cellar. Many more novels followed and he won the Whitbread Book Award in 1987 for *The Child in Time* and the Booker Prize in 1998 for *Amsterdam. Atonement* (2002) also won high critical acclaim.

Melvyn Bragg (1939–), well known to the British public as a radio and TV presenter, is also a prolific novelist, having published novels regularly since the 1960s. Many of his stories draw on his Cumbrian roots and are set against a background of English social history. Bragg has won awards for *Without a City Wall* (1968), *The Hired Man* (1969) and *The Soldier's Return* (1999). He has published non-fiction books about the English language and was made a life peer in 1998.

Martin Amis (1949–), the son of Kingsley, began publishing in the 1970s. One of his most highly praised novels is *Money* (1984), which is concerned with the materialism and greed of England, particularly London, in the 1980s. Michael Bracewell (1958–) also captured the social climate of London in the 1980s. Other writers of note from this era are Julian Barnes (1946–), Will Self (1961–) and the Anglo-Indian Hanif Kureishi (1954–).

The 1970s and 1980s saw a turning away from the down-to-earth realism of the Angry Young Men with the work of British writers who incorporated fantastic unreal elements of **magic realism** into their work. Magic realism was a device employed by Latin American writers such as Jorge Luis Borges, Gabriel Garcia Marquez and Isabel Allende, and can be seen in the work of British writers such as **John Fowles**, **Angela Carter**, **Jeanette Winterson** and the Anglo-Indian **Salman Rushdie**. Rushdie was one of the most prominent writers of the 1980s and 1990s, winning a Whitbread Award and Booker Prize. He had to spend almost a decade living in hiding after Iranian Muslim clerics pronounced a death sentence on him for allegedly insulting Islam in his novel *The Satanic Verses* in 1989. In 1998 the Iranian government finally announced that it would not seek to enforce the fatwa.

Feminism, and the wider exploration of gender roles, has been an important theme, being relevant to varying degrees to the work of **Virginia Woolf**, Margaret Drabble, **Doris Lessing Jean Rhys**, **Angela Carter**, **Jeanette Winterson** and others.

Two broad strands can be distinguished in fiction since the Second World War: traditional and **postmodernist**. Traditional novelists, content with the novel form inherited from the Victorians, include such writers as Somerset Maugham (1874–1965), **Graham Greene** (1904–91) and Sir Angus Wilson (1913–91), while postmodernists would include **John Fowles**, **William Golding**, Anthony Burgess and **Samuel Beckett**.

Postmodernist writers do not accept traditional realism or the Modernist experiments such as the stream of consciousness of **James Joyce** and **Virginia Woolf** as adequate representations of reality, and try to change the perspective of the reader in a number of ways. One way is to disrupt the narrative illusion and remind the reader that he is reading a work of fiction. In *The French Lieutenant's Woman*, for example, John Fowles addressed the reader directly and offered two alternative endings. Fowles's novel also juxtaposed the perspectives of two time periods, the nineteenth and twentieth centuries, as did the highly acclaimed academic, critic and novelist A. S. Byatt (1936–) (sister of Margaret Drabble) in her Booker Prize-winning novel *Possession* (1990). Other postmodernists have turned away from realism by writing 'fabulations' or fables, examples being *Lord of the Flies* by William Golding and *A Clockwork Orange* by Anthony Burgess.

The postmodern attitude also involved looking outwards, beyond the traditional boundaries of 'English Literature' to the literature of other countries, and this theme points us towards another development in literature of the late twentieth century and back to a subject we mentioned at the beginning – the Empire.

Kipling's novel *Kim* (1901) presented a complacent view of the strength of the British Empire. One might even call it a blinkered view, since it dismissed the Great Mutiny of 1857 as 'a madness', apparently oblivious to the tide of resentment against British occupation which was stirring in India. Conrad's *Heart of Darkness* (1902) presented a more worrying and ambivalent picture of the morality and sustainability of the Empire, and the picture had changed radically by 1924, for in spite of this being the year of the great Empire Exhibition, this was also the year of the publication of E. M. Forster's novel *A Passage to India*, which caused controversy with its openly critical portrayal of the Raj and its suggestion that perhaps it was time for the British to think about getting out of India altogether.

Nationalist ambitions in the colonised countries had become pronounced after the First World War and even more so after the Second World War, and throughout the 1940s, 1950s and 1960s the Empire steadily broke up as country after country achieved independence. Writers in those countries began to produce a literature in English, and it is now more appropriate to talk of 'literature in English' than 'English literature' because some of the most important writing in English is being produced by these **postcolonial** writers.

Contributors: Ian Mackean, Bram de Bruin

The poetry of the First World War

Of the varied literary output of the twentieth century, few kinds of writing have been more influential in shaping cultural memory and public imagination than the poetry of the First World War. The mythic landscape of the Western Front, pitted with shell holes and rent by fire, is one of the most enduring images of the modern era. The two major protagonists in this theatre were Siegfried Sassoon, the conscientious objector turned bitter satirist, and Wilfred Owen, the quintessential war poet with his 'pity of war'. Just a few weeks before his death on 4 November 1918, Owen wrote to Sassoon about his 'excellent little servant Jones':

[...] the boy on my side, shot through the head, lay on top of me, soaking my shoulder, for half an hour.

Catalogue? Photograph? Can you photograph the crimson-hot iron as it cools from the smelting? This is what Jones's blood looked like, and felt like. My senses are charred.[1]

Horror, pity, maternity and a diffuse eroticism are fused and confused in that 'half an hour' of bodily contact. Owen's letter points to a paradox that lies at the heart of First World War poetry: the world's first industrial war brutalised the male body on an unprecedented scale, but also fostered the most tender and intimate of human bonds. The 'human' element regularly, powerfully drowns the formal qualities of the verse: First World War poetry seems to be one of the last refuges of the inviolate bond between literature and life, largely resistant to the 'linguistic turn' in postmodern critical thought, as if the free play of signs would undermine its terrible and tragic reality.

The war poetry we have inherited consists of a powerful but relatively small body of pacifist verse – in fact antiwar poetry – by 'soldier-poets': men such as Owen, Sassoon, Ivor Gurney, Edmund Blunden, Edward Thomas, Robert Graves and Isaac Rosenberg, all of whom went through the line of fire. Personal experience stamps these poems as 'authentic', yet, with the exception of Sassoon, few of these men published their verse during the war years. Owen saw only five of his poems in print during his lifetime; the first edition of his *Poems* was prepared only after his death, by Sassoon in 1920.

During the actual war years, far more popular was the now discredited but still powerfully romantic figure of Rupert Brooke. Well connected and strikingly handsome, feted at both Rugby and Cambridge, Brooke might be said to have forged the very concept of 'soldier-poet' in December 1915 with his five patriotic 'war sonnets': 'Peace', 'Safety', two called 'Dead' and 'The Soldier'. The opening line of Brooke's 'Peace' – 'Now, God be thanked Who has matched us with His hour' – catches the early mood of optimism of August 1914 following the declaration of war. On Easter Sunday 1915, the Dean of St Paul's incorporated 'The Soldier' in his address to the congregation, noting that 'the expression of a pure and elevated patriotism has never found a nobler expression'. With Brooke's early death on a troopship bound for Gallipoli, burial on the romantic island of Skyros, and the glowing valediction that appeared in *The Times* over the initials of Winston Churchill, he passed into myth, crystallising the heroic ideals, fears and pathos of a war-time England. Published in 1915, Brooke's *1914 and Other Poems*, together with his *Collected Poems*, sold 300,000 copies over the next decade.

At the time, war poetry poured out from civilian writers in newspapers, periodicals and anthologies. Prominent literary figures such as Thomas Hardy, the Poet Laureate Robert Bridges, Rudyard Kipling, Edmund Gosse, Laurence Binyon and John Masefield all felt compelled to write about the war, many of them for patriotic or propaganda purposes. In August 1914 about a hundred poems a day arrived at *The Times*; three anthologies of war poetry appeared in September 1914, another in November, twelve in 1915, six more in 1916. Catherine Reilly's bibliography of First

World War poetry lists over 3000 works by 2225 English poets; of these, only 417 were in uniform and around 532 were women.[2] More than half of the war poetry was thus produced by male civilians and a quarter by women, including prominent poets such as Margaret Postgate Cole, Rose Macaulay and Jessie Pope. What needs to be grasped is that English poetry of the First World War is a huge and varied corpus of works, drawing on various cultural, linguistic and literary traditions, though, with time, the focus has tended to rest on a handful of 'soldier-poets'.

In spite of the overwhelming emphasis on 'experience', the poetry of the trenches is not of virgin birth. In his seminal work *The Great War and Modern Memory* (1975), Paul Fussell has documented the active literary milieu among the middle-class officer-poets whose works have come to define trench poetry: it was a remarkably 'literary' war. Sassoon writes, 'I didn't want to die – not before I had finished *The Return of the Native* anyhow'; in the trenches, Owen was reading *Gitanjali* by the Indian poet **Rabindranath Tagore** while sitting in a pillbox; and Blunden enjoyed Edward Young's *Night Thoughts on Life, Death and Immortality*.[3] War poetry is dense with literary allusions: the *Oxford Book of English Verse* would be a regular item in the haversacks of these public-school officer-poets. Trench poetry thus developed not only out of the terrible experience of modern warfare but also through a constant negotiation with earlier genres, traditions and poets. Owen's 'Strange Meeting' derives its title from Shelley's *The Revolt of Islam*, while the idea of an underworld encounter, reminiscent of Dante's *Inferno*, provides a brilliant framework to explore certain polarities that came to structure the experience of war: life and death, friend and enemy, love and hate, poet and murderer. Too much emphasis on 'war realism' or mere echo-hunting, however, tends to obscure the psychological complexity and linguistic density of the best of First World War verse. Consider, for example, Owen's 'Dulce et Decorum est' – the title of which is an allusion to Horace's patriotic sentiment, known to most contemporary schoolboys:

> Bent double, like old beggars under sacks,
> Knock-kneed, coughing like hags, we cursed through sludge,
> Till on the haunting flares we turned our backs
> And towards our distant rest began to trudge.
> Men marched asleep. Many had lost their boots
> But limped on, blood-shod. All lame went; all blind;
> …
> Gas! Gas! Quick, boys! – An ecstasy of fumbling
> Fitting the clumsy helmets just in time;
> But someone still was yelling out and stumbling,
> And flound'ring like a man in fire or lime…
> Dim, through the misty pains and thick green light,
> As under a green sea, I saw him drowning.
> …
> In all my dreams, before my helpless sight,
> He plunges at me, guttering, choking, drowning.
> …

If you could hear, at every jolt, the blood
Come gargling from the froth-corrupted lungs,
Obscene as cancer, bitter as the cud
Of vile, incurable sores on innocent tongues, –
My friend, you would not tell with such high zest
To children ardent for some desperate glory,
The old Lie: Dulce et decorum est
Pro patria mori.[4]

This is the quintessential example of the First World War poetry of protest, in which the broken male body in all its horrific sensuousness is evoked to challenge the abstract language of honour and patriotism. In this poem, we seem to find a validation of Owen's famous manifesto: 'My subject is War, and the pity of War. The Poetry is in the pity.'[5] Poetry is thus refashioned as testimony, as missives from the trenches. In a letter to Susan Owen about *Dulce*, he writes, 'Here is a gas poem, done yesterday (which is not private, but not final). The famous Latin tag [from Horace, Odes, III.ii.13] means of course *It is sweet and meet to die for one's country Sweet! and decorous!*[6] Though the gas attack is at the centre of the poem, Owen here combines three separate experiences – a night march, a gas attack and war trauma, or 'shell shock' as it was known – along almost a single bodily axis for maximum effect. At the level of literary form, the lyric with its intimacy and intensity is used to counter the heroic claims of the epic.

In the manuscript version of the poem, Sassoon underlined the ambiguous word 'ecstasy' and put a question mark beside it. How can a horrific gas attack, rooted in historical reality, produce ecstasy? Is Owen hinting at a perceptual confusion at a moment of panic, or is there a validation, in the trenches of the First World War, of Freud's dictum that 'feelings of apprehension, fright or horror' have a 'sexually exciting effect'?[7] Yet, in a poem that explores the complicity of language in violence – of Horace's Latin phrase – the word 'ecstasy' may stand, consciously or unconsciously, for narrative perversity itself: poetic language, asked to describe violence, touches itself through alliteration and echo (ecstasy/clumsy/misty) and experiences exhilaration, replacing real-life horror with linguistic pleasure. For the excessive music of the rhyme in the second stanza, conspiring with labials and sibilance – oddly reminiscent of the decadent verse of Swinburne – creates a sonic realm that obscenely mimes, if not aestheticises, the spectral space created around the charred body through its own jerky, erratic movements as it flounders in fire or lime. Owen, thus criticising the sweetness of Horace's dictum, seems to be trapped insidiously in the sweetness of the lyric form itself. But at the same time, the compulsive rhyme of the present continuous suggests the eternal now of the trauma victim, the shell-shocked soldier doomed to repeat past experience as a perpetual present.

It is important to note that the focus of the poem moves from the actual gas attack and its victim to its traumatic effect on the narrator: 'in all my dreams'. The First World War was the first war in which mental breakdown played a substantial role. Fear, anxiety and horror, as well as the repressive regime of Victorian masculinity, often led to a complete mental collapse among the soldiers on an unprecedented scale. The most common symptoms were stammering, muteness, nightmares, limping, even paralysis. According to the distinguished neurologist W. H. R. Rivers, who treated Sassoon at Craiglockhart War Hospital, soldiers repressed painful sights and sounds which would later haunt them as dreams and nightmares. Owen suffered from war trauma or shell shock and was admitted to Craiglockhart Hospital in Scotland. In 'Dulce et Decorum est', the war protest is voiced not only through horrific sensuous details but also through the traumatised subjective consciousness of the narrator.

Owen, through a strange manipulation of sound, seduces us into moments from which we would otherwise flinch: moments when limbs are sliced off ('limbs knife-skewed', 'shaved us with his scythe'), the flesh is ripped apart ('ripped from my own back/In scarlet shreds', 'limped on, blood-shod') or the mouth starts bleeding ('I saw his round mouth's crimson deepen as it fell').[8] This eroticisation of violence continues from early decadent pieces such as 'Has Your Soul Sipped' and 'Greater Love', and 'The Kind Ghosts' – a poem written or revised as late as July 1918. The perverse aestheticisation often conflicts with the overt political aim of the war poems, creating a strange tension. Even in a poem as avowedly political as 'Disabled' – a bitter satire about a war veteran who lost all his limbs – the language ends up aestheticising the leg wound: 'And leap of purple spurted from his thigh.'[9] Pity is there in ample measure, but there is also a distinct visceral thrill. The strange power of his verse lies in this combination of music, eros and real-life violence. Pain and theatricality define the body, hovering around moments when we no longer know where the *is* ends and the *was* begins. In 'Asleep' the 'aborted life' is still 'quaking', while in 'Futility' the limbs are 'still warm'. A rigorous Protestant ethic, suppressed homoeroticism, the influence of decadent writers and hatred of warfare combine to produce these tortured, masochistic images: the male body that cannot be touched, legally or morally, can only be mutilated in Owen's poetry.

The friendship between Owen and Sassoon at Craiglockhart – given a fresh lease of life by Pat Barker in *Regeneration* (1991) – is one of the most poignant and productive friendships in English literary history. Sassoon, the gallant soldier-officer, had gained notoriety in July 1917 when, disenchanted with the way the war was being conducted, he drafted his letter of 'wilful defiance of military authority' which gained attention in the House of Commons and received a good deal of publicity from the press. He was forcibly admitted to the war hospital at Craiglockhart, primarily to avoid his being court-martialled. Owen, the shy provincial boy with a war stammer, immediately fell under the spell of this good-looking, upper-class rebellious officer who was also a published poet. While Sassoon checked the decadent excesses of Owen, his own poetry remained largely confined to the bitter, ironic mode, intended to expose the horrors of warfare, as in 'Counter-Attack':

> And naked sodden buttocks, mats of hair,
> Bulged, clotted heads slept in the plastering slime.
> And then the rain began, – the jolly old rain![10]

Describing himself as a 'visual' poet, Sassoon's poems were largely trench portraits with realism and satire as his twin weapons. Often published in the *Cambridge*

Magazine, one of the few anti-war journals of the day, Sassoon's war poems such as 'Attack', 'Fight to a Finish', 'Their Frailty' and the harsh 'Glory of Women' were calculated to shock civilians out of their apathy. What made them immensely powerful and effective during the war – descriptions of soldiers floundering in the mud, a mother being fed lies about her son's death, the indifference of the military authority or 'Bart gone syphilitic' – sadly dates many of these poems. While drawing, like Owen, on Victorian poetic conventions – metre, rhyme, syntax – Sassoon however was one of the earliest poets (along with Charles Hamilton Sorley) to forge a new language to convey contemporary violence. His regular use of colloquialism such as 'splosh', 'muck', 'bloody' introduced a new language which reconfigured the male body from the aestheticism of decadent verse into the messy corporeality of trench reality. Highly respected as a gallant officer and known as 'Mad Jack' for his suicidal offensives into No Man's Land, he suffered a severe shoulder injury but came back to the trenches for the 'love' of comrades: 'Love drove me to rebel./Love drives me back to grope with them through hell.'[11] This 'love' would no doubt have held particular poignancy and intensity for a self-confessed homosexual like Sassoon whose elegy 'The Last Meeting', written for his friend David Cuthbert Thomas, remains a powerful evocation of homoerotic longing and loss.

In the trenches of the First World War, the relationships between men changed profoundly: mutilation, mortality, darkness and the constant strain of bombardment led to a new level of intimacy and intensity. Men nursed and fed their friends when ill, bathed together, and during the long winter months wrapped blankets round each other. The theme of comradeship is central to war writing, informing some of the best-known prose works such as Erich Maria Remarque's *All Quiet on the Western Front* (1929), Robert Graves's *Goodbye to All That* (1929) and Sassoon's *Memoirs of an Infantry Officer* (1930). A new world of physical tenderness and intimacy was opening up in which pity, thrill, affection and eroticism merged into each other, defying the established civilian categories of gender and sexuality. First World War poetry, in order to evoke the world of camaraderie, almost obsessively dwells on such moments of physical intimacy: 'I clasp his hand' (Brooke, 'Fragment'), 'sides/full-nerved, still warm' (Owen, 'Futility'), 'the warm passionate lips/of his comrade' (Read, 'My Company') or 'My comrade, that you could rest/Your tired body on mine' (Nichols, 'Casualty'). This use of sensuous, aestheticised language to describe same-sex intimacy was the result not just of private passion – as partly with Owen and Sassoon – but also of a conjunction of class politics, literary history and the culture of mourning. Jon Silkin's enormously popular *The Penguin Book of First World War Poetry* (1979) shows that what has come to be regarded as First World War poetry was largely built on the works of public-school officer-poets, many of whom had, as Graves writes, 'sentimental and chaste' but distinctly 'homosexual' crushes at school.[12] Moreover, from the aestheticism of Walter Pater to the pastoral poignancy of *A Shropshire Lad* by A. E. Housman, to the Uranian poetry of William Johnson Cory, English poetry at the turn of the century was suffused with what Fussell calls a tradition of 'warm homoeroticism' through which the youthful male body was endlessly aestheticised, idealised and eulogised.[13] Even non-homoerotic poets such as Herbert Read and Robert Nichols drew on this language to reconfigure battalions as units of love.

A very different but powerful voice is that of Isaac Rosenberg, perhaps the only working-class poet in the war canon. The son of Lithuanian Jewish immigrants and brought up amidst poverty in the East End of London, Rosenberg enlisted as a private not out of any patriotic motive but to earn money. The sense of war community that we find in Owen or Sassoon is absent in Rosenberg's verse. Instead of the angry outbursts of Sassoon or the pathos of Owen, Rosenberg's protests are articulated as complex ideas or symbols, marked by a deceptive detachment, as in 'Break of Day in the Trenches':

> Droll rat, they would shoot you if they knew
> Your cosmopolitan sympathies.
> Now you have touched this English hand
> You will do the same to a German.[14]

Immediate and sensuous, the poem is nonetheless acutely political. Rosenberg identifies himself as 'English' but the very mention of nationalities points beyond such oppositions. Racially, socially, even physically marginalised (he could enlist only in the Bantam regiment because of his short stature) throughout his life, the ultimate empathy of Rosenberg, the isolated Jewish infantryman, is for the rat, the abject, despised creature. However, by an imaginative stroke, the rat is transformed into a sophisticated, wonderfully transgressive traveller with 'cosmopolitan sympathies' which echo Rosenberg's own pacifist commitments. In an excised line from the poem, Rosenberg wrote: 'A shell's haphazard fury. What rootless poppies dropping?' Rosenberg would have been aware that 'rootless poppies' were dropping on either side of No Man's Land: Jewish poets were fighting and killing other Jewish poets (the German war poet Franz Janowitz came from immigrant Jewish parents).

Meanwhile, the rat, exulting in its freedom, flees the trenches to announce itself in the 'rat's alley' of *The Waste Land* by **T. S. Eliot**, extending the very scope and definition of war poetry; indeed, part of the impetus behind Eliot's **Modernist** classic was the death of his close friend Jean Verdenal who was killed in the war.

While the poems of Owen, Sassoon and Rosenberg have come to define the 'inner' core of First World War verse, other important soldier-poets would include Charles Sorley, Ivor Gurney, Robert Graves, Edmund Blunden, Francis Ledwidge, Ford Madox Ford, Herbert Read, Edward Thomas and David Jones. There has been a recent revival of interest in the poetry of Ivor Gurney and Edward Thomas, who are as much nature poets as war poets. A talented musician and poet, Gurney was wounded and gassed out of the war and spent the last 15 years of his life amidst misery in a mental asylum. In one of his poems he writes, 'There are strange Hells within the minds War made.'[15] Haunting and song-like, Gurney's war poems are full of quick, quiet observations about the humdrum, everyday details of military life – 'Books, cakes, cigarettes in a parish of famine' ('Laventie') or the 'Infinite lovely chatter of Bucks accent' ('The Silent One') – often informed by an almost overpowering nostalgia for his childhood Gloucestershire. Gurney was an ardent admirer of Edward Thomas who was an established literary critic and 36 years old when the war broke out. Written in England before he left for France, Thomas's 'war poetry', like

Gurney's, resists assimilation into the war canon. The war is more of an absence than a presence; evolved into a state of consciousness rather than depicted as an event, it is represented not as death or injury on the battlefield but in the way it effects, ruffles, marks the English countryside, the work of the ploughman, the nesting habits of birds; or the way flowers are strewn beneath the tree, as in 'In Memoriam (Easter 1915)':

> The flowers left thick at nightfall in the wood
> This Eastertide call into mind the men,
> Now far from home, who, with their sweethearts, should
> Have gathered them and will do never again.[16]

A married man, Thomas includes in his war elegy the plight of women, whom Sassoon and Owen so unfairly ignored or derided. His poignant lines, about the 'sweethearts' having no one to whom to give flowers, receives tragic intensity in Margaret Postgate Cole's 'Praematuri': 'We are left alone like old men; we should be dead/But there are years and years in which we shall still be young.'[17]

Women's writing of the First World War has, until very recently, been largely ignored. Unfortunately, the First World War 'woman' was conflated with Sassoon's or Graves's jingoistic version of woman, while women's wartime verse has been dismissed as patriotic and sentimental. As with men's poetry, the quality varies and there are different voices. Catherine Reilly notes, 'Women such as Mary Gabrielle Collins, S. Gertrude Ford, May Herschel-Clark and Winifred M. Letts were writing protest poetry before Wilfred Owen and Siegfried Sassoon.'[18]

At the outbreak of war, thousands of women volunteered as nurses, caring for the wounded soldiers in England, France and Mesopotamia, and many of them wrote powerfully about their experiences. For the hundreds of thousands of women left behind in England, the war was no less 'real': the war changed their lives, teaching them to survive as bereaved mothers, daughters, widows or lovers. In her memoir *Testament of Youth* (1933), Vera Brittain writes of how she lost all her male companions: her lover, her brother and her two close male friends. Even when romantic or sentimental, their works remain valuable testimony to contemporary violence while a few show a maturity and complexity that compare with the best of the male poets. Consider Margaret Postgate Cole's 'Afterwards':

> And if these years have made you into a pit-prop,
> To carry the twisting galleries of the world's reconstruction
> (Where you may thank God, I suppose
> That they set you the sole stay of a nasty corner)
> What use is it to you? What use
> To have your body lying here
> In Sheer, underneath the larches?[19]

The desolate tone is achieved partly through a complex negotiation with the genre of pastoral elegy. Instead of the harmonious assimilation of the lover into a romantic landscape (as for example in Sassoon's 'The Last Meeting'), he is imagined as a 'pit-prop'. Any idealisation or solace is denied through the reiterated question 'What use . . . ?' which has the same tragic intensity as Owen's 'Futility': 'Was it for this the clay grew tall?'

With the gradual inclusion of women's and working-class voices in the canon of First World War poetry, we are now more alert to the heterogeneity and diversity of war experience. Similarly, it is important to consider the American poetry of the Great War and the verses about the war written in English from different parts of the Empire, such as the works of the Irish poet Francis Ledwidge.

The verse of the period remains one of the most powerful means by which the memory of the First World War seems perpetually to renew itself. In a way, First World War poetry continues to be produced. Poets such as **Ted Hughes**, Michael Longley and **Seamus Heaney** were drawn powerfully to the Great War, viewing it as a complex historical process, in their different ways, through which to view the present. As fresh wars continue to wreak havoc and bring more suffering, the War Poets seem to beckon us from the past with their verse, not just to console but, as Owen envisaged, to actively 'warn'.

References

1. **Owen, Harold and Bell, John** (eds) (1967) *Wilfred Owen, Collected Letters.* Oxford: Oxford University Press, p. 581.

2. **Reilly, Catherine W.** (1978) *English Poetry of the First World War: A Bibliography.* London: George Prior Publishers, p. xix.

3. *See* **Fussell, Paul** (1975) *The Great War and Modern Memory.* Oxford: Oxford University Press, pp. 155–190.

4. **Stallworthy, Jon** (ed.) (1990) *The Poems of Wilfred Owen.* London: Chatto and Windus, p. 117. Henceforth referred to as Owen *Poems.*

5. **Owen** *Poems,* pp. 117–118.

6. **Owen** *Collected Letters,* pp. 499–500.

7. **Freud, Sigmund** (1953) 'Infantile Sexuality' in *The Standard Edition of the Complete Psychological Works of Sigmund Freud.* Volume VII. Trans. James Strachey. London: Hogarth, p. 203.

8. **Owen** *Poems,* pp. 143, 142, 155, 117, 100.

9. **Owen** *Poems,* p. 152.

10. **Sassoon, Siegfried** (1984) *Collected Poems 1908–1956.* London: Faber, p. 68.

11. **Sassoon** 'Banishment' in *Collected Poems,* p. 86.

12. **Graves, Robert** (1929) *Goodbye to All That.* Harmondsworth: Penguin. 1988, p. 23.

13. **Fussell** *Great War,* pp. 270–286.

14. **Parsons, Ian** (ed.) (1979) *The Collected Works of Isaac Rosenberg*. London: Chatto and Windus, p. 103.

15. **Walter, George** (ed.) (1996) *Ivor Gurney*. London: Everyman, p. 60.

16. **Thomas, R. George** (ed.) (1978) *The Collected Poems of Edward Thomas*. Oxford: Oxford University Press, p. 58.

17. **Reilly, Catherine** (1997) *The Virago Book of Women's War Poetry and Verse*. London: Virago, p. 22.

18. Ibid, p. viii.

19. Ibid, p. 22.

Further reading

Fussell, Paul, *The Great War and Modern Memory*. Oxford: Oxford University Press, 1975. Some of the other exciting works on First World War poetry are: Jon Silkin, *Out of Battle: Poetry of the Great War* (1972; Basingstoke: Macmillan, 1998), Desmond Graham, *The Truth of War: Owen, Blunden and Rosenberg* (Manchester: Carcanet, 1984), Adrian Caesar, *Taking it Like a Man: Suffering, Sexuality and the War Poets* (Manchester: Manchester University Press, 1993), Simon Featherstone, *War Poetry: An Introductory Reader* (London: Routledge, 1995) and Jon Stallworthy, *Anthem for Doomed Youth: Twelve Soldier Poets of the First World War* (London: Constable, 2002). Also see Trudi Tate, *Modernism, History and the First World War* (Manchester: Manchester University Press, 1998).

Contributor: Santanu Das

The Bloomsbury Group (c. 1905–41)

The Bloomsbury Group, whose best-known member was **Virginia Woolf**, had a considerable influence on literature, philosophy and art during and after the First World War. They were rebels in that they paid little heed to the social, religious or political norms of their day, and were experimental and innovative in their work, in which they had a serious purpose: to redefine the parameters of art and literature. The painters and art critics among them were influential in bringing modern art to England, while in literature, reacting against the formal rigidity and **realist** approach of the nineteenth century, Virginia Woolf became a key figure of **Modernism**.

E. M. Forster said he considered the group to be the only genuine movement in English civilisation. The members of the Bloomsbury Group were, however, true Europeans. They travelled widely on the Continent and beyond, and they loved the art and literature of Europe, which must be seen as the background to their own work. They saw the shadow of Fascism falling over the countries they knew and loved, and tried to warn the world.

In both world wars, Bloomsbury Group member Bertrand Russell, the philosopher, came to public attention as a pacifist, and after the Second World War, as a member of CND. Russell exerted a strong influence on the group's attitude to war and politics.

The group originally consisted of a few close friends who, from around 1905, began to meet for debate and discussion in the Bloomsbury area of London. The prime movers were the four children of Sir Leslie Stephen and his wife Julia, who had been brought up in the sternly literary family household at 22 Hyde Park Gate. The two boys, Thoby and Adrian, went to Trinity College, Cambridge, but the girls, Vanessa and Virginia, were, as was usual for the time, educated at home and helped to entertain their father's friends there after the death of their mother. When Sir Leslie died in 1904 the family house was sold and the children of the family moved into 46 Gordon Square, Bloomsbury, a more bohemian area of London.

Vanessa held informal meetings on Thursday evenings and when Thoby left Cambridge he and his friends began to attend. Several of them had belonged to the exclusive Cambridge society The Apostles, who considered themselves to be seekers after truth and were some of the keenest and liveliest minds of their generation. The Apostles was founded in the 1820s and membership was by election only, making it, to an extent, a secret society. It was a forum for discussion and the pursuit of truth, where candour and wit had equal place. Members included graduates as well as undergraduates, so a certain gravitas balanced the livelier tone of the younger members.

Bloomsbury Group members Leonard Woolf, Lytton Strachey, Saxon Sydney-Turner, Thoby Stephen and Clive Bell had been contemporaries at Trinity College, Cambridge. All were close friends, though only the first three became Apostles, Leonard Woolf being the first Jew to be elected to the society. Bertrand Russell was also an Apostle, while Thoby Stephen and Clive Bell were part of another group, The Midnight Society, founded by Bell, whose members met at midnight on Saturdays to read aloud plays and discuss them.

Leonard Woolf, in a volume of his autobiography, mentions how he and Strachey developed a method of questioning their friends in what he terms a 'third-degree psychological investigation', the theory being that this in-depth knowledge of each other would greatly improve personal relationships. This kind of interrogation was carried over into the later discussions of the Bloomsbury Group, and the constant probing of feelings and motives both united the group and made its members intimidating to outsiders.

Woolf cites G. E. Moore, philosopher and fellow of Trinity, as the one great man he had ever known. The ideas expressed in Moore's *Principia Ethica* (1903), with their emphasis on the importance of human relationships and the pursuit of beauty in all its forms, were to become the guiding principles of the Bloomsbury Group. John Maynard Keynes, the economist who studied at King's College, Cambridge, called *Principia Ethica* the bible of his generation's new religion. Bertrand Russell published his influential *Principles of Mathematics* in the same year. Both men were later to become involved with the Bloomsbury Group, as was E. M. Forster, who was also at King's College at this time and an Apostle. Though only ever a peripheral member of Bloomsbury, his comments on Virginia Woolf's novels were eagerly awaited and always considered seriously by her.

The gatherings held at Gordon Square were presided over by Vanessa and Virginia. The participants were all aesthetes, as well as being concerned with feelings and the expression of feelings. Their outlook was serious, but their conversation was light-hearted and, on occasion, even bawdy. They were of good social standing, but had turned their backs on their conventional backgrounds, and their idiosyncratic views and lifestyles later led them to be ostracised by more conventional members of society – something which delighted them and bound them more closely together.

Thoby Stephen died in 1906, at the age of 26. A year earlier, Clive Bell, who counted Thoby as his first real friend, had proposed to Vanessa but she had refused him. However, two days after her brother's death, Vanessa agreed to marry Bell, who, though not an intellectual, had a passion for art and literature.

Leonard Woolf, who fell deeply in love with Virginia, came from a liberal Jewish family. He was an outstanding writer with a clear, lucid style and a man of very deep feelings. After leaving Cambridge, he went to Ceylon, where he served in the Colonial Civil Service for seven years, during which time he developed a keen dislike of imperialism. On his return, Woolf renewed his acquaintance with his Cambridge friends and shared a house, 38 Brunswick Square, also in Bloomsbury, with Virginia and her brother Adrian, Duncan Grant and J. M. Keynes, who several years later married Lydia Lopokova, a dancer with the Russian Ballet.

In August 1912 Leonard Woolf and Virginia Stephen were married, even though she had previously been unsure of her feelings for him. With the second Bloomsbury marriage, the Stephens and their Cambridge friends were forever firmly intertwined. As time went on, more erotic complications were to follow, as the loving friends of the Bloomsbury Group displayed more startling and diverse patterns of relationships and behaviour.

The two Stephen sisters were always very close, and although Virginia was at first upset by her sister's marriage to Clive Bell, the deep affection between them rarely wavered. From childhood, they had mapped out their separate paths, Vanessa to be an artist and Virginia to be a writer, and they remained true to their early ambitions.

The Stephens, Woolf and Strachey all came from large families of intellectuals, but as members of 'Old Bloomsbury', as Leonard Woolf later called them, they turned their backs on the established order and, in a sense, made their own family of highly gifted individuals. Desmond MacCarthy, the critic, and his wife, Molly MacCarthy, were also considered members of 'Old Bloomsbury' though they lived in Chelsea, and it was Molly MacCarthy who in 1910 wittily named the group 'The Bloomsberries'.

'Old Bloomsbury' came into being around 1910 and it could be argued that it ended in 1918. But according to Leonard Woolf, it transformed into 'newer Bloomsbury' which, in addition to the original members, included Vanessa Bell's children, Julian (who was killed in the Spanish Civil War), Quentin and Angelica, and David Garnett, a successful novelist, who later married Angelica. At about this time, Bloomsbury became more closely involved with Lady Ottoline Morrell and her guests at Garsington, which were to include **Aldous Huxley**, **D. H. Lawrence**, **Katherine Mansfield** and John Middleton Murry, the critic, whom Mansfield married in 1918.

Virginia Woolf is undoubtedly seen as the member who had the greatest influence on modern literature. Her literary output was tremendous, and the intensity and precision of her writing was highly regarded. Woolf's genius came at a high price. She had always been mentally unstable and she suffered her first nervous breakdown at the age of 13, precipitated by her mother's death. Subsequently, the completion of her novels was often followed by episodes of madness. It is believed that in her later childhood and indeed her whole life she was also adversely affected by her domineering father and by the incestuous advances of her half-brother, George Duckworth.

As Virginia Stephen she received several proposals of marriage and although she was fond of Leonard Woolf, whom she finally agreed to marry, she stated that she felt no physical attraction for him. However, the marriage was a successful one and even though Virginia had several more breakdowns and eventually committed suicide, Leonard Woolf was her support and guide throughout her life and helped her to remain creative even at her lowest moments.

At the time of her marriage, Virginia Woolf was already working on her first book, *The Voyage Out*, which was published in 1915. This novel and her second, *Night and Day* (1919), were both conventional in form, but her later major works, such as *Jacob's Room* (1922), *Mrs Dalloway* (1925), *To The Lighthouse* (1927) and *The Waves* (1931), changed the course of fictional writing. In those works Woolf left behind the traditional form of the novel to explore the tenets of **Modernism**, whereby character and plot are of less importance than the flow of thought passing through the minds of the main protagonists. The narrative technique became known as **stream of consciousness** and had its roots in **Freudian** psychology. In this way, Woolf's writing was allied to the novels of **James Joyce** and the poetry of **T. S. Eliot** (who praised her work) and **Ezra Pound**. The Cambridge critic F. R. Leavis, however, was sternly antagonistic to what he saw as the elitism and self-indulgence of the Bloomsbury Group, exemplified in Woolf's writing.

Orlando (1928) explored the androgyny of the human psyche set against a keenly felt historical background and was inspired by the affair between Virginia Woolf and Vita Sackville-West, whose love for her family home, Knole, and sexual ambiguity provided the twin themes of the book.

Virginia Woolf kept a journal for most of her life and often used it to analyse the aims and pitfalls of her work in progress. Her habit was to plan each novel for many months before she began to write. But she wrote to a rhythm, not a plot, and the poet in her was often more important than the novelist. Her last novel, *Between the Acts*, was published posthumously in 1941, four months after her suicide. The novel is divided not into chapters but into a series of scenes, and in her diary Woolf said she was planning to present a rambling but unified whole. F. R. Leavis considered the novel to be formless and of extraordinary pointlessness, while others found it baffling but beautiful.

Between the Acts is set on a June day in 1939, in a remote English village. The history of England is told satirically in a village pageant in the grounds of a big house, the pageant itself becoming part of the narrative. In the last scene of the pageant, 'Present Time', the actors, who are the people of the village, hold up mirrors so that the audience see themselves. Perspectives shift throughout the novel, the reader often sharing the **point of view** of the village audience. The last speech is interrupted by the sound of military aircraft. After the pageant the family of the house sit alone, in darkness. The last line of the novel is: 'Then the curtain rose. They spoke.'

Woolf was to speak no more through her fiction. Fearing another bout of madness, on a day in March 1941 she walked through her garden at Monk's House and drowned herself in the River Ouse.

Virginia Woolf had always been an accomplished essayist and *A Room of One's Own* (1929) and *Three Guineas* (1938) have become important landmarks in the development of **feminist** literature. They call for women to claim their own literature and proclaim to the world of masculine writers that they have only been held back from achieving their true literary potential by the confining circumstances of their lives.

In *Three Guineas* Woolf makes her points in the light of the political situation of the time, commenting on the diverse battles being fought by socialists, pacifists, anti-fascists, Jews, Irish rebels and feminists, urging them to unite their efforts in a common cause. Also, returning to a theme she had explored in *Orlando*, she deals with a statement made by Coleridge – that a truly great mind is androgynous.

Three Guineas had very mixed reviews and was castigated by Q. D. and F. R. Leavis, who continued to dislike what they saw as Woolf's elitism. Their critical standpoint, which held sway through the 1940s and 1950s, was that art should be separated from politics – a point of view which was anathema to the Bloomsbury Group.

Woolf's books were published by the Hogarth Press, which was started by Leonard Woolf in a very modest way in 1917, with a printing press on the kitchen table at Hogarth House, Richmond, where the Woolfs were then living. The Woolfs taught themselves the basics of printing and the venture was conceived as a therapeutic activity for Virginia, although it later became another source of stress. The Hogarth Press printed some of the most interesting and seminal writing of the time, including T. S. Eliot's 'The Waste Land', and the novels of E. M. Forster.

Vanessa Bell was closely involved with the Hogarth Press, illustrating many of her sister's books and designing dust-covers for them. She was a serious artist whose paintings, in particular her portraits and colourful abstracts, helped to revolutionise English art in its move from Post-Impressionism to Modernism. She was strongly influenced by her relationship with her husband, and by Clive Bell, Roger Fry and Duncan Grant. She often painted the same subjects as Grant, and the interior of Charleston, the house in Sussex which she bought in 1916, was decorated by the pair in a way that has come to typify the artistic exuberance of the Bloomsbury Group.

The art critic and painter Roger Fry, as well as being a great influence on Vanessa Bell, was instrumental in bringing the art and ideas of Post-Impressionism to England. His first exhibition, 'Manet and the Post-Impressionists', took place in London in 1910 and was followed by a similar one in 1912. Virginia was as impressed by Fry as her sister was, calling him the plume in Bloomsbury's cap.

Clive Bell, in his book *Art* (1914), emphasised the importance of significant form, which he defined as relations and combinations of lines and colours, and Fry was passionately interested in the twin aesthetics of art and poetry, a juxtaposition which typified the many-stranded thinking of the Bloomsbury Group. Fry was very supportive of Virginia Woolf's writing and she, in turn, was to write his biography.

The painter Duncan Grant, who lived with Vanessa Bell from 1916 to her death in 1961, was a co-director with her and Fry of the Omega Workshops and was a great influence on all the members of the group. In fact the group was once humorously defined as 'people all in love with Duncan Grant'. He himself was the cousin of Lytton Strachey, who had been deeply infatuated with him in 1905–6.

The biographer Lytton Strachey was to become one of the most important members of the Bloomsbury Group. He came from a family of eccentrics and was indeed eccentric himself. Physically weak and very tall and thin, he cut an odd figure, but after an unhappy childhood, the small circle of intimate friends he had made at Cambridge gave him confidence. Strachey was living with his mother in the early days of Bloomsbury, but often returned to Cambridge in an attempt to re-ignite the excitement of his undergraduate days. As well as his strange appearance, later accentuated by a red beard, Strachey had an odd and very individual way of speaking and his speech patterns and high-pitched tones were sometimes copied by other members of the circle.

Strachey craved success as a writer and published his first book, *Landmarks in French Literature,* in 1912. It was an important work, but received little critical attention. It was his next book, *Eminent Victorians* (1918), that brought him both fame and notoriety. The four Victorian worthies, Cardinal Manning, Florence Nightingale, Thomas Arnold and General Gordon, were given no respect in Strachey's biographical essays, and the book's iconoclastic wit brought its writer acclaim. It was followed by the well-constructed and elegantly written *Queen Victoria* (1921). *Elizabeth and Essex* (1928) was composed in a more highly charged style and the protagonists were portrayed in a Freudian light. Although these books contained inaccuracies and biased judgements, they heralded a new kind of biographical writing, by which the Bloomsbury Group itself was later evaluated, in the wealth of critical writing that it generated.

Strachey also sought love, sometimes homo-erotic, sometimes platonic, but always with a passionate intensity. Although he had had several homosexual affairs at Cambridge, he actually proposed to Virginia Stephen before Woolf returned from Ceylon. The proposal was hastily retracted, however, to the relief of both parties.

Strachey fell in love with a variety of artists, among them Duncan Grant, Henry Lamb and, most importantly, Dora Carrington. Carrington, although she married Ralph Partridge after a series of affairs, including one with the artist Mark Getler, lived with Strachey in a *ménage à trois* in his house, Tidmarsh, in Berkshire. Her feelings for Strachey were so deep that she killed herself a few weeks after his death in 1932.

Charleston, home of Vanessa Bell from 1916, and later Monk's House, which became the home of the Woolfs in 1919, had taken the Bloomsbury Group to Sussex, and both houses became important to the group. Charleston, in particular, has become a centre of artistic excellence and is now a place of pilgrimage for all lovers of the Bloomsbury Group.

The Bloomsbury Group survived two world wars, and most of its members were conscientious objectors or pacifists. During the First World War the former were able to work on a farm near Charleston and at Garsington Manor, Oxfordshire, the home of Lady Ottoline Morrell and her MP husband, Philip.

Lady Ottoline, who had an affair with Bertrand Russell, was closely involved with the Bloomsbury Group but was never entirely accepted by them. In their treatment of her they showed the most unpleasant aspects of their group psyche which so infuriated D. H. Lawrence. They were willing to accept her lavish hospitality but were reluctant to take her seriously as an intellectual equal. Lady Ottoline was, indeed, no intellectual, but the group were only too happy to bite the hand that fed them so generously, making fun behind her back of her increasingly eccentric behaviour.

Today, as in their own time, the Bloomsbury Group are either loved or loathed. Whatever one's opinion, they cannot be ignored. They continue to inspire biographers, artists and film-makers and their influence on the literature, art and thought of the twentieth century cannot be denied.

Selected works:

Virginia Woolf Novels: *The Voyage Out* (1915); *Night and Day* (1919); *Jacob's Room* (1922); *Mrs Dalloway* (1925); *To The Lighthouse* (1927); *Orlando* (1928); *The Waves* (1931); *Flush* (1933); *The Years* (1937); *Between the Acts* (1941). Essays: *A Room of One's Own* (1929); *Three Guineas* (1938). Journals and letters.

Leonard Woolf Novel: *A Village in the Jungle* (1913); Autobiography in five volumes (1960–69).

Lytton Strachey. *Landmarks in French Literature* (1912); *Eminent Victorians* (1918); *Queen Victoria* (1921); *Elizabeth and Essex* (1928).

Further reading

Gadd, David, *The Loving Friends*. The Hogarth Press, 1974.

Holroyd, Michael, *Lytton Strachey and the Bloomsbury Group*. Penguin, 1971.

Holroyd, Michael, *Lytton Strachey: A Biography*. Penguin, 1971.

Hussey, Mark, *Virginia Woolf A–Z*. Oxford University Press, 1995.

Lee, Hermione, *Virginia Woolf*. Chatto and Windus, 1996.

Contributors: Margaret Tarner, Ian Mackean

British writers of the 1930s

The leading British writer of the 1930s was **W. H. Auden** and closely associated with him were four other writers of significance: Christopher Isherwood (1904–86), Stephen Spender (1909–95), Louis MacNeice (1907–63) and Cecil Day-Lewis (1904–72). They began writing during a turbulent period in European history, encompassing the Spanish Civil War and Hitler's rise to power in Germany, and feeling a need to respond made their left-wing political views central to their work. They were influenced in literature by the **Modernist** writers, in politics by **Karl Marx** and in psychology by **Sigmund Freud**.

Documents released from the National Archives in November 2003 showed that Auden, Spender and especially Day-Lewis were under the surveillance of MI5 and

MI6 before the Second World War. Day-Lewis came to MI5's attention after adding his name to an anti-war manifesto in 1933. His mail, including a cheque he sent as a donation to the Communist Party of Great Britain, was subsequently intercepted and photographed, and when he and Spender attended a Paris conference of the Society of International Authors, MI5 sent a brief to MI6 which included the passage:

> Like his close associates Stephen Spender and W. H. Auden, Day Lewis is an intellectual communist, but of the three he is definitely the most convinced and practical party man, the others, as you know, being communists of a highly ideal-istic and literary brand.[1]

Christopher Isherwood collaborated with Auden on three plays, *The Dog Beneath the Skin* (1935), *The Ascent of F6* (1936) and *On the Frontier* (1938), which used a variety of dramatic techniques to explore political and psychological themes. They also collaborated on an account of their journey to China, *Journey to a War* (1939), and in the same year emigrated to the United States, subsequently taking on US citizenship. Isherwood settled in California and became a celebrity through advancing Indian religion and homosexual rights.

Christopher William Bradshaw-Isherwood, to give him his full name, was born into a family of minor landed gentry, owners of Wyberslegh Hall in Cheshire. He met Auden at school in Hindhead and later they were at Oxford University together in the mid-1920s, although two years separated them. Both pursued their private literary interests rather than university studies, with the consequence that Auden barely managed to obtain a Third Class degree and Isherwood failed to take a degree at all.

Isherwood's first novel, *All the Conspirators*, is characterised by a conscious use of Modernist techniques, following the inner thoughts and perceptions of the characters and jumping from viewpoint to viewpoint with no omniscient narrator to function as an intermediary between the reader and characters. The novel was published in 1928 and in the same year, having graduated from Oxford, Auden visited Berlin. Isherwood followed and stayed in Germany for almost four years, teaching English, writing and translating.

During this period Isherwood met Stephen Spender, E. M. Forster and Leonard Woolf (husband of Virginia Woolf), having been introduced to the latter by Auden. He also began work on a film script and continued to write for the stage and screen throughout his literary career.

Leonard Woolf had set up the Hogarth Press with the intention of publishing modern writers, one of the first being James Joyce. Hogarth Press published several books by Isherwood, including *Mr Norris Changes Trains* (called *The Last of Mr Norris* in the USA) in 1935 and *Goodbye to Berlin* in 1939. In these novels Isherwood used a more conventional form of narration than he had in his first novels.

Isherwood had moved to the United States before *Goodbye to Berlin* appeared; he took up Hinduism and worked for the MGM film studio in Hollywood. When the USA entered the Second World War in 1941 he registered as a conscientious objector and assisted German refugees until 1943, when he returned to California. There he became closely associated with Swami Prabhavananda and Aldous Huxley, while working on the translation of Hindu texts and a film script. Another close friend was the writer Gore Vidal.

Isherwood's Berlin stories, based on his experiences in Germany during the rise to power of the Nazi party, were adapted for the stage in 1951 by John van Druten and played on Broadway as *I Am a Camera*, subsequently filmed with Laurence Harvey in 1955. Ten years later the play was readapted as a musical, *Cabaret*, staged in 1966 and filmed in 1972 with Liza Minnelli and Michael York in the starring roles.

In 1953 Isherwood met the artist Don Bachardy and became engaged in the promotion of homosexual liberation and equality. Bachardy remained with Isherwood until his death from prostate cancer at the age of 83.

Stephen Spender came from a literary family; his uncle, J. A. Spender, was a journalist and biographer, and Stephen had already determined on a literary career by the time he attended University College London in 1927. After one year he transferred to Oxford University where he met Auden, Day-Lewis, MacNeice and Isherwood. In 1928 Spender printed Auden's first small volume of poetry on a hand press, followed by a similar book of his own in 1930. Spender's poetry is characterised by a modern sensibility and social conscience, and his second book, *Poems,* 1933, contained 'The Pylons', which was taken up by the literary press as the name for the group – the **Pylon Poets**.

Spender used industrial and mechanical imagery, in contrast to the style of the **Georgian Poets**, in which the countryside was presented as an anodyne environment from which modern reality had been banished. To John Masefield, for example, the then Poet Laureate, electricity pylons did not enter into poetic vocabulary. Spender pointed out that they criss-crossed the landscape and could not be ignored. The 'lightning's danger' is not the scourge of the present but of the past; and the 'quick perspective of the future' is not only a rapid snapshot of things to come but quick in the sense of alive – unlike the dead poetry of the past and its idealised vision of the countryside, 'with its gilt and evening look'. When read aloud, one might hear the word 'guilt'; guilt perhaps for outworn certainties, self-deception and bourgeois complacency.

The word 'bourgeois' was characteristic of the vocabulary of the politically orientated writers of the 1930s, along with words such as 'revolution', 'socialism', 'progressive', 'class struggle', 'fascism' and 'imperialism'. But these young writers themselves came from the well-to-do ranks of the bourgeoisie. The Pylons march forward with the revolutionary and futuristic confidence of a Soviet propaganda slogan, such as 'Communism is Soviet power and electrification of all the country' (Lenin). But although Spender remained committed to his left-wing views, MacNeice later felt that the group's political stance was remote from reality, implying that the 'facts' of 'guns and frontiers and factories' (see below) were seen from a naïve undergraduate perspective.

From 1930 to 1933 Spender made several visits to Germany where he stayed with Christopher Isherwood, who introduced him to the German poetry of Rainer Maria Rilke and the Spanish verse of Federico García Lorca. He wrote two volumes of poetry, a verse play, short stories and a novel in the mid-1930s, and after visiting Spain, collaborated with Cyril Connolly in founding the literary magazine *Horizon* in 1939.

Like many other left-wing writers and sympathisers Spender was drawn to Spain in support of the Republican cause during the Civil War. Auden went as a stretcher-bearer and Spender went with the intention of making broadcasts in English from a Spanish radio station, but found that the station had ceased to operate.

On the outbreak of the Second World War Spender registered as a conscientious objector and served with the London Fire Brigade during the Blitz. His writing became more subjective, dealing with his own experiences and reactions to external events. He wrote his autobiography *World Within World* in 1951 and became editor of *Encounter*, an influential political and literary journal, in 1953. By the mid-1960s, however, he was questioning the finances that supported *Encounter* and resigned the editorship in 1967, believing that the money originated from a United States propaganda fund controlled by the CIA.

During the 1960s he lectured in the USA and spent a year as poetry advisor to the Library of Congress from 1965 to 1966, following which he became professor of English at University College London in 1970 and professor emeritus in 1977. He also founded *Index on Censorship*, an organisation dedicated to assisting writers living under repressive political regimes. His work was recognised with a knighthood in 1983.

Shortly before his death, Spender accused the novelist David Leavitt of having reproduced material from his autobiography *World Within World* without permission. This led to a law suit and considerable publicity in *The New Yorker* and other literary journals. Spender remained in the literary news until his end.

Louis MacNeice was born in Belfast, Northern Ireland, the son of a Protestant clergyman, and grew up in Carrickfergus, Co. Antrim. At Marlborough College he met influential friends – Anthony Blunt, who subsequently became a spy for the Soviet Union, and John Betjeman, who later became Poet Laureate. At Oxford University he studied Classics and produced his first volume of poetry, *Blind Fireworks*, in 1929, which shows the strong influence of left-wing thought.

McNeice's poetry has a wry quality and lacks the magisterial references of Auden, perhaps because MacNeice was truly a Classical scholar and possessed a degree of plain common sense denied to Auden. In his poem 'The Suicide' he captures the directness of Greek tragedy, without ostentatious display of learning, and translates it into a twentieth-century idiom.

During the 1930s he taught Classics at Birmingham University, where he married. Later he moved to Bedford College London after separation from his wife. He accompanied Auden on a trip to Iceland, after which they jointly wrote *Letters From Iceland* in 1937. The following year he went to Spain with Anthony Blunt. He continued to write poetry and translations from the Greek.

In spring 1939 he lectured in the United States and visited Auden in New York. At the outbreak of war in Europe he attempted to enlist in the British army but was refused on medical grounds. He then returned to the United States and remained there until December 1940 when he crossed the Atlantic in a troop ship in order to take up an appointment with the BBC.

His first broadcast on 15 February 1941 was *Word From America*, modelled on the reports of the influential American broadcaster Edward Murrow. He continued to work at the BBC for the remainder of his life, writing many radio plays, until he contracted a cough and chill while making acoustic recordings in a Yorkshire mine shaft. Heavy drinking had undermined his frail health and viral pneumonia was not immediately diagnosed, with fatal consequences. He died at the age of 55.

Like the others, MacNeice took a firm left-wing stance in his early poetry, but by the end of the Second World War his ideas had changed and he came to regard the poetry of social commitment as a pretence.

> If the war made nonsense of Yeats's poetry and of all works that are called 'escapist', it also made nonsense of poetry that professes to be 'realist'. My friends had been writing for years about guns and frontiers and factories, about the 'facts' of psychology, politics, science, economics, but the fact of war made their writing seem as remote as the pleasure dome in Xanadu. For war spares neither the poetry of Xanadu nor the poetry of pylons.
>
> [*The Poetry of W. B. Yeats*]

Cecil Day-Lewis is not as well remembered as the other writers of the 1930s, despite having been Poet Laureate for the four years prior to his death, and is omitted from the *New Penguin Book of English Verse* (2001). Perhaps his poetry lacks memorability or he led too respectable a life. He was a communist in 1930 but a grand establishment figure 40 years later, by which time he had five children by two wives and a mistress (one of the sons being the famous actor, Daniel Day-Lewis) and enjoyed a steady income from his side-line in writing detective stories.

The son of a Protestant clergyman, he grew up in London and showed considerable academic ability which won him a scholarship to Wadham College, Oxford. His first volume of poetry, *Beechen Virgil,* appeared in 1925 and gained him the attention of Auden, with whom he subsequently worked on *Oxford Poetry* in 1927.

In 1928 Day-Lewis married the daughter of a public school-master and then taught in schools for the next seven years. Although he wrote and edited many books, his income at that time was barely sufficient to support his growing family and he found himself unable to pay for repairs to the roof of his cottage in 1935.

Day-Lewis's solution to his poverty was to write a detective story under the pseudonym Nicholas Blake, creating the character Nigel Strangeways. Nineteen popular novels followed, characterised by highly literate text and intelligent plot. Long before Oxford-based Inspector Morse, the detective created by Colin Dexter, Nigel Strangeways was able to quote Blake, Keats, Clough and **A. E. Housman**.

In 1935 Day-Lewis published *Revolution in Writing* which had more to say about Marx than the Muse and trumpeted the names of Auden, MacNeice, Spender and Day-Lewis as a sort of Intellectual Revolutionary Command Council. 'A good poem enters deep into the stronghold of our emotions: if it is written by a good revolutionary, it is bound to have a revolutionary effect on our emotions, and therefore to be essentially – though not formally – propaganda.'

Day-Lewis became disillusioned with communism by the end of the Spanish Civil War and worked for the Ministry of Information from 1941 to 1945. After the Second World War he became a senior editor and then a director of the publishing firm Chatto & Windus. He linked his middle and surnames to become C. Day-Lewis, in part, so he claimed, to avoid confusion with the Oxford scholar and writer C. S. Lewis.

Day-Lewis's novel *The Beast Must Die* (1938), written under the name of Nicholas Blake, was filmed by Claude Chabrol under the French title *Que la Bête Meure* which in the English subtitled version became *Killer!* The title is from the Book of Ecclesiastes. 'The beast must die, the man dieth also, yea both must die.'

His steady literary output earned him a reputation as both poet and critic and he was Professor of Poetry at Oxford from 1951 to 1956, immediately prior to Auden. He was made Poet Laureate in 1968 on the death of John Masefield.

Day-Lewis lectured at many universities, was President of the Arts Council, Vice-President of the Royal Society of Literature, a member of the Irish Academy of Letters and an honorary member of The American Academy. After such an august career, one may wonder why his poetry is not better recollected, but the same question can be asked of John Masefield who was Poet Laureate for 36 years.

Day-Lewis died suddenly while visiting the house of **Kingsley Amis** in 1972 and was buried at Stinsford churchyard, in Dorset, close to the grave of Thomas Hardy, whom he had greatly admired.

References

1. **Norton-Taylor, Richard** (2003) 'MI5 spied on future laureate Day Lewis.' Guardian Unlimited, 14 November. www.guardian.co.uk (Accessed 16 November 2003.)

Selected works

Christopher Isherwood: *All the Conspirators* (1928); *The Memorial* (1932); *Mr Norris Changes Trains* (1935); *The Dog Beneath the Skin* – with W. H. Auden (1936); *The Ascent of F6* – with W. H. Auden (1936); *On the Frontier* – with W. H. Auden (1938); *Journey to a War* – with W. H. Auden (1939); *Goodbye to Berlin* (1939); *Jacob's Hands* – with Aldous Huxley (1944); *The Condor and The Cows: A South American Travel Diary* (1949); *The World in the Evening* (1954); *Down There on a Visit* (1962); *An Approach to Vedanta* (1963); *A Single Man* (1964); *A Meeting by the River* (1967); *A Meeting by the River* – with Don Bachardy (1972); *Christopher and His Kind* (1976); *My Guru and His Disciple* (1980).

Stephen Spender: *Twenty Poems* (1930); *The Destructive Element* (1935); *Trial of a Judge* (1938); *The Still Centre* (1939); *Ruins and Visions* (1942); *Poems of Dedication* (1946); *World Within World* (1951, reissued 1994); *The Creative Element* (1953); *The Struggle of the Modern* (1963); *Selected Poems* (1965); *The Year of the Young Rebels* (1969); *Love-Hate Relations* (1974); *Recent Poems* (1978); *The Thirties and After* (1978).

Louis MacNeice: *Blind Fireworks* (1929); *Poems* (1935); *Letters From Iceland* – with W. H. Auden (1937); *The Earth Compels* (1938); *Autumn Journal* (1939); *Plant and Phantom* (1941); *The Poetry of W. B. Yeats* (1941); *The Dark Tower and Other Radio Scripts* (1947); *Solstices* (1961); *The Burning Perch* (1963); *Collected Poems* (1966).

Cecil Day-Lewis: *Transitional Poems* (1929); *A Hope For Poetry* (1934); *A Question of Proof* (1935); *Overtures to Death and Other Poems* (1938); *The Beast Must Die* (1938); *The Poetic Image* (1947); *The Lyric Impulse* (1965); *Thomas Hardy* (1965); *A Need For Poetry* (1968); *Poems of C. Day-Lewis 1925–1972* (1977); *Posthumous Poems* (1979).

Further reading

McDonald, Peter, *Louis MacNeice: the Poet in His Contexts*. Clarendon Press, 1991.

McKinnon, William T., *Apollo's Blended Dream: A Study of the Poetry of Louis MacNeice*. Oxford University Press, 1971.

Wade, Stephen, *Christopher Isherwood* (Modern Novelists Series). Palgrave Macmillan, 1991.

Contributors: Stephen Colbourn, Ian Mackean

The Liverpool Poets

In Liverpool you're a poet one minute, but the next minute you're talking about football, or you're buying bus tickets, or someone's kicking your head in outside a pub. It's all part of living.[1]

The Liverpool poets, Adrian Henri (1932–2000), Roger McGough (1937–) and Brian Patten (1946–) began their careers in poetry by giving readings in the clubs and coffee bars of Liverpool in the 1960s and gained recognition in print in *Penguin Modern Poets 10: The Mersey Sound* (1967)[2] and *The Liverpool Scene* (1968)[3]. The works of other poets were included in *The Liverpool Scene*, but it was Henri, McGough and Patten who were featured in *The Mersey Sound* and went on to fame as the Liverpool Poets.

They were writing at a time when the poetry of **The Movement** was prominent, but their roots and aims were different from those of established poets. They wrote their poetry to be read aloud and their audiences were young Liverpudlians who might normally have attended pop concerts but were now finding that poetry could be equally accessible and appealing.

The kids didn't look on it as Poetry with a capital 'P', they looked on it as modern entertainment, part of the pop movement.[4]

By opening poetry to a wider audience the Liverpool Poets were part of the democratisation of the arts which was also taking place in painting and sculpture in the **pop art** movement of the 1950s and 1960s. Their poems deal with ordinary people in everyday situations ('I'm concerned about the person next door, and the person next to me'[5]) and are filled with images of their environment, such as streets, cafes, buses, parties, cinemas and chip shops. They also drew on popular culture, such as pop music, comic books and television, and made references to casual sexual relationships and the 'recreational' drugs of the era such as cannabis and LSD. Political issues of the day, such as the Vietnam war, CND (the Campaign for Nuclear Disarmament), the Cold War, racial intolerance (see Patten's 'I'm Dreaming of a White Smethwick') and 'the bomb', also make an occasional appearance in their poems. 'The bomb' was a prominent topic of discussion in that Cold War era, and perhaps the pervasive background fear associated with the nuclear threat contributed to their impulse to write poetry to be performed in the here and now. Live for today, because we could all be annihilated at the push of a button tomorrow, was part of the mind-set of the generation growing up in the wake of Hiroshima.

Their Liverpool location was significant for two reasons, firstly because it was the home of The Beatles and other Merseybeat pop groups, whose music was taking Britain and America by storm, making Liverpool famous, and secondly because it was provincial – away from the influence of London. Much of their work may have been loosely, even carelessly structured – poetic entertainment rather than serious poetry – but that mattered far less in Liverpool than it did in London, and if established literary critics did not consider them as serious poets that was of little concern to them.[6] They were proud of their working-class backgrounds and provincial status and felt no need to worry about what the literary highbrows of London might think.

> I think of it as a Liverpool thing as opposed to a London thing, or a capital thing, or a public school thing . . . We've got no literary or dramatic heritage . . . We haven't got people to bow down to. The Beatles were like that.[7]

Their disdain for the establishment and determination that their art should be for ordinary people is reflected in Henri's poem 'Adrian Henri's Last Will and Testament':

> I leave my paintings to the Nation with the stipulation that they must be exhibited in Public Houses, Chip Shops, Coffee Bars and the Cellar Clubs throughout the country.

The list is notable for the conspicuous absence of art galleries or any other kind of official building.

Their main influences were the **Beat poets** of America, particularly **Alan Ginsberg**, who impressed them when he visited Liverpool, and French **Symbolist poetry**, such as that of Baudelaire and Rimbaud. They were not interested in imitating the form or subject matter of the writers they admired, but were, rather, inspired by the mood and tone of their poems and by their power to make an immediate emotional impact on the reader.

> I suddenly realised that when I was reading about people like Rimbaud and Baudelaire, I felt as they felt. I recognised a kindred spirit, and therefore I must be a poet.[8]

Their other influences were many and various. In Adrian Henri's poem 'Me' he lists people he admires, and alongside Burroughs, Rimbaud and Mallarmé we find pop, jazz and classical musicians, radical political figures, film directors, artists, and poets and novelists from all eras. The concept of this poem has something in common with the cover of The Beatles' *Sergeant Pepper's Lonely Hearts Club Band* album of 1967, being a catalogue of diverse influences and showing the levelling effect of pop culture in bringing together the 'high' and 'low' arts.

Henri dedicated the poem 'Mrs Albion You've Got a Lovely Daughter' to Ginsberg and on the death of the leading figure of **Modernist** poetry, **T. S. Eliot**, in 1965 paid tribute to him in 'Poem in Memoriam to T. S. Eliot', likening him to 'a favourite distant uncle'.

And it was as if a favourite distant uncle had died

. . .

For years I measured out my life with your coffeespoons
Your poems on the table in dusty bedsitters

Henri was a painter as well as a poet, and both he and Roger McGough were also musicians. Henri led a group called *Liverpool Scene* and McGough was part of the pop group *The Scaffold* along with Michael McCartney, brother of Beatle Paul.

Although the poetry of all three had aims and attitudes in common, they also had their own distinctive styles, both in performance and on the page, Brian Patten being the most serious and intense. Comparing McGough's and Patten's live performances, Grevel Lindop says:

McGough . . . is meticulously controlled: the moods of the poems are carefully varied, McGough keeping an entirely straight face throughout even the most comic ones . . . Patten on the other hand seems both more spontaneous and less relaxed. He appears moody, even inarticulate between poems, and the audience is excited, probably, not only by the enormous passion with which he reads (or rather intones, or chants) his poems, but also by the suspicion that at any moment he may be going to pick a quarrel with someone.[9]

In Henri's poems we typically find whimsical **surrealism**, gentle humour and wistful **romanticism**. We also find, reflecting his other artistic endeavours, frequent references to painting and borrowings from pop music.

In McGough's poems we find a more extreme and jarring form of surrealism (*see* for example, 'You and Your Strange Ways') and typographical experiments such as the use of lower-case letters throughout a poem, in the manner of e e cummings, and the formation of evocative neologisms by the running together of words.

you are the underwatertree
around which fish swirl like leaves
['What You Are']

The point made above, about the poetry of The Liverpool Poets being written with little regard for posterity, needs to be qualified in relation to the later works of McGough and Patten. Of the three, Patten has emerged as the most serious poet and was concerned even at the time of *The Liverpool Scene* about the distinction between poetry and poetic entertainment.

It's just got to last longer than me. I'm involved with the poetry and music scene, and the entertainment . . . I mean I believe in poetic entertainment, but poetic entertainment is not poetry.[10]

Patten's poems were more considered and carefully crafted than those of the others. His poems were powered by feelings rather than ideas and he had a deeper, more serious underlying purpose. Martin Booth wrote of him:

> Of the Liverpool poets, it was Brian Patten who became the leader, and it is he who has maintained his artistic hold and development, leading his ideas and muse on from earlier work to later progressions.[11]

References

1. **Roger McGough**, in Lucie-Smith, Edward (ed.) (1968) Introduction. *The Liverpool Scene.* New York: Doubleday (hereafter referred to as *The Liverpool Scene*).

2. *Penguin Modern Poets 10: The Mersey Sound.* Penguin, 1967, revised and enlarged 1974.

3. **Lucie-Smith, Edward** (ed.) Introduction. *The Liverpool Scene.*

4. **Roger McGough**, in *The Liverpool Scene.*

5. Ibid.

6. See *The War With the 'Establishment'*, in Chapter 2 of Cookson, Linda, *Brian Patten* (1997). Northcote House.

7. **Roger McGough**, in *The Liverpool Scene.*

8. Ibid.

9. **Lindop, Grevel** (1997) *Poetry Rhetoric and the Mass Audience: The case of the Liverpool poets. British Poetry Since 1960.* Ed. G. Lindop and M. Schmidt. London: Carcanet, 1972. Quoted in: Cookson, Linda, *Brian Patten.* Plymouth: Northcote House.

10. **Brian Patten**, in *The Liverpool Scene.*

11. **Booth, Martin** (1985) *British Poetry 1964–84: Driving Through the Barricades.* Routledge & Kegan Paul.

Selected works:
Compilations: Lucie-Smith, Edward (ed.) *The Liverpool Scene.* Doubleday (1968); *Penguin Modern Poets 10: The Mersey Sound* (1967, revised and enlarged 1974).
Adrian Henri: *Tonight at Noon* (1968); *City* (1969); *Autobiography* (1971); *I Want* (1972); *Environments and Happenings* (1974); *The Best of Henri* (1975).
Roger McGough: *Watchwords* (1969); *After the Merrymaking* (1971); *Out of Sequence* (1972); *Gig* (1973); *Sporting Relations* (1974); *In the Glassroom* (1976); *Frinck; A Life in the Day of* (1978); *Summer with Monika* (1978); *Holiday on Death Row* (1979); *Waving at Trains* (1982); *Melting into the Foreground* (1986); *Nailing the Shadow* (1987); *Helen Highwater* (1989); *Selected Poems 1967–1987* (1989); *You at the Back: Selected Poems 1967–87* (1991); *Defying Gravity* (1992); *Penguin Modern Poets 4* (Liz Lochhead; Roger McGough; Sharon Olds) (1995); *The Way Things Are* (1999); *Everyday Eclipses* (2002); *Collected Poems* (2003).

Brian Patten: *Little Johnny's Confession* (1967); *Notes to the Hurrying Man* (1969); *The Irrelevant Song* (1971); *Vanishing Trick* (1976); *Grave Gossip* (1979); *Love Poems* (1981); *Storm Damage* (1988); *Grinning Jack* (1990); *Armada* (1996).

Bibliography and further reading

Booth, Martin, *British Poetry 1964–84: Driving Through the Barricades.* London: Routledge & Kegan Paul, 1985.

Cookson, Linda, *Brian Patten.* Plymouth: Northcote House, 1997.

Lindop, Grevel, *Poetry Rhetoric and the Mass Audience: The case of the Liverpool poets. British Poetry Since 1960.* Ed. G. Lindop and M. Schmidt. London: Carcanet, 1972.

Lucie-Smith, Edward (ed) *The Liverpool Scene.* New York: Doubleday, 1968.

Penguin Modern Poets 10: The Mersey Sound. Penguin, 1967.

Thwaite, Antony, *Poetry Today: A Critical Guide to British Poetry: 1960–1984.* London: Longman, 1985.

Contributor: Ian Mackean

Canadian literature

A survey of Canadian literature in English of the twentieth century

Canadian literature in English came of age in the twentieth century. The nineteenth century had witnessed the beginnings of a literary consciousness in small magazines and newspapers and the development of a growing body of literature that at first imitated its closest western models: the United Kingdom and the United States. By the end of that century, the political emancipation of the country (British North America Act, 1867) was mirrored by the achievements of a new generation of authors who attempted to express the themes and aesthetic values of a new Canadian identity through both poetry and fiction.

1900–50: International connections

In the first half of the twentieth century, Canada made a successful transition from a frontier nation to a modern industrialised society. The standard of living and legal status of most social groups improved substantially. Women were enfranchised after the First World War. But Native Canadians were a notable exception. For them, this period was one of strict white control of the reservations by the Department of Indian Affairs. They lived in extreme poverty and strove to fight against the loss of their culture, language and traditions.

New cultural institutions emerged in order to promote and disseminate Canadian writing. Literary magazines such as *The Dalhousie Review* (1920) were established and literary awards created, among them the prestigious Governor General's Awards (1937) for the best Canadian works published every year in both English and French. Academics started shaping a corpus of Canadian literature in anthologies and critical essays. The first courses in Canadian literature were introduced in universities in the inter-war period.

Canadian writers felt the pull of issues similar to those occupying their contemporaries elsewhere. Social problems pervade the literature of this period: the impact of the two world wars in Canada, the poverty and misery of the Depression, the rise of Fascism, Communism and anti-Semitism.

Poetry

Canadian poets started to look outside their borders and to relate to artistic movements in America and Britain. Those most influenced by the **Modernists**, such as

W. B. Yeats, **T. S. Eliot**, **Ezra Pound** and **W. H. Auden**, were the Montreal Movement, a group of poets in the 1920s and 1930s centred around the influential academic A. J. M. Smith (1902–80). They were critical of the previous generation for what they saw as their Victorianism and conservatism and for their endless repetition of poetic topics such as Canadian nature. They sought new and less mechanical verse forms and a freer structure and diction for their poems. Together with Smith, the poets involved in this search were F. R. Scott, A. M. Klein, Leo Kennedy and Leon Edel. The Montreal Movement rejuvenated Canadian poetry, publishing first in literary magazines and later in anthologies, such as *New Provinces* (1936, edited by the Toronto poets E. J. Pratt and Robert Finch) and *The Blasted Pine* (edited by Smith and Scott in 1957).

Poetry became increasingly politicised in the following years and the shift in approach influenced the writers of the Montreal Movement. Scott (1899–1985) wrote against social vices, while Klein (1909–72) explored his Jewish heritage at a time of intense racial trauma, and in the context of bicultural Montreal, in works such as *Hath Not a Jew* (1940) – the title being taken from Shylock's famous speech in Shakespeare's comedy *The Merchant of Venice*.

Two other prominent poets of this period, Dorothy Livesay (1909–96) and Earle Birney (1904–95), shared a left-wing approach to political injustice and the theme of the harsh experience of the working class, which surface in their publications of the 1940s. Both received two Governor General's Awards for Poetry in that decade: Livesay for *Day and Night* (1944) and *Poems for People* (1947) and Birney for *David and Other Poems* (1942) and *Now is Time* (1945). Livesay's work is also renowned for her uninhibited portrayal of women's sexuality, which opened new paths for later women writers, while Birney's radical pessimism was accompanied by experimentation with new and old poetic forms.

Perhaps the most famous poet of this period was E. J. Pratt (1882–1964), who won the Governor General's Award for Poetry three times. Most at home with narrative verse, he produced long epic poems describing episodes from Canadian history. Examples of his interest in patriotic themes are *Brébeuf and His Brethren* (1940), about the seventeenth century Jesuit missionaries among the Hurons, and *Towards the Last Spike* (1952), documenting the construction in the nineteenth century of the transcontinental railway.

Fiction

Fiction writers, caught up in the social transformation of their country, aimed to depict it realistically. In the early years of the century they concentrated on displaying the local colour of their communities, as seen especially in the popular novels of Lucy Maud Montgomery, who made Prince Edward Island famous in *Anne of Green Gables* (1908). Stephen Leacock was more critical and less idealistic in his portrayal of Ontario's small-town life in *Sunshine Sketches of a Little Town* (1912).

This period in Canadian literature is characterised by the rise of regionalism, particularly as a new region, the Prairies, now became a frequent setting for fiction. A good example is Frederick Philip Grove's *Settlers of the Marsh* (1925), which explores the harshness of pioneer life in the prairies, describing the life of farmers and the vast expanses of grain. Similarly, Martha Ostenso's novel *Wild Geese* (1925) conveys the tensions within a family in which the father refuses to acknowledge other members' desires and interests, demanding instead that they submit to the never-ending toils of farm life.

Like other Canadian provinces, the Prairies were home to immigrants of various origins and not exclusively from the British Isles. Laura Salverson's *The Viking Heart* (1923) is among the earliest novels to record the plight of non-British pioneers, in this case the first Icelandic colony's problems in the lake area of Manitoba. The Eurasian sisters Edith and Winnifred Eaton gave literary expression to the lives of other ethnic groups in Canada. Edith published short stories, such as her volume *Mrs Spring Fragrance and Other Stories* (1912), under her Chinese pen-name Sui Sin Far, and Winnifred described her mixed upbringing in Montreal in her fictionalised autobiography *Me: A Book of Remembrance* (1915) under the Japanese pen-name Onoto Watanna.

Like poetry, fiction opened up to new themes in response to the socio-economic crisis of the 1930s. Morley Callaghan (1903–90) and Sinclair Ross (1908–96) shared an interest in the material, moral and psychological effects of marginality and poverty. In *Such is My Beloved* (1934) Callaghan tells the story of two prostitutes and the efforts of a Roman Catholic priest to help them out of their situation. Ross's *As For Me and My House* (1941) remains a masterpiece, mostly because of the power of the narrative voice of Mrs Bentley, the parson's wife, who in her diary entries portrays small-town Saskatchewan life during the Depression.

Two other major fiction writers, Gwethalyn Graham (1913–65) and Hugh MacLennan (1907–90), published novels in the 1940s touching on a theme of strong national relevance. Graham's *Earth and High Heaven* proved to be extremely controversial on its publication in 1944. A Romeo-and-Juliet kind of romance between a young woman belonging to the Anglophone élite of Montreal and an obscure Jewish man, the novel probed underlying tensions between different ethnic groups in French Canada in the stressful atmosphere of the Second World War. MacLennan used similar materials for the construction of his novel *Two Solitudes* (1945), which follows the lives of three generations of French-Canadians and English-Canadians in Quebec throughout the first half of the twentieth century, even-handedly recording their mutual distrust and frequent misunderstandings. MacLennan's dramatisation is considered so accurate that the term 'two solitudes' has entered everyday language to signify the uneasy relationship between the two 'founding nations' of Canada.

Drama

During the 1920s, inspired by the nationalist example of the Abbey Theatre in Dublin, established during the **Irish Cultural Revival**, the Little Theatre movement in Canada was set up to offer national alternatives to the entertainment provided by touring British and American companies, and to promote Canadian plays. This movement offered suitable venues for the work of playwrights such as Merrill Denison and Herman Voaden. The 1930s, however, favoured political drama of the kind exemplified by *Eight Men Speak* (1933), authored by several members of the Workers' Theatre using agit-prop techniques. Regional settings, characters and concerns featured in the plays of Gwen Ringwood (1910–84), such as *Still Stands the House* (1939).

Other forms of entertainment, such as radio and motion pictures, tempted many Canadian artists. Some left their country to try their luck in Hollywood. Mary Pickford (1893–1979), Louis B. Mayer (1885–1957) and Jack Warner (1892–1978) founded Hollywood studios between 1919 and 1924.

1950–80: Nationalism and after

Canadian nationalism became a much stronger force after the Second World War, affecting all cultural institutions. Canadians were concerned about the pervading influences from abroad, especially from the United States, and set out to develop ways to protect national culture from an excess of such influences. In the 1950s the government took several important initiatives. The first Canadian Broadcasting Corporation stations opened in 1952 and the Canada Council was founded in 1957, both with the mission of promoting Canadian content and talent. Nationalist preoccupation became even stronger in the 1960s as the nation prepared for the celebration of its first centenary. A new Canadian flag was adopted in 1964, followed by a national anthem in 1967. Other national concerns, such as the relationship between the two founding nations, were partially solved by new policies on equal partnership, which brought about the official adoption of bilingualism in 1969.

Canadian literature rose in status and began to be taught in most Canadian universities. A new school of critics formulated theories on its main features. Because it was mainly concerned with the most distinctly national themes to be found in Canadian writing, it was known as 'thematic criticism'. Conferences discussed the literary canon and several important academic journals were founded in these decades, such as *Canadian Literature* (1959), *Essays on Canadian Writing* (1974) and *Studies in Canadian Literature* (1976). Small presses arose to cater for a growing readership and the New Canadian Library paperback series (1958) attempted to make the best of Canadian literature accessible to the average citizen. Canadian writers found recognition at home and beyond.

Poetry

After the Second World War there was a remarkable increase in the amount of poetry published in Canada. Making the transition from the writing of the 1940s to the nationalist revival of the 1960s were three important poets, whose unbroken production in the second half of the century proved influential on later generations: P. K. Page, a writer who combined her interest in words with the visual arts; Phyllis Web, who pursued formal innovation; and Irving Layton, who, like A. M. Klein before him, drew from his Jewish Montreal background.

The poets who came into prominence in the 1960s and 1970s expanded the subject matter of Canadian poetry to include local history, personal and family history conveyed in a **confessional** mode, politics, popular culture and fantasy. There was continued interest in Canadian landscape, including the wilderness, but seen from fresh perspectives. On the West Coast the innovatory impulse centred on the poetry magazine *Tish*, published in Vancouver throughout the 1960s, which focused on the search for new diction and forms, as seen for example in the poetry of George Bowering and Frank Davey. bill bissett, who prefers to write his name phonetically and therefore does not use capital letters, is well known for experimenting with the oral nature of poetry in his phonetic poems. Daphne Marlatt felt the pull of *écriture féminine*, while another West Coast poet, Robert Bringhurst, often draws on the Native cultures of the area.

In the Prairies a strong sense of the past pervades the writing of John Newlove, deeply interested in the history of the land, and of Robert Kroetsch, who interweaves myth and autobiography. Lorna Crozier's ear is also tuned to the landscape and nature, though like Livesay, some of her writing has caused controversy due to its outspoken sexuality. B. P. Nichol (1944–88) wittily played in his poetry with words and images, long and short forms, sound and syntax.

From the Maritimes came two contrasting writers. Elizabeth Brewster displays a fine sense of place and roots in her poetry, especially in her early work, whereas Milton Acorn's **Marxist** approach is linked to the political approach of earlier poets of the century. Native poets such as the Mi'kmaq writer Rita Joe started to attract some attention in the 1970s.

Other major poets came to the fore in Ontario and the English-speaking areas of Quebec. Al Purdy (1918–2000) had a fine ear for the conversational and the sardonic and excelled at short lyric poems with an edge of humour. **Margaret Atwood**, though now better known as a fiction writer, first wrote poetry and has continued to publish poetry regularly. Her gender politics brought a fresh approach to topics of nation and representation. Leonard Cohen, a poet, novelist and renowned singer, follows up on Klein's and Layton's representations of the Montreal Jewish experience.

Fiction

Immigrant fiction continued its rise, in particular that depicting immigrant experiences in the urban world. Two important novels of the 1950s fictionalised the troubles of immigrant communities in Winnipeg. Adele Wiseman's *The Sacrifice* (1956) used the Biblical story of Abraham's willingness to sacrifice his son as a backdrop for the plight of Jewish Ukrainians. John Marlyn's *Under the Ribs of Death* (1957) displayed the transformation of the humble Hungarian boy Sandor Hunyadi into the Canadian businessman Alex Hunter. Also dealing with ethnic communities in urban Canada were two novels by Mordecai Richler (1931–2001), *Son of a Smaller Hero* (1955) and *The Apprenticeship of Duddy Kravitz* (1959). They centred on the problems of Anglophone Jewish life in multicultural Montreal. Richler explored this topic throughout his long career, raising challenging questions about Canadian (particularly Quebecker) identity and the Jewish community's role within it. More experimental in language and structure was Sheila Watson's *The Double Hook* (1959), which critics consider a cornerstone of Canadian modernist aesthetics, while the rural landscapes of Nova Scotia inspired the mood of Ernest Buckler's *The Mountain and the Valley* (1952).

The Prairies continued to provide writers with powerful topics and settings in the 1960s and 1970s. Margaret Laurence (1926–87) developed her own fictional world in a series of novels starting with *The Stone Angel* (1964), where she masterfully portrayed elderly Hagar Shipley's attempt to retain her independence and individuality as she lies dying. Linked to this novel through the common setting of the prairie town of 'Manawaka' are the novels *A Jest of God* (1966), *The Fire-Dwellers* (1969), *A Bird in the House* (1970) and *The Diviners* (1974). In them, Laurence engaged such issues as the conflict between community and individual, as well as between parents and children, and the power of memory, ancestry and myth. Due to her creation of a contained fictional world, Manawaka, Laurence, often compared to **William Faulkner**, attained a place of honour in Canadian writing of the twentieth century.

Other major writers of the Prairies, similarly innovative in subject matter and style, are Rudy Wiebe and Robert Kroetsch. Wiebe broke new ground with his portrayal of the Mennonite community into which he was born, in two novels of the 1960s, *Peace Shall Destroy Many* and *The Blue Mountains of China*. These were followed by an empathetic representation of Aboriginal life in *The Temptations of Big Bear* (1973) and *The Scorched-Wood People* (1977), which hinge on the treaty-signing period of the late 1800s. Kroetsch, also a poet and critic, is deeply concerned with the connections between storytelling and myth and legend. The Canadian landscape he depicts in novels such as *The Studhorse Man* (1969), *Badlands* (1975) and *What the Crow Said* (1978) is always layered with a number of cultures, stories, memories and ancestries, sometimes leading to a blurring of the border between fact and fiction. Jack Hodgins, from British Columbia, displays similar **postmodernist** characteristics in fictional pieces such as *Spit Delaney's Island* (1976) and *The Invention of the World* (1977).

In Ontario, too, writers of this generation achieved international acclaim. Robertson Davies (1913–95) started out in the 1950s as a playwright but later became better known for his fiction and as a brilliant professor at Massey College (University of Toronto). His fame rests above all on the Deptford Trilogy (*Fifth Business*, 1970, *The Manticore*, 1972 and *World of Wonders*, 1975), set in Canada and Europe and following the interconnected fates of three Ontario men. **Margaret Atwood** started her long career with *The Edible Woman* (1969) and *Surfacing* (1972). As her fame grew in the 1980s, her name became closely associated with formal innovation and provocative issues. Timothy Findley (1930–2002), a fellow postmodernist writer, also entered the literary scene in the 1970s with *The Wars* (1977), a novel focusing on Canadian participation in the First World War. In *Famous Last Words* (1981) his gaze shifted to the Second World War, while *Not Wanted on the Voyage* (1984) rewrote the Biblical episode of the Flood. Throughout his long and successful career, Findley remained interested in a postmodernist blend of history, myth and fiction.

The short story was the chosen form of Montreal-born Mavis Gallant from the publication of *The Other Paris* (1956), and she has regularly published collections ever since, from her home in France. *Home Truths* (1981) selected some of her best work, often deploying international settings and subject matter or dwelling on the comparison between North American and European values and lifestyles. **Alice Munro** also appropriated the genre in the 1970s, with three very strong, woman-centred collections. *Lives of Girls and Women* (1971) gained immediate acclaim for its cyclical structure and *bildungsroman* plot. *Something I've Been Meaning to Tell You* (1974) and *Who Do You Think You Are?* (1978) established her as a seminal writer of short stories in English, a place of honour she holds to this day, along with Gallant.

The civil rights movements empowered Native writers. The turning point came in 1969 with the publication of the first anthology of Native Canadian Literature under the title *I Am an Indian.* This was followed by an upsurge of autobiographical writing, in which writers recorded the marginal existence of the Native community, as, for example, Maria Campbell did for the Métis of Saskatchewan in *Halfbreed* (1973). Others, like Basil Johnston (Ojibway), collected traditional materials and wrote short stories, paving the way for a later generation.

Drama

Government support contributed to the growth of Canadian drama through the creation of major professional theatres. Social issues permeated the plays of the 1960s, as seen particularly in John Herbert's prison drama *Fortune and Men's Eyes* (1967), about homosexuality and prison life, and George Ryga's *The Ecstasy of Rita Joe* (also 1967), with its powerful condemnation of white oppression of British Columbian Natives. Based on the true story of the murder of a young Native woman in Vancouver, the play adopted the structure of a trial that, though formally against Rita Joe, ended up condemning the moral insensitivity of white society.

The 1970s saw the rise of alternative theatres, such as Toronto's Theatre Passe Muraille and the Tarragon, where a new generation of writers found success. David French's 'Mercer trilogy', starting with *Leaving Home* (1972), dealt with the problems of a Newfoundland family adjusting to the urban lifestyle of Toronto. French, one of Canada's most accomplished playwrights, has also achieved recognition for lighter plays like *Jitters* (1979), a comic metatheatrical piece. Alternative theatres also favoured experimentation in form and content, such as the bilingual dialogue of David Fennario's *Balconville* (1979). Developing the already familiar theme of the two solitudes of Canada, Fennario adds to his picture of ethnic and linguistic conflict an element of class struggle.

Other playwrights were drawn to historical episodes for their materials, like James Reaney, whose trilogy *The Connollys* (1973–75) was based on incidents that occurred in Ontario in the 1880s. Sharon Pollock turned to the same period in *Walsh* (1973), in order to criticise Canada's hypocritical policies concerning Native affairs in their handling of the Sioux community after the Battle of Little Big Horn in the United States. Pollock also maintained this kind of documentary approach and subject matter in *The Komagata Maru Incident* (1976), on the racist rejection of South Asian immigrants in Vancouver in 1914, while in *Blood Relations* (1980) she presented feminist issues once more with a historical backdrop.

1980–2000: Emergence of 'other' Canadian literatures

From the 1970s, most new immigrants to Canada came from areas other than Europe, such as the Caribbean islands, Africa and the Indian subcontinent. They changed the demographic make-up of the country, and their increased visibility in all social arenas has raised meaningful questions about the main features of Canadian culture and society. For instance, the fact that their works often deal with settings and characters outside Canada has challenged the implicit notion that in order to be considered 'Canadian', the work has to be set in Canada. As the title of one anthology suggested, the 'two solitudes' frame has expanded to include 'other solitudes'.

At the same time that many of these so-called 'new' Canadian authors made their mark on the literary world, two critical movements entered academic circles: **feminism** and **postcolonialism**. Feminist criticism in Canada has denounced the male bias of the relatively young Canadian canon, while postcolonial criticism has pursued comparative studies of Canadian writing with that of other (settler) colonies, particularly Australia, moving away from the more traditional comparative approaches associated with the literatures of the United States and Great Britain. Native Canadian literature has increased its visibility and its appeal to both critics and readers.

Poetry

Throughout this period most of the poets mentioned above have continued to write and to win awards. Among the younger writers to attain recognition in the 1980s and 1990s, Erin Mouré deserves to be mentioned for her innovative approach to language from a gendered perspective.

Michael Ondaatje's poetic production, like that of Margaret Atwood, has run a parallel course to his fiction writing. Though often of a lyric, autobiographical nature, Ondaatje's most interesting work is perhaps to be found in longer poems such as *The Collected Works of Billy the Kid* (1970). The Afro-Caribbean poets Claire Harris, Marlene Nourbese Philip and Dionne Brand are often cited together because of a commonality of themes, most importantly race and gender, though Brand also highlights issues of class and sexual orientation (*No Language is Neutral*, 1998) and Philip the politics of silence and voice in a postcolonial context (*She Tries Her Tongue, Her Silence Softly Breaks*, 1989). In the Maritimes, the poets George Elliott Clarke (*Whylah Falls*, 1990) and Maxine Tynes have successfully recorded the world-view of Black Nova Scotians.

An Anthology of Canadian Native Literature in English (1992), edited by Daniel David Moses and Terry Goldie, contributed to the dissemination of the work of many interesting poets. Marilyn Dumont (Métis) and Lenore Keeshig-Tobias (Anishinabe) write strong, committed poems against racism. Louise Bernice Halfe (Cree) and Gregory Scofield (Métis) give voice to their ancestors in *Blue Marrow* (1998) and *I Knew Two Métis Women* (1999), respectively.

Fiction

The last 20 years of the century witnessed the increasing popularity of several major writers, such as Wiebe, Atwood, Munro and Findley, and the rising fame of some newcomers. The outstanding narrative skills of **Carol Shields** (1935–2003) came under the spotlight in the 1980s, particularly with *Swann* (1987), and became known worldwide with the publication of *The Stone Diaries* (1993), a postmodern blend of genres that covered most of the twentieth century by way of telling the story of an average woman. Jane Urquhart and Aritha Van Herk belong to a younger generation. Urquhart's novels, from *The Whirlpool* (1986) to *The Stone Carvers* (2001), display a strong historical flavour, often spanning the nineteenth century and the First World War, while also interweaving writing with the visual arts, both in technique and subject matter. Aritha van Herk's work tends to connect gender issues to space and geography, as seen in such novels as *No Fixed Address* (1986) and *Restlessness* (1998).

The most remarkable feature of the period, however, was the emergence of a generation of Canadian writers of non-European origin, of whom Joy Kogawa is often seen as the forerunner. Indeed, her novel *Obasan* (1981) raised important questions about the Canadian government's treatment of the Japanese Canadian community during the Second World War, an issue that later writers such as Kerri Sakamoto (*The Electrical Field*, 1998) have continued to address. The long-standing presence of Chinese immigrants in Canada, especially in British Columbia, has been the subject matter of such novels as *Disappearing Moon Café* (1990) by Sky Lee and *The Jade Peony* (1995) by Wayson Choy.

Equally notable has been the participation of writers from the Indian subcontinent, such as Michael Ondaatje and **Rohinton Mistry**. Ondaatje's work started by being fairly autobiographical (*Running in the Family*, 1982), but later opened up to include multicultural experiences in Toronto (*In the Skin of a Lion*, 1987) and even later international settings in *The English Patient* (1992), which won the Booker Prize and obtained wide recognition as a film. Mistry's interest continues to lie closer to his origins, the Parsi community in India, which has featured prominently in his fiction since the short story collection *Tales from Firozsha Baag* (1997).

Also of South Asian background, though born in Kenya, is M. G. Vassanji, who won acclaim in the 1990s with novels such as *Uhuru Street* (1992) and *The Book of Secrets* (1994). Cyril Dabydeen and Neil Bissoondath are likewise of South Asian ancestry though Caribbean-born. Their fiction has developed issues of displacement and exile, Bissoondath's essays on immigrant identity and assimilation proving very controversial. Also from the Caribbean comes another acknowledged forerunner of ethnic Canadian writing, Austin Clarke, who has recorded Caribbean immigrant experiences in Toronto from the 1950s, bringing attention to issues of racism, poverty and marginality.

Native writers have managed to interest a widening readership while holding on to issues and conventions uniquely their own. The Okanagan storyteller and poet Jeannette Armstrong reflected on the evolution of Native communities in the 1960s and 1970s in her famous novel *Slash* (1985), which followed a young boy's path towards the recovery of Native identity and pride through his involvement in the civil rights movement. Lee Maracle (Métis-Salish) is also in the frontline for her protest writing in the autobiographical *I Am Woman* (1988), though she has published short stories and novels too. Thomas King's work has received critical praise for the way he handles postmodernist techniques and approaches together with traditional elements of Native storytelling, such as the trickster figure, which surface in his short stories (*One Good Story, That One*, 1993) as well as in his longer fiction such as *Green Grass, Running Water* (also 1993).

Drama

A similar multiplicity of topics and approaches has reached the Canadian stage. Native Canadian drama has shown particular strength. The Cree playwright Tomson Highway brought innovation to the theatre of the 1980s with two remarkable blendings of tradition and modernity, *The Rez Sisters* (1986) and *Dry Lips Oughta Go to Kapuskasing* (1989), both set in the fictional reservation of Wasaychigan Hill. By focusing first on the women characters and later on the male characters, Highway provided a rich picture of the gender and racial conflicts affecting Native Canadian communities. The Ojibway playwright Drew Hayden Taylor has focused on the historical grievances of his people in plays such as *Someday* (1993) and *Only Drunks and Children Tell the Truth* (1998), dealing with cases of forced adoption of Native children by white families, which split family units and resulted in uprooting and displacement. Daniel David Moses, a Delaware, has powerfully staged closely related issues of assimilation and resistance to acculturation in his plays, such as *Almighty Voice and His Wife* (1992) and *Big Buck City* (1998).

Writers of Caribbean origin have also made an important contribution. Djanet Sears's two plays, *Afrika Solo* (1990) and *Harlem Duet* (1997), have addressed the problems of the representation of Black identity, especially in the latter, which has **intertextual** links with Shakespeare's *Othello*.

Shakespeare's plays *Othello* and *Romeo and Juliet* provide further intertextual basis for the award-winning play *Goodnight Desdemona (Good Morning Juliet)*, by Anne-Marie MacDonald, originally performed in 1988 by the feminist company Nightwood, which also staged plays by other notable women playwrights, such as Margaret Hollingsworth. Other playwrights, such as Guillermo Verdecchia, have experimented with agit-prop techniques in the tradition of political drama. His solo play *Fronteras Americanas/American Borders* (1993) raised questions about immigrant identity and national borders.

Further reading

Benson, Eugene and L. W. Connolly, *English-Canadian Theatre.* Toronto: Oxford University Press, 1987.

Keith, W. J., *Canadian Literature in English.* London: Longman, 1985.

Kroller, Eva-Marie (ed.) *The Cambridge Companion to Canadian Literature.* Cambridge: Cambridge University Press, 2003.

New, William H., *A History of Canadian Literature.* Montreal and Kingston: McGill-Queen's University Press, 1989.

New, William H. (ed.) *An Encyclopedia of Literature in Canada.* Toronto: University of Toronto Press, 2002.

Petrone, Penny, *Native Literature in Canada: From the Oral Tradition to the Present.* Toronto: Oxford University Press, 1990.

Toye, William and Eugene Benson (eds) *The Oxford Companion to Canadian Literature,* 2nd ed. Toronto: Oxford University Press, 1998.

Contributor: Pilar Cuder Domínguez

Caribbean literature

Identity and Caribbean literature[1]

In his introduction to *Party Politics in the West Indies*, C. L. R. James, one of the most distinguished thinkers of the modern Caribbean, made the following statement about the people of the Anglophone (English-speaking) Caribbean:

> People of the West Indies, you do not know your own power. No one dares to tell you. You are a strange, a unique combination of the greatest driving force in the world today, the underdeveloped formerly colonial coloured peoples; and more than any of them, by education, way of life and language, you are completely part of Western civilization. Alone of all people in the world you began your historical existence in a highly developed modern society – the sugar plantation.

> All those who would say or imply that you are in any way backward and therefore cannot in a few years become a modern advanced people are your enemies, satisfied with the positions that they hold and ready to keep you where you are forever.

James made this statement in 1961, as part of the explanation of why he left the People's National Movement. Some years later, David Lichenstein reminded us of the contention of *Britannica Online* that the Caribbean possessed 'no indigenous tradition' in writing:

> The civilization that was to replace the Indians, made up of several different West African peoples brought to the West Indies as slaves, did not possess a written tradition of it own – nor was it allowed to develop one while it suffered in bondage. But the Africans did in some measure pass on a culture of orality, of storytelling and song – a culture that writers like Kamau Brathwaite point to as evidence of an African heritage in the Caribbean.

Lichenstein goes on to argue that the first breakthrough in Caribbean literature came in the French and Spanish islands in the works of Aime Cesaire of Martinique, Luis Pales Matos of Puerto Rico, Jacques Roumain of Haiti, Nicolas Guillen of Cuba and Leon Damas of French Guyana:

. . . the first to carve out a distinctive Caribbean literary identity. This identity was based not on European ideals but on links between black communities in the Caribbean. The British West Indies did not really pick up this challenge until after World War II. With the growth of newly independent states like Barbados, Trinidad, and Jamaica, Anglophone writers finally began to develop a tradition that focused on a distinctly Caribbean consciousness.

Pioneers in this movement, he argued, include Vic Reid (*New Day,* 1949), George Lamming (*In the Castle of My Skin,* 1953) and **V. S. Naipaul** (*A House for Mr Biswas,* 1961).

If we follow these two contradictory points of view (of C. L. R. James and *Britannica Online*), we identify two approaches to the literature: one that asserts the uniqueness of the Caribbean story and another that suggests that nothing indigenous came out of the Caribbean until the 1930s. More importantly, the latter interpretation makes a great distinction between the oral and written traditions, placing little value on the oral tradition. Such a dramatic distinction is not especially meaningful since many aspects of the oral tradition appear in the written work and are much more meaningful to the masses than they are to the literati. More importantly, in the Caribbean, one must define what one means by literature and how it manifests itself in our context.

In *Beyond Boundaries: The Intellectual Tradition of Trinidad and Tobago in the Nineteenth Century* I have suggested that a tradition of Anglophone writing began much earlier than the 1930s and it is one which involves a much more complex imbrication of the oral and the written. Suffice it to say that the tradition is much deeper and more complex than most critics suggest. Necessarily, any new criticism within the field must revolve around an understanding of what constitutes literature, especially as we try to understand our position in the global economy. Indeed, if literature mirrors or signifies the emotional consciousness of a people, then an examination of the literature raises the question: how have we depicted our situation in our new world through our literature?

In speaking of identity and the Anglophone Caribbean literary experience, it is necessary to emphasise that all such discussions/analyses should include the experiences of all of the groups and their unique experiences of the Caribbean. The groups did not experience the Caribbean in the same way, nor, for that matter, did they respond in exactly the same way. So while one can speak of a Caribbean experience or a Caribbean identity, it is necessary to be aware of the nuances of experience of each specific group and how it manifested itself in the region. Such an understanding of Caribbean experiences has implications even for today, with respect to how these groups express their Caribbeanness. Any analysis of Caribbean literature should produce a new reading of our condition. It should tell us how those varied groups negotiated their Caribbeanness, how it prepared them to occupy their contemporary space, and how the Caribbean crucible of experience modified their experiences. Much of this essay will be concerned with identifying moments in this continuing drama of identity in the Caribbean.

Anglophone Caribbean literature is an offshoot of African oral literature (most island inhabitants having come from West Africa). Its Amerindian provenance, together with its Asian and European roots, also contributed to its ultimate contours. Thus, the earliest literature of the Anglophone Caribbean can be traced to the proverbs, riddles, kheesas (tales) of African and Indian literature. Although there are poems written in the later part of the eighteenth century (such as 'The Sorrows of Yamba; Or, The Negro Woman's Lamentation') and the work of the Latinist and schoolmaster, Francis Williams, we can begin to locate an identifiable, indigenous tradition as beginning in Jean Baptiste Philippe's *Free Mulatto* (1824), one of the earliest works in Anglophone Caribbean literature that speaks specifically of our place in society and the unjust manner in which we are treated in this new environment.

This narrative revolved around a plea to the colonial government in which a Caribbean man sought to define the place of the mulatto (or the coloured person) within the context of his Trinidadian reality. The contradiction inherent in his situation (that of a free coloured man owning slaves, yet pleading for the freedom of his coloured brethren) did not seem to detract much from his urgent demand that his people be treated fairly on the basis of their capacity for reason, virtue and good breeding. This stance was part of the Enlightenment ideal.

The slave narratives, *The History of Mary Prince* (1831), the *Narrative of Ashton Warner* (1831), the *History of Abu Bekr* (1834), the *Narrative of James Williams* (1838), *The Interesting Narrative of Maria Jones* (1848) and the *Narrative of John Monteith* (1853), spoke of the inhuman conditions in which Africans in the Caribbean lived. Although the conditions described in Jamaica were not always identical to those of the other Caribbean islands (Trinidad, for example, had a milder form of slavery), a reading of these narratives gives one a sense of the hardship Africans endured as they strove to acclimatise themselves to the unfortunate circumstances in which they found themselves.

The next major narrative that examined the African condition in a critical manner was Maxwell Philip's *Emmanuel Appadocca: A Tale of the Boucaneers* (1854), although Kamau Brathwaite, the Barbadian poet and critic, suggests that the anonymous narrative, *Hamel the Obeah Man* (1827), offers the first complex portrayal of the African in Anglophone Caribbean literature. *Emmanuel Appadocca*, the first known novel written by a Caribbean person in the Anglophone Caribbean, makes a moral case against a person (his father) and two systems (slavery and colonialism) that make him an orphan. The novel examined the implications of the *lex talionis* (the principle of 'an eye for an eye, a tooth for a tooth') in this new Caribbean environment. In an illuminating introduction to a recent edition of *Emmanuel Appadocca*, William Cain argues that the narrative should be seen as a companion piece to such manifestly antislavery texts as *Uncle Tom's Cabin* and Douglass's *The Heroic Slave*. Moreover, *Emmanuel Appadocca* inaugurated a tradition in fiction of creative resistance and defiance of the combined forces of slavery, colonialism and dispossession that I examined in *Resistance and Caribbean Literature* (1980).

The Wondrous Adventures of Mary Seacole in Many Lands (1857), another pivotal work in this tradition of critical self-examination, recounts Seacole's development as she travelled and worked in many lands where she practised medicine and engaged in business. Comfortable in her womanhood (she averred that she chose not to remarry), she struck out independently in the colonial and coloniser's world, secure in the conviction that women could navigate life on their own. This conviction and enormous bravery alert us to the independent existence that many of our women were forced to lead in the islands and abroad.

This tradition of resistance and courage was demonstrated once more in the works of the poets and dramatists in the second half of the nineteenth century. The two out-standing works of the period were Horatio Nelson Huggins's *Hiroona*, an epic poem that recounted the Black Carib War against the English in St Vincent at the end of the nineteenth century. Although the work was not published until 1937, evidence suggests that it was composed around 1885. Literary critic Paula Burnett calls *Hiroona* 'the Caribbean's first epic poem'. Of equal interest and demonstrating the heteroge-neous nature of the Caribbean experience was Jean-Ch de Saint Avir's *The First Two Martyrs of Trinidad* (1885), which was serialised in a Trinidadian newspaper and even-tually published as a book. Like *Hiroona*, this tragedy of the faith of two Roman Catholics fathers who came to serve among the Amerindians in the early part of the sixteenth century suggests the complexity of the region's history and the varied expe-riences that shaped its cultural and intellectual presence. Not to be outdone were the various forms of Hindu and Islamic drama (seen in the performance of the remlee-las and the hosay) that were being performed in the outdoors and which gave expres-sion to the oral literary forms that our Indian ancestors brought with them to the islands.

If the written literature of the nineteenth century was imbricated with the pressure of the oral literary forms, the early twentieth century saw a more sustained attempt to examine the peasant life of those inhabitants who had to make the Caribbean their home. Thus, the first 30 years of the century saw the publication of several interest-ing literary works. The Jamaican poet and novelist Thomas MacDermot (better known as Tom Redcan) published *Beeka's Buckra Baby* (1903) and *One Brown Girl and ¼* (1909). Within this period, three other significant novels appeared, including *Rupert Gray: A Tale of Black and White* (1907) by Stephen Nathaniel Cobham, who became a fervent follower of Sylvester Williams, the father of Pan Africanism. In 1913, Herbert de Lisser published *Jane's Career*, the life of a peasant woman of Jamaica, while A. R. F. Webber published *Those That Be in Bondage: A Tale of Indian Indenture and Sunlit Western Waters* which contrasted the opposing ideological visions vis-à-vis the European world that the Asians brought to the Caribbean.

Significantly, both de Lisser and Webber were intensely involved in politics and press freedom. They worked together to form the first West Indian Press Association, of which de Lisser was president, while T. A. Marryshow from Grenada and Webber were members of the Management Committee. The works of the authors of this peri-od paved the way for a Caribbean renaissance of the 1930s in which one saw the flow-ering of the islands' arts and culture and a more self-assertive Caribbean presence. Necessarily, this movement was tied to the growing self-assertiveness of the Caribbean nationalist parties, the decolonisation process and the increased agitation of the labour unions.

Coming on the heels of the Wall Street Crash of 1929 and the Great Depression in the United States, and a rise in the social and political consciousness of Caribbean people, the Caribbean Renaissance offered a deeper and more penetrating exploration of our history. During this time Caribbean people felt a greater sense of being at home and the need to examine what this sense of home implied. Relying on a mixture of **naturalist** and **realist** tendencies – depicting social conditions rather than psychological issues – these novels played an important role of delineating the issues that confronted society. Beginning with Alfred Mendes's *Black Fauns* (1935) and C. L. R. James's *Minty Alley* (1936), this period culminated in the achievement of political independence and a formal conclusion to colonialism. It certainly was a period in which the people played a more active role in their affairs.

Nadi Edwards observes:

> Trinidad popular culture was appropriated by the writers of the 1930s in order to initiate a decolonized literary and cultural practice. The barrack-yard culture of Port of Spain, with its expressive vehicles of picong, calypso and Carnival, provided local aesthetic models that enabled C. L. R. James, Alfred Mendes and others to produce a self-consciously local literature.

Necessarily, this period of more intense political activity (the societies achieved adult suffrage in the 1940s) ushered in a writing that bore all the marks of the political aspirations of the people. Not only were they prepared to examine issues of personhood, they also examined the impact that colonialism had on their lives. It is within this period that the literary names such as Edgar Mittleholzer, Seepersad, **V. S. Naipaul**, Vic Reid, Roger Mais, Sam Selvon, Martin Carter, George Lamming, Wilson Harris and **Derek Walcott** began to appear. Many of these writers published their first works in the new magazines (*Trinidad, The Beacon, Bim, Focus* and *Kyk-Over-Al*) which appeared in this period. These writers also explored areas of experience that were not previously subjected to literary expression. Seepersad, Naipaul and Selvon examined the Asian aspect of our identity; Mittleholzer considered the mixed nature of our identity; while Harris looked within the heart of the South American landscape to understand how that aspect had shaped our present condition. After the 1960s, literary production proceeded apace. Apart from the writers above, most of the writers with whom Anglophone Caribbean has become associated began to take their place in the literary firmament.

The publication of V. S. Naipaul's *A House for Mr Biswas* (1961) was a significant achievement. I argue in another context that it sought to retell the Ramayana, the Hindu epic, in a Caribbean context. As a statement of identity, it chronicled how the Indians adapted to the rigours of their New World. Wilson Harris's *History, Fable and Myth in the Caribbean and Guianas* was also of special importance. Published in 1970, it sought to explore what can be called 'the subconscious reality' of the Caribbean experience. In the process, he argues that 'a philosophy of history may well lie buried in the arts of the imagination' and notes that 'whether the emphasis falls on limbo or vodun, on Carib bush-baby omens, on Arawak zemi, on Latin, English inheritances – in fact within and beyond these emphases – my concern is with epic stratagems available to Caribbean man in the dilemmas of history which surround him'.

In *Season of Adventure* (1963), George Lamming also sought to push deeper into our unconscious level of reality, drawing upon Haitian vodun and the Ceremony of the Souls. It would seem that he used this religio-cultural practice to warn society that as a people we could not be free unless we came to terms with a past that we scorned and neglected. Written when most Caribbean countries were assuming formal independence (Trinidad and Tobago and Jamaica in 1962, Guyana and Barbados in 1965), the contempt of Powell, the protagonist, seems to capture the angst that many Caribbean people felt about their new condition but were not bold enough to articulate:

'Change, my arse,' he shouted, 'is Independence what it is? Is one day in July you say you want to be that there thing, an' one day in a next July the law says all right, from now you's got what you askin' for. What change can that be? Might as well call a dog a cat and hope to hear him mew. Is only words an' name what don' signify nothing.'

Although literary historian Lloyd Brown placed the birth of modern Anglophone Caribbean poetry in the 1940–60 period, the 1970s saw the emergence of **Derek Walcott** and Kamau Brathwaite, two of our strongest poetic voices. Yet the voices could not be more different. While the former honed the poetic language of the master and made it his own, the latter hankered after the rhythm and cadences of African ancestors. One critic notes that Brathwaite's 'poetry, prose fiction, historiographical essays and literary criticism all reflect a scheme of thought wherein language is seen as a means of communication, a vehicle of cultural identity [and] a principal instrument for liberation from the vestiges of the colonial master'. Walcott, on the other hand, aware of a much more complex heritage, uses the language of his poetry and his plays to tease out the varied nuances of Caribbean life. His excursion into folk culture and his adaptation of the coloniser's culture to serve his own ends (as in *Omeros*, his epic poem which draws its inspiration from Homer) make him a voice that much of the English-speaking world can relate to. Both Walcott and Brathwaite, in their own ways, plumb the depths of the Caribbean experience and its ancestral past to come to terms with the challenge of the present.

Reference

1. This essay was originally delivered as a lecture by Selwyn R. Cudjoe to the Japanese Black Studies Association at Nara Women's College, Nara, Japan.

Contributor: Dr Selwyn R. Cudjoe. This article was originally published on www.trinicenter.com/Cudjoe

Indian literature in English

Rabindranath Tagore's English *Gitanjali*:
Defining Modernity in the East

> *He came and sat by my side and I woke not. What a cursed sleep it was,*
> *O miserable me!*
> *He came when the night was still; he had his harp in his hands, and*
> *my dreams became resonant with its melodies.*
> *Alas, why are my nights all thus lost? Ah, why do I ever miss his sight*
> *whose breath touches my sleep?*[1]

When **Virginia Woolf** asserted, 'In or about December, 1910, human character changed' in a lecture to the Heretics at Cambridge on 18 May 1924,[2] she was referring to the first Post-Impressionist exhibition in London, curated by Roger Fry. Unknown to her and most of the West, human identity also underwent a change in the East around the same time. In 1910 Rabindranath Tagore's *Gitanjali* was published in Bangla. In 1913 the Nobel Committee of the Swedish Academy conferred that year's Prize for Literature on Tagore for the poet's English version of the same work, *Gitanjali: Song Offerings* (1912).

Despite the difficulties of defining and interpreting terms such as 'Modernity' or '**Modernism**' in Western art and literature, it is possible to associate its beginnings with a range of historical events and dates. The Post-Impressionist exhibition was certainly significant, although for practical purposes 1914, the beginning of the Great War, is often taken as a signpost of the start of the 'Modern' era. But when we look farther afield, to the East and to Africa, it becomes notoriously difficult, perhaps even impossible, to find a convenient marker, a date to signify the beginning of Modernity. In this respect the English *Gitanjali* offers us a convenient handle, a *terminus a quo,* of Modernity in the East. Historically it is close to European Modernism and it is a book that for the first time compelled the world to take note of 'other' Englishes, started the ongoing process of rewriting the script of the Empire. Critically, it is the *Ur* text of **postcolonial** discourse.

The Nobel Prize in Literature being awarded to a non-white person startled the West, or certainly its press. The Swedish correspondent of *The Times* reported from Stockholm under the 14 November dateline, 'The newspapers this morning express some surprise at the unexpected decision of the Swedish Academy to confer the

Nobel Prize for Literature on the Indian poet Rabindranath Tagore.'[3] The *Los Angeles Times* flagged up the news: 'The Ignoble Decision: Hindu Poet Unworthy of the Nobel Prize', and the *New York Times*, while failing to get his name right, calling him Babindranath Tagore, sought consolation in the fact that the poet, 'if not exactly one of us, is, as an Aryan, a distant relation of all white folk'.[4]

Translation and translatability are core issues in postcolonial estimates of other literatures in English today. One argument is that all writers who chose to write in English and not their native languages are in a state of perpetual translation. Not only are these authors translating cultural tokens, they themselves lead a translated existence. In *Gitanjali* Tagore foreshadows these problems and in so far as he fails to provide a way out, and even complicates the original problems, *Gitanjali* is a **postmodern** text. A leading postcolonial theorist and critic, Harish Trivedi, has this to say of Tagore's translation of his poems from the original Bangla to English: 'Tagore was merely anticipating the hegemony of the English language and Western culture which continues to flourish and proliferate in India nearly half a century after the end of imperial rule.'[5]

The English version of *Gitanjali*, prepared by Tagore and published in November 1912 by the India Society in London, contained only 53 poems from the Bangla original. The remaining 51 poems were culled from a range of other publications, including a song that subsequently became part of a play. In this sense the English *Gitanjali* is Tagore's own selection. Its textual hybridity and complex genesis are, therefore, crucial to the work's assessment.[6]

W. B. Yeats commended the musicality of the English *Gitanjali* in his introduction to the 1912 volume and a number of these verses were set to music in Europe soon after its publication, particularly in Germany and the Scandinavian countries. Conversely, a number of Tagore's musical compositions were given lyrics in European languages at around the same time.

The Nobel citation praised Tagore's 'profoundly sensitive, fresh and beautiful verse by which . . . he has made his poetic thought, expressed in his own English words, a part of the literature of the West'. The wording of this citation, which thrust Indian writing in English into the limelight long before the likes of G. V. Desani, **Salman Rushdie**, **Arundhati Roy** or **Jhumpa Lahiri** were born, is interesting. It condemns, by condoning, Tagore's English, his 'own English words' and the attempt to absorb his work into an implicitly better or higher tradition of 'literature of the West' sounds either naïve or racist today, depending on one's perspective.

Like the English novels of Raja Rao and **R. K. Narayan**, *Gitanjali* in English made Tagore accessible not just to the West but to readers throughout India. Then, as now, English was not the most widely spoken language in India, but it was the language of the multi-ethnic and multi-lingual nation's intellectuals and fledgling political leadership, a language well on the way to becoming the favoured medium of instruction in higher education.

Exalted to the high pedestal of a cultural shibboleth, *Gitanjali*'s presence in the Bengali way of life is pervasive, almost insidious. Some of the best-known Rabindrasangeet, or Tagore Songs, are from *Gitanjali*. It's well nigh impossible to spend a day in Bengal without coming across snatches of lines from the collection from one source or another. Apart from the usual suspects – the state-owned radio and television channels – the songs are played incessantly on the PA systems in Kolkata's Metro Rail and can frequently be heard being hummed by thoroughly incompetent amateur exponents of the complex art form. Lines from the poems are used in advertising copy, newspaper headlines and, recently, to adorn T-shirts, saris and kurtas! In sharp contrast, the English *Gitanjali* exists largely in Bengali minds, and on bookshelves, as an academic curiosity, its literary essence unsullied by other cultural modes. Revered but seldom read, it leads a lone and insular existence.

The view that Tagore's English was not contemporary, and perhaps less than adequate for literary representation, is not new; it surfaces every time a new translation appears. While Tagore was himself acutely conscious of the inadequacy of his English, he was extremely touchy about any criticism of it.[7] Part of the problem originates from the fact that almost all the poems are devotional in substance, their tone and content similar to the mystical verses of Kabir and Soor Das. Frequently, they are addressed to God, the beloved, and as in the cases of Kabir and Soor, most verses in the Bangla *Gitanjali* can also be read as secular love poems. This alternative secular reading is possible largely because in Bangla the third person singular pronoun is gender neutral.

In English, however, Tagore is compelled to use the gender-specific 'Him' or 'He'. At times this practice results in a clash of metaphors and confusion of tones: frequently the tropes of masculine love are employed to address a male lover. Tagore appears to be aware of this problem and in many verses he explicitly assumes the role of the female admirer/devotee, most memorably in Verse 41:

Men going home glance at me and smile and fill me with shame. I sit like a
beggar maid, drawing my skirt over my face, and when they ask me, what it is I
want, I drop my eyes and answer them not.

This reversal of gender roles is a reworking of an established tradition in Vaishnavite literature from Bengal. It represented a break from Christian devotional or mystic literature for the English *Gitanjali*'s Western readers.

The practice also results in a curious androgynous quality in some poems, such as the passionate devotion depicted in Verse 26, which reveals the Tagore Bengal adores:

HE CAME AND sat by my side and I woke not. What a cursed sleep it was,
O miserable me!
He came when the night was still; he had his harp in his hands, and
my dreams became resonant with its melodies.
Alas, why are my nights all thus lost? Ah, why do I ever miss his sight
whose breath touches my sleep?

There is no perceptible authorial design in the arrangement of the 104 verses that make up the English *Gitanjali*, but often a cluster of poems can be observed to trace tentatively a theme. For instance, in Verses 22 to 27, one can detect a progression in time, from night to day to night again, with corresponding changes in the mood of the narrator.

At times Tagore appears to break a thematic continuity deliberately, as in the placing of Verse 35, one of the most frequently quoted verses from the book:

WHERE THE mind is without fear and the head is held high
. . . into that heaven of freedom, my Father, let my country awake.

The aggressive tone and nationalist fervour is unique to this collection, yet curiously 'modern' in the specific Indian context. The assertion of national identity evident in this verse would, by the 1920s, find its political voice in Mahatma Gandhi and the Indian National Congress (both Gandhi and Nehru, India's first Prime Minister, addressed Tagore as Gurudev, or the Master, a term of high veneration), eventually leading to India's independence on 15 August 1947.

A few poems display a conflict between Tagore the Poet and Tagore the Mystic. In Verse 73, for once, it appears that the poet shakes off the mantle of mysticism and frolics in earthly delights:

DELIVERANCE IS not for me in renunciation. I feel the embrace of freedom in a thousand bonds of delight . . . Yes, all my illusions will burn into illumination of joy, and all my desires ripen into fruit.

The arrangement of lines, the rhythm and the tempo of the verses can often make it difficult for a reader to ascertain whether the book is meant to be read as one single poem or as a collection. Specifically, in the middle section (Verses 41 to 61) the book gives the impression of being arranged in prose form and the free verse style that Tagore adopted throughout *Gitanjali* often reads like prose poems. But at times he uses rhymes and subtle rhythms to create a startling effect, as in Verse 30, lines 4–5:

He makes the dust rise from the earth with his swagger; he adds his
loud voice to every word I utter.

The verses in which Tagore uses the parable form are decidedly better than the rest. For example, Verse 50 which begins:

I HAD GONE a-begging from door to door in the village path, when thy golden chariot appeared in the distance like a gorgeous dream and I wondered who was this King of all kings!

The cadence and innate musical quality of this particular verse stands out among the rest. In Bangla, Tagore weaves music so intricately that one tends to overlook it. In English, Tagore rarely strikes that rhythm, at times using weary and worn-out phrases and displaying a fastidious, almost Victorian adherence to English syntax and grammar.

In its mood and diction, *Gitanjali* resembles Tennyson's *In Memoriam* more than any other work in English literature, and the similarity of Verse 39 ('WHEN THE HEART is hard and parched up, come upon me with a shower of mercy') to Verse L (50) of *In Memoriam* is striking ('Be near me when my light is low . . . be near me when my faith is dry). In Bangla, the opening line of Verse 58 is almost a direct translation of Tennyson's phrase 'faith is dry'.

In spite of its obvious limitations, the English *Gitanjali* remains a landmark publication, and not simply because it won the Nobel Prize. It is the finest document of the complex negotiations that one of the most gifted literary minds had to make with the politics of reception simply because he wasn't 'to the language born'.

If Bengali readers such as myself miss out on the lyrical element of the verses in the English *Gitanjali*, this may well be down to our inadequate appreciation of the rhythms and nuances of English. Irrespective of linguistic and cultural affiliations, a reading of the English *Gitanjali* can be a personal and intimate engagement with the spectres of a postcolonial world order, a probing of issues central to the problems of translation and translatability. Engaging with Tagore's own version of *Gitanjali* remains an act of faith for the acolytes of Indian writing in English.

References

1. Verse 26. All extracts from the English *Gitanjali* are from the edition published by Macmillan India in 2002.

2. Printed originally as 'character in Fiction' in *The Criterion* 11,8 (July 1924) and then revised and reprinted as 'Mr Bennet and Mrs Brown' in a pamphlet by the Hogarth Press the same year. Source: *A Modernist Reader: Modernism in England 1910–1930*, ed. Peter Faulkner, London: B.T. Batsford, 1986.

3. *The Times*, Saturday 15 November 1913; p. 13; Issue 40370; col F. The Times Digital Archives, accessed on 30 March 2004, 15.10 BST.

4. Quoted by Farida Majid, 'Tagore's Own Translations: Blindness and Hindsight' in *Revisioning English in Bangladesh*, eds Fakrul Alam, Niaz Zaman and Tahmina Ahmed, University Press, Dhaka, 2001. Majid quotes from *Passage to America: The Reception of Rabindranath Tagore in the United States, 1912–1941*, Sujit Mukherjee, Bookland, Calcutta, 1964.

5. Introduction, *Rabindranath Tagore: Poet and Dramatist* by Edward Thompson, Oxford University Press, 1991, p. a25.

6. These issues have been traced adequately in the introduction and notes that accompany *The English Writings of Rabindranath Tagore*, Volume I (Sahitya Akademi, New Delhi, 1994), edited by Sisir Kumar Das.

7. For a fuller discussion of this strange dichotomy in Tagore, see Harish Trivedi's 'Introduction', mentioned above.

Further reading

The English writings of Rabindranath Tagore (three volumes). Edited by Sisir Kumar Das. Sahitya Akademi, New Delhi, 1994–96.

Kripalani, Krishna, *Rabindranath Tagore: A Biography*. Oxford University Press, London, 1962.

Rabindranath Tagore: Universality and Tradition. Edited by Patrick Colm Hogan and Lalita Pandit, Associated University Presses, London, 2003.

Thompson, Edward, *Rabindranath Tagore: Poet and Dramatist*. Oxford University Press, New Delhi, 1948. A new paperback edition, also by OUP, brought out in 1991 has an excellent introduction by Harish Trivedi.

Contributor: Debanjan Chakrabarti

Modern Indian women writers in English

Introduction

The efforts of several generations of Indian authors writing in English have resulted in international success, particularly since the publication of *Midnight's Children* (1981) by **Salman Rushdie**, and the Indian novel in English has finally been accepted as an important literary endeavour. Indian women writers have begun to gain recognition, largely thanks to **Arundhati Roy** winning the Booker Prize for *The God of Small Things* in 1997. Behind this success lies a social history and a body of other work to which little critical attention has yet been paid.

Traditionally, the work of Indian women writers has been undervalued due to patriarchal assumptions about the superior worth of male experience. One factor contributing to this prejudice is the fact that most of these women write about the enclosed domestic space and women's perceptions of their experience within it. Consequently, it is assumed that their work will automatically rank below the works of male writers who deal with 'weightier' themes. Additionally, Indian women writers in English are victims of a second prejudice, vis-à-vis their regional counterparts. Since proficiency in English is available only to writers of the intellectual, affluent, educated classes, a frequent judgement is made that the writers, and their works, belong to a high social stratum and are cut off from the reality of Indian life. The majority of these novels depict the psychological suffering of the frustrated housewife, this subject matter often being considered superficial compared with the depiction of the repressed and oppressed lives of women of the lower classes that we find in regional authors writing in Hindi, Bengali, Malayalam, Urdu, Tamil, Telugu and other native languages.

English formal education in India

English education was introduced to India in the nineteenth century, serving as an ideological force behind social reform and control. There was an imperial mission of educating colonial subjects in the literature and thought of England, a mission that in the long run served to strengthen Western cultural hegemony. Thomas Babington Macaulay's *Education Minute* of 1835 is regarded as a crucial document in this history. His arguments were based on an assumption of the innate superiority of English culture, a key sentence in his *Minute* being:

> [we] must at present do our best to form a class of interpreters between us and
> the millions whom we govern; a class of persons Indian in blood and colour, but
> English in taste, in opinions, in morals and in intellect.

The establishment of English colleges in India led to the creation of an English-educated, and predominantly Hindu, élite, who eventually became critical of both their own religious orthodoxies, such as the caste system and child brides, and of British rule. The British-style education also had the effect of linking Indian writers to literary traditions of the West, enabling Indian writers writing in English to reach an audience in Europe as well as in India.

In the nineteenth century, both progressive and orthodox reformers supported female education in India, believing that social evils could be eliminated through education. However, the concept of education was limited to producing good home-makers and perpetuating orthodox ideology, as women were believed to support the traditional values of Indian society. Christian missionaries and British rulers, especially in Bengal where the British had made their first inroads in the mid-nineteenth century, started girls' schools, and in the 1880s, Indian women started to graduate from universities. The vast majority of girls, however, did not attend school, as education for women was confined mainly to the larger towns and cities.

The English language in India

Many critics see the use of the English language in India as one among many post-colonial mimic activities, resulting from the imposition of the English language as a part of British colonialist intervention in Indian education, language and literature. In India, some critics see the hegemony of English language and literature as a form of continuing cultural imperialism. Others argue that the widespread use, prestige and expansion of English in India in recent decades are attributable to the post-war hegemony of the United States rather than to the British Empire, that is, its growing global currency as a medium of communication.

However, the English language can alienate a text from its culture of origin, a view put forward by the Indian author Shashi Deshpande. She bases her argument on the idea that the English language is in some ways harmful to Indian culture not because it is the language of the former colonisers but because it has become the language of the privileged, élite classes in India. She admits that when she writes in English she is aware that her work will reach out to only a few English-speaking readers, most of whom will be thinking the way she does. The problem is that if an author writes in English with the purpose of changing social traditions, the language excludes the women whose involvement is most needed, English having no place in those women's daily lives. Another problem is the fact that writing in English also means using a language which most, or at least many, of one's characters do not speak. However, for many Indian authors English is no more than the medium through which they express themselves and through which they can reach an international audience.

Indian women authors

Prior to the rise of the novel, many Indian women composed poetry and short stories in Hindi, Punjabi, Bengali, Urdu, Tamil, Malayalam and Kannada. Women were the chief upholders of a rich oral tradition of story-telling, through myths, legends, songs and fables. Once literacy began to filter through society, those stories were transformed into poetry and drama. The novel was not at first a common form, perhaps because the majority of women had less access to education than men. It was not until prose began to be used in the late nineteenth century by Bengali writers who had been exposed to European culture that the novel form took hold in India.

The volume of Indian literature written in English is smaller than that written in the various regional languages and spans a smaller range of time, having commenced only with the spread of the English language and education. But in the last two decades there has been an astonishing flowering of Indian women writing in English, the literature of this period being published both in India and elsewhere. The authors are mostly western educated, middle-class women who express in their writing their discontent with the plight of upper-caste and class traditional Hindu women trapped in repressive institutions such as child-marriage, dowry, prohibitions on women's education, arranged marriages, suttee and enforced widowhood.

Poetry

Toru Dutt (1856–77) was the first Indian woman poet to write in English. Her work depicts archetypes of Indian womanhood, such as Sita and Savitri, showing women in suffering, self-sacrificing roles, reinforcing conventional myths in a patriotic manner. Her first book, published when she was 20, was a book of verse translations from French, *A Sheaf Gleaned in French Fields: Verse Translations and Poems* (1876).

Kamala Das originated a vigorous and poignant feminine *confessional* poetry, in which a common theme is the exploration of the man-woman relationship. This style was subsequently taken up by other women poets such as Gauri Deshpande, Suniti Namjoshi and Chitra Narendran.

The predicament of a single woman, spinster or separated, has also been a prominent theme in women's poetry. Tara Patel shows in *Single Woman* (1991) that in the harsh reality of the world, the quest for companionship without strings is a difficult one. Anna Sujata Matha in *Attic of Night* (1991) writes of the trauma of separation and the travails of a separated woman. Poetry for her seems to be an act of transcendence of agony, in the name of survival. But the image of woman she projects is strong and determined and she argues for a sense of community, justice and companionship.

While in women's poetry we hear the voice of the New Woman's definition of herself and a quest for her own identity, we hear the conventional male voice and see a conventional, often negative portrayal of women in men's poetry. An example is the six volumes of Nissim Ezekiel's poems, which depict women as mother, wife, whore, sex object or seductress.

Novels

Many Indian women novelists have explored female subjectivity in order to establish an identity that is not imposed by a patriarchal society. Thus, the theme of growing up from childhood to womanhood, that is, the **Bildungsroman**, is a recurrent strategy. Santha Rama Rau's *Remember the House* (1956), Ruth Prawar Jhabvala's first novel *To Whom She Will* (1955) and her later *Heat and Dust* (1975) which was awarded the Booker Prize, and Kamala Markandaya's *Two Virgins* (1973) are good examples. Sex is implied in these novels, but depicted more explicitly in *Socialite Evenings* (1989) by Shobha De, in which she describes the exotic sex lives of the high society in Mumbai.

As in poetry, the image of the New Woman and her struggle for an identity of her own also emerges in the Indian English novel. Such a struggle needs support structures outside the family to enable women to survive. Nayantara Sahgal uses this theme as the nucleus of *Rich Like Us* (1986). Other novels, such as Rama Mehta's *Inside the Haveli* (1977), look more towards issues of traditional Indian culture, particularly the debate on female education. Another example of the western-educated female protagonist's quest for her cultural roots is Githa Hariharan's *The Thousand Faces of Night* (1992).

A number of Indian women novelists made their debut in the 1990s, producing novels which revealed the true state of Indian society and its treatment of women. These writers were born after Indian independence, and the English language does not have colonial associations for them. Their work is marked by an impressive feel for the language and an authentic presentation of contemporary India, with all its regional variations. They generally write about the urban middle class, the stratum of society they know best.

Many of these authors, such as Chitra Banerjee Divakaruni in *The Mistress of Spices* (1997), use **magic realism** in their novels. Suniti Namjoshi stands out for her use of fantasy and surrealism, and Anuradha Marwah-Roy's *Idol Love* (1999) presents a chilling picture of an Indian dystopia in the twenty-first century. Other novels deal with various aspects of college life, such as Meena Alexander's *Nampally House* (1991) and Rani Dharker's *The Virgin Syndrome* (1997). Another theme to emerge is that of the lives of women during India's struggle for independence, as seen for example in Manju Kapur's *Difficult Daughters* (1998).

In the field of regional fiction, four women writers, Arundhati Roy, Anita Nair, Kamala Das and Susan Viswanathan, have put the southern state of Kerala on the fictional map, while the culture of different regions has been represented by other women writers.

Anita Desai, in her psychological novels, presents the image of a suffering woman preoccupied with her inner world, her sulking frustration and the storm within: the existential predicament of a woman in a male-dominated society. Through such characters, she makes a plea for a better way of life for women. Her novels have Indians as central characters and she alternates between female-centred and male-centred narrative. Her later novels, written since she moved to the USA, reveal all the characteristics of diasporic fiction, that is, a concern with the fate of immigrants and a growing distance from the reality of India, which is viewed from the outside.

As early as 1894 in *Kamala*, Krupabai Satthianadhan explored the cultural clash suffered by a Hindu woman who is given a western education in India, and the experience of being caught between two cultures has remained a prominent theme in writing by Indian woman. There are many Indian women writers based in the USA, Canada, Britain and other parts of the world. Some are recent immigrants, while others, such as **Jhumpa Lahiri**, are second-generation immigrants. These authors write about their situation in cross-cultural contexts – states of 'in-betweenness'.

Expatriate representation has been questioned on several counts. Most expatriate writers have a weak grasp of actual conditions in contemporary India and tend to recreate it through the lens of nostalgia, writing about 'imaginary homelands'. Distancing lends objectivity, but it can also lead to the ossification of cultural constructs, and even if memory is sharp and clear, the expatriate is not directly in contact with the reality of India.

The East/West confrontation, or the clash between tradition and modernity, is the impulse behind the works of acclaimed migrant writers, such as Meera Syal, Anita Rau Badami, Shauna Singh Baldwin, Uma Parameswaran, Chitra Banerjee Divakaruni, Anjana Appachana and Kiran Desai.

The theme of migration that leads to self-discovery, with a negation of the traditions of the country of origin, is a recurrent one among migrant authors, Bharti Kirchner's *Shiva Dancing* (1998), Ameena Meer's *Bombay Talkie* (1994) and Bharati Mukherjee's *Jasmine* (1989) being good examples.

Short stories

Alongside poetry and novels, many collections of short stories and anthologies of works by Indian women around the world have appeared, such as *Truth Tales* (1986), *Right of Way* (1988), *Truth Tales 2: The Slate of Life* (1990), *The Inner Courtyard* (1990), *Other Words: New Writing by Indian Women* (1992) and *Flaming Spirit* (1994).

Conclusion: the changing image of women in Indian fiction

The Hindu moral code known as *The Laws of Manu* denies woman an existence apart from that of her husband or his family, and since the publication of Bankim Chandra Chatterjee's *Rajmohan's Wife* in 1864 a significant number of authors have portrayed Indian women as long-suffering wives and mothers silenced by patriarchy. The ideal of the traditional, oppressed woman persisted in a culture permeated by religious images of virtuous goddesses devoted to their husbands, the Hindu goddesses Sita and Savitri serving as powerful cultural ideals for women. In mythical terms, the dominant feminine prototype is the chaste, patient, self-denying wife, Sita, supported by other figures such as Savitri, Draupadi and Gandhari. When looking at these narratives, silence/speech can be a useful guide to interpreting women's responses to patriarchal hegemony. Silence is a symbol of oppression, a characteristic of the subaltern condition, while speech signifies self-expression and liberation.

The image of women in fiction has undergone a change during the last four decades. Women writers have moved away from traditional portrayals of enduring, self-sacrificing women towards conflicted female characters searching for identity, no longer characterised and defined simply in terms of their victim status. In contrast to earlier novels, female characters from the 1980s onwards assert themselves and defy marriage and motherhood.

Recent writers depict both the diversity of women and the diversity within each woman, rather than limiting the lives of women to one ideal. The novels emerging in the twenty-first century furnish examples of a whole range of attitudes towards the imposition of tradition, some offering an analysis of the family structure and the caste system as the key elements of patriarchal social organisation. They also re-interpret mythology by using new symbols and subverting the canonic versions. In conclusion, the work of Indian women writers is significant in making society aware of women's demands and in providing a medium for self-expression and, thus, re-writing the History of India.

Contributor: Antonia Navarro-Tejero

For more on Indian literature see: Lahiri, Jhumpa; Mistry, Rohinton; Narayan, R. K.; Roy, Arundhati; Rushdie, Salman; An Introduction to Postcolonial Literature; Postcolonial Feminist theory: an overview.

Irish literature

The Irish Cultural Revival, W. B. Yeats and postcolonialism: two perspectives

Frantz Fanon and cultural nationalism in Ireland

Only recently has Ireland been included in the study of **postcolonial** societies. The fact that we are geographically close to Britain, racially identical, speak the same language and have the same value systems makes our status as postcolonial problematic. Some might argue that it is impossible to distinguish between Irish and British, while for others to mistake Irish for English is a grave insult.

An examination of Ireland's position in the light of the theories of the West Indian social philosopher Frantz Fanon (1925–61), put forward in his seminal work of anti-colonialism, *The Wretched of the Earth* (1961), can help to determine whether Ireland should be considered a postcolonial nation.

Fanon's observations on the rise of cultural nationalism in colonised societies suggest that the events which took place in Ireland at the end of the nineteenth century bore the hallmarks of a colonised people's anti-colonial struggle. The struggle was seen not only in the insistence on self-government but also in the revival of a culture that attempted to assert difference to the coloniser.

The years 1870 to 1890 saw a fervent battle for home rule for Ireland, led by Charles Stewart Parnell and his Home Rule party. Their aim was that Ireland should have its own parliament to deal with internal affairs, while remaining under the control of Westminster in international affairs. It was not yet the desire for a full separation from Britain; this would come later. By 1890, however, problems in Parnell's personal life had led to a breakdown in communication with the Prime Minister and a split in the Home Rule party.

As M. E. Collins points out, this failure left a void in Irish politics and social life which was filled by a new cultural awareness and a concern with Irish identity: 'the new movements were different. They stressed the importance of Irish identity, Irish race and Irish culture' (Collins, p. 170). In this context, the views Fanon put forward in *The Wretched of the Earth* are relevant to Irish history. In the chapter 'On National Consciousness' he stresses the colonised natives' fears of being totally assimilated into the culture of the coloniser – of being 'swamped' (Fanon, p. 169). This was the concern which occupied the minds of the Irish people after the failure of home rule. They began to be anxious about what Collins terms 'the distinguishing marks of

Irishness . . . a culture and language that was different to Britain's'. This culture and language 'was now disappearing fast. Ireland was developing an English culture that was indistinguishable from that in Britain' (Collins, p. 170).

Towards the end of the century, Ireland saw the rise of movements that attempted to reverse the process of 'cultural obliteration' (Fanon, p. 190) at the hands of the colonising power and to deAnglicise Ireland. In 1884, with the setting up of the Gaelic Athletic Association, distinctly Irish games were organised, with nationwide rules and competitions. A revival of the Irish language started in 1893 with the founding of the Gaelic League, a body which attempted to revive spoken Irish. The revival of the language was directly linked by some to a sense of national identity; you were not really Irish if you did not speak it. In the later 1890s, however, a new movement began which attempted to revive Irish literature without the necessity of the Irish language. This was the National Literary Society, led predominantly by **W. B. Yeats** and responsible for setting up the Abbey Theatre.

Fanon's theories are also seen to be relevant when considering Yeats and his involvement in the **Irish Cultural Revival**, particularly in the light of Yeats's choice of subject matter in his poetry after the 1880s. Fanon remarks on the use of a pre-colonial past to fight against the cultural hegemony of the coloniser: 'because they [the natives] realise that they are in danger of losing their lives and thus becoming lost to their people, these men . . . relentlessly determine to renew contact with the oldest and most pre-colonial springs of life' (Fanon, p. 169). Yeats revived and used Irish legends, associated with the pre-colonial, oral culture, as signifiers of a new contemporary national culture. In this way Yeats mirrors Fanon's theories on the use of the past (imagined or not) to restore a distinct identity and construct a homogenous national culture, different from and equal to the culture of the coloniser.

Tales of the heroic exploits of such characters as Cuchulainn and Na Fianna, which were predominant in Yeats's work, celebrated Ireland's past and endowed it with 'dignity, glory and solemnity' (Fanon, p. 169), as opposed to the savage picture imposed by Britain. Yeats was an example of Fanon's idea of the 'native intellectual' who 'decided to go back further and to delve deeper down' (Fanon, p. 169).

Fanon observes that it is difficult to have a distinct and separate national culture without having a distinct and separate nation: 'In the colonial situation, culture, which is doubly deprived of the support of the nation and the state, falls away and dies. The condition for its assistance is therefore national liberation and the Renaissance of the state' (Fanon, p. 197). In this way Fanon links the revival of a culture with the violent struggle for freedom in colonised societies. Yeats also makes this link, though in a more narcissistic way: 'did that play of mine send out/Certain men the English shot?' It is not known whether Yeats's play *Caitlin Ni Houlihan* (1902) (about self-sacrifice for the freedom of Ireland) was directly responsible, but subsequent to the revival of a distinct and glorified idea of Irish national culture, by the Gaelic League and the National Literary Society, home rule was no longer sufficient for Ireland.

'An Ireland not Gaelic merely, but free as well' (Collins, p. 178) was now demanded. In 1916, a bid was made for this independence, followed by a more successful one in 1919. Thus Fanon's theory, 'the claims to a national culture in the past . . .

rehabilitate that nation and serve as a justification of a future national culture' (Fanon, p. 169) is clearly exemplified by turn-of-the-century Ireland.

Yeats's preoccupation with reviving Irish folk culture allowed him to participate in a new construction of Irish nationality. He was, however, part of the Protestant ascendancy and it was believed by some that this qualified him as anything but Irish. Many did not want to define their identities by the cultural signs resurrected by Yeats and those who shared his views, causing a divide in Ireland that has repercussions to the present day.

Contributor: Jayne Lendrum

Edward W. Said and W. B. Yeats

In 1988 'Field Day', a cultural arts group founded by the dramatist Brian Friel and the actor Stephen Rea, and associated with **Seamus Heaney**, Seamus Deane and Tom Paulin, published 'Yeats and Decolonization', an article by the influential Palestinian-American literary critic Edward Said (1935–2003). The pamphlet proved to be an important catalyst for the study of Irish literature and culture in terms of postcolonial theory.

The premise of this seminal study is that Yeats was a poet of decolonisation, expressing the Irish experience of subjugation at the hands of the colonial power of Britain. Rather than reading Yeats's poetry from the conventional perspective of European high **Modernism**, Said writes, 'he appears to me, and I am sure many others in the Third World, to belong naturally to the other cultural domain' (Said, p. 3).* Said argues that Yeats's work towards the construction of a national Irish identity was an act of decolonisation. Further, he places Yeats within a global framework of anti-imperialism, drawing parallels between him and Third World writers and theorists such as Frantz Fanon, Pablo Neruda and **Chinua Achebe**.

Although this was in many ways an important and influential article, some of Said's underlying assumptions are questionable. Said links Ireland with territories such as India, South America, Africa and Malaysia, as a site of colonial contention. In doing so he emphasises Ireland's position (and thus the position of its literature) in colonial history as belonging to the peripheral Third World. According to Said's view, 'bog dwellers' are the Irish counterpart to 'niggers . . . babus and wogs' (Said, p. 6). But this argument does not stand up to scrutiny and Denis Donoghue, for example, has condemned this aspect of postcolonial theory for adopting a global paradigm of colonial experience which treats all empires as homogenous.

Displaying many of the pitfalls critiqued by Donoghue, Said's article offers a simplistic formulation of colonial experience – a formulation convenient for the nationalist politician and the scholar searching for an uncomplicated postcolonial framework in which to examine Irish literature. But the view is centrally flawed in that it is insensitive to the variations in individual national and regional encounters with imperial powers. Said does acknowledge the complex relationship between Ireland and Britain: 'It is true the connections are closer between England and Ireland than between England and India' (Said, p. 15) and the complexity of Yeats's own position: 'He belongs . . . to the Protestant Ascendancy whose Irish loyalties . . . were confused'

---

*Citations are from Said's essay 'Yeats and Decolonization' as published by Bay Press.

(Said, p. 13), but it seems that he does so only to gloss over such glaring problems with his thesis.

Furthermore, Said wishes to present Ireland as a Third World nation, as England's poor 'other' and as belonging to the 'cultural domain' of the developing world. But to refer to 'Ireland's backwardness' (Said, p. 14) and Third World status is to ignore the historical and economic fact that Ireland was, and is, a relatively wealthy member of the First World. As Liam Kennedy points out, even if Ireland is less wealthy as a nation than Britain or France, to consider Ireland as an underdeveloped peripheral nation is farcical:

> Average incomes in Ireland, even half a century earlier in time than in the case of African and Asian countries, belonged to a different economic league. That league was a West European one, with Ireland enjoying much the same average living standards as countries like Spain, Norway, Finland, Italy. (Kennedy, p. 110)

What makes the Irish example so challenging for the postcolonial theorist is the fact that Ireland was victim, accomplice and beneficiary of British and European imperialism. The sense of hybridity in postcolonial culture, that 'cultures are never unitary in themselves, nor simply dualistic in relation of Self to Other' (Bhabha, p. 207), is essential to an understanding of Irish identity. Eight centuries of movement between Ireland and Britain has produced some of the most complex cultural identities possible, which can be seen to manifest themselves today in the North as enigmatically as they ever have in Irish–British relations.

In spite of the shortcomings of Said's thesis, it remains the case that an imperial relationship did exist between Britain and Ireland and Said's article is significant for the dual effect it had of bringing postcolonial theory into Irish cultural criticism and moving the perception of Ireland closer to the postcolonial arena.

The most positive aspect of Said's essay is his placing of Yeats as an important artist in the context of Irish nationalist aspirations and decolonising enterprises. Said depicts Yeats's 'insistence on a new narrative' for Irish people as central to the emergence of Irish nationalism. The ideal of the reclaiming of Ireland, the geographical space and the notion of a community, in his poetry, is seen as a countermeasure against colonialism.

For Said, Yeats's Poem *Leda and the Swan* represents Yeats 'at his most powerful', where 'he imagines and renders' (Said, p. 24) the outcome of the colonial relationship between Ireland and Britain. The poem has been further discussed in this vein by Declan Kiberd, who interprets the 'swan as the invading occupier and the girl as a ravished Ireland' (Kiberd, p. 315).

Leda and the Swan was composed in September 1923, a fact Kiberd finds significant in suggesting a meaning behind the subject matter and imagery relating to the Irish Civil War of 1922–23. The final lines of the poem are particularly relevant in this respect:

> Being so caught up,
> So mastered by the brute blood of the air,
> Did she put on his knowledge with his power
> Before the indifferent beak could let her drop?

If one takes the swan to be colonial Britain and Leda a feminised and subjugated Ireland, Yeats might seem to be offering a prophetic commentary on the consequences of colonialism. According to Greek mythology, following the rape of Leda, Clytemnestra, who would later kill Agamemnon, was born. Yeats, perhaps, suggests that the new nation of Ireland which would emerge after the withdrawal of England (the dropping from the 'indifferent beak') was destined for a chaotic and violent future: anti-colonial nationalism based on a colonial model of state, searching for a return to a pre-colonial Ireland without acknowledging the hybridity of the new Irish culture, would inevitably lead to civil war. Yeats does not offer a solution to the problems of reasserting an Irish nation after colonialism, but if this reading of the poem is correct he does offer an insight to the problems Ireland might encounter as a postcolonial nation.

Postcolonial discourse has begun to contribute to Irish culture and to an understanding of that culture. As this process continues, with the publication of works by scholars such as David Lloyd and Declan Kiberd, the case of Ireland should refine the current models of postcolonial thought.

Contributor: Andy Morrison

References

(with annotations by Aidan Fadden and Andy Morrison)

Bhabha, Homi K. (1988) 'The Commitment to Theory', *New Formations*, 5: 5–23. Reprinted in part as 'Cultural Diversity and Cultural Differences' in *The Postcolonial Studies Reader*. Ed. Bill Ashcroft, Gareth Griffiths and Helen Tiffin. London: Routledge, 1995, 206–209.

Collins, M. E. (1993) *History in the Making: Ireland 1868–1966.* Dublin: Education Company of Ireland.

Deane, Seamus (1997) *Strange Country: Modernity and the Irish Nation – Irish Writing Since 1790.* Oxford: Clarendon Press.

Donoghue, Denis (1998) 'Confusion in Irish Studies': Queen's University of Belfast English Society Lecture. The Queen's University of Belfast. 5 March. *(A controversial lecture which posits a critique of the limitations of postcolonial theory in relation to the study of Ireland with a consideration of Kiberd and Deane.)*

Fanon, Frantz (2001) *The Wretched of the Earth.* London: Penguin Classics. (First published as *Les Damnes de la Terre*, 1961, and as *The Wretched of the Earth*, 1963.)

Kennedy, Liam (1992/93) 'Modern Ireland: Postcolonial Society or Postcolonial Pretensions?' in *The Irish Review*, 13, Winter: 107–121. *(Excellent study of Ireland's economic status which answers the assertion that Ireland may be considered a Third World nation. An objective sociological and economic analysis vital to any scholar wishing to discuss Ireland from a postcolonial perspective.)*

Kiberd, Declan (1996) *Inventing Ireland: The Literature of the Modern Nation.* London:

Vintage. *(Kiberd's approach is a broadly canonical and sequential treatment of Ireland's literature and history. He offers strong insight in a form which is less jargon oriented than some criticism in the field. He views Ireland in some ways as an accumulation of postcolonial personalities in an interesting opposition to Elmann's emphasis on modernity.)*

Lloyd, David (1993) *Anomalous States: Irish Writing and the Post-colonial Moment.* Dublin: The Lilliput Press. *(Excellent postcolonial study of Irish literature which pre-dates Kiberd's text and provided the impetus for future work. The essay on Seamus Heaney is very good.)*

Said, Edward W. (1989) 'Yeats and Decolonization' in *Remaking History,* ed. Barbara Kruger and Phil Mariani. *Dia Art Foundation: Discussions in Contemporary Culture.* 4. Seattle: Bay Press. *(An early attempt to appropriate Ireland into mainstream postcolonial theory. A little clumsy in its tendency towards essentialist formulations, it nevertheless raises valid questions regarding the complex case of Ireland in postcolonial studies.)*

These articles are edited version of articles which were originally published on The Imperial Archive, a project supervised by Dr Leon Litvack, School of English, Queen's University, Belfast. www.qub.ac.uk/en/imperial/imperial.htm

See also: A survey of modern British, Irish and American drama; Beckett, Samuel; Heaney, Seamus; Joyce, James; Yeats, W. B.

South African literature

A survey of modern South African literature

South Africa has a rich history of literary output. Until relatively recently, **realism** dominated South African fiction, perhaps because authors felt an overriding concern to capture the country's turbulent history and the experiences of its people. Fiction has been written in all of South Africa's 11 official languages – with a large body of work in Afrikaans, in particular – but this survey focuses primarily on fiction in English, though it also touches on major poetic developments.

The colonial adventure

The first fictional works to emerge from South Africa were produced by immigrants who often felt alienated from the South African landscape, even if fascinated by its harsh beauty. These colonial writers were unsettled and intrigued by what they perceived to be exotic elements of indigenous cultures. Their attitude to indigenous South Africans was, at best, ambivalent, if not outright hostile. This is especially true of the writers of adventure-type stories, in which colonial heroes are romanticised and the role of black South Africans is reduced to that of enemy or servant.

One such writer was Rider Haggard, who wrote many mythical and adventure stories, beginning in the early 1880s. His most famous book is *King Solomon's Mines* (1886), a best-seller in its day (and filmed several times up to the 1980s). Like subsequent novels such as *Allan Quartermain* and *She* (both 1887), its central character is the hunter Allan Quartermain, Haggard's ideal of the colonial gentleman. These novels follow his adventures in the 'darkest Africa' of the European imagination, fixated on mysterious white queens and hidden treasures in ancient cities (built, of course, by someone other than black people). The **point of view** is that of the heroic Englishman, and indigenous peoples are portrayed either as dangerous savages or given the role of the faithful servant (Quartermain's Zulu retainer eventually gives his life for his master). Although Haggard wrote many other adventures and fantasies, it is his highly coloured African works that are still read today.

Truly South African voices

Olive Schreiner's novel *The Story of an African Farm* (1883) is generally considered to be the founding text of South African literature. Schreiner was born on a mission station and worked as a governess on isolated Karoo farms, an experience that informed the novel. It tells the story of several characters representing aspects of South African society of its day. Lyndall, the young heroine, is the focus of Schreiner's **feminist** concerns. Bonaparte Blenkins is a portrait of the 'imperial rogue' and thus allows Schreiner to express her nascent anti-colonial ideas (she later supported the Boers in their war of freedom against Britain). There is also Tant Sannie, the Boer woman, the kindly German Uncle Otto and Otto's son Waldo, who expresses the universal themes of the novel in his concern with spiritual meaning. The novel draws on the post-**Romantic** sensibility of *Wuthering Heights* and depicts rural South African life with authenticity and brio. It has been criticised for its silence with regard to the black African presence in South Africa, but it is still a key text in the formation of a truly South African voice. Schreiner's other work includes a critique of Cecil John Rhodes's brutal form of colonialism, *Trooper Peter Halkett of Mashonaland* (1897), and the polemical *Women and Labour* (1911).

Douglas Blackburn had a certain amount in common with Schreiner, though he was writing from a very different standpoint. He was a maverick British journalist who went to South Africa when the Transvaal was still a Boer republic and stayed during the Anglo-Boer War and beyond. In several newspapers, he denounced British colonial attitudes as well as satirising Boer corruption. He wrote two novels set in this world, *Prinsloo of Prinsloosdorp* (1899) and *A Burgher Quixote* (1903), capturing with a great deal of sly humour the personality and situation of the Boer at the time.

His later novel *Leaven* (1908) is a moving denunciation of 'blackbirding' and other iniquitous labour practices and is one of the first South African novels to portray what life was really like for peasants forced into urban labour. *Love Muti* (1915) attacks British colonial attitudes. Blackburn is not read much today, but his work is an important contribution to a developing South African literature – and style. Herman Charles Bosman, for one, seems to have learned from Blackburn's ironic humour.

Emergence of black writing

It was not until the twentieth century that literature by black South Africans emerged, with the first generation of mission-educated African writers seeking to restore dignity to Africans by invoking and reconstructing a heroic African past.

The first novel by a black South African was *Mhudi* (completed in 1920 but only published in 1930), by Solomon (Sol) Thekiso Plaatje. This epic story follows the progress of the Tswana people during and after their military encounter with the Zulus under Shaka, the Zulu conqueror of the nineteenth century, and encompasses their earliest encounters with the white people moving into the interior.

Viewed as the founding father of black literature in South Africa, Plaatje was also the first secretary general of the then South African Native National Congress (now the African National Congress) at its foundation in 1912. His *Native Life in South Africa* (1916) was a seminal text in the study of land dispossession in South Africa. He also wrote a diary of the siege of Mafeking during the Boer War and translated Shakespeare into Setswana language.

While Plaatje's *Mhudi* related the history of the Tswana people, Thomas Mofolo's

Chaka reinvents the legendary Zulu king (commonly referred to as Shaka). Mofolo portrays him as a heroic but tragic figure, a monarch to rival Shakespeare's Macbeth. He is concerned to find in African history characters to rival those of the European literary tradition, which is based on the epics of ancient times, with their gods and heroes. Mofolo, however, also invests Shaka with a complex personality, in which good and evil are at war – in contrast to white colonial historians who made him a simplistic monster of tribal savagery. Completed in 1910, the novel was published in 1925 and the first English translation came out in 1930.

Shock and satire

Just as Olive Schreiner had drawn fire from the colonial élite for her liberal views, so William Plomer, decades later, shocked colonial society with his novel *Turbott Wolfe* (1926), written when he was only 19 years old. It tackled the highly sensitive issue of inter-racial love, though it is hardly a roistering sexual chronicle. It was, however, an indictment of white South African attitudes at the time – a mere suggestion that there might be some human sympathy, let alone sexual attraction, between a white person and a black person, horrified many. There is also open discussion of the political and racial situation in South Africa. Along with his contemporaries and sometime collaborators Laurens van der Post and Roy Campbell, Plomer left South Africa soon after the publication of his novel. He settled finally in Britain, where he became known primarily as a poet.

Between the wars

Perhaps the dominant figure of South African literature in the period between the two world wars was Sarah Gertrude Millin, whose reputation has faded considerably since her death. This is due to her politics: she was initially a devout supporter of Jan Smuts's government, but later became something of an apologist for Apartheid. Her views on the 'tragedy' of racial miscegenation were put forward in *God's Stepchildren* (1924). Seen in terms of racial hierarchies, with whites at the top and blacks at the bottom, Millin's views represented those held widely at the time. Her later novels continued to deal with the 'predicament' of coloured (mixed-race) people in South Africa or attempted to describe the world of indigenous peoples.

The 1940s

The 1940s saw the beginnings of a flowering of literature by black South Africans, as a generation of mission-educated Africans came of age. Among them was H. I. E. Dhlomo, whose work preached a 'return to the source' – the wisdom of finding traditional ways of dealing with modern problems. His work includes several plays and the long poem 'The Valley of a Thousand Hills' (1941). Poets such as B. W. Vilakazi, who wrote in Zulu, gave new literary life to their indigenous languages.

Peter Abrahams, an important voice who began writing in the 1940s, was of mixed-race descent. His early novel, *Mine Boy* (1946), was published in the same year in which a large miners' strike was violently suppressed by Smuts's government. *Mine Boy* depicts life in black areas of the time and dramatises the problems of rural people in a depressed urban environment – a theme that was referred to as the 'Jim comes to Jo'burg' phenomenon in South African literature. Later works by Abrahams (who left South Africa and settled in Britain before finally moving to Jamaica) include *The Path of Thunder* (1948), which deals with interracial love; *Return to Goli* (1953), about his journey back to report on life in Johannesburg; and his autobiography *Tell Freedom* (1954).

Another South African writer who emerged in the 1940s, Herman Charles Bosman, has become one of the country's best-loved authors, particularly for his short stories set in the Groot Marico farming district. These tales, first published in the late 1940s, are a sometimes-gentle-sometimes-savage portrait of Afrikaner storytelling skills and social attitudes. Bosman uses the voice of **unreliable narrators** such as Oom Schalk Lourens who relate the stories as if from their own **viewpoint**, but in a way that allows the reader to see through their prejudices and blind spots. Among the most famous are 'Unto Dust' and 'In the Withaak's Shade'. Bosman's first collection of stories, *Mafeking Road*, was published in 1947. A colourful character, who was jailed for the mysterious murder of his stepbrother, Bosman also wrote poetry, novels and much journalism, often satirical. One of his best works, *Cold Stone Jug* (1949), is a semi-fictionalised account of his time in jail. All his books were reissued in new 2001 editions to coincide with the 50th anniversary of his death.

Bosman had satirised social attitudes in South Africa, but it was the work of Alan Paton, a former schoolteacher – published in the very year in which the Afrikaner Nationalists came to power and established Apartheid – that brought the world's attention to the situation of black people in South Africa. And it was written by a white man. *Cry, The Beloved Country* (1948) is possibly the most famous novel to have come out of South Africa. When it was first published, it was an international best-seller, launching Paton to worldwide fame. The novel put South Africa on the map of international politics by making visible to Western audiences the effects of racial prejudice and the oppression of black people.

Cry, The Beloved Country is the story of a black priest who travels to Johannesburg in search of his son, who has fallen victim to the corrupting influence of the city. The novel explores themes of corruption and forgiveness, putting forward a liberal-humanist view of South Africa's racial politics, as well as Paton's deeply felt Christianity. The novel has a poetic language, with extensive use of Biblical cadences, though Paton has also been criticised for a possibly condescending portrayal of black people.

Paton later got involved in South African politics through the Liberal Party, of which he was a leader. He opposed the Apartheid state while refusing to countenance the use of violence against it. He also wrote biography, much journalism, poetry and two further novels.

The *Drum* decade: urban black life

The 1950s was the decade in which the African National Congress and its alliance partners launched the massive Defiance Campaign, a huge, peaceful challenge to white supremacy. It was the decade in which the Freedom Charter, the central document of the anti-racist movement, was written on the basis of contributions from all over the country. And it was the decade in which the Apartheid state responded with massive treason trials for those who defied it.

The 1950s also saw a new generation of black writers talking about the conditions of their lives in their own voices – voices with a distinctive stamp and style. The popular *Drum* magazine in the 1950s was their forum and encouraged their emergence. It depicted a vibrant urban black culture for the first time – a world of jazz, shebeens (illegal drinking dens) and flamboyant gangsters (tsotsis). Reportage blurred into fiction: there were satirical stories ridiculing the discriminatory and repressive policies of the state, while others provided harrowing details of the effect of Apartheid legislation on people's lives. These writers recorded urban deprivation, but also the resilience of people who survived 'without visible means of subsistence'.

Es'kia (formerly Ezekiel) Mphahlele later described the style of *Drum* writers as 'racy, agitated, impressionistic, it quivered with a nervous energy, a caustic wit'. These writers may have been politically cynical rather than directly involved in politics (and their sexism has been noted by many), but they did create a vibrant voice that speaks in the truly original tones of the urban black experience in South Africa, and for that alone they are highly valued. Their work ranged from the investigative journalism of Henry Nxumalo to the witty social commentary of Todd Matshikiza; others such as Nat Nakasa, Can Themba and Mphahlele moved towards embodying their visions of black South African life in poetry or fiction.

Later, Nakasa edited a literary journal, *The Classic*, which published work such as Themba's story *The Suit* (1963), now regarded as a classic of South African literature. It has been adapted for the stage and has toured the world in Peter Brook's production. Themba was banned by the Apartheid state and died in exile, an alcoholic, in 1968, but others such as Mphahlele pursued their literary careers (see below).

Lewis Nkosi became a noted literary critic in Europe and the United States. Other notable writers connected in some way to *Drum* include William Bloke Modisane, Arthur Maimane, Dyke Sentso, James Matthews, Peter Clarke, Richard Rive, Jordan Ngubane, Alex La Guma and Casey Motsisi. Modisane wrote the autobiography *Blame Me on History* (1963), Matthews has written much poetry and a novel, and Rive wrote *Buckingham Palace, District Six* (1986), about life in that coloured Cape Town area, and two novels about South African states of emergency, decades apart, *Emergency* (1964) and *Emergency Continued* (1989).

E'skia Mphahlele's autobiographical *Down Second Avenue* (1959) is a landmark in the development of South African fiction. Set in a village and a township near Pretoria, the text records in evocative language the resilience of various female characters in Mphahlele's life, who defy poverty and urban squalor to bring him up. At the same time, they are presented with complexity and depth – his grandmother, for one, is a rather tyrannical figure.

Mphahlele went on to write critiques, *The African Image* (1962), short stories, *Man Must Live* (1946), *In Corner B* (1967), as well as further novels, including *The Wanderers* (1971). In some ways an extension of the autobiographical form of *Down Second Avenue, The Wanderers* articulated his own experiences, first as an adult in South Africa and then his move into exile (he settled in Nigeria in 1957, returning to South Africa in 1977). He also wrote poetry and autobiography. Taken as a whole, Mphahlele's oeuvre represents one of the most important views of the life experience and developing views of a politically aware South African; this is the work of a black man taking the urban scenario as his subject matter and moving beyond the sometimes contradictory messages of the mission-educated generation.

Gordimer: from liberalism to radicalism

At the same time as the *Drum* generation was creating the first urban black voice, one of South Africa's most important white writers was beginning her long, distinguished career. Nadine Gordimer published her first short stories in the early 1950s; in 1991 she was awarded the Nobel Prize for Literature. Between those two dates, her many novels and short stories articulated key issues for white South Africans sympathetic to the plight of disenfranchised blacks, as well as providing for the outside world a devastating picture of what it was like to live under Apartheid.

In her fiction, Gordimer moves from the position of a white liberal with a perhaps mildly or unconsciously paternalistic attitude towards her black compatriots, to a much more radical position that attempts to give voice to the black liberation movement, while at the same time articulating the contradictions in which white liberals and radicals were often caught.

Her second novel, *A World of Strangers* (1958), shows the first fruitful but often frightening encounters between white and black people in the heady days of Sophiatown. By the time of *The Late Bourgeois World* (1966), Gordimer was dealing directly with the effects of the black liberation movement on white South Africans, showing the divided soul of the white liberal in a morally ambivalent situation. *The Conservationist* (1974) pits Afrikaner land hunger against the indigenous population in an often phantasmagoric narrative. *Burger's Daughter* (1979) depicts the involvement of radical white activists in the liberation struggle. *July's People* (1981), perhaps Gordimer's most powerful novel, projects into the future the final collapse of white supremacy and what that might mean for white and black people on an intimate level. Her other works (and her short stories are regarded as among her finest work) deal with issues such as love across the colour line and, more recently, the emergence of South Africa into a democracy after the release of Nelson Mandela in 1990 – a society still dealing with myriad contradictions.

Figures of the 1960s

In the early 1960s, the State of Emergency used by the Apartheid state to crack down on dissidents, the banning of political organisations such as the African National Congress and the Pan African Congress, and the jailing of leaders such as Nelson Mandela, sent many black writers into exile. Among them was Alex la Guma, a Marxist and ANC leader who saw the purpose of his work as the exposure of the dreadful conditions of South Africa's oppressed. His novella *A Walk in the Night* (1962) shows the life of crime to which slum inhabitants are driven, while *And a*

Threefold Cord (1967) contrasts the existence of a black worker in a white home with her employer's affluent life. The later novel, *In the Fog of the Season's End* (1972), possibly his best, shows the developing consciousness of a man dedicated to the underground struggle for freedom. As a 'listed person', little of la Guma's work was available in South Africa until 1990, when the ban on the liberation movements was lifted.

At the same time, in the 1960s, the Afrikaans literary scene had a rush of new blood, as writers such as Jan Rabie, Etienne Leroux, Breyten Breytenbach and Andre Brink emerged. Publishing first in Afrikaans, these writers were increasingly politicised by the situation in South Africa and their contrasting experiences overseas.

Breytenbach, who began as one of the most linguistically radical new poets in Afrikaans, left South Africa in 1960 where he had become a vocal critic of the Apartheid state. Later, in the 1970s, he returned to South Africa and was arrested and jailed for work he was doing for the liberation movement. From this experience came his extraordinary prison memoir, *True Confessions of an Albino Terrorist* (1996). It is as much interior monologue as it is a record of his prison years, mixing **surreal** visions and Zen attitudes. His return visits to South Africa are recorded, mixing reportage and imaginative commentary, in *A Season in Paradise* (1976) and *Return to Paradise* (1993). His prison poetry was published in English in *Judas Eye* (1988). Breytenbach remains as caustic about politics and power under an ANC government as he was under a Nationalist one. His essays have been published in *The Memory of Birds in Times of Revolution* (1996).

Andre Brink stayed in South Africa to see his novels become the first Afrikaans works banned by the government. He began to write in English as well as Afrikaans and his novels have become as important a part of South African English-language literature as they are in Afrikaans. Having published several novels in Afrikaans during the 1960s, it was his novel *Looking on Darkness* (1973) that was first banned. His immensely powerful novel *A Dry White Season* (1982), focused on the death in detention of a black activist and caused great irritation to the Apartheid state, while stirring the conscience of many white South Africans. It was also banned, then the ban was lifted. Later novels by this prolific novelist include *An Act of Terror* (1991), dealing with an Afrikaner dissident turned 'terrorist', and *On the Contrary* (1993), a playful reworking of South Africa's colonial history.

During this period, Bessie Head emerged as a leading South African woman writer, with the role of women as a central concern. Of mixed blood, and with a traumatic family history, Head left South Africa to avoid its racial policies and lived in Botswana, where she felt more at ease. Her novels show a marked sympathy with ordinary peasant women; her heroines are poor but strong-willed, women who have to face up to various forms of prejudice. Her first novel was *When Rain Clouds Gather* (1968), followed by *Maru* (1971), *A Question of Power* (1973) and *The Collector of Treasures* (1977). *The Collector of Treasures* is her most autobiographical work, dealing with the traumas of her illegitimate mixed-race birth, her mother's suicide and her own nervous breakdown.

Another writer to make his name in the 1960s was Wilbur Smith, South Africa's most popular literary export. He is a worldwide best-selling author who now stands in the ranks of the money-making élite as far as popular fiction is concerned. In many ways he is the heir to the tradition of Rider Haggard – some would say politically as well. His long, fast-moving adventure stories deal in sex and violence, often set against a backdrop of political turmoil. It is here that Smith reveals attitudes that were not out of place in Apartheid South Africa. As with Haggard, black characters are often either menacing or servile; there are few who are treated simply as human beings with full interior lives to match those of his sexy, strong white heroes.

Smith's earliest novels are probably his best: *Where the Lion Feeds* (1964) and *The Sound of Thunder* (1966) are set in the era of the foundation of gold-mining in South Africa. Others go as far afield as the state of Israel, Ethiopia during the Italian invasion, piracy in the age of sail or, more recently, investigate the pharaonic times of Ancient Egypt. There is no doubt that Smith has a propulsive narrative gift; some readers, though, may be irked by his often sexist and racist assumptions, as well as repelled by the frequent blood-letting.

The 1960s also saw the emergence of a new generation of white South African poets, among them Douglas Livingstone, Sidney Clouts, Ruth Miller, Lionel Abrahams and Stephen Gray. Their work ranges from powerful apprehensions of natural life (Livingstone) to more interior, meditative considerations (Abrahams) and a sardonic socio-political sensibility (Gray). Gray has also written novels, plays and much criticism. Abrahams has written two semi-autobiographical novels, *The Celibacy of Felix Greenspan* (1977) and *The White Life of Felix Greenspan* (2002).

The Soweto poets

In the 1970s, South Africa experienced a literary revival of black voices that had been silenced by repression. The 1970s are widely regarded as a defining period for the development of political consciousness among black South Africans, with the rise of the Black Consciousness (BC) movement, of which the martyred Bantu Steve Biko was a leading figure, and the schoolchildren's revolt of 1976.

BC advocated an affirmation of black cultural values and a racial solidarity in the face of state oppression. Literature became a vehicle to promote the political ideals of anti-Apartheid popular movements. Many of these productions were designed to mobilise audiences against state policies, and the genres of drama and poetry were utilised for their immediacy of impact. The most notable writers from this period are Mongane (Wally) Serote, Sipho Sepamla, Oswald Joseph Mbuyiseni Mtshali, Christopher van Wyk, Mafika Gwala and Don Mattera. Couched in graphic language designed to arouse the emotions of listeners, their poems were often performed at political rallies.

While Mtshali's poems, first published in 1971 in *The Sound of a Cowhide Drum*, asked for generalised sympathy for the plight of poor black people, and Sepamla was at first considered a 'contemplative' poet, the tone soon changed. By the time of *The Soweto I Love* (1977), Sepamla's poetic persona is fully identified with the oppressed. Sepamla also wrote a novel of this turbulent time, *A Ride on the Whirlwind* (1981). Sepamla, apart from being a leading arts teacher, has written several other novels and his *Selected Poems* was published in 1984.

Serote's early poems, in volumes such as *Yakhal'inkomo* (1972) and *Tsetlo* (1974), are short and sharp. They deal with the life and attitudes of a politically aware black person, looking at his society and its discontentment. In later volumes, Serote begins to develop an epic, incantatory voice, with the long poems of *Behold Mama, Flowers* (1978) and *Come and Hope with Me* (1994), winner of the Noma Award for Publishing in Africa.

Serote (who became an ANC leader) is also the author of the novel *To Every Birth Its Blood* (1981), a remarkable account of political activity in the 1970s. It graphically recreates state violence, initial black apathy and ultimate black involvement in 'liberatory' violence. Serote's later novel, *Gods of our Time* (1999), reconstructs civil and military campaigns which led to the demise of Apartheid. These novels do not simply record the grim life of people in the ghetto but go on to celebrate the resilience of the human spirit in the face of adversity.

Other interesting fiction to deal with the Soweto revolt and subsequent political activity includes Miriam Tlali's *Amandla* (1980) and Mbulelo Mzamane's *The Children of Soweto* (1982). Don Mattera has written an account of life in Sophiatown and its destruction, *Memory is the Weapon* (1987).

The emergency years

Increasing internal and external pressure on the Apartheid state led, in the 1980s, to its most repressive measures yet. While sanctions were imposed from outside, a mass democratic movement, based on the ideals of the Freedom Charter, arose within the country. The state responded with successive states of emergency that brought white troops to the townships; a state of civil war existed in all but name.

In the face of this, the driving need for politicised work was felt, as it had been in the 1970s. Poets such as the orator Mzwakhe Mbuli reached vast audiences, while novelists such as Menan du Plessis and Mandla Langa engaged with the business of resistance to Apartheid. Yet at the same time, some felt the need for a move away from rhetoric and towards the depiction of ordinary life. In his 1986 essay, *The Rediscovery of the Ordinary*, Njabulo Ndebele expressed this view, seeing politically determined work as inimical to a full depiction of rounded humanity in fiction. His own fiction, in the award-winning collection *Fools and Other Stories* (1983), demonstrated that it could be done with grace. Although written in the wake of township rebellion, the book is not polemical but evokes township life with subtlety. It probes the formative experiences of young men growing up in a township, vividly evoking the rhythms and speech of township life. The main story, 'Fools', was later reworked into a movie with an all-South African cast.

J. M. Coetzee, one of South Africa's most lauded writers, began publishing in the 1970s, but achieved prominence in the 'emergency years'. Like Ndebele, he eschewed fiction of direct political statement, though his complex **postmodern** work deals in subtle ways with issues of power, authority and history. One of the key works of recent South African writing, Coetzee's novel *Waiting for the Barbarians* (1980), tackles issues germane to South Africa by telling the story of an official at the outpost of an unidentified empire, one under stress from a barbarian threat that may or may not be imagined. His next novel, *Life and Times of Michael K* (1983), won the Booker Prize in Britain. This story of a poor man of colour trying to survive in a civil-war situation, never taking sides, is very powerful, as is *Age of Iron* (1990), which takes the perspective of a white academic who is dying even as the townships explode with violence.

Coetzee's novel *Disgrace* (1999) won him a second Booker Prize and caused huge debate in South Africa over its depiction of a post-Apartheid reality in which the wounds of the past have not been healed – and new ones are being inflicted. Coetzee is also an illustrious literary academic (*Doubling the Point* (1992)) and has published a memoir of growing up in South Africa, *Boyhood* (1998).

After Apartheid

Questions were asked of writers as Apartheid came to an end with the release of Nelson Mandela in 1990 and over the transitional period leading up to the democratic election in 1994. What, they were asked, will you write about now that Apartheid and racial tension, your primary topics as South African writers, have gone? Well, Apartheid may have died, but its effects linger on, and as writers such as Coetzee have demonstrated, the issues of power that haunted the Apartheid era are still with us in many ways. Certainly, while there has been no sudden post-Apartheid renaissance, there are many important writers dealing with South Africa today and processing its past.

Among them, one of the most acclaimed is Zakes Mda, who worked for many years as a playwright and poet before publishing his first novels in 1995. He started with a bang – with two novels, *She Plays with the Darkness* and *Ways of Dying*. The latter, the story of a professional mourner, won the M-Net Book Prize. His next novel, *The Heart of Redness* (2001), won the Commonwealth Prize; it contrasts the past of the nineteenth century, when the prophetess Nongqawuse brought ruin to the Xhosa people, with a present-day narrative.

Ivan Vladislavic is another author pushing into the post-Apartheid future, with distinctly **postmodern** works that play with the conventions of fiction as much as they speak about contemporary realities in South Africa. He has published two collections of stories, *Missing Persons* (1990) and *Propaganda by Monuments* (2000), and two novels, *The Folly* (1993) and *The Restless Supermarket* (2001).

Lesego Rampolokeng came to prominence in the 1980s, through the Congress of South African Writers. His is one of the most irreverent voices to hit the South African literary scene in recent years. Using a vibrant mix of rap-styled poetry and township idiom, he displays no loyalty to any figures of authority. His poems were published in *Horns for Hondo* (1991) and *End Beginnings* (1993). A powerful live performer of his work, he has collaborated with musicians as well.

K. Sello Duiker is a young novelist who made a name for himself in South Africa, with two novels, *Thirteen Cents* (2000) and *The Quiet Violence of Dreams* (2001), coming out in quick succession. Both have won him awards and critical acclaim. Set in the urban landscape of Cape Town, the novels see the world through the eyes of the underdog, a street kid in the first and an ostracised gay student in the second.

Mark Behr has been one of the most compelling and controversial additions to the South African literary canon. His first novel, *The Smell of Apples* (1997), was published first in Afrikaans. It tells of white South Africans who were brainwashed by the Apartheid system, and went on to win several prizes. Soon after that, Behr admitted that he had been a spy for the Apartheid police while a student activist; a graphic illustration, if one were needed, of the divided loyalties felt by many whites in that period. Behr's second novel, *Embrace* (2000), deals with the formative experiences of a young homosexual.

There are many contemporary South African writers worthy of attention. Many are still dealing with the legacy of Apartheid and the struggle against it, as South Africa finds a new national – and hybrid – identity. One is Zoe Wicomb, whose novel, *David's Story* (2001, winner of the M-Net Book Prize), interrogates the past and present of an anti-Apartheid activist, as does Achmat Dangor's *Bitter Fruit* (2001).

Mike Nicol's first novel, *The Powers That Be* (1989), brought a **magic realist** sensibility to South African literature and his latest, *The Ibis Tapestry* (1998), is a **postmodern** take on the secrets of South Africa's Apartheid abuses. Among Afrikaans writers now translated into English, notable works have come from Etienne van Heerden, particularly the marvellous *Ancestral Voices* (1989), and from Marlene Van Niekerk, with the hilarious and horrifying *Triomf* (1994). Phaswane Mpe's *Welcome to Our Hillbrow* (2001) is a critically acclaimed view of the physical and moral decay in both the rural areas of Tiragalong and the urban ghetto of Hillbrow. Kgafela wa Magogodi is a poet who probes issues such as AIDS in his collection *Thy Condom Come* (2000).

This essay by Thomas Thale was originally published on 'South Africa.info' at www.safrica.info

Part 4

Reference materials

Glossary of terms

Abstract expressionism

A form of art in which the artist expresses himself or herself purely through the use of form and colour. It is non-representational, or non-objective, art, which means that there are no concrete objects represented. It was one of the first purely American art movements and is usually associated with New York in the 1940s to 1960s.

In terms of art history, the movement can be broadly divided into two groups: action painters such as Jackson Pollock and Willem de Kooning who put the focus on the physical action involved in painting, and colour field painters such as Kenneth Noland and Mark Rothko who were primarily concerned with exploring the effect of pure colour on a canvas.

Abstract expressionism is closely linked to several literary movements, particularly **Imagism** and **Postmodernism**. The **New York School** of writers, led by poets John Ashbery, Kenneth Koch and Frank O'Hara, were actively involved in the appreciation and promotion of Abstract expressionism in America. Many of their poems attempt to replicate in lyric form what the painters were doing on canvas. [Jonathan Ellis]

Aestheticism

The doctrine that aesthetic values – judgements about beauty – are the most important in assessing a work of art and that art is an end in itself and does not require a religious, moral or didactic purpose. The outlook, encapsulated in Theophile Gautier's dictum 'l'art pour l'art' ('art for art's sake'), was popular in France through much of the nineteenth century and gave rise to the English Aesthetic Movement of the late nineteenth century, influenced particularly by the critic and Oxford University tutor Walter Pater (1839–94). Oscar Wilde (1854–1900) was one of the most outspoken proponents of the movement, which influenced the poetry and painting of the pre-Raphaelites and the early poetry of **W. B. Yeats** (1865–1939).

Alliteration

In poetry: the repetition of sounds in closely associated words. The term is usually applied to the repetition of consonants, particularly when they are the first letter of the words, but can apply to any stressed consonants. The term is sometimes used to refer to repeated vowel sounds, though the term more often used in this case is '**assonance**', e.g. O wild West Wind.

Angry Young Men

A term coined by literary journalists in the 1950s to describe the writers at the forefront of a new trend of social realism and anti-establishment attitudes in fiction and drama. The phrase *Angry Young Man* was used in 1951 as the title of the autobiography of Leslie Allen Paul, a co-founder of the Woodcraft Folk youth movement, but its application in 1956 was inspired by the title of John Osborne's play *Look Back in Anger*, which struck the keynote for the new trend. Other writers often grouped under this heading are Arnold Wesker, **Kingsley Amis**, John Braine, John Wain and **Alan Sillitoe**.

Antihero/antiheroic

A protagonist in a work of literature who lacks, and may be opposed to, traditional heroic virtues such as courage, confidence and virtue, and may have characteristics traditionally associated with a villain. He or she may be a flawed character who fails where a conventional hero would succeed, or his or her attitudes might be intended to subvert the idea of a literary hero or of what society might consider to be heroic.

Examples are Jimmy Porter in John Osborne's *Look Back in Anger* (1956) and many of the protagonists in the works of the **Angry Young Men**, particularly Smith in *The Loneliness of the Long Distance Runner* (1959) by **Alan Sillitoe**. Absurdist antiheroes appeared in the **Theatre of the Absurd**, for example Vladimir and Estragon in *Waiting for Godot* (1952) by **Samuel Beckett**, and their counterparts, Rosencrantz and Guildenstern, in *Rosencrantz and Guildenstern are Dead* (1966) by **Tom Stoppard**.

Assonance

In poetry: a repetition of similar vowel sounds in words of close proximity, particularly in stressed syllables. A form of imperfect rhyme, where the vowels rhyme but not the consonants, e.g. know – home – goat – go.

Beat literature/Beat writers/Beat Generation

A style of literature which emerged in America in the 1950s, influenced by the poet **Allen Ginsberg** (1926–97) and the novelist **Jack Kerouac** (1922–69), two of the best-known works being Ginsberg's *Howl* (1956) and Kerouac's *On the Road* (1957). They themselves were influenced by William Burroughs (1914–77), best known as the author of *The Naked Lunch* (1959). Beat writers had little regard for the formal conventions of literature and put all the emphasis on spontaneity and self-expression, their loosely structured style reflecting the influence of the jazz music of the time. The term's origins are variously said to be the 'beatitude' of the state of mind to which they aspired, the 'beat' of jazz music or 'beaten' as in 'worn out' or 'defeated'.

The movement was associated with the idea of 'dropping out' of materialistic middle-class life to pursue a form of freedom and spiritual exploration. They were forerunners of the **hippie** counter-culture of the 1960s. Ginsberg visited England in the 1960s and his spontaneous style and emphasis on poetry as live performance influenced the **Liverpool Poets**.

Bildungsroman

A German word meaning a 'novel of education', referring to a novel taking as its theme the development of an individual from childhood to adulthood, following the protagonist's search for his or her own identity. The form was common in German literature, the archetype being Goethe's *Wilhelm Meister Lehrjahre* (1795–6). In English literature the term is more applicable to novels of the nineteenth century, such as *David Copperfield* by Charles Dickens, but can also be applied to *A Portrait of the Artist as a Young Man* (1916) by **James Joyce**.

Black Mountain Poets

A group of avant-garde American poets writing during the 1950s that included Charles Olson, Robert Duncan and Robert Creeley. These poets shared ties to Black Mountain College in North Carolina, an experimental school of art that operated from 1933 until its closing in 1956, and to its literary review, *The Black Mountain Review*. The poets are also sometimes referred to as **'projectivist'** poets because of their shared interest in Charles Olson's 'projectivist verse'. [Trenton Hickman]

Bloomsbury Group, The

A group of writers, artists and critics centred around Vanessa and Virginia Stephen (later Vanessa Bell and **Virginia Woolf**) and their home in the Bloomsbury area of London in the early years of the twentieth century. Opposed to the social constraints of their age, they had a modernising liberal outlook and made significant achievements in their fields, though they were accused by some of élitism.

Chicana/Chicano

See *Latino/a literature.*

Confessional poetry

An approach to poetry in which the poet employs his or her own life and feelings as subject matter, often using verse as an outlet for powerful emotions. The attitude was a break from the view that poetry should be impersonal, advocated by **T. S. Eliot**. The style emerged in America with Robert Lowell's volume *Life Studies* (1959), other practitioners being John Berryman (1914–72), Anne Sexton (1928–74) and **Sylvia Plath** (1932–63).

Constative

The use of language to indicate a state of affairs which exists, in contrast to language used 'performatively' – to initiate an action. See *Performative.*

Dadaism

A European art movement, characterised by an anarchic protest against bourgeois society, founded in 1916 by the Rumanian-born French poet Tristan Tzara (1896–1963). Part of the motivation behind the movement was the wish to express a sense of outrage in response to the First World War and the culture which had brought it about. The main centre of Dadaism was Paris, but it also flourished in America, the main proponents of the two centres being Marcel Duchamp (1887–1968) and Man Ray (1890–1976) respectively. The movement was superseded by **Surrealism** from around 1922.

Deconstruction/deconstruct

A concept originating in **poststructuralist** critical theory, deriving from the work of Jacques Derrida (1930–), which is used in many ways. It refers to the analysis of a text taking into account that its meaning is not fixed but can vary according to the way in which the writer, and reader, interpret language. Instead of looking for meanings, deconstruction aims to analyse concepts and modes of thought to expose the pre-conceived ideas on which they are founded.

Dystopia/dystopian

A Greek term which means a bad place, or the opposite of **Utopia**. The negative characteristics of a dystopia serve as a warning of possible social and political developments to be avoided. Examples of modern novels which depict dystopias are *Nineteen Eighty-four* by **George Orwell** (1903–50) and *Brave New World* by **Aldous Huxley** (1894–1963).

Existentialism/Existential

A European movement in philosophy which became particularly influential after the Second World War. Some of the leading proponents were Martin Heidegger (1889–1976), Albert Camus (1913–60) and Jean-Paul Sartre (1905–80). The existentialist world-view sees human existence as ultimately meaningless – a situation which causes 'angst' or dread – but at the same time emphasises the importance of each individual taking responsibility for his or her own choices concerning decisions and actions. Existentialism was a direct influence on the dramatists of the **Theatre of the Absurd**, such as **Samuel Beckett**, and on the British novelists **Iris Murdoch**, **John Fowles** and Muriel Spark.

Feminist/womanist

Feminist writing and criticism highlights the position of women in literature, society and world culture, emphasising that the roles and experiences of women tend to be marginalised by patriarchal societies. Feminist writers and critics attempt to redress the balance by writing literature and criticism from the point of view of women. A key feminist work from the modern period is *A Room of One's Own* (1929) by **Virginia Woolf**.

The term 'womanist' is sometimes used to refer to black feminists, to distinguish their approach from that of mainstream white middle-class feminism.

Formalism

An artistic and critical sensibility in American and British literature and criticism which reached its greatest influence between 1930 and 1950 and which promoted a view of art as 'objective' – that is, that the work in itself was more important than the subjective contexts of its artistic production. In formalism, the proper focus of artistic creation and criticism is the art object itself rather than the author or artist's thoughts, intentions or other personal sensibilities. In the case of literature, formalism assumes that well-wrought form (the structure of the literary piece, its constituent images, metaphors and other 'building blocks') can carry the most important dimensions of content from the author to the reader without reference to contextual elements. Much of post-war literature in both Britain and the United States can be seen as a reaction to this extreme view, as poets and writers actively sought to reintroduce subjectivities into literary production and study as a way of reclaiming the 'personal' in literary experience. [Trenton Hickman]

Freud, Sigmund/Freudian

By revolutionising our understanding of the inner workings of the human mind, the process of personality development and the motives behind human behaviour, the Austrian psychoanalyst Sigmund Freud (1856–1939) was a major influence on twentieth-century thought. Freud showed the importance of the unconscious in all aspects of human life and developed techniques of psychoanalysis and dream interpretation as ways of gaining access to it. In art Freud was a direct influence on **Surrealism**, and in English literature was a direct influence on **W. H. Auden**, **D. H. Lawrence** and **Iris Murdoch**.

Georgian Poets

Poets active during the early part of the reign of George V (1910–36), including Rupert Brooke, Edmund Blunden, Walter de la Mare and Edward Thomas. They wrote delicate, lyrical poetry, often concerned with nature. Their style was a break from the poetry of the late nineteenth century and the decadence which had evolved from **aestheticism**. In the 1920s they were overshadowed by the **Modernist** innovations of **Ezra Pound** and **T. S. Eliot**.

Gothic/Southern Gothic

Gothic literature deals with macabre, supernatural subject matter, aimed at inducing fear and a sense of dread. The form became popular in the late eighteenth and early nineteenth centuries, classics of the genre being *The Castle of Otranto* (1765) by Horace Walpole (1717–97), *The Mysteries of Udolpho* (1794) by Ann Radcliffe (1764–1823), *The Monk* (1796) by Matthew Gregory Lewis (1775–1818) and *Frankenstein* (1818) by Mary Shelley (1797–1851).

In the context of modern literature the term is still used to describe literature with macabre, horrifying subject matter, such as much of the work of **Beryl Bainbridge**.

In modern American literature the term **Southern Gothic** is applied to works by writers from the Southern states of the USA, whose stories are often set in that region and include macabre or fantastic incidents in their plots. Examples are **William Faulkner** (1897–1962), **Tennessee Williams** (1911–83), Carson McCullers (1917–67), **Flannery O'Connor** (1925–64) and **Harper Lee** (1926–).

Group, The

A name sometimes given to a group of British poets who in the late 1950s and 1960s wanted to take poetry in a new direction by liberating it from the restraints favoured by **The Movement**. The main poets were **Ted Hughes**, Peter Porter, George Macbeth, Peter Redgrove and Alan Brownjohn.

Harlem Renaissance

A flourishing of African-American literature which took place in the 1920s and was centred around the Harlem district of New York City. The movement took African-American life and culture as its subject matter, some of its major writers being James Weldon Johnson (1871–1938), Zora Neale Hurston (1903–60), **Langston Hughes** (1902–67) and Countee Cullen (1903–46).

Hippie/Hippie movement

A movement of young people in America and Europe in the 1960s who rejected conventional values and morality and adopted a rootless or communal style of living. Many used, and advocated the use of, psychoactive drugs, such as marijuana and LSD, to achieve altered states of awareness. Their ideals were those of peace and love and they congregated at rock festivals, culminating in the Woodstock festival of 1969. Their main art forms were psychedelic music, posters and light shows. The American writers **Allen Ginsberg** and **Ken Kesey** were associated with the movement.

Imagism/Imagist

The Imagists were a group of poets who were influenced by **Ezra Pound**, who in turn had been influenced by the French **Symbolist** poets, Japanese haiku and the writings of the poet and critic T. E. Hulme (1883–1917). The Imagist movement, which originated in London and was prominent in England and America from around 1912 to 1917, was crucial to the development of **Modernist** poetry. These poets aimed to free poetry from the conventions of the time by advocating a free choice of rhythm and subject matter, the diction of speech, and the presentation of meaning through the evocation of clear, precise, visual images.

Among the poets associated with Ezra Pound in this movement were Hilda Doolittle, Amy Lowell and William Carlos Williams. Pound later associated himself with **Vorticism** and Amy Lowell took over the leadership of the Imagist movement. Many English and American poets were influenced by Imagism, such as **D. H. Lawrence**, **T. S. Eliot**, Conrad Aiken, Marianne Moore and **Wallace Stevens**.

Intertext

A term used to denote a text referred to within a text. *The Bible*, the works of Shakespeare and Classical myths, for example, are frequently found as intertexts in works of literature. [Julie Ellam]

Intertextuality

A term which can refer to a text's inclusion of **intertexts** but is also a concept introduced by philosopher and semiotician Julia Kristeva and used in **poststructuralist** criticism, according to which a text is seen as not only connecting the author to the reader but also as being connected to all other texts, past and present. Thus there is a limit to the extent to which an individual text can be said to be original or unique and a limit to the extent to which an individual author can be said to be the originator of a text. [Julie Ellam]

Irish Cultural Revival/Irish Literary Revival

Also called Irish Literary Renaissance, Celtic Renaissance or Celtic Revival. A revival of Irish literature in the late nineteenth century, driven primarily by **W. B. Yeats**. The aim was to create a distinctive Irish literature by drawing on Irish history and folklore. In the 1880s the Gaelic League attempted to revive the Irish language, but the use of Gaelic was not a requirement of the revival led by Yeats in the 1890s. The movement developed simultaneously with a rise in Irish nationalism and a growth of interest in Gaelic traditions.

Jung/Jungian

The theories of the Swiss psychiatrist Carl Gustav Jung (1875–1961) grew out of those of **Sigmund Freud**. Having been closely associated with Freud originally, he broke away and developed his own theories, which placed less emphasis on sexuality and more on symbolism, the collective unconscious and archetypes. Many artists, including the British novelist **John Fowles**, have been influenced by Jung's ideas, particularly his emphasis on the importance of myths and symbols.

Latino/a literature

Literature written in English for an English-speaking audience by American writers of Latin-American heritage, such as the Puerto Rican American (sometimes called

'Nuyorican', since many of these writers are 'New York Puerto Ricans'), Cuban-American, Dominican-American and Mexican-American (often called 'Chicano/a') writers. Latino/a ('Latino' if male, 'Latina' if female) writers were the big literary phenomenon of the 1990s in the United States. [Trenton Hickman]

Magic realism

Fiction which displays a mingling of the mundane with the fantastic, giving the narrative dual dimensions of realism and fantasy. One of its purposes is to draw attention to the fact that all narrative is an invention. The technique is mainly associated with South American writers, such as Jorge Luis Borges and Gabriel García Márquez, but has also been used by writers such as the British **Angela Carter** and the Anglo-Indian **Salman Rushdie**.

Marx, Karl/Marxist

The theories of the German social scientist and revolutionary Karl Heinrich Marx (1818–83) have had a profound effect on political and economic thought throughout the world since the mid-nineteenth century. His best-known works are *The Communist Manifesto* (1848), written with Friedrich Engels (1820–95) and *Das Kapital* (1867–95). His writings, based on an analysis of capitalist society in which he saw the workers as being exploited, emphasised the importance of class struggle and change through conflict.

In English literature Marx was an influence on the political dimension of works by writers of the 1930s such as **W. H. Auden** and Cecil Day-Lewis.

Marxist criticism

Literary criticism deriving from the theories of Marx, which emphasises the cultural and political context in which the text was produced.

Metafiction/metanarrative

Fiction about fiction. An approach in which the writer draws attention to the process by which the author and the reader together create the experience of fiction, implicitly questioning the relationship between fiction and reality. This **postmodern** technique was used in *The French Lieutenant's Woman* (1969) and other novels by **John Fowles**.

Modern

The term 'modern' can apply to a wide variety of different historical periods in different contexts. In the context of 'modern literature' it is generally taken to refer to the period from 1914, the outbreak of the First World War, to the present day. When capitalised, 'Modern' can refer to **Modernism**.

Modernism/Modernist

A movement in all the arts in Europe, with its roots in the nineteenth century but flourishing in the period during and after the First World War. The period 1910 to 1930 is sometimes called the period of 'high Modernism'. The war having undermined faith in order and stability in Europe, artists and writers sought to break with tradition and find new ways of representing experience.

Some of the characteristic features of Modernist literature are a drawing of inspiration from European culture as a whole; experimentation with form, such as the fragmentation and discontinuity found in the free verse of 'The Waste Land' by T. S. Eliot; the radical approach to plot, time, language and character presentation as seen in *Ulysses* by James Joyce and the novels of Virginia Woolf; a decrease in emphasis on morality and an increase in subjective, relative and uncertain attitudes; in poetry, a move towards simplicity and directness in the use of language.

Dada, Surrealism, The Theatre of the Absurd and stream of consciousness are all aspects of Modernism.

Movement, The

The name given to a generation of British poets who came to prominence in the 1950s, of whom the best known was Philip Larkin (1922–85). Disliking the free form and emotional tone of poets such as Dylan Thomas and W. S. Graham, they initiated a style of verse which was intellectual, witty and carefully crafted. Their work gained prominence in the anthology *New Lines* (1956), edited by Robert Conquest. Other Movement poets included Thom Gunn, Kingsley Amis, D. J. Enright and John Wain.

Naturalism/naturalist

A term often used interchangeably with realism, but which has a more specific meaning suggesting that human life is controlled by natural forces such as those explored in the natural sciences, particularly those expounded by Charles Darwin (1809–82). Naturalist writers aimed to create accurate representations of characters and their interaction with their environment based on scientific truth. The movement was particularly associated with the nineteenth-century French novelist Emile Zola (1840–1902) and influenced the English writers George Gissing (1857–1903) and Arnold Bennett (1867–1931).

New Apocalypse/New Romantics

Movements in British poetry which flourished in the late 1930s and early 1940s, when Dylan Thomas was the foremost poet. The poets behind the movements were Henry Treece (1911–66), George Granville Barker (1913–91), W. S. Graham (1918–86), J. F. Hendry (1912–86) and Dorian Cooke. They reacted against the politically orientated realist poetry of the 1930s by drawing inspiration from mythology and the unconscious. Their work is generally regarded by critics as having little merit, being vastly inferior to that of Thomas.

New Criticism, The

A movement in literary criticism which developed in the USA in the 1940s and which aimed to approach literary texts in an 'objective' way, as self-contained objects of study, without reference to such contextual factors as the author's biography or intentions. One of the main texts of the movement was *Understanding Poetry* (1938) by Cleanthe Brooks (1906–94) and Robert Penn Warren (1905–89). The movement was influenced by the British critic I. A. Richards (1893–1979) and his books *Principles of Literary Criticism* (1924), *Science and Poetry* (1926) and *Practical Criticism* (1929). Richards, in turn, had been influenced by the critical stance of F. R. Leavis (1895–1978) and **T. S. Eliot** (1888–1965).

New Journalism, The

A mid-twentieth-century American literary aesthetic practised by writers such as Thomas Wolfe and Norman Mailer, which privileges a lively, newspaper-style 'novelisation' of actual events but from a subjective narratorial point of view, fusing the art of novel writing with the quirky accessibility of the journalist as character and participant. [Trenton Hickman]

New York School

A group of American poets who lived and worked in and around New York City during the mid-twentieth century, including Frank O'Hara, John Ashbery, Kenneth Koch and James Schuyler. The aesthetic of these poets evidences a shared interest in **abstract expressionist** art as well as in American popular cultural subjects such as jazz and movies. Their poetry magnifies these interests and elevates them through sophisticated intellectual treatment into smart, witty, verbal 'gymnastics' of verse. [Trenton Hickman]

Omniscient narrator

See *viewpoint*.

Onomatopoeia

In poetry: a word whose sound resembles the sound to which it refers or whose sound suggests the sound of something associated with its meaning, e.g. buzz, splash.

Other/otherness

A concept central to **postcolonial criticism**, referring to the way colonised people and places were seen as alien, subordinate and, implicitly, inferior from the point of view of the colonising culture. The concept can be extended into other areas, such as when feminist criticism sees women as being put in the position of 'other' by a patriarchal point of view.

P.E.N.

International Association of Poets, Playwrights, Editors, Essayists and Novelists. International P.E.N. was founded in London in 1921 by Mrs C. A. Dawson Scott. Its first president was **John Galsworthy**. The only worldwide association of writers, its aims are to: (1) promote intellectual cooperation and understanding among writers; (2) create a world community of writers that would emphasise the central role of literature in the development of world culture; (3) defend literature against the many threats to its survival which the modern world poses. [www.internatpen.org]

Performative/performativity

'Performative' indicates the special qualities brought out through a 'performance' of something (for example, a play text or poem) or in some cases an artistic event which has no originating text (such as in performance art). The 'performance' is a time-and-space-bound event, which is ephemeral (it never happens exactly the same way twice). A further, related meaning (derived from the philosophy of J. L. Austin) is that of doing or making something happen rather than stating or representing it. This leads to the idea that the 'performative' is how symbolic systems (language, art, theatre) both represent things from the world but are also simultaneously making that world.

'Performativity' is a related term. It is the ability of something to be 'performative' or else that it should be seen as constructed through performative means. Judith Butler, the cultural theorist, argues that 'gender', for example, is constructed through performance. [Steven Barfield]

Point of view

See *viewpoint*.

Pop art

Art movement in Britain and America in the late 1950s and 1960s in which elements from everyday life, popular culture and the mass media were used as subject matter. Not always taken seriously by critics or the public, pop art could be seen partly as a liberating attack on more conventional art and partly as a response to a mechanised, media and advertising-saturated, modern world. American pop artists included Andy Warhol and Roy Lichtenstein. British representatives included Peter Blake and David Hockney. Pop art had a direct influence on the **Liverpool Poets**.

Postcolonial criticism

Branch of literary criticism which focuses on seeing the literature and experience of peoples of former colonies in the context of their own cultures, as opposed to seeing them from the perspective of the European literature and criticism dominant during the time of the Empire.

Postcolonial literature

Literature written in the language of former colonisers by natives of their colonies. Usually, literature written in English by writers from former colonies of Great Britain. The term usually applies to literature written after the country has ceased to be a colony, but can also include literature written during the time of colonisation.

Postmodern/Postmodernism

In a general sense, literature written since the Second World War, i.e. after the **Modernist** era. In a more specific sense the concept of postmodernism as a subject of study emerged in the 1980s, applying across many disciplines, encouraging interdisciplinary studies and being interpreted in many ways.

The postmodern outlook is associated with the erosion of confidence in the idea of progress, as a result of such phenomena as the holocaust, the threat of nuclear war and environmental pollution.

In literature one of its manifestations is the attempts by some writers to examine and break down boundaries involved in such issues as race, gender and class, and to break down divisions between different genres of literature. Other aspects of the postmodernist outlook are a spirit of playfulness with the fragmented world, the awareness of fiction as an artifice, and the creation of works as a pastiche of forms from the past. Postmodern writers include Thomas Pynchon, **John Fowles, Angela Carter** and **Salman Rushdie**.

In literary criticism such approaches as **structuralism, poststructuralism, deconstruction** and **postcolonial criticism** are postmodern methods.

Poststructuralism

A **postmodern** approach to literary criticism, and other disciplines, growing out of **structuralism**. Like structuralism, it questions the relationship between language and reality and it sees 'reality' as something socially constructed.

Problematise

To produce or propose a debating point or problem out of given data. [Margaret J-M Sonmez]

Projectivism

A style of poetry innovated by American poet Charles Olson in his 1950 essay 'Projective Verse' and adopted by others of the **Black Mountain Poets**. Olson advocated a poetry that rebelled against the **formalist**, **New Critical** poetry that preceded it by insisting that 'form was never more than an extension of content' and that the poem should emerge line by line, driven by the measure of one's breath and with 'one perception' necessarily 'projecting' itself into 'a further perception'. In this manner, Olson and other projectivists hoped that the speed, immediacy and lack of predetermined poetic form would re-energise the poetry of their time with a spontaneity and improvisational spirit that had been lost over the preceding decades. [Trenton Hickman]

Pylon Poets

A name given to British poets of the 1930s who included industrial artefacts such as pylons in their descriptions of landscape. The poets included **W. H. Auden**, Stephen Spender, Louis MacNeice and Cecil Day-Lewis. The nickname originated in response to Stephen Spender's poem 'The Pylons'.

Realism/social realism/Socialist realism

Broadly, writing about people and settings which could really exist and events which could really happen. In particular the term realism refers to a movement of nineteenth-century European art and literature which rejected Classical models and Romantic ideals in favour of a realistic portrayal of actual life in realistic settings, often focusing on the harsher aspects of life under industrialism and capitalism. Forerunners in literature were the French novelist Honoré de Balzac (1799–1850) and the English novelist George Eliot (1819–80). In the twentieth century the writing of the **Angry Young Men** can be seen as a reassertion of the values of realism.

'Social realism', a term borrowed from art criticism, is often used synonymously with 'realism'. 'Socialist realism' refers to literature or criticism presented from the **Marxist** viewpoint.

Romantic/Romanticism

The term is used both in a general and in a specific way. The specific sense refers to Romanticism, a movement prevalent in European art, music and literature in the late eighteenth and early nineteenth centuries. The style was revolutionary in that it emphasised subjective experience and favoured innovation over adherence to traditional or Classical forms, and the expression of feeling over reason. In English literature, William Wordsworth (1770–1850) and Samuel Taylor Coleridge (1772–1834) were first-generation Romantic poets and Byron (1788–1824), Shelley (1792–1822) and Keats (1795–1821) were second-generation Romantics.

In its more general application the term can refer to an attitude of mind which draws on imagination and emotion rather than reason, and favours subjective, dream-like or exotic experiences over **realism**.

Sprung rhythm

A name given by **Gerard Manley Hopkins** to his technique of breaking up the regular meter of poetry to achieve versatile and surprising rhythms, which retained regularity but more closely resembled speech than did conventional poetry.

Stream of consciousness

Sometimes called 'continuous monologue'. Literary technique developed in the 1920s, as part of **Modernism** which attempts to reproduce the moment-to-moment flow of subjective thoughts and perceptions in an individual's mind. The technique was used by Dorothy Richardson, **James Joyce** and **Virginia Woolf**. The term was originally coined by the American philosopher and psychologist William James in *Principles of Psychology* (1890).

Structuralism

An approach to literary criticism which emphasises that a text does not have one fixed meaning but is open to any number of interpretations, depending on the meanings attributed to words by both the writer and the reader. It is founded on the idea that the meanings of words are ultimately arbitrary and instead of looking for the meaning of a text, structural analysis aims to explore oppositions and conflicts within the text and the underlying structures of thought which produce meanings. The approach is based on the work of the Swiss linguist Ferdinand de Saussure (1857–1913) and has been influential in the humanities since the mid-1950s, being applied not only to literary texts but to a wide range of cultural phenomena.

Surrealism

An artistic and literary movement which grew out of **Dadaism** between 1917 and the 1920s. Influenced by the writings of **Sigmund Freud**, the practitioners explored the world of dreams and the unconscious in their art, emphasising the irrational dimensions of human experience. Leaders of the movement were the French artists Guillaume Apollinaire (1880–1918), who coined the term in 1917, and André Breton (1896–1966).

Surrealists experimented with automatic writing, the technique, analogous to the free association method of psychoanalysis, involving the attempt to achieve a state of mind in which rational thought is disengaged and allowing words to arise spontaneously from the unconscious.

Symbolist/Symbolism

The Symbolist movement originated in France with the volume of poetry *Les Fleurs du Mal* (1857) by Charles Baudelaire (1821–67) and was taken up by such poets as Stéphane Mallarmé, Paul Verlaine, Arthur Rimbaud and Jules Laforgue. They aimed to break away from the formal conventions of French poetry and attempted to express the transitory perceptions and sensations of inner life rather than rational ideas. They believed in the imagination as the arbiter of reality, were interested in the idea of a correspondence between the senses and aimed to express meaning through the sound patterns of words and suggestive, evocative images rather than by using language as a medium for statement and argument.

The Symbolists were a major influence on British, Irish and American writers such as **W. B. Yeats, Ezra Pound, T. S. Eliot, Dylan Thomas**, e e cummings, **Wallace Stevens** and **William Faulkner**.

Theatre of the Absurd

Avant-garde drama movement originating in the 1950s in Europe with dramatists such as **Samuel Beckett** (1906–89), Jean Genet (1910–86) and Eugene Ionesco (1912–94). Influenced philosophically by **Existentialism**, and in particular by *The Myth of Sisyphus* (1943) by Albert Camus (1913–60), they expressed a world-view in which there was no God and life was meaningless. They had no faith in logic or rational communication, feeling that attempts to construe meanings broke down into absurdity – 'absurd' in this context meaning 'out of harmony' rather than 'ridiculous'.

In their approach to the theatre they drew upon a tradition of comedy which can be traced from Roman drama through the music hall and into such as the silent comedies of Charlie Chaplin and the surreal comedies of the Marx Brothers of the 1930s and 1940s.

Unreliable narrator

A fictional narrator whose views do not coincide with those of the author or do not accurately represent what 'really' happened in the story. Henry James was a master of the unreliable narrator technique. Writers use subtle methods to let readers know that they cannot trust what the narrator says, setting up tension between reader and narrative. One extreme example is seen in the novel *Spider* (1990) by Patrick McGrath, in which the narrator, a schizophrenic, is unable to distinguish between reality and fantasy. Without intruding on the first-person viewpoint, McGrath gradually allows the reader to understand that what the narrator thinks is the truth is not the truth at all.

Utopia

A Greek term which means an imaginary perfect place. Even if the imagined place could never be achieved in reality, its positive qualities represent ideals to be striven for. The term was coined by Thomas More (1478–1535) who wrote his *Utopia*, a description of an ideal state, in 1516. Other examples of such descriptions in the history of literature include Francis Bacon's *New Atlantis* (1626) and *The Republic* by Plato (c.427–347 BC).

Viewpoint/Point of view

The viewpoint which the reader shares while reading a narrative. Fiction writers use three main viewpoints: (1) The omniscient (all-knowing) narrator's viewpoint. The narrator of the story theoretically knows everything about all the characters.

Referring to them in the third person, the author can tell us about the characters in an objective way and switch between them at will, showing us what each is doing thinking and feeling at any time. (2) The first-person viewpoint, in which the narrator speaks as 'I' and conveys the story through his/her subjective experience. (3) The viewpoint of the main character, or characters, in the story, but conveyed in the third person. Here the narrative is ostensibly being presented by a narrator, in that we read '*she* did this', or '*he* did that', but the narrator's viewpoint is merged with that of the character(s) so that everything in the story is seen through the subjective experience of the character(s).

Vorticism

An approach to art and literature associated with the abstract artist Percy Wyndham-Lewis (1882–1957) which sought to address industrial processes through art. Although mainly a movement in painting and sculpture, Wyndham-Lewis, influenced by Imagist poetry and collaborating with Ezra Pound, published two issues of a journal named '*BLAST*'.

War Poets, The

Name given to a group of British soldier-poets who became prominent during the First World War, the best-known being Seigfried Sassoon (1886–1967), Rupert Brooke (1887–1915), Isaac Rosenberg (1890–1918) and Wilfred Owen (1893–1918). The main impact of their poetry came through its depiction of the horrors of war, bringing the reality of events home to the British public.

Womanist

See *Feminist*.

Note: This glossary has been compiled by Ian Mackean (except where otherwise credited).

Literary awards, prizes and laureateships

Poets Laureate of England since 1913

A form of poet laureateship was established in England in 1616, with a pension granted to Ben Jonson for his services to the Crown as a poet, but the office as we know it today was formed in 1668, when John Dryden was officially made Poet Laureate. The title-holder becomes a member of the Royal household, receives a small salary and used to be obliged to compose poems to mark state occasions, though this ceremonial duty is no longer obligatory.

1913–1930   Robert Bridges (1844–1930)
1930–1967   John Masefield (1878–1967)
1967–1972   Cecil Day-Lewis (1904–72)
1972–1984   Sir John Betjeman (1906–84)
1984–1998   Ted Hughes (1930–98)
1999–   Andrew Motion (1952–)

American Poets Laureate

The United States Library of Congress has appointed consultants in poetry since 1937 and in 1985 the title of the position was changed to 'Poet Laureate'. The appointment is an annual one, the laureate being selected by the Librarian of Congress. Some American states and cities have now started appointing their own Poets Laureate.

1986   Robert Penn Warren
1987–1988   Richard Wilbur
1988–1990   Howard Nemerov
1990–1991   Mark Strand
1991–1992   Joseph Brodsky the first foreign-born laureate
1992–1993   Mona Van Duyn the first woman laureate
1993–1995   Rita Dove the first African-American laureate
1995–1997   Robert Hass
1997–2000   Robert Pinsky
2000–2001   Stanley Kunitz
2001–   Billy Collins

Nobel Prize for Literature

The Nobel Prize was established by the Swedish chemist, inventor and philanthropist Alfred Bernhard Nobel (1833–96) and is administered by the Nobel Foundation. Nobel stated that the prizes should be awarded to 'those who, during the preceding year, shall have conferred the greatest benefit on mankind'. The awards began in 1901, the awards for literature being given by The Swedish Academy.

1901	Sully Prudhomme	1937	Roger Martin du Gard
1902	Theodor Mommsen	1938	Pearl Buck
1903	Bjørnstjerne Bjørnson	1939	Frans Eemil Sillanpää
1904	Frédéric Mistral, José Echegaray	1940	No award
1905	Henryk Sienkiewicz	1941	No award
1906	Giosuè Carducci	1942	No award
1907	Rudyard Kipling	1943	No award
1908	Rudolf Eucken	1944	Johannes V. Jensen
1909	Selma Lagerlöf	1945	Gabriela Mistral
1910	Paul Heyse	1946	Hermann Hesse
1911	Maurice Maeterlinck	1947	André Gide
1912	Gerhart Hauptmann	1948	Thomas Stearns Eliot
1913	Rabindranath Tagore	1949	William Faulkner
1914	No award	1950	Bertrand Russell
1915	Romain Rolland	1951	Pär Lagerkvist
1916	Verner von Heidenstam	1952	François Mauriac
1917	Karl Gjellerup, Henrik	1953	Winston Churchill
	Pontoppidan	1954	Ernest Hemingway
1918	No award	1955	Halldór Kiljan Laxness
1919	Carl Spitteler	1956	Juan Ramón Jiménez
1920	Knut Hamsun	1957	Albert Camus
1921	Anatole France	1958	Boris Pasternak
1922	Jacinto Benavente	1959	Salvatore Quasimodo
1923	William Butler Yeats	1960	Saint-John Perse
1924	Wladyslaw Reymont	1961	Ivo Andric
1925	George Bernard Shaw	1962	John Steinbeck
1926	Grazia Deledda	1963	Giorgos Seferis
1927	Henri Bergson	1964	Jean-Paul Sartre
1928	Sigrid Undset	1965	Michail Sholokhov
1929	Thomas Mann	1966	Samuel Agnon, Nelly Sachs
1930	Sinclair Lewis	1967	Miguel Angel Asturias
1931	Erik Axel Karlfeldt	1968	Yasunari Kawabata
1932	John Galsworthy	1969	Samuel Beckett
1933	Ivan Bunin	1970	Alexander Solzhenitsyn
1934	Luigi Pirandello	1971	Pablo Neruda
1935	No award	1972	Heinrich Böll
1936	Eugene O'Neill	1973	Patrick White

1974	Eyvind Johnson, Harry Martinson	1989	Camilo José Cela
1975	Eugenio Montale	1990	Octavio Paz
1976	Saul Bellow	1991	Nadine Gordimer
1977	Vicente Aleixandre	1992	Derek Walcott
1978	Isaac Bashevis Singer	1993	Toni Morrison
1979	Odysseus Elytis	1994	Kenzaburo Oe
1980	Czeslaw Milosz	1995	Seamus Heaney
1981	Elias Canetti	1996	Wislawa Szymborska
1982	Gabriel García Márquez	1997	Dario Fo
1983	William Golding	1998	José Saramago
1984	Jaroslav Seifert	1999	Günter Grass
1985	Claude Simon	2000	Gao Xingjian
1986	Wole Soyinka	2001	V.S. Naipaul
1987	Joseph Brodsky	2002	Imre Kertész
1988	Naguib Mahfouz	2003	J.M. Coetzee
		2004	Elfriede Jelinek

Man Booker Prize for Fiction

The 'Booker Prize', as it was originally called, is administered by the Booker Prize Foundation and regarded as the most prestigious of the awards available to British novelists. The prize has been awarded since 1969 and was originally sponsored by Booker-McConnell plc, a food wholesaling company. Sponsorship has now been taken over by the Man Group, a London-based international stockbroking firm, and the title changed to the Man Booker Prize for Fiction. Any full-length novel written in English and published in the United Kingdom by a citizen of the Commonwealth or Republic of Ireland is eligible for the prize. Nominations selected by publishers are submitted to a panel of five judges, consisting of literary editors, novelists, academics and critics.

1969   P. H. Newby, *Something to Answer For*
1970   Bernice Rubens, *The Elected Member*
1971   V. S. Naipaul, *In a Free State*
1972   John Berger, *G*
1973   J. G. Farrell, *The Siege of Krishnapur*
1974   Stanley Middleton, *Holiday*. Nadine Gordimer, *The Conservationist*
1975   Ruth Prawer Jhabvala, *Heat and Dust*
1976   David Storey, *Saville*
1977   Paul Scott, *Staying On*
1978   Iris Murdoch, *The Sea, The Sea*
1979   Penelope Fitzgerald, *Offshore*
1980   William Golding, *Rites of Passage*
1981   Salman Rushdie, *Midnight's Children*
1982   Thomas Kneally, *Schindler's Ark*
1983   J. M. Coetzee, *Life and Times of Michael K*
1984   Anita Brookner, *Hotel du Lac*

1985   Keri Hulme, *The Bone People*
1986   Kingsley Amis, *The Old Devils*
1987   Penelope Lively, *Moon Tiger*
1988   Peter Carey, *Oscar and Lucinda*
1989   Kazuo Ishiguro, *The Remains of the Day*
1990   A. S. Byatt, *Possession*
1991   Ben Okri, *The Famished Road*
1992   Barry Unsworth, *Sacred Hunger*. Michael Ondaatje, *The English Patient*
1993   Roddy Doyle, *Paddy Clarke Ha Ha Ha*
1994   James Kelman, *How Late It Was, How Late*
1995   Pat Barker, *The Ghost Road*
1996   Graham Swift, *Last Orders*
1997   Arundhati Roy, *The God of Small Things*
1998   Ian McEwan, *Amsterdam*
1999   J. M. Coetzee, *Disgrace*
2000   Margaret Atwood, *The Blind Assassin*
2001   Peter Carey, *True History of the Kelly Gang*
2002   Yann Martel, *Life of Pi*
2003   D. B. C. Pierre (pen name of Peter Finlay), *Vernon God Little*
2004   Alan Hollinghurst, *The Line of Beauty*

The Whitbread Book Awards

The Whitbread awards were founded in 1971 and are administered by the Booksellers Association of Great Britain. Sponsored by Whitbread Breweries, the awards are considered by some to be of almost equal prestige to the Booker Prize. Only authors who have lived in Great Britain or Ireland for over three years are eligible and the panel of judges is selected from prominent authors, booksellers, critics and sometimes politicians. There are now five categories of Whitbread award: best novel, best first novel, best biography, best book of poems and best children's book, from which one is chosen as Whitbread book of the year.

1971   Novel Gerda Charles, *The Destiny Waltz*
        Poetry Geoffrey Hill, *Mercian Hymns*
1972   Novel Susan Hill, *The Bird of Night*
1973   Novel Shiva Naipaul, *The Chip Chip Gatherers*
1974   Novel Iris Murdoch, *The Sacred and Profane Love Machine*
1975   Novel William McIlvanney, *Docherty*
1976   Novel William Trevor, *The Children of Dynmouth*
1977   Novel Beryl Bainbridge, *Injury Time*
1978   Novel Paul Theroux, *Picture Palace*
1979   Novel Jennifer Johnston, *The Old Jest*
1980   Novel David Lodge, *How Far Can You Go?* *
1981   Novel Maurice Leitch, *Silver's City*
        1st Novel William Boyd, *A Good Man in Africa*

1982   Novel John Wain, *Young Shoulders*
        1st Novel Bruce Chatwin, *On the Black Hill*

1983   Novel William Trevor, *Fools of Fortune*
        1st Novel John Fuller, *Flying to Nowhere*

1984   Novel Christopher Hope, *Kruger's Alp*
        1st Novel John Buchan, *A Parish of Rich Women*

1985   Novel Peter Ackroyd, *Hawksmoor*
        1st Novel Jeanette Winterson, *Oranges Are Not the Only Fruit*
        Poetry Douglas Dunn, *Elegies* *

1986   Novel Kazuo Ishiguro, *An Artist of the Floating World* *
        1st Novel Jim Crace, *Continent*
        Poetry Peter Reading, *Stet*

1987   Novel Ian McEwan, *The Child in Time*
        1st Novel Francis Wyndham, *The Other Garden*
        Poetry Seamus Heaney, *The Haw Lantern*

1988   Novel Salman Rushdie, *The Satanic Verses*
        1st Novel Paul Sayer, *The Comforts of Madness* *
        Poetry Peter Porter, *The Automatic Oracle*

1989   Novel Lindsay Clarke, *The Chymical Wedding*
        1st Novel James Hamilton Paterson, *Gerontius*
        Poetry Michael Donaghy, *Shibboleth*

1990   Novel Nicholas Mosley, *Hopeful Monsters* *
        1st Novel Haneif Kureishi, *The Buddha of Suburbia*
        Poetry Paul Durcan, *Daddy, Daddy*

1991   Novel Jane Gardam, *The Queen of the Tambourine*
        1st Novel Gordon Burn, *Alma Cogan*
        Poetry Michael Longley, *Gorse Fires*

1992   Novel Alisdair Gray, *Poor Things*
        1st Novel Jeff Torrington, *Swing Hammer Swing!* *
        Poetry Tony Harrison, *The Gaze of the Gorgon*

1993   Novel Joan Brady, *Theory of War* *
        1st Novel Rachel Cusk, *Saving Agnes*
        Poetry Carol Ann Duffy, *Mean Time*

1994   Novel William Trevor, *Felicia's Journey* *
        1st Novel Fred D'Aguiar, *The Longest Memory*
        Poetry James Fenton, *Out of Danger*

1995   Novel Salman Rushdie, *The Moor's Last Sigh*
        1st Novel Kate Atkinson, *Behind the Scenes at the Museum* *
        Poetry Bernard O'Donoghue, *Gunpowder*

1996   Novel Beryl Bainbridge, *Every Man for Himself*
        1st Novel John Lanchester, *The Debt to Pleasure*
        Poetry Seamus Heaney, *The Spirit Level* *

1997   Novel Jim Crace, *Quarantine*
        1st Novel Pauline Melville, *The Ventriloquist's Tale*
        Poetry Ted Hughes, *Tales from Ovid* *

1998   Novel Justin Cartwright, *Leading the Cheers*
        1st Novel Giles Foden, *The Last King of Scotland*
        Poetry Ted Hughes, *Birthday Letters* *
1999   Novel Rose Tremain, *Music and Silence*
        1st Novel Tim Lott, *White City Blue*
        Poetry Seamus Heaney, *Beowulf* *
2000   Novel Matthew Kneale, *English Passengers* *
        1st Novel Zadie Smith, *White Teeth*
        Poetry John Burnside, *Asylum Dance*
2001   Novel Patrick Neate, *Twelve Bar Blues*
        1st Novel Sid Smith, *Something Like a House*
        Poetry Selima Hill, *Bunny*
2002   Novel Michael Frayn, *Spies*
        1st Novel Norman Lebrecht, *The Song of Names*
        Poetry Paul Farley, *The Ice Age*

(*Book of the Year)

The Orange Prize for Fiction

The Orange Prize for Fiction is open only to women writers and is judged by a panel of women judges. Sponsored by the Orange Telecommunications company, it was launched in 1996 in the United Kingdom to raise public awareness of women writers, who were under-represented on the other major prize lists.

1996   Helen Dunmore, *A Spell of Winter*
1997   Anne Michaels, *Fugitive Pieces*
1998   Carol Shields, *Larry's Party*
1999   Suzanne Berne, *A Crime in the Neighborhood*
2000   Linda Grant, *When I Lived in Modern Times*
2001   Kate Grenville, *The Idea of Perfection*
2002   Ann Patchett, *Bel Canto*
2003   Valerie Martin, *Property*

Commonwealth Writers' Prize

The Commonwealth Writers' Prize, awarded by the Commonwealth Foundation, was begun in 1987. For the purposes of the award the Commonwealth is divided into four regions:

■ **Africa:** Botswana, Cameroon, The Gambia, Ghana, Kenya, Lesotho, Malawi, Mauritius, Mozambique, Namibia, Nigeria, Seychelles, Sierra Leone, South Africa, Swaziland, Tanzania, Uganda, Zambia, Zimbabwe.
■ **The Caribbean and Canada:** Antigua and Barbuda, The Bahamas, Barbados, Belize, Canada, Dominica, Grenada, Guyana, Jamaica, St Kitts and Nevis, St Lucia, St Vincent and The Grenadines, Trinidad and Tobago.

■ **Eurasia:** Bangladesh, Cyprus, India, Maldives, Malta, Pakistan, Sri Lanka, United Kingdom.

■ **South East Asia and South Pacific:** Australia, Brunei Darussalam, Fiji Islands, Kiribati, Malaysia, Nauru, New Zealand, Papua New Guinea, Samoa, Singapore, Solomon Islands, Tonga, Tuvalu, Vanuatu.

A shortlist is drawn up from the winner in each region and each of the 53 countries takes turn to host the final judging and award ceremony.

Best book

1987   Olive Senior *Summer Lightning* (Jamaica)
1988   Festus Iyayi *Heroes* (Nigeria)
1989   Janet Frame *The Carpathians* (New Zealand)
1990   Mordechai Richler *Solomon Gursky Was Here* (Canada)
1991   David Malouf *The Great World* (Australia)
1992   Rohinton Mistry *Such a Long Journey* (Canada)
1993   Alex Miller *The Ancestor Game* (Australia)
1994   Vikram Seth *A Suitable Boy* (India)
1995   Louis de Bernieres *Captain Corelli's Mandolin* (United Kingdom)
1996   Rohinton Mistry *A Fine Balance* (Canada)
1997   Earl Lovelace *Salt* (Trinidad)
1998   Peter Carey *Jack Maggs* (Australia)
1999   Murray Bail *Eucalyptus* (Australia)
2000   J. M. Coetzee *Disgrace* (South Africa)
2001   Peter Carey *True History of the Kelly Gang* (Australia)
2002   Richard Flanagan *Gould's Book of Fish* (Australia)

Best first book

1989   Bonnie Burnard *Women of Influence* (Canada)
1990   John Cranna *Visitors* (New Zealand)
1991   Pauline Melville *Shape-Shifter* (Guyana)
1992   Robert Antoni *Divina Trace* (the Bahamas)
1993   Gita Hariharan *The Thousand Faces of Night* (India)
1994   Keith Oatley *The Case of Emily V* (United Kingdom)
1995   Adib Khan *Seasonal Adjustments* (Pakistan)
1996   Vikram Chandra *Red Earth, Pouring Rain* (India)
1997   Ann-Marie MacDonald *Fall on your Knees* (Canada)
1998   Tim Wynveen *Angel Falls* (Canada)
1999   Kerri Sakamoto *The Electrical Field* (Canada)
2000   Jeffrey Moore *Prisoner in a Red-Rose Chain* (Canada)
2001   Zadie Smith *White Teeth* (United Kingdom)
2002   Manu Herbstein *Ama, a Story of the Atlantic Slave Trade* (South Africa)

Pulitzer Prizes

Pulitzer Prizes are awarded annually by Columbia University, New York City, in recognition of outstanding public service and achievement in American journalism, letters and music. Originally established by Hungarian-born journalist Joseph Pulitzer (1847–1911), publisher of the *New York World*, they have been awarded since 1917 on recommendation of the Pulitzer Prize Board. There are many categories of Pulitzer Prize. The list below shows the winners in fiction, drama and poetry. (Until 1947 the category now called 'fiction' was called 'novel'.)

Fiction

1917	(No Award)
1918	His Family by Ernest Poole
1919	The Magnificent Ambersons by Booth Tarkington
1920	(No Award)
1921	The Age of Innocence by Edith Wharton
1922	Alice Adams by Booth Tarkington
1923	One of Ours by Willa Cather
1924	The Able McLaughlins by Margaret Wilson
1925	So Big by Edna Ferber
1926	Arrowsmith by Sinclair Lewis
1927	Early Autumn by Louis Bromfield
1928	The Bridge of San Luis Rey by Thornton Wilder
1929	Scarlet Sister Mary by Julia Peterkin
1930	Laughing Boy by Oliver Lafarge
1931	Years of Grace by Margaret Ayer Barnes
1932	The Good Earth by Pearl S. Buck
1933	The Store by T. S. Stribling
1934	Lamb in His Bosom by Caroline Miller
1935	Now in November by Josephine Winslow Johnson
1936	Honey in the Horn by Harold L. Davis
1937	Gone With the Wind by Margaret Mitchell
1938	The Late George Apley by John Phillips Marquand
1939	The Yearling by Marjorie Kinnan Rawlings
1940	The Grapes of Wrath by John Steinbeck
1941	(No Award)
1942	In This Our Life by Ellen Glasgow
1943	Dragon's Teeth by Upton Sinclair
1944	Journey in the Dark by Martin Flavin
1945	A Bell for Adano by John Hersey
1946	(No Award)
1947	All the King's Men by Robert Penn Warren
1948	Tales of the South Pacific by James A. Michener
1949	Guard of Honor by James Gould Cozzens

1950   The Way West by A. B. Guthrie, Jr.

1951   The Town by Conrad Richter

1952   The Caine Mutiny by Herman Wouk

1953   The Old Man and the Sea by Ernest Hemingway

1954   (No Award)

1955   A Fable by William Faulkner

1956   Andersonville by MacKinlay Kantor

1957   (No Award)

1958   A Death In The Family by the late James Agee

1959   The Travels of Jaimie McPheeters by Robert Lewis Taylor

1960   Advise and Consent by Allen Drury

1961   To Kill A Mockingbird by Harper Lee

1962   The Edge of Sadness by Edwin O'Connor

1963   The Reivers by William Faulkner

1964   (No Award)

1965   The Keepers Of The House by Shirley Ann Grau

1966   Collected Stories by Katherine Anne Porter

1967   The Fixer by Bernard Malamud

1968   The Confessions of Nat Turner by William Styron

1969   House Made of Dawn by N. Scott Momaday

1970   Collected Stories by Jean Stafford

1971   (No Award)

1972   Angle of Repose by Wallace Stegner

1973   The Optimists Daughter by Eudora Welty

1974   (No Award)

1975   The Killer Angels by Michael Shaara

1976   Humboldt's Gift by Saul Bellow

1977   (No Award)

1978   Elbow Room by James Alan McPherson

1979   The Stories of John Cheever by John Cheever

1980   The Executioner's Song by Norman Mailer

1981   A Confederacy of Dunces by the late John Kennedy Toole

1982   Rabbit Is Rich by John Updike

1983   The Color Purple by Alice Walker

1984   Ironweed by William Kennedy

1985   Foreign Affairs by Alison Lurie

1986   Lonesome Dove by Larry McMurtry

1987   A Summons to Memphis by Peter Taylor

1988   Beloved by Toni Morrison

1989   Breathing Lessons by Anne Tyler

1990   The Mambo Kings Play Songs of Love by Oscar Hijuelos

1991   Rabbit At Rest by John Updike

1992   A Thousand Acres by Jane Smiley

1993   A Good Scent from a Strange Mountain by Robert Olen Butler

1994   The Shipping News by E. Annie Proulx

1995   The Stone Diaries by Carol Shields
1996   Independence Day by Richard Ford
1997   Martin Dressler: The Tale of an American Dreamer by Steven Millhauser
1998   American Pastoral by Philip Roth
1999   The Hours by Michael Cunningham
2000   Interpreter of Maladies by Jhumpa Lahiri
2001   The Amazing Adventures of Kavalier & Clay by Michael Chabon
2002   Empire Falls by Richard Russo
2003   Middlesex by Jeffrey Eugenides

Drama

1917   (No Award)
1918   Why Marry? by Jesse Lynch Williams
1919   (No Award)
1920   Beyond the Horizon by Eugene O'Neill
1921   Miss Lulu Bett by Zona Gale
1922   Anna Christie by Eugene O'Neill
1923   Icebound by Owen Davis
1924   Hell-Bent Fer Heaven by Hatcher Hughes
1925   They Knew What They Wanted by Sidney Howard
1926   Craig's Wife by George Kelly
1927   In Abraham's Bosom by Paul Green
1928   Strange Interlude by Eugene O'Neill
1929   Street Scene by Elmer L. Rice
1930   The Green Pastures by Marc Connelly
1931   Alison's House by Susan Glaspell
1932   Of Thee I Sing by George S. Kaufman, Morrie Ryskind and Ira Gershwin
1933   Both Your Houses by Maxwell Anderson
1934   Men in White by Sidney Kingsley
1935   The Old Maid by Zoe Akins
1936   Idiots Delight by Robert E. Sherwood
1937   You Can't Take It With You by Moss Hart and George S. Kaufman
1938   Our Town by Thornton Wilder
1939   Abe Lincoln in Illinois by Robert E. Sherwood
1940   The Time of Your Life by William Saroyan
1941   There Shall Be No Night by Robert E. Sherwood
1942   (No Award)
1943   The Skin of Our Teeth by Thornton Wilder
1944   (No Award)
1945   Harvey by Mary Chase
1946   State of the Union by Russel Crouse and Howard Lindsay
1947   (No Award)
1948   A Streetcar Named Desire by Tennessee Williams
1949   Death of a Salesman by Arthur Miller

1950   South Pacific by Richard Rodgers, Oscar Hammerstein, 2nd and Joshua Logan
1951   (No Award)
1952   The Shrike by Joseph Kramm
1953   Picnic by William Inge
1954   The Teahouse of the August Moon by John Patrick
1955   Cat on A Hot Tin Roof by Tennessee Williams
1956   Diary of Anne Frank by Albert Hackett and Frances Goodrich
1957   Long Day's Journey Into Night by Eugene O'Neill
1958   Look Homeward, Angel by Ketti Frings
1959   J. B. by Archibald Macleish
1960   Fiorello! Book by Jerome Weidman and George Abbott, music by Jerry Bock
        and lyrics by Sheldon Harnick
1961   All The Way Home by Tad Mosel
1962   How To Succeed In Business Without Really Trying by Frank Loesser and
        Abe Burrows
1963   (No Award)
1964   (No Award)
1965   The Subject Was Roses by Frank D. Gilroy
1966   (No Award)
1967   A Delicate Balance by Edward Albee
1968   (No Award)
1969   The Great White Hope by Howard Sackler
1970   No Place To Be Somebody by Charles Gordone
1971   The Effect of Gamma Rays on Man-In-The-Moon Marigolds by Paul Zindel
1972   (No Award)
1973   That Championship Season by Jason Miller
1974   (No Award)
1975   Seascape by Edward Albee
1976   A Chorus Line. Conceived, choreographed and directed by Michael
        Bennett, with book by James Kirkwood and Nicholas Dante, music by Marvin
        Hamlisch and lyrics by Edward Kleban
1977   The Shadow Box by Michael Cristofer
1978   The Gin Game by Donald L. Coburn
1979   Buried Child by Sam Shepard
1980   Talley's Folly by Lanford Wilson
1981   Crimes of the Heart by Beth Henley
1982   A Soldier's Play by Charles Fuller
1983   'Night, Mother by Marsha Norman
1984   Glengarry Glen Ross by David Mamet
1985   Sunday in the Park With George. Music and lyrics by Stephen Sondheim,
        book by James Lapine
1986   (No Award)
1987   Fences by August Wilson
1988   Driving Miss Daisy by Alfred Uhry
1989   The Heidi Chronicles by Wendy Wasserstein

1990   The Piano Lesson by August Wilson
1991   Lost in Yonkers by Neil Simon
1992   The Kentucky Cycle by Robert Schenkkan
1993   Angels in America: Millennium Approaches by Tony Kushner
1994   Three Tall Women by Edward Albee
1995   The Young Man From Atlanta by Horton Foote
1996   Rent by the late Jonathan Larson
1997   (No Award)
1998   How I Learned to Drive by Paula Vogel
1999   Wit by Margaret Edson
2000   Dinner With Friends by Donald Margulies
2001   Proof by David Auburn
2002   Topdog/Underdog by Suzan-Lori Parks
2003   Anna in the Tropics by Nilo Cruz

Poetry

1922   Collected Poems by Edwin Arlington Robinson
1923   The Ballad of the Harp-Weaver: A Few Figs from Thistles: Eight Sonnets in
       American Poetry, 1922. A Miscellany by Edna St. Vincent Millay
1924   New Hampshire: A Poem with Notes and Grace Notes by Robert Frost
1925   The Man Who Died Twice by Edwin Arlington Robinson
1926   What's O'Clock by the late Amy Lowell
1927   Fiddler's Farewell by Leonora Speyer
1928   Tristram by Edwin Arlington Robinson
1929   John Browns Body by Stephen Vincent Benet
1930   Selected Poems by Conrad Aiken
1931   Collected Poems by Robert Frost
1932   The Flowering Stone by George Dillon
1933   Conquistador by Archibald Macleish
1934   Collected Verse by Robert Hillyer
1935   Bright Ambush by Audrey Wurdemann
1936   Strange Holiness by Robert P. Tristram Coffin
1937   A Further Range by Robert Frost
1938   Cold Morning Sky by Marya Zaturenska
1939   Selected Poems by John Gould Fletcher
1940   Collected Poems by Mark Van Doren
1941   Sunderland Capture by Leonard Bacon
1942   The Dust Which Is God by William Rose Benet
1943   A Witness Tree by Robert Frost
1944   Western Star by the late Stephen Vincent Benet
1945   V-Letter and Other Poems by Karl Shapiro
1946   (No Award)
1947   Lord Weary's Castle by Robert Lowell
1948   The Age of Anxiety by W. H. Auden

1949   Terror and Decorum by Peter Viereck

1950   Annie Allen by Gwendolyn Brooks

1951   Complete Poems by Carl Sandburg

1952   Collected Poems by Marianne Moore

1953   Collected Poems 1917–1952 by Archibald MacLeish

1954   The Waking by Theodore Roethke

1955   Collected Poems by Wallace Stevens

1956   Poems-North & South by Elizabeth Bishop

1957   Things of This World by Richard Wilbur

1958   Promises: Poems 1954–1956 by Robert Penn Warren

1959   Selected Poems 1928–1958 by Stanley Kunitz

1960   Heart's Needle by W. D. Snodgrass

1961   Times Three: Selected Verse From Three Decades by Phyllis McGinley

1962   Poems by Alan Dugan

1963   Pictures from Breughel by the late William Carlos Williams

1964   At The End Of The Open Road by Louis Simpson

1965   77 Dream Songs by John Berryman

1966   Selected Poems by Richard Eberhart

1967   Live or Die by Anne Sexton

1968   The Hard Hours by Anthony Hecht

1969   Of Being Numerous by George Oppen

1970   Untitled Subjects by Richard Howard

1971   The Carrier of Ladders by William S. Merwin

1972   Collected Poems by James Wright

1973   Up Country by Maxine Kumin

1974   The Dolphin by Robert Lowell

1975   Turtle Island by Gary Snyder

1976   Self-Portrait in a Convex Mirror by John Ashbery

1977   Divine Comedies by James Merrill

1978   Collected Poems by Howard Nemerov

1979   Now and Then by Robert Penn Warren

1980   Selected Poems by Donald Justice

1981   The Morning of the Poem by James Schuyler

1982   The Collected Poems by the late Sylvia Plath

1983   Selected Poems by Galway Kinnell

1984   American Primitive by Mary Oliver

1985   Yin by Carolyn Kizer

1986   The Flying Change by Henry Taylor

1987   Thomas and Beulah by Rita Dove

1988   Partial Accounts: New and Selected Poems by William Meredith

1989   New and Collected Poems by Richard Wilbur

1990   The World Doesn't End by Charles Simic

1991   Near Changes by Mona Van Duyn

1992   Selected Poems by James Tate

1993   The Wild Iris by Louise Gluck

1994   Neon Vernacular: New and Selected Poems by Yusef Komunyakaa
1995   The Simple Truth by Philip Levine
1996   The Dream of the Unified Field by Jorie Graham
1997   Alive Together: New and Selected Poems by Lisel Mueller
1998   Black Zodiac by Charles Wright
1999   Blizzard of One by Mark Strand
2000   Repair by C.K. Williams
2001   Different Hours by Stephen Dunn
2002   Practical Gods by Carl Dennis
2003   Moy Sand and Gravel by Paul Muldoon

The Governor General's Award

The Governor General's Award has been awarded annually since 1936 and is regarded by many as the most prestigious literary award in Canada. The awards were created by the Scottish politician and writer Lord Tweedsmuir (1875–1940), also known as John Buchan, who was Governor General of Canada from 1935 to 1940 and the author of *The Thirty-Nine Steps* (1915). Books by Canadian authors, or published in Canada, are eligible. Administered by the Canada Council, the award comprises many categories, covering writing in both English and French. The list below shows the winners for Fiction in English.

1936   Bertram Brooker, *Think of the Earth*
1937   Laura G. Salverson, *The Dark Weaver*
1938   Gwethalyn Graham, *Swiss Sonata*
1939   Franklin D. McDowell, *The Champlain Road*
1940   Rinquet (Phillipe Panneton), *Thirty Acres*
1941   Alan Sullivan, *Three Came to Ville Marie*
1942   G. Herbert Sallans, *Little Man*
1943   Thomas H. Raddall, *The Pied Piper of Dipper Creek*
1944   Gwethalyn Graham, *Earth and High Heaven*
1945   Hugh MacLennan, *Two Solitudes*
1946   Winifred Bambrick, *Continental Revue*
1947   Gabrielle Roy, *The Tin Flute*
1948   Hugh MacLennan, *The Precipice*
1949   Philip Child, *Mr Ames Against Time*
1950   Germaine Guevremont, *The Outlander*
1951   Morley Callaghan, *The Loved and the Lost*
1952   David Walker, *The Pillar*
1953   David Walker, *Digby*
1954   Igor Gouzenko, *The Fall of a Titan*
1955   Lionel Shapiro, *The Sixth of June*
1956   Adele Wiseman, *The Sacrifice*
1957   Gabrielle Roy, *Street of Riches*
1958   Colin McDougall, *Execution*

1959   Hugh MacLennan, *The Watch that Ends the Night*
1960   Brian Moore, *The Luck of Ginger Coffey*
1961   Malcolm Lowry, *Here Us O Lord from Heaven Thy Dwelling Place*
1962   Kildare Dobbs, *Running to Paradise*
1963   Hugh Garner, *Hugh Garner's Best Stories*
1964   Douglas LePan, *The Deserter*
1965   No Award
1966   Margaret Laurence, *A Jest of God*
1967   No Award
1968   Alice Munro, *Dance of the Happy Shades*
1969   Robert Kroetsch, *The Studhorse Man*
1970   Dave Godfrey, *The New Ancestors*
1971   Mordecai Richler, *St Urbain's Horseman*
1972   Robertson Davies, *The Manticore*
1973   Rudy Wiebe, *The Temptations of Big Rear*
1974   Margaret Laurence, *The Diviners*
1975   Brian Moore, *The Great Victorian Collection*
1976   Marian Engel, *Bear*
1977   Timothy Findley, *The Wars*
1978   Alice Munro, *Who Do You Think You Are?*
1979   Jack Hodkins, *The Resurrection of Joseph Bourne*
1980   George Bowering, *Burning Water*
1981   Mavis Gallant, *Home Truths*
1982   Guy Vanderhaeghe, *Man Descending*
1983   Leon Rooke, *Shakespeare's Dog*
1984   Josef Skvorecky, *Engineer of the Human Souls*
1985   Margaret Atwood, *The Handmaid's Tale*
1986   Alice Munro, *The Progress of Love*
1987   M. T. A. Kelly, *A Dream Like Mine*
1988   David Adams Richards, *Nights Below Station Street*
1989   Paul Quarrington, *Whale Music*
1990   Nino Ricci, *The Lives of the Saints*
1991   Rohinton Mistry, *Such a Long Journey*
1992   Michael Ondaatje, *The English Patient*
1993   Carol Shields, *The Stone Diaries*
1994   Rudy Wiebe, *A Discovery of Strangers*
1995   Greg Hollingshead, *The Roaring Girl*
1996   Guy Vanderhaeghe, *The Englishman's Boy*
1997   Jane Urquhart, *The Underpainter*
1998   Diane Schoemperien, *Forms of Devotion*
1999   Matt Cohen, *Elizabeth and After*
2000   Michael Ondaatje, *Anil's Ghost*
2001   Richard B. Wright, *Clara Callan*
2002   Gloria Sawai, *A Song for Nettie Johnson*

Contributor: Ian Mackean

Time chart

Date	A selection of publications	Historic and political events	Social history, popular culture, science and technology
1914	Theodore Dreiser: *The Titan* James Elroy Flecker: *The King of Alsander* Robert Frost: *North of Boston* Thomas Hardy: *Satires of Circumstances* Henry James: *Notes of a Son and Brother* James Joyce: *Dubliners* Joyce Kilmer: *Trees and Other Poems* D. H. Lawrence: *The Prussian Officer* Sinclair Lewis: *Our Mr Wrenn* Carl Sandburg: *Chicago* W. B. Yeats: *Responsibilities*	**First World War**: Austrian Archduke Franz Ferdinand assassinated in Sarajevo by Serbian gunman. **First World War starts.** First Battle of Ypres. **UK**: Irish Home Rule Bill passed, warnings of possible civil war. **Panama**: Canal opened.	**UK**: Suffragettes protest for votes for women. Huge recruitment campaign for the Army. **Art**: *Blast*, manifesto of Vorticist group published by Wyndham Lewis. **Classical music**: Vaughan Williams, *London Symphony*.
1915	Rupert Brooke: *1914 and Other Poems* Willa Cather: *The Song of the Lark* Joseph Conrad: *Victory* Theodore Dreiser: *The Genius* T. S. Eliot: *The Love Song of J. Alfred Prufrock* Ford Madox Ford: *The Good Soldier* D. H. Lawrence: *The Rainbow* W. Somerset Maugham: *Of Human Bondage* Ezra Pound: *Cathay* Isaac Rosenberg: *Night and Day* Herbert Read: *Songs of Chaos* Dorothy Richardson: *Pointed Roofs* Edith Sitwell: *The Mother and Other Poems* Virginia Woolf: *The Voyage Out*	**First World War**: Second Battle of Ypres. Germans use poison gas for first time. Sinking of SS *Lusitania*. Dardanelles Campaign – to Jan 1916. **USA**: National Association for the Advancement of Colored People boycotts the film *Birth of a Nation*.	**UK**: Government appeals for women to work in factories to help war effort. Emmiline Pankhurst calls off suffragette campaign. Lawrence's *The Rainbow* withdrawn and destroyed. **Science**: Einstein proposes General Theory of Relativity (in addition to the Special Theory of Relativity of 1905). **Cinema**: D. W. Griffith, *Birth of a Nation*.

Date	A selection of publications	Historic and political events	Social history, popular culture, science and technology
1916	Sherwood Anderson: *Windy McPherson's Son* Harold Brighouse: *Hobson's Choice* Hilda Doolittle (H. D.): *Sea Garden* Robert Frost: *Mountain Interval* Wilfrid Wilson Gibson: *Battle, and Other Poems* James Joyce: *A Portrait of the Artist as a Young Man* Ring Lardner: *You Know Me* D. H. Lawrence: *Amores* Katherine Mansfield: *Prelude* Eugene O'Neill: *Bound East* Ezra Pound: *Lustra* Charles Hamilton Sorley: *Marlborough and Other Poems* Mark Twain: *The Mysterious Stranger*	**First World War**: Battle of the Somme. Gallipoli Campaign. **UK**: David Lloyd George appointed Prime Minister. Lord Kitchener killed at sea by mine. **USA**: President Wilson calls for a 'league of nations'. **Ireland**: Easter rising, rebels executed, Roger Casement hung. **Russia**: Rasputin murdered.	**UK**: Conscription introduced. Daylight saving time introduced. **Art**: Start of Dada movement in Zurich. **European influence**: Franz Kafka, *Metamorphosis*. **Popular music**: The term *Jazz* starting to be used.
1917	J. M. Barrie: *Dear Brutus* T. S. Eliot: *Prufrock and Other Observations* Wilfred Wilson Gibson: *Livelihood* Robert Graves: *Fairies and Fusiliers* Ivor Gurney: *Severn and Somme* Thomas Hardy: *Moments of Vision* Ralph Hodgson: *Poems* D. H. Lawrence: *Look! We have Come Through!* Sinclair Lewis: *The Job* Edna St Vincent Millay: *Renascence and Other Poems* Robert Nichols: *Ardours and Endurances* Siegfried Sassoon: *The Old Huntsman* George Bernard Shaw: *Heartbreak House* Edward Thomas: *Poems* Alec Waugh: *The Loom of Youth* Edith Wharton: *Summer*	**First World War**: Third Battle of Ypres, Passchendaele. T. E. Lawrence's campaigns in Arabia. USA declares war on Germany, sends forces to Europe. **UK**: Balfour declaration on establishment of Jewish state. **USA**: East Saint Louis Race riot. **Russia**: Mar: First Russian Revolution – Tsar abdicates. Nov: Bolshevik Revolution led by Lenin – Soviet Federative Socialist Republics created.	**UK**: Royal family adopts name *House of Windsor*. **Art**: France: *Parade*, a circus ballet by Jean Cocteau, designed by Picasso, music by Erik Satie. Appolinaire describes it as 'Surrealism'. Holland: 'De Stijl' movement, Piet Mondrian. **UK**: Paul Nash, *We are making a new world*. **USA**: Start of Pulitzer Prizes. Start of draft. Death of William Cody, 'Buffalo Bill'.
1918	Rupert Brooke: *Collected Poems* Willa Cather: *My Ántonia* Gerard Manley Hopkins: *Poems*, edited by Robert Bridges Aldous Huxley: *The Defeat Of Youth* James Joyce: *Exiles*	**First World War**: Mar: Second Battle of the Somme, 'Red Baron' shot down. Nov: **Armistice ends First World War.** Influenza pandemic begins.	**UK**: Women over 30 get vote. *Married Love* by Dr Marjorie Stopes published. Food rationing. **Art**: Imperial War Museum commissions paintings of the war.

Date	A selection of publications	Historic and political events	Social history, popular culture, science and technology
	D. H. Lawrence: *New Poems* Katherine Mansfield: *Prelude* Ezra Pound: *Pavannes and Divagations* Siegfried Sassoon: *Counter-Attack* Lytton Strachey: *Eminent Victorians* Booth Tarkington: *The Magnificent Ambersons* Edward Thomas: *Last Poems* Edith Wharton: *The Marne*		**European influence**: Luigi Pirandello, *Six Characters in Search of an Author.* **Classical music**: Holst *The Planets* first performed. **Popular music**: First US Jazz band visits UK.
1919	Sherwood Anderson: *Winesburg, Ohio* Joseph Conrad: *The Shadow Line* T. S. Eliot: *Poems* John Galsworthy: *A Saint's Progress* Ivor Gurney: *War's Embers* W. Somerset Maugham: *The Moon and Sixpence* Ezra Pound: *Homage to Sextus Propertius* Herbert Read: *Naked Warriors* Carl Sandburg: *Cornhuskers* Siegfried Sassoon: *War Poems* Virginia Woolf: *Night and Day* W. B. Yeats: *The Wild Swans at Coole*	Treaty of Versailles. Many monarchies replaced by republics. League of Nations created. Influenza kills millions in Europe. **USA**: Chicago race riots and Ku Klux Klan lynchings. **Ireland**: Rebellion led by Sinn Fein. Lloyd George announces partition plan. **Italy**: Mussolini forms Fascist party. **India**: Jallianwala Bagh massacre.	**UK**: Nancy Astor first woman MP. **Technology**: Splitting of the atom by Rutherford. Air service links London and Paris. First flight across Atlantic. **Art**: Bauhaus founded by Gropius. **European influence**: Marcel Proust wins Prix Goncourt. Hermann Hesse, *Demian.* **Cinema**: Fritz Lang, Das *Kabinet den Doktor Caligari.* *United Artists* formed.
1920	Sherwood Anderson: *Poor White* Hart Crane: *My Grandmother's Love Letters* F. Scott Fitzgerald: *This Side of Paradise* Robert Frost: *Mountain Interval* Sinclair Lewis: *Main Street* Katherine Mansfield: *Bliss* Edna St Vincent Millay: *A Few Figs From Thistles* Eugene O'Neill: *Beyond the Horizon* Wilfred Owen: *Poems* Ezra Pound: *Hugh Selwyn Mauberley* Carl Sandburg: *Smoke and Steel* Siegfried Sassoon: *Picture Show* H. G. Wells: *The Outline of History*	**USA**: President Wilson boycotts first meeting of League of Nations. **Germany**: Adolf Hitler, spokesman of National Socialist German Workers Party, publishes plan for Third German Reich, and campaign against Jews. **Ireland**: Civil war. **India**: National Congress adopts Gandhi's programme of non-co-operation.	**UK**: Miners' strike. First radio broadcast. **USA**: Start of prohibition. Women get vote. Ponzi swindle. Roscoe 'Fatty' Arbuckle charged with murder. **Art**: Dadaist exhibitions throughout Europe: Marcel Duchamp, Tristan Tzara, Andre Breton, Paul Elouard, George Grosz, Max Ernst, Kurt Schwitters, Francis Picabia.

Date	A selection of publications	Historic and political events	Social history, popular culture, science and technology
	Edith Wharton: *The Age of Innocence* W. B. Yeats: *Michael Robartes and the Dancer*		
1921	Agatha Christie: *The Mysterious Affair at Styles* John Dos Passos: *Three Soldiers* F. Scott Fitzgerald: *Flappers and Philosophers* D. H. Lawrence: *Women in Love* Aldous Huxley: *Crome Yellow* Walter de la Mare: *The Veil* Marianne Moore: *Poems* Eugene O'Neill: *Anna Christie* Ezra Pound; *Instigations* Lytton Strachey: *Queen Victoria* W. B. Yeats: *Four Plays for Dancers*	**USA**: Warren Harding, Republican, becomes President, rejects League of Nations. **Ireland**: Truce. **Russia**: famine. **China**: Communist Party formed. **India**: All-India Congress party boycotts visit of Prince of Wales. Gandhi organises burning of foreign cloth.	Foundation of P.E.N. **Technology**: First helicopter flight. **UK**: Unemployment over one million. First birth control clinic. **Classical music**: Sibelius's *Fifth Symphony* performed in London. **Cinema**: Rudolph Valentino, *The Sheik*, Charlie Chaplin, *The Kid*.
1922	Willa Cather: *One of Ours* E. E. Cummings: *The Enormous Room* T. S. Eliot: *The Waste Land* F. Scott Fitzgerald: *Tales of the Jazz Age* James Joyce: *Ulysses* D. H. Lawrence: *Fantasia of the Unconscious* Sinclair Lewis: *Babbitt* Katherine Mansfield: *The Garden Party* W. Somerset Maugham: *On A Chinese Screen* Eugene O'Neill: *The Hairy Ape* Virginia Woolf: *Jacob's Room*	**Ireland**: Eire formally gains independence. Irish Free State under Michael Collins. Ulster to remain British. Collins shot dead. **Russia**: USSR proclaimed. **Italy**: Fascist government under Mussolini. **India**: Gandhi sentenced to six years in jail.	**UK**: BBC makes first broadcast. **USA**: *Reader's Digest* first published. **Philosophy**: Wittgenstein, *Tractatus Logico-Philosophicus*. **European influence**: Bertolt Brecht, *Drums in the Night*. Herman Hesse, *Siddhartha*.
1923	Arnold Bennett: *Riceyman Steps* Willa Cather: *A Lost Lady* E. E. Cummings: *Tulips and Chimneys* James Elroy Flecker: *Hassan* Aldous Huxley: *Antic Hay* Walter de la Mare: *Come Hither* D. H. Lawrence: *Birds, Beasts, and Flowers* Katherine Mansfield: *The Doves' Nest and Other Stories* John Masefield: *Collected Poems*	**UK**: Stanley Baldwin becomes Prime Minister. **USA**: Warren G. Harding dies, Calvin Coolidge, Republican, becomes President. Ku Klux Klan claims million members. **Germany**: First Nazi rally in Munich. Hitler jailed after abortive attempt to seize power. **India**: Plan to restore salt tax.	**Popular music**: **USA**: Opening of *Cotton Club*. Craze for marathon dancing. **Cinema**: Harold Lloyd, *Safety Last*. **USA**: *Time* magazine founded.

Date	A selection of publications	Historic and political events	Social history, popular culture, science and technology
	Sean O'Casey: *The Shadow of a Gunman* Laura Salverson: *The Viking Heart* Edith Sitwell: *Façade* Wallace Stevens: *Harmonium*		
1924	Noel Coward: *The Vortex* F. Scott Fitzgerald: *The Beautiful and Damned* Ford Madox Ford: *Some Do Not* E. M. Forster: *A Passage to India* Robert Frost: *New Hampshire* Katherine Mansfield: *Something Childish and Other Stories* John Masefield: *Sard Harker* Herman Melville: *Billy Budd, Foretopman* Sean O'Casey: *Juno and the Paycock* George Bernard Shaw: *St Joan* Mark Twain: *Autobiography* Edith Wharton: *The Old Maid* P. G. Wodehouse: *The Inimitable Jeeves*	**UK**: Feb: First Labour government under J. Ramsay MacDonald. Nov: Stanley Baldwin becomes Prime Minister, with Winston Churchill Chancellor. **Russia**: USSR constituted. Death of Lenin, Stalin is effective leader. **India**: Gandhi on hunger strike over Hindu-Moslem riots. Spread of plague.	**UK**: Empire Exhibition. Imperial Airways formed. **Technology**: wireless communication between UK and Australia. **Classical music**: George Gershwin, *Rhapsody in Blue*. Sir Edward Elgar made 'Master of the King's Musick'. **Cinema**: First Disney cartoon.
1925	Willa Cather: *The Professor's House* Noel Coward: *Hay Fever* John Dos Passos: *Manhattan Transfer* Theodore Dreiser: *An American Tragedy* F. Scott Fitzgerald: *The Great Gatsby* Ford Madox Ford: *No More Parades* Ernest Hemingway: *In Our Time* C. Day-Lewis: *Beechen Virgil* Sinclair Lewis: *Arrowsmith* Amy Lowell: *What's O'clock* Thomas Mofolo: *Chaka* Ezra Pound: *A Draft of XVI Cantos* Ben Travers: *A Cuckoo in the Nest* William Carlos Williams: *In the American Grain* Virginia Woolf: *Mrs Dalloway* W. B. Yeats: *A Vision*	**USA**: State of Tennessee bans teaching of evolution, 'Monkey trial' case. **USSR**: Stalin ousts Trotsky from leadership. **South Africa**: Law banning blacks from skilled jobs. **Germany**: Hitler publishes *Mein Kampf*. **Shanghai**: Riots against British Imperialism.	**Art**: First Surrealist exhibition in Paris. Jacob Epstein, *Risen Christ*. Beginning of Art Deco. **European influence**: Franz Kafka, *The Trial*. **Popular music**: *Charleston* dance craze comes to UK from USA. **Cinema**: Eisenstein, *Battleship Potemkin*, Charlie Chaplin, *The Gold Rush*.
1926	Willa Cather: *My Mortal Enemy* Ford Madox Ford: *A Man Could Stand Up*	**UK**: Commonwealth of Nations established, reduction of Empire.	**UK**: General strike. **Technology**: Logie Baird demonstrates first TV system.

Date	A selection of publications	Historic and political events	Social history, popular culture, science and technology
	Ernest Hemingway: *The Sun Also Rises* Langston Hughes: *The Weary Blues* T. E. Lawrence: *Seven Pillars of Wisdom* Hugh MacDiarmid: *A Drunk Man Looks at the Thistle* Archibald MacLeish: *Streets in the Moon* Sean O'Casey: *The Plough and the Stars* William Plomer: *Turbott Wolfe* Ezra Pound: *Personae*	**Ireland**: Foundation of Fianna Fail. **India**: Severe rioting between Hindus and Moslems.	Plans for electric trains to replace steam trains. First rocket propelled by liquid fuel. **Cinema**: Fritz Lang, *Metropolis*.
1927	Willa Cather: *Death Comes for the Archbishop* E. M. Forster: *Aspects of the Novel* Ernest Hemingway: *Hills Like White Elephants* James Joyce: *Poems Pennyeach* Jean Rhys: *The Left Bank and Other Stories* Thornton Wilder: *The Bridge of San Luis Rey* Virginia Woolf: *To the Lighthouse* W. B. Yeats: *October Blast*	**Ireland**: Kevin O'Higgins, vice-president of Irish Free State, shot. **USSR**: Stalin ousts Trotsky from Communist party.	**Technology**: First solo flight across Atlantic. **Science**: Heisenberg's Uncertainty principle. **Philosophy**: Heidegger, *Being and Time*. **Classical music**: Yehudi Menuhin, ten years old, performs in Paris. **Cinema**: First 'talkie', *The Jazz Singer*, starring Al Jolson.
1928	W. H. Auden: *Paid On Both Sides* Ford Madox Ford: *Last Post* E. M. Forster: *The Eternal Moment and Other Stories* Aldous Huxley: *Point Counterpoint* Christopher Isherwood: *All the Conspirators* D. H. Lawrence: *Lady Chatterley's Lover* Compton Mackenzie: *Extraordinary Women* W. Somerset Maugham: *Ashenden* Anthony Powell: *The Barnard Letters* Siegfried Sassoon: *Memoirs of a Fox-Hunting Man* R. C. Sherriff: *Journey's End* Allen Tate: *Mr Pope and Other Poems* Evelyn Waugh: *Decline and Fall* Virginia Woolf: *Orlando* W. B. Yeats: *The Tower*	**USA**: Herbert Clark Hoover, Republican, becomes President. Wall Street share prices plunging.	**UK:** Women over 21 get vote. Thames floods, killing 14 and damaging pictures at Tate. Start of Flying Scotsman rail service between Edinburgh and London. **Technology**: Logie Baird demonstrates first colour TV system. **Science**: Discovery of penicillin by Alexander Fleming. **Cinema**: First moving pictures in colour. Disney: Mickey Mouse, *Steamboat Willie*.

Date	A selection of publications	Historic and political events	Social history, popular culture, science and technology
1929	Robert Bridges: *The Testament of Beauty* G. K. Chesterton: *Everlasting Man* C. Day-Lewis: *Transitional Poem* William Faulkner: *The Sound and the Fury* Robert Graves, *Goodbye to All That* Ernest Hemingway: *A Farewell to Arms* Richard Hughes: *A High Wind in Jamaica* Sinclair Lewis: *Dodsworth* Louis MacNeice: *Blind Fireworks* Sean O'Casey: *The Silver Tassie* Rebecca West: *Harriet Hume: A London Fantasy* Thomas Wolfe: *Look Homeward, Angel* Virginia Woolf: *A Room of One's Own* W. B. Yeats: *The Winding Stair*	**USA**: Wall Street Crash, 'Black Thursday'. St Valentine's Day massacre by Al Capone's gang. Capone jailed. **South Africa**: Term *Apartheid* (separate development) first used. **Italy**: Fascists 'win' single party election. **Yugoslavia** formed. **India**: Continuing riots between Hindus and Moslems.	**UK**: Margaret Bonfield first Cabinet minister. Police seize nude paintings by D. H. Lawrence. **USA**: Academy Awards started. Death of Wyatt Earp. **Science**: 'Big bang' theory put forward. **Art**: Second Surrealist Manifesto, Dali joins group. Opening of Museum of Modern Art, New York. **European influence**: Jean Cocteau, *Les Enfants Terribles.*
1930	W. H. Auden: *Poems* Samuel Beckett: *Whoroscope* Noel Coward: *Private Lives* Hart Crane: *The Bridge* T. S. Eliot: *Ash-Wednesday* William Faulkner: *As I Lay Dying* Robert Frost: *Collected Poems* Dashiell Hammett: *The Maltese Falcon* Langston Hughes: *Not Without Laughter* W. Somerset Maugham: *Cakes and Ale* Sol Thekiso Plaatje: *Mhudi* Stephen Spender: *Twenty Poems* Evelyn Waugh: *Vile Bodies* Thornton Wilder: *Woman of Andros*	World Economic Depression. **USA**: Al Capone released from prison. **Germany**: Nazis come second in election, attacks on Jewish traders. **India**: Gandhi's 300-mile march in protest against salt tax. Gandhi arrested, civil protests.	**UK**: two million unemployed. **Science**: Invention of Nylon. discovery of Pluto. **Cinema**: Hitchcock's *Blackmail*, his first talking picture. Marlene Deitrich, *The Blue Angel*. Rene Clair, *Sous les Toits de Paris*.
1931	Samuel Beckett: *Proust* John Betjeman: *Mount Zion* Pearl S. Buck: *The Good Earth* Noel Coward: *Cavalcade* A. J. Cronin: *Hatter's Castle* William Faulkner: *Sanctuary* Langston Hughes: *Dear Lovely Death*	**UK**: MacDonald resigns and all-party government formed in face of economic crisis. Sir Oswald Mosley forms the 'New Party'. **USA**: Al 'Scarface' Capone sentenced to 11 years in prison.	**Classical music**: William Walton, *Belshazzar's Feast*. Yehudi Menuhin's first London performance. **Cinema**: Boris Karloff, *Frankenstein*, Bela Lugosi, *Dracula*, Charlie Chaplin, *City Lights*.

Date	A selection of publications	Historic and political events	Social history, popular culture, science and technology
	Aldous Huxley: *The World Of Light* Nancy Mitford: *Highland Fling* Anthony Powell: *Afternoon Men* Jean Rhys: *After Leaving Mr Mackenzie* Nathanael West: *The Dream Life of Balso Snell* Virginia Woolf: *The Waves*	**India**: Continuing riots between Hindus and Moslems. Gandhi asks Britain for Indian independence.	
1932	Pearl S. Buck: *Sons* Willa Cather: *Obscure Destinies* T. S. Eliot: *Sweeney Agonistes; Selected Essays* William Faulkner: *Light in August* John Galsworthy: *Forty Poems* Graham Greene: *Stamboul Train* Thomas Hardy: *Collected Poems* Ernest Hemingway: *Death in the Afternoon* Aldous Huxley: *Brave New World* Christopher Isherwood: *The Memorial* Compton Mackenzie: *Greek Memories* Nancy Mitford: *Christmas Pudding* Evelyn Waugh: *Black Mischief*	**UK**: Sir Oswald Mosley forms British Union of Fascists. **USA**: Franklin Roosevelt, Democrat, becomes President. **India**: Gandhi arrested in action against 'Gandhi's Cabinet'.	**UK**: Bill to abolish whipping of children under 14. Riots against unemployment. **Classical music**: Founding of London Philharmonic Orchestra by Sir Thomas Beecham. **European influence**: Bertolt Brecht, *The Mother*. **Cinema**: Shirley Temple, *Red-Haired Alibi*. First *Tarzan* film. The Marx Brothers, *Horse Feathers*.
1933	W. H. Auden: *The Dance of Death* C. Day-Lewis: *The Magnetic Mountain* Walter Greenwood: *Love on the Dole* D. H. Lawrence: *Last Poems* Sean O'Casey: *Within the Gates* Eugene O'Neill: *Ah, Wilderness!* George Orwell: *Down and Out in Paris and London* Gertrude Stein: *The Autobiography of Alice B. Toklas* H. G. Wells: *The Shape of Things to Come* Nathanael West: *Miss Lonelyhearts* Virginia Woolf: *Flush*	**USA**: Roosevelt's New Deal. **Germany**: Hitler becomes Chancellor. Persecution of Jews, burning of books, attacks on unions, banning of opposition. First concentration camp at Dachau. **India**: Gandhi leaves jail, and hospital, after hunger strike.	**UK**: Slum clearance programme in progress. Battersea power station built. **USA**: Prohibition ends. **Arts & music**: Jewish artists flee from Germany. **Popular music**: Duke Ellington's UK debut. **European influence**: Andre Malraux, *La Condition Humaine*
1934	Samuel Beckett: *More Pricks than Kicks* William Carlos Williams: *Collected Poems*	**UK**: Oswald Mosley addresses mass meeting of British Union of Fascists. Fascist and Anti-Fascist	**UK**: Driving tests introduced. Liner *Queen Mary* launched. **USA**: Bonnie and Clyde caught and killed by police. **European**

Date	A selection of publications	Historic and political events	Social history, popular culture, science and technology
	T. S. Eliot: *Burnt Norton* F. Scott Fitzgerald: *Tender is the Night* Robert Graves: *I, Claudius; Claudius the God* Henry Miller: *Tropic of Cancer* Dylan Thomas: *18 Poems* Evelyn Waugh: *A Handful of Dust*	demonstrations. **France**: General strike against Fascism.	**influence**: Jean Cocteau, *La Machine Infernale*.
1935	W. H. Auden and Christopher Isherwood: *The Dog Beneath the Skin* Pearl S. Buck: *A House Divided* Ivy Compton-Burnett: *A House and its Head* T. S. Eliot: *Murder in the Cathedral* Christopher Isherwood: *Mr Norris Changes Trains* Louis MacNeice: *Poems* John Masefield: *Box of Delights* R. K. Narayan: *Swami and Friends* Clifford Odets: *Waiting for Lefty* George Orwell: *Burmese Days; A Clergyman's Daughter* Katherine Anne Porter: *Flowering Judas and Other Stories* Wallace Stevens: *Ideas of Order*	**UK**: Ramsay MacDonald resigns, Stanley Baldwin becomes Prime Minister. King George V's Silver Jubilee. 'Government of India Bill' gives limited home rule. **USA**: Second round of New Deal legislation. **Germany**: Nuremberg Rally, persecution of Jews intensifies, build-up of arms brings fears of war in Europe. **Italy**: Mussolini invades Abyssinia.	**UK**: Craze for keep-fit classes. 'Green belt' around London established. Penguin books founded, start of paperbacks. **Science**: Development of radar. **Classical music**: George Gershwin *Porgy and Bess*. Alban Berg, *Violin Concerto*. **Popular music**: Count Basie rise to fame, Benny Goodman orchestra formed. **Cinema**: Hitchcock, *The 39 Steps*. Astaire and Rogers in *Top Hat*.
1936	W. H. Auden: *Look Stranger!* W. H. Auden and Christopher Isherwood: *The Ascent of F6* Willa Cather: *Not Under Forty* Robert Frost: *A Further Range* Graham Greene: *A Gun For Sale* Aldous Huxley: *Eyeless in Gaza* C. L. R. James: *Minty Alley* James Joyce: *Collected Poems* Arthur Miller: *Honors at Dawn* Dorothy Parker: *Not So Deep as a Well* Ayn Rand: *We, the Living* John Steinbeck: *In Dubious Battle* Dylan Thomas: *Twenty-Five Poems* Rebecca West: *The Thinking Reed*	**UK**: Death of King George V, accession of Edward VIII, abdicates to marry Mrs Wallis Simpson. Clashes between Fascists and Anti-Fascists. **Spain**: Start of civil war. **India**: Further clashes between Hindus and Moslems.	**UK**: Unemployed from Jarrow march on London. Legal grounds for divorce widened. BBC starts TV broadcasts, Pinewood film studio opens. **Art**: Surrealist exhibition in London. **Popular music**: Start of the 'Swing' era with Benny Goodman 'King of Swing'. **Cinema**: Charlie Chaplin, *Modern Times*.
1937	W. H. Auden and Louis MacNeice: *Letters from Iceland* John Betjeman: *Continual Dew* A. J. Cronin: *The Citadel*	**UK**: Coronation of King George VI. Public Order Act curbs Mosley's fascist organisation. Stanley	**UK**: *Ark Royal* launched. Green belt proposed. Plans to build air raid shelters. **USA**: Strikes in car industry. Hindenburg

Date	A selection of publications	Historic and political events	Social history, popular culture, science and technology
	Ernest Hemingway: *To Have and Have Not* Arthur Miller: *No Villain / They Too Arise* R. K. Narayan: *The Bachelor of Arts* George Orwell: *The Road to Wigan Pier* Ezra Pound: *Polite Essays* John Steinbeck: *Of Mice and Men* Wallace Stevens: *The Man with the Blue Guitar* J. R. R. Tolkien: *The Hobbit* Virginia Woolf: *The Years*	Baldwin resigns, Neville Chamberlain becomes Prime Minister. Plan to partition Palestine to create homeland for Jews. **Spain**: Volunteers flock to help in civil war. German bombers attack Guernica in support of Franco.	airship disaster. **Art**: Picasso, *Guernica*. Hitler bans modern art as 'degenerate'. **Cinema**: Jean Renoir, *La Grande Illusion,* Judy Garland and James Mason, *A Star is Born*.
1938	Samuel Beckett: *Murphy* Elizabeth Bowen: *The Death of the Heart* William Faulkner: *The Unvanquished* Robert Graves: *Count Belisarius* Graham Greene: *Brighton Rock* Ernest Hemingway: *The Fifth Column and the First Forty-Nine Stories* Louis MacNeice: *The Earth Compels* Vladimir Nabokov: *Invitation To A Beheading* R. K. Narayan: *The Dark Room* George Orwell: *Homage to Catalonia* Ezra Pound: *The Fifth Decade of Cantos* John Steinbeck: *The Blood is Strong* Evelyn Waugh: *Scoop* Virginia Woolf: *Three Guineas* W. B. Yeats: *Last Poems*	**UK**: Chamberlain signs 'Munich Agreement'. IRA bombs London, Manchester, Birmingham. **USA**: Fair Labor Standards Act. **Germany**: Germany annexes Austria, gets part of Czechoslovakia. Further persecution of Jews. **Spain**: Franco takes Barcelona and Madrid.	**UK**: Sigmund Freud moves to London to escape Nazis. **USA**: Orson Welles's radio broadcast of H. G. Wells's *The War of the Worlds* causes public panic. **Science**: Hahn and Strassman demonstrate splitting of atom in nuclear fission. **European influence**: Jean Paul Sartre, *La Nausée*. **Cinema**: Disney, *Snow White and the Seven Dwarfs*, first feature-length cartoon.
1939	Pearl S. Buck: *The Patriot* T. S. Eliot: *The Family Reunion* Ernest Hemingway: *The Snows of Kilimanjaro* Christopher Isherwood: *Goodbye to Berlin* James Joyce: *Finnegan's Wake* Arthur Koestler: *The Gladiators* Louis MacNeice: *Autumn Journal* Flann O'Brian: *At Swim-Two-Birds*	**Second World War**: Mussolini and Hitler sign 'Pact of Steel'. Germany annexes Czechoslovakia and invades Poland. **Second World War starts.** **UK and Eire**: Crackdown on IRA. IRA bombs Coventry. **Spain**: Civil war ends.	**UK**: Children evacuated from cities. **Technology**: First jet aircraft. **Classical music**: Béla Bartók, *String Quartet No. 6.* William Walton, *Violin Concerto*. **Popular music**: Vera Lynn, *We'll Meet Again*. **Cinema**: *Gone With the Wind*. John Ford, John Wayne, *Stagecoach*.

Date	A selection of publications	Historic and political events	Social history, popular culture, science and technology
	Jean Rhys: *Good Morning, Midnight* John Steinbeck: *The Grapes of Wrath* Dylan Thomas: *The Map of Love* Nathanael West: *The Day of the Locust*		
1940	W. H. Auden: *New Year Letter* Willa Cather: *Sapphira And The Slave* T. S. Eliot: *East Coker* Graham Greene: *The Power and the Glory* Ernest Hemingway: *For Whom the Bell Tolls* A. M. Klein: *Hath Not a Jew* Carson McCullers: *The Heart Is a Lonely Hunter* C. P. Snow: *Strangers and Brothers* John Steinbeck: *A Letter to the Friends of Democracy* Dylan Thomas: *Portrait of the Artist as a Young Dog* Richard Wright: *Native Son*	**Second World War**: Germany invades Denmark, Norway, Belgium, Holland and France and Channel Islands. General de Gaulle leads French resistance movement. **UK**: Winston Churchill becomes Prime Minister of coalition government, 'their finest hour' speech. Oswald Mosley arrested. Evacuation of troops at Dunkirk, 'blitz' on London, 'Battle of Britain'.	**UK**: Food rationing. 'Careless talk costs lives' campaign. Women war workers demand equal pay and conditions to men. William Joyce, 'Lord Haw Haw', makes broadcasts from Germany. **Art**: UK: Official war artists appointed, including Paul Nash and Stanley Spencer. **Cinema**: Charlie Chaplin in *The Great Dictator*. Disney, *Fantasia*.
1941	Noel Coward: *Blithe Spirit* A. J. Cronin: *The Keys of the Kingdom* H. I. E. Dhlomo: *The Valley of a Thousand Hills* T. S. Eliot: *The Dry Salvages* F. Scott Fitzgerald: *The Last Tycoon* Arthur Koestler: *Darkness at Noon* W. Somerset Maugham: *Up at the Villa* Vladimir Nabokov: *The Real Life of Sebastian Knight* George Orwell: *The Lion And The Unicorn* Sinclair Ross: *As For Me and My House* John Steinbeck: *The Forgotten Village* Eudora Welty: *A Curtain of Green* Virginia Woolf: *Between the Acts*	**Second World War**: Germany invades Russia, transports Jews to ghettos. Japanese attack American ships at Pearl Harbor, USA and Britain declare war on Japan. Japan advances in S. E. Asia. **USA**: Racial discrimination outlawed in defence industry.	**UK**: Meeting place of Bloomsbury Group bombed in blitz, Virginia Woolf drowns herself. **Science**: Start of 'Manhattan project' to develop atomic bomb. **European Influence**: Bertolt Brecht, *Mother Courage and her Children*. **Cinema**: Orson Welles, *Citizen Kane*. John Huston, *The Maltese Falcon*, start of *Film Noir*.
1942	Earle Birney: *David* Taylor Caldwell: *The Strong City*	**Second World War**: British victory in N. Africa. Japanese	**Science**: Atomic bomb tested. First nuclear reactor.

Date	A selection of publications	Historic and political events	Social history, popular culture, science and technology
	T. S. Eliot: *Little Gidding* William Faulkner: *Go Down, Moses* Robert Frost: *A Witness Tree* Langston Hughes: *Shakespeare in Harlem* Patrick Kavanagh: *The Great Hunger* Ezra Pound: *Carta Da Vista* Stephen Spender: *Ruins and Visions* John Steinbeck: *Bombs Away* Wallace Stevens: *Parts of a World* Evelyn Waugh: *Put Out More Flags* Thornton Wilder: *The Skin of Our Teeth*	take Singapore. USA bombs Tokyo, lands troops in N. Africa. **Germany**: Wannsee Conference on 'The Final Solution', extermination camps established in Poland. **India**: Britain offers Gandhi plan for Indian self-government. Gandhi imprisoned before disobedience campaign.	**European influence**: Albert Camus, *The Outsider*. **Popular music**: Vera Lynn, *White Cliffs of Dover*. Frank Sinatra rise to fame. **Cinema**: *Casablanca*.
1943	Raymond Chandler: *The Lady In The Lake* Walter de la Mare: *Love* Robert Graves: *Wife to Mr Milton* Graham Greene: *The Ministry of Fear* Kate O'Brien: *The Last of Summer* Ayn Rand: *The Fountainhead* Herbert Read: *Education Through Art* Betty Smith: *A Tree Grows in Brooklyn* John Steinbeck: *The Moon is Down* Dylan Thomas: *New Poems*	**Second World War**: **Poland**: Nazi massacre of Jews in ghetto. **Italy**: Mussolini deposed. Allied invasion of Italy. Italy declares war on Germany. German 6th Army surrenders at Stalingrad.	**Science**: Properties of LSD discovered. **Philosophy**: Jean Paul Sartre, *Being and Nothingness*. **Popular music**: George Formby. Gracie Fields. Rogers and Hammerstein, *Oklahoma*.
1944	Saul Bellow: *The Dangling Man* John Betjeman: *New Bats in Old Belfries* Joyce Cary: *The Horse's Mouth* Walter de la Mare: *Collected Rhymes and Verses* Hilda Doolittle (H. D.): *Trilogy* T. S. Eliot: *Four Quartets* Dorothy Livesay: *Day and Night* W. Somerset Maugham: *The Razor's Edge* James McAuley: *'Ern Malley' hoax* Katherine Anne Porter: *The Leaning Tower and Other Stories*	**Second World War**: British and Americans advance in Italy, liberate Rome. American Pacific assault. 'D Day' Allied landings in Normandy, liberation of Paris. Death camps found in Poland. **UK**: German doodlebug and V2 flying bombs hit London.	**UK**: Pre-fabricated houses developed. **Science**: discovery of DNA. **European influence**: C. G. Jung, *Psychology and Religion*. Jean Paul Sartre, *In Camera*. **Classical music**: Michael Tippett, *A Child of Our Time*. **Popular music**: Charlie Parker, 'bebop'.
1945	W. H. Auden: *Collected Poetry* Earle Birney: *Now is Time*	**Second World War**: Allies reach Berlin. Hitler kills	**Art**: Henry Moore sketches underground shelters. Paul

Date	A selection of publications	Historic and political events	Social history, popular culture, science and technology
	Robert Frost: *A Masque of Reason* Henry Green: *Loving* Philip Larkin: *The North Ship* Norman Mailer: *The Naked and the Dead* Arthur Miller: *Grandpa And The Statue* R. K. Narayan: *The English Teacher* George Orwell: *Animal Farm* John Steinbeck: *Cannery Row* Evelyn Waugh: *Brideshead Revisited* Tennessee Williams: *The Glass Menagerie*	himself. German surrender, death camps liberated. Atomic bombs on Hiroshima and Nagasaki, **Second World War ends.** **UK**: Labour government under Clement Attlee. **USA**: Harry S. Truman, Democrat, becomes President. **India**: Gandhi and Nehru ask Britain to leave India. Britain promises home rule.	Nash. John Piper. Graham Sutherland. **European influence**: Jean Paul Sartre, *The Age of Reason.* Bertolt Brecht, *The Caucasian Chalk Circle.* **Classical music**: Benjamin Britten, *Peter Grimes.* **Popular music**: Charlie Parker, *The Charlie Parker Story.* **Cinema**: David Lean, *Brief Encounter.* Rossellini, *Rome, Open City.*
1946	Peter Abrahams: *Mine Boy* Elizabeth Bishop: *North & South* William Carlos Williams: *Paterson* Walter de la Mare: *The Traveller* Graham Greene: *The Little Train* Philip Larkin: *Jill* Robert Lowell: *Lord Weary's Castle* W. Somerset Maugham: *Then and Now* Carson McCullers: *The Member of the Wedding* Eugene O'Neill: *The Iceman Cometh* Robert Penn Warren: *All the King's Men* Terence Rattigan: *The Winslow Boy* Henry Reed: *A Map of Verona* Dylan Thomas: *Deaths and Entrances* Eudora Welty: *Delta Wedding*	Nuremberg trials. League of Nations dissolved. United Nations established. **UK**: Churchill warns of Iron Curtain and Communist tyranny. **India**: Demonstrations against British rule. Moslems demand state of Pakistan. Violence between Hindus and Moslems.	Term 'Third World' began to be used. **UK**: Arts Council founded. Radio 3 starts. Heathrow Airport opened. Plans for 'New towns'. **Science**: research links smoking to cancer. **Technology**: IBM develops electronic calculator. Ball point pen developed. **Cinema**: Jean Cocteau, *La Belle et la Bete.*
1947	Saul Bellow: *The Victim* Herman Charles Bosman: *Mafeking Road* Ivy Compton Burnett: *Manservant and Maidservant* Ralph Ellison: *Invisible Man* Anne Frank: *The Diary of a Young Girl* Philip Larkin: *A Girl in Winter* Malcolm Lowry: *Under the Volcano* W. Somerset Maugham: *Creatures of Circumstance*	**UK**: Britain agrees to leave Palestine after Jewish terrorism campaign. UN partitions Palestine. **USA**: Crusade against communism begins. House Committee on Un-American Activities. **India**: India and Pakistan gain independence, Nehru becomes Prime Minister, partition leads to massacres.	**UK**: Coal industry and road transport nationalised. Feb: severe weather causes crisis. Food rationing, austerity cuts. School leaving age raised to 15. **European influence**: Albert Camus, *The Plague.*

Date	A selection of publications	Historic and political events	Social history, popular culture, science and technology
	Compton Mackenzie: *Whisky Galore* Louis MacNeice: *The Dark Tower* Stephen Spender: *Poems of Dedication* Tennessee Williams: *A Streetcar Named Desire*		
1948	Peter Abrahams: *The Path of Thunder* John Betjeman: *Selected Poems* Winston Churchill: *The Gathering Storm* William Faulkner: *Intruder in the Dust* Christopher Fry: *The Lady's Not For Burning* Robert Graves: *The White Goddess* Graham Greene: *The Heart of the Matter* Norman Mailer: *The Naked and the Dead* Alan Paton: *Cry the Beloved Country* Ezra Pound: *Pisan Cantos* Anthony Powell: *John Aubrey and His Friends* Terence Rattigan: *The Browning Version* Irwin Shaw: *The Young Lions* Evelyn Waugh: *The Loved One* Thornton Wilder: *The Ides of March* Tennessee Williams: *One Arm And Other Stories*	**UN** forms WHO and adopts Declaration of Human Rights. **USA**: Armed forces desegregated. **USSR** blockades Berlin, **beginning of Cold War**. **Czechoslovakia**: Communist coup. **Burma**: Gains independence. **Israel**: Creation of state of Israel. **India**: Gandhi assassinated, rioting erupts.	**UK**: National Health Service begins. Plans for comprehensive schools. Birth of Prince Charles. 'Baby boom', birth rate rises steeply. Railways nationalised. **Science**: First heart operation. **Art**: Bill Brandt, *Camera in London*. Jackson Pollock, *Composition No. 1*, Abstract Expressionism. **Popular music**: Julie Andrews. **Cinema**: Italian neorealism: Vittorio de Sica, *Bicycle Thieves*.
1949	Nelson Algren: *The Man with the Golden Arm* Elizabeth Bowen: *The Heat of the Day* Herman Charles Bosman: *Cold Stone Jug* Paul Bowles: *The Sheltering Sky* Pearl S. Buck: *The Angry Wife* William Faulkner: *Knight's Gambit* Langston Hughes: *One-Way Ticket* Arthur Miller: *Death of a Salesman* Nancy Mitford: *Love in a Cold Climate*	**USA**: President Truman tries to quell anti-Communist hysteria. **Ireland**: Eire gains republic status. **China**: Communist regime under Mao Tse-tung takes over. **South Africa**: Further implementation of Apartheid, race riots. **USSR**: First atomic bomb tests.	**UK**: Iron and steel industries nationalised. End of clothes rationing. Popularity of cinema falls as popularity of TV rises. **USA**: First colour TV system. **Technology**: Seven-inch records available. First jet airliner. **Art**: RA president attacks modern art of Picasso, Matisse and Henry Moore. **Cinema**: Carol Reed, Orson Welles, *The Third Man*.

Date	A selection of publications	Historic and political events	Social history, popular culture, science and technology
	R. K. Narayan: *Mr Sampath: The Printer of Malgudi* George Orwell: *Nineteen Eighty-four* Ezra Pound: *The Cantos Of Ezra Pound* Rebecca West: *The Meaning of Treason*	**NATO** formed.	
1950	W. H. Auden: *Collected Shorter Poems* Pearl S. Buck: *The Child Who Never Grew* T. S. Eliot: *The Cocktail Party* Ernest Hemingway: *Across the River and into the Trees* Langston Hughes: *Simple Speaks his Mind* Jack Kerouac: *The Town and the City* Doris Lessing: *The Grass is Singing* Ford Madox Ford: *Parade's End* Ezra Pound: *Seventy Cantos* Carl Sandburg: *Complete Poems* John Steinbeck: *Burning Bright* Wallace Stevens: *The Auroras of Autumn* Dylan Thomas: *Twenty-Six Poems* Derek Walcott: *Henri Cristophe* Evelyn Waugh: *Helena*	**USA**: Senator Joseph McCarthy launches crusade against alleged Communist infiltration of Federal government. **Korea**: Start of war, Communist North invades South, USA and UK send troops, China sends in troops. **Tibet**: China invades Tibet.	**UK**: End of petrol rationing brings motoring boom. **Science**: First kidney transplant. USA plans to build hydrogen bomb. **Technology**: BBC's first broadcast from overseas. **Popular music**: Frank Sinatra's London debut. **Cinema**: Marilyn Monroe in *The Asphalt Jungle* and *All About Eve*. Jean Cocteau, *Orphee*. Akira Kurosawa, *Rashomon*.
1951	Samuel Beckett: *Molloy* William Faulkner: *Requiem for a Nun* E. M. Forster: *Two Cheers for Democracy* Langston Hughes: *Montage of a Dream Deferred* James Jones: *From Here to Eternity* Nicholas Montsarrat: *The Cruel Sea* Anthony Powell: *A Question of Upbringing (A Dance to the Music of Time* to 1975) J. D. Salinger: *Catcher in the Rye* William Styron: *Lie Down In Darkness* Derek Walcott: *Henri Dernier*	**UK**: Conservative government under Winston Churchill. **South Africa**: Coloured (mixed race) people denied the vote. **Egypt**: Fighting between British and Egyptians in Canal Zone.	**UK**: Festival of Britain. First electricity from atomic energy. Burgess and MacLean suspected of being Soviet spies. **Science**: First H-bomb tests. **Art**: Henry Moore, *Reclining Figure*. **Classical music:** Benjamin Britten, *Billy Budd*. Igor Stravinsky, *The Rake's Progress*.

Date	A selection of publications	Historic and political events	Social history, popular culture, science and technology
1952	Pearl S. Buck: *The Hidden Flower* Agatha Christie: *The Mousetrap* A. J. Cronin: *Adventures in Two Worlds* Ralph Ellison: *Invisible Man* Ernest Hemingway: *Old Man and the Sea* Aldous Huxley: *The Devils of Loudun* Arthur Koestler: *Arrow in the Blue* Doris Lessing: *Martha Quest* R. K. Narayan: *The Financial Expert* Anthony Powell: *A Buyer's Market* Terence Rattigan: *The Deep Blue Sea* John Steinbeck: *East of Eden* Evelyn Waugh: *Men at Arms* *(Sword of Honour series* to 1961)	**UK**: Death of King George VI. **USA**: Dwight D. Eisenhower, Republican, becomes President. **South Africa**: Demonstrations against Apartheid laws.	**UK**: First test of atomic bomb. London trams taken out of service. **Science**: First contraceptive pill. First artificial heart. USA tests first hydrogen bomb. **Popular music**: Term 'Rock and Roll' being used. **Classical music**: John Cage, *4'33"* **Cinema**: Gene Kelly in *Singin' in the Rain*.
1953	Peter Abrahams: *Return to Goli* Kingsley Amis: *A Frame Of Mind* James Baldwin: *Go Tell It on the Mountain* Samuel Beckett: *Waiting for Godot* Saul Bellow: *The Adventures of Augie March* William Burroughs: *Junkie* A. J. Cronin: *Beyond This Place* T. S. Eliot: *The Confidential Clerk* E. M. Forster: *The Hill of Devi* Louis MacNeice: *Autumn Sequel* Arthur Miller: *The Crucible* Nancy Mitford: *Madame de Pompadour* J. D. Salinger: *Nine Stories* Wallace Stevens: *Collected Poems* Dylan Thomas: *Under Milk Wood* John Wain: *Hurry On Down*	**UK**: Coronation of Queen Elizabeth II. **Russia**: Death of Stalin, rise of Nikita Khrushchev. **Korea**: End of Korean War.	**UK**: Plans for commercial TV. *The Goon Show* and Tony Hancock popular. **USA**: *Playboy* first published. **Science**: Polio vaccine developed. Watson and Crick propose double helix structure of DNA. **Philosophy**: Ludwig Wittgenstein, *Philosophical Investigations*. **Cinema**: Fritz Lang, *The Big Heat*. Fred Zinnemann, *From Here to Eternity*. Federico Fellini, *I Vitelloni*.
1954	Peter Abrahams: *Tell Freedom* Kingsley Amis: *Lucky Jim* John Betjeman: *A Few Late Chrysanthemums* William Golding: *Lord of the Flies* Thom Gunn: *Fighting Terms* George Lamming: *The Emigrants* Iris Murdoch: *Under the Net* Terence Rattigan: Separate Tables Jon Silkin: *The Peaceable Kingdom*	**USA**: US Supreme Court declares racial segregation in schools unconstitutional. H-bomb tests at Bikini Atoll. **Vietnam**: Battle of Dien Bien Phu leads to French colonial loss of Indo-China. Beginning of Vietnam wars. **Algeria**: Beginning of Algerian War of Independence.	**UK**: End of food rationing. US evangelist Billy Graham holds massive meetings in London. **Classical music**: Britten, *The Turn of the Screw*. Schoenberg, *Moses and Aron*. **Popular music**: Rock and Roll era: Bill Haley and the Comets, *Rock Around the Clock*.

Date	A selection of publications	Historic and political events	Social history, popular culture, science and technology
	John Steinbeck: *Sweet Thursday* J. R. R. Tolkien: *The Lord of the Rings* (to 1956)		
1955	Kingsley Amis: *That Uncertain Feeling* James Baldwin: *Notes of a Native Son* J. P. Donleavy: *The Ginger Man* W. S. Graham: *The Nightfishing* Graham Greene: *The Quiet American* Philip Larkin: *The Less Deceived* Arthur Miller: *A View from the Bridge* Vladimir Nabokov: *Lolita* R. K. Narayan: *Waiting for the Mahatma* Flannery O'Connor: *A Good Man is Hard to Find* Anthony Powell: *The Acceptance World* Evelyn Waugh: *Officers and Gentlemen* Rebecca West: *A Train of Powder* Patrick White: *The Tree of Man*	**UK**: Anthony Eden becomes Prime Minister. **USA**: Rosa Parks arrested for refusing to move to Negro section of a bus, start of Martin Luther King's civil rights movement. **Warsaw Pact** signed. **South Africa**: Blacks removed from areas designated 'white only'. ANC issues 'Freedom Charter'.	**UK**: Upsurge in immigration from West Indies. *Waiting for Godot* gets poor reception. Start of ITV. **USA**: James Dean dies in car crash. **Technology**: First mass-produced transistor radios. **Cinema**: Richard Brooks, *The Blackboard Jungle*. Nicholas Ray, James Dean, *Rebel Without a Cause*.
1956	Kingsley Amis: *A Case Of Samples: Poems 1946–1955* Saul Bellow: *Seize the Day* John Berryman: *Homage to Mistress Bradstreet* Allen Ginsberg: *Howl* William Golding: *Pincher Martin* Langston Hughes: *The First Book of the West Indies* Norman Mailer: *The White Negro: Superficial Reflections on the Hipster* Eugene O'Neill: *Long Day's Journey Into Night* John Osborne: *Look Back in Anger* Robert Penn Warren: *Promises* Angus Wilson: *Anglo-Saxon Attitudes*	**USA**: Race riots. **Egypt**: Suez crisis. **USSR**: Insurrection in Hungary crushed.	**UK**: 'Teddy Boys' rioting in cinemas to *Rock Around the Clock*. **Popular music**: Elvis Presley *Heartbreak Hotel*. **Technology**: Transatlantic telephone service started. **Cinema**: Dirk Bogarde, Brigitte Bardot, *Doctor at Sea*. Grace Kelly, Louis Armstrong, Bing Crosby, Frank Sinatra, *High Society*.
1957	Samuel Beckett: *Endgame* John Braine: *Room at the Top*	**UK**: Harold Macmillan becomes Prime Minister.	**UK**: Harold Macmillan's 'never had it so good' speech.

Date	A selection of publications	Historic and political events	Social history, popular culture, science and technology
	John Cheever: *The Wapshot Chronicle* Lawrence Durrell: *Justine* Thom Gunn: *The Sense of Movement* Ted Hughes: *The Hawk in the Rain* Jack Kerouac: *On the Road* Colin MacInnes: *City of Spades* Bernard Malamud: *The Assistant* John Osborne: *The Entertainer* Harold Pinter: *The Room* Anthony Powell: *At Lady Molly's* Ayn Rand: *Atlas Shrugged* Stevie Smith: *Not Waving but Drowning* Muriel Spark: *The Comforters* Keith Waterhouse: *There is a Happy Land* Patrick White: *Voss*	**USA**: School desegregation enforced by troops. **Europe**: EEC formed. **Africa**: Ghana gains independence. **Malaya**: Malaya gains independence.	**USA**: Start of 'Beatnik' era. **Technology**: UK tests nuclear bomb. USSR launches first satellite, Sputnik. **Popular music**: Bill Haley and the Comets' first London performance. Tommy Steele and other British rock and roll bands start up.
1958	Chinua Achebe: *Things Fall Apart* Kingsley Amis: *I Like it Here* Samuel Beckett: *Acte Sans Paroles* John Betjeman: *Collected Poems* Truman Capote: *Breakfast at Tiffany's* Shelagh Delaney: *A Taste of Honey* Lawrence Durrell: *Balthazar* Lawrence Ferlinghetti: *A Coney Island of the Mind* Nadine Gordimer: *A World of Strangers* Graham Greene: *Our Man in Havana* Malcolm Lowry: *Lunar Caustic* Iris Murdoch: *The Bell* R. K. Narayan: *The Guide* Harold Pinter: *The Birthday Party* Alan Sillitoe: *Saturday Night and Sunday Morning*	**France**: De Gaulle given powers to deal with French colonial crisis in Algeria, end of Fourth Republic.	**UK**: CND founded – mass rally. Race riots in Notting Hill and Nottingham. Beatnik movement comes to UK. UK launches its first satellite. First parking meters. First stereo recordings. **Popular music**: Miles Davis, 'progressive jazz'. Oscar Peterson. *My Fair Lady*. **Cinema**: Hitchcock, *Vertigo*. Jacques Tati, *Mon Oncle*. Ingmar Bergman, *Wild Strawberries*.
1959	John Arden: *Sergeant Musgrave's Dance* Brendan Behan: *The Hostage* Saul Bellow: *Henderson the Rain King* William Burroughs: *The Naked Lunch*	**USA**: Protests against desegregation of schools. **Cuba**: Fidel Castro comes to power. **Tibet**: Chinese repression of nationalists, Dalai Lama flees to India.	**UK**: Two-thirds of population now own a TV, cinema audiences declining. 'Mini' car launched. Aldermaston demonstration against nuclear weapons. First section of M1 motorway built. **USA**: Buddy

Date	A selection of publications	Historic and political events	Social history, popular culture, science and technology
	Lawrence Durrell: *Mountolive* William Faulkner: *The Mansion* William Golding: *Free Fall* Robert Lowell: *Life Studies* James A. Michener: *Hawaii* E'skia Mphahlele: *Down Second Avenue* Vladimir Nabokov: *Invitation to a Beheading* V. S. Naipaul: *Miguel Street* Harold Pinter: *The Dumb Waiter* Philip Roth: *Goodbye, Columbus* Alan Sillitoe: *The Loneliness of the Long Distance Runner* W. D. Snodgrass: *Heart's Needle* Terry Southern: *The Magic Christian* Keith Waterhouse: *Billy Liar* Arnold Wesker: *Roots* Tennessee Williams: *Sweet Bird of Youth*	**India**: Indira Gandhi elected President of Congress Party.	Holly dies in plane crash. **Technology**: USA and USSR put satellites in space, monkeys survive space flight. **European influence**: Gunther Grass, *The Tin Drum*. **Popular music**: Tamla Motown label formed. **Cinema**: French New Wave. Alain Resnais, Francois Truffaut. Laurence Harvey in *Room at the Top*.
1960	W. H. Auden: *Homage to Clio* Stan Barstow: *A Kind of Loving* John Betjeman: *Summoned by Bells* Robert Bolt: *A Man for All Seasons* Lawrence Durrell: *Clea* Ted Hughes: *Lupercal* Jack Kerouac: *The Scripture of The Golden Eternity* Harper Lee: *To Kill A Mockingbird* Flannery O'Connor: *The Violent Bear It Away* Harold Pinter: *The Caretaker* Sylvia Plath: *The Colossus* Anthony Powell: *Casanova's Chinese Restaurant* David Storey: *This Sporting Life* John Updike: *Rabbit Run*	**USA**: Start of sit-in movement, black college students insist on service at segregated lunch counter. **Africa**: Nigeria gains independence. **South Africa**: Sharpeville massacre, mass protests against Apartheid.	**UK**: Macmillan's 'wind of change' speech about African nationalism. CND and anti-Apartheid demonstrations. Lady Chatterley trial. Foundation of Royal Shakespeare Company. **European influence**: Eugene Ionesco, *Rhinoceros*. **Popular music**: The Beatles performing in Hamburg. **Cinema**: Alfred Hitchcock, *Psycho*. Ken Russell, *Sons and Lovers*.
1961	Edward Albee: *The American Dream* Samuel Beckett: *Happy Days* Thom Gunn: *My Sad Captains* Joseph Heller: *Catch 22* Malcolm Lowry: *Hear Us O Lord In Heaven Thy Dwelling Place* Iris Murdoch: *A Severed Head*	**USA**: John F. Kennedy, Democrat, becomes President. **Germany**: Berlin Wall constructed. **Cuba**: Bay of Pigs crisis. **South Africa** leaves Commonwealth.	**UK**: *Beyond the Fringe* revue, and *Private Eye* magazine begin. Contraceptive pill on sale. 'Ban the bomb' demonstrations. **Science**: Yuri Gagarin first man in space. **Art**: Beginnings of Pop Art, David Hockney, Peter Blake,

Date	A selection of publications	Historic and political events	Social history, popular culture, science and technology
	V. S. Naipaul: *A House for Mr Biswas* John Osborne: *Luther* Walker Percy: *The Moviegoer* Anthony Powell: *Venusberg* J. D. Salinger: *Franny and Zooey* Alan Sillitoe: *Key to the Door* Muriel Spark: *The Prime of Miss Jean Brodie* John Steinbeck: *The Winter of Our Discontent*	**OPEC** formed.	Allen Jones. **Popular music**: Bob Dylan performing in New York. **Cinema**: Alain Resnais, *L'Année Dernière à Marienbad*. François Truffaut, *Jules et Jim*.
1962	Edward Albee: *Who's Afraid of Virginia Woolf?* A. Alvarez: *The New Poetry* Elizabeth Bishop: *Brazil* Anthony Burgess: *A Clockwork Orange* William Carlos Williams: *Pictures from Brueghel* William Faulkner: *The Reivers* Robert Frost: *In the Clearing* Ken Kesey: *One Flew Over the Cuckoo's Nest* Alex la Guma: *A Walk in the Night* Doris Lessing: *The Golden Notebook* Vladimir Nabokov: *Pale Fire* Flannery O'Connor: *Wise Blood* Anthony Powell: *The Kindly Ones* Anne Sexton: *All my Pretty Ones* John Steinbeck: *Travels with Charley: In Search of America* Kurt Vonnegut: *Mother Night* Derek Walcott: *In a Green Night*	**UK**: Commonwealth immigrants act. End of National Service. **USA**: Martin Luther King jailed, then released. Violent protests against enrolment of black student in college. **Africa**: Independence of Algeria and Uganda. **South Africa**: Nelson Mandela jailed. **West Indies**: Independence of Jamaica and Trinidad.	**UK**: *That Was The Week That Was* launched. **USA**: Death of Marilyn Monroe. **Technology**: John Glenn first American to orbit Earth. First communications satellite; Telstar. **Art**: Andy Warhol's Campbell's soup cans. **Popular music**: Bob Dylan, *Blowin' in the Wind*. **Cinema**: John Schlesinger, *A Kind of Loving*. David Lean, *Lawrence of Arabia*. Stanley Kubrick, *Lolita*, Tony Richardson, *A Taste of Honey*.
1963	Kingsley Amis: *One Fat Englishman* James Baldwin: *The Fire Next Time* Taylor Caldwell: *Grandmother and the Priests* Nell Dunn: *Up the Junction* John Fowles: *The Collector* William Bloke Modisane: *Blame Me on History* Iris Murdoch: *The Unicorn* V. S. Naipaul: *Mr Stone and the Knights*	**UK**: Alec Douglas-Home becomes Prime Minister. **USA**: John F. Kennedy assassinated, Lyndon Baines Johnson, Democrat, becomes President. Martin Luther King's 'I have a dream' speech at 'Jobs and Freedom' march. **Africa**: Kenyan independence.	**UK**: Profumo affair. Great train robbery. CND demonstrations. **USA**: Timothy Leary expelled from Harvard for experimenting with psychedelic drugs. **Science**: First kidney transplant. **Popular music**: Beatles, *Please Please Me* album – 'Beatlemania'. **Cinema**: Alfred Hitchcock, *The Birds*. First James Bond film: *Dr No*.

Date	A selection of publications	Historic and political events	Social history, popular culture, science and technology
	Sylvia Plath: *The Bell Jar* Wole Soyinka: *The Lion and the Jewel* Tom Stoppard: *A Walk on the Water* Can Themba: *The Suit* Kurt Vonnegut: *Cat's Cradle*		
1964	Chinua Achebe: *Arrow of God* Saul Bellow: *Herzog* John Berryman: *77 Dream Songs* John Betjeman: *Ring of Bells* Edward Bond: *Saved* John Braine: *The Jealous God* Leonard Cohen: *Flowers for Hitler* William Golding: *The Spire* Ernest Hemingway: *A Moveable Feast* Philip Larkin: *The Whitsun Weddings* Robert Lowell: *For the Union Dead* Vladimir Nabokov: *The Luzhin Defense* Joe Orton: *Entertaining Mr Sloane* John Osborne: *Inadmissible Evidence* Anthony Powell: *The Valley of Bones* Richard Rive: *Emergency* Peter Shaffer: *The Royal Hunt of the Sun* Gore Vidal: *Julian* Tom Wolfe: *The Kandy-Kolored Tangerine-Flake Streamline Baby*	**UK**: Labour government under Harold Wilson. Malawi and Zambia gain independence. **USA**: Johnson brings in Civil Rights Act against racial discrimination. Race riots in New York. Bombing of Vietnam begins. **South Africa**: Nelson Mandela sentenced to life imprisonment. **India**: Death of Nehru.	**UK**: Start of pirate radio stations. **Art**: 'OP' art – geometric designs which give illusion of movement. **Popular music**: Beatles perform in USA. Rise of The Rolling Stones. **Cinema**: Stanley Kubrick, *Doctor Strangelove*. The Beatles in *A Hard Day's Night*.
1965	Edward Bond: *Saved* Margaret Drabble: *The Millstone* Richard Eberhart: *Selected Poems* John Fowles: *The Magus* Seamus Heaney: *Death of a Naturalist* Doris Lessing: *Landlocked* David Lodge: *The British Museum Is Falling Down* Norman Mailer: *An American Dream* Harold Pinter: *The Homecoming* Sylvia Plath: *Ariel* Paul Scott: *The Jewel in the Crown*	**USA**: Step-up in bombing of Vietnam, troops sent in. Martin Luther King leads further civil rights marches. **Africa**: Rhodesia declares UDI, gains independence. **India**: War with Pakistan over Kashmir.	**UK**: Death of Churchill. Beatles awarded MBE. Miniskirts appear in Mary Quant's boutique in King's Road. Post Office Tower opened. Gas discovered in North Sea. **USA**: Allen Ginsberg coins term Flower Power at anti-war rally. **Technology**: First space walk by astronaut. **Popular music**: The Beach Boys, *California Girls*. The Rolling Stones, *Satisfaction*.

Date	A selection of publications	Historic and political events	Social history, popular culture, science and technology
	Jon Silkin: *Nature with Man* Neil Simon: *The Odd Couple* Wole Soyinka: *The Interpreters* Derek Walcott: *The Castaway*		
1966	Chinua Achebe: *A Man of the People* Edward Albee: *A Delicate Balance* Margaret Atwood: *The Circle Game; Expeditions; Speeches for Doctor Frankenstein* Truman Capote: *In Cold Blood* Nadine Gordimer: *The Late Bourgeois World* Graham Greene: *The Comedians* LeRoi Jones: *Black Art* Bernard Malamud: *The Fixer* Nancy Mitford: *The Sun King* Joe Orton: *Loot* Anthony Powell: *The Soldier's Art* Jean Rhys: *Wide Sargasso Sea* Tom Stoppard: *Rosencrantz and Guildernsterne are Dead* Jacqueline Susann: *Valley of the Dolls* Patrick White: *The Solid Mandala*	**USA**: Further race riots. **China**: Cultural revolution under Mao Tse-tung. **Guyana**: Guyana gains independence. **India**: Indira Gandhi becomes Prime Minister.	**UK**: 'Swinging London', Carnaby Street fashions, hippies. England wins World Cup. Aberfan disaster. **Technology**: First space docking. First moon landing. **Art and popular music**: Velvet Underground perform multi-media shows with Andy Warhol. Bob Dylan introduces electric guitars and back-up band. **Cinema**: Michael Caine in *Alfie*. David Lean, *Dr Zhivago*. Andrei Tarkovsky, *Andrei Rublev*.
1967	Angela Carter: *The Magic Toyshop* Margaret Drabble: *Jerusalem the Golden* Allen Ginsberg: *TV Baby Poems* Anthony Hecht: *The Hard Hours* Ted Hughes: *Wodwo* Langston Hughes: *The Panther and the Lash* Alex la Guma: *And a Threefold Cord* V. S. Naipaul: *The Mimic Men* R. K. Narayan: *The Vendor of Sweets* Peter Nichols: *A Day in the Death of Joe Egg* Joe Orton: *The Erpingham Camp* Harold Pinter: *The Homecoming* Wole Soyinka: *Idanre* William Styron: *The Confessions of Nat Turner* Derek Walcott: *Dream on Monkey Mountain* Thornton Wilder: *The Eighth Day* Angus Wilson: *No Laughing Matter*	**UK**: UK leaves Aden, independence for South Yemen. **USA**: Further race riots. **Israel**: Six Day War.	**UK**: Abortion legalised, homosexuality decriminalised. Flower Power festival. *Oz* magazine launched. Rolling Stones on drugs charges. **USA**: Demonstrations against Vietnam war. **Science**: First heart transplant. Warnings of 'greenhouse effect'. **Technology**: First microwave oven. **Classical music**: Stockhausen, *Anthems*. **Popular music**: The Beatles, *Sergeant Pepper*. Jimi Hendrix, *Are You Experienced?* The Monkees, *I'm A Believer*.

Date	A selection of publications	Historic and political events	Social history, popular culture, science and technology
1968	Alan Bennett: *Forty Years On* Taylor Caldwell: *Testimony of Two Men* Bessie Head: *When Rain Clouds Gather* Norman Mailer: *The Armies of the Night* Liverpool Poets: *The Liverpool Scene* Anthony Powell: *The Military Philosophers* Tom Stoppard: *The Real Inspector Hound* John Updike: *Couples* Gore Vidal: *Myra Breckenridge*	**USA**: Martin Luther King assassinated. Robert Kennedy assassinated. **USSR**: Soviet invasion of Czechoslovakia. **Northern Ireland**: 'Troubles' begin. **France**: Paris: student riots.	**UK**: Capital punishment abolished. Race Relations Bill. Enoch Powell's Birmingham speech. Violent anti-Vietnam war demonstration in Grosvenor Square. Theatre censorship abolished.
1969	W. H. Auden: *City without Walls* Kingsley Amis: *The Green Man* Margaret Atwood: *The Edible Woman* Angela Carter: *Heroes and Villains* Leonard Cohen: *Poems 1956–1968* A. J. Cronin: *A Pocketful of Rye* John Fowles: *The French Lieutenant's Woman* Seamus Heaney: *Door into the Dark* Doris Lessing: *The Four Gated City* Toni Morrison: *The Bluest Eye* Iris Murdoch: *Bruno's Dream* Vladimir Nabokov: *Ada, or Ardor* Joe Orton: *What the Butler Saw* Philip Roth: *Portnoy's Complaint* Kurt Vonnegut: *Slaughterhouse Five*	**USA**: Millions in anti-Vietnam war protests. Richard Milhous Nixon, Republican, becomes President, promises withdrawal from Vietnam. **Northern Ireland**: Rioting, British troops sent in.	**UK**: Free rock concerts in Hyde Park. First Isle of Wight festival. Miners' strike. **USA**: Start of gay rights movement. Start of internet. Woodstock festival. Murder of Sharon Tate. **Technology**: Astronauts walk on the moon. Human egg fertilised in test tube. First flight of Concorde. **Cinema**: *Easy Rider. Women in Love. If.*
1970	Maya Angelou: *I Know Why the Caged Bird Sings* Margaret Atwood: *The Journals of Susanna Moodie* James Dickey: *Deliverance* Graham Greene: *Travels with My Aunt* Germaine Greer: *The Female Eunuch* LeRoi Jones: *It's Nation Time* W. S. Merwin: *The Carrier of Ladders*	**UK**: Conservative government under Edward Heath. **USA**: Anti-war protestors shot at Kent State University, Ohio. **Vietnam**: War spills into Cambodia and Laos. **Women's Liberation Movement** formed.	**Technology**: Computer floppy disks invented. First jumbo jet. **UK**: Equal pay bill. Voting age reduced to 18. Oil found in North Sea. Gay liberation demonstration. New English Bible published. Start of *Play for Today* on TV. **Popular music**: Beatles split up. Jimi Hendrix dies.

Date	A selection of publications	Historic and political events	Social history, popular culture, science and technology
	Toni Morrison: *The Bluest Eye* Michael Ondaatje: *The Collected Works of Billy the Kid* Ezra Pound: *Drafts and Fragments of Cantos CX to CXVII* C. P. Snow: *Strangers and Brothers* Derek Walcott: *The Gulf*		
1971	Maya Angelou: *Just Give Me a Cool Glass of Water 'Fore I Die* Edward Bond: *Lear* Frederick Forsyth: *The Day of the Jackal* Bessie Head: *Maru* E'skia Mphahlele: *The Wanderers* V. S. Naipaul: *In a Free State* Harold Pinter: *Old Times* Anthony Powell: *Books Do Furnish a Room* Wole Soyinka: *Madmen and Specialists* Wallace Stegner: *Angle of Repose* John Updike: *Rabbit Redux* James Wright: *Collected Poems*	**USA**: Lieutenant Calley found guilty of Mylai massacre. **Northern Ireland**: First British soldier killed. Internment introduced. Provisionals break from Official IRA. **South Africa**: Winnie Mandela jailed. **India**: Border war with Pakistan after Bangladesh splits from Pakistan. **Greenpeace** founded.	**UK**: Immigration bill. Decimal currency introduced. Open University opened. **Technology**: Astronauts drive on moon. Intel develops microprocessor. **Cinema**: Stanley Kubrick, *A Clockwork Orange*. Luchino Visconti, *Death in Venice*. Joseph Losey, *The Go-Between*.
1972	Athol Fugard: *Sizwe Banzi is Dead* Ted Hughes: *Crow* Buchi Emecheta: *In the Ditch* LeRoi Jones (as Amiri Imamu Baraka): *Spirit Reach* Thomas Keneally: *The Chant of Jimmy Blacksmith* Maxine Kumin: *Up Country: Poems of New England* Alex la Guma: *In the Fog of the Season's End* Wole Soyinka: *A Shuttle in the Crypt* Tom Stoppard: *Jumpers* Hunter S. Thompson: *Fear and Loathing in Las Vegas*	**USA**: Apr: Increased bombing of North Vietnam. Aug: Combat troops withdraw. Dec: Bombing halted. Watergate, charges against Nixon aides. **Northern Ireland**: Bloody Sunday massacre. Ulster placed under Westminster rule. **Israel**: Olympic compound in Munich stormed by 'Black September' Arab guerrillas.	**UK**: Miners' strike leads to state of emergency. **Technology**: Video cassette recorders introduced. **Classical music**: Harrison Birtwhistle, *The Triumph of Time*. **Popular music**: David Bowie, *Ziggy Stardust*. **Cinema**: Francis Ford Coppola, *The Godfather*.
1973	Martin Amis: *The Rachel Papers* Samuel Beckett: *Not I* Howard Brenton: *Magnificence* Graham Greene: *The Honorary Consul* Bessie Head: *A Question of Power* Iris Murdoch: *The Black Prince*	**UK**: Britain joins European Community. IRA bombs in London. **Ireland:** Power-sharing deal agreed. **USA**: Withdrawal from Vietnam. Watergate – Nixon	**UK**: Energy crisis, power cuts, three-day week. **Popular music**: Pink Floyd, *Dark Side of the Moon*. **Cinema**: François Truffaut, *Day for Night*. Bernardo Bertolucci, *Last Tango in Paris*. Martin

Date	A selection of publications	Historic and political events	Social history, popular culture, science and technology
	R. K. Narayan: *My Days* Anthony Powell: *Temporary Kings* Thomas Pynchon: *Gravity's Rainbow* R. S. Thomas: *Selected Poems* Peter Schaffer: *Equus* Gore Vidal: *Burr* Kurt Vonnegut: *Breakfast of Champions* Derek Walcott: *Another Life* Patrick White: *The Eye of the Storm*	aides found guilty, start of select committee hearings. **Israel**: Yom Kippur War.	Scorsese, *Mean Streets,* Lindsay Anderson, *O Lucky Man.*
1974	W. H. Auden: *Thank You, Fog: Last Poems* Beryl Bainbridge: *The Bottle Factory Outing* Samuel Beckett: *That Time* Charles Bukowski: *Burning in Water, Drowning in Flame* Nadine Gordimer: *The Conservationist* Joseph Heller: *Something Happened* David Jones: *The Sleeping Lord* Philip Larkin: *High Windows* Margaret Laurence: *The Diviners* Vladimir Nabokov: *Look at the Harlequins* Tom Stoppard: *Travesties*	**UK**: Labour government under Harold Wilson. IRA bombs Westminster Hall. **USA**: Watergate scandal, Nixon forced to resign, Gerald Ford, Republican, becomes President. **Ireland**: Power-sharing executive collapses. **India**: First nuclear bomb test.	**UK**: Inflation at 20%. Disappearance of Lord Lucan. **Science**: Experiments towards genetic engineering. Warnings about damage to ozone layer. **Cinema**: Federico Fellini, *Amarcord.* Louis Malle, *Lacombe Lucien.*
1975	Maya Angelou: *Oh Pray My Wings are Gonna Fit Me Well* John Ashbery: *Self-Portrait in a Convex Mirror* Saul Bellow: *Humboldt's Gift* Malcolm Bradbury: *The History Man* Charles Bukowski: *Factotum* E. L. Doctorow: *Ragtime* Athol Fugard: *Statements* Trevor Griffiths: *The Comedians* Seamus Heaney: *North* Kenneth Koch: *The Art of Love* David Lodge: *Changing Places* Harold Pinter: *No Man's Land* Anthony Powell: *Hearing Secret Harmonies* Ruth Prawer Jhabvala: *Heat and Dust*	**UK**: Margaret Thatcher becomes leader of Conservative party. **Africa**: Angola achieves independence. Civil war. **Vietnam**: Khmer Rouge invades Cambodia. Saigon falls to communists. End of Vietnam war. **Lebanon**: Civil war.	**UK**: One million unemployed. First 'bleepers'. Sex Discrimination Bill. North Sea oil on stream. **Technology**: First personal computer marketed in USA. Joint Russian-American space flight. **Latin American influence**: Jorge Luis Borges, *The Book of Sand.* **Popular music**: Bruce Springsteen, *Born to Run.* **Cinema**: Milos Forman, *One Flew Over the Cuckoo's Nest.* Sidney Lumet, *Dog Day Afternoon.* Steven Spielberg, *Jaws.*

Date	A selection of publications	Historic and political events	Social history, popular culture, science and technology
	Stevie Smith: *Collected Poems* Wole Soyinka: *Death and the King's Horseman* Tennessee Williams: *Memoirs*		
1976	Samuel Beckett: *Ghost Trio* Saul Bellow: *To Jerusalem and Back* Elizabeth Bishop: *Geography III* Buchi Emecheta: *The Bride Price* Thom Gunn: *Jack Straw's Castle* Alex Haley: *Roots* James Merrill: *Divine Comedies* Anthony Powell: *Infants of the Spring* Jean Rhys: *Sleep It Off, Lady* Tom Stoppard: *Dirty Linen and New-Found-Land* Gore Vidal: *1876* Kurt Vonnegut: *Slapstick or Lonesome No More!* Derek Walcott: *Sea Grapes*	**UK**: Wilson retires, James Callaghan becomes Prime Minister. **Ireland**: SAS unit sent in. Start of women's peace movement. European Commission accuses Britain of torture. **South Africa**: Soweto riots.	**UK**: Concorde begins service. National Theatre completed. Riots in Notting Hill. **Technology**: Viking spacecraft lands on Mars. **Popular music**: Sex Pistols on Bill Grundy show – the Punk era. **Cinema**: Derek Jarman, *Sebastiane*. Wim Wenders, *Kings of the Road*. Martin Scorsese, *Taxi Driver*.
1977	Samuel Beckett: *Collected Poems in English and French* Stephen Berkoff: *East* Joseph Brodsky: *A Part of Speech* Donald Davies: *To Scorch or Freeze* Margaret Drabble: *The Ice Age* Bessie Head: *The Collector of Treasures* Christopher Isherwood: *Christopher and his Kind* Toni Morrison: *Song of Solomon* R. K. Narayan: *The Painter of Signs* Howard Nemerov: *Collected Poems* J. B. Priestly: *Instead of the Trees* Paul Scott: *Staying On* Sipho Sepamla: *The Soweto I Love* Tom Stoppard: *Professional Foul*	**USA**: James Earl Carter, Democrat, becomes President. **South Africa**: Death of Steve Biko.	**UK**: Queen's Silver Jubilee celebrations. **USA**: Death of Elvis Presley. Execution of Gary Gilmour. **Art**: Opening of Pompidou Centre in Paris. **Popular music**: The Sex Pistols, *Never Mind The Bollocks*. **Cinema**: George Lucas, *Star Wars*. Steven Spielberg, *Close Encounters of the Third Kind*. John Travolta in *Saturday Night Fever*.
1978	Maya Angelou: *And Still I Rise* Beryl Bainbridge: *Young Adolf* A. S. Byatt: *The Virgin in the Garden* Taylor Caldwell: *Bright Flows The River*	**Vietnam**: Vietnamese begin invasion of Cambodia to crush Pol Pot and Khmer Rouge. **Rhodesia**: Plans for black majority rule.	**UK**: 'Winter of discontent', strikes, bad weather. **Technology**: First 'test tube baby'. **Popular music**: Disco music popular, tracks from *Saturday Night Fever* and

Date	A selection of publications	Historic and political events	Social history, popular culture, science and technology
	Graham Greene: *The Human Factor* David Hare: *Plenty* John Irving: *The World According to Garp* David Malouf: *An Imaginary Life* Armistead Maupin: *Tales of the City* Ian McEwan: *The Cement Garden* Iris Murdoch: *The Sea* Harold Pinter: *Betrayal* Dennis Potter: *Pennies from Heaven* Craig Raine: *The Onion, Memory* John Updike: *The Coup*	**Iran**: Millions in demonstrations against Shah. **Guyana**: Mass suicide of members of 'The People's Temple'.	*Grease.* **Cinema**: Christopher Reeve in *Superman.* Elizabeth Taylor in *A Little Night Music.*
1979	Samuel Beckett: *Company* Peter Carey: *War Crimes* Buchi Emecheta: *The Joys of Motherhood* William Golding: *Darkness Visible* Nadine Gordimer: *Burger's Daughter* Seamus Heaney: *Field Work* Ted Hughes: *Moor Town* Norman Mailer: *The Executioner's Song* V. S. Naipaul: *A Bend in the River* Craig Raine: *A Martian Sends a Postcard Home* Philip Roth: *Ghost Writer* Peter Schaffer: *Amadeus* William Styron: *Sophie's Choice* Kurt Vonnegut: *Jailbird* Derek Walcott: *The Star-Apple Kingdom* Tom Wolfe: *The Right Stuff*	**UK**: Conservative government under Margaret Thatcher. **USSR**: Russia invades Afghanistan. **Poland**: Solidarity movement heralds end of Communism. **Rhodesia**: First black Prime Minister. **Iran**: Shah in exile, Ayatollah Khomeini takes over. Supporters of Khomeini take American hostages. **Nicaragua**: Civil war, Sandinista rebels gain power.	**UK**: Airey Neave and Lord Mountbatten killed by IRA bombs. 'Yorkshire Ripper' murders. Anti-racist protestors clash with National Front. **Cinema**: Monty Python's *Life of Brian.* Francis Ford Coppola, *Apocalypse Now.* Robert De Niro in *The Deer Hunter.*
1980	Howard Brenton: *The Romans in Britain* Anthony Burgess: *Earthly Powers* J. M. Coetzee: *Waiting for the Barbarians* Rita Dove: *The Yellow House on the Corner* Penelope Fitzgerald: *Human Voices* William Golding: *Rites of Passage* Graham Greene: *Dr Fischer of Geneva.*	**UK**: Storming of Iranian embassy. **Africa**: Rhodesia becomes Zimbabwe with Robert Mugabe as Prime Minister. **Iraq**: Iran-Iraq war begins. **India**: Sanjay Gandhi killed in plane crash.	**UK**: Unemployment over two million. Recession. Riots in Bristol. **USA**: John Lennon shot. **Technology**: Introduction of the 'walkman'. **Cinema**: John Hurt in *The Elephant Man.*

Date	A selection of publications	Historic and political events	Social history, popular culture, science and technology
	David Lodge: *How Far Can You Go?* Salman Rushdie: *Midnight's Children* Carol Shields: *Happenstance* Miriam Tlali: *Amandla*		
1981	Martin Amis: *Other People: A Mystery Story* Samuel Beckett: *Nohow On* Peter Carey: *Bliss* Raymond Carver: *What We Talk About When We Talk About Love* William Golding: *Rights of Passage* Nadine Gordimer: *July's People* John Irving: *Hotel New Hampshire* Ian McEwan: *The Comfort of Strangers* Toni Morrison: *Tar Baby* Brian Patten: *Love Poems* Sipho Sepamla: *A Ride on the Whirlwind* Mongane Serote: *To Every Birth Its Blood* Paul Theroux: *The Mosquito Coast* D. M. Thomas: *The White Hotel* Gore Vidal: *Creation*	**USA:** Ronald Reagan, Republican, becomes President. Assassination attempt on Reagan. **Ireland:** Riots after death of hunger-striker Bobby Sands.	**UK:** Thatcher government privatising nationalised industries. Prince Charles marries Lady Diana Spencer. Toxteth and Brixton race riots. Social Democrat party formed. Start of Channel 4. **Technology:** Personal computer introduced by IBM. **Cinema:** Harold Pinter's adaptation of *The French Lieutenant's Woman*. Roman Polanski, *Tess*.
1982	Andre Brink: *A Dry White Season* Charles Bukowski: *Ham on Rye* Graham Greene: *Monsignor Quixote* Kazuo Ishiguro: *A Pale View of Hills* Thomas Keneally: *Schindler's Ark* R. K. Narayan: *Malgudi Days* Tom Stoppard: *The Real Thing* Alice Walker: *The Color Purple* Tennessee Williams: *The Bag People*	**UK**: Falklands War. **Poland:** 'Solidarity' outlawed.	**UK**: Unemployment at three million. IRA bomb in Hyde Park. Start of Greenham common anti-missile protests. **Technology**: First CD players. **Popular music**: Michael Jackson, *Thriller*.
1983	Maya Angelou: *Shaker, Why Don't You Sing?* J. M. Coetzee: *Life and Times of Michael K.* Ted Hughes: *River* Norman Mailer: *Ancient Evenings* Ian McEwan: *The Ploughman's Lunch*	**USA**: President Reagan proposes 'Star Wars' defence system.	**UK**: Neil Kinnock becomes Labour leader. IRA car bomb outside Harrods. **Technology**: IBM and Apple producing personal computers.

Date	A selection of publications	Historic and political events	Social history, popular culture, science and technology
	Njabulo Ndebele: *Fools and Other Stories* Salman Rushdie: *Shame* Sam Shepard: *Fool for Love* Graham Swift: *Waterland*		
1984	Martin Amis: *Money* Margaret Atwood: *Interlunar* Iain Banks: *The Wasp Factory* Julian Barnes: *Flaubert's Parrot* Samuel Beckett: *Catastrophe* Saul Bellow: *Him with His Foot in His Mouth and Other Short Stories* Angela Carter: *Nights at the Circus* Don DeLillo: *White Noise* Timothy Findley: *Not Wanted on the Voyage* Seamus Heaney: *Station Island* V. S. Naipaul: *Finding the Centre* Harold Pinter: *One for the Road* Craig Raine: *Rich* Sipho Sepamla: *Selected Poems* Tom Stoppard: *Squaring the Circle* John Updike: *The Witches of Eastwick* Gore Vidal: *Lincoln: A Novel*	**UK**: Policewoman shot outside Libyan embassy. IRA bomb Conservative party conference. Agreement to return Hong Kong to China. **USA**: Bombing of embassy in Beirut. **Lebanon**: Peace keepers quit civil war. **India**: Further Hindu-Moslem riots. Troops storm Golden Temple at Amritsar. Assassination of Indira Gandhi. Riots between Hindus and Sikhs. Gas leak at Bhopal.	**UK**: Miners' strike. Term 'Yuppie' introduced. **USA**: Gunman kills 20 at a McDonald's in California. **Science**: Discovery of AIDS virus. Reports of danger to environment from acid rain and greenhouse effect. **Technology**: 'DNA fingerprinting' developed. **Popular music**: Boy George. Bob Geldof etc, *Band Aid* single. **Cinema**: Tarkovsky, *Nostalgia*. Wim Wenders, *Paris Texas*.
1985	Peter Ackroyd: *Hawksmoor* Margaret Atwood: *The Handmaid's Tale* Howard Brenton and David Hare: *Pravda* Rita Dove: *Fifth Sunday* John Irving: *The Cider House Rules* Lorrie Moore: *Self-Help* Carol Shields: *Various Miracles* Stephen Spender: *Collected Poems* Anne Tyler: *The Accidental Tourist* Jeanette Winterson: *Oranges are not the Only Fruit*	**UK**: Race riots in London after death of black woman, PC Keith Blakelock killed. **Ireland**: Anglo-Irish Agreement, Ulster Unionist MPs resign from House of Commons. **USSR**: Gorbachev becomes leader of Soviet Union.	**UK**: The Westland Affair. Buses privatised. **Art**: Christo, wrapping public buildings. **Popular music**: *Live Aid* rock concert in USA and UK for Ethiopian famine. Madonna, *Like a Virgin*.
1986	Kingsley Amis: *The Old Devils* J. M. Coetzee: *Foe* Kazuo Ishiguro: *An Artist of the Floating World* Garrison Keillor: *Lake Wobegon Days*	**USA**: Bombing of GI disco in Berlin, air strike against Libya. 'Irangate' begins. **USSR**: Chernobyl nuclear disaster. **South Africa**: White	**UK**: British Gas privatised. Clashes between police and pickets at Wapping print workers' strike. Nissan opens car factory. **USA**: Explosion of Challenger space shuttle.

Date	A selection of publications	Historic and political events	Social history, popular culture, science and technology
	Cormac McCarthy: *Blood Meridian, or the Evening Redness of the West* Iris Murdoch: *Acastos: Two Platonic Dialogues* Anthony Powell: *The Fisher King* Richard Rive: *Buckingham Palace, District Six* Derek Walcott: *Collected Poems*	extremists break up Pik Botha meeting. State of emergency on 10th anniversary of Soweto. Repeal of the Urban Areas Act.	**Technology**: Laptop computers introduced.
1987	Maya Angelou: *Now Sheba Sings the Song* David Edgar: *That Summer* Garrison Keillor: *Leaving Home* Ian McEwan: *The Child in Time* Toni Morrison: *Beloved* Vladimir Nabokov: *The Enchanter* Michael Ondaatje: *In the Skin of a Lion* Salman Rushdie: *The Jaguar Smile: A Nicaraguan Journey* Carol Shields: *Swann: A Mystery* Jeanette Winterson: *The Passion* Tom Wolfe: *Bonfire of the Vanities*	**UK**: Conservatives under Thatcher win election for third time. **Ireland**: Enniskillen Remembrance Day bomb. **USSR**: Gorbachev extending policy of 'perestroika' and 'glasnost' (openness).	**UK**: Terry Waite kidnapped in Beirut. Gunman kills 14 in Hungerford. Black Monday stock market crash. Destructive storms. King's Cross tube fire. *Herald of Free Enterprise* ferry disaster. **Cinema**: Wim Wenders, *Wings of Desire*. Bernardo Bertolucci, *The Last Emperor.*
1988	Kingsley Amis: *Difficulties With Girls* Margaret Atwood: *Cat's Eye* Joseph Brodsky: *To Urania* Charles Bukowski: *The Roominghouse Madrigals* Peter Carey: *Oscar and Lucinda* Raymond Carver: *Elephant* Penelope Fitzgerald: *The Beginning of Spring* Graham Greene: *The Captain and the Enemy* Philip Larkin: *Collected Poems* R. K. Narayan: *My Dateless Diary: An American Journey* Harold Pinter: *Mountain Language* Alan Sillitoe: *Three Poems* Tom Stoppard: *Hapgood*	**UK**: Formation of Liberal Democrat party. IRA members shot by SAS in Gibraltar. **USA**: George Herbert Walker Bush, Republican, becomes President. American missile shoots down Iranian airliner in Gulf. **USSR**: Estonia moves towards self-determination. Troops begin withdrawal from Afghanistan. **Kosovo**: Serbs and Albanians fight.	**UK**: Piper Alpha disaster in North Sea. Clapham train crash. Lockerbie disaster. Start of Comic Relief. **Technology**: Serious attacks by computer viruses. **Popular music**: Michael Jackson on UK tour. **Cinema**: Martin Scorsese, *The Last Temptation of Christ*. Pedro Almodovar, *Women on the Verge of a Nervous Breakdown.*
1989	Martin Amis: *London Fields* Beryl Bainbridge: *An Awfully Big Adventure* Rita Dove: *Grace Notes* Buchi Emecheta: *Gwendolen*	**UK**: IRA bomb at Deal barracks. Resignation of Nigel Lawson. **USA**: Earthquake in San Francisco.	**UK**: Start of Sky satellite TV. Hillsborough football stadium disaster. Plane crashes on M1. **USA**: First woman bishop consecrated. **Popular music**:

Date	A selection of publications	Historic and political events	Social history, popular culture, science and technology
	Frederick Forsyth: *The Negotiator* Janet Frame: *The Carpathians* John Irving: *A Prayer For Owen Meany* Kazuo Ishiguro: *The Remains of the Day* Richard Rive: *Emergency Continued* Salman Rushdie: *The Satanic Verses* Alice Walker: *The Temple of My Familiar* Jeanette Winterson: *Sexing the Cherry*	Europe: Berlin Wall dismantled, **end of Cold War**. Revolutions in Eastern Europe. **Iran**: Fatwa declared against Salman Rushdie. **China**: Tiananmen Square protest.	Kylie Minogue. Jason Donovan. Acid House Rave parties. **Classical music**: Michael Tippett, *New Year*.
1990	Maya Angelou: *I Shall Not be Moved* Charles Bukowski: *Septuagenarian Stew* A. S. Byatt: *Possession* J. M. Coetzee: *Age of Iron* Penelope Fitzgerald: *The Gate of Angels* Hanif Kureishi: *The Buddha of Suburbia* Alice Munro: *Friend of My Youth* V. S. Naipaul: *India* Thomas Pynchon: *Vineland* Salman Rushdie: *Haroun and the Sea of Stories* Ivan Vladislavic: *Missing Persons* Derek Walcott: *Omeros*	**UK**: Margaret Thatcher loses leadership of Conservative party, John Major becomes Prime Minister. Iraq takes British hostages. **Germany**: Reunification. **South Africa**: End of ban on anti-apartheid parties. Nelson Mandela freed. **Kuwait**: Iraq invades Kuwait.	**UK**: Anti-poll tax riots. BSE crisis. Violent storms. Strangeways prison riot. **Science**: First human gene experiment. Hubble Space Telescope launched. **Cinema**: David Lynch, *Wild at Heart*. Martin Scorsese, *GoodFellas*.
1991	Alan Bennett: *The Madness of George III* Andre Brink: *An Act of Terror* Anthony Burgess: *Mozart and The Wolf Gang* Peter Carey: *The Tax Inspector* Angela Carter: *Wise Children* Roddy Doyle: *The Van* Bret Easton Ellis: *American Psycho* Graham Greene: *Reflections* Arthur Miller: *The Ride Down Mount Morgan* Rohinton Mistry: *Such a Long Journey* Ben Okri: *The Famished Road*	**Kuwait**: Gulf war liberates Kuwait. **UK**: IRA fires mortars at Downing St. Poll tax abandoned. **Russia**: Gorbachev ousted in short-lived coup. USSR dissolved. Croatia and Slovakia declare independence from Yugoslavia. **South Africa**: End of Apartheid. Winnie Mandela sentenced to prison. **India**: Assassination of Rajiv Gandhi.	**UK**: Inner city riots. Magazine *Viz* a best-seller. Release of Terry Waite from Beirut. Death of Robert Maxwell. Helen Sharman, first British astronaut, in Soyuz spacecraft. **Classical music**: Pavarotti performs in Hyde Park. **Popular music**: Nirvana, *Nevermind*, 'Grunge' music.

Date	A selection of publications	Historic and political events	Social history, popular culture, science and technology
	Lesego Rampolokeng: *Horns for Hondo* Alan Sillitoe: *Leonard's War* Tom Stoppard: *In the Native State* James Tate: *Selected Poems*		
1992	Margaret Atwood: *Good Bones* Angela Carter: *Expletives Deleted* Roddy Doyle: *Paddy Clarke Ha Ha Ha* Thom Gunn: *The Man with Night Sweats* Ted Hughes: *Shakespeare and the Goddess of Complete Being* Ian McEwan: *Black Dogs* Rohinton Mistry: *Tales from Firozsha Baag* Toni Morrison: *Jazz* Michael Ondaatje: *The English Patient*	**USA**: William Jefferson Clinton, Democrat, becomes President. **Serbia**: Prison camps, 'ethnic cleansing'. **India**: Rioting after destruction of Babri Masjid mosque.	**UK**: Over two million unemployed. Recession. Exit from ERM. Drought. Resignation of David Mellor. Windsor Castle fire. Church of England allows women priests. Polytechnics become universities. **USA**: Race riots in LA.
1993	Martin Amis: *Visiting Mrs Nabokov and Other Excursions* Andre Brink: *On the Contrary* Angela Carter: *American Ghosts and Other World Wonders* Yusef Komunyakaa: *Neon Vernacular* Lesego Rampolokeng: *End Beginnings* Vickram Seth: *A Suitable Boy* Tom Stoppard: *Arcadia* Ivan Vladislavic: *Folly*	**UK**: IRA bomb in Warrington. EEC single market comes into force. **Russia**: Yeltsin crushes hard-line rebellion. **India**: Bombings in Bombay.	**UK**: Queen agrees to pay tax. Floods. Murder of Stephen Lawrence. Murder of Jamie Bulger. **USA**: Lorena Bobbitt case. **Cinema**: Jane Campion, *The Piano*. Steven Spielberg, *Jurassic Park*.
1994	Edward Albee: *Three Tall Women* Carol Ann Duffy: *Selected Poems* James Kelman: *How Late It Was, How Late*. Philip Levine: *Simple Truth* Arthur Miller: *Broken Glass* Alice Munro: *Open Secrets* V. S. Naipaul: *A Way in the World* Craig Raine: *History: The Home Movie* Salman Rushdie: *East, West* Mongane Serote: *Come and Hope with Me* Stephen Spender: *Dolphins*	**UK/Ireland**: IRA and Loyalist cease-fires. Northern Ireland peace process begins. **Russia**: Troops enter Chechnya. **South Africa**: Nelson Mandela becomes President. **Rwanda**: Tribal massacres. **India**: Phoolan Devi freed. Pneumonic plague epidemic.	**UK**: Channel tunnel opened. National Lottery launched. Sunday trading legalised. **USA**: Earthquake in LA. O. J. Simpson arrested. **Science**: Discovery of 'top quark'. **Art**: Damien Hirst, *Away from the Flock*. **Cinema**: Steven Spielberg, *Schindler's List*.

Date	A selection of publications	Historic and political events	Social history, popular culture, science and technology
1995	Martin Amis: *The Information* Kate Atkinson: *Behind the Scenes at the Museum* Angela Carter: *Burning Your Boats* Rita Dove: *Mother Love* Kazuo Ishiguro: *The Unconsoled* Zakes Mda: *She Plays with the Darkness; Ways of Dying* Rohinton Mistry: *A Fine Balance* Salman Rushdie: *The Moor's Last Sigh* Tom Stoppard: *Indian Ink* Jeanette Winterson: *Art Objects*	**UK/Ireland**: Peace plan launched. **USA**: Oklahoma bomb. **Bosnia**: Bosnian crisis, UK and USA ready to intervene. **Tokyo**: Poison gas attack on underground. **Afghanistan**: Taleban fighters taking power. **AIDS**: WHO reports over one million cases of AIDS.	**UK**: Barings Bank bankrupted by Nick Leeson. Scott Inquiry into government involvement in arms sales to Iraq. Start of first DNA database. **Popular music**: Oasis, *(What's the Story) Morning Glory*. **Cinema**: *Toy Story, Batman Forever.*
1996	Margaret Atwood: *Alias Grace* Beryl Bainbridge: *Everyman for Himself* A. S. Byatt: *Babel Tower* Allen Ginsberg: *Selected Poems* Seamus Heaney: *The Spirit Level* Alice Munro: *Selected Stories* Harold Pinter: *Ashes to Ashes* Arundhati Roy: *The God of Small Things* Meera Syal: *Anita and Me*	**USA**: 'Whitewater' scandal. O. J. Simpson trial begins. **Afghanistan**: Taleban capture Kabul.	**UK**: Prince Charles and Lady Diana divorce. Dunblane school massacre. BSE scare damages beef industry. Completion of re-built Globe Theatre. First Orange Prize for fiction by female novelists. **Cinema:** *Trainspotting.*
1997	Kate Atkinson: *Human Croquet* Peter Carey: *Jack Maggs* Ian McEwan: *Enduring Love* Philip Roth: *American Pastoral*	**UK**: New Labour government under Tony Blair. Hong Kong handed back to China.	**UK**: Princess Diana dies in car crash in Paris.
1998	Julian Barnes: *England, England* J. M. Coetzee: *Boyhood* John Irving: *A Widow for One Year* Cormac McCarthy: *Cities of the Plain* Ian McEwan: *Amsterdam* Toni Morrison: *Paradise* Andrew Motion: *Selected Poems* Alice Munro: *The Love of a Good Woman* Tom Wolfe: *A Man in Full*	**UK/Ireland**: Northern Ireland peace plan, 'Good Friday Agreement'. Omagh bomb. **USA**: Embassy bombings. **Iraq**: Disarmament crisis. USA and UK threaten military action.	European ban on human cloning. **USA**: Monica Lewinsky scandal; President Clinton charged with perjury and obstruction of justice.
1999	J. M. Coetzee: *Disgrace* Seamus Heaney: *Beowulf* Frank McCourt: *'Tis* Salman Rushdie: *The Ground Beneath her Feet* Mongane Serote: *Gods of our Time*	**UK**: Scottish parliament and Welsh Assembly start. **USA**: Columbine high school massacre. **Balkans**: Balkans war.	**UK**: Millennium Dome built. **Cinema**: *Star Wars: The Phantom Menace. The Matrix. American Beauty.*

Date	A selection of publications	Historic and political events	Social history, popular culture, science and technology
2000	Kate Atkinson: *Emotionally Weird* Peter Carey: *True History of the Kelly Gang* Seamus Heaney: *The Midnight Verdict* Philip Roth: *The Human Stain* K. Sello Duiker: *Thirteen Cents* Zadie Smith: *White Teeth* Ivan Vladislavic: *Propaganda by Monuments*	Stock market crash of dot.com companies. **USA**: Navy ship attacked by suicide bombers. **France**: Concorde crashes in Paris. **Iraq**: Rejects new weapons inspection programme.	**UK**: Tate Modern gallery opens. **Science**: Completion of draft of the sequence of the human nuclear genome.
2001	Achmat Dangor: *Bitter Fruit* John Irving: *The Fourth Hand* David Lodge: *Thinks ...* Zakes Mda: *The Heart of Redness* Salman Rushdie: *Fury* K. Sello Duiker: *The Quiet Violence of Dreams* Amy Tan: *The Bonesetter's Daughter* Anne Tyler: *Back When We Were Grownups* Ivan Vladislavic: *The Restless Supermarket* Zoe Wicomb: *David's Story*	**USA**: George W. Bush, Republican, becomes President in controversial election. September 11th attack on World Trade Center and Pentagon. Anthrax attacks in mail. **India**: Gujarat earthquake kills 30,000 and leaves 200,000 homeless.	**UK**: Lord Jeffrey Archer jailed. Ronald Biggs, train robber, gives himself up. **Cinema**: *The Lord of the Rings, part 1.*
2002	Lionel Abrahams: *The White Life of Felix Greenspan* Edward Albee: *The Goat, or Who Is Sylvia?* Kate Atkinson: *Not the End of the World* Margaret Atwood: *Negotiating with the Dead* Michael Frayn: *Spies* Yann Martel: *Life of Pi* Ian McEwan: *Atonement* Ann Patchett: *Bel Canto* Richard Russo: *Empire Falls* Carol Shields: *Unless*	**USA**: US-led action in Afghanistan against Taleban and al Qaeda. Sniper attacks on the public in Washington. **Ireland**: Power-sharing suspended. **Bali**: Terrorist bombing of night-club. **Iraq**: Disarmament crisis continues. UN Security Council Resolution 1441.	Introduction of euro banknotes and coins in some European countries. **UK**: Party in the Palace for Queen's Golden Jubilee. **USA**: Department of Homeland Security established. **Science**: Odyssey Mars probe finds evidence of water ice. **Cinema**: *The Lord of the Rings, part 2.*
2003	Margaret Atwood: *Oryx and Crake* Pat Barker: *Double Vision* Peter Carey: *My Life as a Fake* Nilo Cruz: *Anna in the Tropics* Jeffrey Eugenides: *Middlesex* Valerie Martin: *Property* Toni Morrison: *Love* Paul Muldoon: *Moy Sand and Gravel* D. B. C. Pierre: *Vernon God Little*	**UK**: State visit by George Bush. **Iraq**: USA, Britain and coalition invade Iraq. **Turkey**: Terrorists bomb synagogues, and British interests. **Iran**: Earthquake kills 30,000.	**UK**: Concorde supersonic aircraft taken out of service. **Technology**: NASA experimenting with laser-powered model aircraft. **Cinema**: *The Lord of the Rings, part 3.*

The following sources are acknowledged for assistance in compiling this time chart:

Bloom, Clive and Day, Gary (eds) *Literature and Culture in Modern Britain. Volume Three: 1956–1999.* Longman, and imprint of Pearson Education, 2000.

Brannigan, John, *Orwell to the Present: Literature in England 1945–2000.* Palgrave Macmillan, 2003.

Compact Chronology of World History. Penguin Hutchinson Reference Library. Helicon Publishing and Penguin Books Ltd, 1996.

Department of English at the University of Toronto: A *Time-Line of English Poetry 658–2001* http://eir.library.utoronto.ca/rpo/display/indexpoet.cfm

Mercer, Derrik (ed.) *Chronicle of the 20th Century.* Dorling Kindersley, 1995.

Microsoft Encarta 99 Encyclopedia. Microsoft Corporation. 1993–1998.

Wikipedia www.wikipedia.org/wiki/

Contributor: Ian Mackean

Author index

Index

Authors in bold blue type are authors about whom there is an article in the A–Z section in Part 1. Page numbers in bold type represent the page on which the main entry on a topic can be found.